The Extreme Right in France

From Pétain to Le Pen

J. G. Shields

Routledge
Taylor & Francis Group

LONDON AND NEW YORK

First published 2007
by Routledge
2 Park Square, Milton Park, Abingdon, Oxon OX14 4RN

Simultaneously published in the USA and Canada
by Routledge
270 Madison Ave, New York, NY 10016

Routledge is an imprint of the Taylor & Francis Group, an informa business

© 2007 J. G. Shields

Typeset in Baskerville by
Taylor & Francis Books
Printed and bound in Great Britain by
TJ International Ltd, Padstow, Cornwall

British Library Cataloguing in Publication Data
A catalogue record for this book is available from the British Library

Library of Congress Cataloging in Publication Data
A catalog record for this book has been requested

ISBN 978–0–415–09755–0 (hbk)
ISBN 978–0–415–37200–8 (pbk)
ISBN 978–0–203–96754–6 (ebk)

The Extreme Right in France

The Front National (FN) is France's third political party and the most notable far-right force in Europe; its leader, Jean-Marie Le Pen, contested the 2002 presidential election run-off with 5.5 million votes. What do Le Pen and the FN represent? What are their historical roots, their values and their policies? Who votes for them and why? And what has been their impact on the political agenda in France?

Adopting an essentially chronological approach, this wide-ranging and authoritative study traces the political lineage of Le Pen and the FN through key figures, movements and events on the French extreme right from the Vichy regime to the present, providing a detailed historical perspective for understanding the FN today.

Part I of *The Extreme Right in France* examines:

- the Vichy regime, collaboration and 'collaborationism'
- the aftermath of Liberation and the post-war extreme right
- the Poujadist movement and the politics of populism
- the Algerian War as a catalyst for change
- the 'Nouvelle Droite' and the search for doctrinal renewal
- old and new forms of extreme-right ideology and activism.

Part II of the book provides a comprehensive study of the FN, analysing:

- the party's early development and electoral rise
- its evolving programme and strategy
- the factors underlying its popular appeal
- the geography and composition of its electorate
- its exercise of local power and regional influence
- its defining impact on the national political agenda.

The FN, it is argued, represents both the latest manifestation of a long tradition of authoritarian nationalism and a complex new phenomenon within the changing social and political dynamics of contemporary France.

Drawing on extensive research, this scholarly book is an essential resource for academics, students and all readers with an interest in French and European politics and modern history.

J. G. Shields is Senior Lecturer in French Studies at the University of Warwick.

To my four pillars
Lena, Johnny, Dallal, and Britta

Contents

List of maps and tables

Maps

Tables

Acknowledgements

This book is the fruit of a long labour; in writing it, I have incurred many debts of gratitude. I wish firstly to acknowledge those bodies which funded research leave or enabled me to undertake a number of extended research trips to France: the Arts and Humanities Research Board, the British Academy, the Nuffield Foundation, and the Institut Francophone de Paris are thanked for their generous support. I am grateful to the University of Warwick for study leave and supplementary funding, to Liese Perrin for her research support service, and to the Department of French Studies for providing a conducive working environment. My project could not have progressed far without the assistance of the University Library, in particular that of Peter Larkin and the Document Supply team, and of the Fondation Nationale des Sciences Politiques in Paris, whose library and press holdings constitute an invaluable resource for students of French politics and whose staff have been consistently helpful.

I have been fortunate to be granted interviews by important witnesses to some of the events and issues discussed in these pages. I am especially indebted to the late Pierre Poujade and to Jean-Marie Le Pen for submitting to exhaustive interviews and for their generous hospitality; I am further indebted to M. Poujade for many briefer exchanges by correspondence over a number of years and for providing some rare documents relating to the Poujadist movement. I am grateful to Georges Moreau, Jean-François Jalkh and Pierre Descaves of the Front National for their insights, to Carl Lang and Alain Vizier for party publications, and to officials of the FN, MNR, RPR, UDF, UMP, PS, PCF and other political movements who readily provided documentation on request.

Among those many colleagues from whose scholarship and support I have benefited, special acknowledgement is due to Joseph Algazy, David Bell, Alistair Cole, John Gaffney, Paul Hainsworth, Stanley Hoffmann, Nonna Mayer, the late Peter Morris, Robert Paxton, Pascal Perrineau, Martin Schain, and, for his defining influence and sustained encouragement, Christopher Thompson. I am particularly grateful to Professor Paxton for his enlightening correspondence and for very kindly reading and helpfully commenting on the manuscript of Chapter 1. Neither those named here nor the many other scholars whose work I have consulted in the course of this study bear responsibility for the judgements offered or the errors committed.

My appreciation is due to Routledge for commissioning the book, to Craig Fowlie, Nadia Seemungal, Neil O'Regan and Marianne Bulman for seeing it through so patiently to publication, and in particular to Mark Ralph for his obligingly sensitive copy-editing and Ulrike Swientek for her good-humoured efficiency at the production stage. Chapters 3, 9 and 10 draw in places on material from articles published in the journals *French Politics and Society* (vol. 13, no. 2, 1995; vol. 15, no. 3, 1997), *Modern and Contemporary France* (vol. 8, no. 1, 2000) and *The European Legacy* (vol. 1, no. 2, 1996). The Center for European Studies at Harvard University and Taylor & Francis publishers are thanked for permission to incorporate this material in amended form here. My thanks are due also to Professor Rod Kedward and Penguin publishers for kindly allowing me to adapt Maps 1 and 2 from R. Kedward, *La Vie en bleu: France and the French since 1900* (London, Penguin/Allen Lane, 2005). Unless otherwise indicated, all translations from French are my own.

Finally, I thank those friends, close colleagues and relatives who helped in diverse ways: Bill, Cécilia, Joël and Richard for their dispatches from the front; Jerry, Jacques and Ali for covering during periods of leave; Tom for his personal communications, Leslie for occasional counsel, Craig for the book loans, Paul and Mary for the coastal retreat, John for his timely visits, Gordon and Jasp for staying true, Helena and Charlie as always. My appreciation is also extended to the undergraduate and postgraduate students at Warwick who have shared in my enthusiasm for French history and politics. Above all, I record here my gratitude to my parents, Lena and Johnny Shields, for an interest in my work undimmed after all these years; to Dallal for so much moral, practical and other support; and to Britta, for putting up with those curtailed weekends and for all her unfailing interest and help. It is to them that this book is affectionately dedicated.

James Shields
January 2007

List of abbreviations

AA	Alsace d'Abord
ADMP	Association pour Défendre la Mémoire du Maréchal Pétain
AF	Action Française
AGRIF	Alliance Générale contre le Racisme et pour le Respect de l'Identité Française
AN	Alleanza Nazionale
ANFANOMA	Association Nationale des Français d'Afrique du Nord, d'Outre-Mer et de leurs Amis
ARLP	Alliance Républicaine pour les Libertés et le Progrès
BNP	British National Party
BVA	Brulé, Ville et Associé
CAD	Centre d'Action et de Documentation
CAPS	Comités d'Action Politique et Sociale
CAR	Comités d'Action Républicaine
CDPU	Centre de Documentation Politique et Universitaire
CDS	Centre des Démocrates Sociaux
CESPS	Centre d'Etudes Supérieures de Psychologie Sociale
CEVIPOF	Centre d'Etude de la Vie Politique Française
CFTC	Confédération Française des Travailleurs Chrétiens
CGQJ	Commissariat Général aux Questions Juives
CGT	Confédération Générale du Travail
CNI(P)	Centre National des Indépendants (et Paysans)
CNPI	Conseil National des Populations Immigrées
CPE	*Contrat première embauche*
CPNT	Chasse, Pêche, Nature et Traditions
CSA	Conseils Sondages Analyses
CSAR	Comité Secret d'Action Révolutionnaire
CSG	*Contribution sociale généralisée*
DL	Démocratie Libérale
DPS	Département Protection et Sécurité
DRP	Deutsche Reichspartei
EC	European Community
EEC	European Economic Community

ENA	Ecole Nationale d'Administration
EU	European Union
FAF	Front de l'Algérie Française
FAN	Front d'Action Nationale
FANE	Fédération d'Action Nationale et Européenne
FC	Front des Combattants
FEN	Fédération des Etudiants Nationalistes
FER	Fédération des Etudiants Réfugiés
FLN	Front de Libération Nationale
FN	Front National
FNAF	Front National pour l'Algérie Française
FNC	Front National des Combattants
FNF	Front National Français
FNJ	Front National de la Jeunesse
FNUF	Front National pour l'Unité Française
FPÖ	Freiheitliche Partei Österreichs
GAJ	Groupe Action Jeunesse
GENE	Groupe d'Etudes pour une Nouvelle Education
GMR	Groupes Mobiles de Réserve
GNR	Groupes Nationalistes-Révolutionnaires
GRECE	Groupement de Recherche et d'Etudes pour la Civilisation Européenne
GUD	Groupe Union Droit/Groupe d'Union et de Défense/Groupe Union Défense
IEQJ	Institut d'Etude des Questions Juives
IFOP	Institut Français d'Opinion Publique
IGF	*Impôt sur les grandes fortunes*
INSEE	Institut National de la Statistique et des Etudes Economiques
JE	Pour une Jeune Europe
JIP	Jeunes Indépendants de Paris
JPS	Jeunesses Patriotes et Sociales
LCR	Ligue Communiste Révolutionnaire
LICA	Ligue Internationale Contre l'Antisémitisme
LICRA	Ligue Internationale Contre le Racisme et l'Antisémitisme
LO	Lutte Ouvrière
LVF	Légion des Volontaires Français contre le Bolchevisme
MCR	Mouvement Français de Combat Contre-Révolutionnaire
MDC	Mouvement des Citoyens
MEP	Member of the European Parliament
MJR	Mouvement Jeune Révolution
MNP	Mouvement Nationaliste du Progrès
MNR	Mouvement National Républicain
MNR	Mouvement Nationaliste Révolutionnaire
MP 13	Mouvement Populaire du 13 Mai
MPF	Mouvement Populaire Français

MPF	Mouvement pour la France
MRAP	Mouvement contre le Racisme et pour l'Amitié entre les Peuples
MRP	Mouvement Républicain Populaire
MSE	Mouvement Social Européen
MSI	Movimento Sociale Italiano
MSR	Mouvement Social Révolutionnaire
MSUF	Mouvement Socialiste d'Unité Française
NATO	North Atlantic Treaty Organisation
NOE	Nouvel Ordre Européen
NPD	Nationaldemokratische Partei Deutschlands
NRF	*Nouvelle Revue Française*
OAS	Organisation Armée Secrète
OSS	Organisation du Svastika
OVF	Organisation des Vikings de France
PACS	*Pacte civil de solidarité*
PARIS	Pour l'Avenir et la Réforme Institutionnelle et Sociale
PCF	Parti Communiste Français
PFN	Parti des Forces Nouvelles
PNP	Parti National Populaire
PNSOF	Parti National-Socialiste Ouvrier Français
PPF	Parti Populaire Français
PPNS	Parti Prolétarien National-Socialiste
PPR	Parti Patriote Révolutionnaire
PQJ	Police aux Questions Juives
PR	Parti Républicain
PRUP	Parti Républicain d'Unité Populaire
PS	Parti Socialiste
PSF	Parti Social Français
REL	Rassemblement Européen de la Liberté
RMI	*Revenu minimum d'insertion*
RN	Rassemblement National
RNP	Rassemblement National Populaire
RPF	Rassemblement du Peuple Français
RPF	Rassemblement pour la France
RPR	Rassemblement pour la République
SERP	Société d'Etudes et de Relations Publiques
SFIO	Section Française de l'Internationale Ouvrière
SMIC	*Salaire minimum interprofessionnel de croissance*
SOFRES	Société Française d'Enquêtes par Sondage
SOL	Service d'Ordre Légionnaire
SPAC	Service de Police Anticommuniste
SRMAN	Service de Répression des Menées Antinationales
SSS	Service des Sociétés Secrètes
STO	Service du Travail Obligatoire

TNS-SOFRES	Taylor Nelson Sofres
UDAF	Union de Défense des Agriculteurs de France
UDC	Union de Défense des Combattants
UDCA	Union de Défense des Commerçants et Artisans
UDF	Union pour la Démocratie Française
UDJF	Union de Défense de la Jeunesse Française
UDL	Union de Défense des Lycéens
UDPILA	Union de Défense des Professions Intellectuelles, Libérales et Associés
UDR	Union des Démocrates pour la République
UDT	Union Démocratique du Travail
UDTF	Union de Défense des Travailleurs Français
UFBS	Union des Français de Bon Sens
UFDR	Union Française pour la Défense de la Race
UFF	Union et Fraternité Française
UGT	Union Générale des Travailleurs
UMP	Union pour la Majorité Présidentielle/Union pour un Mouvement Populaire
UN	United Nations
UNEF	Union Nationale des Etudiants de France
UNESCO	United Nations Educational, Scientific and Cultural Organization
UNIR	Union des Nationaux Indépendants et Républicains
UNR	Union pour la Nouvelle République
URC	Union du Rassemblement et du Centre
ZEP	*Zone d'éducation prioritaire*

Key
• Regional prefecture
— Regional boundaries

Map 1 The regions of metropolitan France

Map 2 The departments of metropolitan France

Introduction

Un passé qui ne passe pas

On 21 April 2002, Jean-Marie Le Pen created arguably the greatest electoral shock in the history of the French Republic. Winning almost 17 per cent of the presidential poll, the support of some 4.8 million voters, the leader of the Front National (FN) beat the Prime Minister and Socialist front runner, Lionel Jospin, to challenge the neo-Gaullist incumbent, Jacques Chirac, for France's highest political office. The predicted run-off between centre-right and centre-left was thus converted into a perceived contest between the Republic and the extreme right, with French streets becoming the theatre for the most extensive public protest to be orchestrated against a political figure in France. The 'Republic' won the second ballot resoundingly, but Le Pen's participation in it and his capacity to attract – and retain – the support of over one voter in six represented the strongest performance ever by a far-right candidate or party in a French national election.

Some weeks later, as the re-elected President Chirac took part in the traditional Bastille Day parade on the Champs-Elysées, a shot was discharged from a small-bore rifle. The would-be assassin, it transpired, was a neo-Nazi sympathiser, a reader of Brasillach and Drieu La Rochelle, with a history of involvement in some of the most radical activist groups on the French extreme right. It also transpired that the same individual had stood as a candidate in the 2001 municipal elections for the Mouvement National Républicain (MNR), the party formed by Bruno Mégret in 1999 following his removal from the post of delegate-general of the FN.[1] The wayward attempt on the President's life by a maladjusted loner was a parody of the concerted assassination attempts mounted by right-wing extremists and dissident army officers against Chirac's predecessor, Charles de Gaulle, at the height of the Algerian crisis in the early 1960s; but it revived the spectre of political violence in France and threw light onto the shadowy fringes of the contemporary extreme right.

Two other events of note occurred in the weeks following Le Pen's passage to the presidential run-off. The first was the sixtieth anniversary, on 16 July 2002, of the round-up by French police of almost 13,000 Jews in occupied Paris, most of whom were herded into the Vélodrome d'Hiver sports stadium before being deported via French holding camps to Auschwitz. Though a further 60,000 foreign and French Jews would be similarly deported to their deaths, the '*rafle du Vel d'Hiv*' stands as the starkest monument to Vichy France's active collaboration with Nazi Germany from 1940 to 1944. The solemn ceremony of remembrance contrasted with the outcry which greeted the announcement, in September 2002, that the 92-year-old Maurice Papon was to be released on grounds of ill health after serving only three years of his 10-year prison sentence for complicity in crimes against humanity. As Secretary-General of the Gironde Prefecture between 1942 and 1944, Papon had overseen the deportation of Jews from the Bordeaux area. He was sentenced in 1998 after one of the longest trials in French legal history, describing himself – in a remark laden with historical significance – as 'the Dreyfus of modern times'.[2]

Though bearing no immediate relation to one another, the events described here mark out some of the contours of this book. It is a study of the French extreme right in historical and contemporary perspective, and it rests on two simple propositions: first, that the extreme-right tradition constitutes an important component of French political culture and warrants serious academic study; second, that its continued, if modified, expression in France today can be understood only by close reference to the past. Since the Second World War, the political conscience and to a large extent the political institutions of western Europe have been shaped by the legacy of German National Socialism and Italian Fascism as the dominant nationalist ideologies spawned in those febrile years 1919–39 and which are today designated by the generic term 'fascism'. The experience of France in the inter-war years, under Nazi occupation, and in relation to this fascist legacy since 1945 remains a much contested area of modern French political history, while the sustained electoral challenge of a far-right party in France today imposes with urgency the need to understand the ideological hinterland from which it emerges and the values which it represents. The importance of a historically informed appreciation of the FN arises not just from the 5.5 million votes won by Le Pen in the second round of the 2002 presidential election; it arises also, and perhaps more imperatively, from the influence which he and his party have brought to bear on the political agenda in contemporary France, despite the institutional obstacles which have prevented them from playing a role commensurate with their electoral support.

When, in his final pre-election rally of April 2002, Le Pen invoked the Vichy trilogy '*Travail, Famille, Patrie*' ('Work, Family, Motherland') as 'values without which there is no viable society', he defied a taboo that had endured in France since the Liberation and endorsed the value system of the most infamous regime in modern French history.[3] The outrage provoked by his later assertion, in an interview for the extreme-right weekly *Rivarol*,[4] that the Nazi occupation 'was not particularly inhumane' and that France should dispel 'the lies about her history' demonstrated the extent to which the wartime collaboration remained a live issue not only for the FN leader but for a France seeking still to come to terms with its role as auxiliary to Hitler's Reich. Other examples abound of the import of history. In lamenting the neglect of France's overseas territories, it is to 'the tragedy of French Algeria' that the FN points today still as a wound unhealed by the passage of time. Equally, when the FN calls for a 'Nuremberg trial' of communism, it yields to an impulse undiminished by the demise of its one-time great demon, the Soviet Union; but it also aspires more generally to redress the moral imbalance which it holds to have prevailed in Europe to the benefit of the left and the detriment of the right since the victors' justice of 1945.[5] The past is ever present in the world view articulated by Le Pen and his party, and the decades that have elapsed since the defining events of the 1940s have brought little closure.

Outline of the book

Adopting an essentially chronological approach, this book explores the political lineage of Le Pen and the FN through key figures, movements and events on the French extreme right since 1940. Part I devotes chapters to the Vichy regime, the aftermath of the Liberation, the Poujadist movement, the Algerian War, the Nouvelle Droite (New Right), and changing patterns of extreme-right ideology and activism in the 1950s and 1960s. Part II provides a detailed study of the FN from its formation in 1972 to the present day. These chapters chart the FN's progression from fringe movement to third political party in France, assessing its significance within the wider context of contemporary French politics and society. They examine the nature of the party in the light of its antecedents, and seek to explain how it has developed its electoral appeal, adapted its ideology to changing circumstances, and amplified its influence on political debate and the policy agenda in France.

The space accorded to Vichy in Part I reflects the importance of this regime as the single period in modern French history when government bore the stamp of the extreme right. It is too sweeping to label the entire Vichy project 'extreme-right', and quite inaccurate to label it 'fascist'; but it was a regime wide open to extreme-right influences and where avowed fascists acceded to power over time. From its inception, Vichy was determined by opposition to what had preceded it – the perceived 'decadence' of the parliamentary Third Republic – and by the catastrophic military defeat which had brought it into being. It set the liberal, democratic, assimilationist model of French republicanism in reverse: it was authoritarian, repressive and exclusionist, drawing on a xenophobic nationalism which had found expression through Charles Maurras and his Action Française movement among others. Anti-Semitism had a long history in France and had been a feature of right-wing nationalist discourse since the Dreyfus affair of the 1890s. Following the election in 1936 of the left-wing Popular Front under France's first Jewish premier, the Socialist Léon Blum, powerful political animosities compounded the anti-Semitism that would become official policy for a Vichy regime dedicated to undoing the malign influence of the 'Jewish Republic'.

Embodying legislative, executive and even some judicial powers, Marshal Philippe Pétain as 'Head of the French State' at Vichy returned France to a form of *ancien régime* despotism. Those who argued for a *fascisme à la française* found in this not the strength but the critical weakness of the regime: its backward-looking, ultra-conservative, narrowly nationalist character and failure to construct a vigorous 'new order' at one with Hitler's Europe. While the distinction between state collaboration and pro-Nazi 'collaborationism' remains essential for understanding the dynamics of France under occupation, the boundaries were permeable. Though Vichy did not from the outset erect the infrastructure of the fascist state nor formulate a coherently fascist ideology, it did exhibit certain features of fascism, and it did evolve into a police state more closely aligned with the methods of Nazism. Collaborators and collaborationists alike succumbed in the end to the same error and the same delusion: the error was to interpret French administrative authority as a surrogate sovereignty and to aspire to recover national grandeur under military occupation; the delusion was to overestimate the value of France to Germany and to misread Hitler's intentions for the French in a post-war European order. Both of these misconceptions would find symbolic expression in the raising of a French volunteer legion, then a Waffen-SS division, to make a futile contribution to the German war effort on the eastern front.

All of these issues are addressed in Chapter 1, which discusses the Vichy regime as a laboratory for the cultivation of extreme-right ideas and policies. It considers the intellectual and political background to Vichy, its project of a 'National Revolution', its progressive radicalisation, the tensions between collaboration and collaborationism, and the ultimate difficulty of defining Vichy as a political regime. Chapter 2 focuses on the aftermath of Vichy and the Fourth Republic. In the moral and political climate of the post-Liberation years, extreme-right groups were largely forced underground, where they conceptualised themselves as a new 'resistance'. Engaging in apologias for Vichy and crude variations of neo-Nazism, they could achieve neither the critical mass nor the popular support required to weigh in the political balance. Early attempts to construct a fascist 'International' to rival that of communism were more theatre than substance; but the tenacity of some apologists ensured the propagation of Pétainism, neo-Nazism and a historical revisionism denying the justice of the post-war tribunals. Meanwhile, the developing Cold War, the war in Indo-China and the threat of communist expansionism caused collaboration and resistance gradually to recede as the defining distinction in political identification in France.

The Fourth Republic saw the birth and rapid growth of a new 'ism'. Poujadism was a mass movement of lower middle-class opposition to economic modernisation in the France of the 1950s. Located by most commentators on the extreme right, Poujadism was denounced by some as a renascent fascism. Chapter 3 subjects that interpretation to scrutiny and finds a movement resistant to conventional classification, incorporating two distinct and opposing French political traditions: the conservative-nationalist and the revolutionary-republican. Poujadism restored anti-parliamentarism, anti-Semitism and aggressive nationalism to public discourse but at the same time drew on a pantheon of popular left-wing values and references. Though extreme-right elements infiltrated this populist movement, they failed to take control and turn it to their advantage, confirming both the highly syncretic nature of Poujadism and the continued weakness of the French extreme right a decade on from Vichy.

The opportunity for rehabilitation which eluded the extreme right at home would be found for a time overseas. In championing the cause of *Algérie Française*, extreme-right groups were able to renew their claim to patriotism and effect the transition from a retrograde cult of Vichy to a political sensibility more attuned to the world around them. That world was now conceived above all by the nationalist right in terms of a West under threat from communist imperialism, with the humiliation of Indo-China looming large over the struggle to retain Algeria. Extreme-right movements proliferated in this period and were active in the defining events of the Algerian conflict, expanding their support beyond Pétainists and Nazi sympathisers to former and serving soldiers, colonial settlers, and those (among them many former resisters) committed to the preservation of the French Union. When all of this came to naught with the granting of independence to Algeria in 1962, diehard elements sought to assassinate President de Gaulle and to bring down the Fifth Republic. Their campaign of terror in France and Algeria merely served to bolster de Gaulle in power and to alienate the last vestiges of public support for their cause.

While the loss of Algeria constituted a failure of politics on the extreme right, Chapters 4 and 5 argue its importance as a critical point in the development of ideology and strategy. A French nationalism that had been expressed historically in territorial terms (Alsace-Lorraine, the empire, *Algérie Française*) required now to be redefined. As a result, some on the nationalist right who could no longer glory in France's imperial power began to fashion a post-colonial ideology with an emphasis not on France but on Europe. Central to this new ideological enterprise was the publication in 1961 by Maurice Bardèche of his *Qu'est-ce que le Fascisme?*, to become for many the handbook of French and European neo-fascism. Chapter 4 considers this landmark publication and its attempt to restore a dehistoricised fascism to political respectability. In his Europeanist pretensions, Bardèche contributed to the development (by the Europe-Action movement notably) of a less narrowly Gallic nationalism which stressed the shared origins, ethnicity, civilisation and interests of European peoples faced with the conjoined threats of global communism, Third World nationalism and demographic decline. Though European supremacism had long underpinned the extreme right's world view, not least in the arguments of the wartime collaborationists, the attempt to theorise, extend and bring new scientific legitimacy to the idea of a 'European nationalism' would constitute a major shift in French extreme-right thinking in the 1960s. For those movements that occupied centre stage prior to the FN – Jeune Nation, Europe-Action, Occident, Ordre Nouveau – French identity came to be defined increasingly in terms of European kinship, Western culture and racial specificity. The development of a strong anti-Arab sentiment was a further legacy of the Algerian War which, compounded by growing hostility to North African immigrants in France, would gain prominence in extreme-right discourse.

Ideological renewal in the 1960s was accompanied by a strategic rethink. Algeria had failed to provoke a revolution in France and had shown that power could not be won by overthrowing the regime. Leading thinkers on the far right now recognised the need to build popular support for their ideas if they were to have any hope of acceding to political power. While think-tanks were set up to bring a new ideological rigour and relevance to nationalist doctrine, grass-roots infiltration and cultural entryism were advocated as methods of disseminating it. In this way, a sustained attempt would be made to challenge the intellectual, cultural and moral ascendancy of the left, with selective recourse to the biological and behavioural sciences to lend authority to anti-egalitarian, anti-liberal propositions. This process would be taken to new levels of refinement by the Nouvelle Droite, which became the engine of ideological modernisation on the far right in the 1970s and whose metapolitical strategy of cultural infiltration is examined in Chapter 6.

The other major innovation of the 1960s was the development in some quarters of the French extreme right of a commitment to electoral politics. This ran counter to a deep-seated tradition of anti-parliamentarism but was embraced as a necessary means to an end. The candidacy of Jean-Louis Tixier-Vignancour in the 1965 presidential election is given detailed consideration in Chapter 5. The Tixier-Vignancour campaign was intended to launch a new, broad-based nationalist party; instead, it exposed the political, ideological and personal tensions within the extreme right under the early Fifth Republic and demonstrated the difficulty of adjusting to the democratic process. The real impetus to 'democratise' would come from a less likely source, the self-styled 'revolutionary' movement Ordre Nouveau, which brought together a younger generation of right-wing radicals with the old guard of the collaborationist and *Algérie Française* extreme right. Ordre Nouveau applied to political strategy the renovation that Europe-Action and others had brought to ideology. It is examined as a crucial transition between the violent activism and anti-system ethos of its predecessors, Jeune Nation and Occident, and the electoralist vocation of its eventual successor, the FN.

The formation of the FN in 1972 ushered in a new era in the history of the French extreme right. Its defining purpose was to be a legitimate parliamentary party appealing to a broad constituency. As the latest in a succession of attempts to create a far-right 'front', the new party would bring together ultra-nationalists and Euro-nationalists, Pétainists and collaborationists, Poujadists and Tixierists, colonialists, neo-fascists, monarchists, fundamentalist Catholics, neo-pagans and others. While ideological compromise was the first principle of the 'frontist' strategy, the FN drew inspiration from the intellectual renewal undertaken by earlier movements and combined this with a resolute commitment to participation in elections.

Chapter 7 examines the electoral programmes and campaigns of the FN in the 1970s and traces its early political and organisational evolution through a number of formative phases. Dispensing with the anti-republican references that had made the extreme right unelectable, the FN found itself bereft of a distinctive message. Though vocal in its anti-communism (which it shared with the centre-right), it was initially muted on the issues from which it would eventually make its electoral capital: immigration and law and order. In promoting its anti-immigrant message in the later 1970s, moreover, the FN would not set the agenda but would respond to an agenda already set at the highest levels of government. The most notable ideological development in these early years was the conversion from neo-corporatist to neo-liberal economics. In this, it is argued, the FN broke important new ground, casting off part of its extreme-right heritage, catching the turn of the tide towards neo-liberalism, and giving economic expression to two central elements of its politics: belief in natural hierarchies and radical opposition to communism. The chapter considers the endemic tendency to division among the early FN's diverse components and detects a major influence of the Nouvelle Droite in the party's evolving political philosophy.

Through detailed study of electoral results, analyses and polling data, Chapters 8–10 chart and seek to explain the increasing electoral strength of Le Pen and the FN since the early 1980s – from fewer than 45,000 votes in 1981 to 2.2 million in 1984, 4.57 million in 1995, and 5.5 million in May 2002. These chapters measure the FN's performance through several cycles of legislative, regional, municipal, cantonal and European elections, reflecting its adaptation to the demands of electoral competition at all levels, while analysis of Le Pen's presidential campaigns of 1988, 1995 and 2002 shows the success with which the FN leader exploited the highly personalised nature of presidential elections under the Fifth Republic. Discussion of the FN is framed within that of the wider political, social and economic conditions which allowed it to prosper. The new terms in which immigration came to be addressed in the 1980s and the new salience of '*insécurité*' as a public concern were not attributable solely to the FN but would be crucial in helping the party to gain and retain its audience. The success of the FN in attracting recruits from the centre-right allowed it to grow and to press its claim to respectability, while its rapid progression to the National Assembly did much to advance its institutional legitimacy and give it leverage over political debate and policy-making on its favoured issues. The strategic dilemmas raised both within the FN and across the centre-right are discussed, as is the split inflicted on the party in 1999 by the departure of Mégret to form his own rival party.

Together, these chapters offer soundings on the composition of the FN electorate from one election to another and over the longer span. They show FN voting to have a complex dynamic of its own, with a strong pull to the left, rather than being merely a radicalised right-of-centre vote. The strength of the FN in many areas with no history of extreme-right voting, and its penetration into traditionally right-wing and left-wing constituencies alike, confronted analysts with a party for which they had no ready model. Despite their sociological diversity, FN voters emerged as the most consistent in their voting motivation; they displayed a recurrent element of protest in their vote yet proved the most loyal from one election to the next. While opinion polls indicated an electoral potential beyond the FN's actual achievement, other polls showed Le Pen and his party to be hampered by a serious credibility deficit even among their own supporters. These ambiguities are explored through survey data which identify a high degree of attitudinal affinity among FN voters, revealing them to be distinctive in their response to social and economic issues and at variance with other voters in their political priorities.

The 1980s drew an electoral map that would broadly reflect the FN vote thereafter, with support concentrated in departments of the north, north-east and east, in parts of the Ile-de-France and Rhône-Alpes regions, and across the Mediterranean littoral. These are largely the most urbanised and industrialised departments of France, with the most severe socio-economic problems, the highest levels in places of recorded crime, and the highest concentrations of non-European immigrants. Though studies of voting patterns at sub-departmental and intra-urban levels found that the FN vote could not always be correlated with the immediate presence of immigrants, FN voters consistently cited immigration (linked to law and order, and more loosely to unemployment) as their foremost concern. While the analysis offered in these chapters confirms the geographical pattern of FN voting outlined above, it also considers the FN's progressive implantation in areas where immigration was not a determining factor. In the 1988 presidential election, Le Pen exceeded 10 per cent in 76 of France's 96 metropolitan departments; in 2002, he achieved this in 93 departments (rising to 95 in the second round). Immigration and law and order were unarguably the FN's two most electorally profitable themes, but it learned to feed off disenchantment of different sorts, whether over specific issues (unemployment, taxation, Europe, globalisation) or through rejection of other parties. The growth in support from workers (especially blue-collar), the unemployed, and those classing themselves as disadvantaged was the most significant development within the FN's electorate, making it by the mid-1990s the leading party of the working class in France. This traditionally left-leaning constituency combined with voters from the traditionally right-leaning sector of shopkeepers, artisans and small entrepreneurs to give the FN electorate a distinctive character and set the party the challenge of adapting its policies to a socio-economically hybrid support base.

The FN's successive programmes are examined to reveal a number of distinct phases of evolution. The 1990s saw two particularly important shifts: the first, from a neo-liberal to a protectionist and (in some aspects) welfarist agenda; the second, from measured pro-Europeanism to outright anti-Europeanism. After the fall of the Berlin Wall in 1989 and the Maastricht referendum in 1992, Europe replaced the collapsed Soviet Union for the FN as the prime threat to France, an open door to immigration being only one element of that perceived threat. At the same time, the increase in support for the FN among the most economically vulnerable sections of society was accompanied by the party's conversion, in some of its rhetoric at least, to the politics of social welfare. This was a major departure from the unrestrained neo-liberalism articulated in the 1980s (and now associated with the spectre of Europe), returning the FN to a position closer to its 'third way' posture of the 1970s. It is argued that such shifts on issues as critical as the economy and Europe reveal incoherence at the heart of the FN's programme, the price of promoting electoral opportunism over rigorous policy.

The one arena in which the FN was called upon to make the transition from policy to practice was in its government of four sizeable towns after 1995. Examination of this experiment in local government shows FN mayors straining at the bounds of constitutional legality on some issues and cutting a more moderate, if studiously populist, image on others. The election to municipal power even on this limited scale marked a further stage in the institutionalisation of the FN, while the re-election of three of these four mayors in 2001 was arguably of greater significance still than their initial election.

The exercise of real power by the FN at the municipal level aroused only a fraction of the consternation provoked by Le Pen's victory over Prime Minister Jospin to qualify for the presidential run-off in 2002. Chapter 10 provides an analysis of this 'seismic' event, a vindication of the electoralist strategy embraced by the FN leader over 30 years. Behind the national angst generated by his 0.68 per cent margin over Jospin, however, lay other statistics that scarcely suggested the Republic was in danger: a gain by Le Pen of less than 2.5 per cent of the vote in 14 years, an increase since 1988 of fewer than half a million votes from an electoral register exceeding 41 million. The FN leader was propelled in 2002, it is argued, less by his own dynamism than by the complacency and miscalculation of others; and there was not the remotest prospect that he would be elected President of the Republic.

The book concludes with a chapter considering events and elections since 2002. Chapter 11 casts a view back across the period covered by the preceding chapters and identifies some of the potential opportunities and obstacles in the path of an FN anticipating its *après*-Le Pen. As a point of conclusion this is apt, since Le Pen incarnates not only the history of the FN but largely that of the French far right throughout the entire post-war period. From the early attempts to regroup in the aftermath of Vichy, through the series of causes espoused over the next two decades (Indo-China, *Algérie Française*, Poujadism, the Tixier-Vignancour campaign), to the formation of the FN and the sustained pursuit of electoral legitimacy, Le Pen has been a constant presence. Noted in Paris police files in 1948 for hawking the Maurrassian, pro-Pétain weekly *Aspects de la France*, he played a part in 1951 in the election campaign of Jacques Isorni's Pétainist UNIR party. More than half a century later, Le Pen is a faithful witness still to the memory of Vichy and, in his political longevity and enduring importance, the principal protagonist of this book.

A word on terminology

There are two preliminary problems with entitling a book *The Extreme Right in France*. The first relates to range, the second to classification. In the period covered by this book, the French extreme right has been host to hundreds of movements, many of them small, short-lived and born from mutations of others. It has been estimated that, over the course of the Algerian War alone, as many as a thousand extreme-right groups jostled within the *Algérie Française* lobby. The most prominent of these figure among the dizzying array of parties, movements and propagandist organs inventoried by Henry Coston in 1960.[6] In their more recent survey, Jean-Yves Camus and René Monzat recorded several hundred extreme-right parties, clubs and associations, together with a prodigious output of periodicals.[7]

This book deals with only a small sample of such movements, selected on account of their significance, their influence or their representative value. It is concerned primarily with movements having some discernible impact on wider politics in France; it is not concerned with the many arcane sects that have shown an astonishing capacity to flourish on the extreme right, or with those radical activist groups which operate on the fringes of legality. In a report to the Interior Ministry in January 2005, prompted by an escalation in racist and anti-Semitic attacks in 2004, French intelligence services listed some 20 such activist groups, deploying up to 3,500 militants in all and divided into the five categories of skinheads, racists, ultra-nationalists, neo-Nazis and hooligans. Subsequent moves by the government to impose banning orders on these groups observed a clear category distinction between them, as 'a threat and a danger' to the constitutional order, and the FN as a legitimate political party 'compatible with the values of the Republic'.[8]

This raises the second preliminary problem, that of classification. Defining political movements on the extreme right is notoriously difficult, the more so when such movements exhibit, as they often do, characteristics that can be ascribed to quite different political traditions. A relatively recent review of the literature on right-wing extremism found 26 distinct definitions combining 58 defining features.[9] As such definitions have proliferated, so too have the terms employed to encapsulate them. A brief list of terms applied by commentators to the FN alone – 'extreme-right', 'far-right', 'radical-right', 'new radical-right', 'nationalist', 'populist', 'national-populist', 'neo-populist', 'radical right-wing populist', 'fascist', 'neo-fascist', 'third wave right-wing extremist' – highlights the problem of affixing labels that are not themselves tightly sealed to movements that can respond to some or all of these descriptors in varying degrees.[10] It also anticipates the difficulties that may be encountered when considering a range of such movements over a span of time.

With the caveat, then, that there exist countless and very diverse extreme-right movements in the period under study here, it is proposed to use the collective term 'extreme right', or 'far right',[11] as encompassing figures, movements and currents of thought that display some degree of commonality and a core of shared dispositions. The FN itself provides the model of a broadly unified party forged from a wide diversity of component tendencies. While the inadequacy of the term 'extreme right' to convey any nuance or reservation is acknowledged, it offers the most comprehensive cover term for the range of parties, movements and figures considered in this study. The latter fall essentially into three types: those which openly proclaim their extreme-right heritage or evince a sufficiently authoritarian, anti-democratic or ethnocentrically nationalist/Europeanist character to qualify themselves outright; those which have their origins in the anti-republican tradition even if they move towards a more democratically Republican posture, or whose anti-liberal, anti-egalitarian elements remain so pronounced as to outweigh more mainstream conservative characteristics (such movements or figures, while paying lip service to democracy, may seek to delegitimise its processes and institutions); and those to which commentators have applied the label 'extreme-right' in sufficient numbers and with sufficient insistence that they require to be considered, and re-evaluated, in that context. Two features can be said at the outset to be common to all of these movements and figures, at some point in their development at least: the strength of their opposition to certain left-wing political values, whether it be expressed in anti-republican or anti-communist form (or both); and the fact that they are located outside the moderate political consensus and defined as 'extreme-right' or 'far-right' in relation to a mainstream-right norm and coalition bloc (traditionally represented under the Fifth Republic by the Gaullist and centrist parties, and designated in this book by the term 'centre-right').

The borders defining this spatial differentiation, however, are not fixed. In a French and west European political environment where liberal democracy is now effectively unchallenged, far-right and far-left parties, if they are to have any prospect of success, must adapt and appeal to voters beyond their own marginal constituencies. From its creation in 1972, the FN renounced both the organised violence and the 'revolutionary' discourse of previous extreme-right movements and projected itself as a conventional party in search of democratic legitimacy; though it was still firmly positioned on the extreme right, this set it apart even from its immediate predecessor, Ordre Nouveau. As the FN has sustained its engagement with the democratic order, renewing its personnel, modifying its programme over time and gaining a large electoral audience, and as other parties have echoed or co-opted parts of the FN's agenda, the gravitational centre of much political debate in France has shifted and with it the border separating 'moderate' from 'extreme' right. This closing of the distance between the FN and the centre-right parties, together with the process of institutionalisation which Le Pen and the FN have undergone since the mid-1980s and their consolidation of a sociologically diverse support base around issues of central public concern, make the FN an extreme-right party that has become progressively less 'extreme'. This poses problems for classifying the FN today, leading some commentators to speak of its 'normalisation' and effective integration into the constitutional culture of contemporary France, while others continue to view it as an unreformed 'fascist' party. It is beyond the purview of this study to enter the fascism(s) debate and venture a further definition to add to the many already forged by scholars dedicated to conceptualising fascism as a political 'genus', or 'ideal type', independent of historical moment; but the discussion will draw in places on a number of defining features which, by scholarly consensus, can be ascribed to inter-war fascism as the essential paradigm and which argue for more rigour than is applied at times in the use by some commentators of the epithet 'fascist'.

The Vichy regime, Poujadism, the Nouvelle Droite, and other movements and currents examined here pose similar problems of classification to those presented by the FN. As will be seen, each of these is problematic enough to define within its own terms to prompt wariness of any common designation; and

Part I

Lost opportunities and lost causes

1 The Vichy regime

A laboratory for the extreme right

The path of collaboration

In May and June 1940, the lightning invasion of France by German panzer divisions brought about the worst military catastrophe in the country's history. In the shock of defeat, parliament voted its own disempowerment and, in search of an *homme providentiel*, vested full constituent powers on 10 July 1940 in the First World War hero of Verdun, Marshal Philippe Pétain. This was not a vote of confidence in what history would come to know as the Vichy regime, but rather an expression of support for the paternalistic 84-year-old chosen to head it, with even a majority of Socialists and Radicals in favour.[1]

Pétain's route to power had been as short as France's to defeat. He had been brought into Paul Reynaud's government as deputy premier on 18 May 1940, within a week of the German advance across the Meuse; on 16 June, with military collapse imminent, he had replaced Reynaud at the head of a crisis government. Foreclosing the prospect of further military resistance, the new premier's immediate priority was to conclude an armistice with Hitler in breach of a Franco-British agreement struck some weeks earlier that no such negotiation would be sought. The armistice saw France divided into two zones: a *zone occupée* centred on Paris and including the more developed northern half of the country together with the entire Atlantic seaboard, and an unoccupied southern *zone libre* to be governed from the spa town of Vichy in the central Allier department.[2]

The 24 clauses of the armistice convention laid the contractual grounds for collaboration. Signed on 22 June 1940 in the same railway carriage at Rethondes where the armistice had been dictated to Germany in 1918, its terms were onerous and humiliating. The French army, navy and air force were to be demobilised, with the retention of only a small armistice army for the maintenance of order in the unoccupied zone and a limited naval force for the defence of overseas territories. Though the docked fleet was to remain in French hands, aerodromes, military installations and armaments were to be handed over to German control. The French administration in the occupied zone was required to cooperate fully with the German military authorities; the French treasury would assume all maintenance costs for the troops of occupation; and, most infamously, France would agree to surrender on demand German nationals who had taken refuge there from the Nazi regime. As surety, more than 1.5 million French prisoners of war would remain in German camps, until it later became expedient to trade some of them against a French volunteer – then conscript – labour force.

From abject defeat, the new regime in embryo extracted its own putative victory. In his radio broadcast of 25 June 1940, Pétain announced that much of the country was to be 'temporarily occupied', but 'honour has been saved' and 'France will be administered only by Frenchmen under a government that remains free'.[3] Soon the term 'occupation', with its connotations of defeat and passivity, would give way to a quite different term suggesting that France could remain at the helm of its own destiny. In a radio broadcast of 30 October 1940, Pétain reported on his recent meeting with Hitler as 'the first step towards our country's recovery', exhorting his listeners 'in the interests of French unity' to follow him down 'the path of collaboration'. Four months on from total military and political collapse, France had contrived its salvation as self-appointed partner in the Nazi project of constructing a 'new European order'.[4]

The foremost concern of those who had sought an armistice was that France should be spared the indignity of 'Polonisation', or rule by an appointed governor. Despite the demarcation line between occupied and unoccupied France, the French government retained nominal authority over the whole of France and its overseas territories (with the exception of Alsace-Lorraine, where three departments were annexed and run by *Gauleiter*). In his broadcast of 30 October 1940, Pétain acknowledged the 'numerous obligations' imposed on a defeated France, but presented the paramount objective as having been secured: 'At least she remains sovereign.'[5] By contrast with other countries under Nazi occupation, a semblance of French national sovereignty was thus preserved – for a time. In November 1942, the southern zone too would be occupied, reducing the whole of France to a satellite of the Third Reich, despite the continued pretence of an 'Etat Français' governed from Vichy.

From democracy to despotism

By the time Pétain shook Hitler's hand to seal the policy of collaboration at Montoire on 24 October 1940, the parliamentary Republic in France had given way to a profoundly anti-democratic regime. The 'National Revolution'[6] ushered in by Pétain owed much to a French right-wing tradition of anti-parliamentarism dating back to the Revolution of 1789. It repudiated the liberal, humanistic rationalism of the Enlightenment and preached a reactionary, authoritarian nationalism. It drew inspiration in particular from the ideas of Charles Maurras and his Action Française movement, with their sustained assault on the democratic values and institutions of the Third Republic as inimical to the culture, traditions and interests of the French nation.

The change of regime was signified in the replacement of the universalist principles '*Liberté, Egalité, Fraternité*' by the slogan '*Travail, Famille, Patrie*' ('Work, Family, Motherland').[7] For the Vichy authorities, these represented the natural, concrete, time-honoured bonds that held organic communities together, as opposed to fictitious abstractions. What sense, ironised Pétain, could 'liberty – the abstract concept of liberty – have for an unemployed worker or a ruined small employer in 1940, except the liberty to suffer helplessly amidst a defeated nation?' Equality – that 'false idea of a natural equality between men' – was scorned in similar terms as a vacuous notion that had no place within a regime proclaiming itself 'authoritarian and hierarchical'.[8] The various strata of the democratic state were removed, with the dissolution of elected departmental and (in all but the smallest communes) municipal councils. Elite appointments by decree replaced elections, since responsibility in public life was now to be determined by 'weighing up value' rather than merely 'counting votes'.[9]

The constitutional law of 10 July 1940 consigning full political authority to Pétain marked the passage from the Third Republic to the Etat Français.[10] It was adopted by a National Assembly of deputies and senators improvised in the Grand Casino at Vichy. The overwhelming vote of 569 to 80, with 17 abstentions, was the final act of a 70-year-old Republic.[11] This was followed on 11 July by constitutional acts to suspend both chambers of parliament indefinitely, depose the sitting President (Albert Lebrun) by abolishing his function, install Pétain formally as '*chef de l'Etat français*', and affirm the new Head of State's extensive legislative and executive powers. These gave him authority to appoint and dismiss all members of the government, promulgate and implement legislation, control key appointments of state, determine budgetary and fiscal policy, negotiate international agreements, and command the armistice army. Declaration of war was the only initiative that Pétain could not undertake without the approval of parliament. In a further constitutional act of 12 July, Pétain arrogated to himself the power even to designate his own successor (namely the *vice-président du Conseil*, Pierre Laval). As his *chef de cabinet* observed, the head of Vichy would shortly come to enjoy 'more powers than Louis XIV'.[12] So much that had been achieved in France since 1789 (and that had been celebrated only a year before in the 150th anniversary of the Revolution)[13] was undone at a stroke, with government under Pétain effected by diktat. To his powers as supreme legislator and head of the executive were added special judicial prerogatives, making Pétain the very embodiment of the despot as conceived by Montesquieu in the mid-eighteenth century.

The symbol of the new regime was the *Francisque*, a double axe-head on a marshal's baton, linking Pétain with the ancient warrior Gauls and serving as the decoration bestowed by Vichy on its favoured servants.[14] The emphasis on service and fidelity in the oath sworn by recipients of the *Francisque* reflected the shift in official discourse from the notion of rights to that of duties. In morality at large, the regime sought to foster a new spirit of asceticism, preaching solidarity and sacrifice and denouncing the pleasure-seeking ethos of liberal individualism. Accordingly, the Declaration of the Rights of Man and of the Citizen, the founding document of the French Republic dating from 1789, was replaced by newly drafted Principles of the Community. Sixteen in number, these aped the format of the Declaration, with the first setting the tone: 'Nature bestows upon man his fundamental rights, but these are guaranteed only by the communities around him: the family by which he is raised, the profession by which he earns his living, the nation by which he is protected.'[15] Such precepts, together with a welter of Pétain's utterances collected in diverse publications, were invoked as a new moral code. René Jeanneret's *Maxims and Principles of Marshal Pétain Drawn from his Messages to the French People*, with its dictum for every day of the year, was a classic example of this quasi-catechismal genre.[16] The cult of *Maréchalisme* reached its apogee in the hymns to Pétain's glory and even the paraphrasing of the Lord's Prayer in his name (culminating in the plea: 'And deliver us from evil, oh Maréchal').[17]

Healthy minds and healthy bodies

The National Revolution was to take root in the schools. For those in power at Vichy, the war had been lost not so much on the battlefield as in the classroom, where French youth had been inculcated with a corruptive individualism at the hands of decadent primary school teachers. Appointed Minister of War in the government of Gaston Doumergue in 1934, Pétain claimed that he would have preferred the Education Ministry in order to 'deal with communist teachers' and reform an education system that was 'destroying State and society'.[18] In 1940, in his self-assigned role as national educator-in-chief, he seized his opportunity. Under Vichy, the teacher training institutes (*écoles normales d'instituteurs*), reviled as 'evil seminaries of democracy', were abolished, and a purge was undertaken of communists and other 'elements of disorder' within the teaching profession.[19] Those teachers who remained would be required to swear an oath of loyalty to Pétain. Schoolchildren were taught to honour the Marshal and encouraged in their millions to send him letters and drawings. The assiduity of his office in replying to these (with a personalised message and photograph of Pétain) signalled how seriously it took this aspect of its propagandist mission. As government and clergy propounded their shared ideals of order, discipline and duty, a close alliance of interest and ideology made the Church a pillar of the National Revolution and an important political player in France for the first time in over half a century. Religious instruction, banished by the secular laws of the 1880s, returned (for a time) to the curriculum; religious orders regained their right to teach; state subsidies were granted to Catholic schools; and crucifixes reappeared, alongside Pétain's portrait, in state schools.

The new moral hygiene was to be accompanied by a hygiene of the body. Measures were taken to promote physical education and sports in schools. Vichy did not create a single youth movement on the Nazi model, but it placed a premium on reforming youth culture. Two notable movements, the Chantiers de la Jeunesse (Youth Work Sites) and Compagnons de France (Companions of France), were launched with the purpose of instilling in the young an ethic of duty and service.[20] Structured along quasi-militaristic lines, these movements organised camping, hiking, sporting and community activities, and exalted the virtues of self-discipline, hard work and the traditional rural life. A surrogate form of military service, the eight-month spell on the Chantiers de la Jeunesse, became compulsory for all 20-year-olds in the unoccupied zone, while both the Compagnons and the Chantiers were banned from the occupied zone as potentially dangerous expressions of chauvinistic fervour. Prominent among youth movements north of the demarcation line were the Jeunes de l'Europe Nouvelle (Youth of the New Europe) and the Jeunes du Maréchal (Marshal's Youth). Drawn largely from lycée and university students, these were small but strongly collaborationist movements evincing National-Socialist sympathies and admiration for the *Hitlerjugend*.[21]

While measures were set in place to combat symptoms of social degeneracy such as venereal disease and alcoholism, youth affairs were entrusted to such paragons of sporting prowess as the pelota specialist Jean Ybarnégaray and the tennis champion Jean Borotra. The family was invested with a pre-eminent role as the 'essential cell and very foundation of the social edifice'.[22] Family mores were centred on a celebration of motherhood, with mothers of three or more children being granted a priority card for first access to some public services. Similarly, fathers of large families were favoured in the workplace in terms of job prospects and, following the statute on state employees of September 1941, pay. Draconian legislation was introduced against abortion, with abortionists facing life imprisonment and even the death penalty; divorce was made more difficult and forbidden within the first three years of marriage; and a law was passed barring married women from employment in the public sector.[23] At the same time, Pétain sought to construct national unity through a paternalist discourse that projected him not just as *chef* but also as *père*.

In the early days of the regime, all of these concerns were brought together in a single Ministry for Youth, the Family and Sport under Ybarnégaray. In December 1942, a law of a quite different tenor was passed obliging couples to undergo a pre-marital medical examination to screen for congenital defects. This was the most overtly eugenicist measure implemented by the Vichy regime, which described it as 'only a first step' that might eventually be extended. It never was. Fear of depopulation kept the emphasis of the regime firmly on procreation, despite voices calling for a full-blown programme of interventionist eugenics. The pre-marital examination law remained largely symbolic, since no secondary legislation was introduced to prevent questionable marriages, and it was left to the 'conscience and responsibility' of couples to determine whether or not to have children; but it occupied a space where two of Vichy's foremost concerns – the family and public health – continued to intersect after youth had been relocated to a separate secretariat within the Ministry of Education.[24]

The collective health of society too had to be restored. This would begin in the workplace, where worsening labour relations and the rise of the industrial left under the Third Republic were held to have sapped national unity. In order to make France again 'what she should never have ceased to be, an essentially agricultural nation',[25] incentives were introduced to encourage a return to the land and the artisan's workshop. The economy as a whole was reorganised along broadly corporatist lines, with 'organisation committees' taking control of each sector and the state adopting the role of honest broker between professional interests.[26] The workplace was to become a theatre of unity rather than division, the foundation on which a 'balanced and harmonious' France would be rebuilt. Class and interest-group affiliations were to be replaced by loyalty to *métier*. As Pétain pointedly declared in his May Day address of 1942, 'There is no possibility of class struggle in the artisan's workshop.'[27]

Redefining the national community

Just as the Vichy regime sought to rediscover 'Frenchness', it sought also to preserve it from contamination by alien influences. The assimilationist model of French republicanism was inverted. Legislation was introduced as early as July 1940 to exclude naturalised French citizens from public office and prominent professions. With strictly defined exceptions (notably for those who had fought in the French army and their immediate offspring), naturalised citizens were progressively disqualified from serving as government officials, civil servants, teachers, doctors, dentists, pharmacists, lawyers, vets, and even architects.[28] As Pétain intoned in his address of 13 August 1940, 'too many freshly made Frenchmen' had 'wormed their way' into positions of responsibility in a public administration which now had to be 'purged'.[29] At the same time, a commission was set up to review all naturalisations granted since 1927, when procedures for acquiring French nationality had been relaxed. The commission examined some 500,000 dossiers; it removed citizenship from over 15,000 people, some 6,300 of them Jews who would be exposed subsequently to easy deportation as a result.[30] It says much about the complexity of assigning guilt or innocence to participation in Vichy's programme that the chief prosecutor at Pétain's trial in 1945, Judge André Mornet, served on this commission.[31]

In a diluted version of the Nuremberg Laws of September 1935, the exclusionary legislation imposed on naturalised citizens was soon extended to French Jews. Again with strictly defined exceptions for *anciens combattants*, this barred Jews from positions of authority in the political hierarchy, civil service, judiciary and armed forces, and from 'professions allowing them to exert a manifestly pernicious influence over our public administration, public opinion and youth', notably teaching and the media.[32] Separate legislation imposed employment quotas (normally of 2 per cent) on Jews across a range of liberal professions (doctors, lawyers, pharmacists, architects and others), while a 3 per cent quota was set for Jews in higher education.[33] A special office, the Commissariat-General for Jewish Affairs (CGQJ), was set up in March 1941 to coordinate anti-Jewish policy. Its first head, Xavier Vallat, saw himself as a surgeon called upon to 'take up the scalpel' and excise a Jewish influence which had brought France 'to the brink of death'.[34] After his first six months in office, Vallat could point to some 3,000 civil servants who had been removed from their posts, with a similar order of dismissals from the media and other influential professions.[35] Official government figures for March 1942 showed that the majority of dismissals in the public sector were of teachers, with 685 sacked in the unoccupied zone and 426 in the occupied zone. In all, by March 1942, 3,424 Jews had been dismissed from the public service in France, with a further 2,531 in Algeria.[36]

On 18 October 1940, a memorandum from the Ministry of Foreign Affairs at Vichy to the French ambassador in the United States sought to justify the regime's earliest anti-Semitic legislation before a potentially hostile American public. The memorandum lamented the 'preponderant influence' exercised by Jews in France and stressed the urgency of removing from public life 'elements whose racial characteristics make them dangerous when they become too closely involved in politics and public administration'.[37] That a document intended to assuage concern could refer to Jews in these terms indicates the depth of the anti-Semitism at work in Vichy. The definition of Jewishness on which the new exclusionary measures were based was overtly racial, applying to 'any person with three grandparents of the Jewish race or two grandparents of the same race if also married to a Jew'.[38] This was a reiteration of the essential definition of Jewishness to be found in the 1935 Nuremberg Laws on Citizenship and Race. It was to be distinguished from the German ordinance of 27 September 1940 instituting a register of Jews in the occupied zone, which (in deference to French public opinion) did not use the term 'race' and defined Jewishness instead by religious practice.[39]

While French Jews were subject to two major statutes (of October 1940 and June 1941) and a host of discriminatory laws and decrees, prefects were empowered to intern 'foreigners of the Jewish race' in 'special camps'.[40] Internment camps had been used under the Third Republic to hold refugees from the civil war in Spain and other asylum seekers. Under Vichy, the network of camps was greatly extended as foreign Jews found themselves interned in large numbers alongside Spanish republicans, other displaced foreigners, political opponents (notably communists), common criminals and suspects. By the end of 1940, the internment camps of France housed some 50–60,000 inmates, often in atrocious conditions.[41]

The CGQJ was empowered to 'instigate against Jews all policing measures dictated by the national interest'.[42] Once equipped with its brief to enforce anti-Jewish legislation and oversee a programme of economic expropriation of Jews ('Aryanisation'), it operated with equal purpose in both zones, drawing foreign and French Jews throughout France into the five-stage process described by Philippe Burrin as 'registration, despoliation, segregation, concentration, deportation'.[43] One of the CGQJ's first tasks in summer 1941 was to conduct a census of Jews in the unoccupied zone, following an earlier census in the occupied zone. The register to which this gave rise prepared part of the ground for arrests carried out by Vichy police in summer and autumn 1942, as the unoccupied zone yielded up some 10,000 of the 42,000 Jews deported from France in that year. In the occupied zone too, French police, under the orders of the Secretary-General for Police, René Bousquet, played the major role in arresting Jews – most infamously in the *rafle du Vel d'Hiv*. This was the round-up in Paris on 16–17 July 1942 of almost 13,000 Jews, the majority of whom were held for several days in the Vélodrome d'Hiver sports stadium before being deported via French camps to Auschwitz.[44] At such a price, the retention of French control over policing was assured by a regime concerned to preserve every morsel of administrative 'sovereignty' to which it could cling.

Almost all of the Jews deported from France in 1942 were foreign. This was part of the deal brokered by Laval and Bousquet with the German authorities. As Laval declared to the Council of Ministers, a distinction had to be observed 'between French Jews and the rubbish sent here by the Germans themselves'.[45] Vichy therefore contrived to meet its initial quota from foreign Jews interned in French camps, other foreign Jews arrested in round-ups, and denaturalised Jews.[46] In this way, the regime practised a grotesque form of 'national preference' which saw the preservation of French Jews as an issue of national sovereignty and the victimisation of foreign Jews as a policy both less reprehensible and less likely to cause public disquiet.[47] Not that public reaction was the paramount consideration. To objections raised by religious leaders Bousquet replied dismissively that it was 'the role of public opinion to register feelings, and that of government to make choices'.[48]

The paranoid character of the Vichy regime was evident from the outset. In August 1940, legislation was implemented to outlaw secret societies and specifically Freemasons, towards whom French Catholic conservatives had long harboured animosity and suspicion. All state employees in mainland France and the overseas territories were now required to swear that they had no connection with a secret society and that they would never join one.[49] Measures were also enacted against other potentially traitorous elements within French society. As Pétain asserted in a radio broadcast of 9 October 1940, 'the search for those responsible for our disaster' was one of the first steps to be taken in the 'purification' and 'reconstruction' of France.[50] Those who in the run-up to war had led France politically (Blum, Daladier, Reynaud, Mandel) and militarily (Gamelin, La Chambre) were arrested and tried. Significantly, the period under investigation at their brief trial was 1936–40, focusing Vichy's revanchism on the left-wing Popular Front government and its aftermath and allowing Pétain's own record as Minister of War in 1934 to escape scrutiny.[51]

Those tried for treason by Vichy were held to belong to that community which Charles Maurras decried as 'internal foreigners'.[52] Through his Action Française, Maurras propounded an embattled nationalism which envisaged France at the mercy of a variety of aliens, denouncing immigrants, Jews, foreign interests and unpatriotic Frenchmen as the causes of social disorder and national decline. The Manichaean terms in which Vichy in turn conceived of its mission in this respect were spelled out by Pétain in August 1940: 'There is no possible neutrality between truth and falsehood, between good and evil, between health and illness, between order and disorder, between France and anti-France.'[53]

The National Revolution: a paradoxical project

The National Revolution, in sum, was to restore order and greatness to France, promoting national unity to the detriment of individualism, authority to that of

The Vichy regime 23

liberalism, hierarchy to that of equality. As a political regime, Vichy struck out into territory uncharted by a French history forged through monarchy, empire and republic. Despite the strong Maurrassian influence at work in Vichy, there was no question of going back to the monarchy or any other *ancien régime*; nor was the 'new order' to be brought about, in Pétain's words, through 'servile imitation of foreign experiments'.[54] But where foreign experiments were concerned, it was clear where Pétain's preference lay. 'Liberalism, capitalism, collectivism, are in France foreign, imported products which France restored to herself quite naturally rejects', he argued, declaring himself more ready to accept 'as a part of our national heritage the national-socialist idea of the primacy of toil and its essential reality as compared to the fiction of monetary values'.[55]

The objective, in principle at least, was to fashion a new political and social regime overseen by a new governing elite. Here Vichy would quickly succumb to an unyielding paradox: that of seeking to construct a 'new order' on the basis of age-old French values. The gravamen of the criticism levelled against Pétain's regime by the more radical proponents of a French fascism would be its back-ward-looking character, its populist nostalgia for ancestral traditions and failure to generate an invigorated new society turned towards the future. In its rural Catholic emphases and mythology of a lost heritage to be restored, it owed more to the 'Estado Novo' of Salazar's Portugal than to Italian Fascism or German National Socialism.[56] From the outset, the National Revolution heralded itself as a '*re*making of France', a project of '*re*construction' and '*re*juvenation', a '*re*storation of the State', a '*re*discovery of the finest traditions', a '*re*turn' to the rural France of former times.[57] This was hardly the language of fascist millenarianism.

A further, equally unyielding paradox lay in Vichy's aspiration to effect this return to the sources of a pure Frenchness – to 'think exclusively French', as the future deputy head of government, Admiral François Darlan, would urge[58] – while bowed under the yoke of German occupation. In late 1941, the propaganda office of the Secretariat-General for Youth issued a booklet to instruct French youth in the National Revolution. Consisting largely of extracts from Pétain's speeches, this exhorted France's young to 'reconstitute the national soul' and rebuild the nation's past grandeur 'on the unshakable rock of French unity'. It also acknowledged, however, that little could be achieved while France remained bound by its armistice obligations to Germany and Italy. Only if the Germans knew how to 'rise above their victory', it meekly conceded, would the French be allowed to 'rise above our defeat'.[59]

In the public discourse of the regime from the start, there was no recognition of these inherent contradictions. While the outgoing Under-Secretary of State for Defence, General de Gaulle, projected a lone voice of resistance from London, Pétain's incoming deputy head of government, Laval, set out with stark clarity the direction for France: 'Since parliamentary democracy undertook and lost the fight against Nazism and Fascism, it must disappear. A new, bold, authoritarian, social and national regime must take its place. [. . .] There is no other way forward than through loyal collaboration with Germany and Italy.'[60]

Laying the ground for Vichy

The Vichy regime did not materialise *ex nihilo*. In its guiding principles and policies, Pétain's administration drew on a long tradition of opposition to the
parliamentary Republic. Prior to 1870, France had known only two brief experiments in Republican government (1792–1804 and 1848–52). In its earliest form,
anti-republicanism had expressed itself in calls for the restoration of the
monarchy; by the later nineteenth century, however, the competing claims of
Bourbon, Orleanist and Bonapartist dynasties made monarchism a complex, and
ultimately self-defeating, cause.[61] After the collapse of the Second Empire in the
Franco-Prussian War (1870–71) and the declaration of the Third Republic, the
anti-parliamentary right mounted a virulent opposition to the regime, deriving
its ideological impetus less from monarchism than from an authoritarian nationalism infused with desire for revenge against Germany, whose annexation of
large tracts of Alsace and Lorraine struck at the heart of French national pride.

France's recovery, it was argued on the nationalist right, could never be
achieved under a corrupt and enfeebled Republic. Paul Déroulède, founder in
1882 of the ultra-nationalist Ligue des Patriotes (League of Patriots), decried
parliamentarians as the enemy within, declaring that 'before liberating Alsace
and Lorraine', it was 'necessary to liberate France'.[62] The short-lived populist
adventure of Boulangism in the late 1880s drew its sustenance from the same
source. The figurehead of revanchist nationalism, General Georges Boulanger,
denounced the ills of the parliamentary Republic and (a century before Jean-
Marie Le Pen) called for a strong presidential regime and a plebiscitary
democracy based on popular referenda. Pope Leo XIII's injunction to the cardi-
nals of France to reconcile themselves to the Republic, and the condemnation of
Action Française by his successor Pius XI, diminished the legitimacy of anti-
parliamentarism among some French Catholic monarchists in particular,[63] but
not among those most committed to seeing democracy eradicated.

At a time when both Darwinian and Pasteurian ideas were in the ascendant, a
metaphoric discourse was fashioned whereby the health of the nation state could
be likened to the health of the living organism. Advances in the knowledge of
disease causation and management brought a new dimension to nationalist
discourse, figuring the nation as an organism susceptible to infection from
'foreign bodies'. 'A people', wrote the sociologist Gustave Le Bon, was 'an
organism forged from the past', an organism whose health was determined by its
'mental constitution' and the 'institutions, beliefs and arts' that flowed from it.[64]
Within the perspectives of psychological and racial determinism which this
opened up (and which were developed by others such as Jules Soury and Georges
Vacher de Lapouge), the anti-parliamentary right could argue that liberal
democracy was a foreign graft onto the French 'organism', a vitiating influence
undermining the nation in its struggle for survival.[65]

In keeping with this rationale, the intellectual ground for Vichy was laid by a
number of writers and propagandists who peddled variations on Maurras'
theme of a Republic sold out to 'four confederated estates' – Jews, Freemasons,
Protestants and wogs (*métèques*). The concepts and language of pathology were

deployed as images of disease and decomposition abounded in polemics against the Third Republic. Edouard Drumont and Maurice Barrès cursed the 'pestilential' nature of parliamentary democracy, the latter likening its effects on the French people to those of 'alcoholism, lead-poisoning or syphilis'. In the interwar years, Pierre Drieu La Rochelle would denounce the same 'syphilitic power' in France, while Léon Daudet portrayed parliamentarians as blood-sucking parasites on the body politic.[66] Colonel François de La Rocque, leader of the militantly nationalist ex-servicemen's Croix de Feu (Cross of Fire), railed against a government dying of 'poisoning' and a 'lying party system' that had entrusted power to 'custodians who were unworthy of their responsibilities'.[67] Early apologists of fascism in France such as Georges Valois joined in this chorus of vilification and called for a new regime led by a vigorous new elite. Thus too Marcel Bucard, head of the Francisme movement, who longed for the 'beneficent and salutary advent of the fascist Revolution'. Sending telegrams of solidarity to Mussolini and Hitler, the Francistes called for 'the establishment of fascism in France' and 'an entente with National-Socialist Germany' as the only way to overcome the decadence afflicting France.[68]

Closely allied to this theme of decadence was that of conspiracy, and in particular Jewish conspiracy, predicated on the notion of a France at the mercy of its internal – and therefore external – enemies.[69] The most infamous dramatisation of this paranoia was staged in the 1890s, when the Jewish army captain Alfred Dreyfus was wrongfully convicted of passing intelligence to the Germans. His trial, sentencing and subsequent acquittal galvanised an anti-Dreyfus alliance of militarists, nationalists, monarchists and militant Catholics, while some more rabidly anti-Semitic voices (such as the self-styled 'most anti-Jewish newspaper in France', *La Croix*) called for all Jews to be stripped of their citizenship.[70]

The Dreyfus affair gave political expression to an anti-Semitism that had been gaining ground in the late nineteenth century, aided by the popularising of race-science and Aryan mythology. It supplemented older forms of (religious and economic) anti-Semitism which had long been part of the public discourse in France. As Christophe Prochasson reminds us, anti-Semitism in *fin-de-siècle* France was just 'one opinion among many', with its place in 'the area of legitimate opinions that could be aired'.[71] And aired it was. Not least by that hero of the Socialist left and defender of Dreyfus, Jean Jaurès, who could still in 1898 denounce 'the power of the Jews' and draw a tight connection between 'the Jewish race', with its 'feverish desire for profit', and the 'exploitative, lying, corrupt and extortionate workings of capitalism'.[72]

This late nineteenth-century anti-Semitism found its most mordant expression in Edouard Drumont's *La France juive*, an anti-Semitic best-seller published in 1886 which by 1914 had run to its 200th edition. Drumont also used his newspaper, *La Libre Parole*, to insist on Dreyfus's guilt and to propagate the theme of an international Jewish conspiracy against France. With his assertion that 'Everything starts with the Jew, and everything comes back round to the Jew', Drumont offered an all-encompassing explanation for the evils of the modern world. For Drumont as for Barrès, Dreyfus's guilt was 'a question of race'; no further evidence was required. Maurras in turn saw in 'this providential anti-Semitism' not just a patriotic imperative but a means of binding French society, a sure point of reference around which national identity could be defined. Drumont's book would be re-issued in yet a further edition in 1941, when he would assume a sage-like status (hailed by Robert Brasillach as 'the brilliant precursor of a French national-socialism') in a France ready to derive government policy from his diatribes.[73]

The Dreyfus affair marked a watershed. A judicial case became a conflict between two entire value systems, liberal humanitarianism (championing justice and the rights of man) and reactionary nationalism (wedded to order, authority and *la raison d'Etat*). The rejection of anti-Semitism only became an imperative for the Republican left during and in the wake of the Dreyfus affair; conversely, its espousal now became a preserve of the nationalist right. Like the military capitulation at Sedan in 1870, the affair was interpreted by anti-Dreyfusards as a national humiliation. They saw the campaign mounted in defence of Dreyfus by some of France's intellectual and political elite as yet another symptom of the country's decadence. Those who, like Admiral Darlan, ascribed the weakness of the Republic to its 'Judaeo-Masonic political habits'[74] equated the consolidation of liberal democracy with instability and corruption (highlighted in the crash of the Catholic Union Générale bank in 1881, the Panama scandal of the 1890s and the Stavisky affair of the 1930s). Following the failures of President Mac-Mahon and General Boulanger to impose themselves as providential leaders, elements of the French right longed for a strong man to arrest the degeneracy induced by a parliamentary Republic that saw close on a hundred successive governments rise and fall with an average lifespan of a few months. In the 1930s, some argued the need for a Hitler or a Mussolini *à la française*; others called for a President in the mould of Salazar; yet others, more prescient, invoked the name of Marshal Pétain.[75]

What they witnessed instead was a Popular Front government set up in June 1936 and headed by France's first Jewish premier, the Socialist Léon Blum. A formerly prominent defender of Dreyfus, Blum led a coalition of left-wing and centre-left forces resolved to face down the threat of fascism at home and abroad. The fact that Blum and several members of his administration (notably the Education Minister, Jean Zay) were of Jewish descent offered a pretext for denouncing the disproportionate influence of Jews in government. With a Jewish father and a Protestant mother, Zay was not a Jew in strict terms nor even within the later Vichy definition of Jewishness; but as a Radical-Socialist and a Freemason too, he was, like Blum, easily portrayed as a suspect foreigner by the Catholic nationalist right.[76] 'France under the Jew', spat the headline of *L'Action Française* following the formation of Blum's first government on 4 June 1936.[77] In the same vein, the future head of Vichy's CGQJ, Xavier Vallat, publicly deplored the 'historic moment' when this 'ancient Gallo-Roman country' was for the first time to be governed by a 'subtle Talmudist'.[78] The journalist Jean-Pierre Maxence accused the Popular Front leader of being 'foreign to the last fibre of his being', while the extreme-right press around him engaged in a 'pogrom' which, as Michel Winock puts it, 'was still confined to paper'.[79]

The stimulus which Blum's premiership (1936–37, then again briefly in 1938) gave to anti-Semitism may be measured by the fascist intellectual Lucien Rebatet's observation, in *Je suis partout* of 1 April 1938: 'Anti-Semitism in France is enjoying a remarkably vigorous revival.'[80] Rebatet would later reflect on the years 1936 and 1937 as 'the golden age of invective' for this politico-literary weekly, 'one of the few healthy and robust cells within the nation capable of combating the bacillus' rampant under Blum.[81] Even when the Popular Front had run its course in autumn 1938, Blum remained an emblematic figure, berated in the extreme-right press as a rootless traitor to French national interests. The slogan 'Rather Hitler than Léon Blum' signified that, here at least, hatred of the 'Jewish Republic' finally outweighed that of another traditional enemy, Germany.[82] The writer Louis-Ferdinand Céline (Destouches), author in 1937 of the viciously anti-Semitic pamphlet *Bagatelles pour un massacre*, declared that he 'would prefer a dozen Hitlers' to one Blum, 'the worst enemy'.[83]

The 'divine surprise'

For some on the French extreme right, therefore, the German invasion and the collapse of the Third Republic were a victory to be savoured, a fitting backlash against the triumph of the parliamentary Republic and growing power of the left. The disaster of 1940 was seen as retribution in particular for the Popular Front and the emergence of the PCF as a significant parliamentary force. René Rémond sums up the counter-revolution effected overnight: 'No more elections, no more deliberative assemblies, no more political parties, no more freedom of the press or right of assembly: those who had never accepted [17]89 and liberalism had their revenge at last.'[84] Maurras greeted Pétain's leadership as an 'extraordinary surprise' with a 'divine' quality, while Rebatet rejoiced in a 'dream' come true, heralding 'the absolute obliteration of our past, such that there should be no vestige left of a Jewish, democratic France, with all its vileness and stupidity [. . .] in the France of the armistice, punished but purified'.[85] Others such as Pierre-Antoine Cousteau, a leading journalist with the *Je suis partout* team, would call unequivocally for 'Power to the fascists!' Reflecting in 1958 on his support for collaboration, Cousteau would explain this not as an opportunistic political stance but as the expression of an ideological conviction with an explicitly racist core: 'It was because I wanted the victory of Germany' as 'the last chance of the white man', while democracy represented quite simply 'the end of the white man'.[86]

Many of a less radical temper also found Pétain's regime to be more in tune with their sympathies than a parliamentary Republic run by careerist politicians and widely held to have failed.[87] The Republic – 'the old slut' (*la gueuse*), as it was crudely dubbed by its detractors – stood accused of political divisiveness, financial mismanagement and corruption, and of fostering individualism and social unrest. The writer Paul Claudel condemned the armistice as a 'terrible, shameful' event, particularly in its stipulation that France surrender its refugees; but he drew consolation from 'the end of this foul parliamentary regime that for years has been eating away at France like a generalized cancer. At least this is the end of the Popular Front, the CGT [a communist-led trade union], the processions with raised clenched fists, the manifestos signed by communists and Catholics alike, the foul tyranny of the bars, freemasons, foreigners, and little schoolmasters. At least, let us hope so!'[88] Even among resisters, including de Gaulle himself, the Third Republic could claim few advocates in its defence.[89]

In its initial phase, by contrast, the Vichy administration commanded massive popular sympathy, or at least acquiescence.[90] In particular, it attracted the support of those conservative forces for whom 'the Republic was no longer conservative enough'. These included 'an appreciable fraction of nonsalaried social groups (farm owners and operators, heads of business, shopkeepers and artisans, members of the professions) and "cadres", a smaller percentage of public and trade-union officials, office workers, and independent workers'.[91] One can add to these the greater part of the Church and military hierarchies, who viewed with consternation the rise of the left-wing parties, especially the PCF. To such groups, Vichy offered the preservation of a social order that had long been stable but was now under threat. In that spirit, Pétain was glorified as the embodiment of traditional France, a quasi-monarchical, quasi-mystical symbol of national unity above divisive politics.

Such, at least, was the fiction. In reality, the new *rassembleur* lost no time in announcing that the disaster of June 1940 was 'simply the reflection, on a military level, of the weaknesses and defects of the old political regime'.[92] Going further, Maurras' *L'Action Française* newspaper proposed that 'a stake should be erected to burn the declaration of the Rights of man together with the works of Rousseau, Kant and Blum'. Embodying 'all the Jewish vices', the latter was cast as the very personification of culpability, the man who had 'consciously and satanically laid the ground for our defeat', who had through his social legislation (the 40-hour working week, collective bargaining, paid holidays) 'injected the virus of laziness into the blood of a people'.[93] To compound his guilt, Blum had also been prominent among the 80 who voted against granting full powers to Pétain on 10 July 1940. He would be the main defendant when those judged responsible for the debacle were arraigned before a special court at Riom in February 1942, in a trial which the Germans quickly suspended as being more detrimental than helpful to the collaborationist cause.

Though technically still an enemy, Nazi Germany was reconfigured – in line with a hasty redefinition of French national interest – as the foundation block of a new Europe and, after June 1941, a bastion against the Bolshevik peril. It was within this Europeanist perspective that Pétain justified his meeting with Hitler to agree the principle of collaboration in October 1940; within this perspective, too, that Laval notoriously declared, in June 1942, 'I desire victory for Germany because, without it, Bolshevism would become established everywhere. France cannot remain indifferent in the face of the immensity of the sacrifices made by Germany in order to build a Europe in which we must take our place.'[94]

The securing of an armistice in June 1940 had seemed to confirm the Marshal's protective impulses, while the cult that grew up around him was the closest occupied France came to forging a form of national unity. The popular image of Vichy as a rampart against the worst excesses of military occupation and the conduit to a new Franco-German partnership placated public opinion only for a time, however. The popularity of the regime ebbed away as early as autumn 1940, when relief at the cessation of hostilities was replaced by the aggravations of occupation.[95] These would be exacerbated by the occupation of the southern zone in November 1942 and by German demands for French conscript labour from February 1943, giving impetus to de Gaulle's self-proclaimed government-in-exile and the Resistance in France. By then, the global balance of the war had shifted decisively with Hitler's ill-fated invasion of the Soviet Union and the engagement of the United States. Summer 1941 marked an important turning-point, as the PCF abandoned its 'neither Pétain nor de Gaulle' stance and committed its resources to the Allied effort and the Resistance. As disenchantment grew towards the Vichy regime and mounting German exactions, and as the balance of the war tipped in the Allies' favour, the repressive face of collaboration became more pronounced, with the escalating execution of hostages providing a bloody barometer of the worsening climate.[96]

Pétain's radio broadcast of 12 August 1941, in which he spoke of an 'ill wind' blowing through France and called for renewed commitment to collaboration, was in response to a campaign of sabotage against the occupying authorities which translated into action the PCF's new stance of resistance. Pétain's sombre message was also informed by extensive intelligence from Vichy's post and telecommunications censors, the Service des contrôles techniques.[97] It showed a regime patently on the defensive. So too did the oath of personal allegiance to Pétain required from high-ranking public officials and extended by a series of decrees in August 1941.[98] A booklet issued by the Vichy propaganda ministry in the same month listed this measure with the others outlined in Pétain's *rappel à l'ordre*, including increased powers for the police and a clampdown on political activity in the unoccupied zone. The title of this booklet and others like it – *Le Maréchal Pétain décide* – indicated well how policy was determined and implemented at Vichy.[99]

Collaboration and collaborationism

The precise political nature of the Vichy regime remains an issue of debate among historians;[100] likewise the extent to which collaboration constituted a pragmatic rather than an ideological posture, a means of sparing France the harsher impact which direct rule from Berlin might have brought. A common claim among later defenders of Vichy was that Pétain had served as the 'shield' to de Gaulle's 'sword', and that both had been essential to France's preservation. This was the defence put forward by Pétain himself at his trial in July 1945.[101] It was in line with his long-standing reputation, endorsed by none other than Léon Blum, as France's 'noblest and most humane soldier', who had repulsed the German forces at Verdun and exhibited a tireless concern for the welfare of those under his command.[102] As a former Minister of War and ambassador to

General Franco's Spain, however, Pétain was no political innocent, and his predilection for autocratic government was clear. His political leanings had been evident in his approval of La Rocque's authoritarian-nationalist Croix de Feu as 'one of the healthiest elements in our country'.[103] It was from this movement and its successor, the Parti Social Français (PSF), that Vichy would derive its slogan '*Travail, Famille, Patrie*' and much of its political tenor.

In view of the later opprobrium attaching to this regime, it is important to recall that other key figures at Vichy too had inhabited the respectable ranks of the Third Republic. Neither Laval nor his interim replacement as deputy head of government, Admiral Darlan, had exhibited any active tendency to right-wing extremism in the inter-war years. Having entered politics as a Socialist, Laval was a maverick parliamentarian whose moral compass was expediency and who had held a succession of major ministries, including several spells as premier. Darlan, too, had begun his political itinerary on the left; he was a calculating operator whose sympathies had nonetheless been thought to lie with the Republic. Going beyond these main protagonists and seeking to define the regime over which they presided, historians have observed a crucial distinction between state collaboration (the official policies emanating from Vichy) and 'collaborationism' (the utterances or activities of Nazi sympathisers, fascist ideo-logues and assorted opportunists in occupied Paris mainly).[104] Though there were significant, and increasing, overlaps, it is on this essential distinction that any nuanced understanding of France in the years 1940–44 rests.

The Germans did not dictate, and appeared to care little about, the type of regime which would assume the government of France under Pétain, provided it ensured full compliance with the terms of the armistice. The defining features of the team which signed up to collaboration at Vichy were, in the first instance, its heterogeneity and improvised nature. Its overriding objectives were to secure the best possible conditions for France under occupation and to reserve a leading place for the French in a post-war Europe dominated by Nazi Germany. To those ends, Vichy was conceived as an essentially temporary arrangement, an interregnum between the Third Republic and a new regime to be defined by a constitution, endorsed by popular approval and implemented by newly created assemblies (none of which would materialise).[105] The decision to break with the Constitution of the Third Republic and redefine the institutional bases of France was imposed neither by the occupying Germans nor by a cabal of French right-wing opportunists: it was supported by 624 to 4 members of the outgoing parliament at Vichy on 9 July 1940 and, more widely, reflected French public opinion at large.[106]

Though its centre of gravity was decidedly to the right, the Vichy administra-tion incorporated elements, as Philippe Burrin observes, from 'almost every political family of the prewar era'.[107] In the converted hotels of the spa town, staunch anti-republicans shared ministries with remnants of the Republican elite, (pro-German) fascist sympathisers with traditional (anti-German) nation-alists, authoritarians with liberal conservatives, clericals with anti-clericals, corporatists with syndicalists and even some few leftists drawn to Vichy through their anti-communism (notably the prominent trade unionist René Belin, Vichy's first Minister of Labour and Industrial Production). The strongest ideological imprint on the new regime was that of Maurras' integral-nationalist Action Française, with its counter-revolutionary, anti-republican, Catholic-monarchist doctrine. This current was prominently represented by Raphaël Alibert (the first Minister of Justice and author of the Jewish Statute of October 1940), Xavier Vallat (the first head of the CGQJ), and architects of the National Revolution such as René Gillouin, Henri Massis and Henri du Moulin de Labarthète. Not all such figures had been Action Française militants but they embraced an authoritarian Catholic conservatism summed up in Vallat's attendance each year at a Mass to commemorate the execution, on 21 January 1793, of Louis XVI.[108] They wielded their influence at Vichy alongside conservatives of an arguably more Republican bent such as Lucien Romier and Joseph Barthélemy. Added to all of the foregoing were political careerists of less firm conviction and a large number of high-ranking technocrats drawn from public administration or business and brought into ministries less for their ideas than for their expertise. Dynamic young figures like Jean Bichelonne and François Lehideux represented a strong modernising current which amplified the efficiency but also the tensions within economic planning at Vichy. There was enough common ground between all of these different sensibilities to create some basis for consensus around Pétain's leadership; but this did not prevent the economist Charles Rist from observing acidly that the ideology of Vichy was less 'integral nationalism' than 'integral confusionism'.[109] François Mitterrand, who as a former official in Pétain's administration was well placed to know, would describe government at Vichy as '*une pétaudière*', or pandemonium.[110]

The result in policy-making was that ministries sometimes pursued divergent and even opposing policies, while some ministries changed hands at a rate reminiscent of the governmentally unstable Third Republic. While the Secretariat of State for Labour held trade unionism to be an important pillar of social organisation, others sought to reduce the unions to impotence and even to abolish them. The same tensions were evident in youth policy over the question of whether the Etat Français should have a single youth movement or foster pluralism. More marked still was the confrontation in economic planning between Vichy's back-to-the-land ethos and the promotion of industry and a rationalised modern economy. The key document in economic planning was the Labour Charter of October 1941. Its drafting was, in Richard Kuisel's description, a 'fiasco', pitting corporatists against syndicalists and giving rise to a muddled, cumbersome system welcomed by no-one.[111]

If those at Vichy struggled to balance their political leanings with pragmatism, the 'collaborationists', in contrast, were unconstrained by the exigencies of government or by any promptings of moderation. The first recorded use of the term '*collaborationniste*' was by Marcel Déat in his organ *L'Œuvre* of 4 November 1940, distinguishing already between that more radical stance and the practical '*collaboration*' for which Pétain had called just a few days before in his radio broadcast of 30 October.[112] A disparate group of militants and intellectuals concentrated in occupied Paris, the collaborationists acted as the apologists of fascism and kept up a constant pressure to radicalise on the more traditionalist and cautious Vichy regime. The collaborationists fell broadly into four (sometimes overlapping) groups: journalists ready to ply their trade in the service of their new Nazi masters; intellectuals committed to the cause of fascism; activists fascinated by the trappings and practices of the Nazis and wedded to totalitarian political methods; and defectors from the anti-communist and pacifist left who embraced collaborationism as the least of the evils now open to them.[113]

In the main, the collaborationists called for a reinvigorated France to take its place in a fascist European order, seeing Hitler as a latter-day Charlemagne uniting Europe against the perils of international Jewry and Bolshevism. They promoted a cult of force, were seduced by the image of dynamic leadership, and – obsessed by the moral and physical decadence they perceived around them – longed for the genesis of a 'new man'.[114] Nor did they shrink from advocating violence as a means to that end. Some sought preferment within Pétain's regime before denouncing its ideological timidity. One such was the writer and journalist Lucien Rebatet, who aspired to a key role in the Vichy propaganda machine before returning aggrieved to the Paris offices of the collaborationist weekly *Je suis partout*. Rebatet would later write that, 'with a few isolated exceptions', 'all those who had any "fascist" and anti-Jewish convictions returned to Paris'.[115]

Literary collaborationism: Drieu La Rochelle and Brasillach

Pierre Drieu La Rochelle likewise returned from Vichy to Paris 'disgusted' by the 'archaic spirit' and 'decrepitude' which he found in Pétain's timid regime.[116] Arguably the most influential exponent of French literary fascism, Drieu became an ardent advocate of collaboration with Nazi Germany, which he came to see as the only means of rescuing France from decadence. In a string of books in the 1920s and 1930s, Drieu had argued against the narrow nationalism of Maurras and Barrès. He called for a strong European federation as a third force, both political and economic, capable of resisting the expansionist designs of the United States and the Soviet Union. He was one of the earliest and most vigorous proponents in France of a Europeanism to replace the outmoded, chauvinistic nationalism that had led to the First World War, in which he had seen action at Charleroi and Verdun.[117]

Having served his ideological apprenticeship with Maurras' Action Française, Robert Brasillach (Drieu's junior by some 16 years) was one among a number of young right-wing intellectuals drawn to fascism in the 1930s who, like Drieu, came to embrace collaborationism in the wake of the defeat of 1940. A product of the elite Ecole Normale Supérieure, Brasillach was a precocious talent as a literary critic, novelist, poet and journalist. He became literary editor then editor-in-chief of *Je suis partout*, moving beyond his early Maurrassism towards a fascination with the fascist mystique and a conception of fascism as the 'highest artistic creation' of the age. In the columns of *Je suis partout* and other publications,

Brasillach gave expression to the pro-Nazi sentiments that would see him executed at the Liberation for 'intelligence with the enemy' and as the exemplar of literary collaborationism. His was the pen that contrasted the ordered beauty of Nazi Germany with the 'wrinkled' and 'decrepit' French Republic, a 'syphilitic strumpet, smelling of cheap perfume and vaginal discharge', whose embrace had rendered Frenchmen 'rotten to the bone'. The same Brasillach called as early as June 1938 for a review of naturalisations and a special statute excluding Jews from the national community. He urged that Blum and other '*assassins de la patrie*' be shot, and declared in September 1942 that France 'must remove the Jews as a whole and not keep any of the little ones'.[118]

Drieu proclaimed his adherence to fascism in his *Socialisme fasciste* of 1934, advocating an authoritarian regime to regenerate French physical and moral fibre. Like Brasillach, he envisaged the creation of a 'new man', the antithesis of 'the bent backs, the slumped shoulders, the swollen stomachs, the small thighs, the flabby faces' of the Frenchmen around him.[119] Fascism for Drieu, as for Brasillach, had a strong aesthetic appeal. Both were captivated by the youthful energy of National Socialism as paraded at the Nuremberg rallies, though both had reservations about the distinctly unheroic personage of Hitler as its leader. Drieu was critical of Hitler's 'vulgarity' and Brasillach thought him a 'sad, vegetarian *fonctionnaire*'.[120] By contrast, Drieu's enthusiastic support in 1936 for Jacques Doriot and his newly formed Parti Populaire Français (French Popular Party, PPF) was in part an aesthetic response, a cult of virility dedicated to no 'potbellied intellectual' but to an athlete embracing the debilitated body of France 'who breathes into it his own bursting health'.[121] From his encomia on Doriot it is clear that this 'great herculean brother' was the street fighter whom Drieu would have liked to be, had he had the physical prowess to put himself to it. Brasillach was similarly drawn to the Belgian Rexist leader Léon Degrelle as the embodiment of virile energy and a 'poet of action'.[122]

Such manifestations of health and vigour were for Drieu and Brasillach the antidote to a hedonistic, materialist, modern France which, they held, had fallen under the corrupting influence of the Jew – 'the France of sitters, fishers, Pernod drinkers, and the babblers of committees, unions, and salons'. This rejection of modern 'decadence' and nostalgia for more Spartan values was an essential ingredient in the aesthetic appeal of fascism. 'Thanks to us', proclaimed the future Vichy minister Paul Marion, 'the France of camping, of sports, of dances, of voyages, of collective hiking will sweep away the France of aperitifs, of tobacco dens, of party congresses and of long digestions.'[123]

Hoping at first that the French could develop their own fascist alternative, Drieu and Brasillach had not looked to Germany to impose it; indeed, Drieu broke with Doriot in autumn 1938 over the latter's support for the Munich agreement. Following the defeat of 1940, however, Drieu came to see Nazism as an irresistible force and the only means of forging European unification. It was better, he reasoned, to have the importation of a foreign fascism than no fascism at all. 'The Germans are honest invaders', he would write in August 1941. 'Long before they imposed themselves, four million Jews had subjected me to the agonising spectacle of occupation.'[124]

Entrusted with editorship in occupied Paris of France's most prestigious literary journal, the *Nouvelle Revue Française* (NRF), Drieu used this largely as a forum for literary collaborationism. He contributed to more expressly collaborationist periodicals such as *Je suis partout* and *La Gerbe*, wrote a number of pro-fascist works, and dismissed Vichy as a regime of reactionary conservatives. Together with Brasillach and some other French writers, Drieu lent his literary prestige to Nazism by attending a congress of European writers at Weimar in October 1941. In January 1943, he would explain in forthright terms why he had opted for collaboration with the Nazis: 'I am a fascist because I have measured the progress of decadence in Europe. I saw in fascism the only means of containing and reducing that decadence, and [. . .] I saw no other recourse than that of the genius of Hitler and Hitlerism.'[125] Even when disabused of his faith in collaboration as the prelude to a new fascist Europe, he could still reflect in summer 1943: 'If I had not been too old to leave my books, I should have joined the SS.'[126] Progressively, however, Drieu's private and political disenchantment led him to renounce all hope of a new Europe, to abandon his editorship of the NRF and to take his own life in March 1945 before a hostile justice could pass its sentence.

French 'Führer': *Doriot, Déat, Darnand*

Drieu's fascism, like that of Brasillach, remained intensely subjective, ethereal and remote from practical politics: the aesthetic of an elite rather than an ideology for the masses. Other collaborationists traded in a less rarefied currency. They operated mainly through a variety of parties and movements, some of which adopted the trappings of fascism in their uniforms, Nazi-style salutes and rallies. Party membership in this period is impossible to determine with precision. It is estimated that at their height (until the end of 1942) such groups commanded a combined membership in the region of 150,000, and that they might have attracted up to 250,000 in all over the entire period of the Occupation.[127] Their wider support base is even more difficult to quantify, though Philippe Burrin advances the broad hypothesis, on the basis of estimated readership figures for collaborationist periodicals across both zones, that 'at least one or two million French people leaned toward collaborationism'.[128] This is too wide an estimate to be helpful, but it indicates well the difficulty of measuring such undocumented commitment. The parties which gave political expression to this position set themselves up, in Bertram Gordon's phrase, as 'a kind of alter ego of the Vichy regime', seeking to lead France 'further in the direction of the one-party state, mass mobilization in the fascist manner, and alliance with the Axis than Vichy was willing to go'.[129] Prominent here were the leaders of the three most important collaborationist organisations in France: Jacques Doriot, Marcel Déat and Joseph Darnand.

Doriot was a charismatic communist-turned-fascist, mayor of the industrial Paris suburb of Saint-Denis and founder in 1936 of the PPF.[130] Attracting many other communist dissidents together with members of the right-wing inter-war 'leagues', this movement resulted, in Berstein and Milza's terms, from 'a fusion of revolutionary leftism and anti-parliamentary nationalism, the same two currents which had come together to form Italian fascism'.[131] Membership of the PPF was predominantly young, male, urban working-class and lower middle-class, with strong representation among the unemployed and socially disadvantaged and some bases of support beyond the Paris region. Founded only a few weeks after the electoral victory of the Popular Front in May 1936, the PPF was arguably the closest inter-war France came to spawning a genuinely fascist party. As Malcolm Anderson notes, its essential components were 'virulent anti-Communism, social radicalism, anti-parliamentary authoritarianism, vague anti-Semitism (although it was not part of the official programme until the defeat), a leadership cult, a disciplined team of militants and a popular clientèle'. What it lacked was a rigorous, practicable programme – or even a 'coherent set of principles' – to give substance to the demagogic appeal of its leader.[132]

Such as it was, the PPF's programme expressed a rudimentary version of 'third way' politics, attacking the abuses of capitalism and communism both; but the party was in essence more reactionary than revolutionary, with strong links to employers' organisations and an aptitude for strike-breaking. Seen for a time as a bulwark against the Popular Front and the advance of communism, the PPF attracted donations from some financial and business concerns, with a symbolic contribution from Mussolini. The collapse in 1938 of the Popular Front removed part of the PPF's *raison d'être*, and with it much of its membership and funding. Doriot's calls for appeasement in the build-up to war brought a further demobilisation, prompting accusations of defeatism and the departure of a number of the party's leading lights. These included the industrialist backer Pierre Pucheu and prominent intellectuals such as Drieu La Rochelle and Alfred Fabre-Luce.

Doriot's wavering policy line has been described as '*ni Berlin ni Moscou* in 1937, pro-Munich in 1938, anti-German nationalism in 1939, Collaborationist at the defeat'.[133] The rupture of the Nazi–Soviet pact and the German invasion of the Soviet Union in June 1941 brought a new ideological dimension to the war – and a new opportunity to the PPF. It released Doriot from an unwelcome constraint (that of tempering his opposition to Moscow) and allowed him to rebuild his PPF support base on a virulently anti-communist platform. At its peak, Doriot's party claimed a membership of 300,000, a figure which some commentators have taken at face value. Although 50–60,000 seems a more plausible estimate, with some 10–15,000 hardcore militants, it has been suggested that the party could have had up to 300,000 sympathisers within its 'sphere of influence' (including readers of its weekly, *L'Emancipation nationale*, and later its daily, *Le Cri du Peuple*).[134] The cry against the Popular Front, 'Rather Hitler than Léon Blum', was converted with ease to the new slogan, 'Rather Hitler than Stalin'. Rallying to the Nazi model, the PPF called for a 'totalitarian' France, 'national, socialist, imperialist, European and authoritarian'.[135]

Barred from a role in the Vichy administration, Doriot would concentrate on organising the Légion des Volontaires Français contre le Bolchevisme (Legion of French Volunteers Against Bolshevism, LVF) and fighting with it on the Russian front. The LVF was launched on the initiative of the Paris collaborationists in the weeks following the German invasion of the Soviet Union in June 1941. Among some 2,250 volunteers signed up in the first months of recruitment, it attracted pro-Nazi and anti-communist ideologues as well as its share of adventurers and mercenaries. It was incorporated into the Wehrmacht (whose uniform LVF members wore) and used mainly to engage partisan groups behind the German lines. It would be complemented in 1943–44 by the raising of a French Waffen-SS brigade, and both would be absorbed in late 1944 into the Waffen-SS Charlemagne Division, which saw some 7,500 Frenchmen deployed against the Soviet offensive in Pomerania in February 1945.[136] Though enlistment in the LVF or Waffen-SS represented the ultimate act of collaborationism, prominent collaborationists with few exceptions (Doriot, Clémenti) contented themselves with 'defending Western civilisation' by being part of the LVF's organisational apparatus in Paris (Déat, Deloncle).[137]

Like Doriot and others in the pro-fascist camp, Marcel Déat began his political career on the left, as a Socialist deputy then minister under the Third Republic. Where Doriot was a demagogue, Déat was an intellectual. Having advocated an arrangement with Nazi Germany (most notoriously through his article 'Why Die for Danzig?'),[138] he viewed the military defeat and occupation as a providential force to sweep away the structures of a politically, socially and morally decadent France. In July 1940, he urged in the collaborationist newspaper *L'Œuvre*: 'Like all those other peoples who have carried out their revolution, who have effected their transformation, whether Italy, Germany or Russia, we too need a party, a single party, to define and direct our shared aspirations.'[139] In February 1941, Déat co-founded the Rassemblement National Populaire (National Popular Rally, RNP) with Eugène Deloncle, former leader of the Cagoule (or 'Hood', a violently anti-Marxist organisation specialising in political terrorism in the late 1930s).[140] Like Doriot's PPF, the RNP was a fusion of radical left-wing and right-wing elements which anticipated an end to traditional political cleavages through the creation of a single mass party on the Nazi model.[141] Promoting a form of 'left-wing fascism' with an appeal to former Socialists and syndicalists, it rejected Vichy as a 'capital of reaction' run by a 'consortium of old men'.[142] The RNP argued the need for France to modernise and, by replacing liberal capitalism with rigorous state planning, assume its place in an industrialised Europe. To this end, it articulated what Berstein and Milza describe as a form of 'national, corporatist, authoritarian and popular socialism, tinged with racist ideology and closer to early-day National Socialism than to the Vichy government'.[143] Attracting a mixed membership estimated at some 20,000,[144] the RNP had notable representation among the urban (mostly Parisian) middle class, including teachers, civil servants and liberal professionals. In addition, Déat reached a much wider audience through his editorship of *L'Œuvre*, with its reported sales figures approaching 130,000.[145]

Though bitter rivals, Doriot and Déat had in common their pro-Nazi sympathies, their support for authoritarian government and a single mass party (which each aspired to lead), their penchant for corporatist solutions, their staunch anti-communism and, to a degree, their anti-Semitism (less pronounced in Déat than in Doriot). The shortcomings of Vichy, with its backward-looking Maurrassian ideas, were harshly judged by these would-be National Socialists. Doriot accused the Vichy regime of being an obstacle to real social change in its conservative *attentisme*; Déat and his RNP were even more defiantly critical: 'Vichy wants to restore an outdated past and ridicules us with its parody of revolution. Vichy plots with Jews and international freemasons, with financiers and American arms dealers who are laying down the law.'[146] Such denunciations of Vichy were commonplace in collaborationist circles. As Maurice Bardèche would later recall, 'To those who genuinely wished for a *national revolution* based on the principles of fascism, the regime of the *Etat Français* seemed like a return to the authoritarian republic of Marshal Mac-Mahon.'[147] A bastion of traditional conservative interests, Pétain's regime was for the apologists of fascism no more than 'a counter-revolution, but one which *called* itself a revolution'.[148]

Unlike the PPF and RNP, the Milice Française (French Militia) was a paramilitary police force set up by Laval in January 1943 as an arm of the Vichy government and outgrowth of ex-servicemen's organisations (notably the Légion Française des Combattants and its more radical offshoot, the Service d'Ordre Légionnaire, SOL).[149] Its leader was Joseph Darnand, a decorated veteran of both world wars, former member of Action Française and the Cagoule, and head of the Alpes-Maritimes branch of the Légion Française des Combattants. Darnand had nothing of the charismatic Doriot or the cerebral Déat, but his credentials as a courageous man of action were well attested. His ambition was also to transform his force into the unitary state party that Pétain had denied the PPF and RNP leaders. Darnand's conversion to collaborationism after Montoire had been confirmed by the German invasion of the Soviet Union, which allowed him to channel his fierce anti-communism into zealous support for the Nazi cause. Conceived as a sort of palace guard for Vichy, the Milice evolved into a trained and armed paramilitary force under the aegis of the SS. As such, it was used increasingly to combat Resistance activity, though it identified no shortage of other enemies within. The 21-point oath of the Milice served as a mirror held up to the illiberal, anti-republican values of the regime. In addition to repudiating 'futile freedom for true freedom', 'egalitarianism for hierarchy' and 'democracy for authority', the Miliciens swore to fight 'against Gaullist dissidence and for French unity, against Bolshevism and for nationalism, against Jewish leprosy and for French purity, against pagan freemasonry and for Christian civilisation'.[150]

The Milice, like the PPF, drew much of its membership from the working and lower middle classes, with a strong appeal among former soldiers, police and certain sections of the young, including students; it also attracted its share of thugs, criminals and desperados. Unlike the collaborationist parties, it had significant numbers of rural recruits. In terms of ideological affinity, it was firmly of the authoritarian nationalist right, attracting many recruits with backgrounds in Action Française, the Cagoule or the inter-war leagues such as Pierre Taittinger's Jeunesses Patriotes, as well as political parties like Doriot's PPF and La Rocque's PSF. Among them were diehard anti-communists and militant Catholics.

By 1944, the Milice had expanded to an estimated 30,000 volunteers and was engaged in a form of civil war against the Resistance. Meanwhile, its leader had been made a *Sturmbannführer* in the Waffen-SS and had sworn an oath of personal allegiance to Hitler, 'the Germanic and reforming Führer of Europe'.[151] Having been banned in the northern zone due to German suspicion of paramilitary organisations, the Milice was eventually supplied by the SS with money and arms and authorised to operate throughout France. An American intelligence report dated 30 August 1944 identified the Milice as the most formidable pro-fascist organisation in Vichy France.[152] At his trial in October 1945, where he would be sentenced to death, Darnand would keep faith with himself. As defiant as he was honest, he declared: 'I am not one of those who will tell you: "Monsieur le Premier Président, I played a double game." I marched. I simply marched. I am proud of what I did. I was mistaken but I acted in good faith. I believe that I, too, served.'[153]

Pernicious outsiders

Besides the PPF, RNP and Milice, there were many other collaborationist movements. These included Alphonse de Chateaubriant's Groupe Collaboration (with upwards of 40,000 members), Eugène Deloncle's Mouvement Social Révolutionnaire (MSR) (with its membership of up to 20,000), Marcel Bucard's Parti Franciste (with its estimated 10,000 members), and other smaller, idiosyncratic movements such as Maurice-Bernard de La Gatinais' Croisade Française du National-Socialisme (French Crusade for National Socialism) or Pierre Costantini's Ligue Française d'Epuration, d'Entraide Sociale et de Collaboration Européenne (French League for Purification, Mutual Social Aid and European Collaboration).[154] In practical terms, such movements had a limited and largely futile function: when they were not brawling with each other, as Julian Jackson puts it, 'they distributed tracts and papers, destroyed busts of Marianne, defaced Republican street names, denounced people to the authorities, or smashed up Jewish shops. In short, they remained outsiders, even after 1940.' Outsiders perhaps, but no less pernicious for that. Costantini's newspaper, *L'Appel*, published a series of articles in 1941 on the question: 'Should the Jews be Exterminated?'[155]

It was here that the collaborationists arguably had their greatest effect: in the Nazification of the popular and intellectual press in occupied France. Drawing on German subsidies, they controlled a string of daily and weekly publications (*Paris-Soir, Le Petit Parisien, Le Cri du Peuple, L'Œuvre, Les Nouveaux Temps, Je suis partout, La Gerbe, Au Pilori*, and many others). In all, there were around a dozen French dailies and some 18 weeklies preaching collaborationism and support for fascism. Through these means, and through publishing houses such as Gallimard, Grasset and Denoël, the so-called literary fascists exerted their influence unrestrained. Brasillach became the 'poet' of collaborationism and Drieu, as editor of Gallimard's NRF, one of its most prominent literary exponents. Céline gave expression to a rabid anti-Semitism rivalled only by that of Rebatet, who laid claim to the best-seller of the Occupation with *Les Décombres*, a work which proclaimed total commitment to the Nazi cause.[156] Other writers such as Henry de Montherlant, Jacques Chardonne (Boutelleau), Marcel Jouhandeau and Alfred Fabre-Luce peddled variations on the same themes of collaborationism, anti-Semitism and 'new order' Europeanism.

The failure of these groups and individuals to realise their ideological programme lay partly in their irremediable divisions, and partly in the fact that it was not the Germans' purpose to concede as much to a defeated France. Hitler's intention, it became clear, was to keep the collaborationist groups sufficiently strong to exert pressure on Vichy, but not strong enough to join forces in a movement capable of mobilising mass popular support. The collaborationists were to be 'a sword of Damocles suspended over the Vichy government – threatening enough to keep it in line, never strong enough to unseat it (unless the Germans wished)'. Berlin's instructions on this point were explicit, exhorting that 'everything must be done to encourage the internal divisions and thus the weakness of France'.[157] Certainly, had the collaborationists paid heed to the fate reserved for France by the German Propaganda Ministry in July 1940 ('a greater Switzerland, a country of tourism . . . and fashion'),[158] they would have had fewer illusions about their place in the New European Order. Göring's reported conception of collaboration was savage in its irony: 'I see collaboration with Messieurs les Français in the following fashion: let them deliver up everything that they can until they can deliver up no more. If they do it voluntarily, I shall say that I collaborate.'[159] Goebbels, too, consigned to his diary in April 1942 the reflection that France offered nothing beyond material support: 'I consider the French people sick and worm-eaten. No notable contributions towards the reconstruction of Europe can be expected from them.' The same entry concluded that 'the Führer's policy towards France' (that of simple exploitation) had been 'absolutely right'.[160]

Collaborators and collaborationists were in this sense similarly deluded, both over-estimating France's prospective value to Hitler. The ultimate failure of the collaborationists, however, was not so much political as philosophical. It lay in their inability to resolve the dilemma at the heart of the Occupation, that of reconciling ardent nationalism with abject servility. Nationalism itself became an unstable concept, at once buttressed and undermined by the Europeanism which collaboration with Nazi Germany implied. To this problem the collaborationists could offer no solution, intellectual or practical. While Brasillach, for all his fascination with the Germany of Nuremberg, had argued that the 'only way to overcome foreign fascism is with French fascism, the only true fascism', others called for uncritical emulation of Hitler's Reich. 'I wish the victory of Germany because her war is *my* war, *our* war', declared Rebatet, while Déat exhorted the French to prove themselves 'possible partners' of Nazism. In this as in so much else, Drieu was incoherent, arguing first that the French should build their 'own fascism' lest they be 'fascisized from outside', then, under the Occupation, urging the simple necessity to 'impress the Germans at all costs'.[161]

Porous boundaries

While the distinction between collaboration and collaborationism is essential for any appreciation of the dynamics at work in occupied France, it risks obscuring the porousness of the boundaries between these two positions. The Pétain administration viewed many *collaborationnistes* with suspicion and kept them away from the levers of power (the most notable case being that of Jacques Doriot, seen from Vichy as a dangerous political adventurer).[162] Others were admitted to influential posts, such as Vichy's Delegate-General to the Occupied Zone, Fernand de Brinon, and the Education Minister, Abel Bonnard, both enthusiastic collaborationists brought into government after Laval's return to power in April 1942. Figures such as Jacques Benoist-Méchin and Paul Marion, in charge of relations with Germany and propaganda respectively, also testified to a distinctly pro-fascist presence at Vichy, while some aides and second-rank officials shared a common past as members of Doriot's PPF. Other fascist ideologues were admitted belatedly and under German duress to prominent positions within the Vichy government. Chief among later appointments were Déat (Minister of Labour), Darnand (Secretary-General for the Maintenance of Order), and the militant Catholic, ex-Milicien and Radio Vichy broadcaster, Philippe Henriot (Secretary of State for Information and Propaganda).

Pétain's inner circle harboured pronounced anti-Semites such as his doctor, Bernard Ménétrel, and his first Justice Minister, Raphaël Alibert. The latter was an Action Française supporter whose hard-line Catholic proclivities underpinned the regime's earliest anti-Jewish legislation. In May 1942, the CGQJ passed into the hands of the notorious anti-Semite, Louis Darquier de Pellepoix, who outdid the zeal even of his predecessor, Xavier Vallat. In the pre-war years, Darquier had been a Paris city councillor and extreme-right journalist (directing, among other publications, *L'Antijuif*). A violent political agitator, he had been president of the Association des Blessés et Victimes du 6 Février 1934 (Association for the Wounded and Victims of 6 February 1934), the occasion when an anti-parliamentary riot orchestrated mainly by right-wing nationalist organisations had left 15 dead and several hundred injured outside the Chamber of Deputies. Darquier had served a spell in prison for incitement to racial hatred, having founded in 1937 the Rassemblement Antijuif (Anti-Jewish Rally), to be replaced in 1940 by the Union Française pour la Défense de la Race (French Union for the Defence of the Race, UFDR). He had called openly for Jews in France to be 'expelled or massacred', and had greeted the news of *Kristallnacht* in November 1938 with the exclamation '*Bravo, Fritz!*'[163] Among his proposals on coming to office were the exclusion of Jewish children from schools and the obligation on Jews to wear a yellow star before this was imposed even in the occupied zone, both of which measures were resisted by Vichy. Anti-Semitic propaganda was increased and a number of pseudo-scientific bodies were given official support for their propagation of race theory (barely disguised under such labels as 'Anthropo-Sociology' and the 'Study of Jewish and Ethno-Racial Questions'). Racists and anti-Semites such as René Martial and Georges Montandon, authors respectively of *La Race française* (*The French Race*) and *Comment reconnaître le Juif?* (*How to Recognise the Jew*), attained new prominence as ethnological experts under Darquier's patronage.[164]

It has been argued that appointments such as those of Darquier, de Brinon and Bonnard, and later those of Déat, Darnand and Henriot, carried the policy of collaboration 'to its logical conclusion', completing 'the transformation of the Vichy regime into a thoroughgoing fascist state'.[165] Other historians dispute this analysis, arguing that even at its most repressive, when declared fascists had acceded to power in the final phase, Vichy was 'a police state, not a fascist State'.[166] A conclusion common to both interpretations is that these later appointments did mark a serious radicalisation of Pétain's regime. They also exposed the 'National Revolution' for the sham it was, since the custodians of France's new moral order were scarcely paragons of the virtues on which it purported to rest – Darquier as a wife-beating dissolute, Bonnard as a renowned homosexual, de Brinon with his Jewish divorcee wife, even Pétain himself as an erstwhile philanderer married also to a divorcee.

Above all, the Vichy regime in its later stages illustrated the divisions and tensions at work across the wider far-right community, which remained in occupied France as riven and factionalised as it had been in the inter-war years – and as it would continue to be in the post-war period. The lines of opposition were not drawn simply between Vichyites and Paris collaborationists: they ran through both camps, dividing traditionalists from radicals, diehard nationalists from 'new order' Europeanists, Germanophobes from Germanophiles, monarchists from supporters of a fascist-style dictatorship, intellectual sympathisers with Nazism from *jusqu'au-boutistes* prepared to die in Waffen-SS uniforms on the battlefields of the eastern front. Such divisions had a generational dimension too, as younger radicals took issue with the perceived timidity of their elders and forebears. Hence the ironic dismissal by Rebatet and others of Maurras' 'Inaction Française' and the growing impatience with Vichy's temporising; hence the regret in Brasillach's judgement of Charles Péguy as a nationalist and a socialist but 'unfortunately not a racist'; hence, too, the criticisms levelled by some against the insufficiency of Maurras' anti-Semitism – his 'horror of racism', as Rebatet, himself a scion of Action Française, complained.[167]

As Stanley Hoffmann has observed, the personal and ideological relations among the collaborationists, and between them and Vichy, were of such 'byzantine complexity' as to form 'a tangled web compared with which parliamentary politics look eminently Cartesian'.[168] Quarrels were rife among individuals and groups united more by what they opposed than by what they supported. In this sense, too, the failure of collaborationism was portended from the outset. When Déat set up a committee in July 1940 to lay the ground for the creation of a single mass party, the members (including representatives from Doriot's PPF and other advocates of a fascist solution) could not agree sufficiently among themselves to advance a coherent proposal. Their deliberations were cut short in late August by the decision from Vichy to merge all war veterans' associations in the Légion Française des Combattants. Called upon to serve as the 'eyes and ears of the Marshal', the Legion by early 1941 boasted over half a million members, together with a newspaper and daily radio slot.[169] The legionnaires were to be the embodiment of Vichy's values, responsible for 'promoting, defending, if necessary imposing' the National Revolution.[170] Representing a specific category only of the population, however, the Legion fell a long way short of constituting a mass party. Despite its later expansion to incorporate non-veterans (as the Légion Française des Combattants et des Volontaires de la Révolution Nationale), it marked from the earliest a clear divide in intent between Pétain's administration and the proponents of a 'fascist' France.

Nor did such divisions lessen over time. In the final weeks of the war, when the leading collaborationists had fled to Germany, a French governmental delegation – a sort of Vichy-in-exile – was set up in the small German town of Sigmaringen. Headed by the former Delegate-General to the Occupied Zone, Fernand de Brinon, it included hard-line collaborationists like Darnand and Déat but not Doriot, who continued to see himself as the true spokesman for French interests. Though there was nothing left to govern, Doriot set up his own organisation with a radio service and newspaper to rival those of de Brinon's delegation. Before this farce could be played out to conclusion, Doriot was killed by a strafing aircraft, at which point Déat too promptly formed his own organisation to undermine the delegation of which he himself was a member.[171]

Vichy: a fascist regime?

From all of the foregoing it is clear that Vichy was not a 'fascist' regime in any rigorous sense of the term. It did not erect the infrastructure of fascism, resisting from the outset the model of the single-party state and retaining a pluralism at odds with the centralising drive of fascism. In economic planning, youth policy and much else, Vichy remained – at least until its final throes in 1944 – a 'pluralist dictatorship'.[172] It failed to mobilise mass support around a clearly conceived political project, finding its unifying force mainly in nostalgic reverence for Pétain and generalised antipathy to the Third Republic. In October 1941, the postal censors reported that 'only the personality of the Head of State is holding together an entirely artificial unity'; in September 1942, a prefect's report likewise observed: 'The majority of the population continue to revere the Marshal but they follow him less as a Leader than as a legendary personage, a magnificent old man of astonishing capacity and virtue.'[173] The members of the governing team at Vichy were not even themselves united in support of the National Revolution, which dwindled to near-extinction as a programme in the later stages of the regime. Seen through the eyes of a Paris collaborationist like Brasillach, the National Revolution held out the hope of real change for 'at least two months' before turning into an 'immense farce'.[174] The appointment to government of hard-line collaborationists (especially from January 1944) would serve belatedly to create, in Stanley Hoffmann's image, a sort of fascist bridgehead at Vichy; but the regime collapsed before this ground could be consolidated and converted into a fascist victory.[175]

Born of defeat, installed in a provincial spa town and led by an octogenarian, the Vichy regime offered a hastily improvised solution for a 'France in parenthesis'.[176] Though army and navy officers were prominent in the upper echelons at Vichy, they were leaders with nothing left to lead. With an armistice army of no more than 100,000 men at its disposal (until November 1942, when even that was disbanded), the regime was denied the militarism that constituted an important component of fascism. Nor did Vichy embrace the long-term vision of fascism, the commitment to a thoroughgoing transformation of state and society. Despite lip service to a 'new European order' and some genuinely progressive modernisers within the governing apparatus at Vichy, the dynamic, transformative, revolutionary dimension of fascism was absent from a regime whose loudest voices preached instead archaic values and an anachronistic social model. While Italian Fascism and German National Socialism invoked the past, with its attendant mythologies, in order better to dominate the future, Vichy sought to recover the past for its own sake. Roger Griffin has argued the importance of this distinction as a general principle in defining fascism:

> Fascism's essentially palingenetic, and hence anti-conservative, thrust towards a *new* type of society means that it builds rhetorically on the cultural achievements attributed to former, more 'glorious' or healthy eras in national history only to invoke the regenerative ethos which is a prerequisite for national rebirth, and not to suggest socio-political models to be duplicated in a literal-minded restoration of the past. It thus represents an alternative modernism rather than a rejection of it.[177]

It was precisely in its ideological rejection of modernism and its attempt to restore the past (most marked in its back-to-the-land agenda and its rural Catholic ethos) that Vichy was most sharply at odds with the fascist project. If it could be argued to meet in substantial measure the anti-Marxist, anti-liberal, ultra-nationalist or third-way criteria central to some definitions of the 'fascist minimum', it had nothing of the latter's anti-conservatism and essential radicalism.[178] Pétain's Etat Français represented the triumph of ultra-conservatism and reaction in a specifically French (counter-Revolution, anti-Republic) idiom. It was a heterogeneous and essentially temporary regime lacking in political coherence and profoundly lacking in an element of fascism not to be overlooked: imagination. Despite aligning itself objectively with the Third Reich, as Griffin avers, 'Vichy was far from fascist in its inspiration'; it was a 'Babel of illiberal nationalisms' converging on a First World War hero who was more Hindenburg than Hitler.[179]

If the attitude evinced by Berlin and the chorus of criticism directed by the Paris collaborationists against Vichy were not enough to persuade us of this, then the retrospective judgement of a fascist *maître à penser* such as Maurice Bardèche might. An outspoken champion of the Etat Français in the immediate post-war years, Bardèche reflected in his later book *Qu'est-ce que le Fascisme?* on the regime in defence of which he had been imprisoned. He rehearsed again here his 'esteem for the men who governed France in those dramatic years'; but he judged Vichy itself, in its lack of radicalism and unwillingness to effect a transformation of French society, to have been 'the opposite of what we call fascism'.

The prudent, 'tranquillising' values on which it rested – *Travail, Famille, Patrie* – were values worthy of the Swiss, emasculated values privileging obedience over the raw energy and pioneering spirit that were the driving force of the fascist for Bardèche. '*Work* means submission to the rich; *Family*, submission to the moral code; *Patrie*, submission to the gendarme.'[180]

That Vichy did not fit neatly into a fascist typology, however, did not prevent it from displaying certain features of fascism. It was an authoritarian-nationalist, repressive, exclusionary, anti-Semitic regime – 'the apotheosis of undemocracy in France'.[181] In its leadership cult, its propagandism, its anti-materialism, its corporatist leanings, its visceral anti-communism and moral Manichaeanism, it also exhibited strong traits of fascism. More significantly still, Vichy participated actively in the wider fascist project for Europe. It supported the Nazi war effort through money, materials and programmes of voluntary then forced labour, helping to draft some 650,000 French workers into service in German factories.[182] The bulk of the Vichy government's revenue went to meet the costs of the occupying forces, while French industrial production became primarily geared to German needs. Most importantly perhaps, in its maintenance of law and order and its increasing tendency to repression, Vichy saved the Germans from having to divert much larger forces from military deployment elsewhere.

Finally, for all that Vichy was and all it became, it would be wrong to see it as instituting a brutal transition from a tolerant, liberal Republic to a totalitarian regime. The Third Republic in its final phase had not been so liberal, and Vichy could not without substantial qualification be classed as totalitarian (except arguably in its most repressive phase after January 1944, when Darnand and his Milice came into their own). Many of the attitudes and predispositions which informed policy-making at Vichy had long roots, and some of the ground on which the National Revolution was founded had been prepared by the preceding administration of Edouard Daladier (1938–40). In its legislation against 'undesirables', its anti-communist measures, its use of internment camps, its interception of mail and telecommunications, its family policy and preoccupation with *la dénatalité* (falling birth rate), and its emphasis on national renewal, Vichy merely went further than the regime it succeeded; but it did go further, and in some cases much further.

Collaboration in acts: an increasingly compliant partner

Beyond such areas of broad overlap with the outgoing Third Republic, Vichy served as a laboratory for the development and implementation of extreme right-wing ideas and policies. It restricted liberties, abolished democratic institutions, passed racial laws, persecuted designated groups (communists, Jews, Freemasons) and ruthlessly pursued the outlaws of the Resistance. The ever-present paranoia of the regime was reflected in the proliferation of special police services – among them a 'Jewish Police' (PQJ), a 'Secret Societies Police' (SSS) and an 'Anti-Communist Police' (SPAC), the latter evolving into the more generalised 'Service for the Repression of Anti-National Activities' (SRMAN).[183] The same paranoia was manifest in the extensive censorship of post and telecommunications under Vichy, resulting in almost 3,000 arrests for the month of July 1941 alone, when growing hostility towards Vichy and collaboration could be detected.[184] The call for strong government that had reverberated through the ranks of the anti-republican right in the inter-war years found itself answered in a regime which colluded in the detention, torture, execution or deportation of French civilians as resisters, hostages, enemies of the state, or on account of their 'race'. Extensive archival work undertaken by the Fondation pour la Mémoire de la Déportation (Foundation for Preserving the Memory of the Deportation) has yielded a figure of almost 87,000 men and women deported from France for resistance in one form or another to the Occupation. When added to almost 76,000 foreign and French Jews of all ages, this puts at over 160,000 the total number of *déportés*.[185]

The high point of Vichy repression was reached in early 1944 when, in what Robert Paxton calls 'the final paroxysm of a moribund dictatorship',[186] Darnand assumed responsibility for law and order in the face of a growing threat from the Resistance. By a law without parallel in modern French history, he was vested with the power to create special courts martial to mete out summary justice against those caught engaging in terrorist acts, whether directed against French or German targets. Darnand had personal authority over the selection of the three judges who sat (often masked to conceal their identity) on these tribunals and who were usually members of the Milice or tactical police reserve units (Groupes Mobiles de Réserve, GMR). They took the place of regular judges who were increasingly subject to reprisals for convicting members of the Resistance. No records were kept of their impromptu hearings, which resulted in immediate execution in cases of 'clearly proven guilt', with the accused having a right to neither legal counsel nor appeal.[187] Together with this state-sponsored disregard for due process went a number of assassinations by Miliciens of high-profile political adversaries (among them the prominent Dreyfusard and former president of the League of the Rights of Man, Victor Basch, the former Popular Front Education Minister, Jean Zay, and the former conservative minister and vocal opponent of the armistice, Georges Mandel – all three of Jewish descent).

Thus, over its four-year lifespan, the Vichy regime underwent a process of radicalisation, moving from a paternalistic dictatorship focused on the person of Pétain towards an administration more closely aligned with the methods of Nazism. The year 1942–43 marked a critical transition. Following Laval's return to power in April 1942, this was the period when active collaboration was stepped up.[188] In addition to being '*chef du Gouvernement*' with explicit control over all policy areas, Laval was also Minister of the Interior, of Information, and of Foreign Affairs. After the German invasion of the southern zone in November 1942, a further constitutional act gave him authority to promulgate legislation in his own name, a power until then reserved to Pétain, who became an increasingly disengaged Head of State.[189] Dictatorship at Vichy had effectively changed hands. By then, the constitutional reforms envisaged in the law of 10 July 1940 no longer had the remotest prospect of realisation; the belated attempt by Pétain in autumn 1943 to promulgate a new constitution reinstating elected assemblies – in anticipation of a potential Allied liberation – was blocked by the Germans.[190] Berlin now tightened its grip on Vichy. By the end of 1943, all French legislation would be subject to German scrutiny and the Germans would impose their own government appointments (Darnand, Henriot, and later Déat).[191] As the regime's room for autonomous manoeuvre was reduced, Laval used his power not only to bargain as ever with the occupying authorities, but also to intensify France's commitment to the German war effort. Thus, in December 1943, he compounded his earlier expression of unequivocal support by declaring: '[T]he victory of Germany will prevent our civilisation collapsing into communism. The victory of the Americans would be the triumph of the Jew and of communism.'[192]

The turn of the year 1942–43 saw the agreement to raise a French conscript labour force to support the war effort in Germany, in contravention of international law on forced labour. In June 1942, Laval had launched the relief scheme (*relève*) whereby one French prisoner of war would be returned for every three skilled workers sent to Germany; by February 1943, the voluntary *relève* had become the Service du Travail Obligatoire (Compulsory Labour Service, STO), making young men born between January 1920 and December 1922 liable for up to two years' work in Germany.[193] Where propaganda had sought to persuade, the French police would now oblige. The same period saw the setting up, in January 1943, of the Milice (which, like the growing Resistance movement, would offer an alternative outlet for some young men seeking to escape the STO). Since Laval as head of government was also head of the Milice, Vichy was complicit from the outset in the excesses to which Darnand's organisation would lend itself, just as the Milice would serve as the very expression of Vichy's paranoia and prejudice. Annexed to the law of 30 January 1943 by which it was founded, the three primary conditions which Miliciens had to fulfil were: '1. To be French by birth; 2. Not to be a Jew; 3. To be a member of no secret society.'[194] At the same time, Vichy implicated itself further in the Nazi war effort by authorising, in summer 1943, the formation of a French unit in the Waffen-SS which would become a component in the later Charlemagne Division.

The intensification of Vichy's collaboration over this period had its deepest roots not in mounting German pressure, which there was, but paradoxically in the notion of French government as enshrined in Article 3 of the armistice convention. This had stipulated that the French would exercise administrative authority over all occupied and unoccupied French territory, an administrative authority that soon came to be prized as a surrogate sovereignty. Since France was not denuded of its resources from the outset – retaining its 'free zone', its overseas territories, its fleet and armistice army – collaboration was not a static affair but rather a process of continual negotiation.[195] While Vichy had these assets to protect and potentially lose, and while Germany continued to hold over a million French prisoners of war, Pétain's administration proved an increasingly compliant partner, acceding to a series of concessions that went far beyond the requirements of the armistice. The consequence of this was to draw the Vichy regime ever deeper into a cycle of repressive collaboration, for fear that the Germans would assume administrative control themselves or install an alternative French government of their own choosing, for which there was no shortage of willing candidates among the Paris collaborationists. That French governmental authority was nothing more than a device manipulated from Berlin was confirmed by Hitler's message to officers of the Wehrmacht in December 1942, barely a month after the occupation of the entire French mainland: 'French sovereignty will be maintained but only in so far as this serves our interests. It will be suppressed the moment it proves irreconcilable with military necessities.'[196]

This did not prevent Vichy, in an exaggerated appreciation of its own status, from seeking to make a more active contribution to the German war effort. A test of whose side the Etat Français was on militarily came as early as September 1940, when French forces repelled an attempted British-Gaullist seizure of the West African port of Dakar. A similarly spirited, if less successful, opposition by Vichy troops to an Allied assault in Syria was mounted in June–July 1941.[197] Despite its official neutrality, moreover, Vichy pursued negotiations with Germany over limited military collaboration; these took the form of the 'Paris Protocols', hatched by Darlan in May 1941 and abandoned when the political concessions for which Vichy pressed were judged excessive.[198] When in August 1942 German coastal defences withstood an attempted British–Canadian landing at Dieppe, Pétain wrote to congratulate Hitler and appealed that the French be allowed to participate in their own defence and in 'the safeguard of Europe'. While Vichy propaganda newsreels celebrated the liberation by Germany of some 750 prisoners of war from Dieppe in recognition of the town's steadfastness, Hitler seems not to have thought Pétain's overture worthy even of a reply.[199]

When Allied forces landed on the beaches of Normandy on 6 June 1944, Pétain called upon the French to take no part in their own liberation and to observe the 'strictest discipline' in complying with the requirements of the German army. He had agreed with the German authorities in August 1943 that, in the event of an Allied landing, he would issue an instruction to keep the French population 'quiet and orderly'. He described these first actions of the Liberation as an attack 'against our country', espousing to the end the logic of collaboration.[200] By the same logic, Darnand instructed his Miliciens in June 1944 to consider Resistance fighters supporting the Allied invasion as 'enemies of France'.[201] By then, the Milice had become an auxiliary force for the German military command, as demonstrated by the bloody engagement on the Glières plateau in Haute-Savoie in March 1944. There, in a pitched battle against the Resistance which cost heavy casualties on both sides, the armed wing of the Milice, the Franc-Garde, fought alongside Wehrmacht troops to wipe out a major *maquis* stronghold and strategic base for Allied airdrops.[202] This engagement and others (notably on the Vercors plateau near Grenoble in July 1944) completed the transformation of the Milice into an internal equivalent of the LVF, an armed volunteer force of Frenchmen at the service of the Reich – only here their fire was directed against their fellow countrymen.

Collaboration in ideas: the 'Jewish peril'

No area of Vichy's activity demonstrates the regime's slide into repression more than its treatment of Jews. Anti-Jewish legislation was enacted by Vichy as early as summer 1940, and estimates of foreign Jews already interned by the start of 1941 in concentration camps in the unoccupied zone ranged as high as 45,000, with up to 15,000 more in North Africa.[203] The creation of the CGQJ in March 1941 was undertaken in order to retain French authority over the Jewish question and preclude the setting up of an office under German control. Similarly, Vichy lent itself with a will to the programme of expropriating Jewish businesses ('Aryanisation'), lest the Germans establish an administrative monopoly over this and reap the economic rewards. As of June 1942, Jews in the occupied zone were obliged to wear a yellow star; though the same was not imposed in the unoccupied zone, Jews there were required, from December 1942, to have their identity and ration cards stamped with the word '*Juif*', and were thereby exposed more readily to detection and arrest.[204] French collusion in the Holocaust dated from spring and (more actively) summer 1942, and here motivations were tightly bound up with concern both to reduce the numbers of refugees in France and to preserve French authority over the highly sensitive issue, for Vichy, of policing in the occupied zone.[205] It was French police, aided by gangs of PPF volunteers, who conducted the major round-ups that would see 75,721 Jews (around a quarter of the total population) deported to Nazi concentration camps over the next two years, of whom 2,566 would be recorded survivors.[206]

Of all the attitudes that Vichy held in common with Nazism (*völkisch* nationalism, anti-communism, authoritarianism, belief in natural hierarchies), that of anti-Semitism casts the longest, darkest shadow over the regime. The illusion has long been dispelled that French persecution of Jews was undertaken in response to German pressure.[207] Just as in Nazi Germany, Jews in Vichy France were from the outset 'the official pariahs of the nation', with powerful political animosities in the wake of the Popular Front compounding a historic anti-Semitism on the French right dating back to the Dreyfus affair and even the Revolution of 1789.[208] The catastrophic defeat of 1940, with the charges that the 'Jewish Republic' had led France into a war against Germany that it was ill-equipped to fight, sharpened further the vengeful anti-Semitism that would find official expression under Vichy.

In October 1946, Pétain's former *chef de cabinet*, Henri du Moulin de Labarthète, declared that Vichy's anti-Semitic legislation had been 'spontaneous', 'home-grown' and developed independently of Germany.[209] Independently perhaps, but not without Germany in mind. The Vichy administration was less than a week old when Pierre-Etienne Flandin, a former premier who was to serve briefly as Laval's successor in 1941 (and not the most noted anti-Semite), made plain his view that collaboration would require France 'completely to rid herself' of Jewish influence.[210] The first Jewish Statute of 3 October 1940 was enacted within a week of the anti-Jewish ordinance of 27 September imposed by the Germans in the occupied zone. This early synchronisation of anti-Jewish policy allowed Vichy not only to address an urgent internal 'problem' but also to prove itself a worthy, and willing, partner of Nazi Germany.[211] Occupation did not constitute the reason for state anti-Semitism under Vichy, but it did provide the pretext.

The Paris collaborationists pressed their Vichy counterparts for ever stronger measures. Vying with Rebatet's anti-Semitic excesses, Céline called hysterically for 'Supreme racism! Disinfection! Cleansing! Only one race in France: the Aryan', declaring the 'real enemies' to be 'Jews and Masons'.[212] As already stated, a number of convinced anti-Semites operated close to the centre of power at Vichy, wielding either personal influence over Pétain (Ménétrel) or political influence over decision-making (Alibert, Vallat, Darquier). For those who promoted it, anti-Semitism was a means of keeping faith with what Vallat approvingly described as a 'long national tradition' – a French tradition, he held, that had always been in conflict with an 'unassimilable Jewish tradition'.[213] As though to illustrate the point, one of Vallat's successors as head of the CGQJ would be Charles Mercier du Paty de Clam, offspring of the Commandant du Paty de Clam who had arrested Dreyfus in 1894.

An anti-German nationalist as well as an anti-Semite, Vallat was a *grand mutilé* of the 1914–18 conflict who had been prominent in right-wing veterans' associations and militant Catholic circles in the inter-war years. He even saw potential for competition between French and German anti-Semitism, dismissing the SS officer in charge of Jewish affairs in France, Theodor Dannecker, as a mere novice: 'I am an older anti-Semite than you. I could be your father in these matters.'[214] At his trial in 1947, Vallat would defend himself against the charge of collaboration on the grounds that he had always been anti-Semitic: his anti-Semitism, he protested, had a French rather than German pedigree, 'inspired by my personal conception of the Jewish problem'. Vallat's personal conception was clearly that anti-Semitism ranked some way behind collaboration as an incriminating posture.[215]

Anti-Semitism was a regular feature in the daily radio broadcasts of the Légion Française des Combattants, while Pétainist propaganda trumpeted the 'defensive measures' taken by the regime against the 'Jewish peril'. Such measures against Jews were described as 'a first very necessary and very gentle sweep of the brush after the harm they have done to us'.[216] As a symbol of their national exclusion, Jews were barred from the Allier department in which Vichy was located. In summer 1943, when Pétain visited the small spa town of La Bourboule in the neighbouring Puy-de-Dôme department for a thermal cure, Jewish residents and other 'undesirables' (332 persons in all, many of whom had been resettled there as refugees) were forcibly removed in advance and relocated. Similar measures were taken on behalf of other Vichy notables in Châtel-Guyon, Aix-les-Bains and elsewhere.[217] When, from March 1942, the regime became complicit in the deportation of Jews to the Nazi camps, Laval defended its action as a form of 'national prophylaxy'.[218] Likewise, Darquier justified the *Vel d'Hiv* round-up of July 1942 as a measure 'in the province of public hygiene', a first step in clearing the way for 'an aristocracy of young men, rid of this Jewish scum, who will be able to conduct France toward its true destiny'.[219]

Callously pragmatic, Laval persuaded the Germans to include children in the initial deportations, ostensibly to keep families together but more plausibly to prevent them falling as a charge on the government. As early as June 1941, Laval's replacement as deputy head of government, Admiral Darlan, had urged that 'the foreign Israelites currently held in centres of accommodation or concentration camps' should be kept isolated from the wider community, and that 'everything should be done to bring about their departure from France'.[220] By February 1942, just weeks before the first mass deportations, the German authorities needed no further persuading of how representative was this attitude. In a communication to his Consul-General, Rudolf Schleier, the embassy official entrusted with Jewish affairs, Carl-Theo Zeitschel, noted that 'the French government would be happy to get rid of the Jews somehow, without attracting too much attention'.[221] Once this was in train, moreover, Laval would make no secret of his satisfaction to be relieved of an unwelcome community in France's foreign Jews.[222]

The extent to which Vichy knowingly collaborated in the Nazi genocide has never been conclusively determined, and Laval 'bargained' hard to limit deportation to non-French Jews. To the SS police chief in France, Karl Oberg, he protested in September 1942 that Jews could not simply be 'handed over as in a discount store, as many as you like and all at the same price'.[223] This grotesque remark appears to obviate the charge (at least) of persecution on purely racialist grounds and points, as Robert Paxton argues, to an 'exclusionary rather than exterminationist' rationale, the corollary of a French anti-Semitism based largely on criteria of assimilation as distinct from the more biological conception that underpinned Nazism.[224] The exemptions extended to *anciens combattants* and holders of the *Légion d'honneur* in the Jewish Statutes of October 1940 and June 1941, following hard upon an explicitly racial definition of Jewishness, had illustrated from the outset the ambiguous nature of Vichy's anti-Semitism.[225]

Only through an effort of will, however, could those at Vichy have remained ignorant of the reports circulating, from as early as autumn 1941, of atrocities committed against Jews in the occupied territories of eastern Europe and early evidence suggesting a programme of extermination. The inclusion of elderly and infirm Jews in the deportation convoys, moreover, made forced labour an implausible objective. Vichy nonetheless conspired in the fiction that the Jews deported from France were being resettled in eastern Europe; and neither Laval nor Bousquet, in their macabre negotiations with SS police chief Oberg, appear to have asked too many importuning questions about the real destination of the convoys. On one occasion, Laval pressed Oberg for clarification not of what was actually happening to deported Jews but of what the German authorities were *claiming* to be happening – to ensure that the line from Vichy remained consistent with this.[226]

One of the first pieces of Republican legislation to be repealed by Vichy was the Marchandeau decree, introduced in April 1939 to restrain the extreme-right press in its expression of racism and anti-Semitism. This permitted a number of popular dailies and weeklies to urge support for state persecution of Jews. They called for sweeping anti-Jewish sanctions and a 'fight to the death' that would purge the country of its last remaining Jew.[227] In March 1941, the stridently anti-Semitic *Au Pilori* called for 'Death to the Jew!', declaring that Jews were 'not men' but 'stinking beasts' deserving of the same treatment as 'fleas', 'epidemics' and 'invasive microbes'.[228] Proclaiming that 'Jews should pay for the war or die', *Au Pilori* appealed to the basest motives of its readers, encouraging them to denounce their Jewish neighbours by letter to the editor or directly to the authorities.[229] At the same time, the Paris-based and German-financed Institut d'Etude des Questions Juives (Institute for the Study of Jewish Questions, IEQ J) launched a touring 'exhibition' on the Jews and France at the Palais Berlitz, and published a series of brochures with titles such as *The Jews and Parasitism in Nature*, *Judaism Against Aryan Humanity*, *The Real Power of the Jews*, and *No, The Jews Are Not Men Like Us!*.[230] That publications such as *Au Pilori* and the pro-Nazi *La Gerbe* or *Je suis partout* should have enjoyed circulation runs of 65,000, 140,000 and up to 300,000 respectively says much about the ambient anti-Semitism in which, from across the demarcation line, Vichy sought to pass this 'essential test of collaboration'.[231]

2 The Vichy legacy

The extreme right in post-war France

Liberation and retribution

At the Liberation, Vichyites and collaborationists reaped what they had sown in the years 1940–44. 'The revulsion which collaboration provoked – even among those conservatives who had originally backed Vichy – benefited the very enemies whom Vichy and collaborationists had wanted to destroy: the Republic, the democrats, and above all the Communists.'[1] With the left in the ascendant and many communists boasting distinguished Resistance records, the political climate was inimical to those tarred with the legacy of collaboration. The Constitution of the Fourth Republic reasserted the 'inalienable and sacred rights' that had been abolished by Vichy, reconnecting France to the heritage of the Revolution and the Republic. It restored the motto '*Liberté, Egalité, Fraternité*' and defined further rights that would have been anathema to Vichy, in the areas of racial and sexual equality, industrial relations, political asylum and freedom of conscience. It enshrined not only Republican principles of governance and social protection but collectivist principles of economic management antithetical to the ethos of Vichy.[2]

Of those elected to the first Constituent Assembly charged with laying the foundations of the new Republic, over 80 per cent claimed service in the Resistance; conversely, none of the 569 deputies and senators who had voted full powers to Pétain were eligible to stand.[3] In the elections of October 1945 (to the Constituent Assembly) and November 1946 (to the National Assembly), the PCF emerged as the most powerful party in France, winning between a quarter and a third of the votes and seats. Having taken no part in the infamous vote of 10 July 1940 and promoting itself as the party of the Resistance, it increased its electorate from 1.5 million in 1936 to 5.5 million in 1946.[4] Taken together, the Communists, Socialists and Mouvement Républicain Populaire (MRP) accounted for some three-quarters of the votes and seats in these elections, dramatising the surge of support in the immediate post-war period for parties claiming to represent the antithesis of Vichy.

Many alleged collaborators met with rough justice in the early phase of the Liberation before the legal framework of de Gaulle's provisional government took effect in autumn 1944. The finer distinctions between collaboration and collaborationism were largely lost in the settling of scores that took place throughout France. The extreme-right historian François Duprat advances the figure of 15,000 'national militants' summarily executed in the *épuration* (purge), and 250,000 deprived of their civic rights; others put the executions at over 100,000, drawing comparisons between the Liberation and the Terror of 1793.[5] The findings of modern historians and official estimates argue for some 9,000 summary executions carried out during the *épuration sauvage* (the period immediately preceding and following the Liberation), 767 executions after due process, and a further 770 death sentences handed down by military tribunals. Of over 300,000 cases of alleged collaboration considered, around 170,000 went to trial, resulting in some 40,000 sentences of imprisonment and some 50,000 of 'national degradation' (loss of civic rights and exclusion from public office). Added to these were possibly 10,000 women who had their heads shaved in public humiliation as a punishment for alleged '*collaboration horizontale*'.[6]

Staged in late July and early August 1945 in the Palais de Justice in Paris, the trial of Pétain was that of the entire collaboration process. Before a courtroom packed with observers and journalists, Pétain's defence was submitted to a jury composed of 12 former parliamentarians of the Third Republic and 12 representatives of the Resistance. The selection of jurors was politically loaded, drawn by lot from those parliamentarians who had voted against granting full powers to Pétain in July 1940 and from a list of names provided by the Resistance. The ghosts of Vichy were present not only in the dock. The presiding judge at the trial was Judge Pierre Mongibeaux, president of the Cour de Cassation (Court of Cassation), who had sworn allegiance to Pétain in 1941 and applied himself to upholding the laws of Vichy. The chief prosecutor, Judge André Mornet, had been part of the Vichy commission that had stripped over 15,000 citizens of their naturalised status; he had also offered his services to the Riom court set up in February 1942 to prosecute Léon Blum and other Third Republic leaders for treason.[7]

When, on 30 October 1940, Pétain had announced for the first time to the French people that he was 'embarking down the path of collaboration', he had stressed his personal responsibility. 'This policy is mine. The ministers are answerable to me alone. It is me alone whom history will judge.'[8] When history did come to judge him, he was less accepting of its right to do so. He refused to cooperate with the court proceedings, declaring in a preliminary statement that he had been entrusted with power by legitimate means in a context of national emergency and that he did not recognise the right of this court to try him now. He had served as a 'shield' to France, he protested, and 'struggled daily against the enemy's demands, with a dagger held to my throat'. He would not, he declared, answer any questions of his accusers.[9]

With Pétain essentially a spectator at his own trial, his defence was conducted by the young lawyer Jacques Isorni, who had acted for Robert Brasillach at his trial some months earlier. Testimonies were heard from a host of witnesses, major players from the Third Republic and Vichy concerned primarily to absolve themselves. At the end of it all, Pétain was sentenced to death with a recommendation that, on account of his 89 years and previous record of service to France, this be commuted to life imprisonment and national degradation. The recommendation was accepted by de Gaulle, and Pétain spent the last six years of his life as a prisoner on the Ile d'Yeu, where his remains lie still despite an energetic campaign by his supporters to have them transferred to the fort at Douaumont, which had been central to the defence of Verdun in 1916.

The most dramatic intervention in Pétain's trial was the unexpected appearance as witness of Pierre Laval, who had failed to secure political asylum in Spain. Laval's spirited testimony was a dress rehearsal for his own trial some weeks later. He argued that Pétain had been complicit in everything the Vichy regime had done and that he, Laval, had not been the evil genius behind an essentially innocent Head of State. At his own trial, Laval would respond defiantly to the charges brought against him, but he was damned in advance by his collaborationist policies and his unequivocally stated wish that Germany should win the war. Laval's trial was an ignominious affair, degenerating into a slanging match between the accused and his jurors before the inevitable death sentence was passed. Having attempted to poison himself, Laval had his stomach pumped with sufficient effect to allow him to be dragged, more dead than alive, before a firing squad on 15 October 1945.[10]

Among high-level collaborationists executed by the Liberation tribunals were the head of the Milice, Joseph Darnand, Vichy's Delegate-General to the Occupied Zone, Fernand de Brinon, the head of the Press Corporation, Jean Luchaire, the Radio Paris broadcaster, Jean-Hérold Paquis, and the head of the pro-fascist Parti Franciste, Marcel Bucard. Others were more fortunate. The death sentence handed down to Jacques Benoist-Méchin was commuted to life imprisonment, while Xavier Vallat, former Commissioner-General for Jewish Affairs, was sentenced to 10 years in prison (a sentence that took account of the severe wounds which he bore from the 1914–18 war). Among those who eluded the justice of the courts, Henriot was assassinated by the Resistance and Doriot was killed when his car was strafed in Germany; Déat escaped to Italy, Bonnard and Darquier de Pellepoix to Spain; Céline took refuge in Denmark and Chateaubriant in the Austrian Tyrol. From an 'index' of 160 collaborationist writers, a few were sentenced to death while most were given prison sentences or acquitted.[11] Though de Brinon was tried and executed as late as March–April 1947,[12] it was not long before the focus of the Liberation courts shifted from retribution to the restoration of national unity. Whereas Georges Suarez (editor of the pro-Nazi newspaper *Aujourd'hui*) was executed in November 1944 and Robert Brasillach in February 1945, Henri Béraud, Lucien Rebatet and Pierre-Antoine Cousteau had their death sentences commuted and were among the many condemned to prison or hard labour. 'If Drieu agrees to remain hidden two years in a cellar', quipped the collaborationist writer Marcel Jouhandeau, 'he'll end up as a minister.'[13] While Drieu evaded the verdict of the courts by taking his own life in March 1945, Céline would be sentenced *in absentia* in February 1950 to a year's imprisonment and a fine. The recycling of some prominent Vichy officials through the administrations of the Fourth and Fifth Republics would give a wry prescience to Jouhandeau's remark.

Unlike many of his fellow collaborationists, Brasillach did not attempt to flee. His death sentence represented the act of atonement for literary collaborationism at large. Brasillach was executed by firing squad on the highly symbolic date for the extreme right of 6 February 1945 (11 years to the day after the anti-parliamentary riot recalled by many as a *coup d'état manqué*). This despite a petition for clemency signed by over 50 intellectuals of diverse political persuasions and delivered in person to de Gaulle, as head of the provisional government, by the novelist François Mauriac.[14] The signatories included Mauriac himself, Paul Valéry, Jean Anouilh, Jean Cocteau, Paul Claudel and, after much hesitation, Albert Camus. Reflecting on Brasillach's end, Simone de Beauvoir articulated the ambivalence of those who called down justice on their fellow writers while acknowledging the danger of turning due process into martyrdom: 'We wanted the death of the editor of *Je suis partout*, not the death of this man who was completely absorbed in dying well.'[15] De Beauvoir was among those who had refused to sign the petition on Brasillach's behalf.

Brasillach's execution exacerbated the feeling among Vichyites and collaborationists that they were the victims of rank injustice at the Liberation. Their organisations were proscribed and their publications banned from circulation. This led partly to a denial of the 'right-wing' label, with a preference for more anodyne appellations such as 'national opposition', and partly to a recourse to clandestinity in extreme-right activism during the immediate post-war years. Coming to terms with their crushing defeat, Vichyites and collaborationists who had escaped the *épuration* could only look on in dismay as the hated institutions of the Third Republic were replicated in the constitutional framework of the new Fourth Republic. This provided for the concentration of power in parliament rather than a strong executive, and for elections on a list system of proportional representation – both factors which, in seeking to guarantee protection from authoritarianism, heralded a return to the party-dominated regime of the pre-war years. In these circumstances, some Vichy sympathisers bowed to the inevitable and fell in behind the democratic parties; others waged a bitter rear-guard action to keep alive their disgraced politics, fostering an ideological counter-culture as the 'Opposition Nationale' within the new Republic. As one contemporary observed, the underground had shifted camps.[16]

Following the trial, commuted death sentence and imprisonment of Marshal Pétain and the execution of Laval, Darnand and others, the initial reflex of the extreme right as a whole was to mount a retrospective defence of the Vichy regime. From as early as summer 1944, clandestine notices were circulated in support of Pétain and collaboration. A handbill with the names and addresses of the 24 jurors at Pétain's trial called for revenge in the case of a guilty verdict. These notices soon gave way to better organised bulletins and periodicals such as René Malliavin's *Ecrits de Paris*.[17] With a reported circulation of some 30,000, this served as a forum for neo-Pétainism, publishing contributions from prominent Vichy officials and apologists, including Pétain's defence counsel, Jacques Isorni, the former minister for relations with Germany, Jacques Benoist-Méchin, and the former Commissioner-General for Jewish Affairs, Xavier Vallat.[18] Representatives of the extreme right in this period were almost exclusively *anciens* – former Vichyites and collaborationists, ex-Miliciens or LVF volunteers. Their model was predominantly Nazism, though Italian Fascism, Belgian Rexism and Spanish Falangism provided other reference points. Writing a decade and a half after the Liberation, Maurice Bardèche would reflect upon the rapidity with which extreme-right militants resumed their activities 'amid the maelstrom of defeat and persecution'. While those less fortunate faced the verdicts of the courts, these 'heroes of desperate hours' regrouped 'in the shadows of injustice and hatred'. They were, as Bardèche put it, a scattered army bereft of its commanding officers, 'living off roneotyped pamphlets and meetings where the stirring marching songs of Hitler's divisions were sung and where the fires of the summer solstice burned'.[19]

Defending the indefensible: Maurras and Bardèche

If Pétain was held accountable for the policies implemented by Vichy, it was elsewhere that the courts looked to pass sentence on the regime's underlying ideology. The trial of Charles Maurras in January 1945, though focused on his conduct during the Occupation, was also the trial of the political ideology for which he had long stood and which had been an important influence on Vichy policy-making. In the inter-war years, Maurrassism had exerted a similarly powerful influence on the right to that exerted by communism on the left in the post-war years, predisposing many young right-wing intellectuals against the Republic.[20] A leading anti-Dreyfusard and anti-democrat as well as a distinguished *littérateur* and Academician, Maurras had lent the prestige of his pen to supporting Pétain's regime, though his uncompromising 'France alone' nationalism conserved its anti-German core and kept him at some remove from the Paris collaborationists. 'The revenge of Dreyfus!' is how Maurras would greet his sentence to life imprisonment and national degradation after a trial in which he refused to acknowledge the merest modicum of guilt.[21]

In response to the arrest and sentencing of Maurras, there appeared a series of clandestine pamphlets, the *Documents nationaux*, in defence of the Action Française leader. These rehearsed familiar pro-Vichy themes, condemned the Resistance as 'terrorists', and lamented the 'illness called Democracy' to which France had once more succumbed. The same period saw the appearance of other publications dedicated likewise to the shades of Vichy, venting their authors' spleen against the post-war judicial process and their savage opposition to the incipient Fourth Republic. Such publications demanded an amnesty for convicted collaborators, severe sanctions against the PCF, and a successful conclusion to the war now being waged by the French army in Indo-China – a conflict seen as one more stage in the relentless advance of communist imperialism.[22]

Beyond the spectacle of an unbowed Maurras in the dock and a defiant, if small, following still at large, the most notorious and influential defence of Vichy was articulated by Maurice Bardèche. A university professor best known for his literary studies of Balzac and Stendhal, Bardèche had been imprisoned for six months at the Liberation on account of his close association with Robert Brasillach, his brother-in-law with whom he had published an *Histoire du cinéma* and a pro-Franco *Histoire de la guerre d'Espagne*. Recalling the petition submitted by François Mauriac in favour of the condemned Brasillach, Bardèche's first major polemic, published in 1947, was the *Lettre à François Mauriac*. Here he argued the fundamental legality of the Vichy regime and the illegitimacy of the Resistance, taking issue with the 'lie' at the heart of the post-war judicial process: that '[w]hoever was not a member of the Resistance was a bad Frenchman'. The post-war consensus with its anti-Vichy animus, he declared, rested on 'a lie from beginning to end'. Pétain's regime had entered into collaboration with Nazi Germany as a 'vital necessity'; it had been right to exterminate its enemies in the pursuit of national unity. The Vichy administration had preserved France from extinction, while its Jewish Statutes had done more to protect than to endanger French Jews. The post-war tribunals, Bardèche insisted, did not have 'the *right* to condemn a single one of those men who had served the *legitimate* government of France'.[23]

In a further book published the following year, *Nuremberg ou la terre promise*, Bardèche turned his attentions to Nazi war crimes and the victors' justice meted out at Nuremberg. Using a similar line of argument, he challenged the authority of the war crimes tribunals and sought to rehabilitate 'the moral virtues enshrined in Fascism and National Socialism: civic engagement, discipline, the desire to serve, total commitment to an ideal, be it good or bad'.[24] Bardèche accused the Allies of largely fabricating the case against Nazi Germany and pointed the way for later revisionists by casting doubt on the evidence of the Holocaust: 'in the pious hope of appearing more plausible', he claimed, the Allies 'built *extra* crematoria at Auschwitz and Dachau, for example, in order to allay the scruples that might have arisen in the minds of some mathematicians'. Bardèche would go on to argue elsewhere that the Holocaust was a 'lie' and that there had been 'no deliberate extermination of Jews in the concentration camps'.[25]

While the *Lettre à François Mauriac* had outraged a section of public opinion, it had brought no legal proceedings against its author. As an apology for Nazism and a denial of Nazi war crimes, *Nuremberg ou la terre promise* was banned and saw Bardèche brought to trial. Defended by the former counsel for Pétain and Brasillach, Jacques Isorni, he was sentenced in 1954 to a year's imprisonment, after a series of trials and appeals. He served only days of his sentence before being pardoned by President René Coty, in view of his earlier imprisonment and his pressing family situation as a father of five children.[26] Echoing the campaign mobilised to defend him on grounds of freedom of expression, Bardèche would later reflect: 'I was thrown into prison under unbelievable conditions. It was the first time in forty years that a writer had been put in prison because of his ideas. Not because of his political actions but because of his ideas.'[27]

Bardèche's writings and imprisonment marked him out as the egregious voice of French and European neo-fascism. At the same time, others were busy propagating a range of themes that went beyond the narrow defence of Vichy. Though their freedom of public expression was restricted, such propagandists circulated publications on monarchism, ultra-nationalism, anti-parliamentarism, anti-communism, anti-capitalism, militant Catholicism, anti-Semitism, racism and European supremacism, to name but some of the causes espoused. The defining feature of the extreme right in this period was its heterogeneity. Even in the withering climate of post-Liberation France, the outer fringes of the right threw up what Bardèche would describe as an 'anarchic proliferation' of factions and coteries, many of them knowing successive incarnations under different names (a classic means of overcoming proscription) despite very limited membership.[28]

Smouldering embers

Mediated through the events of 1940–44, the ideological inspiration for these movements lay in a variety of pre-war sources: Maurras' Action Française, the right-wing 'leagues' of the inter-war years, and the writings of authors such as Drieu, Brasillach, Rebatet and Céline – without going back to Drumont, Barrès and others of an earlier generation. Among those in post-war France evincing an intellectual affinity with such sources, two names are worthy of brief note: René Binet and Charles Gastaut, alias Luca, the in-law nephew of Marcel Déat. A communist-turned-fascist who had served in the Waffen-SS Charlemagne Division, Binet became one of the French extreme right's most energetic and venomous propagandists in the immediate post-war years. Through his books *Théorie du racisme* (*Theory of Racism*) and *Contribution à une éthique raciste* (*Towards a Racist Ethics*), and through a series of ephemeral publications (*Le Combattant européen*, *La Sentinelle*, *Le Nouveau Prométhée* and others), he proclaimed the 'absolute superiority' of the white European race over 'Semitic, Mongoloid and Negroid dross'. Postulating the 'inequality of the human races' on grounds not of culture but of blood, Binet called for a 'racist revolution' and the creation of an 'ethnic elite' through a state-sponsored programme of eugenic engineering.[29]

As early as 1946, Binet helped to launch the Parti Républicain d'Unité Populaire (PRUP), with its slogan '*La France aux vrais Français!*' ('France for the Real French!').[30] Hostile to American and Soviet hegemony alike, the PRUP was an ideological hotchpotch mixing nationalism with Europeanism and socialist themes with collaborationist sympathies. Given its tiny membership (estimated by Duprat at around 150), the PRUP joined forces with Julien Dalbin's Rassemblement Travailliste Français to contest the 1947 municipal elections. Following its dismal electoral performance, Binet converted the PRUP in 1948 into the Mouvement Socialiste d'Unité Française (MSUF), described by Duprat as 'the first real movement implacably opposed to the order emerging from the Allied victory in 1945, and the first after that date to profess a thoroughgoing racism and explicit anti-Semitism'.[31] Styling itself loosely under the intellectual aegis of Bardèche, the MSUF used its weekly *L'Unité* to call for an amnesty for convicted collaborators, a Europe unified against the Soviet Union and the United States, and the reversal of the 'African invasion' by returning all North African Arabs to their countries of origin.[32] Though it, too, attracted only a tiny membership (some 250 at most, according to Duprat), the MSUF provoked sufficient concern to be proscribed in 1949. Undeterred, Binet turned to other channels, such as the journal *La Sentinelle*, to promote his conceptions of 'national socialism' and 'scientific racism' while advocating the creation of a 'fascist international'.[33] Until his early death in 1957, the European supremacist ideology to which he gave crude expression, calling for the 'purification of the French race of the elements which pollute it',[34] constituted a tireless assault on the humanitarian values reaffirmed at the Liberation and enshrined in the Constitution of the Fourth Republic.

At the same time as Binet was propagating his 'social-racism' through his shadowy movements and publishing outlets, Charles Luca was seeking to lay the ground for 'an authentic National Socialism' in France, boldly declaring: 'The century in which we are living will be that of Fascism.'[35] Founder of a succession of militaristic movements between 1947 and 1960 (Commandos de Saint-Ex, Mouvement National Citadelle, Parti Socialiste Français, Phalange Française, Mouvement Populaire Français), Luca placed his emphasis on discipline and combat readiness; he claimed several hundred, mostly young, adherents and dressed his 'troops' in quasi-Nazi garb procured from army surplus stores. Beneath the theatricality (Nazi-style salutes, swearing of oaths, presentation of arms, etc.) lay an ideology close to that of Binet, which called for the defence of the 'white race' and of Western civilisation by 'a revolutionary elite selected solely on grounds of their biological worth'. Like Binet, Luca denounced both Anglo-Saxon and Soviet imperialism, arguing for a 'liberated' and 'independent' Europe united around a 'Socialist, Nationalist and Racist revolutionary programme'. The designated enemies were familiar: 'inferior races', 'half-breeds', 'degenerates', 'universalist doctrines', 'the farce of parliamentary democracy', 'Mongol Russian communism', 'Jewish international capitalism', and 'the Negro peril'. In their journal, *Fidélité*, Luca and his collaborators expressed support for the policy of apartheid in South Africa ('the bastion of white peoples against degeneration') and for the persecution by white racists of blacks in the American southern states, including the 'summary justice of "lynch-law"'. Racism, they proclaimed, 'is the reflex of a nation that does not wish to die, the antidote to the virus of democracy'.[36]

The 'Fascist International'

The importance of Binet, Luca and their circles lay not in the few hundred malcontents and misfits whom they attracted but in the fact that they stoked, as one historian put it, the 'smouldering embers' of right-wing extremism during these early post-war years.[37] In so doing, they helped to set the terms of a neo-fascism that did not just hark back to the heroes of the past in Pétain, Laval, Brasillach and others: it also sought to take account of the new world order emerging from Yalta and to respond to contemporary issues such as the Cold War and decolonisation. It was this need to adjust to a changing global environment that delivered the impetus to found a neo-fascist 'International'. Against the backdrop of a world rent into East and West, such an International was to be centred on a 'new Europe', defined in André Mutter's *Paroles Françaises* as a '[c]ommunity of free peoples, sharing the same civilisation, the same religion, the same blood, and the same destiny'.[38] Though there was nothing essentially new in this idea, the vigour with which it was propounded made it one of the defining features of the post-war French and European extreme right. Binet put the issue most forcefully in his journal, *La Sentinelle*: 'DOWN WITH THE EUROPE OF STRASBOURG, DOWN WITH THE EUROPE OF THE FEDERALISTS, DOWN WITH THE EUROPE OF THE LACKEYS OF RUSSIAN OR AMERICAN IMPERIALISM.' The objective, he urged, was to 'forge the links between nationalists across the whole of Europe which will enable us to form THE ALLIANCE OF NATIONAL WORKERS' STATES OF EUROPE, while preserving the dignity and independence of each of our peoples'.[39]

Such a Europe of nationalist states, constituting a third force between the superpower blocs, was the objective at the heart of an international conference of neo-fascists held in the Swedish town of Malmö in May 1951 and hosted by Per Engdahl, leader of the Swedish Nysvenska Rörelsen (Movement for a New Sweden). This followed a preliminary meeting held the previous year in Rome under the auspices of Giorgio Almirante's Movimento Sociale Italiano (MSI), showing that defeat and opprobrium had done nothing to dampen the ambitions of a hard core of European neo-fascists. Among the participants at the Malmö conference were Maurice Bardèche at the head of the French delegation (which included Binet and Luca), the English fascist Oswald Mosley, and around a hundred other delegates from the main German, Austrian, Italian, Spanish, Hungarian and Swedish neo-fascist groups. The outcome was the creation of a European Social Movement (MSE), an international organisation focused on anti-communism, national-corporatism and 'third force' Euro-peanism. In its manifesto, the MSE envisaged a 'European Empire' with a 'central government', common army and economic identity. Though it proposed to bring about a 'spiritual regeneration of man, society and the State', it found itself having to temper its radicalism, retaining residually democratic controls on power such as plebiscitary elections. At a moment when the memory of fascist dictatorship overlapped with the fear of Soviet totalitarianism, a full-scale assault on democracy was not the means by which to exert popular appeal.[40]

Despite support from established names on the French extreme right such as Doriot's former lieutenant, Victor Barthélemy, and the former Vichy propagandist, Jean-Louis Tixier-Vignancour, the MSE was soon exposed to the centrifugal pressures so typical of national neo-fascist movements. Dissatisfied with its restrained programme, a number of more radical members broke away in September 1951 to form the rival New European Order (NOE), an organisation distinguished by its pronounced racism, anti-Semitism and propagation of social Darwinism. Led by René Binet and the Swiss Guy Amaudruz, the NOE called at its founding congress in Zurich for a 'European racial policy' to control ethnic inter-marriages and improve the white European gene pool through medical and scientific intervention. The 'decline of Europe' was to remain an obsessive concern of the NOE, which also articulated a virulent anti-Semitism and a revisionist dismissal of the Holocaust as 'a few thousand Jews and degenerates who died of typhus in the labour camps'.[41]

For all the prolific activity of figures such as Bardèche, Binet and Luca, two overriding features continued to characterise the movements which they launched in the late 1940s and early 1950s: their weakness in terms of numbers and real political influence, and their tendency to scission and internecine conflict. Despite attempts to find common cause around a number of key themes, the landscape of the extreme right in post-war France remained a 'backwater in which small activist groups proliferated' without achieving 'the merest semblance of unity'.[42] The radical nature of the views expressed by some of these groups, moreover, had an inverse effect upon their ability to attract popular support, consigning them to a self-perpetuating isolation on the fringes of French politics.[43] The high-profile campaigns to rehabilitate Pétain or defend Bardèche, the efforts to construct a 'Fascist International', and the production of publications designed to contest a place among the mainstream French press (such as René Malliavin's *Rivarol* and Bardèche's *Défense de l'Occident*)[44] testified to a small but dedicated reservoir of support for what remained nonetheless 'the most unpopular cause in France'.[45]

Le Pen: an apprenticeship in politics

It was into this world that Jean-Marie Le Pen stepped to take up his law studies in autumn 1947. Born in 1928, Le Pen had spent his childhood in a modest, conservative Breton family of small farmers and fishermen, an environment which he would describe as being of the 'popular and patriotic right'.[46] Educated in part by the Jesuits at the college of Saint-François-Xavier in Vannes, he was to be remembered by teachers and fellow pupils as a precocious, recalcitrant child. In 1942, he became a *Pupille de la Nation* (war orphan) when his father's fishing boat struck a mine. This, Le Pen would argue, marked him out from an early age as 'more French than the others', as both a natural and an adopted son of the nation.[47]

Frustrated in his ambition to become a naval officer by the decimation of the French fleet, Le Pen obtained his '*Bac philo*' and enrolled on a slender state grant to study law in Paris. There he quickly assumed a leading role in student politics, gaining election in 1949 (and re-election in 1950) as president of the Corporation de Droit (Law Students' Union), a right-leaning component of the National Union of Students (UNEF). Le Pen's arrival in the Latin Quarter took him to one of the centres of political engagement in post-war Paris, while his role in the Corpo de Droit and UNEF provided some of his earliest lessons in political action.[48] He would later describe himself at that time as apolitical – 'I had no involvement in politics in those days' – and his approved biographies make little of his interests beyond his student union activities.[49] Thus with his first mention in *Le Monde*, which he earned leading a student demonstration outside the National Assembly on 15 March 1951, protesting against the Pleven government's austerity programme and its effect on the newly launched students' social security scheme. Le Pen was singled out in this report for having kept the students in order and prevented their protest from degenerating into violence.[50]

Beyond this aspect of his student days, there was evidence of Le Pen's wider political sympathies and involvement. Following the 'Revolution of 1945', he would later recall, 'the right looked dead and buried. Stripped bare, insulted and reduced to nothing, it was kept alive in the minds and hearts of an ardent and generous few.'[51] Of no fixed abode within the fragmented landscape of the post-war right, Le Pen seems to have found most affinity with the 'integral nationalism' of Charles Maurras which had exerted such an important influence on the Vichy regime. Fellow students Paul Anselin and Claude Chabrol would recall the young Le Pen's vocal defence of Pétain and Vichy, and his aversion in equal measure to communism and Gaullism; others remembered him as a 'declared A[ction] F[rançaise] supporter'; others still, as a *grande gueule* (loud-mouth) lacking any real depth of engagement with political issues.[52] In any case, in November 1948, Le Pen found his way into police records as a 'monarchist militant' for hawking the Maurrassian, pro-Pétain weekly *Aspects de la France* on the Rue de la Sorbonne.[53] While this may seem no more significant than a young Jacques Chirac selling the communist daily *L'Humanité*, it pointed to a commitment that would endure far beyond Le Pen's student years.

Though in essence a Catholic-monarchist ideology, Maurrassism offered a synthesis of many elements of French right-wing thought that chimed with Le Pen's early political dispositions. Whatever his reservations on its Catholicism or its monarchism,[54] he would have found here ample expression of an authoritarian, ultra-nationalist politics, channelling bitter grievance against a variety of enemies: the PCF, de Gaulle, the Republic, the foreigner, the Freemason and the Jew chief amongst them. Maurrassism stressed the decadence and moral decline of modern France and called for a return to order and traditional values under the binding institutions of Family, Church, State and Nation.[55] Though Le Pen avoided locating himself within any single ideological tradition, his name would appear in the mid-1950s among the earliest contributors to *La Nation Française*, an offshoot of *Aspects de la France* founded by the Maurrassian philosopher Pierre Boutang.[56]

The strength of the PCF in the immediate post-war period assured its prime place within the demonology of the right, setting the terms of an ideological conflict that would endure until the collapse of the Soviet Union almost half a century later. With the Cold War (and the war in Indo-China) gathering momentum, the late 1940s were a period of often violent confrontation between radical left-wing students and those (Vichy sympathisers, ultra-nationalists, neo-fascists, monarchists, and even Gaullists) who could be marshalled under the umbrella of the 'right' and whose rallying point was their anti-communism. Though de Gaulle remained the nemesis of Vichy, his resignation as head of the provisional government and muscular opposition to the Fourth Republic made him also now an objective 'ally'. More widely, it was de Gaulle and his Rassemblement du Peuple Français (Rally of the French People, RPF), not the splintered components of the 'Opposition Nationale', that were seen by the left as potentially the most serious 'fascist' threat to the restored Republic. The future leader of the Front National would recall bringing together in an 'embryonic front' Maurrassian monarchists (Pierre Boutang, Jean-Marc Varaut) with other right-wing agitators (Jean Bourdier, Alain Jamet) and Gaullist students under Jacques Dominati to wrest the Latin Quarter from 'the grip of the Marxists'.[57] Le Pen would also forge links in this period with names (Pierre Durand, Jacques Peyrat, the same Alain Jamet) that would feature half a century later in the apparat of the FN.[58]

With several citations in police records of the time on charges of public disorder and affray,[59] the young Le Pen soon developed a reputation as a verbal and physical bruiser: ideal credentials, it transpired, for participating in the security service of Jacques Isorni, head of the Pétainist Union des Nationaux Indépendants et Républicains (Union of Independent and Republican Nationalists, UNIR), who contested a Paris seat in the legislative elections of June 1951. Le Pen's role here involved mainly engaging in violent confrontations with communist 'commando' groups, protesters from the Ligue Internationale Contre l'Antisémitisme (International League Against Anti-Semitism, LICA), and at times Gaullist adversaries. Though Le Pen's autobiographical recollections make no mention of this episode, Isorni's own memoirs record the highly charged nature of UNIR's campaign and the violence of one particular confrontation ('led by Jean-Marie Le Pen and the chevalier d'Orgeix') with protesters. As reported by both Isorni and *Le Monde*, an election rally in the Salle Wagram in Paris two days before the poll saw a three-hour pitched battle, with tear-gas grenades, substantial material damage and over a hundred wounded.[60]

As a prominent lawyer who had defended Pétain and Brasillach at their trials in 1945, Isorni played a leading role in the campaign for Pétain's rehabilitation, notably through the Association pour Défendre la Mémoire du Maréchal Pétain (Association to Defend the Memory of Marshal Pétain, ADMP) which was set up following the latter's death in 1951.[61] He was one of the few Pétainists eligible to stand for election prior to the amnesty of 1953. The significance of UNIR's presence in the 1951 campaign was that it marked the first – and last – attempt to gain electoral legitimacy on an openly pro-Pétainist platform. It demanded a blanket amnesty for all those on whom sentence had been passed at the Liberation, with the restoration of their full civic and political rights; constitutional reform to strengthen the executive over the chamber of deputies; and the banning of the PCF. The movement also demanded 'that the French flag remain solidly implanted in Indo-China as in Africa'.[62] The issue on which it campaigned most vigorously, however, was that of 'a man unjustly imprisoned'; Isorni's principal objective in standing, he would later write, was to press within the National Assembly for a comprehensive amnesty law and 'the rehabilitation of the victor of Verdun'.[63]

The impact of the UNIR campaign was slight: it fielded too few lists to qualify as a 'national party' and its candidates fared badly, with barely a quarter of a million votes and only four elected deputies (among them Isorni and the former Vichy Agriculture Minister, Jacques Le Roy-Ladurie).[64] As a small isolated unit in parliament, the UNIR deputies were quickly absorbed by the conservative right in the form of Roger Duchet's Centre National des Indépendants (CNI). That Isorni's hastily constituted party should have contested the election at all, however, signalled the change in climate that was underway. Already in June 1949, a poll in *Le Figaro* had shown a strong majority of respondents to be in favour of an amnesty for former collaborators.[65] Of some 40,000 imprisoned in 1945, only 4,000 were still serving their sentence in 1951. The amnesty law of January 1951 reduced these to 1,570; a further amnesty law passed in July 1953 would see the figure drop to 62 by 1956 and 19 by 1958; by 1964, all remaining detainees had been released.[66]

These laws marked important stages in the rehabilitation of Vichyites and collaborationists. The first coincided with the launch, in January 1951, of René Malliavin's Pétainist weekly *Rivarol* (self-styled '*Hebdomadaire de l'Opposition Nationale*'), which rallied to UNIR and opened its columns to Isorni. The light sentences handed down by the High Court of Justice to many leading officials of Pétain's regime, together with the shift of emphasis from retribution to reintegration, helped to gloss over the crimes of Vichy and to allow *Maréchalisme* relatively free expression by the early 1950s.[67] Le Pen's involvement with Isorni would certainly have brought him into contact with Vichy ultras and other extreme-right elements while signalling an aspect of his own political temper (the UNIR list drew support notably from René Binet).[68] With Isorni's Paris seat secured, Le Pen emerged with valuable experience from this first sortie into the world of real, rather than student, politics. He had also confirmed his political affinities, since there is evidence that he would continue to frequent Pétainist and Maurrassian circles throughout the 1950s.[69]

Isorni was not alone in championing the Pétainist cause and denouncing the crimes of the Liberation. Bardèche, as has been noted, deployed his considerable literary talent to that end. Within the landscape of post-war French politics, other figures such as the anti-Semitic and anti-Masonic polemicists, Henry Coston and Jacques Ploncard d'Assac, and the former Milicien, François Brigneau, would come into their own as impenitent apologists for Vichy and collaboration. Scions of Action Française and self-appointed heirs to the legacy of Edouard Drumont, Coston and Ploncard, according to Jean-Yves Camus, 'inspired more militants in the 1950s and 1960s than the combined influence of all other radical-right groupings'.[70] Coston had followed Drumont as editor throughout the 1930s of *La Libre Parole* and headed a racist and anti-Semitic propaganda unit under Vichy, the Centre d'Action et de Documentation (Centre for Action and Documentation, CAD).[71] Imprisoned at the Liberation, Brigneau became a prominent journalist with several extreme-right publications (among them *Rivarol* and *Minute*) before going on to contribute a regular column to the FN's *National Hebdo*. Others, such as Maurice-Ivan Sicard (alias Saint-Paulien), would continue in the 1950s and 1960s to defend the Frenchmen who had enlisted to fight in Hitler's army in the name of European fascism. In a similar vein, the former LVF and Waffen-SS volunteer, Marc Augier (alias Saint-Loup), would justify collaboration as nothing less than 'the continuation of Europe', considering French veterans of the Wehrmacht and Waffen-SS as 'crusaders for the West'.[72] Such were the voices that continued to propagate a collaborationist message in the years following the Liberation and to chip away at the taboos erected by the post-war tribunals.

By the time Le Pen concluded his studies in 1953, the extreme right in France had seen out its most desperate hours. The amnesty laws signified the reintegration of Vichyites and collaborationists within the national community. Pétain had died in July 1951, Maurras in November 1952. Vichy had begun to recede as the defining factor in political identification, as Cold War tensions and the excesses of left-wing totalitarianism mounted. Excluded from government as early as 1947, the PCF increasingly became a target of political opprobrium, tempering the discredit of the extreme right. At the same time, the influential review *Paroles Françaises* (under the former PSF activist and Resistance leader, André Mutter) argued for national reconciliation between *collabos* and *résistants* in the interests of a united front against the communist threat.[73] The loss of Indo-China and the outbreak of the Algerian War in 1954 would provide the platform for a rehabilitated French nationalism – defined this time not in relation to Germany, as it had historically been, but in relation to France's colonies and the perceived threat of global communism. In decolonisation, the extreme right would find a redemptive *casus belli*.

Indo-China: an apprenticeship in arms

The defeat of Japan in 1945 left a power vacuum in the former French colonial territories of Indo-China (Cambodia, Laos, and in particular Vietnam). In the wake of the Japanese surrender, the nationalist Vietminh led by the communist Ho Chi Minh moved swiftly to forestall a return to the French colonial rule that had prevailed in Vietnam for almost a century. The French meanwhile harboured the illusion that they could win back not just Vietnam but also Cambodia and Laos, which they proposed to bring together in an Indo-Chinese federation within the French Union. When the delicate negotiations broke down in 1946 between Ho's self-proclaimed revolutionary government and French officials anxious to preserve their hold on Vietnam, France was left with the choice of endorsing the new power structures in Indo-China or embarking on a war of colonial reconquest.

The protracted war which followed saw French political opinion split between advocates of a negotiated settlement and those who called for military escalation. Vietnam was a far-off land with a very small French settler community and, unlike the later conflict in Algeria, this was a war fought by a professional rather than a conscript army. During the war, the French population in Vietnam was estimated at no more than 100,000, only a third of whom were civilians; though metropolitan French personnel formed the core of the military presence, the great majority of the serving soldiers were drawn from Indo-Chinese and African units.[74] An important dimension was added to the conflict by the political fault lines that ran through it. As the Cold War deepened, the Soviet Union and

China came out in support of Ho Chi Minh's independent Vietnamese Republic, just as the United States came to support and bear part of the economic burden for the French war effort. Though the Vietminh were a coalition of different nationalist currents, Indo-China was evoked as an outpost of the free world under threat from communist expansionism. Opposite sides of the debate in France were represented by calls from colonialists for increased American subsidies and an expanded expeditionary force to prosecute the war, and by the PCF's vigorously anti-colonial stance and the attempts by dockers, under the communist-led Confédération Générale du Travail (CGT) trade union, to block the shipment of French military materials.[75]

A further important aspect of this war lay in the ideologically driven strategy of the Vietminh. Theirs was a war of insurgency fought with revolutionary guerrilla tactics. Under the command of General Giap, the Vietminh forces exemplified the close relationship between patriotic fervour, political commitment and military action which constituted for military theorists the essential ingredients of successful insurgent warfare. The French army in Indo-China faced an enemy whose psychological tenacity would prove in the end their most effective weapon.

Having demonstrated as a student in support of French rule in Indo-China, Le Pen enlisted in November 1953 to help 'prevent the reds from seizing control of French Asia', as his biographer, Roger Mauge, tells us.[76] After accelerated training, he arrived in Indo-China in early July 1954, too late to witness the disastrous siege of Dien Bien Phu, where a few weeks earlier his battalion (the First Parachute Battalion of the Foreign Legion) had been part of the French garrison overrun by Vietminh forces under General Giap. Traumatic in its impact on the French army, this defeat marked the effective end of an eight-year war, leaving the new government of Pierre Mendès-France with little option but to conclude a ceasefire. The peace was formalised in the Geneva Agreements of 21 July 1954, which divided the peninsula into a communist north and a non-communist south, laying the ground for the entanglement of American forces in the two decades to come.

Dispatched for war, Le Pen's unit was now charged with enforcing a peace which he and others of like mind saw as a political sell-out, an abject surrender to international communism. 'I had come to understand', he would later write, 'that Indo-China was just the theatre of active engagement in a war which, elsewhere, was being conducted by secret, insidious means, the war that communism has waged relentlessly against the world for fifty years.'[77] Le Pen also subscribed to a view commonly held by veterans of Indo-China: that their defeat was due to a failure of political will in Paris which had undermined the gallant efforts of the soldiers on the front line. Three decades later, Le Pen would trace his calling to active politics in the fall of Dien Bien Phu: 'On that day I realised that it takes more than soldiers and courage to win wars, that wars are not lost on the battlefield but elsewhere. I swore to myself that if I got back, I would devote my life to politics.'[78]

After several months spent in security operations, Le Pen was transferred to Saigon to work as a journalist compiling news reviews for the military weekly, *La*

Caravelle. Here he had occasion to read about a popular movement that was gathering momentum in France under a young man named Pierre Poujade. Le Pen's imagination appears to have been caught by the Poujadist phenomenon, and he claimed to have dedicated an issue of *La Caravelle* to it.[79] There is no record of this in the military archives of Vincennes, where an incomplete collection of *La Caravelle* survives. In the issue of 15 March 1955, however, we do find the contours of Poujadism briefly sketched – as an anti-parliamentary movement, a symptom of the need for reform in France, gaining a national audience for a protest that had moved beyond tax reform to challenge the political regime itself. The anti-Semitic tenor of the movement was also signalled.[80]

In August 1955, Le Pen returned home resolved to channel his energies in a new direction. 'The humiliation of Indo-China and the first wounds inflicted in the Algerian War', he would later recall, 'were to determine my political engagement.'[81] Back in the Latin Quarter and his old Law Faculty circuit, he took charge of his first 'party', the Jeunes Indépendants de Paris (JIP), a small band of nationalist malcontents who had decided to 'scream our anger in the country's face'. That anger was directed 'against the political class and the Fourth Republic, which had wallowed in defeat in Indo-China and was proving incapable of controlling the dramatic events now unfolding across the whole of North Africa'.[82] The JIP was more a loose militant grouping than a properly constituted political party, but it brought Le Pen into contact with several prominent extreme-right agitators, including the self-proclaimed National Socialist Charles Luca and others such as Jean-Gilles Malliarakis, who would play a leading role in extreme-right activism under the Fifth Republic. Courting Vichyites, monarchists, veterans of Indo-China and Gaullists beyond his own political microforce, Le Pen signalled again his early aspirations as a federator, privileging activism over ideology and arguing that political engagement was worthless if it did not extend beyond the Latin Quarter and lead to real political influence.[83] In the weeks that lay ahead, events were to take a providential turn.

3   The Poujadist movement

A false dawn for the extreme right

The birth of an 'ism'

As a political movement which would harness the hopes of the French extreme right a decade on from Vichy, Poujadism was born of inauspicious beginnings. The movement was launched in July 1953 as a localised protest by small shop-keepers against the punitive effects of an anachronistic tax system and the high-handedness of government inspectors in clamping down on tax fraud. Pierre Poujade was no politician, but a stationer and municipal councillor from the small town of Saint-Céré in the southern Lot department. Raised in a deeply conservative, Catholic household of Maurrassian disposition, Poujade had flirted in his youth with Doriot's PPF then been a section leader in Vichy's Compagnons de France.[1] When the southern zone was occupied in November 1942, he had escaped via Spain and North Africa to enlist as a Free French volunteer in the Royal Air Force in England. Having returned to set up his small business in Saint-Céré after the war, he won a seat as a Gaullist (RPF) candidate on a Radical list in the 1953 municipal elections. From this modest platform, the then 32-year-old Poujade would be pitched into a national leadership role as his movement became the conduit for an upsurge of popular grievance against economic restructuring under the Fourth Republic.

Poujadist protest spread quickly from the Lot to neighbouring departments, then to other regions, reflecting the fears of 'static' France confronted with the onset of modernisation.[2] The decade since the Liberation had seen a concerted effort by government planners to transform a still largely archaic and fragmented socio-economic base into a modern, dynamic economy. These were years of rapid industrial development and urbanisation, announcing the end of small-scale agriculture and commerce as the defining features of the French economy. With the expansion of new, industrial and town-centred employment, and the attendant growth of middle- and working-class *salariés*, came rural depopulation and the decline of the peasantry. This 'rural exodus' was most keenly felt in the agricultural central and south-western departments of France, the seedbeds of Poujadism. Provincial shopkeepers and artisans, many of whom lived off slim profit margins, were not only hit by this dislocation of their traditional consumer base; they were also adversely affected by the end of post-war rationing, which had guaranteed a degree of commercial security by tying customers to their local shops for some basic goods. More seriously, they lost through the reining back of inflation, which had allowed them to sell their stock at steadily increased prices and turn a depreciating currency to benefit in backpayments to their creditors and the Revenue. In the mid-1950s, an inordinately high proportion of the French earned their living as small retailers, with one shop per 62 inhabitants, compared with a ratio of 1:89 in Britain and 1:91 in the United States.[3] The modernisation of the commercial sector, with its drive towards larger retail outlets and new modes of commercial production and distribution (retail chains, cooperatives, department stores, mail order – and, on the horizon, the dreaded supermarket), threatened the *raison d'être* of these small dealers.

When all of this was compounded by a new government resolve to curb the widespread practice of tax evasion,[4] the Poujadists' response was direct, brutal and effective. They obstructed treasury officials, mobilised demonstrations and rallies, and called for a general tax strike and the withdrawal of savings from state banks. They articulated their demands (for a fairer tax system, an end to tax inspections, parity of social security rights, an amnesty for Poujadist offenders, and the convocation of an Estates-General to address popular grievances) in a language notable for its aggression. Their enemies were clearly identified: tax officials, politicians, corporate capitalists, technocrats, intellectuals, uncomprehending journalists – so many cosy, metropolitan elites conspiring against the honest toilers of France in the name of 'progress'.[5]

The movement's founding charter was the eight-point Gramat Programme, drawn up in October 1953 and focusing exclusively on tax and social security issues. Its Constituent Assembly, held in Cahors in November 1953, launched the Union de Défense des Commerçants et Artisans (Union for the Defence of Shopkeepers and Artisans, UDCA), which held its first national congress in Algiers in November 1954. By summer 1955, the UDCA enjoyed substantial representation in Chambers of Commerce, Trade and Agriculture. It had an organisational network across France and Algeria, had set up a cadre school and boasted a paying membership of 356,160, comparable to that of the Gaullist RPF at its height in the late 1940s.[6] It ran a press producing information sheets, propagandist tracts and two newspapers, the monthly *L'Union* then the weekly *Fraternité Française*, which would report subscription figures of up to 435,000 and 240,000 respectively.[7] Supplements were provided for different departments, with *Fraternité Française* recording a print run of 15 million on occasion.[8] In an attempt to broaden the movement's appeal, a number of 'parallel unions' were also founded: a Union for the Defence of French Farmers (UDAF), a Union for the Defence of Liberal, Intellectual and Associated Professions (UDPILA), a Union for the Defence of French Workers (UDTF), a Union for the Defence of Servicemen (UDC), and a Union for the Defence of French Youth (UDJF).

In January 1955, a mass rally at the Porte de Versailles in Paris attracted more than 100,000 supporters from all over France, despite floods and the refusal by the Minister of Transport to lay on special trains and buses.[9] In March 1955, a Poujadist delegation presented itself at the National Assembly to press Edgar

Faure's new centre-right government into a number of concessions, including the abrogation of the so-called 'Dorey Amendment', a piece of legislation from August 1954 that had made the obstruction of tax auditors an imprisonable offence. By July 1955, the movement had transcended its original mission of defending shopkeepers and artisans to 'take henceforth in its charge the general interests of the French Nation', beginning with a robust commitment to 'save the French Union' by opposing decolonisation.[10]

From protest to politics

With deep political divisions at home and a worsening situation in Algeria, the Faure government was defeated in late November 1955 by a vote in the National Assembly. Since this was the second time in 18 months that a government had been defied by a majority of the deputies, Faure resorted to a constitutional sanction that had not been used since 1877. He dissolved the National Assembly, bringing forward to January the legislative elections set for June 1956. In so doing, Faure's declared intention was to call for a new mandate to resolve the Algerian conflict and the other problems (not least Poujadism) with which his administration had wrestled; his undeclared intention was to wrong-foot the centre-left opposition, led by Pierre Mendès-France and Guy Mollet, and leave little time for them to mount an effective campaign.

The parties contesting the election fell broadly into four groups: the right and centre-right supporting Faure; the left and centre-left led by Mendès-France and Mollet; the PCF; and the Poujadists, who found themselves presented with the opportunity to stage their most spectacular protest yet. In order to appeal to the grievances of specific sectors of the electorate, they ran three separate lists: one for shopkeepers and artisans (Union et Fraternité Française, UFF), one for small farmers, peasants and wine-growers (Défense des Intérêts Agricoles et Viticoles), and one for consumers, incorporating salaried workers, liberal professionals and other groups less readily attracted to Poujadism (Action Civique de Défense des Consommateurs et des Intérêts Familiaux). By forming alliances between these lists in certain constituencies, the Poujadists would contravene the electoral law of 1951 and find a number of their eventual gains invalidated.[11]

Faure's calculation in calling the election failed to take account of the momentum that had built up behind Poujade's movement and its ability to mount an energetic electoral campaign at short notice. The UDCA had been on a permanent campaign footing for some two years already, with Poujade himself reported to have held over 800 public meetings in that period.[12] The Poujadists targeted their campaigning as far as possible on local issues, producing a plethora of tracts and local supplements to their national publications. With their slogan '*Sortez les sortants!*' ('Kick Out the Outgoing Lot!'), they ran a rowdy, negative campaign which appealed to popular dissatisfaction with the incumbent administration.[13]

The avowed objective of the Poujadists was not to win power and become one of the institutional parties they so despised, but to clear the way for an

Estates-General (a representative body last convened on the eve of the Revolution). Poujadist propaganda railed against the 'fraud' of parliamentary democracy and 'exploitative gangs' growing fat on the toil and suffering of the people.[14] In a language redolent of the radical right *and* radical left of the 1930s, it espoused the cause of the small man, attacking big capital and the self-serving politicians who promoted it. 'BEWARE! THIS MAN IS DANGEROUS', warned an election poster projecting a smiling Poujade as the embodiment of respectability, turning to rhetorical advantage attempts by the mainstream parties to brand him a dangerous demagogue. The same poster denounced politicians of 'left, right and centre', 'financial powers', 'anonymous and exploitative employers', 'stateless trusts', 'the parties of government', and 'those who exploit the misery of the people for political ends'.[15] Poujade's party was to be above sectarian politics, above political ambition itself. A national circular called on its candidates to 'Remember at all times that we promise nothing, except to fight against stateless trusts and the gang of vultures.'[16] An electoral tract addressed to the 'Peasants of France' stressed this anti-political mission:

> Our sole objective is to sweep the house clean and allow for the voice of the people to be heard in the convocation of the Estates-General. Those of us who are elected will think of themselves not as deputies but as delegates of the French peasantry charged with bringing about [this] vast popular consultation [. . .]. Once this has been achieved through our unstinting efforts, we will resign.[17]

An alliance of convenience

Not all of the recruits to Poujadism fought so shy of political engagement. As a law student in Paris and president of the Corpo de Droit, Jean-Marie Le Pen had earned a reputation as a militant nationalist and strident anti-communist. Having completed his studies and a tour of duty as a volunteer in Indo-China, Le Pen was casting around for his entry to politics at the moment when Poujade was looking to expand his support base and inject new blood into his movement. In November 1955, in a meeting arranged by Roger Delpey, head of the Association of Veterans of Indo-China, the two men were introduced, in the company of another ex-paratrooper and nationalist agitator, Jean-Maurice Demarquet. Nothing could have seemed further from Le Pen's martial propensities than this uprising of small shopkeepers from *la France profonde*. Though a stranger to Poujade's professional concerns, Le Pen nonetheless subscribed to much that Poujadism represented, with its imprecations against a corrupt system and emphasis on traditional French values. There were temperamental similarities too between the two men: in their early Maurrassian and Pétainist leanings, their demagogic talents and their preference for activism over ideology. Above all else, though, Le Pen had reason to be drawn by Poujade's robust espousal of the nationalists' paramount cause, the retention of French Algeria. By the time Le Pen came into contact with Poujadism, the movement had thrown its full weight behind the defence of the French Union, with a marked shift towards a more nationalistic discourse. It had, as René Rémond notes, crossed the border from being a socio-economic interest group to becoming 'a right-wing, even an extreme right-wing force'.[18]

In signing up to the Poujadist cause and quickly showing his mettle as a public speaker, Le Pen was made an '*orateur national*' and entrusted with one of the movement's parallel associations, the UDJF youth wing, into which he integrated his own JIP. With television still in its infancy, French election campaigns in the 1950s were conducted largely through public meetings, with the practice of *contradiction*, or right of intervention from the floor, a prominent feature. Given the restricted social base of the audiences attracted to UDCA meetings, the disruption of opponents' meetings was a forceful (if unwelcome) way of putting the Poujadist message across to a wider audience. Philip Williams recounts how Poujadist rowdies would simply drown speakers' voices 'by shouts – or by cowbells, drums, loudspeakers, hunting horns, and alarm clocks', while elsewhere others 'were bombarded with eggs, fruit and vegetables, and even cream cakes'.[19] The former and outgoing Prime Ministers, Pierre Mendès-France and Edgar Faure, and the former Interior Minister, François Mitterrand, were among the favoured targets for this Poujadist tactic, which often took a violent turn. As Williams observed, however, these demonstrations, for all their rowdiness, 'were more like student "rags" than like fascist brutality'.[20]

An electoral sensation

On 2 January 1956, the hastily constituted Poujadist party (UFF) and its allied lists sent a shock wave through the political establishment: with no formal electoral programme and a slate of unknown candidates, it gained 11.6 per cent of votes cast in metropolitan France (2.48 million) and 52 seats in the National Assembly (Table 3.1). The election was conducted on a single ballot with a high degree of proportionality in the distribution of seats. It was won by a 'Republican Front' of left-wing and centre-left parties under the Socialist Guy Mollet, who succeeded Faure as Prime Minister (and who would set the record, at 16 months, for the longest premiership of the Fourth Republic). The Poujadists contested seats in 82 departments, with only the PCF and Socialist SFIO (Section Française de l'Internationale Ouvrière) fielding a larger number of lists.[21] The Poujadist vote represented predominantly the poorer, underdeveloped and economically stagnant departments of central, southern and south-western France, with a strong showing also in the western regions of Pays de la Loire and Poitou-Charentes and in the south-eastern Rhône-Alpes, Languedoc-Roussillon and Provence-Alpes-Côte d'Azur. The Poujadist lists attracted over 15 per cent of registered voters (*inscrits*) in the central and western departments of Mayenne, Maine-et-Loire, Indre-et-Loire, Deux-Sèvres and Charente-Maritime; in the southern departments of Tarn-et-Garonne, Tarn and Aveyron (where the Poujadists were supported by 18.7 per cent of *inscrits*); and in the south-eastern departments of Isère, Hérault, Gard, Bouches-du-Rhône-2

Table 3.1 The 1956 legislative elections (metropolitan France)

	Votes cast	*%*
Communist Party (PCF)	5,494,673	25.6
Socialist Party (SFIO)	3,301,457	15.4
Radicals	2,885,931	13.4
MRP	2,365,535	11.0
Conservatives	3,109,771	14.5
Social Republicans (Gaullist)	934,867	4.4
Poujadists	2,482,406	11.6 (52 of 596 seats)
Extreme Right	251,264	1.2

Source: *Journal Officiel* (R. Pierce, 'The French Election of January 1956', *Journal of Politics*, vol. 19, no. 3, 1957, p. 410).

and Vaucluse (where Poujadist support reached its high point of 22.4 per cent of the electoral register). By contrast, the movement attracted less than 10 per cent in the more industrially developed, economically robust departments of the north and north-east of France (with a low of 3.6 per cent in the Alsatian department of Bas-Rhin).[22]

Shopkeepers, artisans, small farmers, peasants, café proprietors, wine-growers and *bouilleurs de cru* (home distillers) provided the bulk of the Poujadist electorate, which was predominantly male, middle-aged, modestly to poorly educated, and markedly lower middle-class in its profile. Support was drawn mostly from the established right-wing parties, including part of the authoritarian protest vote that had gone to the Gaullists in 1951 and the votes of ex-servicemen responsive to the patriotic posturings of the movement. Though the two electorates differed in geographical spread and socio-professional make-up, the Poujadists replaced the Gaullists in this election as the main party of opposition to the Fourth Republic on the right. Cross-party appeal was one of a number of similarities between Poujadism and early-day Gaullism, together with their nationalism, anti-communism and highly personalised leadership; there were similarities, too, in their calls for a popular *rassemblement* and hostility towards established parties and politicians. Though described by some as 'the poor man's de Gaulle', Poujade attracted strong support in areas where the Gaullists had been weak in 1951. Whereas Poujadist strength was concentrated among the less educated lower middle classes in declining provincial areas, Gaullism was backed by better educated, more affluent sections of the middle classes and was strongest in the more economically developed northern and north-eastern regions of France.[23]

Support for Poujade's party came also from the left, including the communist electorate as the PCF found itself challenged in its traditional tribune function by this new protest force. The Poujadists drew substantial support, too, from former abstentionists and first-time voters seduced by the anti-parliamentary tenor of their campaign.[24] Though they attracted some communist support, the presence of the Poujadists in this election favoured the PCF by splitting the right-wing vote and amplifying communist representation in the new National Assembly, where the PCF emerged as the largest group.

The Poujadist deputies were in the main an unlikely assemblage of *petits commerçants*, with more than half their number having no previous political experience and among whom were found sympathisers of every major party except the PCF.[25] In *Le Monde* of 5 January 1956, a breakdown of the Poujadist deputies by occupation showed them to be almost entirely shopkeepers, artisans and small entrepreneurs, with – incongruously – an ex-police commissioner (Dides) and two 'students' (Le Pen and Demarquet). By what would later be judged a miscalculation, Poujade himself did not contest a seat, preferring to manage his 'delegates' from outside parliament and preclude accusations of self-advancement or compromise with the regime. He had with difficulty persuaded his movement to field candidates at all, such was their hostility to the party system and concern to preserve their apolitical stance.[26]

This reluctance to engage with 'the system' was belied by the double-page photograph published in *Paris Match* of the Poujadist group bedecked in their parliamentary sashes in the foyer of the Fontainebleau Theatre.[27] Without question, Poujade was the media event of this election. In its issues of December 1955, *Paris Match* had reflected the rowdy nature of the Poujadist campaign. Now it focused on the identity of these overnight celebrities, savouring the humble origins of each in a roll-call of their occupations: butcher, baker, upholsterer, seed merchant, bicycle repair man . . . Presented here, too, under the label 'law student', we find 'Jean le Pen' ('former parachute officer in Indo-China' and 'avant-garde of Poujadism') pictured in his Paris bedsit following his election as deputy for the first sector of the Seine.[28]

Behind enemy lines

Elected on a rousingly negative platform, the Poujadists were ill-adapted to their new institutional role. With no parliamentary experience and few ready allies, they fell easy prey to the procedural pitfalls of the National Assembly and the manoeuvrings of the established parties. On the testimony of one witness, Jacques Isorni, the Poujadists were 'incapable of drafting a formal proposal or delivering a speech'.[29] The political declaration which the UFF group lodged with the Bureau of the National Assembly on 23 January 1956 was no more than a brief statement of principle couched in the most general terms and calling for an Estates-General 'to give the French people their say'.[30] Even on their central issue of tax reform, the Poujadists failed to advance any coherent proposal or contribute constructively to the parliamentary process.[31]

Conspicuous as an exception to this ineptitude, Le Pen proved a feisty orator and emerged as effective *porte-parole* for the UFF parliamentary group. He used his experience as a Poujadist candidate and deputy to hone his political skills and to learn early lessons in the management of a national political movement.[32] As a Poujadist, Le Pen engaged in a form of populism that would remain thereafter at the core of his political style, appealing to the good sense and interests of the people in opposition to a corrupt and self-serving political class. He learned lessons, too, in political marketing and in the role of personal image in mobilising electoral support. The Poujadist experience would strengthen and extend Le Pen's personal network, bringing him into contact with a number of figures who were much later to occupy prominent positions in the FN.[33] Once in parliament, however, Le Pen would quickly discover alternative mentors with whom he was more in tune. Though he lent his voice for a time to the campaign for an Estates-General, the vacuity of the Poujadists' programme and the immobilism of their parliamentary group would not long satisfy his ambitions. Those whom Poujade described fondly as 'my sausage merchants' were soon mocked by Le Pen as 'these cretins who are going to save France'.[34]

In January 1956, Poujadism nonetheless offered a valuable launch pad. With his Paris seat secured after only six weeks on the political circuit, Le Pen became, at 27, the youngest deputy in the legislature. Elected, too, were Demarquet and the ex-police commissioner Jean Dides, forming with Le Pen the hard core of militant nationalism within the Poujadist group. The most heated exchanges (including a punch-up on the floor of the National Assembly between Poujadist and PCF deputies) took place in February 1956, when 11 of the group were disqualified for irregularities in the election campaign,[35] then in March with the debates on Algeria. These occasions saw the Poujadists lambasted from the left-wing benches as 'Fascists' and 'Nazis', an image reflected in the seating plan of the Assembly, where the Poujadist deputies were consigned – despite their protests – to the benches on the far right of the chamber. 'In order to play on people's fears', Poujade would later write, 'we were tarred with the brush of the extreme right, when in reality we had nothing to do with it.'[36]

While Poujade continued to resist such labelling, pretending to an increasingly untenable posture of apoliticism for his movement, Le Pen sought from the outset to politicise his role. His declarations in the National Assembly articulated a strident anti-communism and authoritarian nationalism. As one of his earliest parliamentary utterances, the *Journal Officiel* records a pointed address to the PCF benches in February 1956: 'The Poujadist deputies have brought with them into the Assembly the ghosts of 80,000 victims of the Indo-China War. Your allies did not silence me with their sub-machine guns [...] and you have not heard the last of me here!'[37] Invoking the 'solemn warning' of Dien Bien Phu in the debates on Algeria the following month, Le Pen argued forcefully against any move towards Algerian self-government. He denounced 'the same half measures, the same absence of political vision, the same lack of will' in the handling of the Algerian crisis, calling for a more ruthless clampdown on Algerian nationalist terrorism, restrictions on the freedom of a 'defamatory and demoralising' press, and sanctions against the PCF.[38]

Dissent and disintegration

Such interventions, together with his appointment to the parliamentary committees on defence and foreign affairs, indicated well Le Pen's conception of his
parliamentary mandate. Conversely, his silence on economic and social questions
(statutory holiday pay, agricultural policy, pensions, etc.) signalled the limits of
his *poujadisme*. This would become a source of concern for Poujade, who came to
see Le Pen's hard-line political orientation and at times intemperate pronouncements as a liability. For it was Le Pen's clear ambition to transform the UFF into
a full-blown political party and a pole of attraction for the ultra-nationalist
right – those precisely whom Poujade dismissed as 'nationalists by profession', 'a
group of narrow-minded right-wing extremists cut off from political and popular
reality'.[39]

In the months following the election, Poujade determined to re-centre his
movement, returning it to its original – 'pure and wholesome' – objectives.[40] At
an extraordinary congress held in late April 1956, he instructed the Poujadist
deputies to suspend their contributions to the work of the National Assembly
and warned them against contagion from extreme-right elements in parliament.
This was a pointed response to overtures from ultra-nationalists like Jean-Louis
Tixier-Vignancour and ultra-conservatives like Edouard Frédéric-Dupont, with
whom Le Pen in particular had struck up cordial relations.[41] In a further move to
cut ground from under Le Pen, Poujade now declared the role of deputy to be
incompatible with that of directing a parallel association. In effect, this applied
only to Demarquet, head of the servicemen's union, and Le Pen with his UDJF
youth wing, which he had built up as a forum for nationalist students and a
personal power base.

The Poujadist congress of spring 1956 was symptomatic of a movement that
was slipping from the control of its leader and losing its direction. Though it
retained strong professional support, its political edge had been blunted by its
ineffectual absorption into parliament. The oath of loyalty which the Poujadist
deputies had sworn now rang hollow as internal dissent mounted. This came to a
head over the Suez crisis, when Dides led a breakaway faction against Poujade's
opposition to armed intervention, and the worsening situation in Algeria, which
brought the radical militancy of Le Pen and Demarquet into conflict with
Poujade's more moderate stance.[42] In January 1957, Poujade attempted to regain
control of his parliamentary group by contesting a Paris by-election. If it had
been an error not to contest a seat the previous year, it was an error compounded
by running for election now, when the Poujadist tide was on the ebb and the other
parties had taken the measure of the UFF as an adversary. Poujade was heavily
beaten, attracting under 20,000 votes in the same first sector of the Seine where
Le Pen's list had won over 35,000 in January 1956.[43] His defeat, and the open
opposition which he was now facing from prominent elements within his group,
marked the inexorable decline of the movement. Le Pen and Demarquet, who
had taken parliamentary leave in September 1956 to enlist as reservist volunteers
in Algeria, now came out against Poujade and were formally excluded from the
UDCA at its congress in May 1957.[44]

The final break-up of the Poujadist movement occurred over de Gaulle's return to power the following year. United in their opposition to the Fourth Republic, Gaullists and Poujadists entered into negotiations in the run-up to the critical events of May 1958.[45] In addition to its strength in mainland France, Poujadism had many adherents in Algeria, some of whom held open the possibility that Poujade might lead a revolutionary government there. Poujade, for his part, reacted with caution to the evolving events in Algeria. His Cornelian dilemma, as he put it, remained one of reconciling the original socio-economic objectives of the UDCA with the national political issues in which it had become increasingly entangled.[46] Wooed, it seems, by the prospect of a ministry under de Gaulle, Poujade opted to support the latter's investiture, only to withdraw his support on sensing that he had been outmanoeuvred and that Poujadist concerns were being by-passed.[47] Worse still, de Gaulle would preside over precisely those developments (economic modernisation, commercial concentration, industrialisation, an end to French Algeria) against which the Poujadists had campaigned so vigorously.

Poujade's support for the 'no' campaign in the referendum of 28 September 1958 (in the company of his old enemies, the Radical Mendès-France and the PCF) set him at odds with the rank-and-file of his movement, who voted massively in favour of the new Fifth Republic.[48] The Poujadist group disintegrated as its members deserted to other right-wing parties, while in the November 1958 parliamentary elections, the 163 Poujadist candidates (campaigning on familiar themes, with an added anti-Common Market dimension) recorded under 1.5 per cent, just over 300,000 votes.[49] Of the outgoing Poujadist cohort, only Le Pen and Emile Luciani would win re-election, the former as an Independent, the latter as a Gaullist. By the end of 1958, membership of the UDCA had dropped to around 200,000; by the end of 1959, it had fallen to under 100,000, though the movement would continue for a time to enjoy strong representation on professional bodies such as Chambers of Commerce and Trade, and in politics at the municipal level.[50] In the subsequent legislative elections of November 1962, only 40 candidates would run under Poujadist colours, winning a negligible 0.28 per cent of the ballot, little over 50,000 votes.[51] Poujadism as a national political force was spent.

'Poujadolf'

Much has been said about the fascistic nature of Poujadism. François Mitterrand, one of the movement's *bêtes noires*, described it pithily as 'back-shop fascism', while the PCF, renouncing its earlier support, condemned Poujadism as 'a reckless enterprise of a fascist nature'.[52] Following the elections of January 1956, the Ligue Internationale Contre le Racisme et l'Antisémitisme (International League Against Racism and Anti-Semitism, LICRA) launched a public appeal against 'the fascist and racist danger represented by the Poujadist movement'.[53] A number of less engaged commentators concurred with this judgement. Maurice Duverger described Poujadism as 'an elementary, crude, primitive fascism', while others detected echoes of Nazism.[54] One of the defining images of the 1956 elections was the cartoon (by the *Daily Mirror*'s Vicky) which appeared in *L'Express*, depicting 'Poujadolf' holding forth from a podium with the ghost of Hitler whispering in his ear: 'Go on, son! They didn't take me seriously either, at first . . . '[55]

There was much in Poujadism to arouse such concern: its elements of leadership cult, its anti-parliamentarism, its increasing nationalism and xenophobia, its periodic recourse to violence and intimidation. There was much, too, that bore the stamp of a specifically French right-wing tradition, from the overtones of Barrès in Poujade's elevation of 'good sense' and 'instinct' above intellectual reasoning, to the distinction between the *pays légal* (the institutions of state) and the *pays réel* (the people) as prefigured by Maurras.[56] It was in these latter terms precisely that Poujade would proclaim his deputies to be the 'legal as well as real representatives of the French people'.[57] The lamentations over Indo-China and vigorous defence of French Algeria, more pronounced after the Poujadists' first national congress in Algiers in 1954, were redolent of the aggressive nationalism that had characterised the French right in the wake of the Franco-Prussian War. General Boulanger's 'union of malcontents', in its linking of military defeat with the weakness of a decadent regime and its overtones of conspiracy, contained adumbrations of Poujadism.[58]

A further factor giving rise to the charge of 'fascism' was the anti-Semitism on which Poujadism played. The growth of the UDCA in 1954 coincided with the premiership of Mendès-France (June 1954–February 1955). Excoriated for 'selling out' in Indo-China and for persecuting Poujadist protestors through the hated Dorey Amendment, Mendès-France was the butt of the movement's hostility throughout his term of office. While Poujadist propaganda peddled a coded anti-Semitism in its denunciation of 'stateless financial powers with no humanity about them', Mendès-France provided a very human figure on whom the animus could be personalised – as a left-leaning politician, a supporter of modernisation, a decoloniser, and a Jew.[59] When his government launched a campaign against alcoholism with Mendès-France setting the tone by drinking milk at a high-profile reception, he was pilloried by Poujade on behalf of the wine-growers and café owners of France: 'How many billions have certain trusts put up to force our friends out of existence? If you had a drop of Gallic blood in your veins, you would never have dared, in representing our France, a global producer of wines and champagne, to ask for a glass of milk at an international reception! This was, Mr. Mendès, a slap in the face for every Frenchman – even if he is not a drunkard!'[60]

Poujade took to using the mocking sobriquet 'Mendès-Lolo' ('Milky-Mendès'), echoing the treatment handed out in the 1930s to a previous Jewish Prime Minister and head of the Popular Front, Léon Blum, over his habit of drinking water.[61] The projected launch of a 'supermarket experiment' in Corsica in November 1954 was denounced in similarly scathing terms, as a means of forcing French commerce to 'kneel before the golden calf': 'No! Mendès, [. . .] when one is the son of an ancient land like France, one is not made for slavery in any form. [. . .] and if you are so keen on that sort of life, then pack your bag and get out! The people of France did not ask you to come here. They are not holding you back.'[62]

This well-worn theme of the Jew as a malevolent, profit-driven, un-French presence – part of a network of 'national and international conspiracy'[63] – could have been lifted from the pages of Edouard Drumont's *La France juive*, the handbook of anti-Semitism in France from the Dreyfus affair to Vichy. Poujade argued nonetheless that he had 'shaken up a few Israelite ministers because they were ministers, not because they were Israelites'; he had, he objected, attacked non-Jewish ministers just as violently.[64] The defence was a flimsy one, taking no account of those within and around his movement who showed less inhibition, or of the increasingly anti-Semitic line adopted by the official Poujadist press.[65] 'By whom are we governed?', thundered Léon Dupont, leader of an allied farmers' union, at a Poujadist meeting. 'By people who don't even dare to say their names: Mendès-Portugal, from a family of Portuguese Jews and married to an Egyptian Jewess, Salomon Hirsch Ollendorf, otherwise known as Grandval, and Soustelle Ben Soussa. We need to unmask these people and smash in their f . . .'[66]

In its issue of 31 December 1955, on the eve of the parliamentary elections, *Fraternité Française* published an article by Paul Chevallet vilifying each of the other parties in turn, and in particular the Radicals who 'all worship the golden calf; these are people for whom money has no smell, Edgar [Faure] being the prime example, always ready to rake through excrement in search of precious metal. Mendès is another case, only he would rather use his slimy tongue . . .'[67] In the wake of the Poujadist success, Chevallet returned to the attack on Faure and Mendès-France, describing the former as 'a form of chronic tuberculosis' and the latter as 'a virulent form of typhoid' requiring 'urgent treatment'.[68] In its issue of 7 January 1956, the same *Fraternité Française* urged its readers to 'just go and ask people called Isaac Mendès, Servan-Schreiber or Ben Saïd what it is to be a *real* Frenchman!'[69]

As though the Holocaust had not intervened to redefine the boundaries of the permissible in public discourse, these remarks drew upon a stock of invective that had found expression – on both right *and* left – under the Third Republic.[70] They formed part of an old linguistic code that equated Jews with exploitative capitalism, replaying essentially the same anti-Semitism as that of the *petits commerçants* in late nineteenth-century France.[71] The more offensive pronouncements of his associates were at times disavowed by Poujade himself, who continued to deny all accusations of racism.[72] For him, the distinction between 'French' and 'Jew', where it existed, was more social than racial, grounded in the notion of a shared experience of toil, suffering and memory that should form the essential link with the land and the final cement of French identity. His movement, he argued, was there to defend 'with the same courage and the same solidarity' all of those Jews who were 'not ministers but victims of the *fisc*, like the others'.[73] To be – and more especially to suffer – 'like the others' was for Poujade the rite of passage to belonging.

This eschewal of the idea of racial purity in favour of that of social assimilation echoed closely the philosopher Ernest Renan's conception of the nation as 'the culmination of a long past of effort, of sacrifice and of devotion'.[74] Within that perspective, the definition of the Frenchman was not ethnically exclusive but rested rather on a cultural, territorial, historical identity forged through sustained collective endeavour. Like Renan, Poujade would stress the solidarity born of ancestral heritage, cultural bonding, and above all 'common suffering'.[75] 'Gallic blood' might be inherited, but it could – and should – also be earned. In an article in *L'Union* in July 1954, Poujade put the point with force: 'Yes, there is room amongst us for all those who wish to work for their living and, little by little, earn their place as part of the community.' Dismissing racism as a retrograde delusion, he insisted: 'All that counts is the right acquired over generations through toil, sacrifice and sometimes bloodshed.'[76]

The vilification of which Léon Blum had found himself the object in the extreme-right press of the inter-war years cast him not only as the architect of French socialism but as a suspect outsider. Blum did 'not belong amongst us', wrote Georges Suarez in the ultra-nationalist weekly *Gringoire*; in the same publication, Henri Béraud vaunted the land 'for which we have fought, from father to son, this land which neither you [Blum] nor your kin can claim to have cultivated or defended'.[77] Poujade in turn levelled this same charge against a Mendès-France who was likewise figured outside '*la Grande Famille française*', who did not have 'peasant blood' in his veins or 'real French earth' clinging to his shoes, and who had not defended *la patrie* in its hour of need. When Poujade berated Mendès-France for not having fought at Verdun, the reference was purely symbolic, since Mendès-France was aged nine in 1916.[78]

The *sentiment du terroir*, or oneness with the soil, which Poujade invoked as a pre-requisite of Frenchness, played well in a provincial France where local interests predominated; but it could lend itself to distortive simplifications. It underlay the scornful dismissal (with echoes of Pétain) of 'freshly made Frenchmen' and of newly arrived outsiders 'parachuted' into the national community. 'I find it dishonourable', objected Poujade, 'for us to allow people who have been in France for barely a generation to take charge and presume to govern us.' The same rationale explained the requirement of three generations of French ancestry in order to serve on the UDCA's administrative council.[79]

Poujade the Republican

When such evidence is reviewed, it is difficult not to concede something to those who discerned in Poujade's movement the resurgence of a dangerous right-wing extremism. Viewed in its totality, however, Poujadism presents a more complex and equivocal picture: firstly, because so much of its discourse paid homage to the French revolutionary and Republican heritage; secondly, because its supporters were drawn from across the political spectrum, with significant backing for a time from the extreme left; and thirdly, because the nature of the movement, and its political centre of gravity, shifted markedly over a short time, making it difficult to frame a definitive definition.

Poujade insisted that the UDCA was 'neither on the right, nor on the left, nor in the centre'; he appealed to the 'honest people' of France, 'regardless of social condition, ideological conviction or political affiliation'.[80] Though this is a familiar enough posture for right-wing nationalist movements (anticipating the 'Neither Right Nor Left – French!' slogan of the FN in the 1990s), Poujadism claimed a space within French political culture that transcended easy right–left divisions. In its calls for an Estates-General, it embraced a primitive ideal of direct democracy and associated itself with a popular mythology rooted in the Revolution of 1789: the defence of *les honnêtes gens* against an overbearing regime, what Poujade called 'the pure French tradition' of protecting the weak against oppression by the strong.[81] Where Maurras had inveighed against the Revolution and Pétain sought to bury it without trace, Poujade's language abounded with revolutionary imagery, rallying his supporters (in very un-Maurrassian terms) as descendants of those *sans-culottes* 'who did not shirk from guillotining a king'.[82] In the same spirit, Poujade readily invoked the 'great principles' of *Liberté, Egalité, Fraternité*. 'If the authors of the Declaration of the Rights of Man are fascists', he declared to an international press conference in January 1956, 'then Pierre Poujade accepts being taken for a fascist!'[83] By other indicators too, as Seymour Lipset noted, Poujadism leaned towards the 'revolutionary republican tradition'. Whereas much of the anti-republican right exalted the Catholic Church as a bastion of moral leadership, Poujadists were 'more likely to resemble anticlerical leftists in their opinions than right-wing conservatives'.[84]

Mixed in with the Revolution and the Republic were other great moments in the history of France whose authority Poujade invoked in support of his cause. From the siege of Orléans relieved by Joan of Arc to the siege of Verdun relieved by the *poilus*, history provided Poujade with the means to pose as the living embodiment of a national tradition and to proclaim in turn: 'They shall not pass'.[85] The Resistance, too, provided a ready store of myths and symbols for this 'hero of the fiscal liberation'.[86] Thus, in an article in *Fraternité Française*, he declared: 'In 1945 the Resistance liberated France, in 1955 we are going to liberate the French.'[87] Poujade's writings contain frequent reflections on the Resistance as a heroic enterprise and on the Liberation as a horizon of (missed) opportunity, revealing nothing in common with those self-proclaimed fascists who greeted 1940 as a cause for 'jubilation' and 1944 as a 'defeat'.[88] Poujade stressed his 'fundamental attachment to democratic principles' and declared the Republic to be the 'only viable democratic system'.[89] Denouncing the self-serving politicians and administrators who, in the wake of the Liberation, had betrayed the Republic and its honest citizens, he wrote of 'new collaborators' who 'have sold out our country just as shamefully and even more surely than the others did'.[90]

Though there was much in Poujadist discourse that called forth the providential leader, Poujade's express objective was to shake the system up, not to take power himself.[91] His Republic was not a set of institutions but an abstract ideal, with overtones of Rousseau. Hence his care to attack the Fourth Republic, rather than the Republic *per se*, calling not for a new model of government but for 'a return to the most basic principle of the Republic: the people!'[92] While the distinction might have seemed spurious to some of his fellow-travellers and elusive to part of his audience, it was one on which Poujade insisted: 'It matters little that the Fourth Republic should disappear, provided we save the Republic.'[93] The Poujadist slogan 'Forward Towards the Fifth Republic' pointed to the end that lay beyond the interim arrangement of an Estates-General.[94]

Until mid-1955, the Poujadists restricted themselves to demanding legislative reform, escalating to full political action only when Edgar Faure signalled his bad faith, as Poujade saw it, by calling early legislative elections. In their self-appointed mission to reclaim the Republic from those parliamentary mandarins who thought it their privileged preserve, the Poujadists were, as Peter Campbell puts it, exponents of a 'provincial republicanism of the late nineteenth century':

> Its attachment to the Republic and to the principles and symbols of the Revolution place Poujadism in the democratic tradition. Moreover, it is in the tradition of negative democracy: not the totalitarian democracy of the extreme Jacobins wielding the full power of the State to remake society or the authoritarian democracy of Bonapartist caesarism. The language of Poujadism has a Jacobin violence, but the movement is essentially Girondin; like the Girondins, the Poujadists are in revolt against the capital.[95]

In this crucial sense as in others, Poujade was less akin to right-wing nationalist thinkers such as Barrès and Maurras than to the radical nineteenth-century philosopher Alain, with his ideal of direct democracy and deep distrust of political elites.[96] This is but one side of a Poujadism that has another, more anti-democratic aspect; but it is an important side that should not be neglected. Reaching back through history for legitimation, Poujade located his own political ancestry in the same provincial Republican tradition of resistance to the strong centralised state: 'Am I and my movement not, in some sense, the inheritors of all those who have, throughout our history, taken up their picks and pitchforks against the abuses of a centralised power and its tax regime?'[97]

The electoral strength of such an impulse would ultimately prove its political weakness. The success of Poujadism merely exposed its inbuilt obsolescence: having triumphed against 'the system', it could not but compromise its rationale by entering the National Assembly and forfeiting its anti-political role. While it forged for a time a novel solidarity among those traditionally isolated in their trades, its adherents remained too rural, sectionalist and politically disparate to sustain the parliamentary party which they had launched.

Poujadisme and *ultrapoujadisme*

To what extent, then, is Poujadism to be seen as the resurgence of the French extreme right a decade on from Vichy? In order to answer this question, two important distinctions need to be observed: the first, between early Poujadism and the subsequent development of the movement, that is between the issues espoused by *poujadisme* at the outset and the '*ultrapoujadisme*' of some of its later adherents;[98] the second, between a leadership which came to mobilise some of the classic themes of the extreme right and a grass-roots support which remained defined above all by its sectional interests.

Launched against the conservative government of Joseph Laniel, the movement at its inception, as Philip Williams observed, 'was not obviously right-wing'.[99] Another contemporary observer, Jean Touchard, went further, describing Poujadism in its early phase as 'indisputably left-wing', with a strong communist strain.[100] In this sense, the rightward trajectory of Poujadism can be seen to reflect inversely the shifting of its target, as government passed from Laniel's conservative administration (June 1953–June 1954), through the centrist ministries of Mendès-France and Faure (June 1954–January 1956), to the Socialist-led government of Mollet (February 1956–May 1957). The transformation of Poujadism over this period can be seen as a gradual slippage from anti-fiscalism to anti-parliamentarism, from a patriotism with strong Republican resonance to a narrow nationalism with xenophobic tones, from anti-capitalism to anti-Semitism.[101] The first national congress in Algiers in November 1954, the launch of *Fraternité Française* under the wealthy Algiers ultra Paul Chevallet, and the purge of communist influence within the leadership structures all marked stages in the politicisation and rightward shift of the movement.

Whereas the strong communist presence in the early days had precluded recruitment among extreme-right circles, Poujadism now began to serve as a magnet for ultra-nationalists and neo-fascists wishing to destabilise the regime and keen to exploit what they saw as the fascist potentialities of Poujade's movement. As François Duprat noted, these elements believed they had found in this revolt of shopkeepers and artisans conditions similar to those that had permitted the fascism of the 1930s to flourish: the radicalisation of a section of the middle classes threatened with proletarianisation in a context of perceived socio-economic crisis.[102] Thus the influence was increasingly felt through the Poujadist press of figures such as Camille Fégy, Claude Jeantet, Serge Jeanneret and Yves Dautun, all of whom had been collaborationist journalists under Vichy and who brought to *Fraternité Française* a strong extreme-right tenor.[103] As the defining ethos of Poujadism became blurred, it was no longer clear whether it represented 'a form of Jacobinism, a classic expression of xenophobic anti-parliamentarism (of left or right), or a movement bordering on fascism'.[104]

The political opponents of Poujadism showed no such hesitation. The PCF in particular effected an about-turn from active support to vilification. In an editorial in *L'Humanité* of 1 October 1955, the future PCF leader, Waldeck Rochet, deplored the fascist character of the Poujadist movement and placed Poujade in the lineage of La Rocque, Doriot and Dorgères.[105] Following the UFF's electoral success, the PCF's Central Committee on 18 January 1956 echoed this judgement and called on the working class to unite in order to 'block the advance of fascism'.[106] In the March 1956 issue of the *Cahiers du communisme*, Rochet published a more developed philippic, branding Poujade and his inner circle 'a bunch of traitors, Pétainists, renegades, colonialists, Hitlerians and hired hands'. In a superficial (mis)reading of the Poujadist vote, Rochet saw here a massive transfer of the support that had crystallised around de Gaulle before his disengagement from the RPF in 1953. The article trod a careful path between recognising the 'legitimate grievances' of Poujade's supporters and chastising them for harbouring 'some of the bitterest enemies of the working class'; it also, predictably, enumerated all that the PCF had done in support of small retailers and artisans.[107]

Waldeck Rochet provided a statement here of the official PCF line on Poujadism by early 1956. This was clearly informed by tactical as well as ideological considerations. The problem with Poujadism for the PCF lay not just in its 'fascist character', its 'profoundly reactionary politics', its 'ultra-colonialism', its 'Mussolini-style corporatism' or its 'Vichyite leadership'; it lay also, more pressingly, in Poujade's attempt to reach beyond his natural constituency of shopkeepers and artisans and create a mass movement incorporating the working class and peasantry. Among the UDCA's parallel unions was the worker-oriented UDTF. The alliance of the working and middle classes, Rochet insisted, was the 'great task' bequeathed to the Communist Party alone – and he urged the creation of a new 'popular front' to resist once again the rise of fascism.

A missed opportunity

The attentions attracted by the UFF parliamentary group from Tixier-Vignancour in particular seemed to vindicate such concerns. At the same time, the presence of far-right elements in Poujade's own entourage became more marked, like that of the hard-line Peasant Party leader, Paul Antier, and the former Greenshirts' leader and member of Vichy's Peasant Corporation, Henri Dorgères, with whom Poujade concluded a short-lived, pro-*Algérie Française* alliance in 1957.[108] In Algeria itself Poujadism had gained a solid base, with support among the large French settler (*pied-noir*) community and sections of the army, and with Poujade's *pied-noir* wife Yvette providing an influential personal link. As Poujade's campaign for an Estates-General ran out of steam and *Algérie Française* became the mobilising theme, he was drawn into a number of sterile conspiracies with French army and *pied-noir* ultras before being outmanoeuvred here again by de Gaulle.[109]

The fact is, however, that those extreme-right elements drawn to Poujadism imprinted their stamp on the movement but failed – as the communists before them had failed – to take control and re-route it towards their own purposes. Tixier-Vignancour was premature in declaring that Poujadism had opened the 'way back to the masses' for the nationalist right in France.[110] Poujade's resistance to the latter's advances in parliament, his prolonged hesitation over an alliance with Dorgères, and the progressive elimination of the most radical elements from the movement (Le Pen, Demarquet, Dides, Dupont, Chevallet), showed in fact how ill-adapted Poujadism was for a takeover by the extreme right.[111] It matters little whether Poujade's decisions in this regard were born of ideological aversion, pragmatic calculation or a mixture of both: their effect was to leave him sole master aboard and to limit the influence of sectarian politics over a movement whose strongest card was its syncretism – or, in Stanley Hoffmann's phrase, its 'apolitical, anti-political politics'.[112]

This did not deter the extreme-right press from vying for a share, by association, in the Poujadists' electoral success. While *La Nation Française* deemed it a 'healthy and energetic' popular reflex, *Aspects de la France* divined in Poujadism a sub-conscious cry for strong leadership through the restoration of the monarchy, and *Rivarol* saw in it the dawn of a nationalist revival. 'The system has received a blow from which it will never recover', declared an exultant *Rivarol*, announcing its new 'hope and confidence' that a regime of 'criminals, traitors and incompetents' might now be overthrown.[113] Others went further in their attempt to court the UDCA leader. The Phalange Française of Charles Luca (a movement dedicated to 'the implementation of an authentic National Socialism')[114] sought an open alliance with the Poujadists. In its journal, *Fidélité*, the Phalange expressed its 'warm sympathy' for the Poujadists, declaring of their leader: 'He gets through to people with ease, using the same aggressive language as we do – the language of a generation that has read L.-F. Céline.' Heralding the emergence of a new 'National and Popular France', the Phalange called for a 'revolutionary union' with the Poujadists to launch 'the assault that will sweep away the Regime'.[115]

The appeal fell on deaf ears, confirming Poujade's refusal to allow his forces to be pressed into the service of any political cause but his own. And his was not a revolutionary cause. On the eve of the January 1956 election, the swingeing critique in *Fraternité Française* of the 'parties who dupe you' had not spared the extreme right, with its 'few ancient specimens from the anthology of fascism excitedly waving their pitchfork or a copy of the Penal Code'.[116] No sooner was the UFF group elected, moreover, than Poujade showed again his capacity to confound critics and would-be allies alike by denying any intention to be a saboteur and stating his readiness to support the government in most areas in return for tax reform.[117] Small wonder that the same *Fidélité* which had eulogised in March 1956 would, in February 1959, be moved to express its disenchantment by ranging Poujadism among the 'repeated failures' of the nationalist right in France.[118]

Poujadism: a fascist movement?

A more thoughtful contribution to understanding Poujadism rather than merely trying to exploit its success came from another extreme-right journal, Maurice Bardèche's *Défense de l'Occident*, which devoted its May 1956 issue to the Poujadist phenomenon. For Bardèche, Poujadism represented a quintessentially French form of communitarian activism, a *Jacquerie* (peasant revolt) canalising a 'huge groundswell of popular anger' through action rather than ideology. The charge of fascism levelled at Poujade, Bardèche argued, was 'false and absurd'; far from being anti-democratic, Poujadism was a call for 'real democracy as opposed to the perversion of democracy'.[119]

Despite strong personal sympathy for Poujade, Bardèche's refusal to classify Poujadism within a fascist framework was significant. In support of his argument, Bardèche noted the lengths to which Poujade went to effect change through the existing democratic institutions (elected deputies, political parties, parliament) before declaring war on a regime 'deaf to the appeals of the nation'. This was a return to the distinction formulated by Maurras, in his critique of the Third Republic, between the *pays légal* and the *pays réel*. For Bardèche as for Maurras, that distinction rested on an imagined paradigm of 'the Nation' as the embodiment of the real France in opposition to the deficient institutions of 'the Republic'.

Poujade's approach to leadership, too, was quite at odds with fascist models. Where an authentic dictator would seek to impose his ideas on the masses, Poujade had no ideas to offer: he was simply a 'resonance chamber' for the grievances of those he represented, a political leader 'despite himself'. This assessment chimed with Poujade's declared view of himself as nothing more than 'a reflection of public opinion, a loudspeaker, a standard-bearer'.[120] In giving a voice to the people, concluded Bardèche, in focusing his political crusade on the call for an Estates-General, Poujade was 'not combating the Republic but returning it to its source'. If he was to be accused of anything, it was of clinging to an ideal of republicanism that had no place within the existing Republic.[121]

Any attempt to understand Poujadism as a political movement and define it in relation to right-wing extremism or fascism must take account of such objections. Though some of its rhetoric and many of its designated enemies were similar, Poujadism bore no relation in its essential goals to those earlier movements – Georges Valois' Faisceau in the 1920s or Jacques Doriot's PPF in the 1930s – which had called for the overthrow of the Republic by a fascist dictatorship. While Poujade recalled Doriot in his talent for haranguing crowds in shirt-sleeves, his movement never adopted the trappings (uniforms, salutes, parades, etc.) of movements with a fascist bent; nor could the violence of the Poujadists be compared in any real sense to organised fascist brutality. Poujade's avowed republicanism, his caution at every critical juncture (a 'distinctly unfascist' quality, as has been observed),[122] and his reluctance to lend his movement a more sharply defined political vocation argue against comparison along such lines. In his involvement with *Algérie Française* extremists, where he might have played a more determining role, he was circumspect, hesitant and, in the end, ineffec-tual.[123] Even in his anti-communism – that first imperative of fascism[124] – Poujade was belated and tactical rather than driven by ideological principle: the real anti-communist phase of the movement dated from 1955, and its loudest exponents would be Le Pen and Demarquet. Meanwhile, Poujade's fundamental pragma-tism remained undiminished. 'We shared certain positions with the right', he would declare of his parliamentary group, 'but in our opposition to trusts, for example, we ranged ourselves with the communists. We were unclassifiable.'[125]

If we understand one of the essential signifiers of fascism (as of other totali-tarian ideologies) to be, in Stanley Hoffmann's terms, 'a cult of the state, and a belief in the absorption of the whole of society by the state', then Poujadism was no fascism. The base of the movement remained too Girondist to accommodate any sympathy for a totalitarian state, 'too rural, with too many people for whom mass action was a novelty, an exhilarating adventure, but in the long run rather frightening, which cannot be said of those who support totalitarian movements'.[126] Denouncing its agents and incumbent elites, the Poujadists viewed the centralised state as an instrument of oppression, a Moloch to be sated. In its primary expression as a tax revolt and its campaign for an Estates-General, Poujadism was a call for less, not more, state. This backward-looking provincialism, according to Jean-Christian Petitfils, is what most distinguished the Poujadist 'revolt' from a fascist 'revolution'.[127]

Neither was Poujadism 'fascist' in the sense of combining nationalism (which it evinced strongly) with socialism (which it strenuously rejected, aside from its calls for justice in tax and welfare provision). As anti-collectivist as they were anti-capitalist, the Poujadists remained wedded to the defence of small-scale economic liberalism, the micro-capitalism that was their *raison d'être*, along ill-defined corporatist lines.[128] Even the nationalism of the Poujadists had a primitive economic core: the preservation of the 'retail outlets of the Indies', the protection not only of France's greatness 'but also of her prosperity, for the overseas territories are an essential element in our wealth'.[129] The protectionist impulse that was a strong feature of Poujadist nationalism derived from the same source, the defence of France ('the Great France of 140 million inhabitants') against financial speculation, global competition, the Common Market . . . – against modernity, in a word. Whereas fascism embraced the economic necessity of modernisation, notably through industry, Poujadism retained to the end its archaic mentality and opposition to industrial modernisation. It was, as Plumyène and Lasierra conclude, a movement which 'stopped short of modernity' and which remained, in that sense, 'radically different from fascism'.[130]

Peter Campbell makes a notable distinction when he detects in Poujadism a psychology 'very near that of fascism, or, rather, that of the rank-and-file's fascism in contrast to that of the social élite's fascism'.[131] There were certainly elements in this revolt of a threatened lower middle class that justify such a remark (inter-class hostility, the search for scapegoats, chauvinism, xenophobia, anti-intellectualism); but, as Campbell also notes, Poujadism remained in essence an economically reactionary movement, seeking no 'New Order' but pursuing instead a 'politics of rejection' in the face of social and economic change. The Poujadist programme was reducible to the simple formula: 'no social and economic developments at home, and no political developments in the French Union overseas'.[132]

Though survey data for the 1956 elections are localised and fragmentary, they confirm that the vote for the UFF was emphatically a socio-economic vote with limited capacity for wider politicisation. The issues of national grandeur, decolonisation, French Algeria and anti-communism which gave Poujadism its 'high politics' content – and much of its far-right tenor – found not the merest echo among a sample of Poujadist voters interviewed by the Institut Français d'Opinion Publique (IFOP), who explained their vote solely in terms of their professional grievances and general disgruntlement. Interpreting this survey, Jean Stoetzel and Pierre Hassner discovered among Poujadist voters 'no issue that could be properly defined as political, be it right-wing or left-wing'.[133] From post-election correspondence published in *Le Monde*, the same impression emerges of a Poujadist voter exercised, to the exclusion of 'higher' matters, by tax, social security . . . and the development of Prisunic stores.[134]

The lower middle classes gave Poujadism a structured social base, but it was a base of discontent which could not easily sustain a national political party. Apoliticism, moreover, remained a prudent posture for many in the commercial sector anxious to avoid antagonising their clientele. A number of government measures favourable to small business and a relaxing of tax inspection went some way towards addressing the grievances on which Poujadism had thrived. It required only a marked upturn in inflation in late 1956 and 1957, recreating economic conditions which the small retailer could exploit, for the remaining wind to be taken out of the movement's sails.[135] The ineffectiveness of the UFF in parliament, the Mollet government's firm stance on Algeria and the pull of de Gaulle as a new rallying point would in turn render irremediable the disintegration of Poujadism as a political force.

Disparaged for issuing a 'call of the void' with 'as much intellectual content as a scream',[136] Poujade – if his own assertions are to be believed – never in fact sought to do anything more. For this reason, the historian Jean-Pierre Rioux sees in Poujadism not an avatar of fascism but a protection against authentic fascism, a channel for the expression of grievance within the democratic framework. '*Sortez les sortants!*', as Rioux recognises, was a call not to public disorder, as in the 1930s, but to the ballot box.[137] In his *Fascisme français: passé et présent*, Pierre Milza concurs. In the end, he argues, Poujadism had more in common with post-war Italy's L'Uomo Qualunque (Common Man) movement, which saw 30 'popular' deputies elected briefly to the Italian parliament in 1946, than with Italian Fascism or Nazism.[138]

An elusive 'ism'

Though commonly ranged among movements of the extreme right, it is no easy matter to define the essential political nature of Poujadism. For it embodies two distinct and opposing French political traditions, the revolutionary-republican and the conservative-nationalist. It presents itself as a populist movement in defence of lower middle-class interests, mobilising the heritage of the left (Revolution, Republic, Resistance) and of the reactionary right (authoritarianism, nationalism, colonialism) against both left and right alike. Herein lies the ultimate singularity of Poujadism, for it assailed the parties of the left, the trade unions, the welfare state and collectivism as readily as big business, banks, high finance and the established conservative parties, remaining to the end an inchoate mix of the democratic and the authoritarian, the revolutionary and the ultra-conservative.

While the absence of a coherent doctrine made Poujadism seem ripe for exploitation by the extreme right, the political syncretism of its leader and the professional concerns of its supporters proved in the end the most effective barriers against such an enterprise. If Poujadism appeared for a time to mark a turning point of 'unprecedented promise',[139] it ended by merely exposing the continued weakness of an extreme right unable to capitalise on a mass movement of popular protest, a discredited National Assembly, and a transitional economy burdened by successive colonial wars. Dictated more by expediency than ideological kinship, the UDCA's relations with the extreme right replayed its earlier, opportunistic relations with the PCF, which had exerted a strong formative influence in many areas. The charge of fascism levelled so often against Poujade and his movement simply does not hold up. Poujade remained throughout not only impervious but deeply hostile to the imposition of an extreme-right ideology on his movement and resisted attempts to divert it to neo-fascist ends. In their failure to fill the doctrinal void of Poujadism and convert its revolt into revolution, elements within the French extreme right discovered not a new horizon of opportunity but the confirmation of their continued marginality a decade after Vichy.

4 Algeria
Another war, another 'fascism'

The end of '*la grande France*'

In the words of the extreme-right historian François Duprat, the Algerian War of 1954–62 appeared to offer absolution from the 'long penance' imposed at the Liberation on the 'Opposition Nationale'. The war provided a powerful mobilising cause, 'appealing not just to nationalist but to simple patriotic sentiment': the defence of 'a major part of the national territory' and refusal to submit to 'the liquidation of the French colonial empire'.[1] In the decade following Vichy, patriotic sentiment had been unequivocally on the left, the preserve of the Resistance and the Republic; now, the extreme right was able to reclaim the defence of national interest following its forfeiture in the years 1940–44.[2] In the upper ranks of the army and in the French settler community of almost a million in Algeria, right-wing radicals found a ready audience for their intransigent nationalism, while the widespread sympathy in France for *Algérie Française*, in the early part of the conflict at least, gave it a resonance within the very mainstream of French public opinion.

In its history and status, Algeria was like no other territory within the French empire, renamed the 'French Union' in the 1946 Constitution. Annexed in 1830, Algeria was governed not as a colony but as an integral part of France under the jurisdiction of the Interior Ministry. Of its population of 9.5 million in 1954, some 8.5 million were indigenous Arabs denied the social, political and economic privileges of their colonialist (*pied-noir*, or 'black foot') neighbours.[3] While moves towards self-government for Morocco and Tunisia were underway in the mid-1950s (and concluded by 1956), an independent Algeria was a quite different proposition. Given the entrenched interests of the large *pied-noir* community, the support in France for the *Algérie Française* cause, and the initial cross-party consensus to retain Algeria as 'part' of France, the outbreak of the Algerian rebel insurrection in November 1954 was met with a resolve from Paris to defeat the uprising by military means.

In the savage war that followed between the French army and the Algerian National Liberation Front (FLN), French troop levels in Algeria escalated from some 70,000 to 400,000, a predominantly conscript force described by one historian as 'the largest French expeditionary corps since the Crusades'.[4] Trained for conventional military combat, French soldiers were ill-equipped for a guerrilla war against a largely unseen enemy. Algeria was quite unlike Indo-China in the strength of its ties to France, its geographical proximity, the size of its settler population, and the political and economic stakes involved; but it presented a replica of Indo-China in confronting the French army with a mission to subdue forces implacably bent on national liberation. Invoking theories of 'psychological action' and 'revolutionary warfare', French army leaders in Algeria (some of whom had witnessed torture at the hands of the Gestapo or the Vietminh) assented to the widespread use of torture and atrocity to counter the methods of the FLN. Even so, the French authorities refused to acknowledge their engagement in a 'war', maintaining that Algeria presented an internal problem to be resolved internally.

The defence of French Algeria was not in itself an extreme-right cause. The loss of other, lesser colonial territories made Algeria appear as a last bastion to many across the political spectrum. Prime Minister Mendès-France, who had negotiated the peace settlement in Indo-China, saw Algeria as integral to 'the unity and integrity of the French Republic' and deemed Algerians to be 'irreversibly French'. The Interior Minister, François Mitterrand, was more succinct, declaring quite simply '*L'Algérie, c'est la France*'.[5] The majority of those who supported this position even to the point of eventual insurrection had no previous extreme-right affiliation; some, indeed, boasted impeccable records of service in the Resistance. The former resister and Gaullist *fidèle*, Michel Debré, viewed Algeria and the Sahara as France's 'last major assets', without which it would 'cease to have any prospects as a world power'. The future Prime Minister who would help de Gaulle to fashion an exit strategy in the face of violent opposition argued still in December 1957 that 'the abandonment of French sovereignty in Algeria is an illegitimate act', and that 'those who oppose it, by whatever means, are legally defending a legitimate cause'.[6] Only a few weeks after the outbreak of hostilities, Mendès-France had appointed former Resistance leader Jacques Soustelle as Governor-General of Algeria. 'It is precisely *because* we have lost Indo-China, Tunisia and Morocco', declared Soustelle, 'that we must not, at any price, in any way and under any pretext, lose Algeria.'[7]

With the stakes thus defined, there was no shortage of extreme-right agitators and conspirators drawn to defending this 'most French of the provinces of France' and to ensuring that no progress was made towards a negotiated settlement. While nostalgia for Vichy and neo-Nazism had been the dominant themes on the French extreme right in the immediate post-war years, these were superseded in the 1950s and 1960s by an ultra-nationalism that fed off Cold War tensions and crystallised around the highly emotive issue of decolonisation. For the first time since the Liberation, extreme-right groups could now, as Joseph Algazy puts it, 'show themselves for what they were and, without any inhibition, proclaim their existence in public'.[8] According to Del Boca and Giovana, there were 47 extreme-right organisations active during the Algerian War, most of which were formed in 1954.[9] Noting the 'deep and sometimes impenetrable obscurity' in which many such organisations operated, allied to the 'connivance of some sections of the police forces', Malcolm Anderson ventures the much less restrained estimate that 'there were probably over a thousand in total'.[10]

When the newly designated Socialist Prime Minister, Guy Mollet, travelled to Algiers to take matters in hand on 6 February (that date again) 1956, he was pelted with tomatoes by *pieds-noirs* enraged at his apparent willingness to buy peace through political and economic reforms in favour of the Arab population. Confronted with the strength of opposition to any political 'sell-out', Mollet thereupon resorted to a hard-line approach which merely perpetuated the military impasse. The following month, a special-powers law was passed by the National Assembly to increase the army's resources and accelerate 'pacification', a euphemism for crushing the FLN. As the Mollet government gave way to others equally incapable of resolving the crisis, the threat of a military *coup d'état* in Algiers intensified, and with it the threat to the established order in France. On 9 May 1958, three prominent generals (Salan, Jouhaud and Allard) and an admiral (Auboyneau) wrote to President René Coty warning that the armed forces would 'to a man regard as an affront the abandonment of our national heritage', and that their loyalty could be assured only to 'a government firmly resolved to keep our flag flying in Algeria'.[11] Four days later, a violent demonstration organised by *pied-noir* activists resulted in the seizure of the main government building in Algiers and the proclamation of a Committee of Public Safety under General Jacques Massu, commander of the 10th Parachute Division.

The events of 13 May 1958 marked the high point of the threat orchestrated by the ultra-nationalists, who saw Algeria both as an end in itself and as the means of bringing down a hated parliamentary regime in France – a regime they proposed to replace with a 'nationalist, popular, authoritarian and hierarchical State'.[12] Already in 1956, the author Paul Sérant had observed that, 'if by "Fascism" we mean a predilection for authoritarian rule, then there exists in France today a "pre-Fascist" situation far more tense than before the war'.[13] Central to the project of converting this situation into an actual fascist state was a traditionally apolitical French army that had been bearing the weight of France's defeats since 1940.[14] In the wake of the most recent humiliation in Indo-China, the army might now be steered towards revolt. Reflecting on the failure of his administration to forestall this development and resolve the worsening crisis, Guy Mollet would later confess: 'Previous governments, my own included, failed to take seriously the danger posed by fascist organisations. I now say my *mea culpa*.'[15]

As fears grew of a paratroop invasion of Paris and the outbreak of civil war, General de Gaulle used the crisis to effect his return to power. By winning over some key military figures in Algiers and imposing himself on the politicians in Paris, he secured investiture as the last Prime Minister of the Fourth Republic, with authority to draft a new constitution that would reinforce the executive and allow him to govern with a much stronger hand as President (from January 1959) of the new Fifth Republic. While continuing to prosecute the war with vigour, de Gaulle took the steps that no previous administration had dared to take, moving gradually towards resolution of the conflict through a negotiated settlement. His favoured policy of 'association' ('the government of Algerians by Algerians, supported by French aid and in close union with France')[16] was at odds with the demand of the *pieds-noirs* and army ultras that French sovereignty over Algeria be maintained. The result was a concerted endeavour by the latter to derail the peace process, including organised strikes in Algiers, a putsch by army generals, and various attempts on de Gaulle's life by the Organisation Armée Secrète (OAS), a network of army dissidents and diehard extremists who refused to accept the renunciation of French rule in Algeria. Their efforts were in vain. The Evian Agreements of March 1962, ratified by referenda in France and Algeria, granted full independence to Algeria. This brought to a close almost eight years of bloodshed and marked, as one extreme-right publication lamented, the end of '*la grande France* stretching over both shores of the Mediterranean'.[17]

Expanding horizons: Jeune Nation and the FEN

The loss of Algeria dealt a severe blow to the extreme right. What had begun as a promise of rehabilitation ended in a further, painful demonstration of weakness and failure. The prominent role played at the height of the conflict by right-wing nationalist elements within the army and the *pied-noir* community made it harder for these elements to accept their irrelevance as momentum gathered towards a peace settlement. The subsequent challenges to de Gaulle's authority by disaffected ultras and the terrorist campaign waged by the OAS were a desperate rearguard action against the inevitable. As OAS leaders were arrested or took refuge in exile, the signing of the Evian Agreements removed the grounds for their existence. It also dispelled any lingering notion of an identity of sympathy between the extreme right and a French public opinion which had swung overwhelmingly in favour of an end to hostilities, even at the cost of full independence for Algeria. In the referendum of April 1962 on the Evian Agreements, over 90 per cent of those who voted in France did so in support of the peace settlement.

As a mobilising cause, however, Algeria represented a critical phase in the development of the extreme right in post-war France. It provided a unifying focus for activism and a recruiting ground expanded beyond the narrow circuit of Pétainists, Vichy nostalgics and residual fascists towards army veterans, serving soldiers, colonial settlers, and those who saw the defence of the French Union as a patriotic imperative. In this sense, Algeria offered an opportunity for the French extreme right to move beyond its discredited past and pretend to a political sensibility in tune with contemporary concerns. Foremost among these concerns were the fear of global communism in an age of superpowers and the perceived risk of an 'abandoned' Algeria falling under Marxist hegemony. Here the legacy of Indo-China was much invoked, as though the fate of the Western world, jeopardised at Dien Bien Phu, were now being played out in Algiers. Another theme which found currency was the European supremacism that had long underpinned the extreme right's world view, as movements such as Jeune

Nation warned against 'the immense perils threatening the white civilisation of Europe and France'.[18]

Formed during the Indo-China War in 1949 and dissolved finally, after a banning order and change of name, in 1962, Jeune Nation (Young Nation) was the most prominent French neo-fascist movement of the 1950s.[19] This was the vehicle of the Sidos brothers (sons of a Milice leader executed at the Liberation), two of whom, Pierre and Jacques, had been imprisoned until 1949 before standing as candidates for Isorni's Pétainist UNIR party in the 1951 legislative elections. François Sidos was president of Jeune Nation; its chief ideologue and driving force was Pierre, who had served his political apprenticeship under the Occupation in the youth movement of Marcel Bucard's pro-fascist Parti Franciste. With an estimated strength at its height of 3–4,000 militants in France and Algeria, Jeune Nation openly proclaimed its ambition to bring about a 'national insurrection' and replace parliamentary democracy with 'a new State that will be authoritarian and popular, national and social'.[20] It glorified the army, in particular the parachute regiments of the Foreign Legion, in whom it placed its hopes for the overthrow of the Republic. It had as its *idée-force* the defence of the French empire against decolonisation and took as its emblem the Celtic cross 'to combine memories of our nation's distant past with our hopes of an even greater future'.[21]

Acting as a pole of attraction for radical right-wing students and disaffected ex-servicemen from Indo-China, Jeune Nation carried its ultra-nationalist, anti-communist, racist ideology over into violence. It attacked offices of the PCF and the communist-leaning CGT trade union, and visited reprisals on North African workers in France.[22] Terrorist acts attributed to it included the planting of a bomb in a lavatory at the National Assembly on 6 February 1958 (to mark the anniversary of the anti-parliamentary riot of 1934 and the execution of Robert Brasillach in 1945).[23] As the conflict in Algeria neared its denouement, some of Jeune Nation's leaders and activists would find a new channel for their *jusqu'au-boutisme* in the OAS.

In its successive guises, Jeune Nation gave expression to some of the radical aspirations which extreme-right groups sought to pursue through the Algerian crisis: the 'overthrow of the Republic', the suppression of elections and political parties in France, the 'exclusion of wogs [*métèques*] from positions of political and economic responsibility', the punishment of 'those responsible for the needless deaths since 1940 and for abandoning the territories of the Empire'. In economic terms, it called for the abolition of 'stateless capitalism', the establishment of a corporatist system, and opposition to American and Soviet imperialism. It envisaged the construction of a Europe stretching 'from Narvik to Cape Town, from Brest to Bucharest' and 'founded on the common civilisation and destiny of the white race'. Civilisation and race were key notions in the ideology of a movement which demanded 'a review of naturalisations' and 'the removal of rights from undesirable foreigners'. Other proposed throwbacks to the repressive legislation of Vichy included 'the total elimination of capitalism and of international Jewish high finance', and the restriction of women to their 'two most beautiful roles: being a wife and being a mother'. In addition, Jeune Nation called for the replacement of slums by 'solidly built and pleasant blocks of flats' and an all-out war against the 'degenerative social effects of democracy: alcoholism, prostitution, racketeering, begging'. Through the more populist elements of its programme (such as 'housing for all French people'), Jeune Nation sought to attract working-class support and thereby challenge its arch-enemy, the PCF. It aspired to be the single mass party in the fascist mould which the collaborationists had sought to press Vichy into creating – a party whose goal was 'to take power by non-parliamentary means' and embody 'the nationalist State on the march'. Reviving the language of the inter-war extreme right, Jeune Nation denounced the Republic as a 'decrepit "old slut"', called for a 'second French revolution' to overthrow it, and urged that France be 'purified of the villains oppressing her' (a coded call, issued in April 1959, for the assassination of de Gaulle).[24]

Kindred organisations, most notably the Fédération des Etudiants Nationalistes (Federation of Nationalist Students, FEN), sought likewise to turn the Algerian War to the service of their anti-democratic project. Attracting mainly university students, lycée pupils and some budding intellectuals on the far right, the FEN was set up in May 1960 by François d'Orcival and Fabrice Laroche (generally held to be pseudonyms of Amaury de Chaunac-Lanzac and Alain de Benoist). It was conceived as a response to the 'growing Marxist influence within the UNEF' (National Union of French Students)[25] and in particular to the latter's support for a negotiated settlement in Algeria. By 1965, FEN membership was estimated at around 2,500, with sections active in Paris and a number of southern university towns such as Marseille, Aix, Nice and Toulon.[26] The FEN served for a time as a student wing and a legal cover for Jeune Nation following a government banning order. It also provided a more intellectual forum than Jeune Nation and other movements primarily dedicated to violent activism, such as Jean-Baptiste Biaggi's 'commandos' in the Parti Patriote Révolutionnaire (Revolutionary Patriot Party, PPR).

The FEN joined with Jeune Nation militants in public agitation and articulated a message close to theirs in its ultra-nationalism and insistence on the civilising mission of empire. In its 'Manifesto of the Class of 60', the FEN rejected outright 'the democratic conception of man' which 'dragged a Bigeard down to the level of the lowest street-sweeper, a Pasteur to that of an illiterate from the Congo, and a mother to that of a prostitute'. It sought to 'expel Marxism from the universities and schools of France', to keep 'French Algeria territorially bound to the Mother Country', and to found a 'rigorously hierarchical [state] not on election but on selection'. The new governing elite must be of 'European ethnicity', while 'stateless or markedly different elements' were to be kept away from positions of responsibility. For the FEN, the events unfolding in Algeria were a manifestation of a new global tendency, 'the revolt of coloured peoples against the order assured by the imperial sovereignty of white civilisation, a revolt secretly fomented by communism, the masters of high finance and large-scale stateless capitalism'. Only by reasserting the pre-eminence of

'European civilisation' and the 'white man, especially the Frenchman', would the conjoined threats of Marxism and colonial insurrection be overcome and 'the natural order of the world' be restored.[27]

From military to ideological war

Though less notorious than Jeune Nation, the FEN occupies an important place in the development of the extreme right in contemporary France. For it conceived of itself as a forum for rethinking some of the premises of French nationalism in the 1960s and – importantly – for challenging the intellectual ascendancy of the left. It also evinced a new awareness that political activism was futile if the ideas that underlay it did not command popular support. The 'ideological war' on which the FEN embarked was to be waged not in the streets but in 'the biology laboratories, the archives of the National Library [and] the editorial rooms of the mainstream press'. It was to be an insidious war of infiltration and attrition. Its combatants were to 'wear on the outside reassuring labels acceptable to the system, in order not to arouse attention before our war machine is sufficiently strong'.[28]

Following the humiliation of Indo-China and the loss of Morocco, Tunisia and other territories, decolonisation was essentially a *fait accompli*. Despite its commitment to retaining French Algeria, the FEN began to develop a post-colonial ideology with a marked emphasis on Europeanism that foreshadowed the later writings of the Nouvelle Droite (New Right). Hitherto, French nationalism had been expressed largely in territorial terms: Alsace-Lorraine, the colonies, French Algeria. From the outset, by contrast, the FEN saw its nationalism as indissociable from 'the defence of European pre-eminence' and defined the French nation as a 'privileged territory' where 'the main racial branches that make up European ethnicity converge'.[29] It drew on the classic French nationalism of Barrès and Maurras but reserved special praise for those, like Brasillach and Drieu La Rochelle, who had espoused 'nationalism in its European character'. In the post-colonial world, this nationalism would stress the common origins, ethnicity and interests of European peoples and would urge the defence of their superior civilisation against the dangers posed by communism and the Third World. Biology, genetics and the behavioural sciences were pressed into the service of an ideology predicated on inequality and with strong tendencies towards social Darwinism. Through its periodical, *Cahiers universitaires*, the FEN gave expression to the ideas of a younger generation eager to replace nostalgia with a forward-looking, less exclusively Gallic and more Europeanist doctrine of nationalism. Some would go on to play prominent roles in the later 1960s and 1970s and would contribute in particular to the project of ideological renovation undertaken by the Nouvelle Droite. Among the editorial team and contributors of the *Cahiers universitaires* were many of those (Alain de Benoist, Pierre Vial, Jean Mabire, Louis Pauwels and others) who would figure prominently in the Nouvelle Droite's main think-tank, GRECE (Groupement de Recherche et d'Etudes pour la Civilisation Européenne/Research and Study Group for European Civilisation).[30]

Concentrated mainly in Paris, Lyon, Marseille and Algiers, Jeune Nation militants, joined latterly by their FEN counterparts, were active in all of the conspiracies and agitation organised in Algeria and in the campaign of terror waged by the OAS. They took part in the storming of the government headquarters in Algiers on 13 May 1958, and in the demonstrations that followed in France. Calling for parliamentary deputies to be thrown in the Seine, Jeune Nation militants were prominent in the anti-government rally on the Champs-Elysées in Paris – stoking memories of the anti-parliamentary riot of 6 February 1934 and causing the newspaper *Libération* to declare that fascism had 'thrown off its mask'.[31] This led to the movement's dissolution by government decree on 15 May 1958, though it was simply reformed (in October 1958) as the Parti Nationaliste, which continued to propagate its message through the scarcely concealed means of the periodical *Jeune Nation* (which would claim a circulation of 20,000 by the end of 1959).[32] In the editorial for the first issue of *Jeune Nation* on 5 July 1958 (the anniversary of the seizure of Algiers by the French army in 1830), Pierre Sidos made clear the insurrectionary mission of his movement: 'Once again we proclaim that we can look neither to the fatal parliamentary process nor to the Phrygian bonnet to restore to France her rightful place as a great nation. We can look only to the Celtic cross and the parachutist's beret to save France.'[33]

While it opened its columns to some veterans of the extreme right (Coston, Ploncard d'Assac, Tixier-Vignancour), *Jeune Nation* deplored the failures of earlier generations to replace the Republic with a fascist state. Having supported the abortive insurrection at the barricades in January 1960 and the failed generals' putsch of April 1961, the movement saw its struggle to keep 'Algeria forever French' come to nothing.[34] Its leaders were arrested, tried and sentenced for conspiring against the state. By 1963, Pierre Sidos and Dominique Venner had been released from prison and were able to develop their political ideology in new directions. The former would launch the most prominent extreme-right organisation of the 1960s in Occident; the latter would found the review *Europe-Action*, which was to serve as ensign for the political movement of the same name and, like the FEN's *Cahiers universitaires*, as a test bed for ideas that would later find expression in the Nouvelle Droite.

From 1958 until its final dissolution in 1962, Jeune Nation constituted the hard core of subversive action against de Gaulle's Algerian policy and the incipient Fifth Republic. More significantly in the longer term, Jeune Nation and the FEN offered political apprenticeship to a new generation of right-wing radicals, many of them in their teens or early twenties, for whom Vichy was a remote reference point. François Duprat, Alain Robert, Pierre Vial and Jean-Gilles Malliarakis were among prominent militants who would go on to play leading roles in Occident, Ordre Nouveau, the Front National and the Parti des Forces Nouvelles, as well as within GRECE.

Algeria: 'this ultimate Crusade'

Jeune Nation and the FEN promoted in the 1950s and 1960s an elitist, racist, authoritarian ideology that had been kept largely underground since the Liberation. By linking this ideology to the defence of *Algérie Française* and to other factors such as Soviet repression in Hungary in 1956, Jeune Nation projected the French armed struggle in Algeria as a just 'crusade'. The theatre of engagement might have changed, but the struggle against communism remained essentially the same as that undertaken some years earlier by LVF and Waffen-SS volunteers who had enlisted to fight on the Russian front. In Algeria, this global struggle was infused with a more readily racist quality as the anomaly of defending 'national' territory against an indigenous Arab uprising was sustained.

Among those evincing most zeal for such a 'crusade' against communism and its Islamic allies were nationalist Catholics such as Georges Sauge and Robert Martel, with their call to arms in defence of the 'Christian values of civilisation' against the 'legions of Satan'.[35] The legacy of Vichy and the Liberation had been to reconcile many French Catholics to the values of the Republic, and to radicalise yet further those fundamentalist fringes of the Church which refused to have any truck with democracy or the heathen creeds to which post-war liberalism opened the way. Paramount among these was La Cité Catholique, a network of militant Catholics and political reactionaries which, through its periodical *Verbe*, preached an anti-communist, anti-progressivist doctrine that drew on papal encyclicals and the classics of French counter-revolutionary thought (Joseph de Maistre, Louis de Bonald, Antoine de Rivarol). The protagonists of La Cité Catholique recognised a difference of degree only between the evils of liberalism and those of communism, and condemned the revolutions of 1789 and 1917 as equally 'satanic'.[36] For them, Algeria presented an opportunity to win back some of the ground lost at the Liberation and to wage a new holy war in the sign of the cross. Central to their enterprise was the same notion of the Christian warrior that had been evident in the LVF and Milice, whose quasi-sacred oaths and ceremonies had recalled those of medieval crusading knights.[37]

Imbued with the ideas of La Cité Catholique, Sauge, a disaffected communist turned virulent anti-communist, ran a Centre d'Etudes Supérieures de Psychologie Sociale (Centre for Higher Studies in Social Psychology, CESPS) to instruct French army officers in the fight against Marxist subversion. This amounted, in sum, to providing a veneer of legitimacy for the repressive methods used to extract information from suspects and break down the FLN's guerrilla network in Algiers. The sympathy which Sauge commanded among some high-ranking army ultras and some sections of the Church ensured that his fundamentalist Catholic message received a ready audience among the officer corps, especially those engaged in the army's psychological warfare department (the Cinquième Bureau). The latter found in Sauge's writings, seminars and tours of military schools and barracks an aggressively doctrinaire ideology with which to combat the Marxist influence that was seen to lie behind Algerian nationalism. In essence, this could be reduced to the conviction that 'the Cross, enveloped in the folds of the tricolour flag, must wage a holy war against Islam, the ally of Bolshevism'.[38]

Sauge's project was nothing less than to save the modern world from the forces of evil. Within this Manichaean perspective, Algeria offered a providential theatre for 'the Franks and their civilising mission in the service of God'.[39] The same Carolingian echo rang from movements such as Colonel Pierre Château-Jobert's Armée du Christ-Roi (Army of Christ the King), and from Robert Martel's call to the settlers of the Mitidja plain: 'Brandish aloft the symbol of the Heart surmounted by the Cross, and like Father de Foucauld, like Saint Joan of Arc, concentrate your energies in order that the Sacred Heart of Jesus may rule the world.'[40] Standing trial for his alleged role in the assassination attempt by the OAS on de Gaulle at Petit-Clamart in August 1962, Lieutenant Alain Bougrenet de La Tocnaye would declare: 'In defending French Algeria, we were defending Christianity against pan-Arabism and international communism.'[41] At times this struggle was cast in more apocalyptic terms still. In one of his final pronouncements as OAS leader, General Raoul Salan called for resistance to the 'infamous treachery of De Gaulle and his henchmen': 'With our eyes fixed on the example of Saint Joan of Arc, we shall embark on this ultimate Crusade upon which depends the fate of humanity.'[42]

Bardèche: defining Fascism anew

It was in this febrile climate that Maurice Bardèche chose, in 1961, to publish his political credo, *Qu'est-ce que le Fascisme?*. Here, for the first time, Bardèche openly proclaimed himself 'a fascist writer' and sought to theorise a new form of fascism, stripped of the 'errors and excesses' of the Italian and German models.[43] Only thus, reasoned Bardèche, could fascism move beyond its discredited past and reinvent itself as a viable alternative to liberal democracy. As the 'catechism of post-war fascism', the book was to contribute profoundly to the ideological renewal of the French and European extreme right in the 1960s and 1970s. It appeared in a number of editions and translations, and would assume its place alongside 'classics' such as Hitler's *Mein Kampf* for a younger generation of right-wing extremists.[44]

The nature and timing of this publication were highly significant. For it set forth an apologia for fascism at a moment when, as the author asserted, 'fascism is in the air and there are thousands of men who are fascist without knowing it'. The French were even accommodating now to a 'pseudo-fascism' in the form of de Gaulle's presidentialist Fifth Republic, with its 'suppression of essential liberties' and 'feigned respect for the democratic process'.[45] The forthright tone of this work bespoke a new confidence among extreme-right circles – a sentiment which, the historian Joseph Algazy contends, was not entirely misplaced. The convergence of circumstances in the period 1958–62, he argues, with popular support for stronger government and the radicalising effects of the Algerian crisis, made France a country 'open to the dissemination of fascist ideas'.[46]

In a book purporting to define what fascism was, Bardèche was intent to clear the ground by first describing what it was *not*. To pioneer a fascism for the future meant, crucially, to mark a distance from the past. This Bardèche did by reviewing what had been his provocative support in the late 1940s for Vichy and Nazi Germany:

> Along with several others, I defended the Vichy regime; and yet, deep down, I rejected three-quarters of what Vichy had done. I defended those who stood accused at Nuremberg; yet there were some whom, had I followed the promptings of my conscience, I might have condemned. It was not the time to pick and choose. The injustice meted out was indivisible; our response had to be so too. We have reached a point now, however, where we need not shrink from the truth. We must acknowledge that there are aspects of yesterday's fascism from which today's fascism must distance itself.[47]

By so deliberately repositioning himself vis-à-vis the fascism of the 1930s and 1940s, Bardèche sought to rescue some timeless, transcendent essence of fascism 'stripped of the scrub and dead wood that have been choking it'.[48] He showed a marked sympathy for the early popular dictatorship of Mussolini, with its public works, concern for social justice and corporatism, before it lapsed into a remote and sterile Caesarism. German National Socialism, admirable in its galvanising power, had been diverted after only a few years from its reform programme to the prosecution of a global war; it represented the '*strong image* of fascism', but of a fascism hampered by its revanchist impulses and its Germanocentric aspirations.[49] Here, for Bardèche, lay the fundamental weakness of the Italian and German experiments alike: both had foundered on their essential nationalism, failing to attain any truly pan-European or universal stature. Significantly, Bardèche judged Maurrassism in France to have failed on precisely the same grounds that it was too fixed in space and time, too narrow in its nationalism, to have any universal applicability.[50]

The question of Nazi atrocities was addressed here in much more critical terms than in *Nuremberg ou la terre promise*, which had seen Bardèche tried and briefly imprisoned some years before. This, he now argued, had been one of Hitler's major errors, for the 'systematic persecution of the Jews' was nowhere part of the 'fascist contract'.[51] Far from incriminating fascism, however, Bardèche discovered here a means to exonerate it, on the grounds that there was 'no logical, necessary, automatic link between fascism and racism'. National Socialism, in its construction of 'the German' and 'the anti-German', went beyond the 'normal political criteria of the useful, the possible or the necessary' to introduce a biological dimension that had 'no place in true fascism':

> Fascism, as a political system, is no more responsible for the policy of exterminating the Jews than nuclear physics, as a theoretical science, is responsible for the destruction of Hiroshima. We should not therefore have it on our conscience.[52]

The conception of fascism to which National Socialism gave rise was in consequence, for Bardèche, an 'aberrant conception'; yet it '*was and remains*, not just for the enemies of fascism but for fascists themselves, the most powerful image' of fascism. For 'the single party, the SS, the *Führer-prinzip*, authoritarian government and to a certain extent even racism have become the defining characteristics of fascism and, so to speak, the zoological features by which it may be identified'.[53]

Bardèche's impatience with those contemporary parties which pretended to the fascist heritage in Italy and Germany was clear. The MSI 'takes refuge in memories', while the Deutsche Reichspartei (DRP) 'cannot even do that because of legal interdiction'.[54] Hampered by the myopia of electoral politics, neither had a long-term vision that would update, correct and go beyond the projects of Mussolini and Hitler. Their saving grace for Bardèche, and with it their right to call themselves 'neo-fascist', lay in their refusal to accept the new order emerging from 1945, their fundamentally anti-democratic ideology and their vigorous rejection of capitalism and Marxism alike. For it was on these two fronts that the victory of fascism had to be secured: against the 'invisible forces of international capitalism' and the 'invisible battalions waging a war of subversion' upon France and Europe.[55]

Written a decade and a half after the defeat of fascism, Bardèche's book stands as a landmark in the development of the post-war extreme right. For it provided the first sustained critique of Hitler's Germany and Mussolini's Italy from within the French neo-fascist community, and the most self-reflexive statement of the broad values around which this community coalesced. It also offered an opportunity to cast a retrospective judgement on Vichy, which Bardèche deemed to have been far from fascist, likening Pétain's regime to Franco's Spain and de Gaulle's France as a 'pseudo-fascism' only.[56]

Unsurprisingly, Bardèche's fascism remains in the end elusive. It is an 'infinitely less precise', 'infinitely less *scientific*' doctrine than communism, drawing more on sentiment, passion and will than on a set of well-defined principles. The essential elements of fascism as Bardèche apprehends them are nonetheless clear: 'nationalism, socialism, anti-communism and authoritarianism' are the '*fundamental* characteristics' of this syncretic political credo.[57] Such terms, Bardèche insists, are not to be taken in a restrictive sense: 'nationalism' must not preclude the creation of a fascist 'international', and 'socialism' is to be assured only within an anti-democratic, uncompromisingly authoritarian regime.[58]

Such was the socialism of the nationalist right: it had nothing to do with social democracy, little to do with social justice, and everything to do with social order. It was derived from a utilitarian, not a humanitarian, view of the nation. Socialistic reforms there would be, but these would be carried through by a strong central authority, an authority empowered to impose (in Eugen Weber's terms) 'that General Will which, as Rousseau has told us, is not necessarily the will of all, or even that of most'.[59] The socialism for which Bardèche argues may be 'liberating', combating 'the scandalous disparities in standards of living' and 'the exploitation that Marxism rightly denounces', but it is no 'dictatorship of the proletariat'. It is by instituting such a dictatorship that communism (in theory at least) represents, for Bardèche, the very 'culmination of democracy'. His, by contrast, is a social vision devoid of egalitarianism, a socialism 'evidently inseparable from the authoritarian government that is a defining feature of fascism'.[60]

The glimpses of what this fascist socialism might mean in practice point to a combination of economic planning and private enterprise, with an extensive programme of nationalisations (where appropriate, confiscations) and a clampdown on 'anonymous' wealth and big capital. According to Bardèche, democracy is incompatible with such socialism, since democracy is a system dominated by 'pressure groups pursuing their economic interests' and designed to perpetuate 'a class of privileged individuals and parasites whose wealth is a provocation to those who work'. Bardèche is nonetheless careful not to define too narrowly the social base of his fascism. Unlike its privileged enemy, communism, he argues, fascism is not the preserve of any class or social group: it is 'the resort of an angry nation', a 'heroic solution' that calls forth the 'providential man' and thrives in 'periods of crisis'.[61]

Bardèche's *Qu'est-ce que le Fascisme?* was written in response to two clearly perceived imperatives: the first, to draw lessons from the past and avoid a further failure of the fascist project in the future; the second, to confect a sanitised definition of 'moderate' fascism that would restore this ideology to political respectability and promote it as an alternative to the 'sterile confrontation between liberal democracies and communism'.[62] It offered a means to cast off a discredited legacy, to disengage from Hitler and Mussolini while continuing to claim adherence to certain core values of fascism. There was no suggestion here of an electoralist strategy, of participation in 'the farce of parliamentary politics' and the quest for power through 'the temporary approval of a fragile majority': the ideology propounded in 'this *Mein Kampf* of the 1960s' remained resolutely anti-democratic.[63] Bardèche's book nonetheless marks a first important step in the attempted normalisation of the extreme right in post-war France. It pioneered a strategy for dehistoricising fascism and defining anew its place among contemporary political ideologies. It articulated the search for a new way forward that would be taken up by the Nouvelle Droite in the later 1960s and culminate in the formation of the Front National and the pursuit of electoral legitimacy in the 1970s and 1980s.[64]

The extreme right and Algeria: differing responses

Though there was much wishful thinking in Bardèche's reading of the historical moment, the turn of the decade in 1960 did appear to bring together several of the conditions that might conduce to a flowering of neo-fascism: a context of deepening crisis over Algeria, a powerful nationalist ferment, and a sharpening of the perceived conflict between 'the West' and communist expansionism. The closing words of Bardèche's *Qu'est-ce que le Fascisme?* made this global struggle central to the revival of a fascism that remained 'essentially and integrally anticommunist': 'It was Lenin who prophesied that fascism would be the ultimate form of government for the survival of those societies which refused to capitulate without a struggle to the dictatorship of communism.' The Western world, Bardèche concluded, could either 'disappear like a drowning old man' or embrace fascism as 'the last bulwark of Liberty and the sweet joy of living'.[65]

On the Algerian conflict, however, as on Poujadism, Bardèche resisted easy conclusions and articulated a more nuanced position than other extreme-right commentators. The engagement of neo-fascist groups in defence of *Algérie Française*, he argued, had been a purely nationalistic, perhaps even a purely senti-mental, reflex. They had never stopped to question whether they might not thus be furthering the interests of a plutocratic democracy in France, nor whether Algerian nationalism might not itself lead to an Islamic 'fascist' state on the model of Nasser's Egypt, a useful new authoritarian force independent of both Washington and Moscow. 'While the communists immediately posed the Algerian problem in terms of the *Communist International*, the fascist groups did not for a moment think of posing it in terms of the *Fascist International*.'[66] This demonstrated for Bardèche how far post-war fascism remained from its goal of becoming an internationalist ideology capable of forging a 'European Empire', that 'third force' so central to his conception of the fascist project.[67]

Concerned more with universals than with contemporary specifics, Bardèche did not use *Qu'est-ce que le Fascisme?* to develop his position on Algeria; rather, he used the Algerian crisis to argue for the change required in France to bring about his fascist state.[68] In an interview given some two decades after the Algerian War, he would reflect: 'As for *Algérie française*, I was for and against it at the same time.' While sympathetic to the most committed defenders of French Algeria, Bardèche recalled having also 'sided to some extent with the Muslim population in my conviction that colonialism could not continue and that a new type of association had to be sought between France and Algeria, one which would grant a form of independence to the latter while allowing France to retain some beneficial alliance with Algeria that would keep open access to its natural resources'.[69]

This strikingly ambivalent and pragmatic stance set Bardèche at odds with most of his extreme-right contemporaries on the highly charged question of Algeria. It was supported by the conviction that the prospect of granting full French citizenship to the Algerian people was 'utterly aberrant', a 'pure folly' with 'extremely grave' consequences.[70] His refusal to defend *Algérie Française* at any cost was consistent with the broader perspective in which Bardèche interpreted the significance of French involvement in this colonial war. Writing in his journal *Défense de l'Occident* in April 1956, he argued that the wider interests of France were being severely damaged by a war which, coupled with French support for Israel against the Arab states, was alienating France from the entire Muslim world. Algerian nationalism had been 'legitimised by "Resistance" dogma'; it was by holding out against a negotiated independence that the risk was greatest of bringing Soviet Marxist influence into the Mediterranean. Bardèche used this article to argue not only for a mutually beneficial peace settlement between France and Algeria, but for an end to the 'anti-fascist and Jew-loving' Fourth Republic and the suppression of a French Communist Party that was now 'playing the same traitorous role as in Indo-China'. Above all, he concluded, France must retain its attachment to Algeria as a bridge to the Islamic world and an important ally for a Europe hemmed in by Washington and Moscow.[71]

Though there may have been little in such an argument to persuade diehard activists to desist from armed struggle, it expressed a calculated view of the conflict which went beyond the narrow defence of a colonial territory. For Bardèche, the Algerian crisis had to be seen within the wider Europeanist perspective that he had promoted at the 1951 Malmö conference and elsewhere. His fellow delegate at Malmö, René Binet, likewise favoured a form of decolonisation that would allow for continued economic exploitation, arguing that those 'conscious of the value and superiority of their race and civilisation' had nothing to fear from liberated inferiors. As a founding member of the NOE, a radical offshoot of the MSE launched at Malmö, Binet sounded a louder clarion call against the dangers of miscegenation than Bardèche. He based his argument on overtly racist grounds, advocating a 'strict racial segregation' and 'the return of ethnic groups to their originally separate domains'.[72]

Bardèche's geopolitical and Binet's racist arguments for decolonisation pointed the way towards a new anti-colonialism on the extreme right, furnishing the rudiments of a rationale that would be elaborated some years later by the Nouvelle Droite. The issue at stake would no longer be French grandeur as measured by colonial power but French identity as defined through European kinship, Western culture and racial specificity. This current of thought would dispense with the notions around which much of the debate over French Algeria had turned – 'integration' and 'assimilation' – to insist instead on the preservation of difference, and therefore distance, between ethno-cultural communities.[73]

Against this evolving view – embraced by Nouvelle Droitistes such as Jean Mabire and, later, Alain de Benoist – were a host of more simplistic calls for the dogged maintenance of French colonialism. Typical of the irreconcilables were Charles Luca and his MPF. They mounted a strident defence of the colonial cause, urging fidelity to the 'white Aryan ideal' and the formation of an 'International of the white race' to 'reassert the place of the white man in the world'. In particular, the MPF called for 'the establishment of a white dictatorship over a large expanse of Eurafrica' as a 'civilising force against the barbarity welling up from the lowest depths of humanity'.[74] The bellicosity of Luca and his movement was matched by their over-simplification of the issues: 'De Gaulle has destroyed the Empire; the National Socialists swear to reconquer it!'[75]

At the height of the Algerian conflict, it was with this view of the world that many diehards would keep faith. Arraigned before the courts in November 1961 for his part in the 'week of the barricades' (a revolt in January 1960 which had sought to bring the army in Algeria out against de Gaulle), Jean-Jacques Susini, a leading member of the OAS, couched his defence within 'the context of a revolutionary war'. The French army in Algeria, he argued, was 'an army of missionaries and crusaders, of fighters for a revolutionary cause of wider significance'. This cause, for Susini, was none other than the salvation of the West.[76]

OAS: 'the fascism of negation'

De Gaulle's return to power in June 1958 was made possible by the rebellion of 13 May. When, in his radio-televised address of 4 November 1960, he finally declared his intention to hold a referendum on the proposal of an 'Algerian Algeria' with 'its own government, institutions and laws', the response of the ultras was predictable. Violent disturbances broke out in Algeria, orchestrated by radical right-wing groups and *pieds-noirs* who had thought the destiny of Algeria secure in de Gaulle's hands. Undeterred, de Gaulle pressed on with his 'policy of abandonment'.[77] On 8 January 1961, the principle of Algerian self-determination was endorsed by referendum, with a 75 per cent majority in France, Algeria and the overseas territories. In the subsequent referendum of 8 April 1962, over 90 per cent of voters in France and the overseas territories approved the Evian Agreements of March granting full independence to Algeria. On 1 July, the vote of support in Algeria would be little short of 100 per cent.

The referendum of January 1961 opened the way for the final phase of army and *pied-noir* defiance of de Gaulle's proposed Algerian settlement. In April 1961, four army generals (Challe, Salan, Jouhaud and Zeller) staged a putsch in Algiers with the support of the First Parachute Regiment of the Foreign Legion. While de Gaulle invoked his emergency powers under the Constitution and appealed for loyalty, Prime Minister Michel Debré organised blockades of Paris against a possible military invasion. The insurrection failed to win sufficient support across the army as a whole and collapsed within a matter of days, taking with it all hope of reversing the policy of Algerian independence. Opposition would now be pursued, for a time, through the OAS, a clandestine terrorist network that had been formed some weeks before the putsch by army elements and *pieds-noirs* implacably opposed to an independent Algeria.

The OAS engaged in a campaign of bombings and assassinations in Algeria and mainland France, including several attempts on de Gaulle's life. Impossible to measure with precision, its membership was estimated to be between 3,000 and 5,000.[78] It drew to its ranks disaffected soldiers, notably officers who had escaped arrest after the putsch of April 1961, extremist *pieds-noirs* and political irreconcilables opposed to de Gaulle (including General Salan at its head, Jean-Jacques Susini, Joseph Ortiz, Pierre Lagaillarde and Maurice Gingembre). It operated with the support of movements such as the Front Nationaliste, a paramilitary group formed in May 1961 which provided the OAS with armed men and 'commando' units.[79] In Algeria it attacked FLN sympathisers, Arab civilians and Europeans suspected of favouring Algerian independence, while in France its targets were politicians, journalists and intellectuals who supported a peace settlement. It produced a toll, by one count, of some 12,000 victims in France and Algeria.[80]

The OAS issued occasional lists of its victims, accusing them of 'treason' or 'intelligence with the enemy' – thus echoing the charges that had seen numerous collaborators condemned in 1945. The point was not lost on de Gaulle, who detected 'grudges dating from Vichy' behind much *Algérie Française* agitation. As though to illustrate the point, a branch of the Pétainist ADMP was set up in

Algiers in December 1960. In a reversal of the outcome of 1945, it swore to ensure that the 'saviour twice over of *la patrie*' (Pétain) would be duly honoured by having his remains transferred to Douaumont, and that those 'selling out and betraying *la patrie*' (de Gaulle) would be brought to justice before the High Court.[81]

The link with Vichy was one on which the OAS played in other ways. The argument of constitutional legality that had been deployed in defence of Pétain's regime and as a justification for suppressing the Resistance was once again rehearsed in defence of French Algeria. As the supreme custodian of France's 'territorial integrity' (Constitution, Article 5), it was argued, de Gaulle was in breach of his presidential function: insurrection against the Gaullist regime thereby became an urgent national duty. The trials of OAS insurgents in 1962 would echo those of Vichyites in 1945, with de Gaulle accused – again – of placing himself beyond the law and of 'betraying the Constitution, his word and the people by selling off a French province'.[82] Writing more than 20 years later, Le Pen would still denounce de Gaulle's Algerian policy as 'anti-constitutional'.[83] Such an argument, for those who held to it in the early 1960s, conferred a 'right of self-defence' and a 'right of insurrection' – the very terms which de Gaulle's Prime Minister, Debré, had himself once used in support of *Algérie Française*.[84]

Paradoxically, the Resistance also provided a powerful precedent to be invoked in opposition to de Gaulle. The themes of legitimacy and betrayal were again central to the argument. The '*presse de la trahison*' (traitors' press) had been a term used by the left to disqualify collaborationist publications under the German occupation; it was now used by the *Algérie Française* camp against left-wing publications sympathetic to Algerian independence.[85] Those committed to the defence of *Algérie Française*, it has been noted, included many *anciens résistants*. When Georges Bidault founded a National Resistance Council against Algerian independence in 1962, he was clearly invoking the memory of that earlier National Resistance Council which he had taken over from the executed Jean Moulin in 1943. Bidault reflected ruefully that he was beginning a second career in the Resistance in his sixties.[86]

Autumn 1961 saw a sharp escalation of OAS terrorism on the French mainland following the opening of negotiations in summer between the government and the FLN. With cells located in military bases throughout France, the OAS struck in major cities as far apart as Lille, Strasbourg, Marseille and Bordeaux, claiming responsibility for several hundred bombings. The organisation found support not only in the army but also in the ranks of the police, who were a prime target for FLN assassins in France and were brutal in their suppression of anti-OAS demonstrations. On 17 October 1961, in response to a call from the FLN, an estimated 30,000 Algerians staged a demonstration in Paris in defiance of a curfew and in support of independence for Algeria. Over 11,500 were arrested and held in makeshift detention centres; many were savagely beaten by the police; some were clubbed to death and either thrown into the Seine or disposed of in wooded areas around Paris.[87] Just as under the Occupation, Paris public transport was used to facilitate this mass round-up, with sports stadia again serving as holding pens. Despite the recovery of several dozen bodies in the days that followed, the authorities did all they could to cover up this event. The exact death toll on that night has never been established, with estimates ranging from 30 to 300 (contrary to the long-standing official count of only three deaths).[88]

The man with ultimate responsibility for that atrocity was the Police Prefect, Maurice Papon, who would much later (in 1998) be sentenced to 10 years in prison for having overseen the deportation of Jews from the Bordeaux area as Secretary-General of the Gironde Prefecture between 1942 and 1944. It was likewise under Papon's authority that an anti-OAS demonstration in Paris by left-wing parties and trade unions on 8 February 1962 resulted in the death of eight demonstrators at the Métro Charonne.[89] The funerals of these victims of police brutality became a focus of national mourning and did much to complete the shift of French public opinion towards support for a peace settlement in Algeria.

Standing firm against this shift of opinion, the OAS represented, in the words of Malcolm Anderson, 'the apotheosis of the French Algeria extremism'.[90] Following the Evian Agreements of March 1962, it adopted a scorched earth policy of destroying public buildings and amenities in Algeria prior to the exodus to France of almost the entire million-strong *pied-noir* community. Left with only vengeance as its motive, the final, desperate act of the OAS was an assassination attempt on de Gaulle at Petit-Clamart in August 1962. Far from eliminating 'the man who had let Algeria go',[91] this merely served to strengthen de Gaulle's hand, since he used the incident to push through his proposal for a directly elected presidency. As OAS leaders were captured or fled into exile, the last piece in de Gaulle's new Fifth Republic was thus set in place. The execution of Colonel Jean-Marie Bastien-Thiry, who had led the attack at Petit-Clamart, marked the end of the OAS as a subversive threat.

Mobilised exclusively to prevent Algerian independence, the OAS was an organisation which subordinated ideology to activism; it was, in the words of Plumyène and Lasierra, 'the fascism of negation'.[92] It brought together Maurrassians, nationalist Catholics and neo-fascists with former Resistance fighters and some former left-wing militants. It crystallised in action the refusal to compromise that had given this war from the outset such a strongly Manichaean character.[93] 'The OAS is not Fascist', wrote Maurice Bardèche; 'nevertheless there are among its supporters a number of people who are Fascists by temperament, who dream of a regime closely resembling Fascism. In a certain sense they are Fascists without knowing it.'[94] One of the best expressions of the ideas that underpinned OAS activism was provided in 1958 by the joint programme of two among the many *Algérie Française* movements, the Front des Combattants (FC) and Front d'Action Nationale (FAN). A more succinct conspectus of French extreme-right thinking in the late 1950s and early 1960s would be difficult to find:

> *We are nationalists.* [. . .] We believe in the future of France and the greatness of Western civilisation. Faced with the artificial and aggressive forms of

nationalism fomented in our overseas territories by trouble-makers in the pay of foreign powers, we seek to rekindle the nationalism of our time-honoured Frankish nation.

We are Europeans, for we recognise that in the century of the atom and the Sputnik, the peoples of our old European continent will rediscover their economic and political independence only if they unite. [. . .]

We are socialists, for we believe in the need for harmonious collaboration between the different sectors of producers, bosses and employees, managers and workers, city-dwellers and peasants. We are anti-capitalist, for contemporary capitalism is outdated and no longer corresponds to our economic needs. But we are anti-communist, for we reject the class struggle and believe in the need for solidarity within the sectors of the economy as within the national community.[95]

Though too diverse in its make-up and too focused on its practical objectives to formulate a coherent ideological programme, the OAS drew upon such thinking. Its priorities were to root out 'the cancer of communism', defend 'Western civilisation' and forge a 'new France' that would install 'a genuinely popular régime, opposing both the big capitalists and the Communist International; a régime which will safeguard our traditions, restore our links with Africa, rebuild Europe and restore to France her position in a West which will be proud of itself'. The OAS added to this a fundamentalist Catholic dimension in its mission (as expressed by its leader, General Salan) to '*tear down that secular and masonic Republic*' and make France once again 'the solid pillar of Christian Civilisation'.[96] What was noticeably absent from OAS discourse was the customary anti-Semitism. There seem to have been two reasons for this: first, the OAS recruited members and sympathisers among *pieds-noirs* of Jewish origin; second, the hostilities between Israel and the Arab states (some of which provided support for the FLN) made Israel an objective ally for the OAS, as well as a model of military efficiency. As Algazy puts it, 'hatred towards Arabs temporarily outweighed an anti-Jewish sentiment that had to be stifled in the interests of the cause in hand'.[97]

Le Pen and Algeria

For a clear statement of Le Pen's attitude to the war in Algeria, one need look no further than the autobiographical pages of his 1984 publication, *Les Français d'abord*. Like Indo-China, Algeria was 'part of the wider conflict between communist hegemony and the free world'. If France did not 'preserve its African territories at all costs, it would be reduced to a little hexagon in the little Asiatic peninsula of Europe'. Le Pen would describe his decision to enrol for a six-month tour of duty in Algeria as a symbolic gesture of solidarity following the Mollet government's decision to raise military service to 27 months. Reviewing the most dramatic events in the fight to resist de Gaulle's policy of independence, he would recall the week of the barricades as a 'patriotic reflex', the generals' putsch as a misguided and futile gesture too late to be of any use, and the OAS as a 'desperate last stand by doomed soldiers'.[98]

Taking parliamentary leave in September 1956, Le Pen set off to rejoin the First Parachute Regiment of the Foreign Legion serving in Algeria. Initially diverted to Suez during the Canal crisis, he arrived in Algiers in late December just as General Massu was about to assume special powers to wage a campaign of counter-terror against the FLN. From January 1957, the French army in Algiers stepped up repression in its effort to dismantle the network of FLN activists and sympathisers. Le Pen's alleged role in this would later become the most contentious issue relating to his three months of active service in Algeria. In 1985, he would bring a libel case against two newspapers (*Libération* and *Le Canard enchaîné*) which published accounts by individuals claiming to have witnessed or suffered torture at his hands. Le Pen protested that he was the victim of a campaign of defamation mounted by the left, but he had not always, it seems, shown himself to be quite so sensitive on this issue. In May 1957, *Le Monde* reported his open justification of the 'police mission' in which he had been engaged in Algiers, and of the 'harsh methods' and even 'illegal means' employed to accomplish it. Here Le Pen and his companion Demarquet were quoted defending torture as inevitable and just in the circumstances confronting the French army in Algeria.[99] In an interview with the newspaper *Combat* in November 1962, Le Pen would reportedly go further: 'I took part in the Battle of Algiers as an intelligence officer. Much has been said about the Battle of Algiers. I know, and I have nothing to hide. I tortured because it was necessary to do so.' Fearing perhaps the possible repercussions from such a bald assertion, Le Pen published in the same newspaper the next day a 'clarification' in which he denied ever carrying out or witnessing torture as such, claimed that he had always acted on the orders of his superiors, and defended the army's methods as 'legitimate self-defence' in the face of 'revolutionary and subversive warfare'.[100]

The special powers made available to Massu's forces left a wide margin for abuse in their euphemised mission of 'pacification' in Algiers. This amounted essentially to rounding up and interrogating hundreds of suspected FLN terrorists and accomplices in an attempt to break the guerrilla network in the Algerian capital. Torture was routine. The repressive measures yielded results, cutting the monthly total of terrorist acts carried out by the FLN in Algiers from some 4,000 in January 1957 to 1,500 in May 1958;[101] but the gains were bought at a heavy moral price. Barely a decade after Vichy, a Socialist-led 'Republican Front' government in Paris was tacitly sanctioning the use of methods reminiscent of the Gestapo and the Milice.

Though Le Pen's alleged involvement in torture has never been objectively established, it is clear that, as a lieutenant and section head involved in intelligence-gathering under Massu, he played his part in the early weeks of this 'Battle of Algiers'. Nor did Le Pen make any secret of his fierce commitment to defeating the FLN and keeping Algeria French. In this, he showed himself favourable to an integrationist solution, arguing that France should assume its responsibilities vis-à-vis Algeria in terms of economic and technical aid and improved rights for the indigenous Arab population. Algerians should be persuaded to remain by choice, rather than by force, within the French national community.[102] This was a view which set Le Pen at odds with more hard-line militants but which he considered attuned to France's national interests. An independent Algeria would mean the loss of valuable Saharan oil and mark another stage in the 'strategy of withdrawal and abandonment' that had begun in Indo-China, further opening the way for 'the conquest of the world by international Bolshevism'. In early April 1957, Le Pen returned to Paris with the thought that he might do more to prevent this as a politician than as an army officer. 'I knew that this war would be won or lost not in Algeria,' he would later reflect, 'but in France.'[103]

It was back in France that Le Pen would make his most sustained contribution to the cause of *Algérie Française*. Following his expulsion from Poujade's party, he took up his parliamentary seat again in June 1957 as an independent and used his first speech to defend the repressive methods employed by the army and the police in Algeria against the 'revolutionary and subversive warfare' waged by the FLN. The war should be fought, he argued, not in accordance with an 'almost hypercivilised system' of liberal values but by 'using the means necessary to win it'. He called for exceptional legislation to reinforce the army's powers in Algeria and denounced the 'exercise in moral sabotage conducted by the Communist Party and supported by the entire left-wing intelligentsia'.[104]

Just as he had sought to establish an anti-communist 'front' as a student in the late 1940s, Le Pen now set about mobilising an *Algérie Française* 'front', drawing on former members of the JIP and UDJF, disenchanted Poujadists and veterans of Indo-China and Algeria. The resultant Front National des Combattants (FNC) had as its prime objective the retention of Algeria as part of France's vital geopolitical space. It took as its emblem the two-edged sword (insignia of the First Parachute Regiment of the Foreign Legion) and a tricolour flame – anticipating the later emblem of the FN, which would drop the sword and retain the flame. Among its more radical adherents were Jean-Baptiste Biaggi and Georges Sauge. The first initiative of the FNC, in August 1957, was to embark on a 'caravan' tour to raise the consciousness of the holidaying French. The '*Caravane Algérie Française*' secured backing from the Ministry of Defence and some logistical support from the army. It was reminiscent of Poujade's campaign tours, with a convoy of lorries provided by the army, a marquee, loudspeakers, some loudmouths (notably Le Pen, Demarquet, Dides, Biaggi), and banners proclaiming 'Algeria is French and will remain French'. While Dides anticipated 'the triumph of our magnificent army over barbarous pan-Arabism and bloody Soviet dictatorship', Le Pen called (with a resounding echo of Vichy) for a 'national revolution' at home and overseas, a 'new France' founded on the values of '*patrie*', '*famille*' and '*travail*'. Together with belief in God and in authority, he argued, these represented the 'permanent and indisputable values' on which French civilisation rested.[105]

Le Pen would later describe the caravan initiative as a 'great success', with the distribution of 'hundreds of thousands of posters', 'millions of tracts' and 'brochures from the Governor-General of Algeria containing unbearable photos of assassination victims and children with their throats cut'. Above all, he would recall, the caravan tour gave an opportunity to put across to the French the stark message: 'If you do not keep French Algeria, you will have an Algerian France.'[106]

With the parliamentary recess over, Le Pen continued to trumpet his cause in the National Assembly. He renewed his attack on an old enemy, Pierre Mendès-France, 'the man most associated with our defeat in Indo-China', 'the man responsible for our abandonment of Tunisia, our abandonment of Morocco'. In February 1958, Le Pen's virulence towards Mendès-France was inscribed in the parliamentary record of proceedings, as he proclaimed his 'patriotic and almost physical revulsion' at the sight of the former Prime Minister.[107] Those with long memories might have heard an echo of Robert Brasillach in 1936 declaring another Jewish premier (to be), Léon Blum, one of 'the most repugnant specimens' of humanity.[108]

In March 1958, the FNC contested a parliamentary by-election in Paris with a pro-*Algérie Française* candidate. The candidate chosen was an Algerian Arab, Ahmed Djebbour, underlining Le Pen's and the FNC's commitment to an integrationist policy. Djebbour lost the election to Alexis Thomas, candidate of the Centre National des Indépendants et Paysans (CNIP) standing on a 'Union of Nationalists' platform. Thomas took over 40 per cent of the first-round vote to Djebbour's 3.1 per cent, and 57 per cent of the second-round vote to Djebbour's 0.9 per cent, demonstrating the weakness of Le Pen's movement against the serried ranks of the conservative right.[109] In a brawl with opponents during the campaign, Le Pen sustained an injury to his right eye from which he recovered only to lose his left eye to a degenerative cataract several years later.[110]

In the same month of March 1958, Le Pen testified at the trial of four Jeune Nation militants accused of mortally wounding the driver of a van delivering the communist newspaper, *L'Humanité Dimanche*. The event provided evidence that, despite his status as a parliamentary deputy, Le Pen retained links with the most radical anti-parliamentary elements on the extreme right. He submitted a deposition in support of the accused, invoking the memory of 'our soldiers stabbed in the back in Indo-China' and lamenting the freedom with which communist propaganda was disseminated.[111]

Some weeks later, the *pied-noir* and army insurrection of 13 May would leave Le Pen and his FNC on the sidelines. Frustrated in his desire to participate in the events in Algiers, he watched de Gaulle's return to power with more resignation than enthusiasm, believing that therein might lie the best hope for retaining French Algeria.[112] In the referendum of 28 September 1958 on the new Constitution of the Fifth Republic, Le Pen would vote 'yes'. For a time, it seems, he also entertained the thought of participating in the movement in support of the new President, where Gaullists and advocates of *Algérie Française* coalesced under the banner of the Union pour la Nouvelle République (Union for the New Republic, UNR). When no invitation came, he stood in the legislative elections of November 1958 as an independent with backing from the CNIP, under the influence of his erstwhile mentor Edouard Frédéric-Dupont. Le Pen won re-election on a pro-Gaullist platform in the 5th *arrondissement* of Paris, remaining (at 30) the youngest deputy in the National Assembly. In these first elections of the Fifth Republic, the PCF won the largest share of the first-round vote with 18.9 per cent to the UNR's 17.5 per cent, the Socialist SFIO's 15.5 per cent, the CNIP's 13.8 per cent, and the extreme right's 3.2 per cent.[113] Under the aegis of the CNIP, Le Pen would join for a time the ranks of political respectability as part of the centre-right coalition, with appointment once again to the parliamentary committee on national defence.[114]

It would not take long for Le Pen to become disenchanted with de Gaulle.[115] He was arrested and questioned in January 1960 during the 'week of the barricades', having made no secret of his support for the insurgents. This attitude would cost him his place on the parliamentary national defence committee and marginalise him within the centre-right coalition. Undeterred, Le Pen used his parliamentary position to argue for – and ultimately help secure – the release of Pierre Lagaillarde, the Algiers deputy imprisoned for his role in the barricades affair.[116] Nor would it take long for Le Pen to replace his FNC with a new movement and an updated mission. In July 1960, with Colonel Jean-Robert Thomazo (one of the prime movers in the revolt of 13 May 1958), Le Pen founded the Front National pour l'Algérie Française (FNAF). The movement attracted some predictable *compagnons de route* (Tixier-Vignancour, Dides, Sauge, Isorni) and a number of dissident parliamentary deputies (notably Alain de Lacoste-Lareymondie and Bernard Lafay).

The FNAF was conceived as the mainland twin of the Front de l'Algérie Française (FAF), which replaced the Front National Français (FNF), an ultranationalist group in Algiers under Joseph Ortiz and Jean-Jacques Susini with close links to Jeune Nation, whose emblem of the Celtic cross it adopted. Created in order to bring together in a single 'front' all of those radical groups banned by the authorities, the FNF, with its 10–15,000 members, was itself banned following the barricades affair. Its successor, the FAF, was more successful at federating the different *Algérie Française* currents, becoming the most important *pied-noir* activist group in Algeria. With a membership estimated at 100,000 (and even as high as 200,000), armed 'commando' units and a propensity for violence, the FAF has been described as a 'single party in embryo'.[117] It organised riots and, in advance of the OAS, plotted the overthrow and even the assassination of de Gaulle. Embracing the same aims if less overtly violent methods, Le Pen's FNAF also called for the overthrow of the Gaullist regime: 'We believed Algeria to be saved but it is again in grave danger. [. . .] Algeria will not be saved, our *patrie* will not be saved, if we do not smash the System, with its officials, its organisations and its ideologues.'[118]

Together with the FAF, Le Pen's FNAF set up a 'National Committee for Territorial Integrity' to campaign for a 'no' vote in the referendum of January 1961 on Algerian self-determination. Le Pen also sought to radicalise the CNIP in parliament as he had earlier sought to radicalise the Poujadist group. Following violent disturbances sparked by de Gaulle's visit to Algeria in December 1960, both the FAF and the FNAF were banned by government order.[119] It was with his old FNC, ressuscitated for the occasion, that Le Pen would take part in the referendum campaign, where the principle of Algerian self-governance would gain emphatic majority support.

Though Le Pen maintained relations with a roll-call of *Algérie Française* diehards (Salan, Lagaillarde, Demarquet, Susini, Dides, Thomazo, Biaggi, Tixier-Vignancour among others), he did not associate himself actively with the generals' putsch of April 1961, viewing it as a misguided adventure. Nor did he place more faith in the OAS, despite his unfailing sympathy for its cause, his discreet support and his considerable personal contacts here too (among them Captain Pierre Sergent, head of OAS operations in mainland France and future FN parliamentary deputy, and Lieutenant Daniel Godot, head of the Paris cell).[120] With his FNC also banned in the wake of the generals' putsch of April 1961, Le Pen was restricted to mounting a rhetorical opposition against the inevitable in parliament and in public meetings.

The Algerian War consolidated Le Pen's political vocation and his reputation as an uncompromising nationalist. Where Poujadism had been merely a vehicle, *Algérie Française* was a genuine cause. These years strengthened Le Pen's already extensive network of extreme-right associates, bringing him into close contact with major protagonists in the Algerian drama; they would also bring him into contact with prominent international figures such as Otto Skorzeny and the deposed Argentinian dictator, Juan Perón, whom Le Pen met in exile in Madrid alongside fugitives from Gaullist justice.[121] The names of some of those most committed to the retention of French Algeria – Pascal Arrighi, Pierre Sergent, Jean-Pierre Reveau, Pierre Descaves, Edouard Frédéric-Dupont, Roger Holeindre – would reappear a quarter of a century later among the 35 FN deputies elected to the National Assembly in the 1986 legislative elections. Others with whom Le Pen consorted during this period – such as Pierre Durand, Jean-Baptiste Biaggi, the former LVF volunteer André Dufraisse, and the former Doriotist Paul Malagutti – would also go on to occupy important positions within the FN in the 1980s.

Though Le Pen would retain many of his associates from this period, not all of his political impulses then would be consistent with his later utterances. At a moment of surplus employment and despite the worsening crisis in Algeria, we find him in a press interview from 1956 lauding France's 'tradition of offering sanctuary to foreigners': 'We recognise that everyone has the right to come and work here – on condition that they give unmistakable evidence of a real attachment to the French *patrie*.'[122] In the campaign for the legislative elections of November 1962, at the height of his opposition to de Gaulle's 'treachery', Le Pen also signed with other outgoing CNIP deputies a 'manifesto in favour of European integration'. This called for the strengthening of Europe's institutions, closer integration in foreign affairs and defence, and a move to majority voting in the Council of Ministers.[123] No sign here yet of immigration as 'a mortal threat to civil peace' or of European integration as 'the end of France', which were to be core tenets of Le Pen's and the FN's message some 40 years later.[124] Like many of his fellow CNIP deputies, and like the handful of outgoing extreme-right deputies, Le Pen would pay the price of his anti-Gaullism by losing his seat in 1962 to the Gaullist René Capitant. For the first time since January 1956, he would find himself not just without a political cause but without a political mandate.

Back to the ghetto

'With the possible exception of the Vichy period', wrote Malcolm Anderson, 'the eight years of the Algerian War were the most favourable historical context which the extreme Right had enjoyed during the twentieth century.'[125] Following the end of the war, extreme-right groups returned to the political ghetto from which they had temporarily escaped. As revulsion at OAS atrocities alienated public opinion, the loss of the great mobilising cause of Algeria reduced their ranks to so many 'lost soldiers whose only remaining flag was their violent anti-communism'.[126] To this might be added a second flag: that of violent anti-Gaullism. As in 1945, a deep sense of injustice and betrayal accompanied the realisation that a major opportunity had been lost, leaving the extreme right once again with 'little more than a collection of heroes and martyrs in Gaullist prisons'.[127] Two years after the Evian Agreements, the erstwhile leader of Jeune Nation, Pierre Sidos, lamented the loss to French nationalists of 'the formidable leverage that the preservation of a French province used to provide'.[128] A full 10 years after the peace settlement, Jean-Baptiste Biaggi, former leader of the PPR (and future FN regional councillor for Corsica), would have lost none of his bitterness in denouncing before the National Assembly the 'triumph of the Iscariots' creating the 'Algeria of Judas'.[129]

The loss of Algeria thus exacerbated the wounds inflicted at the Liberation. In a radio debate with the Gaullist Alexandre Sanguinetti at the height of the 1965 presidential campaign, Le Pen evoked 'the scores going back more than twenty years' that the nationalist right was 'called upon to settle with General de Gaulle'.[130] In the mid-1960s just as in the late 1940s, campaigns were mobilised on behalf of those imprisoned for insurgency, and retribution was soon followed by attempts to rebuild national unity. In December 1964, an amnesty law saw 173 OAS offenders pardoned, and a further law was implemented in June 1966. Other pardons followed in time, allowing OAS leaders to emerge from prison (Salan) or return from exile (Bidault) before the end of the decade.[131]

Having failed to sustain the necessary base of public support, it seemed, in the words of François Duprat, that 'the Opposition Nationale was now dead and buried'.[132] Once more the period of engagement was followed by one of demobilisation as the many movements formed in support of *Algérie Française* disintegrated and it was left to the most implacable elements to continue their symbolic struggle with no unifying cause other than sterile nostalgia. Deprived of political influence, the extreme right now rediscovered all of its old divisions and rivalries, becoming once again, as Duprat acknowledged, 'the favoured haunt of sub-groups and doctrinal circles with no grip on reality'.[133] The number of 'fronts' formed in defence of French Algeria testified not to the unity of the extreme right in this period but to its irremediable divisions. Even the most focused and resolute of these groups, and the one least encumbered by ideological baggage, the OAS, was so riven by sectarianism that it did not, by its own avowal, have 'any cohesion' between its members or 'any unity of thought beyond the credo: *Algérie française*'.[134]

The Algerian War nonetheless stands as a defining moment in the evolution of the extreme right in France. For it allowed right-wing radicals to begin to modernise both politically (through changing geopolitical imperatives) and ideologically (through Bardèche's *Qu'est-ce que le Fascisme?* and the rethinking of the premises of French nationalism). Over the period 1954–62, extreme-right movements came increasingly to embrace a more internationalist perspective, refashioning their nationalism within a European framework under the perceived threat from international communism and the rise of Third World nationalism. Though disbanded in 1962, Jeune Nation prepared some of the ground – and provided a core of militants – for the most important French nationalist movements of the 1960s, Europe-Action, Occident and Ordre Nouveau. At the forefront of the push towards a Europeanist nationalism would be Europe-Action, founded in 1963 by a former leader of Jeune Nation and editor of its periodical, Dominique Venner. Europe-Action would in turn beget other groups, such as the Mouvement Nationaliste du Progrès (MNP), and would serve as a seedbed for the future Nouvelle Droite and its main organisation, GRECE. Combining European supremacism with anti-communism, these movements would continue to develop their ideology within an internationalist perspective. The war in Algeria heightened support among such movements for other colonial powers (such as Portugal and the regimes in South Africa and Rhodesia) struggling to retain their presence in Africa. More importantly, it fostered a powerful anti-Arab sentiment which, combined with hostility towards France's large North African immigrant population, would come to occupy a prominent place in extreme-right discourse.

With the renewal of its political and ideological *raison d'être* came some renewal, too, of the extreme right's personnel. The years 1954–62 represent something of a transitional phase between the old guard and a new generation. Movements such as Jeune Nation and the FEN served as a training ground for some of the most notable extreme-right figures of the next four decades. They supplemented rather than supplanted an older generation of hard-bitten activists. One such ageing activist and mentor to his younger *confrères* was Jean-Louis Tixier-Vignancour, a former official in the Vichy propaganda ministry who now acquired prominence as defence counsel for two of the most notorious OAS activists, General Salan and Colonel Bastien-Thiry. While the latter was executed for his assassination attempt on de Gaulle at Petit-Clamart in August 1962, Salan was spared the death penalty and imprisoned. Though the OAS leader was also defended by the ever-present Jacques Isorni, former counsel for

5   The extreme right in the 1960s
Ideology and politics

After Algeria: ideological responses

If the Algerian War marked the high point of extreme-right activism in post-war France, the years following it were once again those of disorientation and bitter recrimination. This was also a period of disintegration as the various 'fronts' which had coalesced to defend French Algeria fragmented. While there was a war to prosecute, the immediacy of the cause promoted action over ideology. In the wake of the Evian Agreements, extreme-right groups found themselves challenged to redefine their ideological *raison d'être* – and, in so doing, to reassert their old divisions. In responding to this challenge, these groups fell broadly into three categories: those which groped instinctively for the ideas that had epitomised extreme-right thinking in the post-Vichy years; those which sought to combine these ideas with undying commitment to *Algérie Française*; and those which resolved now to reset their ideological compass, taking account of the new domestic and global realities of the early 1960s.

Fighting lost battles still

Among the first of these groups, Jean-Claude Monet's Parti Prolétarien National-Socialiste (PPNS) warrants brief mention. Launched in September 1961 as the Parti National-Socialiste Ouvrier Français (PNSOF), it would know brief incarnations as the Organisation du Svastika (OSS) and the Organisation des Vikings de France (OVF) before becoming the PPNS in June 1963. Proclaiming its programme through its successive names, the movement staged a crude attempt to re-enact Nazism in its ceremonial trappings (uniforms, swastikas, salutes) and its authoritarian, elitist, racist pronouncements. With echoes of Vichy, it called for a struggle against the 'forces of evil', 'foreign beliefs' and 'anti-natural ideas such as those of equality, liberty and anarchy'. A former member of Charles Luca's Phalange Française, Monet declared himself 'an anti-Semitic and racist National Socialist'. He upheld the 'Nietzschean idea of the superman. The idea of the supremacy of the Nordic race, not only over Negroes and Jews but also over inferior Aryans from the Mediterranean.' Dissenting from the ultra-nationalist mantra of *Algérie Française*, the PPNS called for 'solidarity with our Muslim brothers' against 'Zionist imperialism and Jewish rot'. Through its organ *Le Viking*, it argued that France should cease hostilities in Algeria and foster a global alliance of Nordic Aryans, Slavs and Arabs against the real enemies: Blacks, Orientals and Jews. Europe should unite in a 'federation of ethnic nations' to bring about the 'historic Aryan mission of biological supremacy on a world scale'.[1]

The PPNS denounced capitalism and 'stateless plutocrats' whose 'only guiding principle is their stinking gold'. Seeking to recruit among the working class, the movement attracted a few hundred mainly young, socially disadvantaged malcontents, and was active beyond Paris in cities such as Marseille and Lyon. It also attracted some former Waffen-SS volunteers and members of the Phalange Française and Jeune Nation. Though idiosyncratic in its ideas and parodic in its theatricals, the PPNS claimed sufficient credibility to foster links with neo-fascist movements in Europe, North and South America, and South Africa.

The PPNS stood out by dissociating itself from the struggle for French Algeria and in its crude aping of Nazism. By contrast, the Mouvement Français de Combat Contre-Révolutionnaire (French Movement of Counter-Revolutionary Combat, MCR), or Armée du Christ-Roi (Army of Christ the King), was a movement firmly rooted in the Algerian crisis. It was led by Pierre Château-Jobert, a former Resistance hero and army colonel who took part in the abortive generals' putsch of April 1961 before becoming head of OAS operations in eastern Algeria. Of the same nationalist Catholic persuasion as Georges Sauge and Robert Martel, Château-Jobert saw his mission in simple terms: 'to maintain on African soil the values of Christian civilisation in accordance with the teaching of Christ'.[2] Identifying the lack of a coherent doctrine as a central weakness in the OAS, he set up the MCR in September 1962 to fill this void.

Though it proclaimed its readiness to use violence, the MCR was no OAS and shifted its focus in effect from terrorism to politics. The movement's programme sought, with echoes of Vichy and allegiance to the ideas of La Cité Catholique, to undo the 'politically corrupting' Revolution of 1789 and restore the 'natural Order guaranteeing the rights of workers, of family and of *Patrie*'. Rejecting both 'collectivist and capitalist forms of enslavement', it advocated a corporatist state that would transcend the class struggle. Seeing the loss of Algeria as 'the necessary prelude to the disintegration of France herself', the MCR called for a 'common military defence of the West' and a 'common ideological defence against the attempted incursions of Marxist or liberal thought'.[3]

Château-Jobert combined the influences of dictators such as Portugal's Salazar, nationalist Catholics like Sauge and Martel, the Poujadist corporatist Dr Bernard Lefebvre, and a succession of illiberal Popes. Like Sauge, Martel and Lefebvre agitated for a crusade against the 'legions of Satan' (communists, Freemasons, atheists, 'wogs') and were as strident in their anti-capitalism as in their anti-communism. Lefebvre launched the Mouvement pour l'Instauration d'un Ordre Corporatif (Movement for the Establishment of a Corporatist System), paying nostalgic homage to Vichy. In his more sober moments, he called for a 'great anti-Bolshevik crusade' to restore the 'natural order' based on state authority, the army and militant Christianity; in his less sober moments, he envisaged 'a terrestrial order which will be the image of the divine'.[4] Martel's earlier Mouvement Populaire du 13 Mai (MP 13) had taken as its symbols the Sacred Heart and Holy Cross, and (though weak in mainland France) boasted at its peak a membership of over 10,000 in Algeria. Martel had been involved in political conspiracies stretching back to the Third Republic and had been president of one of the *pied-noir* organisations in Algiers (the Union Française Nord-Africaine), where he had joined Ortiz and Lagaillarde on the barricades in January 1960. He would become Château-Jobert's right-hand man in the MCR before being arrested in January 1963.[5]

Like the PPNS, the MCR was more significant for what it failed to achieve than for what it achieved. Fighting for a cause that had been manifestly lost, Château-Jobert went into exile in Spain and was sentenced to death *in absentia* in 1965. He would be reprieved and return to France in 1968.

Resetting the ideological compass: Europe-Action

A much more meaningful and altogether more lasting contribution to the renovation of the extreme right in the years following the loss of Algeria was made by a group who rallied around the monthly journal *Europe-Action*. Though deeply committed to the cause of French Algeria, they saw the need to refashion radical right-wing ideology from materials other than nostalgia and religiosity, taking account of the new order emerging from decolonisation and the consolidation of de Gaulle's Fifth Republic. The movement was launched in early 1963 by the 27-year-old Dominique Venner, former member of Jeune Nation and founding member of the FEN, who had just served a prison sentence for subversive activities in defence of *Algérie Française*. The essay which Venner wrote in prison and published on his release, *Pour une critique positive* (*For A Positive Critique*, 1962), provided the basis for a reconceptualisation of strategy on the extreme right following the debacle in Algeria. Venner's time in prison had persuaded him that the nationalist right now had to undertake the kind of ideological renewal to which Lenin had exhorted the Bolsheviks after the abortive revolution of 1905. It had also brought him into contact with the former OAS treasurer Maurice Gingembre, who would prove an enthusiastic backer for Venner's new nationalist venture.[6]

For Venner, intellectual persuasion and violence both had their place; but his Europe-Action movement was to privilege ideas over action, recognising 'the sterility of activism alone'.[7] The seeds of this reasoning had been planted in the FEN's 'Manifesto of the Class of 60', which had committed itself to 'action of profound consequence' as opposed to 'sterile activism'.[8] Since political power could not be won by a direct assault on the regime, a revolution of a different sort had to be prepared. This would require nationalists to forge a more coherent doctrine than hitherto and to build popular support for their ideas as a first step on the road to political power. As 'the militants of a white nation', they should seek to infiltrate and win control of organisations (unions, local newspapers, youth hostels, etc.) through which their ideas could be disseminated.[9] Overarching this project of grass-roots infiltration, Europe-Action promoted itself as a think-tank to bring a new ideological rigour and relevance to right-wing nationalist sensibility. It ran its own publishing house, the Editions Saint-Just, and a book-shop, the Librairie de l'Amitié. In this way, Europe-Action sought to redress the anti-intellectualism that had been a major hindrance to the right in the battle of ideas, notably against the Marxist left (though some of its adherents continued to find an outlet for their more violent propensities through other, less cerebral groups). The movement recruited a ready militant base among the students of Venner's FEN. It was particularly active in Paris and in a string of towns across the south of France (Nice, Marseille, Toulon) where many repatriates from Algeria had settled and where the journal *Europe-Action* found a high proportion of its readership.[10]

Between January 1963 and November 1966, Europe-Action served as a politico-intellectual forum for former activists from Jeune Nation and the OAS, members of the FEN, self-proclaimed fascists such as Lucien Rebatet and Maurice Bardèche, and residual Vichyites and anti-Semites like Henry Coston and Jacques Ploncard d'Assac. Most significantly, it attracted a younger genera-tion of right-wing radicals anxious to move beyond the lost causes of the previous two decades. The leading figures of the movement were Dominique Venner, Jean Mabire, Alain de Benoist (alias Fabrice Laroche), Amaury de Chaunac-Lanzac (alias François d'Orcival), Alain Lefebvre and Jean-Claude Rivière.[11] Seeking to assemble as large a constituency as possible and to bridge the pre-war and post-war generations, Europe-Action brought together these up-and-coming names with OAS activists like Maurice Gingembre, collaborationists like Maurice-Ivan Sicard (alias Saint-Paulien), and Waffen-SS veterans such as Pierre Bousquet and Marc Augier (alias Saint-Loup). Beyond its French contrib-utors, the journal also articulated its Europeanism through contributions by such impenitents as Otto Skorzeny, Erich Kern and the Belgian Rexist leader and Waffen-SS veteran, Léon Degrelle.

Europe-Action started from the same premise as Bardèche in his *Qu'est-ce que le Fascisme?*: that fascism had failed to commend itself as a 'coherent political philosophy' and suffered from 'the lack of a sufficiently well-established doctrinal base'. Italian Fascism had relied too heavily on the strong leader, while National Socialism had, despite its 'inspired intuitions', succumbed to its inherent flaws, notably its excessive reliance on the *Führer-Prinzip*, its 'narrow, vengeful, aggres-sive nationalism', and its 'romanticised (unscientific) racism'.[12] In this attempt to diagnose the failings of fascism in practice, the better to rescue an improved conception of fascism in theory, the influence of Bardèche was clear. Like Bardèche too, the monthly *Europe-Action* criticised the 'outmoded nationalism of Barrès' and – in a special issue of May 1963, *Qu'est-ce que le nationalisme?* – viewed the failure of the OAS as 'just the latest in a series of defeats sustained by the "nationalist" right in the pre- and post-war years'. It was no longer enough, Europe-Action argued, to be *anti*-communist, *anti*-Gaullist, etc.: nationalists had to learn to promote the positive ideas for which they stood and to develop the doctrine around which a hitherto fissiparous far right could unite. Bardèche himself set the tone in the first issue of the journal, declaring: 'Our ideas have a bright future, provided we learn to defend them a little less badly.' The difference was that, whereas Bardèche openly proclaimed himself a fascist, Europe-Action shied clear of the term, preferring the label '*révolution nationaliste*' to describe its project.[13]

Despite the resonance of Vichy in this formula, Europe-Action promoted itself as a forward-looking movement. What was most 'revolutionary' about the nationalism propounded in the pages of its journal was its supra-national quality. Francocentric though it inevitably remained, this was a nationalism of Europeanist, and beyond that occidentalist, dimensions. It was a nationalism which called out to be defended against those who, in the name of a fictitious equality, advanced the interests of the Third World and of communism. 'There are "unionist" nationalists among whom we count ourselves and "separatist" nationalists who have lost all sense of the West as a community and of European solidarity, and who concentrate their thought and action on a single fragment of our heritage, whether that be Luxembourg, Scotland or France.'[14]

That heritage was defined above all by one feature: it was white. The editors of *Europe-Action* (which styled itself 'the magazine of Western man')[15] stressed the shared identity of 'white peoples' and elaborated a pseudo-scientific racism which they used to vilify black and Arab immigrant workers in France and to justify support for the racially segregationist regimes of Rhodesia and South Africa. Following a visit to South Africa at the invitation of the white minority government there, two of the journal's leading contributors, Gilles Fournier and Fabrice Laroche (assumed to be Alain de Benoist), issued a publication, *Vérité pour l'Afrique du Sud* (*Truth on Behalf of South Africa*), vigorously defending apartheid and the racist rationale sustaining it. At a time of 'decolonisation and international negrification', they praised the 'white South African nation' for its resolve in maintaining this 'last outpost of the West from which we have sprung'. Returning from a visit to the United States, Laroche conversely deplored the suppression of racial segregation there, anticipating that a *de facto* segregation would nonetheless continue to prevail beyond the law.[16] Another contributor to *Europe-Action*, the Waffen-SS veteran Marc Augier (alias Saint-Loup), even offered to 'raise a legion of combatants to defend the white race and fight along-side our brothers in Pretoria'. Together with Augier, Venner would form a Comité France-Rhodésie to give French support to the white minority regime of Ian Smith, to whom *Europe-Action* dedicated its December 1965 issue.[17]

In its calls for a 'common European nationalism', Europe-Action again exhibited the weighty influence of Maurice Bardèche and of leading figures within the FEN who had been behind the 'Manifesto of the Class of 60'. Espousing the same crude racism and notions of an Aryan mission as the PPNS, it sought to give these more literate expression and to cloak them in an intellectually coherent garb. Though it echoed the MCR's colonialist sympathies and its opposition to Marxism and liberalism alike, Europe-Action had nothing of the latter's religiosity. The 'heritage of the West' so vigorously defended in the pages of its journal was not the Judaeo-Christian heritage, with its 'pernicious' beliefs and 'masochistic' ethic; *Europe-Action* was deeply anti-Christian, advocating an aristo-cratic, neo-pagan ethic freed of bourgeois egalitarianism.[18] With this combination of anti-egalitarianism and anti-Christian animus, *Europe-Action* set itself up, in conjunction with the FEN's *Cahiers universitaires*, as a testing ground for ideas that would later find expression in the Nouvelle Droite and its flagship organisation, GRECE.

The idea of a 'European nationalism' had well-established antecedents. Many of those who had advocated collaborationism or volunteered to fight for Hitler's Reich had in effect lent support to this concept of a nationalism transcending national boundaries. The contribution of Europe-Action was to seek to theorise and extend this idea, redrawing not only national but continental boundaries in the process. 'For us, Europe is a heart which beats with blood in Johannesburg and in Quebec, in Sydney and in Budapest', proclaimed the July–August 1965 issue of the journal, which looked forward to the creation of a 'Western nation-alism, from San Francisco to Vladivostock'.[19] The nationalism of Europe-Action was not geopolitical but racial. It proclaimed 'race' to be 'the new *patrie*, the "*patrie* of the flesh" which should be defended with an animal-like ferocity'.[20] It cultivated links with radical right-wing groups in other European countries, notably Italy, Germany, Belgium, Spain and Portugal;[21] it invoked a 'biological realism' that posited the superiority of 'white civilisation' over 'inferior races'. Deploying the language of biology and genetics, it argued that a hierarchy of intelligence could be established through the measurement in different races of 'cranial capacity', 'brain mass' and 'brain weight', the 'number of neurons', the 'activity of endocrine glands', hereditary characteristics, chromosomes, etc. Proceeding from crude notions of intelligence to equally crude notions of civili-sation, from biology to anthropology, Europe-Action located its gauge of racial superiority in the ability of some communities to master the natural environment through technological progress and the failure of others, due to their inherited make-up, to do so. The result, unsurprisingly, was a scale of human sophistica-tion descending from whites through orientals to blacks and primitive aboriginals.[22]

There was nothing new, of course, in a racism casting around for scientific legitimation. Yet this was the central idea which informed the whole Europe-Action project and underpinned the political orientation of the movement's journal. It advocated racial segregation and denounced miscegenation as 'genetic suicide'; it supported colonialism (synonymous with 'civilisation') and decried 'universalism' and 'globalisation', which 'threatened to submerge the white world' under 'a hideous layer of straw huts, shacks and slums'. It envisaged the creation of a new, genetically improved social elite and the elimination, 'without futile sentimentality', of 'biological scum' – 'not through massacres but through eugenic processes'. *Europe-Action* called for an end to economic aid for former colonies and issued dire warnings against a future France 'occupied by *twenty* million Maghrebi Arabs and *twenty* million Negro-Africans'.[23] Despite the contributions of an unbridled Henry Coston and the pronounced anti-Semitism of the journal, it reserved its most savage attacks not for France's Jews but for the black and Arab immigrant communities. In anticipation of the later FN, *Europe-Action* located in the 'leprosy of immigration' the source of many of France's ills, from venereal disease to violent crime and unemployment. It argued against interbreeding and called for the repatriation of immigrants, especially those of North African origin. 'Our mother country', it proclaimed, 'is the white world, for we consider as our compatriots all of those whose heredity is close enough to our own that we can accept the idea of seeing them marry our sister, our daughter or our niece.'[24] In a further anticipation of the FN, *Europe-Action* warned of North African immigrants in October 1964: 'There will soon be a million of them.'[25]

Though conceived as an intellectual forum, Europe-Action gradually developed the infrastructure of a political movement. In October 1964, 'support committees' were set up, attracting several hundred militants in the university towns where the movement was most active (notably Paris, Lyon, Nice, Marseille and Toulon), with recruitment among students and the better educated rather than workers. These so-called Europe-Action Volunteers were recruited primarily to ensure the dissemination of the journal, with its estimated circulation of 7,500 to 10,000.[26] They were drawn mainly from ex-Jeune Nation and FEN circles, from disbanded movements such as Biaggi's PPR, and from repatriated French Algerians. Of over two hundred Algerian repatriate associations in France in the mid-1960s, the most cohesive, the Fédération des Etudiants Réfugiés (Federation of Refugee Students, FER), fell under the sway of Europe-Action and the FEN, swelling their potential activist base by some 4,500 members concentrated mainly in the south-east, according to François Duprat.[27]

The Europe-Action Volunteers engaged in some violent agitation, disrupting the meetings of political opponents and attacking left-wing newspaper vendors. Europe-Action and the FEN also organised annual school camps, offering lycée pupils and university students a programme of 'physical and intellectual activity' in order to form an 'elite revolutionary cadre'.[28] In the presidential election of December 1965, Europe-Action threw its support behind the nationalist candidate, Jean-Louis Tixier-Vignancour. It used its militants to organise demonstrations demanding a halt to Algerian immigration, and mounted a campaign which the Mouvement contre le Racisme et pour l'Amitié entre les Peuples (Movement Against Racism and For Friendship Between Peoples, MRAP) condemned as racist.[29] The alliance which crystallised around Tixier-Vignancour would collapse in the aftermath of the election, and with it the hopes of Europe-Action's leaders that they might bring radical nationalism in from the margins and become serious players in the political process. The last issue of the journal appeared in November 1966, and the movement folded definitively after a failed attempt to relaunch the publication the following summer. At the same time, Europe-Action's sister movement, the FEN, would also run out of steam, publishing the last number of the *Cahiers universitaires* in January 1967.[30]

After Algeria: political responses

Europe-Action provided the most cogent expression of the ideas fermenting on the French nationalist right in the years following the Algerian War. That such a movement should have committed itself, only three years on from the OAS, to challenging de Gaulle by means of the ballot box rather than the bullet says much about political developments on the extreme right during this period. An explanation of Europe-Action's stance was offered in the December 1965 issue of its journal, which described the presidential election (the first to be contested by universal suffrage) not as 'an end in itself' but as a 'point of departure', a way of 'proving that the nationalist opposition can affirm its political existence by means other than rowdiness and abortive plots'. The votes garnered would 'form the essential basis on which to build a new political movement whose objective will be to win the mass support required in order to take power'.[31]

Here was a clear recognition of the need for change in relation to France's democratic processes and institutions. Extreme-right agitation had been a crucial factor in the downfall of the Fourth Republic; but that regime had been replaced by a Fifth Republic with a much stronger executive and a much more secure base of popular support. The powerful Gaullist movement stretched from the centre to the fringes of the right, forming a bulwark against communism which deprived radical nationalists of part of their vital space and diminished the effectiveness of anti-communism as a mobilising theme. In the legislative elections of November 1962, the Gaullist UNR with its left-leaning ally, the Union Démocratique du Travail (UDT), won a landslide with almost 32 per cent of the first-round vote (and 49 per cent of the seats). The PCF took almost 22 per cent of the first-round vote (and only 9 per cent of the seats, by the distortive logic of the two-ballot majority system).[32] In contrast, those extreme-right elements which contested the election failed to win a single seat, polling under 0.9 per cent in the first round, fewer than 160,000 votes in all.

De Gaulle's betrayal of French Algeria, it has been noted, compounded the deep resentment already felt by many over the perceived injustice of the Liberation. This second abject defeat led some right-wing radicals (such as Pierre Lagaillarde) simply to renounce their struggle.[33] The decision by others in 1965 to challenge de Gaulle on his own terms, by recourse to the electorate, was a clear assertion of the inefficacy of terror and intimidation as a political idiom in post-*Algérie Française* France. Having failed to overthrow the democratic Republic, the extreme right would now seek to capture its highest political office.

The assassination attempt by the OAS at Petit-Clamart in August 1962 had given de Gaulle the pretext to complete his reform of France's institutions by setting in place the direct election of the President. Under the Third and Fourth Republics, the President had been elected by a joint session of the two chambers of parliament; in 1958, de Gaulle himself had been elected by an extended college of some 80,000 elected officials. The proposal to elect the President by universal suffrage was approved by a 62 per cent majority in the referendum of 28 October 1962, and enshrined in the Constitution the following month, opening the way for an entirely new form of presidentialist politics in France.

Within a year of this reform, a Comité d'Initiative pour une Candidature Nationale (Committee to Launch a National Candidate) was set up by Le Pen and the Paris coterie of ultra-nationalists with whom he maintained close links. With some prescience, they recognised that the presidential election would henceforth constitute the ultimate political contest. It provided an opportunity, as Le Pen argued, to disseminate their message at the taxpayers' expense, to exploit the four hours of television and radio airtime allocated to each candidate, and ultimately to measure popular support for the nationalist cause.[34] Scruples about playing the democratic game were outweighed by such pragmatic considerations, and by the prospect that a nationalist candidate might be able to build a base of popular support before mainstream contenders entered the race.

The task was to designate a candidate who could rally maximum support on the extreme right, bridging the gap between older and younger generations, and at the same time reach out to a more moderate constituency. Of the available candidates, the one with the most compelling credentials appeared to be Tixier-Vignancour, the incarnation of *Algérie Française* and, since his defence of Salan and other prominent OAS figures, a lawyer of national renown. Tixier-Vignancour was also a former Vichy official with a long and distinguished record of extreme-right activism. Before qualifying as a barrister at the Paris Court of Appeal in 1927, he had been a militant in the student wing of Maurras' Action Française, going on to take part in the anti-parliamentary riot of 6 February 1934. Having won his first parliamentary seat (for Basses-Pyrénées) in 1936, he was part of a parliamentary group which travelled to Spain to congratulate General Franco on his crusade against the Spanish Popular Front. Present in Vichy's Grand Casino on 10 July 1940, he voted full powers to Marshal Pétain. He went on to serve for a time as Under-Secretary of State (then, briefly, Secretary of State) for Information at Vichy and as director of Pétain's 'Propaganda Committee'.

Among the 'traitors to be punished' listed by the Resistance in January 1944, Tixier-Vignancour was imprisoned by the Allies in the final phase of the war and stripped of his right to stand for public office until his amnesty in 1953.[35] Undeterred, he helped to launch Jeune Nation with Pierre Sidos in 1949 and the 'Eurofascist' MSE with Maurice Bardèche in 1951, collaborating with a variety of extreme-right movements and publications (notably Bardèche's *Défense de l'Occident*) before forming his own short-lived Rassemblement National (RN) in 1954. This was a hard-line nationalist and colonialist movement whose main achievement, despite its anti-parliamentarism, was to propel Tixier-Vignancour into the National Assembly in 1956 as its only deputy (in the same Basses-Pyrénées seat which he had won 20 years before). A long-standing opponent of the Republic ('more nihilist than conservative', in the judgement of Philip Williams), Tixier-Vignancour had earned a reputation as 'the ardent defender of every fascist conspirator against a regime which he skilfully and unscrupulously undermined'. In 1961, he pushed his anti-republicanism to the point of declaring in court: 'I will never use the word legitimacy, for I know it has not existed in France since 21 January 1793 [the date of Louis XVI's execution].'[36]

While some argued for a less notorious figure (such as Alain de Lacoste-Lareymondie) or a younger prospect (namely Le Pen), Le Pen himself threw his weight behind Tixier-Vignancour, protesting that, at 35, he was too young to mount a successful challenge.[37] Although Tixier-Vignancour had been associated with many extreme-right organisations over a 40-year period, he had retained his independent disposition and refused to ally himself too closely with any single party or faction. This was ultimately his strongest asset as the prospective candidate of the nationalist right, the self-styled 'militant of all the nationalist parties whichever they may be'.[38]

As early as November 1963, fully two years before the date of the election, the 56-year-old Tixier-Vignancour publicly announced his candidacy.[39] He was backed by a national 'Tixier-Vignancour Committee', with Le Pen as secretary-general and campaign manager. This coordinated some 80 local 'TV committees' set up throughout the departments of France and ancillary structures organised on the model of the earlier Poujadist networks.[40] One such structure was the Comité Jeunes (Youth Committee) under the former resister and Algerian War veteran Roger Holeindre, just released from his prison sentence for OAS activism. This was a particularly dynamic section supported by leaders of the newly formed Occident movement and quickly attracting several hundred members. When the participation of Occident militants was curtailed by a disagreement between Le Pen and the movement's leader, Pierre Sidos (who did everything thereafter to undermine the Tixier-Vignancour campaign), their place was taken by Venner's Europe-Action Volunteers, despite their own initial reservations about Tixier-Vignancour's candidacy.[41]

The membership of the national 'TV Committee' read like a *Who's Who* of the French nationalist right in the 1960s. As one journalist observed, it comprised 'those nostalgic for Vichy, descendants of Action Française, fundamentalist Catholics, *Algérie française* ultras, the residue of Poujadism, embryonic fascists, and representatives of the liberal right'.[42] This motley assemblage was yet another attempt at a 'front', bringing together former collaborationists like Léon Gaultier and Victor Barthélemy with members of the newly formed Occident movement and, in turn, those of Europe-Action. Here at last might be a basis for the unified nationalist party to which Le Pen had aspired since his days as a Poujadist. With this aspiration to the fore, he and Tixier-Vignancour would undertake a trip to London at the height of the election campaign to contemplate the British Conservative Party as a possible model for a new conservative-nationalist party in France.[43] The common theme around which their makeshift 'front' coalesced, and which constituted the defining principle of Tixier-Vignancour's campaign, was anti-Gaullism. Despite its insistence on national *grandeur*, independence and other values which those around Tixier-Vignancour held dear, Gaullism represented above all for them 'the loss of Algeria, the end of the Empire, the weakening of the army, and closer ties with the communist world'.[44] If it seemed implausible that their candidate could stage 'an electoral Petit-Clamart' by eliminating de Gaulle as President, a victory of sorts would at least be achieved by forcing him to a second ballot.[45]

From bullet to ballot: Tixier-Vignancour

Over the next year, the national 'TV Committee' coordinated a series of rallies around France, drawing enthusiastic support in southern towns from repatriated French Algerians and attracting a sizeable proportion of young participants. The first meeting, held in Paris, drew an audience of some 4,000 and led to violent clashes between Occident militants and the police. By the end of the campaign, it was claimed that Tixier-Vignancour had spoken in every town in France with a population of over 50,000.[46]

The decision to contest the municipal elections of March 1965 brought encouraging results, with 9.6 per cent of the first ballot in Paris (over 90,000 votes) going to Tixier-Vignancour's PARIS list, *Pour l'Avenir et la Réforme Institutionnelle et Sociale* (For the Future and for Institutional and Social Reform). Still more encouraging were poll predictions in the summer which credited Tixier-Vignancour with fully 19 per cent of the presidential vote (before the joint candidate of the left, François Mitterrand, and the centre-right challenger, Jean Lecanuet, entered the fray).[47] To demonstrate the presidential stature of his candidate, Le Pen boasted the signatures of over 500 formal political sponsors, when only 100 were required (drawn from at least 10 departments).[48] Banking on the support of the 1.94 million who had voted 'no' in the referendum of 8 April 1962 to ratify the Evian Agreements, and assured of staunch support among repatriated *pieds-noirs* in particular, the Tixier-Vignancour campaign set a baseline target of 'at least two million' votes.[49] As the election approached, Tixier-Vignancour fostered the illusion of much wider support still, 'drawn from across all of the political parties, even the heartlands of the Communist Party'. He predicted a first-round score of up to 25 per cent, followed by victory in the second round.[50]

In order to raise the profile of his candidate and counter the hostile silence of the mainstream press, Le Pen resorted to a tried and tested method: that of the 'caravan' tour. Throughout the holiday month of August 1965, a convoy of lorries descended on the coastal towns of France, from Dunkerque in the north to Menton in the south-east, disseminating tracts, keepsakes, the campaign periodical *TV-Demain* and, above all, the Tixier-Vignancour message.[51] Meetings were held in a giant marquee with capacity for an audience of 3,000. The organisers of the caravan tour later claimed to have addressed 125,000 people in all, and to have distributed 600,000 copies of *TV-Demain* and two million tracts. Over the course of the campaign, they would claim to have addressed a combined audience of 350,000 and to have disseminated 1.5 million posters bearing the image or the message of their candidate.[52]

Responsibility for propaganda was entrusted to Serge Jeanneret, a former Cagoulard turned resister who had been part of Poujade's inner circle, working now alongside the Waffen-SS veteran Léon Gaultier.[53] With an eye to American-style electioneering, Tixier-Vignancour was marketed as the star of a thousand pens, ashtrays, keyrings and scarves. He took to arriving for meetings in a Citroën DS 19 ostentatiously escorted by a guard of honour on motorcycles. As with Poujade in 1956, a campaign film – *Sept ans de malheur* (*Seven Years of*

Misfortune) – was produced to dramatise the parlous state of France under de Gaulle and offer Tixier-Vignancour as providential saviour. This salvationist dimension was emphasised by the publication in late 1964 of the book *J'ai choisi la défense* (*I Chose to Defend*), a collection of transcripts from Tixier-Vignancour's legal defence of *Algérie Française* activists, copies of which were sold at the end of campaign rallies with the proceeds contributing to campaign funds.[54]

In the manner of an international statesman in pre-presidential mode, Tixier-Vignancour undertook trips to Saigon (to demonstrate his support for American engagement in Vietnam), Bonn (to show himself a good European), Rome (to attest his Catholic credentials), and London (as noted above, to meet members of the British Conservative Party). For all his proven anti-republicanism and his opposition to the seven-year presidential term, his election manifesto articulated in essence a perfectly Gaullist conception of the office for which he was running: 'The presidential function is one of *arbitrage* in normal times and of controlled authority in moments of peril.'[55] The Tixier-Vignancour camp went so far as to argue that the incumbent President had betrayed this conception, and that it was against de Gaulle that the institutions of the Fifth Republic needed to be defended. In an article in *TV-Demain*, Jeanneret declared that, through 'his authoritarianism, his personal conception of power, his contempt for parliament, his haughty nationalism, his mystical worship of the state', 'the main candidate of the extreme right could be General de Gaulle'. For good measure, the same article – entitled 'The Candidates of the Extreme Right' – observed that Lecanuet and Mitterrand were backed by some prominent extreme-right figures and by elements of the extreme-right press.[56] Tixier-Vignancour, the candidate of the 'national and liberal opposition',[57] was by implication the only moderate in the race.

Behind the posturing, the political message was stridently populist and directed by turns at peasants, artisans, liberal professionals, the retired and elderly, female voters, ex-servicemen, students, fishermen, and car drivers. It called for higher wages, lower taxes, better housing and education, retirement at 60, better pensions, price guarantees for meat and milk, the abolition of vehicle tax (to be financed through ending subsidies to Algeria), investment in motor-ways and lower petrol prices.[58] It offered reduced taxes and less state interference to the threatened lower middle classes from whom Poujade had drawn much of his support, and the protection of rural life and values to peasant voters. It criti-cised state *dirigisme*, advocating in the main free-market economics and an ill-defined form of 'popular capitalism'.[59] Tax reductions should be financed by slashing foreign aid and abandoning France's independent nuclear deterrent, the linchpin of de Gaulle's *politique de grandeur*.[60] The statistics which Tixier-Vignancour cited to support his case were highly suspect and chosen at times for their effect rather than their precision. When asked on one occasion how he had arrived at the figure of 11 per cent as a proposed tax cut, he unguardedly replied: 'Because 10 per cent does not come across as a plausible figure.'[61]

In foreign policy, Tixier-Vignancour argued that France should sign up to the multilateral nuclear protection offered by the United States under NATO.

Denouncing de Gaulle as anti-American and anti-European, and evoking the dangers of France's rapprochement with the Soviet Union, he called for an integrated Europe in alliance with the United States as the means of defending the 'humanist and Christian West' against 'communism and its Trojan horse, Gaullism'.[62] France should scale down its commitment to former colonies and the developing world, since 'our country is deprived of stadiums, highways, and schools so that Negro potentates can buy Mercedes for themselves'.[63] One of Tixier-Vignancour's campaign slogans was: 'French money belongs to the French, and [*la Corrèze passe avant le Zambèze*] Corrèze comes before the Zambezi'.[64] At home, he denounced the 'so-called Evian Agreements' and argued that repatriated *pieds-noirs* should be fully compensated for their losses. He declared himself a supporter of '*l'Algérie française*' but not of '*la France algérienne*', proposing that 'strict and rigorously selected quotas' for Algerian immigrants should be set to 'avoid the invasion of France by a multitude of starving mouths, undesirables and invalids with no technical or social education', drawn to France as animals to a trough. He warned that such immigrants would be under the influence of the FLN and used by it 'against France'.[65]

To counter accusations of racism, Tixier-Vignancour suggested that, if elected, he would appoint as Prime Minister the French Guyanese Gaston Monnerville, then President of the Senate.[66] He avoided extremist pronouncements in his television and radio broadcasts in order to strike a more respectable image (reserving for the Portuguese weekly *Agora* his praise of Salazar and for public rallies his denunciation of Prime Minister Georges Pompidou as an agent of the Rothschilds).[67] In his attempt to court moderate support, he rejected the extreme-right label and protested his commitment to Republican democracy. As the first round of the election approached, he issued a rallying call to 'Socialists, Radicals and men of goodwill' to vote for him in the absence of a better alternative.[68]

Despite this studied attempt at moderation, Tixier-Vignancour was supported only by the most radical elements of the right-wing press, such as *Rivarol, Europe-Action, Aspects de la France* and *Minute* (though support from *Rivarol* and *Aspects de la France* was tempered by misgivings over the candidate's apparent conversion to the Republic and to Europe). He drew support, too, from far-right groups such as the FEN, the Fédération des Français d'Algérie, the Maurrassian Restauration Nationale, the Amis d'Antoine Argoud (an OAS leader), and the Convention Paysanne of Henri Dorgères.[69] His call for a review of Pétain's trial and the transfer of his remains to Douaumont, together with a blanket amnesty for those convicted of subversive activities during the Algerian War, were further elements which fixed Tixier-Vignancour's campaign firmly on the far right. As commentators observed, it was 'the alliance of *Algérie française*, Poujadism and the spirit of Vichy'.[70]

On 5 December 1965, to the dismay of his close supporters, Tixier-Vignancour won 5.2 per cent of the first-round vote (Table 5.1). While 1.26 million votes signified an appreciable core of support, it fell far short of expectations. There was meagre comfort only to be had from the fact that de Gaulle faced a run-off against the candidate of the left, the Socialist François Mitterrand. 'My sole objective', declared Tixier-Vignancour, 'was to force General de Gaulle to a second ballot. This has been achieved, and I am happy about it. If he maintains his candidacy, I will do everything possible to ensure his defeat regardless of the candidate standing against him in the run-off.' Between Scylla and Charybdis, the eliminated candidate of '*Dieu et Patrie*' called upon his voters to support Mitterrand against de Gaulle in the second round – a decision taken without consultation which outraged some members of the national 'TV Committee' for whom the prospect of supporting a candidate formally backed by the PCF was anathema.[71]

The map of the Tixier-Vignancour vote showed his strongest support to be concentrated south of a line from Bordeaux to Nice. This replicated to a large extent the highest levels of the 'no' vote in the referendum of April 1962 to ratify the Evian Agreements. It also mirrored the largest concentrations of repatriated French Algerians, from whom Tixier-Vignancour drew the bulk of his support.[72] His share of the vote exceeded 10 per cent in eight departments, clustered mainly in the south-east: Alpes-Maritimes (12.5 per cent), Bouches-du-Rhône (12.5 per cent), Vaucluse (12.2 per cent), Hérault (11.3 per cent), Pyrénées-Orientales (10.4 per cent), Lot-et-Garonne (10.2 per cent), with peaks of 14 per cent in Pyrénées-Atlantiques and Var. The extreme-right candidate beat Lecanuet to finish third behind de Gaulle and Mitterrand in four departments (Alpes-Maritimes, Bouches-du-Rhône, Var, and Corsica with just over 9 per cent). Though the map of support for Tixier-Vignancour matched only patchily that of the Poujadists in 1956, there were similarities in the sociological profile of the vote, with notable support coming from small shopkeepers and artisans.

The call by Tixier-Vignancour for his supporters to vote for Mitterrand in the second round was not exceptional. Jacques Isorni, who had supported Lecanuet in the first round, likewise called for a mobilisation in favour of Mitterrand.[73] The former Governor-General of French Algeria and dissident Gaullist, Jacques

Table 5.1 The 1965 presidential election: first round (metropolitan and overseas France)

	Votes cast	%
De Gaulle	10,828,823	44.65
Mitterrand	7,694,003	31.79
Lecanuet	3,777,119	15.57
Tixier-Vignancour	1,260,208	5.20
Marcilhacy	415,018	1.71
Barbu	279,683	1.15

Source: Constitutional Council (La Documentation Française, *Institutions et vie politique sous la Ve République*, Paris, 2003, p. 177).

Soustelle, and the OAS activist Pierre Sergent, summed up between them the perverse logic of this stance. Soustelle called for a 'useful' vote 'against the regime', a vote 'for Europe, the Atlantic Alliance and an amnesty [for *Algérie Française* offenders]'; Sergent asked: 'Who is likely to be more useful to the communists? De Gaulle or Mitterrand?' His answer: 'Undoubtedly de Gaulle.'[74] Others based their second-round support for Mitterrand on a more simplistic rationale. The *Cri du Rapatrié* (*Cry of the Repatriate*), organ of the Association Nationale des Français d'Afrique du Nord, d'Outre-Mer et de leurs Amis (National Association of North African and Overseas French and their Friends, ANFANOMA), urged its readers to cast their vote for 'anyone except de Gaulle', while Jean-Baptiste Biaggi called bluntly for the latter's elimination.[75]

In the second round of the election, on 19 December 1965, de Gaulle beat his Socialist opponent by 55.2 per cent to 44.8 per cent, dashing all hopes on the extreme right of inflicting defeat on the incumbent President through the ballot box. With those hopes went the illusion that this 'first ever experiment in building a real electoral machine'[76] might lead a unified extreme right to power, or even to an influential position within the political structures of the Fifth Republic.

Defeat, division, dejection

A number of factors accounted for Tixier-Vignancour's relatively poor performance in this election. He did not have behind him the solid party structure that would become a prerequisite for launching *présidentiables* under the Fifth Republic, but was backed by an uneasy alliance of diverse groupings. The unity of purpose around which the 'TV committees' coalesced was severely tested in the course of the campaign by personal rivalries and contentious decisions.[77] The acrimonious departure of Pierre Sidos and his Occident movement, and the fact that others such as Pierre Boutang and *La Nation Française* came out in support of de Gaulle, showed the failure of Tixier-Vignancour's campaign to rally the disparate forces of the far right.[78] A 'National Opposition Liaison Bureau' set up to achieve just that had collapsed at the very outset of the campaign due to factionalism and personal animosity towards Tixier-Vignancour from Poujade and others.[79]

If anti-Gaullism was the single most important unifying factor at the militant level, it was not so at the electoral level, where attitudes were varied and complex. According to one estimation, Tixier-Vignancour succeeded in attracting only 16 per cent of his potential electorate, with 60 per cent voting for de Gaulle and 14 per cent for the centre-right Lecanuet.[80] The same study claimed that only 32 per cent of those who voted for Tixier-Vignancour were of extreme-right persuasion, though the sensitive nature of the question posed here might raise doubts over the reliability of this statistic.[81] What is clear is that the two-round system of electing the President inaugurated by this election placed the mainstream candidates at a distinct advantage over an outsider who had no realistic prospect of progressing and whose performance was subject to the adverse effects of the *vote utile*, or tactical voting.

The fragility of Tixier-Vignancour's appeal was particularly exposed by the late entry of Lecanuet, the young president of the centrist MRP. The decision by Antoine Pinay not to stand had appeared to open inroads for Tixier-Vignancour into the moderate anti-Gaullist right-wing vote; the dynamic campaign mounted at short notice by Lecanuet closed that opportunity and, conversely, opened inroads into Tixier-Vignancour's own support base. A number of prominent figures – among them Jacques Isorni, Georges Sauge, Alfred Fabre-Luce and Jean Dides – diverted their support to Lecanuet, finding here a more effective vote of opposition to de Gaulle. So too did Pierre Poujade and the head of the Mouvement Démocrate et Paysan (Democratic Peasant Movement), Paul Antier, whom Poujade had initially backed as a prospective candidate.[82] Through the traditionalist Catholic organ *La France catholique*, the conservative wing of the Church also declared its support for the centre-right candidate.[83] From his exile in Brazil, the former Prime Minister and *Algérie Française* diehard, Georges Bidault, even prevailed upon the right-wing periodical *L'Esprit public*, hitherto a strident tribune for *Algérie Française*, to shift its support from Tixier-Vignancour to Lecanuet. Like Jacques Soustelle, Bidault was by 1965 more concerned with negotiating his return to France and political re-entry than with fighting yesterday's war.[84]

The effect of Lecanuet's presence on Tixier-Vignancour's electorate, then, was to nullify at a stroke the latter's overtures to the non-Gaullist centre-right and to draw off a significant number of potential voters. Other reasons for Tixier-Vignancour's poor performance lay in the very nature of his campaign. The contradiction was never effectively resolved between a candidacy centred on opposition to de Gaulle (and in that sense sufficient for Tixier-Vignancour's most committed supporters) and the need to elaborate a more constructive political vision (as demanded by the voting public at large). A candidacy based on the narrow – and lost – cause of *Algérie Française* had nowhere else to go once that issue had been ventilated; and it was from that issue alone that Tixier-Vignancour derived the bulk of his support. The SOFRES polling agency estimated that 65 per cent of those who voted for Tixier-Vignancour did so because of his role as 'counsel for the defence of French Algeria'.[85]

This was, moreover, the first election in France in which the new medium of television played a major role, with over six million television sets giving access to an estimated 20 million potential viewers.[86] The 350,000-strong audience which Tixier-Vignancour would claim to have addressed in a year and a half of energetic campaigning was but a fraction of that offered by his allotted two hours of television airtime (alongside two hours of radio). Though a formidable advocate in a courtroom, Tixier-Vignancour proved ill at ease and unconvincing before the television cameras. Despite his effort to project a modernising image as 'TV', his lacklustre performance on television accentuated the ultimate sterility of his campaign, with its more ready focus on the reasons for his candidacy than on his proposals for the future.[87]

There were debilitating tensions, too, within Tixier-Vignancour's own camp. These first stirred over the decision to contest the March 1965 municipal elections.

While Tixier-Vignancour advocated that his PARIS candidates should stand down in the second round in favour of better placed candidates of the centre-right, Le Pen insisted on the more aggressive line of retaining PARIS candidates wherever possible. The disagreement was significant. It weakened the non-Gaullist right in certain constituencies and facilitated the election of a Gaullist or a left-wing candidate. Le Pen's own refusal to withdraw in the 5th and 6th *arrondissements* provoked a three-way run-off which split the anti-Gaullist vote and saw the Gaullist UNR candidate elected.[88] In the short term, this intransigence alienated powerful non-Gaullist conservatives such as Edouard Frédéric-Dupont, Le Pen's erstwhile mentor who had given early support to the Tixier-Vignancour campaign.[89] In the longer term, Le Pen's attitude in these elections betrayed a destructive impulse which would characterise his later dealings with the centre-right in his role as leader of the FN.[90]

Though Tixier-Vignancour was godfather to Le Pen's daughter Marie-Caroline, tensions between the two men worsened over the course of the campaign. These reflected not only a growing personal animosity but a division within the movement between 'moderates' and hard-liners. Like Poujade before him, Tixier-Vignancour came to view Le Pen more as a liability than as an asset, while Le Pen formulated a similar criticism of Tixier-Vignancour to that levelled against Poujade: that he lacked the 'gumption' and 'punch' required to be a 'leader of men'. The final break occurred at a joint meeting in Paris of the national and local 'TV committees' held on 23 January 1966 to plan the way forward following de Gaulle's reinstatement as President. Here Tixier-Vignancour accused Le Pen openly of having weakened his campaign through the tactical miscalculation of dividing the right in the Paris municipal elections and through the release by Le Pen's recording company of a collection of Nazi songs at the height of the presidential campaign – this just as Tixier-Vignancour was straining to cultivate a more respectable image and broaden his appeal.[91]

Ousted from the movement, Le Pen accused Tixier-Vignancour of selling out to the moderate right in the hope of political self-advancement. He pledged, for his part, to go on fighting for 'the unification of the nationalist forces'. He would not be deflected from his objective of bringing to public attention the real nature of de Gaulle's legacy, 'the truth about the political revolution of 1945, when the communists and their allies crushed the right under the charge of Collaboration'.[92] These remarks were telling. For they revealed in Le Pen a political attitude still dictated 20 years later by the events of 1945. De Gaulle's withdrawal from Algeria and his entire foreign policy, Le Pen held, were the direct consequence of his alliance with the communists against the nationalist right at the Liberation.

With Le Pen sidelined, Tixier-Vignancour converted his depleted 'commit-tees' into a new party, the Alliance Républicaine pour les Libertés et le Progrès (Republican Alliance for Liberties and Progress, ARLP). Carrying forward his illusions from the presidential campaign, he now aspired to make this party a viable partner in a future, post-Gaullist majority (formed, as the ARLP proposed, of an expansive coalition 'from Guy Mollet to Tixier-Vignancour').[93] In its manifesto, the ARLP reiterated many of Tixier-Vignancour's campaign themes. It called for the restoration of Pétain's honour, advocated small-scale and family enterprise as a bastion of economic liberalism, and proposed that nationalised industries be converted into joint-stock companies with shares distributed among the victims of decolonisation. It argued for the revision of the Yalta agreement and stressed the importance of European integration and the Atlantic Alliance in the fight against communism.[94]

While Tixier-Vignancour was relaunching his movement under the sign of the Republic, the Europe-Action component of his former support base and its student affiliate, the FEN, reasserted their autonomy by forming the Mouvement Nationaliste du Progrès (MNP) under Dominique Venner.[95] At the same time, many of Tixier-Vignancour's younger supporters broke away to join the OAS-Métro-Jeunes network of Pierre Sergent, soon to become the Mouvement Jeune Révolution (MJR). Having briefly considered launching his own party, Le Pen withdrew from active politics to concentrate on his commercial activities. His 'crossing of the desert' would also be that of close associates such as Jean-Pierre Reveau, Pierre Durand, Dominique Chaboche and Roger Holeindre.

It was a measure of the expectation invested in Tixier-Vignancour's campaign that his 5.2 per cent should have been judged an 'electoral rout' by the extreme-right historian François Duprat, and a 'complete failure' by the political analyst François Goguel.[96] Following the election, an article published in *Le Monde* interpreted this result as marking the end of the French extreme right as a potentially viable electoral force.[97] The election showed clearly that the extreme right in 1965 had no issue on which to mount a campaign, with the exception of an amnesty for *Algérie Française* offenders and compensation for expropriated *pieds-noirs* – and even those demands were echoed by Lecanuet and Mitterrand.[98] The more de Gaulle played on French national independence and *grandeur*, moreover, the less coherent were the attacks upon him by radical nationalists; the more he expressed his belief in a strong executive and his suspicion of political parties and parliament, the more he robbed the same adversaries of other cherished arguments.

Though it helped to inflict on de Gaulle the personal humiliation of a second ballot, Tixier-Vignancour's campaign failed in its two main objectives: to unite the militant forces of the nationalist right and to exert a major electoral appeal. By the first round of voting, as Duprat observed, 'a vast portion of the Opposition Nationale had already quit the Tixier camp'.[99] Of almost six million non-Gaullist and non-Socialist votes registered in the election, barely one in five was cast for the candidate of the nationalist right. On a more modest scale, the latter even fell far short of matching the 'no' vote (9.2 per cent, 1.94 million) in the 1962 referendum on Algerian independence. To complete Tixier-Vignancour's discomfiture, his ARLP went down to a crushing defeat some 15 months later in the legislative elections of March 1967, attracting 0.44 per cent of the ballot, the support of fewer than 100,000 voters throughout France (within a combined score for the extreme right of 0.85 per cent, fewer than 200,000 votes in all).[100] This extinguished the ARLP's principal *raison d'être* along with the extreme right's hopes of achieving success through the ballot box in the 1960s. An electoral irrelevance, Tixier-Vignancour and his party would succumb increasingly to the pull of the Gaullist right, supporting de Gaulle during the events of May–June 1968 and rallying to his successor, Georges Pompidou, the following year.

An instructive interlude

Tixier-Vignancour's presidential campaign provided a brief but instructive interlude in a decade that would see Le Pen consigned to the political wilderness.[101] He had studied law but was never to practise. On losing his parliamentary seat in November 1962, he set up a commercial company, the Société d'Etudes et de Relations Publiques (Research and Public Relations Company, SERP), with his friend Pierre Durand and in association with the former Milicien and Waffen-SS volunteer, Léon Gaultier.[102] The SERP specialised in the reproduction of historical recordings and documents. In this new commercial role, Le Pen continued to court political controversy, launching his venture with bootleg recordings of the trials of General Salan and Colonel Bastien-Thiry (including the salvo from the firing squad at the latter's execution). These and other mementos of the struggle for *Algérie Française* soon had Le Pen himself on trial, charged with illegal recording of public hearings and sympathy for subversive activities, and obliged to withdraw the recordings in question from circulation.[103]

The SERP would go on to publish an extensive collection of recordings dedicated to *Men and Events of the Twentieth Century*, which included tributes to Pétain, Laval, Hitler and Mussolini as well as de Gaulle, Churchill, Lenin and many others. A recording of Nazi speeches and songs as part of this collection (*Voices and Songs of the German Revolution, 1933–1939*), released during the 1965 presidential campaign, would see Le Pen given a suspended prison sentence and fined as an 'apologist for war crimes'. Questioned on the significance of such a recording in the France of the 1960s, he reportedly opined that 'with atheism growing at an alarming rate', the French were 'again in need of moral order'. Within that perspective, he continued, 'the SS soldier with his uniform has become a bit like the priest with his soutane [. . .] a martyr for young people in search of purity, even if it is a purity of evil'.[104]

Though ostensibly a non-political activity, Le Pen's commercial venture kept him in touch with extreme-right circles, to whose diet of nostalgia and resentment he contributed through his recordings. During the 1965 election campaign, the SERP served as a propaganda tool, recording and distributing some of Tixier-Vignancour's campaign speeches along with recordings of other nationalist folk heroes. Commercially, the election provided Le Pen with an opportunity for increased earnings, notably on the caravan tour where his recordings proved highly saleable, especially among repatriates from Algeria who had settled in large numbers along the south coast. Politically, the experience of stage-managing a presidential campaign completed the apprenticeship begun some 10 years earlier under Poujade. Like the latter, Tixier-Vignancour ran a highly personalised campaign with an emphasis on public meetings and with gadgets, keepsakes and memorabilia aplenty. As with the Poujadists before and the FN later, contributions to campaign coffers were collected in a tricolour flag at Tixier-Vignancour's public meetings, which were staged with the efficiency and media awareness that were to become essential features of presidential campaigning under the Fifth Republic.

The 1965 election extended Le Pen's Poujadist experience in another important respect: it gave him further practice as a federator, holding together a motley coalition of nationalists, monarchists, neo-fascists, fundamentalist Catholics and other far-right sensibilities drawn to the Tixier-Vignancour bandwagon. Poujadism had attracted a support base bound together by socio-economic grievances; Tixier-Vignancour's was a more diverse constituency, coalescing mainly around the political issues of French Algeria and anti-Gaullism. The campaign brought together associates from each phase of Le Pen's political career thus far, from the days of the Latin Quarter and JIP (Durand, Varaut, Bourdier, Mamy), from Poujadism (Demarquet, Dides, Jeanneret), and from his time as a parliamentary deputy and defender of *Algérie Française* (Arrighi, Biaggi, Lacoste-Lareymondie, Barthélemy, Thomazo, Holeindre). The 'TV Committee' offered some glimpses, too, of the future leadership of the FN. Of those most actively involved in promoting Tixier-Vignancour's campaign, a number (Le Pen, Arrighi, Holeindre, Reveau, Chaboche, Baeckeroot, Stirbois) would become FN parliamentary deputies in 1986. Some future FN notables, such as Christian Baeckeroot and Jean-Claude Varanne, would prolong their commitment to Tixier-Vignancour by joining the youth section of the ARLP in the wake of the 1965 election campaign. Others, like Jean-Pierre Stirbois and Michel Collinot, would choose instead to join the OAS-Métro-Jeunes then MJR of Pierre Sergent.[105] A former army captain, Sergent had been head of OAS operations in mainland France and was still in hiding in 1966. He would also go on to become an FN parliamentary deputy 20 years later.

Variations on a theme

The formation of the MNP in January 1966 was a rejection, by Europe-Action and the FEN notably, of the personal quarrels and lack of 'clear and coherent political objectives' exhibited by Tixier-Vignancour's presidential campaign. The MNP reasserted the radicalism from which the latter was seen to have departed. Under Venner's leadership, it called for the creation 'not of a conservative party but of a revolutionary movement'. To that end, the MNP represented yet a further attempt, as its manifesto declared, to forge a fissiparous extreme right into a 'homogeneous political movement, based on a nationalist ideology open to Europe, equipped to meet the challenges of the future and effective in its opposition to Marxism and capitalist technocracy'.[106]

At the same time, those behind the launch of the MNP formed another, semi-clandestine organisation, the Centre Nationaliste. This was conceived as a think-tank and liaison centre for diverse nationalist movements. Also under

Venner's direction, the Centre Nationaliste comprised no more than a few dozen carefully chosen members, among them leading lights from Europe-Action and the FEN such as François d'Orcival (Amaury de Chaunac-Lanzac), Fabrice Laroche (Alain de Benoist), Jean Mabire and Jean-Claude Rivière. Other notable figures were the former president of Jeune Nation, François Sidos, the former OAS treasurer, Maurice Gingembre, and the Waffen-SS veteran and future treasurer of the FN, Pierre Bousquet.[107] The Centre Nationaliste was designed to serve as the brains behind the MNP in particular and French militant nationalism in general.

The objective of the Centre Nationaliste and MNP together was to fill the doctrinal gap which had consigned Poujade, the OAS and Tixier-Vignancour to failure and to enable the radical right 'to take power in the service of a nationalist revolution'. Where Europe-Action was dedicated primarily to ideological renewal, the MNP was formed to engage in 'real political action'. As a movement seeking to attract mass support, it played down its debt to 'biological realism' and dropped some of the more extremist tenets of Venner's other movement. Its political mission statement was nonetheless clearly at one with that of Europe-Action: 'To bring about a nationalist Europe and ensure the defence of the white man and of Western culture against the threats posed by coloured peoples and communism.' The MNP also adopted the same stance as Europe-Action against North African immigration, or 'the Algerian invasion of France'; this was a stance increasingly echoed in the extreme-right press, most notably by François Brigneau in the editorial column of *Minute*.[108]

The MNP's inaugural congress was held in Paris on 30 April–1 May 1966. It was attended by over 300 delegates, with a reportedly strong showing among the young. Its leadership was largely that of the Centre Nationaliste (Venner, de Benoist, de Chaunac-Lanzac, Mabire, Bousquet, the OAS veteran Jean-Marcel Zagamé, the former Jeune Nation militant Ferdinand Ferrand, and the FEN activist Georges Schmeltz, alias Pierre Marcenet). It received support from Bardèche's *Défense de l'Occident*, *Rivarol*, *Minute* and *Europe-Action*, which effectively became the MNP's organ just as the FEN (in alliance with the Algerian repatriate FER) became its student section. The recruitment of the FEN and FER gave the MNP ready organisational structures and a militant base in towns with large repatriate communities such as Marseille, Nice, Montpellier, Aix and Toulon.[109]

In order to emphasise the party's Europeanist and internationalist mission, delegations were present at the MNP's inaugural conference from Belgium, Portugal, Spain, Italy, Britain, the United States and Argentina. The white minority government of Ian Smith in Rhodesia sent a Rhodesian national flag which was prominently displayed throughout the conference.[110] In return for its propaganda in favour of colonialism, apartheid and the strong state, the MNP was suspected of receiving financial subsidies from the governments of Rhodesia, South Africa, Spain and Portugal. It also cultivated contacts with extreme-right groups not represented at its inaugural conference, such as the German *Nation-Europa* circle and the Nationaldemokratische Partei Deutschlands (NPD).[111]

Despite claiming a membership of 300,000, the MNP appears to have had no more than some 2,500 members. It nonetheless sought to unite the nationalist right around a more coherent doctrinal base and, like Europe-Action, it propounded a strongly Europeanist version of French nationalism. The term 'Progrès' in the MNP's name also signalled a recognition of the need to modernise the nationalist project, though the continued presence of former collaborationists, Poujadists, Tixierists, OAS activists and other *arriéristes* showed the limits of such ambition in reality.

Though short-lived as a political party, the real importance of the MNP was that, in the wake of Tixier-Vignancour's presidential campaign, it helped accustom the extreme right to the discipline of contesting elections under the Fifth Republic. As a principle, this was far from commanding consensus across an extreme right steeped in anti-republicanism and anti-parliamentarism and traditionally located outside the democratic process. After the rout of Vichy, the false dawn of Poujadism, and the failure of the Algerian crisis to bring down the Republic, Venner acknowledged, in a landmark statement in January 1967, that there was no longer a 'choice of methods' for acceding to power: 'We must take part in the only great political battles of the moment: elections.'[112] Like Tixier-Vignancour's ARLP, therefore, the MNP committed itself to contesting the legislative elections of March 1967. For that purpose, it set up – and in autumn 1966 became – the Rassemblement Européen de la Liberté (European Rally of Liberty, REL). This transition reflected the movement's political mission but also its immaturity, showing yet again the obsessive recourse on the extreme right to self-reinvention through cover movements: the REL was an electoral cover for the MNP, which was itself a political cover for the Centre Nationaliste, which in large part merely replicated the personnel and ideology of Europe-Action and the FEN.

In its programme, the REL called for the suppression of aid to developing countries and a concomitant increase in French workers' pensions; an end to North African immigration and 'the expulsion of elements that pose a danger to public safety and health'; measures to protect French agriculture, artisanal production and industry; and a 'politically unified Europe, with respect for national traditions', equipped to 'resist American or Soviet hegemony and stem the demographic tide from the Third World'. The REL advocated a federal Europe with a European parliament, an integrated European army and diplomatic structure, and a European currency.[113]

Viewing the March 1967 elections as an 'apprenticeship' and a 'first step' only, the leaders of the REL harboured few illusions about effecting an electoral breakthrough. 'Our aim should not be to have deputies elected, but to get ourselves known, to impose our existence', declared Venner in *Rivarol*.[114] Having aspired to put up 75 candidates (and thereby qualify for airtime on radio and television), the REL fielded only 22 candidates who achieved a combined score of fewer than 30,000 votes.[115] Despite the modesty of expectation, this was a blow from which the REL did not recover. After an attempt to restructure the party, Venner, whose Europe-Action had expired some months before, withdrew

from active politics (to re-emerge later in the Nouvelle Droite's GRECE movement). He was succeeded by Pierre Bousquet and Pierre Clémenti, unrepentant
collaborationists who had served in the Waffen-SS and LVF respectively, before
the party finally folded in 1968.[116]

Defending the West: Occident

The collapse of Europe-Action in November 1966 and the electoral failure of
the REL in March 1967 marked the end of the most studied attempt until then
to foster a broad-based nationalist movement with a well-defined ideology and
the capacity to compete within the democratic process. In the two years
preceding Europe-Action's demise, however, it was not Venner's movement
which attracted most public attention on the extreme right, but that of his egregious rival, Pierre Sidos. The Occident movement was formed in April 1964
following a disagreement between Venner and Sidos, and the latter's defection
from Europe-Action with a number of dissidents from the Paris section of the
FEN.[117] Occident appeared at the outset as a remake of Jeune Nation, which
Sidos had also headed and from which the new movement derived its symbol of
the Celtic cross. The violent activism, too, bore the hallmarks of Jeune Nation,
as did the attempts by Occident to recruit among the diehards of the OAS-
Métro-Jeunes network.[118]

While it had a much smaller membership (some 500–600) and far scarcer
resources than Europe-Action,[119] Occident made its mark as the main activist
group on the extreme right in the 1960s. This was due primarily to its
'commando' actions against left-wing students, PCF offices, immigrant associations, anti-colonialists and other 'enemy' targets, such as the Vietnamese
Consulate-General in Paris. The Vietnam War had replaced the Algerian War as
the battleground against communist expansionism, and Occident proclaimed its
mission to 'Defend the West wherever it fights'.[120] Drawing around half of its
membership from Paris, the movement also had sections in other university
towns such as Rennes, Rouen, Bordeaux, Toulouse and Montpellier. Though it
launched raids on cinemas, theatres, bookshops and cafés, its main theatres of
operation were universities and lycées. Occident members provided an intimidating security presence in the early stages of Tixier-Vignancour's presidential
campaign before his break with Sidos. Proclaiming itself 'a violent movement
and proud of it',[121] Occident sought to persuade less through ideas than through
iron bars, teargas grenades and whatever other weapons came to hand. Almost
two hundred broken chairs were the calling card left after the movement's first
'action' in May 1964, when several dozen members ransacked a hall in Paris
where an anti-colonialist meeting was being held by mainly African students.[122]
As one of its leaders acknowledged, the excessive violence of Occident would
earn it the damaging image of 'an organisation of violent thugs with no
brains'.[123]

Though such violence became the stock-in-trade of Occident and the focus of
the attendant media coverage, it was deployed in the service of an ideology of

sorts. With its call to arms in defence of 'the West', Occident effected a rudimentary fusion of nationalism, neo-fascism and social Darwinism. It denounced 'stateless capitalism', international communism and liberalism, calling for an end to class struggle through the development of a corporatist economic regime; it urged the overthrow of 'the Masonic and plutocratic republic' in a 'second French Revolution that will sweep away the pernicious effects of the first'; and it called for a 'new race' of leaders who would emerge from the 'nationalist ranks' not through the 'myth of election' but through 'selection of the best elements from the entire nation'. With its neo-Darwinian overtones, this insistence on 'the principle of selection' as opposed to that of election was a recurrent feature of Occident's discourse. Through its publication *Occident-Université*, it articulated a hierarchical, authoritarian and deeply anti-egalitarian vision of humanity, invoking the eugenicist Alexis Carrel in advocating 'the conservation of the species, the propagation of the race, and the elevation of the spirit' as the 'laws of human life':

> What we reject as unreal is the egalitarian view which claims that humanity is made up of little cubes, each one equal to the others. It is manifestly clear that men are not equal [. . .]. The inequality of men becomes more marked, too, when one moves from the physical domain (strength, speed, nervous energy) to the intellectual and aesthetic domains, and above all to the spiritual domain where inequality is total, transcendent and immeasurable.[124]

The same publication paid tribute to Robert Brasillach – 'that poet of fascism' – and extolled the beneficial effects of fascism on the young. The militants of Occident were themselves young (mostly aged around 20), and it was to the young that the movement looked to bring about 'an immense revolutionary surge' that would fulfil its conception of nationalism as 'the youth in power'.[125] Rehearsing an imagery redolent of fascism, *Occident-Université* evoked 'the mystical blood of Christ, the biological blood of fertilisation, and the blood that is common to all the peoples of Europe'. It denounced 'decadent cosmopolitanism' and set a pseudo-scientific premium on the 'Celtic and pre-Celtic' roots of 'French ethnicity'. The nationalism of Occident (like that of Europe-Action) nonetheless had a markedly Europeanist dimension, recognising 'as brothers the other European nationalist movements that are, like us, engaged in the defence of Western civilisation'. It had an anti-Semitic aspect too, describing the *Protocols of the Elders of Zion* as a 'prophetic' work and – with revisionist echoes of Bardèche – dismissing 'the fable of six million dead'.[126]

Despite its legal registration as a public association, Occident operated in a semi-clandestine way. It changed address frequently and used the cover of parallel associations, such as the laboriously named Centre Universitaire de Documentation et d'Information pour la Renaissance de l'Occident (University Documentation and Information Centre for the Renaissance of the West). Its internal structure was based on provincial sections coordinated by a central secretariat. It attracted mainly university students and some lycée pupils, maintaining close links with the university-based FEN until the latter's disappearance in January 1967. Among its most prominent members were a number of up-and-coming activists such as François Duprat, Gérard Longuet, Alain Madelin, Alain Robert and, for a time, Jean-Gilles Malliarakis. While Longuet and Madelin would go on to occupy prominent positions in the centre-right Union pour la Démocratie Française (Union for French Democracy, UDF) and to become government ministers in the 1980s, others such as Bernard Antony, Michel de Rostolan, Jacques Bompard and Marie-France Stirbois would gravitate to the FN. Robert would become a departmental councillor for the neo-Gaullist Rassemblement pour la République (Rally for the Republic, RPR) and a *chargé de mission* for the future Interior Minister, Charles Pasqua. Other future denizens of the moderate right who cut their teeth in Occident were Patrick Devedjian (RPR), Hervé Novelli (UDF) and Claude Goasguen (UDF).[127] Following the departure of Pierre Sidos, Philippe Asselin became secretary-general in summer 1966, with Duprat, Robert and Longuet in charge of propaganda, operations and doctrine respectively.[128]

Though it sought to exert influence within different student associations and to develop links with radical right-wing groups abroad, notably in the United States, Occident never committed to paper a political programme. Instead, it professed allegiance to a 'strain of thought' summed up in the names 'Barrès, Maurras, Drieu, Brasillach'.[129] A Paris police report of August 1968 noted the ideological confusion of Occident, which it likened more to 'a gang of juvenile delinquents' than a serious political organisation; but it also signalled the movement's racism, its 'carefully cultivated' anti-Semitism, its anti-parliamentarism and echoes of 'fascist mythology' and 'fascist romanticism'.[130]

The ideological impoverishment of Occident meant that it was ill-equipped to respond to the dramatic events of May 1968, when student protests compounded by industrial strikes brought the country to a standstill for a few weeks and threatened to topple de Gaulle's regime. Violent confrontations between extreme right-wing and extreme left-wing student groups contributed significantly to the tensions which found an outlet in these events.[131] Though Occident took part, along with other extreme-right groups, in the first clashes on 3 May, the unfolding crisis and its appropriation by the left soon posed an insoluble dilemma. Should the nationalist right 'join left-wingers in their revolt against the Regime' (which they had vigorously opposed) or come out 'in support of the Regime against Bolshevism' (which they had opposed no less vigorously)?[132] To compound this dilemma, there was much with which the extreme right could sympathise in the rejection by radical left-wing students of bourgeois materialism and their calls for a society structured on a more idealistic set of values. In the end, as Duprat puts it, some extreme-right militants mounted the barricades to fight 'under red flags', while others joined the huge pro-Gaullist rally of 30 May on the Champs-Elysées 'under flags bearing the Cross of Lorraine'.[133] Like most extreme-right movements, Occident finally sided with the regime against the protesting students and striking workers. Though some currents, such as the weekly *Rivarol*, held out against any alliance with the hated Gaullist state, most were motivated by their anti-communism and by the acceleration of an amnesty for *Algérie Française* diehards (which would soon see the release from prison of Salan and the return from exile of Bidault and Soustelle, among others). Threatened by a radicalised left, de Gaulle was not above courting support among radical elements on the right who had once posed the only other serious challenge to his regime.

Once the crisis had been resolved and the Gaullists returned with a landslide victory in the legislative elections of June 1968 (where the extreme right polled 0.13 per cent, fewer than 29,000 votes), Occident sought to impose sense retrospectively on events which had severely tested its coherence. In a pamphlet entitled *Pour une Jeune Nation (For a Young Nation)*, it explicitly distanced itself from both sides of the conflict. The protests, it claimed, had been orchestrated by 'a minority of extreme-left, pro-Chinese, Marxist-Leninist and Trotskyist agitators'; but they had laid bare a profound generational conflict between the young (with whom Occident associated itself) and a 'gerontocracy' dedicated to maintaining the 'established order' of a 'sclerotic society'.[134]

Following the events of May and June 1968, when extreme left-wing groups were dissolved by government order, Occident was spared on the questionable premise that it 'resorted to violence sometimes but has not shown itself to be a subversive movement'.[135] François Duprat claims that between May and October 1968 the movement doubled its support, with some 800 members in Paris and a fast-growing membership in the provinces. Its anti-republican rhetoric and the violence in which it continued to engage, however, were not calculated to secure for long the indulgence of the authorities, who were now anxious to clamp down on all organised breaches of public order. On 31 October 1968, in response to the bombing of a Maoist bookshop in Paris, the government finally imposed a ban on the movement.[136] Whereas 14 extreme-left groups were banned in the five years following May 1968, Occident was the only extreme-right group to incur this measure. Though some of its members continued for a time with sporadic activism, Occident effectively disappeared to be replaced within a year by its successor, Ordre Nouveau (which would in turn be banned for its violence in June 1973).[137]

6 Divergent paths towards the new
The Nouvelle Droite and Ordre Nouveau

The Nouvelle Droite

The year 1968 stands as a watershed in the evolution of the French extreme right. The disappearance of Occident, following that of Europe-Action and the FEN, removed the major channels for militant activism and ideological reflection respectively. The electoral failures of 1965 and 1967 had laid bare an absence of ideas with the capacity to mobilise popular support. The events of May and June 1968 further exposed the political weakness and disorientation of extreme-right movements faced with events which they were powerless to influence and on which they could not even readily determine their own best stance. In supporting de Gaulle as a bulwark against the radical left, many extreme-right groups had, for once, backed the winning side. When the barricades were removed, the need to engage in another battle – that of ideas – was evident to those who had already sought to promote doctrinal renewal through the pages of *Europe-Action* and the FEN's *Cahiers universitaires*. Forsaking the failed methods of street confrontation and electoral competition alike, they turned inward to conduct a re-evaluation of their ideology and to bring about a 'new culture of the right' in France.[1] The moral and intellectual hegemony of the left, they held, had been an established feature of French society since 1945. Even if left-wing parties had known only a brief relationship with political power in that period, left-wing thought had attained a predominant influence in the press, education and the wider intellectual establishment. This cultural power of the left had now been dramatised by a students' and workers' revolt which had taken on the character of a social revolution. The urgency of developing a strategy with which to respond effectively to the cultural ascendancy of the left led to the formation of what would become known as the 'Nouvelle Droite', or New Right.

The prime mover and ideologue-in-chief of the Nouvelle Droite was Alain de Benoist, an erudite Sorbonne graduate who had been a prominent journalist-cum-intellectual in the FEN, Europe-Action and the MNP-REL (commonly identified behind the pseudonyms Fabrice Laroche and Robert de Herte). De Benoist found his model for the renewal of right-wing thought in an incongruous location: on the left, and specifically in the writings of the left-wing political theorist and founding member of the Italian Communist Party, Antonio Gramsci.

Going beyond the Marxist notion that power in capitalist society rested on socio-economic factors bolstered by the agencies of state authority, Gramsci argued that political superstructures themselves were founded on a base of ideas, a hegemonic culture permeating civil society as a whole and propagated by opinion-forming sectors within that society (intellectuals, educationalists, media, etc.). For a revolution to succeed, the ground must first be prepared at the level of ideas – and a new hegemonic culture created – before it could be secured at the level of political power. In other words, people had to be moved to redefine the perceptions and attitudes around which social consensus was structured. As de Benoist neatly put it, 'One cannot have a Lenin without having had a Marx'.[2]

In applying this axiom to a French political culture under the sway of the left, de Benoist aspired to change prevailing assumptions and to fashion a new consensus within which right-wing thought could achieve respectability. The aim, in short, was to create a 'Gramscism of the right'.[3] The conservative revolution in inter-war Germany commended itself as a model of cultural renewal which was no less instructive for being associated with the rise of Nazism.[4] There were other models closer to home from which inspiration could also be drawn. Among these was Charles Maurras, who had argued tirelessly that 'the country needed first to be "monarchised" before any restoration of the king could be contemplated'.[5] Though the Catholic-monarchist Action Française did much to promote right-wing thought and bolster ultra-conservatism in the first half of the twentieth century, the failure of Maurras and others to achieve the necessary intellectual hegemony, it was reasoned, accounted for the ultimate marginality of their ideas. The way forward for de Benoist was therefore not through the 'reactionary' and 'sterile' ideas of 'the old right'. 'The old right is dead', he declared, 'and deserves to be so.'[6] Nor was progress to be achieved through the violent antics of a younger generation of activists. Where Jeune Nation had proclaimed that 'the street belongs to those who go down and take it',[7] the Nouvelle Droite would embark on a very different, more painstaking, long-term project – but with the same ultimate goal in view. They rejected the Maurrassian precept '*politique d'abord*' ('politics first') and replaced it with their own concept of 'metapolitics first'. While the Enlightenment and the 'ideas of 1789' were held responsible for institutionalising an illusory and deleterious egalitarianism, the same forces nonetheless provided 'the perfect example of an intellectual movement which undercut the basis of a political system and provoked a revolution'.[8]

Old ideas in a new style: GRECE

The main forum through which de Benoist and the Nouvelle Droite were to develop their ideas was the GRECE movement, launched in January 1968 following a preliminary meeting in November 1967. The dates are significant in that the movement was formed prior to the events of May 1968 with which its *raison d'être* has commonly been associated. The location of its launch – the Mediterranean town of Nice – was also significant, since Nice had been a regional base of Europe-Action, with a large *pied-noir* repatriate community and a sympathetically disposed mayor in Jacques Médecin. As early as 1965, Europe-Action had in fact created an embryonic version of the movement in its Groupes de Recherches et d'Etudes pour la Communauté Européenne (Groups for the Research and Study of the European Community). Though the name was changed, the contrived Hellenic acronym GRECE – with its connotations of European intellectual heritage and civilisation – was retained.

The new movement was accompanied by a journal, *Nouvelle Ecole*, the first issue of which was dated February–March 1968. From its original typed format, *Nouvelle Ecole* soon evolved into an expensively produced and lavishly illustrated periodical which was aimed at an educated readership and attained a reported circulation of several thousand by the mid-1970s, up to 13,000 by 1979.[9] This was followed by a second, in-house journal, *Eléments pour la Civilisation Européenne* (abbreviated as *Eléments*), by the theoretical review *Etudes et Recherches*, and by a string of books disseminated through GRECE's own publishing house, Copernic. The movement would also develop more specifically targeted publications, such as the periodical *Nation Armée* for the armed forces, and satellite groups with specific interests, such as the Groupe d'Etudes pour une Nouvelle Education (Study Group for a New Education), or – another loaded acronym – GENE. It would finance itself partly through the Club des Mille (Thousand Club), whose members pledged a monthly donation of at least 1,000 francs.[10]

The new style of the GRECE movement was evident from the make-up of its founding committee, a group of doctors, academics, journalists and other highly educated professionals. Behind the style, however, was a somewhat less innovative substance. Among the 40 founding members of the movement in 1968 were prominent figures from Europe-Action and its offshoots, notably the Centre Nationaliste: Alain de Benoist, Jacques Bruyas, Gilles Fournier, Dominique Gajas, Roger Lemoine, Alain Mallard, Georges Schmeltz (alias Pierre Marcenet), Jean-Claude Rivière, Maurice Rollet, Jean-Claude Valla, Dominique Venner (alias Julien Lebel), Pierre Vial and Jean-Marcel Zagamé. Less prominent but no less present were some of the old guard of the collaborationist right, such as Rebatet and Bardèche, whose patronage the new movement secured from the outset.[11] The presence of these superannuated nostalgics suggested that GRECE was, like Europe-Action before it, an attempt to bridge the distance between the generations. It took care, however, to divest itself of the cruder trappings, refusing all overt association with historical fascism and repudiating the activism that had been part of Europe-Action's mission.

Aspiring to a new academicism, GRECE thus envisaged itself not as a militant movement but as an *école de pensée* tasked with redefining the premises of French right-wing thought through its publications, discussion groups and colloquia. Its declared objective was to ensure that 'culture should not remain the "preserve" of the Marxists'.[12] To achieve this, a change of image was essential. A confidential internal circular of February 1969 spelled out to GRECE members the need to be 'very careful about the vocabulary we use. In particular, we must abandon an outdated mode of expression and adopt new habits.'[13] Among the new habits to be adopted was an intellectual bullishness and energetic rebuttal of criticism. Members were urged to respond to adverse press coverage by writing to scotch 'counter-truths' and stress the 'respectability' of GRECE. Their letters, they were advised, should 'denounce misquotations', 'cite those personalities who have lent their support to our organisation', and be signed with the member's 'name, profession and, *where applicable, titles*'.[14]

Despite the makeover, the Nouvelle Droite at its inception had little about it that was genuinely new. Through its journal *Nouvelle Ecole*, it reiterated the anxieties and obsessions of *Europe-Action*, invoking the same themes of 'biological realism', racial and cultural identity, and differentialism.[15] *Nouvelle Ecole* was conceived as a forum not for original thinking but, as its editorial statement declared, for upholding the 'immutable laws of nature, the fundamental values of a 3,000-year-old Western civilisation, or the plain evidence of common sense' against the 'order of the day: that everything is equal to everything else'.[16] The journal publicised developments in the sciences and other fields which could be used to support GRECE's ideological postulates. These denied equality as a basis for social organisation and called for elites selected in accordance with their aptitudes, advancing genetic factors as primary determinants in the moral, social and cultural spheres.[17] Despite the recognised need to be 'very careful about the conclusions to which *Nouvelle Ecole* points', the contributions of its editor-in-chief de Benoist, and of Venner, Fournier and other former members of the editorial team of *Europe-Action*, made it easy to trace the ideological lineage of the new movement.[18]

It would not be long, however, before GRECE would put its own stamp on the ideas propounded in its publications. The doctrinal synthesis to which it gave expression in the early 1970s would pretend to a scientific rigour far beyond that of Europe-Action and kindred movements. It would take account of developments in biology, genetics and ethology, invoking the authority of genetic determinists such as the Austrian zoologist Konrad Lorenz and the American sociobiologist Edward O. Wilson. To its interest in the life sciences it would add an equally vigorous interest in the human sciences of history, psychology and anthropology, drawing on the writings of the Italian thinker Julius Evola, the American educational psychologist Arthur Jensen, the German-born British psychologist Hans Eysenck, and other notable proponents of anti-egalitarianism and racial/cultural differentiation.[19]

In GRECE's publications, a recurrent methodology was to foreground within the text an abundance of quotations and references. This served a double purpose: that of validating the pretension to academic rigour, and that of allowing subjects to speak for themselves with an economy of editorial mediation. De Benoist's *Vu de droite*, which won the Grand Prix de l'Essai from the Académie Française in 1978, is an instructive case. This is essentially a compilation of book reviews, 'A Critical Anthology of Contemporary Ideas' as its subtitle immodestly proclaims, covering fields from biology and the life sciences through psychology, educational theory and sociology to history, philosophy, politics and religion. The book cites liberally from a multitude of selected authors throughout, making de Benoist's own contribution largely one of linking quotations and serving as a mere projectionist for the ideas he chooses to highlight –

ideas such as the claim (in the chapter 'Towards biopolitics') that '[a]ll politics today implies *biopolitics*', and the prediction that one day 'the genetic code will help inform the civil codes'.[20]

From 'race' to 'culture'

At the core of the ideology which GRECE elaborated through its varied publications lay the rejection of the Judaeo-Christian ethical tradition, with its Semitic origins, and the celebration of a lost Indo-European heritage. The Judaeo-Christian values of monotheism, egalitarianism and universalism, GRECE argued, led to totalitarianism and were at odds with an ancient pagan Indo-European culture (as reconstituted by the historian Georges Dumézil) which united communities in their telluric attachments, their bonds of blood and tradition, their myths, and in their hierarchical social order and cult of heroic exploits.[21] Dumézil posited a tripartite division of Indo-European society and culture into the realms of sovereignty (the leadership function), war (the heroic function) and production (the economic function). This rigorously hierarchical model was enthusiastically seized upon by GRECE as the social structure authentic to Europeans, allowing all members of the community to assume rights and responsibilities in line with their natural aptitudes. The diverse branches of primitive Indo-European society, as represented by Dumézil and appropriated by GRECE,[22] were organised into the classes of priest-leader, warrior-hero and peasant-producer, with the harmonious balance between them reflected in their pantheon of gods, their art and their literature. This aristocratic structure promoted ascetic reason and courageous endeavour over appetite and consumption, the latter being relegated to the lowest function.

The indigenous legacy of Europe, GRECE argued, stretched back through Celtic myth, Germanic legend and Nordic saga to the classical cultures of ancient Greece and Rome. This legacy had to be rediscovered and re-evaluated if Europeans were to assume their true identity and reclaim their 'rightful appurtenance' freed of the foreign accretions which had come to overlay it.[23] Replacing narrow French nationalism with this broader Indo-Europeanism, GRECE articulated an untraditional interpretation of French history. It condemned Clovis, the king of the Franks, who converted to Catholicism in the fifth century, thereby 'opening the way to cosmopolitanism' and the end of a distinctive French – and European – identity. In forcibly converting the Saxons, Charlemagne perpetrated one of the atrocities of history.[24] Blurring the boundaries between memory and imagination, GRECE thus envisaged a state of original purity located in the 'furthest reaches of the past'[25] and reminiscent of the remote founding myths which formed the cultural substratum of Nazism. In other words, argues Roger Griffin, 'the old wine of palingenetic ultra-nationalist myth' was 'poured into new bottles, the label originally marked "Aryan" being covered with one marked "Indo-European" or "Traditional"'.[26]

Symbolism had its place in this search for remote cultural roots. GRECE displayed an interest in pre-Christian folk traditions, while the journal *Eléments* carried advertisements for a small Thor hammer necklace as a good luck charm. GRECE also conducted its own neo-pagan ceremonies, such as 'Indo-European' weddings (complete with symbolic exchange of dagger and key), celebration of the winter and summer solstices, and 'pilgrimages' such as that undertaken by GRECE members to Delphi, 'for so long the symbol of our world'.[27]

In terms of its essential doctrine, it is easier to sum up what GRECE was against than to define with precision what it was for. It bore no relation, other than one of outright antagonism, to the Anglo-American 'New Right' with its commitment to neo-liberal, *laissez-faire* economism. It accepted with some reserve the term 'Nouvelle Droite' coined by commentators; though it proclaimed its newness and defined itself on the right in contradistinction to the left, it eschewed traditional categories of right and left and stressed its intellectual as opposed to political vocation.[28] Questions of practical politics such as the form of the regime or the nature of political institutions were studiously shunned or only vaguely adumbrated. GRECE was opposed to the tenets of egalitarianism and of liberalism; it rejected both the collectivist model of the Soviet Union and the capitalist model of the United States, each vying to impose on Europe an alien social system;[29] it disparaged 'Western civilization' (in its American rather than European expression) as a cover for rampant capitalism, a 'system for killing peoples' and destroying local cultures that posed a greater threat than communism; it associated materialism with decadence and spiritual impoverishment, lamenting the dehumanising effects of reducing human beings to units of production or consumers and opposing the notion of an *'organic community'* (pre-Christian Europe) to that of a *'market society'* (quintessentially the United States).[30] Far from being a model of the 'free world', argued de Benoist, the latter was fit only to produce 'happy robots. It is hell with air-conditioning. It kills the soul.'[31]

GRECE held that heredity outweighed environment in the development of human individuals and communities, and (despite strenuous denials) leaned towards sociobiology and racial psychology. It exhibited interest in issues such as birth control, abortion, sterilisation, euthanasia and genetic engineering. The January–February 1971 number of *Nouvelle Ecole* (no. 14) was devoted to 'Eugenics', with other numbers devoted to 'Biology' (no. 7), 'Evolution' (no. 18), 'Ethology' (nos. 25–26), and 'Darwinism and Society' (no. 38). A series of GRECE conferences were dedicated to 'elites', the 'biology of behaviour', the 'illusions of equality', and 'bio-ethics'.[32] In an unusually frank public declaration at a meeting of his Terre et Peuple (Land and People) movement in May 2000, the former secretary-general of GRECE, Pierre Vial, would reiterate all of these same concerns in lamenting the 'ethnic colonisation' of France by non-European immigrant communities with a different 'biological infrastructure'. The 'true cultural revolution', Vial ventured, dispensing with the coded idiom, was 'the ethnic revolution, the revolution of identity'. On the same occasion, another former leading member of GRECE, Guillaume Faye, would describe 'the problem of European identity' as being 'not just cultural and civilisational' but 'anthropobiological'.[33]

GRECE condemned Christianity and Marxism alike, the latter as a secular outgrowth of the former; it argued that each propounded a linear, Messianic view of history (paradise–fall–salvation) and denied the inequalities between human beings and human societies. It claimed that both of these forms of totalitarianism were crumbling at the same time, opening the way for a new, opposing paradigm.[34] Against the Judaeo-Christian and Marxist historical perspectives, GRECE set a pre-Christian, indigenous European conception of history as cyclical, drawing on Nietzsche, Evola and others. In opposition to the cult of humility instituted by Christianity, it advocated an aristocratic ethic, distinguishing between 'mass-men' and 'creative heroes' with strong overtones of Nietzsche.[35] It repudiated the notion of a generic humanity and held that positions of responsibility in society should be reserved for intellectually superior individuals; and, in its most deftly deployed turn of reasoning, it argued a 'right to difference' and to separate cultural identities in configuring the social order. 'There is no such thing as *intrinsic man*', stressed de Benoist, 'there are only *cultures*, each functioning according to its own laws.' For the same de Benoist, the biggest threat to be faced was an '*egalitarian ideology*' which sought to 'consign people to the same level and to reduce all *cultures* to a "global *civilization*" built on the most *common* denominators'.[36]

In arguing as much, GRECE shifted its emphasis from the natural inequalities between individuals and races to the natural differences between cultures, adopting a discourse shorn of crude racism and turning against its left-wing opponents part of their own rationale. As Maurice Bardèche approvingly observed, the 'substitution of the idea of culture for the idea of heredity' allowed the right finally 'to recognise, and even to assert, the diversity of races' while at the same time 'being able even to call itself anti-racist'. As Bardèche also observed, this was more a change of style than a change of substance.[37] It nonetheless allowed the Nouvelle Droite to mount a 'radical critique of *totalitarianism*', seen as a descendant of monotheism, and to posit 'anti-universalism and anti-egalitarianism' as the very foundations of a 'positive tolerance'.[38]

The underlying assumption in the diversity and plurality of cultures as propounded by GRECE was that there existed not just *differences* but a *hierarchy* between individuals and social groups. As de Benoist made clear, 'there is a logical link between recognising the essential diversity of people and recognising the inequality – any difference being in some sense a value judgement – to which this gives rise in concrete terms'. Louis Pauwels, a high-profile right-wing journalist and patron of *Nouvelle Ecole*, expressed the same idea more bluntly by declaring that 'different means unequal'.[39] If difference is thus synonymous with value, the argument could be made not only for a distinct but for an inherently superior European culture; and a superior culture implied a superior genetic stock.[40] From respecting cultural difference, the transition was made to upholding the need for cultural separation. 'Defending the right to difference', wrote de Benoist in the winter 1978 issue of *Eléments*, meant taking a stand 'against social robotisation, against political and philosophical universalism, against the loss of collective identities and the mixing of peoples or cultures'.[41]

'Men are not born equal'

Despite such remarks, de Benoist and the Nouvelle Droite were vigorous in denying all accusations of racism. They projected themselves as 'raciophiles' in their defence of racial diversity. They avoided any explicit assertion of the superiority of one race over another, going so far as to claim that 'each race is superior to others in the realisation of its own particular achievements'.[42] The racists (or 'raciophobes'), they argued, were those who, in the name of equality, sought to destroy ethnic communities through a homogenising universalism. Christian missionaries had attempted this in the name of a one, true God, and Republican ideologues in the name of a civilising mission; both had exhibited the same fear of otherness and embarked on a project of ethnocide.

Those who argued for the assimilation of immigrants into the French national community were equally bent on ethno-cultural genocide. Several carefully framed arguments were put forward by the Nouvelle Droite against immigration. Firstly, 'above a certain *threshold*', it led to 'all sorts of problems: discrimination, segregation, deculturation, delinquency, etc.'; secondly, it was pursued for questionable economic motives which benefited large corporations in the main; thirdly, it provided a ready pool of labour as a substitute for more innovative economic solutions; fourthly, it created an underclass whose demographic expansion outstripped that of the indigenous French; and finally, the problem of illegal immigration showed how difficult it was to regulate migratory flows. The Nouvelle Droite stopped short of calling for the repatriation of non-European immigrants, but its insistence on the incompatibility of different ethno-cultural communities required little elaboration. It declared itself opposed to colonialism and defended 'the right of peoples to self-determination', retaining apparently nothing of the support for white colonialist regimes which some leading Grécistes had proclaimed in the mid-1960s, and nothing of the ardent support which many had lent to the cause of *Algérie Française*. The insistence now was on the need for a '*reciprocal* decolonisation', in other words the right of Europeans in turn 'to preserve their own ethnic heritage' with all its attendant cultural specificity. 'A human race', declared de Benoist, 'is not just a zoological entity. It is also, more broadly, the foundation on which a particular history, culture and destiny are built.'[43]

From recognising differences in 'zoological' and 'cultural' inheritance to positing differences in mental capacity was but a short step. The publication by Copernic of works such as Hans Eysenck's *L'Inégalité de l'homme* (*The Inequality of Man*) or the collaborative *Race et Intelligence* (under the pseudonym Jean-Pierre Hébert) showed how thin was the cultural veil drawn across GRECE's sociobiological outlook.[44] This was evident also in the close affinities between *Nouvelle Ecole* and publications such as *The Mankind Quarterly* in Britain and *Neue Anthropologie* in Germany, journals combining anthropology, psychology, genetics and race-science within a radical right-wing perspective.[45] As early as 1969, *Nouvelle Ecole* embraced the hereditarian theories of the American educational psychologist Arthur Jensen, a former student of Eysenck, following the publication by Jensen of a controversial essay on racially determined intelligence in the

Harvard Educational Review. *Nouvelle Ecole* was swift to promote Jensen's work as a breakthrough in the scientific evaluation of genetic endowment and in the appreciation of racial inequality. In the September–October 1969 issue of the journal, de Benoist published an article entitled 'Educational Integration and Racial Psychology' in which Jensen's findings were summarised. In the 1970s, *Nouvelle Ecole* would continue to defer to Jensen's conclusions, lauding his book *Educability and Group Differences* in 1976 as 'a definitive solution to the problem of differential intelligence-testing between races'.[46] In particular, Jensen was credited with furnishing 'scientific' proof of 'the opposition between the "intuitive reasoning" of the Black African and the "discursive reasoning" of the White European', in other words their respective predisposition to inductive and deductive modes of thought.[47]

To the psychological theories of Eysenck and Jensen, *Nouvelle Ecole* would bring the imprimatur of the Nobel Prize-winning ethologist Konrad Lorenz, with his assertion of the inequalities between individuals as between racial groups, his anxieties over genetic enfeeblement due to miscegenation and the propagation of weaker elements, and the eugenicist implications of such thinking. Alongside these contemporary figures, *Nouvelle Ecole* paid tribute to the founder of eugenics, Francis Galton, 'the father of racist ideology', Arthur de Gobineau, the anti-Semitic inspiration of Nazism, Houston Stewart Chamberlain, and other influential predecessors.[48] In the early issue which it devoted to eugenics, it invoked the authority of Galton, Nietzsche, Georges Vacher de Lapouge, Alexis Carrel, Oswald Spengler and sundry proponents of 'human betterment' by means of favouring the fittest and fostering 'a biological aristocracy through heredity'.[49]

It was this aspect of GRECE's thinking that attracted most comment and most controversy. Though the writings of de Benoist and GRECE rang with calls for creative self-assertion and placed a premium on the will, they promoted the argument of Eysenck and Jensen that human intelligence was determined 80 per cent by hereditary factors and 20 per cent by environmental conditioning.[50] This belief in the primacy of genes and the essentially inherited nature of intelligence opposed GRECE diametrically to the liberal-humanitarian belief that inequalities between individuals and peoples were due primarily to socio-cultural factors and could be redressed through education. GRECE denounced as a pernicious error the Utopian egalitarianism that had installed itself as the unchallenged value system of the Western world, leading to the abolition of elites and the cult of mediocrity. Culture, far from correcting natural inequality, became for de Benoist a further determinant of it; and those who sought to impose equality did so out of horror at their own inferiority, the horror which the sick feel towards the healthy or the weak towards the strong.[51] In all of this, inspiration was drawn by de Benoist and GRECE from the advocate of the *Übermensch*, Nietzsche-Zarathustra, while consolation was derived from the argument that the doctrine of equality had already traversed the three stages of its cycle: the inaugural stage of Christianity, the philosophical stage of the Enlightenment, and the scientific stage of Marxism.[52]

As Julien Brunn observes, biological determinism was not the starting-point of the ideology mediated through *Nouvelle Ecole* and other such publications. The starting-point was rather the uncompromising belief in order and hierarchy as the prerequisites of a well-regulated society. There should be leaders and led. The error in liberal democracies, according to GRECE, was that these leaders should emerge through popular election, with all the arbitrary results and distortions to which this gave rise. The only sure means of appointing the best to lead was to apply scientific criteria free of arbitrariness, opportunism and corruption. Therein lay the role of biology and educational psychology for GRECE, both furnishing proof not only that human beings were unequal but that their inequality was hereditary and therefore definitive. The bases of social organisation quite simply had to be rethought to take account of this predetermined elitism. Invoking the Nobel Prize-winning biophysicist Francis Crick, famous for his work on genetic decoding, de Benoist could boldly declare: 'Men are not born equal. That is plain for all to see. For all except politicians, who have not yet come to this realisation.'[53]

A few thousand . . .

Elitism marked not just the thinking but also the strategy of GRECE. It diverged from the commitment of Europe-Action and other radical right-wing groups to popular recruitment and a political vocation, parading instead its intellectual aloofness. In other ways, too, GRECE made an awkward neighbour for established far-right movements. With its neo-pagan, pan-Europeanist perspective, it drew hostility from traditionalist Catholic and national-monarchist currents. Despite their selective appreciation of its ideas (notably on equality, race and immigration), parties like the FN and Parti des Forces Nouvelles (Party of New Forces, PFN) found GRECE too abstractive and remote from *Realpolitik*. These were not, however, the quarters in which GRECE sought to cultivate approval. Its ambitions were of a different order:

> GRECE will never have a mass membership; we are neither a professional organisation nor a political party. We seek instead to attract those few thousand people who make a country tick. France today is run by thinkers, by professional, cultural, sporting and other associations, by scientists, publicists and administrators who control, influence and impart instruction to millions of individuals. A few thousand is a small number in absolute terms, but with a few thousand people of such importance, if they shared the same thinking and the same approach, a revolution might be possible.

Written in the May 1969 issue of *Eléments* (which remained until 1973 an internal publication for members only), this statement summed up clearly the strategy of intellectual infiltration which lay at the heart of GRECE's metapolitical project.[54] At a time when the movement had around a hundred members only, it nonetheless required new recruits to complete a questionnaire on their education, intellectual interests, reading habits and cultural pursuits. By the late

1970s, membership would rise to perhaps several thousand, organised under the auspices of regional committees and addressed through newsletters, summer schools and discussion groups.[55]

In its quest for elitist influence, GRECE sought to position itself close to the sources of power under de Gaulle's presidential successors, Georges Pompidou (1969–74) and Valéry Giscard d'Estaing (1974–81). It courted opinion-formers and decision-makers in key institutions (government, higher education, the civil service, the media, the army, the upper echelons of industry), 'influential men who occupy their place in the decision-making circles of today and, more importantly, in those of tomorrow'.[56] It attracted the patronage of distinguished academics from France and abroad: anthropologists, historians, biologists, geneticists, sociologists, psychologists, academics from a host of disciplines, and other eminent professionals. It boasted among its patrons members of the Académie Française (Pierre Gaxotte, René Huyghe, Thierry Maulnier), a Nobel Prize winner in Konrad Lorenz, and internationally renowned figures such as the writer Arthur Koestler. It attracted contributions from other prestigious names, such as the Nobel Prize-winning biochemist Jacques Monod. By the late 1970s, it had sympathisers and contact addresses in Belgium, Germany, Italy, Sweden, Greece, Spain, Britain, the United States, Canada, South Africa and South America.[57]

From this sound base, GRECE proceeded to disseminate its ideas to a wider public. De Benoist and others contributed regularly in the 1970s to the periodicals *Valeurs actuelles* and *Le Spectacle du monde*, both part of the media group of the CNIP senator Raymond Bourgine. The most propitious vehicle for the spread of GRECE's ideas, however, was the widely circulated weekend supplement launched in 1978 of the mainstream conservative daily newspaper, *Le Figaro*. The editor of *Le Figaro-Magazine*, Louis Pauwels (like the newspaper's owner, the right-wing press magnate Robert Hersant), was in tune with the ideas of GRECE and part of the same intellectual network.[58] By opening the columns of his magazine to several members of the movement, notably de Benoist and Valla, Pauwels assured them the means of reaching a mass audience on a weekly basis – despite their reservations about the magazine's 'Reagano-Papist' orientation and the *bien pensant* nature of its conservative Catholic readership.[59]

As with people, one can tell a lot about movements from the friends they attract. In 1979, Maurice Bardèche devoted two articles in his *Défense de l'Occident* to GRECE, which he praised as a 'courageous and original intellectual enterprise'.[60] The movement's conclusions on the 'natural inequality between men and between ethnic groups' were, for Bardèche, a 'rehabilitation of good sense', flying in the face of the Marxist intelligentsia and the 'imbecile', 'criminally erroneous' 'dogma of anti-racism'. He commended GRECE's recourse to biology and anthropology as the basis of its 'scientific inquiry', furnishing objective proof of the 'obvious truth' that there are 'fundamental differences between species and between men, along with natural laws governing life which cannot be ignored or infringed without endangering the species as a whole'.

While crediting GRECE with having launched an intellectual initiative 'superior to any other being undertaken on the right', Bardèche was not uncritical. He argued against the movement's too ready dismissal of Europe's Christian heritage, called for more circumspection in its conception of 'culture', and regretted its lack of a 'firm political objective'. Here, in its studied apoliticism, lay the most pronounced weakness of the Nouvelle Droite for Bardèche. Gramsci's cultural offensive had been supported by a whole political network, Bismarck's *Kulturkampf* by the apparatus of the German state; if the Nouvelle Droite did not have the political weaponry with which to consolidate its cultural advance, then the latter might as well not be undertaken. 'One cannot deny the dogma of equality without wishing to change a form of democracy that is founded on that dogma. If this denial of equality and affirmation of the elite are to have any sense, they must be translated into pressure to bring that elite about.' Here Bardèche betrayed a lingering allegiance to the primacy of politics as argued by Maurras and others of an earlier generation. He betrayed, too, a failure to appreciate what the Nouvelle Droite regarded as its most essential political weapon: its cultural entryism.

Friends in high places

GRECE modelled itself on those left-wing think-tanks, or clubs, which had sought to sustain a vigorous ideological culture of the left under de Gaulle, most notably the Club Jean Moulin with which GRECE compared itself directly. The creation in 1974 of the Club de l'Horloge (Clock Club) helped to bring within the Nouvelle Droite's sphere of influence a number of prominent political figures, civil servants, technocrats and academics. Though distinct from GRECE, the Club de l'Horloge became part of the same intellectual network, with some cross-over of personnel and ideas which allowed it to act as a bridge to the Gaullist and Giscardian parties, some of whose members were attracted by the possibilities for ideological renewal offered by these new associations. The members of the Club de l'Horloge were few but influential, drawn initially from graduates of the prestigious Ecole Nationale d'Administration (ENA) and Ecole Polytechnique; it boasted 120 permanent members and several hundred sympathisers in government and industry.[61] Though the commitment by the Club de l'Horloge to free-market economics, Catholic conservatism and the Western Alliance set it at odds with the anti-economism, anti-Christian animus and anti-Americanism of GRECE, a strong kinship was forged by their common rejection of egalitarianism, their scientific pretensions and shared interest in sociobiology, and their anti-communism. Despite their differences and their refusal to acknowledge any formal relationship, their coexistence and informal collaboration testified to a reinvigoration of right-wing thought in France in the 1970s.

Though it was busy extending its influence through these channels, it would take some 10 years for the Nouvelle Droite to come to public attention as a recognisable movement. In summer 1979, it gained prominence by attracting a flurry of articles in the French mainstream press and for the first time provoking public discussion in France and abroad. Its members blamed this long delay in achieving recognition on a conspiracy of silence by the media and left-wing intellectual establishment. They might rather have concluded that their emergence at all from obscurity was due to the public platform which they had acquired in the mass-circulation *Figaro-Magazine*. While denouncing the fanciful nature of much that was said about the Nouvelle Droite, de Benoist described the new attention to which it was subject as a '*historic* development, the first time in at least thirty years that in a European country a current of thought classed "on the right" has made such ground in terms of its ideology and its influence both'.[62]

The ground made by the Nouvelle Droite in the 1970s was due in part to a climate which proved more conducive to the reception of its ideas. The ideological ascendancy of the left in France was shaken by growing disenchantment with the Soviet Union, exacerbated by the publication in 1973 of Solzhenitsyn's *Gulag Archipelago*. The increasingly anachronistic, stolidly Stalinist image of the PCF suffered by association with Soviet repression in eastern Europe, the brutality of the Khmer Rouge in Cambodia and other so-called revolutionary communist regimes. The left was failing in its universal mission. It was failing electorally, too. The inability of the Socialists and Communists in France to use the events of May 1968 as a platform for acceding to power consigned them to opposition throughout the 1970s. The collapse of their Common Programme in 1977 was followed by further defeat in the legislative elections of 1978, despite a strong showing in the municipal elections of 1977 which should have announced their imminent accession to national power.

In a context of deepening economic recession, the progressive hardening under the presidency of Giscard d'Estaing of government policy on law and order, civil liberties and the treatment of immigrants offered the Nouvelle Droite a more amenable environment within which to declaim its anti-egalitarian ideas and its insistence on cultural difference. The overlap between these ideas and utterances by some government ministers and advisers, especially in the fields of education and immigration policy, suggested that the strategy of cultural entryism might be yielding results.[63] The drive by Giscard d'Estaing's administration to return the least 'assimilable' immigrants to their countries of origin, accompanied by a law tightening the conditions for entry and residence, increasing the powers of the police to deal with illegal immigrants, and facilitating expulsion procedures, resonated with some of the Nouvelle Droite's pronouncements on immigration.[64] During the debates preceding the controversial abortion law (*Loi Veil*) of 1975, GRECE was also said to have contributed significantly to the pro-abortion arguments raised in parliament. Its support for abortion would bring it into conflict with other right-wing currents such as traditionalist Catholics, who bitterly opposed the reform.[65]

While it was difficult to measure in concrete terms the impact of the Nouvelle Droite on public policy and legislation, other indicators of its growing respectability could be discerned. In a book published in 1978, following his service as Interior Minister in the governments of Jacques Chirac and Raymond Barre (1974–77), Michel Poniatowski embraced some of the most radical tenets of the Nouvelle Droite. The book located the 'origins of white Western society' among primitive Indo-Europeans, with their tripartite social structure, their distinctive culture, and their 'will to power and taste for heroic and creative enterprise'.[66] In a chapter entitled 'Heredity, Environment and Intelligence', the author argued against the 'egalitarian illusion' fostered by Rousseau that environment outweighed heredity: 'Men are born unequal in intelligence and capacity. Their genetic inheritance gives them different aptitudes.' The former Interior Minister endorsed the conclusion of Eysenck and Jensen (and GRECE) that intelligence was 80 per cent inherited, and denounced 'the artificial organisation of equality, in other words the systematic dragging down of the most able' in society. In opposition to the 'anti-scientific obscurantism' of the egalitarians, this close friend and adviser to President Giscard d'Estaing argued for an education system that would take full account of the heritability of intelligence and harness 'the capacities of the most gifted' to create a hierarchical society led by a natural elite.[67] Reversing the argument of those who might protest that excellence excludes, Poniatowski offered a forceful expression of the Nouvelle Droite's conviction that 'equality is an injustice done to the capable and the better'.[68]

So close was this book to some of the Nouvelle Droite's most controversial positions (and even, in places, its mode of expression) that de Benoist was rumoured to have ghost-written it.[69] Though the ideas expounded here were vigorously opposed by other prominent Giscardians, they contributed to a climate in which the Nouvelle Droite was able to enhance its credibility and to claim a degree of intellectual penetration unthinkable a decade before. The same covert influence was alleged in relation to works published in this period by other leading figures on the right and centre-right, such as the mayor of Nice and Secretary of State for Tourism Jacques Médecin's *Le Terreau de la liberté*, or the former minister Philippe Malaud's *La Révolution libérale*. In a number of other books across the diverse fields of politics, education, history and economics, a real or imagined influence of the Nouvelle Droite could similarly be detected.[70]

There was nothing imagined about the contribution in 1979 by de Benoist and other members of GRECE to a collaborative publication with the President's brother, Olivier Giscard d'Estaing, *La Renaissance de l'Occident?* (*The Rebirth of the West?*).[71] It was even alleged that the President himself might have succumbed to the same influences. In a book published two years into his presidential mandate, Giscard argued that the differences in people's individual situations were due to inequalities in aptitude and endeavour, and that the social hierarchy, while seeking to reduce these inequalities, should nonetheless take account of them.[72] Such was the concern in some quarters of the Giscard camp at the perceived impact of the Nouvelle Droite that in summer 1979 three members of the centre-right Parti Républicain (PR) openly accused GRECE, through the newspaper *Le Monde*, of 'pulling the presidential majority to the right, and weakening it as a consequence'.[73]

Small wonder that Maurice Bardèche should have looked to the strategy of the Nouvelle Droite as 'perhaps the only way left open for us to escape from the "ghetto" in which the right has found itself trapped. [. . .] This breach which has been opened in the front line of intellectual terrorism proves that the time was right to renew our frame of reference and our vocabulary [. . .].'[74] No-one embodied that intellectual and strategic renewal more clearly than Yvan Blot, former president of the Club de l'Horloge and participant in GRECE, who occupied a succession of high-level posts within the civil service and government, notably under Interior Minister Poniatowski and the secretary-general of the neo-Gaullist RPR, Alain Devaquet.[75] Co-founder with Blot of the Club de l'Horloge and a high-ranking member of the PR, Jean-Yves Le Gallou similarly served as an intermediary between the Nouvelle Droite and the centres of political decision-making. While the Club de l'Horloge thus fostered close links with the governing centre-right, seeking to place its members as aides to senior officials, leaders of GRECE, by contrast, remained anxious to stress their intellectual vocation above their political velleities. In an article in *Le Monde* of 24 March 1981, the then secretary-general of GRECE, Pierre Vial, voiced concern that the movement's ideas had been appropriated by the Giscard administration. Vial insisted that the purpose of GRECE was not 'to become in even the remotest sense the ideological laboratory of a political majority'. He further insisted, in *Le Monde* of 28 July 1981, that the Nouvelle Droite and GRECE would not serve as an 'intellectual laboratory for any political operation whatsoever'.

As the influence of the Nouvelle Droite waxed in the late 1970s, so it would wane in the 1980s. The victory of the Socialists in the 1981 presidential and legislative elections represented for the Nouvelle Droite the transition from cultural to political power on the left, and confirmed the cultural and political bankruptcy of the traditional right. The subsequent dilution by the governing Socialists of much of their earlier egalitarianism and social liberalism would remove major arguments against the left from the arsenal of the Nouvelle Droite. Even that popular audience which it had secured would disappear in 1981 when GRECE lost its foothold in *Le Figaro-Magazine*, where its neo-paganism had strained the bounds of the magazine's largely conservative Catholic readership. The rejection by GRECE of liberal economics in a period when neo-liberalism flourished further consigned it to the ideological margins. The electoral successes of the FN from 1983 onwards also refocused public attention away from an esoteric intellectual movement to a noisily prominent political party – which Blot, Le Gallou, Vial and others would eventually elect to join.

Renewing 'revolutionary nationalism': Ordre Nouveau

If GRECE served as a genteel forum for the intellectual, it provided nothing by way of an outlet for the activist. The dissolution of Occident in late 1968 did not leave the extreme right bereft of activist groups. The usual proliferation of self-styled neo-Nazi, neo-fascist and ultra-nationalist movements persisted in the form of Marc Frédriksen's Fédération d'Action Nationale et Européenne (FANE), Jean-Gilles Malliarakis's Action Nationaliste, Pierre Sergent's MJR, Patrick Saint-Bertais' Pour une Jeune Europe (JE), Roger Holeindre's Jeunesses Patriotes et Sociales (JPS) and Parti National Populaire (PNP), and many others. Most of these propagated a form of 'third way' radicalism – 'Neither Marx, nor Coca-Cola, Revolution!', 'Neither banks, nor Soviets, the people!', and other variations on this theme. They were characterised by their ideological sterility, their failure to recruit significant support, and their often intense rivalry.[76]

Among such groups, Pierre Sidos's L'Œuvre Française came closest to repli-cating the crudest ideas of Jeune Nation and Occident, in both of which Sidos had played a leading role.[77] Through its organ *Le Soleil*, L'Œuvre Française proclaimed its opposition to 'Washington, Moscow and Tel-Aviv', locating itself 'at the cutting edge of the nationalist struggle, and of anti-Zionist and anti-Marxist action within the French nation'. It was pointedly anti-Semitic and authoritarian, counting Drumont, Maurras, Brasillach, Drieu La Rochelle and Bardèche among its ideological reference points and Franco, Salazar and Pétain among its political models. In a climate of increasing hostility towards North African immigrants in France, L'Œuvre Française called for 'a halt to the exces-sive number of unassimilable immigrants', the 'automatic return to their countries of origin of unemployed and sick' immigrant workers, and 'stricter controls on naturalisation in order to preserve the homogeneity of the French community'. Here, in essence, were the ideas that would bring the FN to promi-nence a decade and a half later. L'Œuvre Française also anticipated the FN in its slogan '*La France aux Français*' ('France for the French'), which it daubed on walls alongside Sidos's trademark Celtic cross.[78]

Sidos's time as a major player on the extreme right had passed, however, and his movement attracted few militants and little support, especially among the younger generation. Following de Gaulle's resignation in April 1969, Sidos sought to stand as a nationalist and anti-Zionist candidate in the presidential election of June. Unable to secure the 100 signatures of elected officials required by the Constitutional Council, he failed to get his candidacy off the ground – a failure which Sidos blamed on discrimination by Jewish members of the Council.[79] The second round of the 1969 presidential election saw de Gaulle's former Prime Minister, Georges Pompidou, beat the centre-right candidate, Alain Poher, with most extreme-right support going to the Gaullist candidate as the lesser of two evils.[80] Though the failure by Sidos to mount even a token chal-lenge underlined the marginality in the late 1960s of a movement still campaigning on behalf of Vichy and *Algérie Française*, L'Œuvre Française nonetheless pointed the way to the increased emphasis which extreme-right groups would come to place on immigration as a mobilising cause.

The role of filling the void left by Occident fell not to Sidos's L'Œuvre Française but to a movement described by one political historian as 'the most important, the most dynamic and the most dangerous neo-fascist movement in post-war France'.[81] Ordre Nouveau (New Order) was formed in November 1969

from the core of the old Occident, splinters from existing revolutionary nationalist groups, and yet other groups which agreed to be absorbed intact into the
new movement. The most important of these was the Groupe Union Droit
(GUD), a radical right-wing student organisation under the former FEN and
Occident leader, Alain Robert. The GUD (which would soon change its name to
the Groupe d'Union et de Défense, or Groupe Union Défense) continued
Occident's fight 'against Marxist contamination' and 'against decrepit institutions'. It preserved much of Occident's violent ethos too, engaging in running
battles with left-wing groups on university campuses (especially Nanterre and
Assas, whose law faculty became a relative stronghold of the extreme right).
Without relinquishing its own identity, the GUD served as one of the founding
components of Ordre Nouveau, providing the new movement with a ready
reserve of committed activists.

Ordre Nouveau came into being as a result of discussions among a number of
prominent figures on the extreme right, notably the former Poujadist and
Tixierist militant Jean-François Galvaire, the leader of the GUD, Alain Robert,
the former leading members of Occident, Philippe Asselin and François Duprat,
and the former Milicien and editor of *Minute*, François Brigneau. Another ex-
Milicien, Henri Charbonneau, and the former Cagoulard and Pétainist
journalist, Gabriel Jeantet, would act as mentors and serve on the new movement's national council, while the LVF veteran Pierre Clémenti also joined.[82]
Like its predecessors Europe-Action and Occident, Ordre Nouveau thus brought
together a younger generation of right-wing radicals with former collaborationists, Vichyites and OAS veterans. In their common analysis of the failure by
previous and existing extreme-right movements to make a significant impact on
the French political landscape, the founding members of Ordre Nouveau
focused on some familiar causes: 'the total absence of a large, organised, determined, revolutionary nationalist force', and the 'incredible dispersion' of the
nationalist right into so many 'small sectarian groups, scattered, isolated and
completely cut off from reality, consumed by sectarian quarrels where personal
issues and petty resentments count for more than political action'. Attempts to
forge a common ideology, they concluded, had foundered not on major disagree-
ments but 'generally on the smallest of details, and on a preference for division
over unity'.[83]

Such was the problem that Ordre Nouveau was formed to resolve. The idea –
an old one in new guise – was to unite the diverse forces of the far right within a
broad-based 'front' that would lay the foundations for 'a large party, like the
Italian MSI which we are already adopting as our model'.[84] In order to move
beyond the narrow confines of its predecessors and attract 'majority rather than
minority' support, it was essential that Ordre Nouveau should stress its newness
and – here was the innovation – 'abandon all reference to the past'. While recognising its debt to past 'nationalist experiments', it sought to mark itself apart not
just from the 'living fossils' of Nazism and 'diverse sects' of monarchism, but also
from 'the over-simplification of Jeune Nation, the pseudo-philosophical delirium
of Europe-Action, and the unbridled activism of Occident'.[85]

The movement was formally registered with the authorities in Paris in December 1969 under the elaborate name of the Centre de Recherche et de Documentation pour l'Avènement d'un Ordre Nouveau dans les Domaines Social, Economique et Culturel (Research and Documentation Centre for the Advent of a New Order in the Social, Economic and Cultural Spheres). It was initially led by the lawyer Jean-François Galvaire, closely assisted by Alain Robert and a number of other former Occident leaders. It was launched with the aid of an extensive propaganda campaign in which, according to French intelligence services, some 40,000 posters and 150,000 tracts were commissioned for distribution within the Paris region alone. The new movement's call to arms was unambiguous: 'France, wake up! Against Marxism, against the regime, join the fight for a new order.'[86]

Ordre Nouveau's first projected meeting of December 1969 had to be cancelled when a bomb exploded on the premises beforehand; the second, scheduled for February 1970, was banned due to the movement's violent activism and the furore caused by the planned participation of neo-fascist groups from other European countries. The launch was finally achieved at a rally in Paris on 13 May 1970 followed by the movement's constituent congress the next day.[87] The rally of 13 May was attended by some 3,000 people who heard diverse speakers endorse the new strategy of unity on the nationalist right. Reports of the meeting recorded fascist salutes among the audience, cries of 'France for the French!', calls for the philosopher Jean-Paul Sartre to be shot, booing at the mention of de Gaulle and applause at the names of Pétain, Brasillach, Darnand, Céline and other heroes of the extreme right. The addresses from the podium were scarcely more restrained. Bardèche was invoked as a spiritual authority in the fight against 'filthy democraps' (*démocrasouillerie*) and 'cankerous reds'. While Brigneau called for 'a revolutionary party white as our race, red as our blood and green as our hope', Galvaire asserted that, in 'cleansing' France of left-wing 'rabble', 'accounts will have to be settled and execution posts perhaps erected'.[88]

So much for the resolution to cut a new, more acceptable image. The impression created by this inaugural meeting caused concern to one of Ordre Nouveau's leading strategists, François Duprat, who wrote a critical account of the proceedings in the movement's internal bulletin. The terms of Duprat's criticism showed a lucid apprehension of the extent to which the new movement was already at risk of compromising its objective to attract mainstream support: 'Most of the speeches were certainly much too focused on the past. It may not have been useful to devote forty minutes to those martyred in the purges of 1945, or to rehearsing the history of exceptional court proceedings in 1962. But there were more serious problems than this: some of the verbal excesses, some of the incitations to violence, and even to murder, were unhelpful if not dangerous.'[89]

Such self-censure was rare. From the outset, Ordre Nouveau courted controversy by proclaiming its affinity with other extreme-right movements in Europe such as the Italian MSI and the German NPD. It espoused a form of

Europeanist nationalism which it called 'neo-patriotism', since 'the *patrie* of tomorrow is Western Europe'. In this spirit, it called for the creation of 'a new *patrie* stretching from the Atlantic to the marches of the East' as 'the rampart against Bolshevism'.[90] There was nothing here that had not been wished for two decades before at the Malmö conference hosted by Per Engdahl in 1951, which had seen the launch of the 'Eurofascist' MSE. Significantly, Engdahl was among the foreign representatives present at Ordre Nouveau's launch, along with Massimo Anderson of the MSI, which was thought to have provided financial support and which made some of its poster designs available for use by the new French movement.[91]

What passed for an ideology with Ordre Nouveau was a strident discourse of anti-liberalism, anti-capitalism and anti-Marxism. More comfortable with invective than with intellectual debate, it stood on a rudimentary, catch-all programme.[92] It advocated French nationalism and European unity, state intervention and private initiative, industrial development and protection of the peasantry, commercial modernisation and the defence of small shopkeepers and artisans. The very incoherence of this programme, however, was consistent with Ordre Nouveau's resolve to move beyond the narrow, backward-looking issues that had proved so sterile for its predecessors and to seek to maximise its popular appeal.

Following Galvaire's early resignation as head of the movement, Ordre Nouveau was run by a national council of 45 members and a political bureau of 10, including Brigneau, Duprat and Robert. This was soon reduced to a troika of Robert, Duprat and José Bruneau de la Salle. At its height, the movement claimed a membership of around 5,000, concentrated mainly in Paris, with sections in university towns such as Bordeaux, Toulouse, Lille and Lyon, and in the Mediterranean towns of Aix-en-Provence, Nice and Montpellier.[93] It also continued to forge links with kindred movements in other European countries, notably the Italian MSI, the German Aktion Neue Rechte, and the Belgian Ordre Nouveau.

According to an internal survey conducted in June 1970, some two-thirds of Ordre Nouveau's members were university students or lycée pupils aged in the main between 18 and 25. Though the absence of independent verification makes this survey subject to caution, it indicated that almost two-thirds of members came to Ordre Nouveau with no previous political affiliation, again suggesting the youthfulness of the movement's support base.[94] In its political charter, Ordre Nouveau evoked 'the dawn of a new world and a new order'. It looked forward to a 'revolution' in which it would 'take power with the support of the people' and bring about 'the necessary defeat of Marxism'. It rejected violence, though in practice this would become the hallmark of Ordre Nouveau as it had been that of Occident. Most significantly, the new movement committed itself to 'the spread of nationalist ideas through permanent participation in political struggle, including participation where possible in electoral contests'; and it borrowed from the Nouvelle Droite the idea of preparing the ground for political success by infiltrating diverse socio-professional milieux.[95] In the first public appearance of

Ordre Nouveau at a press conference in March 1970, Galvaire proclaimed the movement's intention to 'manoeuvre itself gradually into a position of power' by playing 'the game of parliamentary democracy'.[96]

This clear statement of Ordre Nouveau's electoralist vocation was borne out when it fielded candidates in parliamentary by-elections in Paris and Bordeaux in June and September 1970. It won just over 3 per cent of the vote in the 12th *arrondissement* of Paris and 0.5 per cent in Bordeaux. In March 1971, it entered lists of candidates for the municipal elections, notably in Paris, where it won 2.6 per cent of the ballot (19,529 votes). In Lille, a nationalist coalition with the participation of Ordre Nouveau polled 2.2 per cent, while in Calais a 'National Opposition' list headed by Ordre Nouveau won 22 per cent of the vote in a three-way contest with the combined left and the Gaullist right.[97] With the exception of this aberrational result, due to specific local circumstances, the performance of Ordre Nouveau in these elections made Tixier-Vignancour's national score of 5.2 per cent in the 1965 presidential election seem like a resounding triumph.

Ordre Nouveau combined electoral campaigning with thuggish intimidation. Its hard-core militants dressed in combat fatigues, boots and crash helmets, often marked with the Celtic cross, and carried iron bars and shields as standard 'equipment'. Anticipating one of the FN's favoured themes, it called for stronger law and order measures to ensure the security of citizens – in the absence of which it proposed the organisation of self-defence groups 'wherever safety is not assured'.[98] The huge output of tracts and posters in support of the municipal election campaign raised questions over the movement's funding, to which sympathetic parties and regimes abroad were suspected of contributing. It attracted an audience of some 4,000 to its pre-election rally in Paris on 9 March 1971. They heard Brigneau denounce the 'Algerian invasion' of France and urge the destruction of the 'red beast with the golden calf's head', while Duprat (who had criticised the intemperate language used at the movement's inaugural meeting) called for the country to be 'cleansed of all the low life infesting it' and for the 'return of France to the French'.[99]

The rally was policed by an ostentatiously paramilitary security presence drawn largely from the movement's GUD component. It provoked violent clashes between left-wing protesters and the police. Like its predecessor Occident, Ordre Nouveau enjoyed for a time the indulgence – even, it was alleged, the complicity – of the security services, more exercised in the wake of May 1968 with the threat from radical left-wing groups. Prompted by public concern over Ordre Nouveau's aggressive self-styling, however, a police raid on the movement's headquarters on the eve of the municipal elections uncovered *inter alia* a double-barrel shotgun, some 400 iron bars and 40 wooden shields.[100]

As it prepared for its second national congress in June 1972, Ordre Nouveau published a survey of its membership which (though again subject to caution) appeared broadly to confirm the findings of that cited earlier. The 3,200 members which the survey claimed to cover were predominantly male, aged under 30, and students; the movement attracted some support among salaried employees but almost none among workers or shopkeepers.[101] In an attempt to extend its support base, Ordre Nouveau launched a number of ancillary associations such as the Union de Défense des Lycéens (Union for the Defence of Lycée Pupils, UDL) and the Union Générale des Travailleurs (General Union of Workers, UGT).[102] Though this pseudo-trade union failed to get off the ground, it showed a concern to harness working-class support that would be taken up later and assiduously pursued by the FN. In addition to its monthly publication *Pour un Ordre nouveau*, the movement published a weekly *Ordre nouveau*, a monthly *GUD-Occident université*, a monthly *Jeune Ordre* targeting lycée pupils, and *Travail-Informations* for the workers it sought to attract. This audience-specific approach to disseminating its message was a tactic that would also be embraced by the later FN. Again like its successor, Ordre Nouveau made capital of whatever issues presented themselves. It denounced political corruption, lax morality and mounting criminality. It agitated against the visit to France in October 1971 by the Soviet leader, Leonid Brezhnev, and against disengagement from Vietnam.[103] It soon became clear, however, that it could achieve little as a noisy protest movement more given to violence than to political debate. The need to transform itself into a political party capable of mounting a meaningful challenge in the legislative elections of March 1973 was the theme which dominated the second national congress of Ordre Nouveau in June 1972.

Towards a 'national front'

The June 1972 supplement to the movement's organ, *Pour un Ordre nouveau*, articulated the ambition to become a 'properly organised party' and to employ for the 1973 elections the 'strategy of a national front'. This was motivated not by a genuine conversion to liberal democracy but by the calculation that 'electoral representation allows a revolutionary movement to be infinitely more hard-line since the risks of being dissolved are so much less'. Participation in elections, reasoned the leaders of Ordre Nouveau, would enable the movement to measure its support base, to disseminate its ideas and to build up more solid militant structures at the local level. It would oblige the nationalist right to pull together and to elaborate a more coherent ideology. The 'vast national front' envisaged for the elections of March 1973 would bring together 'the national opposition in its entirety', including those 'nationalist elements cast adrift by the banning of their organisations'. Only once it had attained a foothold through the democratic process would 'all methods' be used to bring about the 'popular nationalist revolution' which remained the openly avowed objective of Ordre Nouveau. This would require 'the overthrow of a decadent regime and its lackeys, and the complete transformation of a society collapsed under the weight of its failings and vices'.[104]

The strategy of a 'national front' which would play 'the card of order and security' and campaign with 'respect for the justice system and rule of law' was, then, a means to an end only. It was put to delegates at the June 1972 congress on the proviso that it would not compromise in any way the 'fundamental ideas' of Ordre Nouveau.[105] The new strategy, it was proposed, should be accompanied by a readiness on the part of the movement to open itself up to support from the mainstream right; this was an argument inspired largely by the MSI's constitution of a 'Destra Nazionale' incorporating diverse (nationalist, monarchist, ultra-conservative) tendencies on the Italian right. The success of Giorgio Almirante's party with its right-wing allies in the Italian elections of May 1972 (8.7 per cent and 56 seats in the Chamber of Deputies, with almost three million votes) proved that such a strategy could pay handsome dividends.

The resolution to emulate the MSI-Destra Nazionale and appeal to a broader right-wing constituency was approved by Ordre Nouveau delegates on a vote of 224 to 52, with eight abstentions. Many of those (GUD militants in particular) who voted against it would leave the movement to join the Groupe Action Jeunesse (Youth Action Group, GAJ) under Jean-Claude Nourry and Patrice Janeau. Other factions such as Pour une Jeune Europe (JE) had already left, accusing Ordre Nouveau of complicity with the regime and its 'bourgeois democracy'.[106] With internal dissidence removed (for the time being at least), the way was clear for the formation of a 'national front' in which Ordre Nouveau reserved for itself the dominant role as 'a centre of united and effective leadership'. There would be no place, it was stressed, for 'pseudo-notables' such as Tixier-Vignancour in a movement whose declared objective was 'the total destruction of the *ancien régime* and the establishment of an entirely new Order'.[107]

With the formation of the Front National in October 1972, a new era in the history of the extreme right in post-war France was inaugurated. In the quarter-century since the trial of Pétain, extreme-right hopes and aspirations had been embodied at different times by very different groups: in the immediate post-war years, by residual Vichyites and Nazi sympathisers; in the mid-1950s, by the lower middle-class categories of *petits commerçants* and artisans; in the late 1950s and early 1960s, by the army and *pieds-noirs*; and in the mid- to late 1960s, by politically radicalised components of the student body. The failure to cultivate a broad base of support that was not contingent on the vagaries of political circumstance had been compounded by the further failure to elaborate a common ideology or agree upon a common strategy. By the early 1970s, there were no fewer than four quite distinct strategies at work on the far right in France: that of Tixier-Vignancour's ARLP, with its attempt to throw off the trappings of extremism and become a respectable part of the mainstream right (an approach also espoused by some individuals such as Alain Madelin, Patrick Devedjian and Gérard Longuet); that of revolutionary nationalist movements implacably wedded to the fight against Marxism through the bomb rather than the ballot box (with some publications even offering instructions on the preparation of home-made explosives); that of Ordre Nouveau, with its incongruous blend of violent activism and electioneering; and that of the Nouvelle Droite, with its eschewal of activism and electoralism both in favour of a metapolitical strategy of cultural infiltration.[108]

It was from the latter two that the FN would draw most of its ideological and strategic impetus. While there was less innovation about the Nouvelle Droite and Ordre Nouveau than their names suggested, they represented separately what the FN would seek to combine: ideological renewal and electoral engagement. If this strategy failed to yield any but the most meagre results in the 1970s, it would be vindicated by the unprecedented success which the party would begin to enjoy in the 1980s.

Part II

Political legitimation and the fruits of electoralism

7 Engaging with democracy
The Front National 1972–81

Strategy

'The Front National will be our opportunity to emerge from the ghetto.' With this buoyant prediction, Ordre Nouveau heralded the formation of the FN in autumn 1972.[1] For some, it was an initiative long overdue. In a special issue of *Défense de l'Occident* published two years before, Maurice Bardèche had delivered an unsparing verdict on the perpetual tendency of the French extreme right towards division and the *groupuscule* culture. Among neo-fascists, Maurrassians, Catholic fundamentalists and a host of others, he charged, the only common denominators were negative: 'anti-communism, anti-Gaullism. There is no understanding between them, and the words they use – revolution, counter-revolution, nationalism, Europe – have different meanings for them.' While the desired end was the creation of a 'large national party', Bardèche caustically observed, the only achievement so far had been the proliferation of ineffectual sects.[2]

The FN was conceived as the solution to this endemic problem. Its originality lay in its new orientation, its ambition to be a modern, forward-looking parliamentary party with a respectable public face and a message calculated to appeal to a wide audience. It brought together in its first phase Ordre Nouveau, Le Pen's nationalist coterie, Roger Holeindre's Parti de l'Unité Française, those grouped around the periodical *Militant* under Pierre Bousquet and Pierre Pauty, some monarchists, Georges Bidault's Justice et Liberté movement, and others. The new party – officially the Front National pour l'Unité Française (National Front for French Unity, FNUF) – was formally launched in Paris on 5 October 1972. Within a week, it suffered its first split as Bidault withdrew his movement, seeing the 'tough nuts' of Ordre Nouveau as an obstacle to nurturing a genuinely electoralist vocation.[3]

In keeping with its emulation of the Italian MSI, the FN adopted the latter's symbol of a tricolour flame, replacing the green with blue. At the outset, it was run by a political bureau of six, elected by a central committee of 30: Le Pen (president), François Brigneau (vice-president), Alain Robert (secretary-general), Roger Holeindre (deputy secretary-general), Pierre Bousquet (treasurer), and Pierre Durand (deputy treasurer). Though small, this group reflected a careful balancing of tendencies on the extreme right – or, as Brigneau would later recall, an 'uneasy marriage' between Le Pen's 'right-wing parliamentary current', Robert's 'revolutionary, pro-European activism', and his own 'counter-revolutionary, Maurrassian stance'.[4] A former Milicien and member of Marcel Déat's RNP, Brigneau was editor of *Minute* and a moving spirit behind Ordre Nouveau; Robert had been a leading figure in Occident, Ordre Nouveau and the GUD; Holeindre was a former resister, OAS veteran and colonialist agitator, founder of a United Front of Support for South Vietnam; Bousquet had been a member of Marcel Bucard's Parti Franciste, a Waffen-SS volunteer, and a militant in Jeune Nation and Europe-Action; Durand was a friend from Le Pen's student days who had been with him in the Poujadist movement, the Tixier-Vignancour campaign and even his commercial venture with the SERP. In his nomination as president, Le Pen enjoyed several advantages: aged 44, he was a former parliamentary deputy, a veteran of Indo-China and Algeria, a well-known militant nationalist and an able speaker. He was also, within the personnel of the extreme right, a relative moderate who could aspire to some degree of political respectability. The factor playing most strongly in Le Pen's favour, however, was a negative one: he was not associated closely enough with any single faction to preclude the unifying leadership which the new movement required.

Against the backdrop of May 1968 and the signing in June 1972 of the Common Programme between the French Socialist and Communist parties, the call for a coherent challenge to the left was given added urgency. The FN stressed from the outset that it was a party of the right, the same 'social, popular and national right' of which Jeune Nation had proclaimed itself the standard-bearer in 1958. This distinguished the FN from other supposedly right-wing parties which, Le Pen protested, had for 15 years 'used the votes of the right to implement the politics of the left'.[5] Financial scandals implicating members of the centre-right majority (not least the Gaullist Prime Minister, Jacques Chaban-Delmas) also brought political corruption to the fore as a charge against the incumbent administration under Gaullist President Georges Pompidou. The FN's earliest slogans, redolent of the 1930s and framing the stage at its first public meeting on 7 November 1972, were 'Let's stop the Popular Front in its tracks' and 'Let's drive the thieves from power'. The central slogan, in giant letters behind Le Pen and the other members of the political bureau, exhorted 'With us, before it's too late!'[6] This rallying cry gave a foretaste of the politics of fear that the FN would make its own. Its main concerns, as expressed in this initial meeting, were the perceived influence of Marxism in the broadcast media and education, and the loss of esteem for 'family', 'army', 'flag' and 'country'.[7]

Much as Dominique Venner had reasoned a decade before, it was acknowledged that the Fifth Republic could not be overthrown by direct revolution; but if support could be recruited among professionals, farmers, shopkeepers and other interest groups, the democratic system might be used to bring down the regime. The purpose of the FN, therefore, was to create a groundswell of public opinion favourable to the nationalist cause, 'widening the scope of nationalist struggle by opening out as broadly as possible'.[8] The new federative structure within which they were called upon to cooperate would mean that members must 'overcome their sectarian quarrels and stop seeking to outdo one another in "revolutionary purity"'.[9] This went to the heart of the problem that had bedevilled extreme-right movements throughout the preceding decades – in Philip Williams' words, their 'mania for division' and 'reactionary sectarianism' which 'closely resembled revolutionary sectarianism in its demand for orthodox purity'.[10] Now, the need for pragmatic compromise over absolutism was seen to be paramount. Ordre Nouveau was moved to redefine for its own membership the very idea of what it was to be a revolutionary political force: 'To be revolutionary is certainly not to live with helmet and boots on, ready to take up arms against our adversaries. [. . .] No, to be revolutionary is to wish to see our ideas come to fruition by what-ever means, provided they ultimately bring about the new social and political order that is the purpose of our fight.'[11]

At the first public meeting of the FN in November 1972, the helmets, weapons and Celtic cross that had been hallmarks of Ordre Nouveau meetings were conspicuous by their absence. Instead, as a journalist from *Le Monde* noted, the meeting was marked by 'a discreet security service, an older audience too, and more accomplished speakers'. The new party, the same observer concluded, was clearly being 'careful to dissociate itself from an image that might disconcert the voting public'.[12] The commitment to this strategy was underlined by Le Pen in an interview on national radio the following month, when he confirmed the presence of Ordre Nouveau as a component of the FN but insisted on the party's rejection of 'violence and the use of methods which I condemn'.[13]

Electoral and political evolution

The 1973 legislative elections

The FN was formed with the express purpose of contesting the legislative elec-tions of March 1973. The result was, in René Chiroux's observation, an 'electoral disaster for the extreme right'.[14] Having set an initial target of 400 candidates for the 490 seats at stake, the new party managed to register only 104, most of them Ordre Nouveau activists.[15] It attracted 108,616 votes, less than 0.5 per cent of the national vote and 1.32 per cent in the constituencies which it contested. Only Le Pen, standing in the 14th *arrondissement* of Paris, exceeded (by a fraction) 5 per cent. His party was outpolled by a breakaway movement from Tixier-Vignancour's ARLP, the Union pour la Majorité Présidentielle (Union for the Presidential Majority, UMP) headed by Jean Barbet, which won 1.59 per cent of the ballot (130,837 votes) in the constituencies where it presented candi-dates. Together with several smaller groups contesting this election, the FN and UMP registered a combined first-round score for the far right of just over a quarter of a million votes.

The FN suffered in this election from its rawness as a party, fielding many candidates with no electoral experience or personal standing in their constituen-cies. It was also squeezed by calls from the centre-right for a tactical vote against the Common Programme of the left. With no prospect of winning seats, Le Pen approached the election as he would approach so many elections thereafter, intent on maximising the FN's influence between the two rounds. Prior to the election, he had declared that his party's objective was to 'bring down communism, bring down the [Gaullist] UDR, and bring down the majority'; in the event, however, he called simply for 'the communists to be blocked at all cost'.[16]

Electoral programme

Despite its poor showing, these elections gave the FN an opportunity to publicise its policies through the allotted seven minutes of radio and television airtime. Those policies were developed more fully in the party's official programme, *Défendre les Français* (*Defending the French*).[17] Here the FN declared France to be in a crisis that was 'less economic and social than moral and political'. With memories of May 1968 still fresh, it denounced contemporary youth culture as 'rotting' under the influence of 'leftism', 'hippiness' and 'drugs'. It identified 'intellectual, moral and physical decadence' as the major evils threatening the individual, the family and the nation; it called for moral regeneration, with the restoration of discipline and sports education in schools; and it warned that the communists were 'at the gates of power'.

The importance of not appearing to be a single-issue party was evident to those who drew up this first electoral programme of the FN. The party defined its primary political objective as 'the defence of the French against foreign designs, subversive activities, class-based selfishness, and oligarchic dictatorship'. It called for a 'truly presidential regime' giving primacy to the executive, with a directly elected President and a National Assembly elected by (regional) proportional representation to act as a check on presidential power. It proposed a 'plural vote' for heads of families with three or more children, and a 'special complementary allowance' for mothers of children under the age of two giving up paid work to devote themselves to child-rearing; the same mothers should later enjoy a 'preferential right to re-employment'. (Though it could clearly be assumed that the mothers in question should be French citizens, the FN did not see the need here to specify this.) Denouncing the politicisation of public services, the programme called for 'political neutrality' in education and the broadcast media, and for an end to 'leftist subversion and corruptive teachers' in schools (through scrapping the 1968 Faure Law which had sought to democratise education at all levels). State education should be secular, though parents should remain free to secure privately for their children a religious education if they so chose.

The FN rejected free-market capitalism as 'an excessive concentration of economic power and profit in the hands of a few large financial groups representing only the interests of a narrow oligarchy'; it also rejected communism as 'a systematic levelling down with punitive effects on work, innovation and savings, bringing economic growth to an inevitable halt'. It outlined an essentially corporatist conception of the economy and labour relations, advocating that organised interest groups should be given 'direct and joint responsibilities' to resolve their common problems. Conflicts between capital and labour would be avoided through the empowerment of 'responsible social partners' (employers' and workers' unions, consumers' associations, a 'collective services corporation'), with the state acting as 'arbiter' to maintain the 'balance of social relations' and 'correct the excesses as required' of employers and employees. The FN declared strong support for the socio-professional groups whom Poujade had championed in the 1950s (shopkeepers, artisans, peasants) against punitive competition and 'those obsessed with expansion'. The lowest wages, it argued, should be raised, taxation rationalised, and savings and investment encouraged. The programme called for antitrust legislation and for the lightening of fiscal and administrative burdens on small and medium-sized business. Among other groups given preferential mention were the police, army veterans and former prisoners of war.

In the most overt reference to its political lineage, the FN called for the renegotiation of the Evian Agreements, an amnesty for offences committed in defence of French Algeria, and full compensation for *rapatriés*. During the campaign, Le Pen also called for a 'gesture of reconciliation' which would allow the transfer of Pétain's remains to Douaumont, as demanded by those seeking to rehabilitate the Marshal's memory.[18] Despite these references, what was most striking in the 1973 programme was its relative moderation. There was no talk of ending the Fifth Republic, let alone democracy. The FN did not strike a posture of isolationist nationalism but called for France to pool its defensive capabilities within a 'European confederation', cooperating on nuclear defence with Britain and the United States. It argued for an end to obligatory national service and the switch to a modern professional army. For a party that would later excoriate President Giscard d'Estaing's Health Minister, Simone Veil, for her legalisation of abortion (a 'genocide of French infants' by a Jew),[19] the FN in 1973 showed surprising indulgence on this issue. It rejected abortion on demand but proposed that a 'socio-medical commission' be set up to determine those cases where it might be appropriate.

More surprising still for today's reader is the restrained reference to immigration, evoked in terms that anticipate only remotely the FN's later focus on this issue. In 1973, the great enemy for the extreme right was still communism, not yet immigration. In its political charter of 1970, Ordre Nouveau had defined the goal of the 'nationalist struggle' as the 'essential defeat of Marxism', without even a passing reference to immigration.[20] Under the heading 'Defence of National Unity', the FN retained this anti-Marxist animus in its programme, declaring French citizenship to be 'incompatible with political subjection to a foreign regime' and demanding 'strict control over the political and economic influence of foreign powers' in French public life. In its only direct references to immigration, it called for an end to 'uncontrolled immigration, which occurs in material and moral conditions that are disastrous for those concerned and a dishonour to our country', and warned of 'the existence of veritable districts or towns of foreigners in France, with its disruptive and destabilising effect on the unity and solidarity of our people'. Outlining measures to increase the birth rate, the FN lamented that, 'due to the insufficiency of its national workforce, France is increasingly obliged to call on foreign workers whose native culture does not allow them to integrate into French society'.

Here the FN did little more than rehearse the conclusions of a government-sanctioned report, published in 1969, distinguishing between 'easily assimilable' (European) and 'unassimilable' (principally North African) immigrants.[21] The party had not yet coined the crude equation between immigration and unemployment that economic recession would later allow it to exploit. In a letter to the newspaper *Le Monde* in February 1973, Le Pen recognised a 'real need' for immigrant workers, but argued that they should be subject to 'quantitative and qualitative controls' – 'especially those of non-European origin' – in order to 'protect French workers and the dignity of foreign workers'.[22] Here again Le Pen merely echoed the terms of the above report, which had advocated 'a strictly selective immigration policy' adapted to 'the real needs of the labour market' and attentive to 'the changes over recent years in the provenance of immigrants, the difficulties of welcoming and housing them, and the evolution of the job situation in France'.[23]

Such was the relative moderation of the first FN programme that René Chiroux could find nothing in essence to distinguish it from that of the mainstream right.[24] One did not have to look far, however, to find a harder edge to the FN's discourse. In its monthly *Front National*, it warned against immigration in more familiar terms:

> It is intolerable that our country should have become a dumping ground for good-for-nothings, degenerates, delinquents and criminals. It is intolerable that insecurity should reign in so many districts where shopkeepers live in fear, where attacks are a daily occurrence, where it is dangerous for a woman to go out alone at night. It is also intolerable that our social services and health care should be wasted on undesirables. To these mounting perils there is only one solution: rigorous control at the borders of would-be immigrants, who should undergo a triple examination – sanitary, professional and judicial.

Once admitted, declared the same publication, immigrants who infringed the 'rules of hospitality' should be subject to a simple sanction: 'immediate expulsion by administrative procedure'.[25]

Scission and reconstitution

Electoral failure had an immediate impact on the new party. It exacerbated tensions between the Le Pen camp, with its commitment to electoralism, and more radical elements in Ordre Nouveau. Within Ordre Nouveau, it sharpened divisions between supporters and opponents of the 'frontist' strategy. At the FN's national congress in April 1973, Le Pen warned against crude activism and urged that the party 'convey its political message through dispassionate language in order to win over the unpoliticised masses'. He warned too against 'sectarian divisions' within the FN and argued for 'total fusion' of the party's diverse currents as the way forward.[26]

Le Pen's calls for restraint and union did not persuade the hard core of Ordre Nouveau. Following its own third national congress in June 1973, the movement determined to revert to a more robust activism. Seizing on what it considered an under-exploited issue, it inveighed against immigration as the 'massive importation of this sub-proletariat', useful politically to the left and economically to the right.[27] It organised a meeting in Paris on 21 June 1973 demanding 'an end to uncontrolled immigration'. The event degenerated into a pitched battle between Ordre Nouveau's security service and members of the Ligue Communiste. Police vehicles were burned and more than 50 police officers were injured in the fighting.[28]

This event prompted the Interior Minister, Raymond Marcellin, to ban both Ordre Nouveau and the Ligue Communiste. The banning order on Ordre Nouveau recorded that a search of the movement's headquarters the day after the riot had yielded a substantial cache of weapons, including '24 pickaxe handles, 41 iron bars and 31 sharpened bamboo poles'.[29] The banning of Ordre Nouveau brought to a head the divisions within the FN, allowing Le Pen to wrest control of the movement from its most important but most unruly faction. Robert and Brigneau were replaced, as secretary-general and vice-president, by Victor Barthélemy and the Le Pen loyalist Dominique Chaboche, who had served his political apprenticeship under Poujade and Tixier-Vignancour. The final act of the split was played out in the courts, where Le Pen won exclusive rights to the party's assets and name, which Robert and Brigneau had sought to use for their new rival movement, Faire Front (Front Up).

This breakaway movement took up where the old Ordre Nouveau had left off, resorting to what *Le Monde* described as 'fighting', 'commando operations' and 'racist attacks'.[30] Iron bars, Molotov cocktails and the Celtic cross became once again part of their political discourse as Faire Front activists sought to draw attention to themselves as the spearhead of radical nationalism. They attacked Socialist and Communist party headquarters, expressed support for Pinochet's military coup in Chile, and called for a united Europe of nationalist states and the defence of 'Western civilisation'. Faire Front also campaigned vigorously against immigration, specifically 'the proliferation of Arabs in France'. Anticipating the FN's later calls for 'national preference', it urged that 'priority be given to French citizens ahead of foreigners' in employment and demanded the deportation of all illegal, unemployed and criminally convicted immigrants, and more generally of 'those who crowd our pavements and hospitals'.[31]

That there should thus be two 'national fronts' competing at a time when unity was the order of the day was symptomatic not only of the FN's difficult beginnings but of the endemic divisiveness of the extreme right. The rift with Faire Front cost the FN a number of its chief protagonists and much of its militant base, but it left Le Pen the uncontested leader of his rump party. This he now refashioned with the aid of two key figures. Born in 1906, Victor Barthélemy had been Doriot's right-hand man in organising the PPF and LVF, before going on to collaborate with Bardèche and Tixier-Vignancour in the 1950s and 1960s.[32] As secretary-general of the PPF, Barthélemy had been entrusted by Doriot in 1940 with the task of attempting to launch a single fascist party in cooperation with Marcel Déat and other collaborationist leaders. Some three decades later, he found himself called upon by Le Pen to reorganise the FN as a national party with a federative structure for which the PPF provided a remote model.[33] Born in 1941, François Duprat represented a younger genera- tion of right-wing radicals and was already a veteran of Jeune Nation, the FEN, Occident and Ordre Nouveau. Though they had been prominent players within Ordre Nouveau, he and his Groupes Nationalistes-Révolutionnaires (GNR) opted for the FN over Faire Front. Until his assassination by a car bomb in March 1978, Duprat would be the leading strategist of the emergent FN, providing much of its intellectual and propagandist energy. Like Le Pen, he was wedded to the 'frontist' strategy and viewed the attainment of electoral credi- bility as the only means of advancing their cause. Just as Ordre Nouveau had argued at the launch of the FN, Duprat insisted: 'The role of the true revolu- tionary is not to bring about the apocalypse that will destroy him, but to advance effectively the cause for which he is fighting. His first duty is to survive.'[34]

A glance at Duprat's political pedigree and writings confirms the cynicism of his electoralist posture. The 'revolutionary nationalism' which he propounded through numerous books, pamphlets and articles was neo-fascism by another name.[35] Duprat collaborated closely with Bardèche and contributed regularly to *Défense de l'Occident* and other fascist-leaning publications. He lauded the anti- Bolshevik crusade of the Waffen-SS, to which he devoted a book, and did much to propagate Holocaust revisionism in France. Well connected among neo-fascist circles in France and Europe, he brought within the FN's orbit most notably Marc Frédriksen's neo-Nazi FANE.[36]

Between 1974 and 1978, the GNR would succeed Ordre Nouveau as the most influential group within the FN, with Duprat's close associate, Alain Renault, becoming secretary-general in 1976. Given their heterogeneity, Duprat argued that the nationalist forces for which the FN served as rallying point should elaborate not so much a unitary ideology as a 'common programme' to rival that of the left. It should address the grievances of 'large sections of the population increasingly affected by the economic and social crisis gripping France'; in short, it should seek to become 'the receptacle of all discontent'.[37] The canvassing of support through democratic channels would be a means to an end only. The objective of Duprat and his 'revolutionary nationalists' remained unequivocal: 'to acquire in the end the necessary strength to bring down the regime and Marxism with it'.[38]

The 1974 presidential election

The death of Georges Pompidou in April 1974 precipitated a presidential elec- tion. As in 1965, the requirements for eligibility were 100 signatures from elected officials in at least 10 departments plus a deposit of 10,000 francs. Le Pen secured the requisite support and stood on the FN's 1973 programme 'to defend the French from the external threat of subversion'.[39]

Like his party in the 1973 legislative elections, however, Le Pen failed to find a mobilising theme. He railed against 'the weakness of the regime, impotent before the tide of decadence unleashed by the leftist intelligentsia (pornography, drugs, violence, delinquency, abortion, youth prostitution, the politicisation of lycées, the blurring of sexual difference etc.)'.[40] Gone was any suggestion of indulgence towards abortion, which Le Pen made one of the major issues of his campaign. He called for an increase in the French birth rate, a reduction in immigration, the establishment of a professional army, and the abrogation of the (now 12-year-old) Evian Agreements. Like Poujade before him, Le Pen presented himself as 'the standard-bearer for the silent and scorned majority'; with echoes too of Pétain, he offered himself to the French as a providential recourse, promoting a 'politics of public salvation [*salut public*] to stop the rot all around and bring about a French and European renaissance'.[41]

Despite being the only nationalist candidate (Pierre Sidos having failed again to muster the requisite signatures), Le Pen was unable to rally the combined forces of the far right. Robert and Brigneau withheld the support of Faire Front and the GUD, preferring the centre-right Valéry Giscard d'Estaing as the non-Gaullist candidate best placed to defeat the united left under François Mitterrand. Dismissing Le Pen's programme as 'absurd', Faire Front even provided a security service for Giscard's campaign meetings. The groups of Georges Bidault and Pierre Sergent, and the journal *Minute*, also supported Giscard. The monarchist vote split between the 'left-leaning monarchist' Bertrand Renouvin (supported by Nouvelle Action Française) and the hard-line conservative Jean Royer (supported by Restauration Nationale). Pierre Sidos's L'Œuvre Française and Catholic fundamentalist groups also declared support for Royer, as did some prominent individuals such as Jacques Isorni. Others, such as the Groupe Action Jeunesse, called for abstention. The Centre de Documentation Politique et Universitaire (Centre for Political and University Documentation, CDPU), a shadowy think-tank in the mould of Europe-Action and with GRECE-like pretensions, ridiculed Le Pen as a 'clownish political nonentity' and called likewise for abstention.[42]

With far-right support thus dispersed, Le Pen found few movements or publications – apart from *Rivarol* and Duprat's *Cahiers européens* – actively on his side. In the midst of the campaign, moreover, his past in Algeria returned to haunt him. The Ligue Communiste Révolutionnaire (LCR, successor to the banned Ligue Communiste), whose leader, Alain Krivine, was also a candidate, published in its organ *Rouge* a denunciation of Le Pen's alleged involvement in torture in Algeria. The affair cast an unsavoury light on the FN leader's faltering campaign, anticipating the much more highly publicised treatment which the same accusations would attract a decade later following the party's electoral breakthrough of 1984.

In the first round of the election on 5 May 1974, Le Pen recorded a derisory 0.75 per cent, the support of fewer than 200,000 voters (Table 7.1). Coming seventh out of 12 candidates, he was outdistanced by the extreme-left Arlette Laguiller and the ecologist René Dumont. Mitterrand (with 43.25 per cent) topped

Table 7.1 The 1974 presidential election: first round (metropolitan and overseas France)

	Votes cast	%
Mitterrand	11,044,373	43.25
Giscard d'Estaing	8,326,774	32.60
Chaban-Delmas	3,857,728	15.11
Royer	810,540	3.17
Laguiller	595,247	2.33
Dumont	337,800	1.32
Le Pen	190,921	0.75
Muller	176,279	0.69
Krivine	93,990	0.37
Renouvin	43,722	0.17
Sebag	42,007	0.16
Héraud	19,255	0.08

Source: Constitutional Council (La Documentation Française, *Institutions et vie politique sous la Ve République*, Paris, 2003, p. 177).

the poll ahead of Giscard (32.6 per cent) and Chaban-Delmas (just over 15 per cent), with Giscard going on to win by a narrow margin in the second round.

Le Pen exceeded 1 per cent in only eight departments, with support most marked in the south, along the Mediterranean littoral and in the Paris region. Even with such a low score, the map of the Le Pen vote fitted broadly that of the 'no' vote in the referendum of April 1962 on Algerian independence, and in places that of the vote for Tixier-Vignancour (who had exceeded 10 per cent in eight departments) in the 1965 presidential election.[43]

Frères-ennemis: *the FN and PFN*

Le Pen's performance was deemed a 'lamentable failure' by his erstwhile allies in Faire Front. In the run-up to the election, they had declared in their journal that the FN leader would win 'a tiny number of votes' and that it was 'therefore utterly useless to support him'.[44] To compound the FN's isolation, Faire Front now set about capitalising on having backed the eventual winner in Giscard d'Estaing. By the end of the year, it had transformed itself into the PFN under Alain Robert, François Brigneau, Jean-François Galvaire, José Bruneau de la Salle, the former Cagoulard Gabriel Jeantet, and Roland Gaucher (pseudonym of Roland Goguillot), who had been a leading member in the youth wing of Déat's RNP under the Occupation. They appointed as secretary-general Pascal

Gauchon, a young history lecturer chosen, at 25, to give the new party a fresh, modernising image. Its effort to cultivate respectability prompted *Le Monde* to report in June 1976 on the lack of aggression exhibited by the PFN compared to its predecessor, Ordre Nouveau.[45] The new party nonetheless retained something of the latter's activism, organising demonstrations against the fall of Saigon in May 1975 and the visit to France by Leonid Brezhnev in June 1977.[46]

Under Gauchon's leadership, the PFN would seek to build bridges with the centre-right majority in the hope of attracting broader right-wing support and insinuating itself as the fourth component of the right, alongside Gaullists, Giscardians and centrists. It sought to nurture relations first with the Giscardians, who kept their distance (except when strong-arm security was required) from a movement declaring itself 'equally opposed to outmoded liberalism and totalitarian Marxism'.[47] Giscard soon proved a disappointment in his failure to overturn the cultural ascendancy of the left or to impose the authority of the state over what the PFN saw as an unruly youth and a workforce too prone to striking. Some of his early liberalising reforms (on abortion notably, and family reunion for immigrants) also alienated his would-be allies in the PFN, who switched their allegiance to Jacques Chirac and the new neo-Gaullist RPR following Chirac's resignation as Prime Minister in 1976. The PFN explained this readiness to seek a rapprochement with the hated Gaullists as a shift from 'systematic opposition' to 'critical opposition'.[48] Though the fruits would be meagre from its cooperation with some RPR lists in the 1977 municipal elections, the PFN projected itself as the major force on the far right under the Giscard presidency. It also flirted with GRECE and the Nouvelle Droite, with whom it had links going back to Europe-Action; and it sought to attract the patronage of intellectuals such as Maurice Bardèche, Louis Pauwels and Jean Raspail.[49] The party's 1979 programme bore the marks of the Nouvelle Droite in its anti-egalitarian themes and even its title, *Propositions pour une nouvelle droite politique* (*Proposals for a New Political Right*).[50]

By comparison, the FN languished in obscurity. In contrast to the PFN's entryism, Le Pen's party displayed a bunker mentality and reluctance to seek any compromise with the regime. Accordingly, it opened itself more to radical elements in the form of Duprat's neo-fascist GNR and Frédriksen's neo-Nazi FANE. Conscious of the tendency of extreme-right parties to disintegrate in the wake of electoral failure, the FN set itself the explicit objective at its third national congress in May 1975 of simply continuing in existence. The party fielded a token 15 candidates in the cantonal elections of 1976, and contested a limited number of council seats (mainly in Paris) in the municipal elections of 1977, which saw the left-wing alliance make important advances throughout France. The FN's 18 'Paris for the Parisians' lists attracted 1.86 per cent of the ballot, just over 15,000 votes, in a contest which saw Chirac elected Mayor at the head of a neo-Gaullist majority.[51]

The 1978 legislative elections

In the legislative elections of 1978, the FN fielded 156 candidates, qualifying comfortably for official campaign slots on radio and television; but it failed to register its application on time, leaving the PFN (with 89 candidates) to relish its seven minutes of national publicity unrivalled. In the first round of the elections on 12 March 1978, the FN attracted 82,743 votes in all, 0.29 per cent of the national ballot.[52] Standing in the 7th *arrondissement* of Paris, Le Pen won 3.9 per cent against his former CNIP mentor, Edouard Frédéric-Dupont, who was elected outright. His lieutenants fared worse, Duprat winning 0.7 per cent, Durand 0.8 per cent, and the secretary-general of the FN, Alain Renault, 1.3 per cent in their respective constituencies. Two other notable results for the FN were those of Frédriksen (1.4 per cent) in Seine-Saint-Denis and Jean-Pierre Stirbois (just over 2 per cent) in Dreux, a town west of Paris which would witness the FN's first landmark success some five years later. The election was a debacle for the far right as a whole. The FN, the PFN and Gérard Furnon's neo-Poujadist Union des Français de Bon Sens (Union of Sensible Frenchmen, UFBS) together polled fewer than 200,000 votes.[53]

On the quite academic question of the stance to adopt for the second round, opinion in the FN was divided. Some held that a left-wing victory might open the door to the FN as the alternative to a discredited centre-right. There was some prescience in this, as events in the early 1980s would attest. Others espoused the traditional line of blocking the left at all cost. 'Given the choice between diarrhoea and cancer', Le Pen crudely declared, the FN would 'choose diarrhoea' and support the centre-right, which held its governing majority against forecasts of a left-wing victory.[54] This perceived collusion with the regime was criticised by some of Duprat's 'revolutionary nationalists', who would soon thereafter defect from the party with other malcontents.

The departure of the 'revolutionary nationalists' was given impetus by a dramatic event. On the eve of the second round of the 1978 elections, Duprat was killed by a car bomb. Le Pen too had been the target of an assassination attempt in November 1976, when his apartment block had been devastated by a bomb (remarkably, without serious injury to any residents).[55] Despite accusations and counter-accusations, the mystery of Duprat's murder was never resolved.[56] The obituary dedicated to him in the FN's newspaper, *Le National*, opened a window onto the paranoia and deep-seated anti-Semitism of the extreme right in the late 1970s. It declared that Duprat had paid with his life for his revisionist writings on the Holocaust, lauded him for challenging 'all of those taboos inherited from the Second World War', and suggested that he had been the victim of a Jewish plot. The same obituary praised Duprat for warning of the 'plan being hatched to carry out genocide on our people' through uncontrolled immigration, campaigns to lower the birth rate and pro-abortion propaganda. His assassination was part of a 'long premeditated assassination attempt' on France itself.[57]

Scission and reconstitution – again

The death of Duprat deprived Le Pen of his chief aide. It left the 'revolutionary nationalists' beset by internal dissensions and weakened within the FN, where their influence was challenged by Stirbois and his 'solidarist' group. The Union

Solidariste, which had joined the FN in autumn 1977, was descended from Pierre Sergent's OAS-Métro-Jeunes and MJR through Nourry and Janeau's GAJ.[58] It included Jean-Pierre and Marie-France Stirbois, Michel Collinot and Jean-Claude Nourry, while others with 'solidarist' sympathies such as Bernard Antony (alias Romain Marie) and Bruno Gollnisch would join the FN later in the 1980s.

'Solidarism' advocated a neo-corporatist third way between capitalism and communism, together with European neutrality towards both the Soviet Union and the United States. It opposed liberal individualism and communism with notions of cross-class solidarity and social justice. It proclaimed itself to be revolutionary, anti-democratic, anti-materialist and communitarian, vigorously anti-Marxist, anti-American and anti-Zionist.[59] Through Bernard Antony, it would open the FN up more to the influence of Catholic fundamentalists and bring within its orbit the ultra-conservative Catholic newspaper *Présent*, together with movements such as Chrétienté-Solidarité (Christianity-Solidarity) and the Comités d'Action Politique et Sociale (Political and Social Action Committees, CAPS).[60]

To the untutored eye, the differences between 'revolutionary nationalists' and 'solidarists' were more of degree than of kind; both were self-proclaimed revolutionary movements, anti-democratic, authoritarian, Euro-nationalist, and treading a well-worn path in their search for a 'third way' between communism and capitalism. Such differences as existed (in the Catholic current within 'solidarism', for example) were intensified by the personal animosities and rivalries in which the French extreme right had long specialised. By 1980, the bulk of 'revolutionary nationalists' had left the FN, together with those grouped around the journal *Militant*, opening the way for Stirbois to succeed Renault as secretary-general and to assert himself as the party's chief organiser and strategist until his own death in a car crash in 1988.

Duprat's murder also provoked the departure of Frédriksen's FANE, who found the FN both too soft and too dominated by the personality of Le Pen. It was to Frédriksen's movement that the 'revolutionary nationalists' would now gravitate, to vie with Malliarakis's Mouvement Nationaliste Révolutionnaire (MNR) in violent, racist or anti-Semitic agitation.[61] Malliarakis had similarly found the FN too lacking in revolutionary resolve, and had broken with Le Pen after the municipal elections of 1977 to form the MNR in early 1979. The FANE and MNR would seek at the turn of the decade to reassert direct activism as a *modus operandi* alongside the FN's and PFN's electoralism and the metapolitics of the Nouvelle Droite.

The 1979 European elections

By then, the remaining electoral test for the FN and PFN in the 1970s had turned to fiasco. The European elections of June 1979 were the first direct elections to the European Parliament in Strasbourg. The 81 seats open to French MEPs were to be contested on the basis of a national list system and proportional representation, with a 5 per cent qualifying threshold. If the task facing the extreme right in this election remained formidable, it nonetheless presented a better chance of gaining representation than the two-round majority system in force for legislative elections.

In response to the development in the mid-1970s of 'Eurocommunism', an initiative was launched under the guiding spirit of Giorgio Almirante, leader of the Italian MSI, to federate the forces of the European extreme right. The first conference of the 'Euro-Right' was held in Rome in April 1978, bringing together the leaders of the MSI, the Francoist Fuerza Nueva, the PFN, and nationalist parties from Belgium, Portugal and Greece. The European elections of June 1979 would be an opportunity for these parties to measure their strength and to mount a campaign on cross-national themes, notably anti-communism.[62]

As the French section of the Euro-Right, the PFN enlisted Tixier-Vignancour to head its campaign. The threat by Le Pen to launch a rival list, and thereby split the already meagre extreme-right vote, was sufficient to bring about a short-lived alliance in May 1979 between the PFN and the FN, which had been invited to play no part in the formation of the Euro-Right. Their joint campaign under the banner 'Union Française pour l'Eurodroite des Patries' collapsed from lack of funds and lack of goodwill. Le Pen was reduced to calling for abstention and disrupting the public meetings of Simone Veil, architect of the 1975 abortion law and head of the Giscardian UDF list. With the FN sidelined, the PFN then proceeded (with support from Almirante's MSI) to enter its own list, headed by Tixier-Vignancour, Gauchon, Robert, and the former *Algérie Française* agitator, Joseph Ortiz. The 1.3 per cent (just over a quarter of a million votes) won by this list confirmed the abject weakness of the extreme right at the end of the 1970s.[63] This was not, however, a restraining consideration for either Le Pen or Gauchon, both of whom declared their intention to stand in the presidential election of 1981.

The 1981 presidential and legislative elections

If the European elections of 1979 were a fiasco for the French extreme right, the presidential election of 1981 was a non-event. A change in the legislation governing eligibility (introduced in 1976) meant that candidates now had to secure the support of 500 rather than 100 elected officials, drawn from 30 rather than 10 departments. This was an obstacle over which neither Le Pen nor Gauchon could pass. With 434 signatures to his name, Le Pen had to resign himself once more to being a spectator, calling on voters to abstain (or, as he put it, to vote for Joan of Arc). Gauchon, for his part, urged a vote for Chirac in the first round and against Mitterrand in the second.[64]

Following Mitterrand's victory with 51.76 per cent of the vote to Giscard's 48.24 per cent on 10 May 1981, the National Assembly was dissolved in a move by the new President to secure a Socialist majority. The legislative elections of June 1981 marked the apogee of the left and the nadir of the extreme right. With more than a third of the first-round vote (over 36 per cent), the Socialists went on to win an outright majority of seats even without their Communist allies (who scored just over 16 per cent). This was the most resounding electoral victory in the history of the French left. The FN and PFN, by contrast, mustered between them some 0.3 per cent, little over 70,000 votes in all.[65]

With three weeks in which to mount its campaign, the FN fielded only 74 candidates in this election, winning 0.18 per cent of the ballot (44,414 votes). Le Pen again recorded the best FN score (4.38 per cent) in the 17th *arrondissement* of Paris. The PFN, with 86 candidates, fared worse still, winning 0.11 per cent (under 27,000 votes), with Gauchon posting the best result of 3.26 per cent in the 7th *arrondissement*.[66] While the FN now dug in for the battles ahead (Le Pen declaring Mitterrand's election to be the 'first day of the national reaction'), the elections of 1981 marked the effective end of the PFN, which had signally failed in its entryist mission.[67] Gauchon gave up politics to pursue his academic career, while Robert and others defected to parties of the mainstream right; yet others would in turn leave to join the FN. Though the PFN continued in existence, it was no longer a contender for the leadership of the far right.

The FN in the 1970s

By 1981, the FN was a quite different party from that launched almost a decade before. Its evolution over this period can be charted in three distinct phases. From the creation of the party in 1972 to Le Pen's presidential campaign of 1974, the FN exhibited all the uncertainty of an extremist party embarking on a new electoralist mission. It sought to strike a relatively moderate posture in its first electoral programme, but had no clear mobilising issues on which to build support. Its major campaigning theme of anti-communism was shared by parties across the centre-right; so too was the insistence on France's national interests, on traditional values and on law and order, while opposition to abortion was also articulated by many on the mainstream right. The mere fact of contesting legislative and presidential elections made the FN appear part of the broad consensus that had crystallised around the institutional structures of the Fifth Republic. The specificity that had distinguished extreme-right movements from the moderate right (anti-republicanism, anti-parliamentarism, diehard colonialism) was precisely what had made them unelectable. In dispensing with these references, however, the FN found itself casting around for a distinctive message. Even the strength of its anti-communism served as an inadvertent endorsement of the centre-right parties.

From 1974 to 1978, under the influence of Duprat and Barthélemy, the FN developed a more cohesive internal organisation, with a federative structure incorporating regional and departmental sections, a national newspaper with targeted local supplements, a youth section (the Front National de la Jeunesse, FNJ, under Christian Baeckeroot), and internal committees to elaborate policy in key areas (defence, the family, institutions, education, economic and social problems). In this period, the growing influence of Duprat and his 'revolutionary nationalists', together with the formation of the PFN as a rival force, had a radicalising effect on the FN. It adopted an increasingly hard-line discourse, notably on the issue that was to become its mainstay: immigration.

Some within the early FN feared that the presence of declared neo-fascists would compromise a party committed to electoralism. Their concerns were not shared by Le Pen, whose priority was to attract militants of any provenance and compensate for the losses inflicted by the split with Faire Front. His 'fervent appeal' in the *Cahiers européens* of June 1974 for 'all revolutionary nationalists' to join him in 'the struggle against a regime as noxious under Giscard as it was under Pompidou and de Gaulle' had a ring both of desperation and of outright pragmatism.[68] The hostility expressed here towards the mainstream right distinguished the FN's isolationism from the entryist aspirations of the PFN. If the adherence of neo-Nazis like Marc Frédriksen would later cause Le Pen some public embarrassment, he was only too ready to welcome them in the mid-1970s as a means of swelling his party's estimated membership of around a thousand. Despite its avowed isolationism, the FN was also prepared to countenance local deals with the 'noxious' Gaullist-Giscardian majority where the opportunity presented itself. In the municipal elections of 1977, such deals were struck in a number of communes between the centre-right parties and the FN and PFN respectively.[69]

The third phase of the FN's evolution was ushered in by the death of François Duprat in 1978, followed by the departure of the 'revolutionary nationalists' and the rise of Jean-Pierre Stirbois and his 'solidarist' faction. The latter exerted an influence which would define the FN over the next decade, preparing it for its electoral breakthrough and its transition from fringe movement to parliamentary party. For this, Stirbois built on the work already undertaken by Duprat, both in party organisation and in the development of a coherent political message. Herein would lie an ever stiffer challenge, as the ideological heterogeneity of the party was stretched by new arrivals from tendencies as sharply opposed as the neo-pagan Nouvelle Droite and Bernard Antony's Catholic fundamentalist associations.

Stirbois' political roots lay in the same soil as those of Le Pen and numerous other recruits to the FN. He had entered politics in defence of *Algérie Française* and had played a leading role in the youth wing of Tixier-Vignancour's presidential campaign before going on to feature in the 'solidarist' movements of the 1960s and 1970s. Having effectively ousted the neo-fascist tendency within the FN leadership, Stirbois became Le Pen's deputy and provided an uncompromising style of party management as a means of maintaining order over the diverse factions, tightening the links between the FN's local federations and its centralised decision-making machinery. The departure of the 'revolutionary nationalists' removed a major obstacle to electoral respectability and altered the complexion of the party. For the second time in its short history, the FN had been purged of its most overtly radical elements. Committed fully to an electoralist strategy, Stirbois placed emphasis on 'working the terrain', especially in constituencies under left-wing control. He himself would turn the town of Dreux west of Paris, with its large immigrant population, high unemployment and attendant social problems, into an experiment in what might be achieved through assiduous cultivation of grass-roots support.

Ideas

Immigration

One issue on which both Duprat and Stirbois squarely agreed was the growing importance and mobilising power of immigration. Duprat had occupied a key role in charge of communication and propaganda, directing with Alain Renault the party's newspaper, *Le National*, and managing the campaigns for the municipal elections of 1977 and legislative elections of 1978. His guiding objective was simple: to capitalise on issues neglected by the mainstream parties and open a space for the FN as a tribune party. Duprat foresaw that immigration would become an increasingly vexed issue. It was not yet a motivating factor in voting, but with the rise of unemployment and economic insecurity, he predicted, it would become one. The slogan 'A million unemployed is a million immigrants too many! France and the French First!' would be used on FN posters for the first time in the 1978 legislative election campaign; but it was to be found already on tracts signed by Duprat and distributed for the municipal elections of 1977.[70] It recalled Nazi posters from the 1930s which had equated numbers of unemployed with numbers of Jews and urged: 'The solution is very simple'. It also resonated with the comment in a televised broadcast in January 1976 of the then Prime Minister, Jacques Chirac: 'A country in which there are 900,000 unemployed but also more than two million immigrant workers is not a country in which the problem of employment has no solution.'[71]

Le Pen came round only gradually to embracing immigration as his privileged campaigning theme. Like Duprat, he recognised the potential propaganda value of an anti-immigrant stance, especially among working-class voters.[72] In a press conference to mark the first anniversary of his party in September 1973, the FN leader deemed France to be 'at its limit in terms of immigration' and warned of 'much more serious racial tensions ahead'. He declared that 'the French should come before others in France', and that Algerian workers in France represented an army of 'some fifty infantry divisions' awaiting their order to mobilise.[73] Anxious to avoid the accusation of crude racism, however, Le Pen played down the issue of immigration in his 1974 presidential campaign. Like the FN in the 1973 legislative election campaign, he preferred to focus his official programme on traditional values and anti-communism, with immigration absent from the 10 headline points of his manifesto. Following the derisory return on this attempt at moderation and under Duprat's influence, the party proceeded to harden its stance on immigration, particularly in the publications addressing its militants. In the December 1974 issue of *Le National*, it warned of the 'dangerous future facing Europe' and predicted 'the bloody effects of a widespread racial war'; in May 1975, the same publication called for 'a systematic reduction in the number of foreign workers, beginning with those who have entered France illegally'.[74]

In the legislative election campaign of 1978, with the worsening economic recession and the sharp rise in unemployment, Le Pen and the FN gave full vent to their anti-immigrant message. The party's election posters called for a 'Halt to unemployment and work for the French'.[75] In an interview on national radio in

February 1978, the FN leader was unequivocal. He warned of the 'demographic crisis' facing France and the 'demographic explosion of the Third World', and – in anticipation of his later policy of *'préférence nationale'* – called for a 'hierarchy' that would 'favour the French above foreigners': 'There is no racism whatsoever in observing, firstly, that there are five million foreigners in France, then in asking whether the million French people who are out of work do not have a greater right than foreigners to work in their own country. [. . .] We think that a million unemployed is a million foreign workers too many.'[76] Adopted as the defining slogan of the FN in the 1978 election campaign, this would be modified as unemployment passed the two-million then three-million marks in the 1980s and 1990s.

Again it is important to note that the FN was not here setting the agenda: it was responding to an agenda already set by the governments of the day. In February 1976, taking his lead from Prime Minister Chirac, the Minister for Employment, Michel Durafour, wrote in the popular daily *France-Soir*: 'There is no concealing the fact that the employment situation in France has an absurd aspect to it. There are a million unemployed; but at the same time there are two million immigrant workers, a significant number of whom have more disposable income than certain salaried employees in the highly coveted tertiary sector. Who can fail to see the contradiction in that?'[77] In April 1977, a voluntary repatriation assistance scheme (*Aide au retour*) was set up by the government of Raymond Barre with the purpose of encouraging immigrants to opt for a subsidised return to their countries of origin. Following the failure of this initiative, the Secretary of State for Manual and Immigrant Workers, Lionel Stoléru, and the Interior Minister, Christian Bonnet, embarked on an attempt to legislate for the mass repatriation of non-Europeans surplus to labour requirements. The government set a target in 1979 of reducing immigrant numbers by up to 100,000 (and even, provisionally, 200,000) a year, before its proposals met with opposition from the Council of State, parliament and human rights groups.[78]

With unemployment now the primary public concern, the FN's fifth national congress in November 1978 amplified the government-endorsed equation between that and immigration. It called for the 'defence of the West' and identified the 'principal cause of unemployment' in 'the massive presence of foreign workers on our soil'. This constituted 'a danger for the security and health of our fellow countrymen, which, along with the drop in the national birth rate, could in time place at risk the very existence of our people'. A special issue of *Le National* devoted to immigration in February 1979 demanded the immediate expulsion of illegal immigrants and those in breach of the law, and a further gradual expulsion of over a million immigrants a year (to bring the level down from 'over five million' to '500,000, of whom 200,000 would be workers'). It claimed that the cost of immigration was 'greater than the revenue from income tax' and 'far greater than the budget of the armed forces'; its reversal would 'relaunch the economy', reducing taxes and welfare charges, stimulating industrial investment and purchasing power while encouraging 'a rise in the birth rate of 20–25 per cent'. *Le National* called for the abrogation of the 1972 Pleven Law on racial discrimination, the imposition of a special tax on companies employing immigrants, and – again – 'priority of employment for the French'.[79]

In an interview published in *Le Quotidien de Paris* in October 1980, Le Pen sought to exonerate himself and his party from the charge of racism. His remarks showed the extent to which the arguments of the Nouvelle Droite were finding a wider resonance on the far right. There was nothing racist, Le Pen declared, 'in recognising that there are different races, different ethnic groups, different peoples, who cannot simply be lumped together, or even in wishing that these races should not be mixed and that they should preserve their identity as an irreplaceable treasure rather than being merged through indiscriminate interbreeding'. It was time, he argued, to dispel the 'carefully cultivated misunderstanding' which deemed such views to be racist.[80] In the early 1970s, Le Pen had restricted his public references mainly to the practical problems associated with illegal immigration, the effect of cheap foreign labour on wages, and the social difficulties of integrating large numbers of North African immigrants.[81] By the turn of the decade, immigration as a threat to national identity and the French genetic pool had come of age within the public discourse of the FN.

Political credo

All of the references that would thereafter characterise the FN's stance on immigration – economic, social, cultural, demographic, racial – are adumbrated in the few extracts quoted above. They formed part of a broader set of ideas which underpinned the party's evolving programme and which again drew upon themes propagated by the Nouvelle Droite through the 1970s. In a contribution to a collective work on the contemporary right published in 1979, Le Pen set out to explain the political philosophy to which he and his party subscribed. Rejecting 'Rousseauistic, humanitarian, Utopian, internationalist' egalitarianism, he declared his party to be 'of the right' – not the false right of Giscard with his 'left-wing philosophy', but the 'popular, social and national right'. The FN, he conceded, could not accede to power within the prevailing system. Its mission was rather to engage in a 'battle of ideas, to exert pressure on all the other parties, and on French political life'.[82]

Some of the ideas which the FN brought to this battle were clearly enunciated here by Le Pen. He rehearsed the Vichy trilogy '*Travail, famille, patrie*', the 'motto of Marshal Pétain and the *Etat français*', as values consigned to opprobrium in the post-war years and now in need of rehabilitation. He outlined a conception of human nature according to which '99.999 per cent of what we are comes from those who have preceded us, whether it be our genes, the colour of our eyes, or that of our hair, the weakness of our liver, our ability to run a hundred metres, and of course our intellectual and emotional capacities'. The real world, he argued, was 'fundamentally inegalitarian', and all human progress had resulted from 'struggle and selection'. He warned against the day when an excessively and disproportionately high number of people will be assisted by the community, outstripping by far the numbers of those who have to look after them. By privileging and over-favouring all of those who are weak in every respect, we weaken the body of society as a whole. We do precisely the opposite of those who breed dogs and horses. I am not against helping those who are suffering, for example the handicapped, but we are at the stage now almost of promoting the handicapped. [. . .] We will reach a point where, if the handicapped can be assured a life of sufficient ease and comfort, it will become desirable for young lads to be mutilated from the age of 18 so as to avoid doing military service, avoid paying taxes, avoid going to work. A people who adopt these methods will be swept away by the barbarians the moment they care to advance.

In the same piece, Le Pen stressed the dangers facing 'not only France but the countries of Europe and the West' from immigration and falling birth rates. Without a 'resolute policy to increase the birth rate', he warned, 'Western civilisation and Western people will be submerged by the demographic tidal wave from Asia and Africa'. Invoking a 'right of self-defence', he urged 'the Whites, the Europeans and the French' to recognise their 'right to exist' and take defensive action.

   The other, still more immediate threat against which defensive action was required was that of a left-wing victory which would bring the Socialist and Communist parties to power in France. The publications and pronouncements of the FN throughout the 1970s projected everywhere this spectre and its dire consequences. It underlay the party's support for figures such as Franco, Pinochet, Salazar and Perón; it also explained the terms in which the FN articulated its apocalyptic fears. 'We are on the eve of a physical confrontation with the Soviet threat', warned Le Pen. 'Between the communist world and the rest of the planet, this confrontation will be a fight to the death which can end only in the annihilation of one or the other.'[83] Asked at a press conference in September 1973 whether the army should intervene in the event of the left coming to power in France, Le Pen replied: 'No, if the left respects the Constitution and our liberties; yes, if, as in Chile, it brings misery, famine and the threat of terror to our country. In that case, the armed forces would have not only the right but the duty to save the situation by restoring order.'[84] In the run-up to the 1978 legislative elections, Duprat would take a less circumspect stance, positively advocating a 'Chilean strategy' for the seizure of power should the ballot box deliver victory to the left.[85]

Economic credo

The neo-Darwinian notion of 'struggle and selection' which informed the FN's politics found expression, too, in the economic policies which Le Pen and his party developed in the late 1970s. Written under the influence of Ordre Nouveau, the FN's 1973 programme had little to say on economics, beyond a few broadly corporatist references. By 1978, the party had rejected corporatism and moved decisively towards a free-market economic stance, reflecting in part

Le Pen's own interests as a commercial entrepreneur. In 1978, it published its economic credo in a programme entitled *Droite et démocratie économique.*[86] Le Pen would later describe this document as a pioneering contribution to liberal economics in its insistence on deregulating the economy, reducing state intervention and privatising the public sector.

The 1978 programme promoted economic freedom as a requisite for political freedom, defining the free-market economy as '*economic democracy*, a *direct* democracy in which the people dictate their wishes without relying on an intermediary to ensure they are fully met'. It called for cuts in tax and welfare charges, particularly in relation to small and medium-sized business. It rejected corporatism as commendable in theory but flawed in practice, advocating instead an inchoate mix of directive management and tightly regulated syndicalism. It called for the Marxist hold over trade unions to be broken and the right to strike severely restricted in the public sector. It proposed a form of popular capitalism in which state-owned companies would be privatised and their shares distributed among French families. It defended the 'profit motive', 'private property' and 'economic inequality' as the 'engines' of a successful economy. The state, it argued, should be restricted to its essential functions: justice, policing, diplomacy and national defence.

The explicit disavowal of corporatism by the FN was highly significant. Since the inter-war years, corporatism had been an article of faith for many movements on the extreme right, a ready refuge for those opposed to communism and capitalism alike. It had been at the core of Mussolini's Fascist project in Italy, and remained an important feature of economic organisation in Franco's Spain and Salazar's Portugal. It was conceived by those extreme-right movements which espoused it as a 'third way' between the individualism of liberal capitalists and the collectivism of socialists. In marking its distance from such a central tenet of the fascist tradition, the FN absolved itself of guilt by association and broke new ground. Its emphatic endorsement of economic liberalism allowed it to engage fully with two essential components of its political philosophy: the belief in natural hierarchies, achieved in economic terms through the laws of the market; and maximal opposition to communism. A decade later, Le Pen would go so far as to claim that the FN's 1978 programme proposed a form of 'Reaganomics' two years before Ronald Reagan's election to the presidency of the United States.[87]

The liberal creed expressed in *Droite et démocratie économique* sat more easily with certain factions within the FN than with 'revolutionary nationalists' sworn to oppose capitalism as vigorously as communism. They held, by contrast, to a strongly interventionist state, with the nationalising of banks and key sectors of production. By 1980, with the 'revolutionary nationalists' and the *Militant* faction under Pierre Bousquet and Pierre Pauty removed (the latter going off to found the Parti Nationaliste Français), the way was clear for Stirbois and his 'solidarists' to take the helm. They, too, were far from being natural economic liberals, but they saw an opportunity to project the FN as a voice of radical opposition to the ascendant Socialist-Communist alliance and its collectivist values.

The politics of the wilderness

It was clear that the enterprise of a 'national front' could not be sustained without a large element of ideological compromise. In addition to the 'solidarist' group, the FN in the late 1970s incorporated ultra-nationalists and Euro-nationalists, Vichy sympathisers and collaborationists, Poujadists and Tixierists, supporters of *Algérie Française*, anti-Gaullists, neo-fascists, monarchists and others. The departure of Renault's 'revolutionary nationalists' and Bousquet's *Militant* group, moreover, was offset by the return of two founding members who had sided with Faire Front in the first major scission, François Brigneau and Roland Gaucher, both former collaborationists with strong influence in Vichyite circles. Others of a similar ilk attracted to the FN showed the long lineage of this fledgling party. They included André Dufraisse (nicknamed 'Uncle Panzer'), a former member of Doriot's PPF and of the LVF who would serve on the FN's political bureau until his death in 1994; Victor Barthélemy, another former Doriotist and PPF leader whose influence on the early FN has been noted; and other former collaborationists such as Pierre Bousquet and Paul Malagutti.[88]

Despite its success in bringing together many of the major currents of the extreme right in post-war France, the FN remained consigned to the wilderness. On the face of it, the mid- to late 1970s might have proved a favourable period. The effects of a deepening economic crisis and the controversial nature of the Giscard administration's early liberalising reforms – in family mores (divorce, contraception, abortion), public mores (relaxing of media censorship, stress on civil liberties), and the rights of immigrants – gave the extreme right campaigning issues which it had lacked under the more conservative Gaullist regimes. A sharp upturn in unemployment and rising levels of crime and delinquency also gave more resonance to the themes of immigration and law and order on which the FN increasingly played. High-profile scandals, too, cast an unfavourable light on mainstream politicians.

For all these potential advantages, the failure of the FN to make any significant ground in the first decade of its existence can be explained by a number of factors. While FN candidates cut inexperienced and marginal figures on the electoral hustings, the threat of a left-wing victory allowed the Gaullists and Giscardians to warn continually against the dangers of a wasted vote on the right. Nor was the extreme right's reputation for violent activism to be dispelled by the simple resolution of a party congress, as mainstream voters continued to be repelled by the ideas and methods of this political fringe. Competition from the PFN prevented Le Pen's party from achieving what it was set up to achieve, the concentration of right-wing nationalist support on one movement. Beyond both of these parties, moreover, the sheer number and diversity of other extreme-right groups gave the FN's mission as *rassembleur* a hollow ring.

Internally, too, the FN was ill-adapted to compete effectively in its first few electoral campaigns. Its heterogeneous nature, as recognised from the outset by its founders, was 'both its strength and its weakness'.[89] For it brought together groups and individuals who could not agree amongst themselves, far less project a coherent message to potential voters. Strategically, the party was caught between outright opposition to the regime and the need to side with the governing centre-right in opposing the left and (as the PFN recognised) in nurturing any prospect of playing a significant role.

The result was incoherence. The PFN's overtures to the centre-right pushed Le Pen to radicalise the FN's anti-system stance. He denounced with equal vigour 'the politics of liberal decadence [and] of Marxist dictatorship'; he accused Giscard of being 'unfit to govern the country' and of implementing 'much of the left's common programme'; but he found himself repeatedly calling on voters to support the incumbent centre-right against the greater enemy, communism.[90] It would take the major shock to the political landscape delivered by the victory of the left in 1981 for the FN to discover a space within which it could assert its own politics to effect and for Le Pen's posturings to be more than an irrelevant sideshow.

8 Electoral breakthrough and consolidation

The Front National 1981–88

The 18th of June is a date writ large in modern French history, marking General de Gaulle's famous *appel* from London in 1940 against surrender to Nazi Germany. On 18 June 1984, memories of that historic event were eclipsed as *Libération* led with the simple banner headline '*Le Choc*' ('The Shock'). Above the image of a sneering Le Pen, the left-leaning daily reported the breakthrough of the FN in the European elections of 17 June. Overnight, the party had emerged as a force in French national politics. With almost 11 per cent of the vote, Le Pen's 'Front d'Opposition Nationale pour l'Europe des Patries' won 10 of the 81 French seats in the European Parliament in Strasbourg, securing the same number of MEPs as the once powerful PCF. In three years, a total of barely 70,000 votes for the FN and PFN combined had swollen to 2,210,334 votes for Le Pen's list, confirming the FN now as the unrivalled party of the extreme right in France.[1]

In subsequent elections, the FN consolidated and extended the ground won in 1984, polling habitually 10–15 per cent of the national vote. It retained its representation in the European Parliament, gained seats for a time in the National Assembly, and won substantial representation in regional and municipal councils throughout France, securing control of the municipalities of Toulon, Orange, Marignane and Vitrolles. In the 1988 and 1995 presidential elections, Le Pen won 14.4 per cent and 15 per cent respectively, the support of 4.38 then 4.57 million voters. In 2002, he would achieve his long-term ambition by winning through to the second round of the presidential election and challenging the neo-Gaullist incumbent, Jacques Chirac, for France's highest political office.

The purpose of the following chapters is to provide a detailed analysis of this unprecedented turn of electoral fortune in the history of the extreme right in France. They will seek to explain why, after years of abject failure, a far-right party should have found fertile terrain for growth in the France of the 1980s and 1990s. The present chapter examines the electoral breakthrough and early successes of the FN and identifies the range of conditions – political, social and economic – which favoured Le Pen and his party. Subsequent chapters will explore how the FN built on the ground gained in the 1980s to extend its electoral appeal, adapt its ideology and amplify its influence on the political agenda in France. Together, these chapters trace the major stages in the FN's electoral advance and progressive institutionalisation, charting some of the changes that have taken place in the party's strategy, programme, support base and political prospects within the electoral framework of the Fifth Republic; they also reflect upon the wider impact that Le Pen and the FN have had on political debate and the policy agenda, on voting patterns, on the party system and the conditions of electoral competition in France.

An unprecedented result

The result of 17 June 1984 was without parallel for the extreme right under the Fifth Republic (Table 8.1). Until then, the high-water marks had been the 'no' vote of 9.2 per cent (1.94 million votes) in the referendum on the Evian Agreements of 1962, and Tixier-Vignancour's 5.2 per cent (1.26 million votes) in the presidential election of 1965.

A further factor distinguishing the FN's performance in this election from previous results lay in the electoral geography. In the 1962 referendum and 1965 election (as in the 1974 presidential election), support for the extreme right had been concentrated mainly in departments across the south of France where many of the million expatriated *pieds-noirs* from Algeria had settled. Support for the FN in 1984 was strong in the departments of the Mediterranean littoral, but also in departments of the east, north-east and north of France which had no tradition of extreme-right voting under the Fourth or Fifth Republics.[2] While the peaks of support occurred in the southern departments of Hérault (15.33 per cent), Pyrénées-Orientales (15.86 per cent), Vaucluse (16.44 per cent), Var (19.96 per cent), Bouches-du-Rhône (19.49 per cent) and Alpes-Maritimes (21.39 per cent), there was marked support too in the north-eastern departments of Haut-Rhin (13.91 per cent), Moselle (14.04 per cent), Belfort (14.77 per cent) and in the central-eastern Rhône (15.86 per cent). The FN vote was also strong in and around Paris, with 14.14 per cent in Hauts-de-Seine, 14.37 per cent in Yvelines, 14.62 per cent in Seine-et-Marne, 14.97 per cent in Val d'Oise, 15.98 per cent in Seine-Saint-Denis and 15.24 per cent in Paris itself.[3]

Table 8.1 The 1984 European elections

	Votes cast	*%*	*Seats*
PCF list (Marchais)	2,261,312	11.20	10
Socialist Party (PS) list (Jospin)	4,188,875	20.75	20
UDF-RPR list (Veil)	8,683,596	43.00	41
FN list (Le Pen)	2,210,334	10.95	10

Source: *Journal Officiel* (La Documentation Française, *Institutions et vie politique sous la Ve République*, Paris, 2003, p. 179).

The same map of support precluded any hasty comparison between the FN vote in 1984 and that of the Poujadists in 1956. In northern and eastern areas where the FN performed strongly, the Poujadist vote had been weakest; conversely, in former bastions of Poujadism the FN recorded some of its poorest scores (with 6.22 per cent in Mayenne, 5.35 per cent in Deux-Sèvres and 5.23 per cent in Aveyron). While Poujadism had been a predominantly small-town and rural movement, the FN attracted support mainly in urban locations beset by quite different socio-economic problems. It registered its lowest scores in the Massif Central departments of Corrèze (4.42 per cent), Cantal (4.65 per cent) and Creuse (4.81 per cent). Regionally, the FN secured its highest score (just over 19 per cent) in the populous Provence-Alpes-Côte d'Azur and its lowest score (just under 5 per cent) in the rural Limousin.

Where a clear echo of Poujadism could be detected was in the strong support drawn by the FN from shopkeepers and artisans (21 per cent). Support was distributed relatively evenly across other socio-professional groups, with 12–13 per cent among farmers and agricultural workers, white-collar workers,[4] middle and senior managers, and liberal professionals. While the FN drew weaker support from blue-collar workers (9 per cent), it registered a notable vote among the unemployed (13 per cent).[5] FN voters were predominantly male, evenly spread through the age ranges, with little discernible distinction between practising and non-practising Catholics.[6] This combination of findings made it difficult to define the early FN electorate in terms of a traditional right/left cleavage and suggested a more eclectic appeal.

As evidence of this, the FN list beat both the Socialist and Communist lists to finish second behind the centre-right alliance in a number of southern towns including Toulon, Aix, Marseille (with 21.42 per cent) and Perpignan (with 21.52 per cent). In the small town of Carmoux in Bouches-du-Rhône, distinguished by having the highest proportion of *pieds-noirs*, one in three voters supported Le Pen's party.[7] The FN outpolled the PCF in some areas of traditional communist strength, such as Lyon, Saint-Etienne and Reims, and in the PCF-controlled Paris suburb of Aulnay-sous-Bois. It was in its national distribution, however, that the FN vote was most remarkable, exceeding 10 per cent in 44 of metropolitan France's 96 departments. Reaching far beyond the traditional heartlands of the extreme right and making inroads into the constituencies of mainstream right and left alike, Le Pen's party confronted political analysts with a new phenomenon for which there was no ready prototype.

Preparing the ground

Though the scale of the FN's success in the European elections of June 1984 came as a shock, there had been isolated signs of a change in the party's fortunes. In the cantonal elections of March 1982, held to elect France's departmental councils (*conseils généraux*), the FN had been able to field only 65 candidates (out of over 7,000 contesting some 2,000 cantonal seats). It polled 25,273 votes, or 0.2 per cent of the ballot overall. This derisory share of the vote concealed a number of strong local results, notably in Dreux, a town west of Paris in the Eure-et-Loir department where Jean-Pierre and Marie-France Stirbois saw their assiduous grass-roots campaigning yield 12.62 per cent in Dreux-West and 9.58 per cent in Dreux-East.[8] Some months later, at the FN's second Fête des Bleu-Blanc-Rouge (an annual jamboree initiated in 1981 to rival the PCF's Fête de l'Humanité), the reported figure of 34,346 participants also suggested a growing audience for the party's ideas.[9]

At a meeting of the FN held in Nice in October 1982, Le Pen outlined the party's strategy within the post-1981 political context. He countenanced the prospect of deals with the mainstream right provided they did not call for a soft-ening of the FN's stance on its key issues of immigration, law and order, unemployment and taxation.[10] In the municipal elections of March 1983, the FN fielded its own lists in towns where its prospects of winning seats appeared strongest (Paris, Nice, Montpellier); in some other towns, it featured on joint lists with the parties of the centre-right. Out of national power and anxious to win back ground from the left where they could, the neo-Gaullist RPR and centrist UDF struck alliances with the FN or PFN in Dreux, Grasse, Antibes, Toulon, Aix-en-Provence, and a number of other locations. In all, extreme-right candi-dates scraped together 0.1 per cent of the vote, winning 211 of over half a million seats distributed across more than 36,000 communes.[11] Even this meagre return was due largely to the element of proportional representation newly intro-duced for municipal elections. The most notable score was the 11.26 per cent (6,788 votes) recorded by Le Pen's list in the populous, multi-ethnic 20th *arrondissement* of Paris, which saw the FN leader elected to a seat on the local council.[12]

The third and most important stage in the FN's advance came in a series of by-elections in autumn 1983. In September, a municipal by-election was held in Dreux, a town which the FN had marked for cultivation with its socio-economic problems and immigrant population of over 20 per cent.[13] The election was due to irregularities in the counting of the March ballot, which the left had won by only eight votes against an RPR-FN list featuring nine FN candidates (and opposed by the UDF).[14] Running its own separate list this time and polling 16.72 per cent against almost 43 per cent for the centre-right, the FN forced the joint RPR-UDF list to choose between a further defeat and a further deal with the FN list under Jean-Pierre Stirbois. The deal was concluded with the approval of the national leadership of the RPR and UDF and few dissenting voices, and the RPR-UDF-FN list won the second round with some 55 per cent of the vote. The RPR leader, Jacques Chirac, who had opposed the alliance in March, now justified it on the grounds that it was 'much more dangerous to support a coali-tion that includes Communists [i.e. the government] than to support a coalition, at the level of medium-sized municipal councils, that includes members of the Front National and is of relatively little importance'.[15]

The relatively important fact for the FN was that it now had a role in governing a town of some 35,000 inhabitants, with Stirbois and two FN colleagues becoming assistants to the neo-Gaullist mayor on issues relating to civil defence, social affairs and culture.[16] In a further municipal by-election held in the rundown Paris suburb of Aulnay-sous-Bois in November 1983, the FN list won 9.32 per cent. The following month, a parliamentary by-election in Le Pen's native Morbihan (which had none of the urban, multi-ethnic character of Dreux or Aulnay-sous-Bois) was the opportunity for the FN leader to claim 12 per cent of the first-round vote, campaigning on the issues of unemployment, taxation and declining morality.[17]

These by-elections kept media attention on the FN and allowed it to pose for the first time as a viable component of the broad right. As a result, in January 1984, Le Pen and the FN made their first appearance in the *Figaro-Magazine*/ SOFRES monthly poll of political popularity, with 9 per cent of respondents holding a 'positive opinion' of the FN and the same proportion wishing to 'see Jean-Marie Le Pen play an important role in the months and years ahead'.[18] This was a milestone passed in terms of political acceptability. A further, arguably critical milestone was passed the following month when Le Pen was invited to appear for the first time on the television channel Antenne 2's prime-time interview programme, *L'Heure de vérité* (*The Hour of Truth*). This gave the FN leader an opportunity to present himself as a reasonable, measured politician, promoting himself as a 'Churchillian democrat' and adeptly turning his interviewers' hostility to his own advantage. So important did Le Pen consider this breakthrough into the mainstream media that he included a transcript of the entire programme in his book *Les Français d'abord*, deeming it 'the hour that changed everything'.[19]

Le Pen also included in the same book extracts from the correspondence with President Mitterrand which had opened the doors of the media to him. Following the first exchange of letters in May and June 1982, in which Le Pen complained of the media boycott of his party, Mitterrand instructed the heads of France's three main television channels to devote equitable coverage to the FN. Within a week, Le Pen was a guest on TF1's late news; more coverage of the FN and further invitations to Le Pen followed on television and radio, before his new media persona was consecrated on *L'Heure de vérité* in February 1984.[20] Mitterrand would later concede that he had underestimated Le Pen, dismissing him at the time as a neo-Poujadist lightweight with no political future.[21] Whether it be ascribed to Republican principle, myopia or political opportunism, Mitterrand's responsibility in promoting Le Pen remains ineluctable.

Though the impact of a television programme cannot be easily measured, it seems clear that Le Pen and his party benefited considerably from that hour. Viewing figures for the programme were notably high, as they would continue to be for subsequent television appearances by the FN leader. A reported rush of applications following the programme swelled (to an implausible 30,000) the membership now claimed by the party.[22] Recruits also began to arrive in numbers from the centre-right parties. More significantly still, polling showed that the 3.5 per cent of respondents declaring an intention to vote for the FN in the European elections rose sharply to 7 per cent, a level sustained from February 1984 onward.[23] In the *Figaro-Magazine*/SOFRES poll the following month, those with a 'positive opinion' of the FN climbed to 13 per cent, while those wishing to 'see Le Pen play an important role' in politics now stood at 16 per cent. These figures would rise further, to 17 per cent and 19 per cent respectively, by July 1984, following the FN's breakthrough in the European elections of June.[24]

Early fruits of success

With no serious rival now on the far right, the FN used the early 1980s to pursue what it had been founded to achieve a decade earlier. Already a mosaic of ideological tendencies, it attracted figures who had hitherto been resistant or even opposed to Le Pen and his party. These included such diverse 'celebrities' as the pretender to the French throne, Sixte-Henri de Bourbon-Parme, the resister turned OAS leader and Catholic 'crusader', Colonel Pierre Château-Jobert, the traditionalist Catholic writer Michel de Saint-Pierre, and the one-time great hope of the nationalist right, Tixier-Vignancour.[25] Despite his ambition to project an image of respectability, Le Pen's attitude to harbouring right-wing radicals of every complexion was similar to that exhibited by Poujade in engaging the services of former collaborationist journalists in the 1950s. Taxed in his February 1984 interview on *L'Heure de vérité* over his close ties with the Waffen-SS veteran and former FN treasurer Pierre Bousquet, Le Pen urged the need for 'reconciliation' and argued that the only question to be asked of such people 40 years after the Liberation was whether or not 'they wish to serve their country'.[26] The same rationale would allow other prominent collaborationists to occupy positions of influence in the rising FN, such as the LVF veteran André Dufraisse, the ex-RNP youth leader Roland Gaucher, and the ex-PPF activist Paul Malagutti, who had been sentenced to death *in absentia* in 1945 for his alleged involvement in the execution of resisters by the Gestapo.[27]

More important still than this extension of the FN's success in federating elements of the far right was its ability to draw sympathisers and recruits from the moderate right. With the centre-right parties struggling to overcome their divisions and adjust to opposition, the emergence of an upwardly mobile FN was too much for some to resist. Le Pen's party now attracted some high-profile defectors from the RPR and UDF, most notably Jean-Marie Le Chevallier, and from the CNIP Olivier d'Ormesson, Gilbert Devèze and Bernard Antony (alias Romain Marie). As former chief of staff to the Giscardian minister and UDF Paris leader, Jacques Dominati, Le Chevallier was a prestigious catch, as was the aristocratic d'Ormesson, son of France's former papal ambassador. Bernard Antony, in turn, brought with him a number of Catholic fundamentalist organisations and their main publication, the daily *Présent*, which supported Monsignor Marcel Lefebvre's revolt against the modernisation of the Catholic liturgy and articulated an authoritarian, anti-Marxist, anti-Jewish ideology.[28] The 81-strong FN list for the 1984 European elections featured 11 significant recruits from the UDF, RPR and CNIP. It included, too, a token Arab and a token Jewish candidate in unwinnable positions, and a woman, Martine Lehideux, in a winnable (ninth) place. The campaign itself was managed by Le Chevallier, hastily promoted to the FN's political bureau as a valuable prize from the respectable right and a counterweight to the growing influence of Stirbois.[29]

The political benefits deriving from the election of 10 MEPs were considerable. Since a minimum of 12 MEPs from three countries were entitled to form a parliamentary group in Strasbourg, the FN combined with the five from the Italian MSI and the single Greek nationalist to form the 'European Right' group, with Le Pen as president. This brought administrative support, invitations to official receptions, speaking time in debates, seats on parliamentary committees and the right to table parliamentary motions. It also gave Le Pen a platform from which to extend his contacts with other European far-right movements. It even opened the door to a collective audience with the Pope.[30]

The transition from obscurity to limelight was accompanied by other changes within the FN. During and following the 1984 European election campaign, the party consolidated its regional, departmental and local bases and refined its communications. The spate of defections by members of the mainstream right continued, bringing influential figures such as Edouard Frédéric-Dupont, Charles de Chambrun, Pascal Arrighi, Michel de Rostolan, Yvon Briant, François Bachelot, Bruno Chauvierre and Bruno Mégret to the FN. The university lecturers Bruno Gollnisch and Jean-Claude Martinez gave a patina of intellectual credibility to the party, while more modest recruits at grass-roots level helped the FN to reorganise and bolster its local sections in a number of departments.[31] The newspaper *National Hebdo* was launched, replacing the earlier *Le National* and *RLP Hebdo*, together with a telephone information service. The youth section (FNJ) was reorganised under Carl Lang and Martial Bild, two activists who would rise loyally through the FN ranks thereafter.[32] A training school for FN cadres was created, offering detailed guidance on all aspects of party activism, and a 'summer school' (*université d'été*) became a fixture in the annual cycle of the FN's internal events. The number of standing committees was increased to develop policy in the areas of agriculture, commerce, industry, defence, education, institutions, health and foreign affairs as well as immigration and law and order.[33] Finally, and importantly, the new resources of militant support on which the FN could draw provided the party with a reservoir of activists and candidates for the forthcoming cantonal and legislative elections.

The wider context: France in the early 1980s

The narrow victory of the Socialist François Mitterrand over the outgoing President Valéry Giscard d'Estaing on 10 May 1981 marked the accession of the left to national power for the first time under the Fifth Republic. The resounding success of the Socialist Party in the subsequent legislative elections, due in part to a demobilisation of the centre-right electorate, appeared to herald the *changement de société* which the left had long promised. Though the formal 'union of the left' had been ruptured in 1977, the government constituted in the wake of the 1981 elections under Mitterrand's first Prime Minister, Pierre Mauroy, included four Communist ministers (as much to insure against potential Communist opposition as to reward the PCF for services rendered in the past). This marked the return of the PCF to national government for the first time since 1947. Such indeed had been the exclusion of the left from power under the Fifth Republic that, of the 44 members of the new governing team, only three had previous experience of ministerial office.[34]

The economy

The incoming government inherited a difficult, and worsening, economic conjuncture. An economic crisis had persisted in France since the first oil shock of 1973, with the trebling of unemployment under Giscard d'Estaing in the period 1974–81 (when it exceeded 1.5 million). After a quarter of a century in opposition, the Socialists' programme (encapsulated in Mitterrand's presidential manifesto, *110 Propositions pour la France*) bore the imprint of their Common Programme with the PCF in the 1970s. They promised to redress the French economy, promote growth and bring unemployment down as part of a radical agenda of economic and social reforms that would inaugurate a 'break with capitalism'. In a changed international environment following the second oil shock of 1979 and with the election of Margaret Thatcher in Britain (1979), Ronald Reagan in the United States (1980), and (soon) Helmut Kohl in West Germany (1982), the French left came to power on an economic programme that was effectively obsolete. A neo-Keynesian policy of reflation was designed to increase purchasing power especially among lower-income households, stimulate domestic demand and relaunch growth – this at a time when other Western economies were resigned to deflationary austerity.

An extensive programme of nationalisation in the industrial and banking sectors, the creation of over 150,000 public-sector jobs, substantial rises in welfare benefits and the minimum wage, and increased loans and subsidies to industry conspired not to break the cycle of recession but to land the government with an unsustainable bill, offset only partly by increased taxes on employers and the imposition of a wealth tax, the *Impôt sur les grandes fortunes* (IGF). In financing these and other reforms, the budget deficit soared. Without protectionist barriers, increased consumer spending worked to the advantage of France's main trading partners, in particular West Germany, and to the detriment of the French balance of payments, as spending on imports rose and French manufacturers found it harder to export goods priced against an overvalued franc. Rises in the minimum wage and in welfare contributions, together with the introduction of a 39-hour working week with no reduction in pay and a fifth week of annual holiday entitlement, increased the cost of labour, reduced company profits and discouraged investment in job creation.

In May 1981, there were 1,794,900 registered unemployed in France; in May 1982, after a year of the 'Socialist experiment', the figure had risen by some 12 per cent to 2,005,000.[35] Nor did the upturn in international economic conditions predicted for 1982 materialise. As a host of negative indicators proclaimed the damage done to the French economy by the public spending programme and the government's failure to curb unemployment and inflation (running at some 14 per cent), Keynesianism was replaced by a policy of austerity – provisionally in June 1982, then definitively in March 1983. This would see two further devaluations of the franc (already devalued in autumn 1981), severe cuts in public spending, a temporary wage and price freeze, the imposition of an income tax surcharge, a selective rise in value-added taxes, special levies on petrol, tobacco and alcohol, higher energy and public transport costs, and increased health charges. A temporary restriction was imposed on the purchase of foreign currency and a ban placed on the use of credit cards abroad. As '*discipline*' and '*rigueur*' became the new watchwords, the austerity plan of the late 1970s, it seemed, had returned in another, arguably worse, guise. More damagingly still, by 1984 unemployment would be pushing up towards 2.5 million, having increased almost by half in the three years of the Socialist administration.[36]

Law and order

The economy was not the only domain in which the new Socialist government set out to implement a radical agenda. Civil liberties and social justice were foremost priorities in Mitterrand's *110 Propositions*. Among the first measures implemented by the Mauroy government were the abolition of capital punishment – in the face of public opinion[37] – and the suppression of the Cour de Sûreté de l'Etat (State Security Court), a special tribunal set up by de Gaulle to deal with state security offences in the wake of OAS terrorism in 1962. Two controversial public order acts – the *Loi anti-casseurs* and *Loi sécurité et liberté* – were repealed, and police powers to stop, search and arrest were more tightly regulated. The legal aid system was improved, and Mitterrand used his presidential prerogative to pardon 6,200 prisoners, some 14 per cent of France's prison population.[38]

Recorded crime had been on the rise in France throughout the two decades preceding the Socialists' accession to power, with an alarming increase in violent crime in the previous decade. By the early 1980s, law and order formed the core of a cluster of issues denoted by the increasingly invoked term '*insécurité*'; this now became a major focus of public concern, reflected by its growing prominence in opinion polls. Already in summer 1981, a poll showed Mitterrand's prisoner amnesty to have been excessively generous in the view of 61 per cent of respondents, including 54 per cent of Socialist and 50 per cent of Communist sympathisers.[39] Despite their own mixed record in this area, the RPR and UDF seized upon the opportunity to attack the Mauroy government for being soft on crime. Following his abolition of the death penalty and moves to reform the justice system, the Minister of Justice, Robert Badinter, was publicly denounced by his Gaullist predecessor, Alain Peyrefitte, as 'the defender of criminals'.[40] Public opinion too remained hostile. A SOFRES poll conducted in April 1983 showed an approval rating of 31 per cent for the government's record in addressing *insécurité*, with 53 per cent judging it unsatisfactory. By April 1984, approval of the government's record in this domain had dropped to 28 per cent and disapproval had risen to 59 per cent, while those declaring themselves favourable to the restoration of capital punishment stood at 64 per cent.[41]

Immigration

Nowhere was the new administration's concern for civil liberties and social justice more pronounced than in the measures proposed to improve the lot of France's immigrant population (recorded by separate measures in 1982 as 3.68 and 4.46 million, 6.8 and 8.2 per cent of the total population).[42] Resolved to exercise tight control over new arrivals, the incoming Socialist government oversaw a sharp rise in the numbers of those refused entry to France, from 28,537 in 1980 to 54,207 in 1982.[43] At the same time, it halted deportations pending under previous legislation and redefined expulsion as a judicial rather than an administrative procedure. Certain categories of immigrant (notably children born in France of foreign parents and those who had lived there since the age of 10) were declared exempt from expulsion. Random identity checks were halted, and the voluntary repatriation assistance scheme (*Aide au retour*) introduced under Giscard d'Estaing was abolished. Some procedural obstacles to family reunion were removed, and full rights of association were granted without the need to seek approval from the Interior Ministry. Dispensing with a requirement that had endured since 1939, this law cleared the way for a proliferation of associations set up to defend the rights and promote the culture of immigrant communities in France. Religious pluralism, too, was accorded a new public space. Since the 1970s, Muslim workers had pressed for prayer rooms in their hostels and prayer breaks in their places of work. The law granting the right of association opened the way for a building programme which saw the number of mosques rise from under a dozen in 1970 to almost 1,000 by the end of the 1980s.[44] Immigrants also benefited from the liberalising of the broadcast media, as numerous radio stations sprang up to articulate the views and cater for the diverse tastes of France's ethnic communities.

In 1946, North Africans had accounted for only 2.3 per cent of the foreign population in France, 88.7 per cent of whom were European (Italian, Polish, Spanish and Portuguese in the main); by 1982, the proportion of Europeans had fallen to 47.6 per cent, while that of North Africans had risen to 38.5 per cent.[45] Under the presidencies of de Gaulle (1959–69) and Pompidou (1969–74), much of the immigrant population was made up of unskilled males from the Maghreb (Algeria, Morocco, Tunisia) recruited on temporary contracts for manual labour in the construction, steel, mining and car industries. This was the pattern advocated in the influential report of 1969 presented by Corentin Calvez to the Economic and Social Council, which recommended that 'the influx of non-European origin, and in particular the current from the Maghreb', should increasingly be treated as a 'temporary immigration for work' only. The same report sounded a warning about 'the very prolific character of Algerian families' and urged that 'precise studies be undertaken to determine the thresholds of tolerance that should not be exceeded in accommodation, schools and the workplace'.[46]

Viewed thus as a short-term economic resource, North African labour migrants lived frequently in hostels close to their places of work and had little impact upon French society at large. The election of Giscard d'Estaing in 1974 marked the end of labour migration of this type to France, and the beginning of a process transforming this largely transient immigrant population into a permanently settled component of French society. It marked the start, too, of the twin-track policy that would be pursued with varying emphases by subsequent governments, balancing tighter immigration controls with attempts to integrate non-European minorities already resident in France.[47]

The recognition in 1976 of family reunion as a right subject to certain conditions was an important factor in changing the composition and character of immigrant communities in France. Where single male migrants had existed on the margins of French society, worked for modest wages and contributed more to social security funds than they derived in return, the arrival of family members placed conspicuous new demands on public services and welfare support. Concentrations of North African families in some social housing estates and of their children in certain schools brought problems of ghettoisation which became linked to rising crime and delinquency in some locations and stoked racial tensions.[48] As noted in Chapter 7, the late 1970s saw an effort by the Barre government to organise the voluntary departure of immigrants and even to legislate for the mass repatriation of non-Europeans surplus to labour requirements. The incoming Socialist government in 1981 inverted the emphasis from repatriation to integration. It set up 'Educational Priority Zones' (ZEP), focusing additional staff and resources on areas with high concentrations of immigrant-born children, and (in 1984) a Conseil National des Populations Immigrées (National Council for Immigrant Populations, CNPI), a consultative body to which all matters relating to immigrant workers and their families could be referred. As the economic recession deepened, however, disadvantages which the government sought to address at one level were compounded at another, as immigrant workers found themselves increasingly joining the ranks of the unemployed.[49] While construction of low-cost social housing was cut back despite growing demand, those high-rise estates that had been thrown up around the *périphériques* of large French towns during the boom years of the 1960s became increasingly symbols of urban decay and of the failure to integrate immigrant communities within the fabric of French society.

The demographic changes described above were accompanied by a growing public perception of the immigrant as specifically North African, a perception reinforced in the early 1980s by the higher public profile of the Arab Muslim community in France. From strikes in the car industry prominently featuring North African workers (Citroën-Aulnay-sous-Bois, Talbot-Poissy, Renault-Billancourt), through the violent protests of immigrant youths in estates such as Les Minguettes outside Lyon, to the marches by young French of North African immigrant parents, or *Beurs*, the immigrant community was forging a more assertive, and for some a more menacing, image. An illustration of this new assertiveness was provided in summer 1984 by the government's decision, in response to pressure from immigrant associations (and the '*Marche des Beurs*' from Marseille to Paris in autumn 1983), to introduce a single residence and work permit valid for 10 years and automatically renewable.

Amid the raft of reforms enacted or proposed by the Socialists in relation to immigrants, two in particular provoked controversy. While seeking to clamp down on the further entry of illegal immigrants, the Mauroy government extended an amnesty to those who had entered France before January 1981 and were in stable employment. Of an estimated 300,000 illegal immigrants in France, 132,000 legalised their status through this *régularisation exceptionnelle* (with the requirement of stable employment being relaxed in mid-process).[50] More potentially far-reaching still was 'Proposition 80' of Mitterrand's manifesto, which envisaged voting rights in municipal elections for immigrants who had been resident in France for five years or more. In this, the President was arguing for an expanded conception of citizenship, a citizenship of community no longer defined exclusively by nationality.

Extending an amnesty to illegal immigrants while at the same time attempting to halt illegal immigration brought charges of laxity and incoherence against the government. In addition, the proposal to grant immigrants even a restricted vote met with concerted opposition from the right. The FN denounced it as an 'insane proposal' which would set 'France on the road to losing its Frenchness'.[51] More importantly, surveys showed public opinion at large to be unsympathetic to the government's pro-immigrant initiatives. In a SOFRES poll conducted in March 1983, 46 per cent of respondents judged that the left had 'done too much for immigrants', as opposed to 34 per cent taking the contrary view. Further polls conducted the following year would show 58 per cent of respondents judging that there were too many foreigners in France, 63 per cent opposed to giving immigrants a vote in municipal elections, and 70 per cent supporting subsidised repatriation. By November 1984, following the prominence given to immigration by the FN's electoral success, the same polling agency would put those opposed to voting rights for immigrants at 74 per cent.[52]

Though bound in principle by this last proposal, the government promptly relegated it to the status of a long-term objective before dropping it altogether. The Socialists had underestimated the potential for anti-immigrant feeling in France and overestimated their ability to carry public opinion with them in their reforms. Following the municipal elections of March 1983, which saw immigration emerge as a major campaign issue, the government proceeded to tighten the legislation on entry and residence and the requirements for family reunion. The identity spot-checks which had been halted in 1981 were brought back into use and stiffer penalties were imposed on the employers of illegal immigrants (with the number of fines rising from 109 in 1982 to 2,266 in 1983 and 2,591 in 1984). A law of June 1983 authorised the urgent deportation of illegal immigrants by court order, effectively denying them a right of appeal. This was followed within a year by the reintroduction, under another name (*Aide publique à la réinsertion*), of the subsidised repatriation scheme which had been deemed an indignity by the incoming government in 1981. As a measure of the change in the government's emphasis, the expulsion rate would rise from 1,950 in 1982 to 12,595 in 1984, while some 50,000 North Africans would be voluntarily repatriated between 1984 and 1986.[53]

The left's fall from grace

On the defensive over its (mis)management of the economy, its approach to law and order, and its immigration policy, and faced with growing industrial unrest and public protest over other aspects of its reform programme (notably the proposed restructuring of the school system),[54] the Mauroy government's fall from grace was precipitous. Following the loss of four parliamentary by-elections in January 1982, a sequence of countrywide elections confirmed the swing of support away from the left – cantonal in 1982, municipal in 1983, European in 1984. In the period from summer 1981 to summer 1984, polls charted the slump of public confidence in the left while the parties of the centre-right saw only a marginal rise in their confidence rating. The personal standing of the President and Prime Minister provided graphic evidence of this collapse in public confidence. In June 1981, 74 per cent of respondents in a SOFRES poll expressed confidence in François Mitterrand to resolve France's problems, while 71 per cent recorded similar confidence in Pierre Mauroy. These were confidence ratings comparable to those enjoyed by General de Gaulle in the early days of the Fifth Republic. By the time of the European elections of June 1984, confidence in Mitterrand had dropped to 41 per cent (sinking further to 37 per cent in the following months), while Mauroy's rating plummeted to 30 per cent in June and 25 per cent in July 1984 before his replacement as Prime Minister by Laurent Fabius.[55]

This was the nadir of the left in government. The replacement of Mauroy by the young, technocratic Fabius and the departure of the PCF from government marked the end of the failed 'Socialist experiment' and confirmed the new orientation of an administration forcibly converted to social democracy and modernisation. This meant in essence the abandonment of old-style socialism and the promotion of economic efficiency over political doxa. The new Fabius government bowed to the contraints of the market and the mixed economy, embraced profitability as a virtue, praised enterprise over state interventionism, restructured French industrial capacity (at the cost of jobs in the steel, coal and car industries), partially privatised firms nationalised by the Mauroy government, and adopted a tough anti-inflationary policy. The new approach yielded positive signs of recovery: a sharp reduction in inflation (down to 5 per cent in 1985), a slowing of unemployment, a reduced budget deficit, higher corporate profits, some modest economic growth, and an increase in industrial investment and purchasing power.

The Socialists could no longer be accused of ideological sectarianism, nor of economic incompetence; but the healthier balance sheet produced by the Fabius government marked a surrender to principles that the left had vigorously condemned in opposition. Its approach to immigration marked a further surrender. In a televised interview in September 1984, the new Prime Minister conceded in a glancing allusion to Le Pen that, while the FN leader offered the 'wrong answers', he was asking the 'right questions'.[56] To acknowledge as much was partially to endorse Le Pen and to suggest that the previous government had not taken sufficient account of the issues on which the FN had effected its electoral breakthrough.

The following month, in a publication devoted exclusively to immigration, the Prime Minister's office gave assurance that there would be no 'uncontrolled and unassimilable influx of immigrants' to France.[57] It announced a series of new and harsher measures to combat illegal immigration and restrict the right to family reunion. Entry points were to be made more secure and 'bogus tourists' apprehended and expelled. These measures were to be accompanied by a renewed effort to combat racism and facilitate the integration of legally resident immigrants; but, with financial incentives now being offered to encourage repatriation, it was clear where the emphasis lay. By the time the Prime Minister met the then leader of the centre-right opposition, Jacques Chirac, in a televised debate in October 1985, there was little in substance or tone to separate them on the immigration issue. As evidence of his government's resolve in responding to this 'undeniable problem', Fabius made no mention of the principles which had informed earlier Socialist policy and proceeded instead to vaunt his government's record on refusal of entry ('over forty thousand'), expulsion ('over twelve thousand') and subsidised repatriation ('fifteen thousand applicants').[58]

On law and order, too, the Fabius government marked a departure from the Socialists' initial refusal to promote the fight against crime to the status of a political priority. In autumn 1984, it acknowledged 'a real feeling of insecurity in France' and announced plans to modernise and re-equip the police force. This led, in summer 1985, to the incongruous spectacle of a Socialist government proposing a massive increase in the police budget at a time of sweeping cutbacks in public expenditure, and pushing it through against opposition from the RPR and UDF (who accused the Socialists of opportunism and foresaw themselves being lumbered with the cost if, as predicted, they were to form the next government).[59]

As the Socialists abandoned the old redoubts of leftist ideology, values traditionally held to be the preserve of the right gained new momentum while those of the left took on increasingly negative connotations.[60] Though the Fabius government succeeded in halting the Socialists' slump, public disenchantment had gone too far to be reversed by a Damascene conversion. Defeat for the left in the cantonal elections of 1985 and continuing expressions of dissatisfaction with Mitterrand in opinion polls suggested that losses in the legislative elections of March 1986 might be so heavy as to call into question the final two years of the President's septennate.

A convergence of causes

It is essential to appreciate this wider context in which the FN effected its electoral breakthrough. Its unexpected success, after a decade of uninterrupted failure, was to be explained by no single cause but by the convergence of a number of crucial factors. The election of the Socialists to power in 1981 and their rapid fall from grace had a destabilising effect on patterns of political allegiance and voting. The 1984 European election was the first national ballot since 1981, contested on a proportional system and offering voters an opportunity to vent their disgruntlement with limited domestic consequences. These circumstantial factors played to the FN's advantage. The crisis of confidence in both the government and the centre-right opposition compounded a sense of alienation expressed by many voters in relation to mainstream politicians and political parties. A succession of opinion polls in the mid-1980s resonated with accusations that politicians were incompetent, dishonest and remote from everyday reality.[61] This divorce between political practice and public opinion opened a space for Le Pen and his party, who capitalised on a vote with a strong element of disenchantment and protest. In this context, unstable voters of the right, and to a lesser extent of the left, shifted support to the FN. Polling data from the 1984 European elections indicated that 55 per cent of FN voters had supported Giscard d'Estaing and 22 per cent Mitterrand in the second round of the 1981 presidential election, while 23 per cent had not voted.[62]

The failure of the centre-right parties to profit from the unpopularity of the governing left allowed the FN to attract those voters and militants most radically opposed to the 'Socialo-Communist' government, whose programme Le Pen denounced as a 'Marxist revolution'.[63] Broadening its message beyond immigration and law and order, the FN attacked the government's nationalisation programme, its raising of taxes, and the bureaucracy and charges that hampered business and job creation. In terms redolent of Poujadism, Le Pen denounced the 'dictatorial imposition of tax by an insolent administration' and a 'system of fiscal inquisition comparable to the Gestapo'; he sought to rally 'those middle classes whose existence and vitality generate national prosperity and promote leadership in society'.[64] With its anti-communist, anti-tax, anti-immigrant and strong-arm law and order rhetoric, the FN capitalised on a convergence of issues whose time had come. Renouncing the tendency of previous extreme-right movements to hold doggedly to their ideas whatever their (lack of) electoral appeal, it showed opportunism in the issues which it prioritised. When a campaign launched by Le Pen to ensure protection of the French in the event of a nuclear conflict failed to spark public interest in autumn 1983, it was promptly dropped. Sensitive to the charge of being a single-issue party, the FN claimed to have just as much to say on 'the international situation, the family, popular share-owning, the intellectual and moral renewal of France, the problems of industry etc.' as it did on immigration and *insécurité*.[65]

For their part, the centre-right parties could be accused of a tactical error in nominating the centrist Simone Veil as head of their joint list for the 1984 elections, given her pronounced Europeanism and the strength of feeling still among sections of the right against her legalisation of abortion in 1975 (combined, for some, with her Jewishness). Veil's social liberalism and pro-Europeanism set her at odds with many right-wing neo-Gaullists in particular. This allowed the FN, with its calls for a '*Europe des patries*', to harvest much of the nationalistic, Euro-sceptic, authoritarian sentiment on the right, at a moment when the RPR leadership was seeking to strike a less nationalistic, more Europeanist tone. A SOFRES exit poll recorded more than one in 10 Chirac supporters having switched their vote to Le Pen's list.[66] The second-order nature of the European elections facilitated this by lessening the need for a disciplined vote on the centre-right and allowing a margin of freedom for protest. Thereafter, the proportional method of attribution ensured that the FN's vote would translate into seats and allow the party entry to the institutional system at a relatively weak point.

The FN's muscular rhetoric struck a chord in other ways. Surveys carried out between September 1983 and January 1984 showed almost one in 10 RPR and UDF supporters wishing to see the centre-right parties 'exceed the bounds of legality in opposing the left'.[67] A poll conducted in May 1984 found over a third of RPR supporters expressing sympathy for Le Pen, along with almost a quarter of UDF supporters. At the same time, the idea of an alliance between the centre-right parties and the FN for the forthcoming legislative elections, including the fielding of joint candidates, found favour with 62 per cent of RPR and 46 per cent of UDF supporters. Again voters and militants from the neo-Gaullist RPR proved more sensitive to the siren calls of a hard-line party to their right. On the specific issues of immigration, law and order, and anti-commu-nism, levels of approval for Le Pen's proposals among RPR supporters reached 45, 47 and 54 per cent respectively.[68] More remarkable still was a survey of dele-gates at the RPR's national congress in 1984, 25 per cent of whom declared themselves more positively disposed to the FN than to their alliance partners in the two main parties of the centre-right UDF confederation, the Centre des Démocrates Sociaux (CDS) and the PR.[69]

This growing acceptability of the FN within a section of the centre-right was enhanced by Le Pen's forceful persona and skilful use of the media, and by his ability increasingly to define the terms of public debate on the issues of immi-gration and law and order. On these issues, the ground had been largely prepared for him by others. In December 1980, the PCF mayor in the Paris suburb of Vitry-sur-Seine dispatched a bulldozer to demolish a newly provi-sioned hostel for immigrant workers on the grounds that Vitry had reached the limit of its capacity to accommodate foreigners. The hostel was to have housed 300 Malians transferred from the UDF-controlled municipality of Saint-Maur-des-Fossés. Charged with racial significance, this incident brought the issue of immigration into the presidential campaign and appeared a blatant attempt by the PCF to mobilise the sort of support on which the FN would soon thrive in similarly sensitive municipalities.[70]

The antagonistic response by the parties of the centre-right to the Mauroy government's pro-immigrant reforms focused attention still further on immigra-tion and its perceived connections to crime and urban insecurity. The 6.78 per cent of the population registered as immigrants in the March 1982 census was barely higher than that recorded in 1931 (6.58 per cent);[71] while the proportion remained the same, however, the nature of immigration itself had changed, and with it public perceptions. In the campaign for the municipal elections of March 1983, the UDF mayor of Toulon, Maurice Arreckx, declared that he would not allow the town to become the 'dustbin' of Europe and Africa, while the future UDF mayor of Saint-Etienne, François Dubanchet, called for 'an end to dark-skinned delinquency'. In Paris, the RPR's Alain Juppé played on the equation between illegal immigration and crime, while RPR and UDF candidates issued a joint tract proclaiming 'This invasion must be stopped!' In summer 1983, the then Mayor of Paris and RPR leader, Jacques Chirac, declared that France 'no longer has the means to support a host of foreigners who abuse her hospitality' and that in Paris 'the threshold of tolerance has been exceeded'.[72] At the same time, the secretary of state with responsibility for immigration, Georgina Dufoix, announced that up to 3,500 *sans-papiers* were detained pending removal and urged on immigrants the need to 'respect French laws and the living habits of French people'. In an interview the following spring, the Interior Minister, Gaston Defferre, went much further, depicting a France 'invaded by foreigners from the four corners of the globe', a haven for bogus North African tourists, black marketeers, criminals and Islamic fundamentalists.[73]

By the time the FN mounted its campaign for the European elections of June 1984, the issue of immigration had thus found a new salience in local and national political debate. The centrepiece of the FN's campaign was its slogan '*Les Français d'abord*' ('The French First'), a variant of the cry that had echoed down through the French extreme right for a century. The arch-anti-Semite Edouard Drumont had first given currency to the call for '*La France aux Français*' ('France for the French'), a call taken up by Charles Maurras and appropriated by the right-wing leagues of the inter-war years. This had been shouted during the anti-parliamentary demonstrations of 6 February 1934 before becoming the guiding principle of the exclusive nationalism promulgated under Vichy.

The opportunity opened up to the FN by the new importance of immigration was evident from polls which showed this to be the main motivating factor in the FN vote. In advance of the elections of June 1984, 64 per cent of those expressing an intention to support the FN cited immigration as their prime concern.[74] Combined with a perceived breakdown in law and order and the ill effects of economic recession, the spectre of a 'foreign invasion' was waved again in the France of the 1980s as it had been in that of the 1930s. Among the electorate at large, the FN attracted 48 per cent of those most concerned about immigration and 22 per cent of those most concerned about law and order.[75] The electoral geography of the FN vote confirmed the party's strong showing in urban, industrially depressed areas where immigrants (especially North Africans) and crime were linked in the experience or the imagination of voters. Roughly one in five voters supported Le Pen's party in towns such as Roubaix, Dreux, Mantes-la-Jolie, Mulhouse, Saint-Etienne, and in the southern conurbations of Marseille, Toulon, Nice and Montpellier. Despite the historical resonances in the FN's discourse, this vote expressed not the backward-looking grievances in which the extreme right had historically traded but the social problems of a modern, urban France in the grip of economic crisis.[76]

Raising the stakes: 1984–88

The FN emerged from the European elections of 1984 with its base of militant support greatly strengthened. Whereas it had struggled to field 65 candidates for the cantonal elections of 1982, it now inflated to 60,000 its claimed membership and presented over 1,500 candidates in the elections of 1985.[77] Cantonal elections renew France's departmental councils (*conseils généraux*) for a six-year term, with half of the 4,038 seats being renewed every three years. They centre on local issues and personalities, making it difficult for a party without local implantation to gain ground. In the elections of March 1982, the FN had attracted 0.2 per cent of the first-round vote; in March 1985, it won on average 10.5 per cent in the three-quarters of renewable cantons which it contested, 8.7 per cent of the vote overall. Support for Le Pen's party soared to over 30 per cent in some pockets of Provence-Alpes-Côte d'Azur (Toulon, Nice, Marseille), placing the FN at times ahead of the RPR and UDF. Due to the two-round majority voting system and the lack of electoral alliances, these results were translated into a single seat (Marseille-2) for the FN out of some 2,000 cantons at stake.

These cantonal elections were important for the FN not so much in themselves but as a trial run for the more significant legislative and regional elections of March 1986. Here the FN's prospects were transformed by President Mitterrand's decision to break with a tradition as old as the Fifth Republic itself and institute a system of proportional representation for a legislative poll. Though anticipated in his 110-point presidential manifesto, this was seen as a calculated move to reduce the Socialists' losses and the centre-right's predicted majority by opening the doors of the National Assembly to the FN. The intention was to increase the President's room for manoeuvre in the likely event of having to 'cohabit' with a centre-right Prime Minister and government until the end of his term in 1988. 'In 1986', Mitterrand would later reflect, 'I considered that a victory for the RPR and its allies represented a greater risk to the country than the election of some Front National deputies.'[78]

As in June 1984, the FN was able in these elections to convert support into seats. Winning 9.8 per cent (2,699,307 votes), it secured 35 seats (some 6 per cent by the rules of the proportional system applied), almost depriving the RPR-UDF alliance of a majority. A party which had had recourse to small ads to constitute its lists for municipal elections only three years before now relished the prospect of having its own parliamentary group. In the regional elections held on the same day (and also on a proportional basis), the FN won 9.7 per cent and 137 seats, gaining representation in 21 of metropolitan France's 22 regional councils, with the sole exception of the rural Limousin. The RPR, UDF and smaller centre-right parties scraped a majority of only two seats in the National Assembly, obviating the need to countenance a parliamentary alliance with the FN. Not so, however, in a number of regional councils, where the support of the FN clinched presidencies for centre-right candidates. These instances saw FN councillors accede to vice-presidential posts in four regions (Haute-Normandie, Picardie, Languedoc-Roussillon and Provence-Alpes-Côte d'Azur) and administrative positions in three others (Aquitaine, Midi-Pyrénées, Franche-Comté), giving the party influence in regional government across the entire Mediterranean littoral and a sizeable section of the north.

The FN's performance in the 1986 legislative elections placed it marginally ahead of the PCF, which won 35 seats on 9.7 per cent of the vote (Table 8.2). This worst electoral performance in over half a century for the PCF was, by contrast, an unprecedented triumph for the FN. With its 35 deputies, Le Pen's party gained the right to representation on parliamentary committees and to a range of other parliamentary privileges.

The legislative and regional elections confirmed the geographical voting pattern that had emerged from the European and cantonal elections. Support for the FN was concentrated largely east of a line connecting the regional capitals of Caen, Lyon and Montpellier, reaching its highest levels in the south-east, the north and north-east, in the greater Paris conurbation and the Rhône valley. The real heartlands were again the Mediterranean coastal regions of Provence-Alpes-Côte d'Azur and Languedoc-Roussillon. In the legislative vote, the FN exceeded 24 per cent in Marseille (where its anti-immigrant message found a ready audience) and 25 per cent in Perpignan (where law and order played strongly). In the populous Bouches-du-Rhône department which Marseille dominates, the FN emerged as the most powerful party of the right with 22.53 per cent (up 3 per cent on 1984). It likewise increased its showing by some 3 per cent in Pyrénées-Orientales (19.08 per cent) and Vaucluse (19.49 per cent), while retaining a strong presence in Alpes-Maritimes (20.88 per cent), Var (17.77 per cent) and Hérault (15.55 per cent).[79] Twenty of the FN's 35 deputies were elected from only three regions (accounting for some 60 per cent of resident foreigners in France): eight from Provence-Alpes-Côte d'Azur, eight from Ile-de-France, and four from Rhône-Alpes.[80]

With 95 FN lists contesting seats attributable on a departmental basis across France, these elections allowed Le Pen's party to work on its national implantation.

Table 8.2 The 1986 legislative elections (metropolitan France)

	Votes cast	*%*
PCF	2,662,244	9.7
PS	8,642,661	31.5
RPR	3,059,124	11.1
UDF	2,316,719	8.4
RPR/UDF (joint lists)	5,859,922	21.4
Various right	1,018,240	3.7
FN	2,699,307	9.8 (35 of 577 seats)

Source: Interior Ministry (La Documentation Française, *Institutions et vie politique sous la Ve République*, Paris, 2003, p. 175).

They also demonstrated the difficulty of passing from a European election to a national election with higher political stakes. The FN exceeded 10 per cent in 31 departments as opposed to 44 in 1984. While the party held its ground in some former left-wing strongholds such as Pas-de-Calais (11.35 per cent), its share of the vote dropped appreciably in a number of departments around Paris and Lyon and in many less urbanised locations. Analysts located the reason for this in the FN's failure to retain many of those centre-right voters who, radicalised by the victory of the left in 1981, had cast a protest vote for the FN in the European elections of 1984. This interpretation was borne out by exit polls in 1986 which showed around a third of the FN electorate of 1984 returning now to the RPR-UDF alliance. The FN maintained its overall share of the vote by attracting in their place new defectors from the centre-right and to a lesser extent the left, together with first-time voters and former abstentionists. With no firm political anchorage, the latter accentuated the already strong element of protest in the FN vote.[81]

The 1986 elections confirmed that the FN vote had a dynamic of its own rather than being merely a radicalised form of right-of-centre voting. Geographically, the electoral maps of the FN and the RPR-UDF were quite distinct. In conservative bastions such as the departments of Mayenne, Vendée or Lozère, where the centre-right commanded up to 60 per cent of the vote, the FN performed very poorly (3–6 per cent). Sociologically, too, there was marked divergence. Whereas the RPR-UDF electorate was composed in its majority of women, those aged 50 or over, and practising Catholics, FN voters were predominantly male, young to middle-aged, and non-practising Catholics or of no religious persuasion. Some four in ten FN voters in 1986 were aged under 35, showing the party's ability to make inroads into the younger electorate.[82]

The capacity of the FN to challenge the left as well as the centre-right was demonstrated by the growing support which it found among blue-collar workers, 11 per cent of whom voted FN in these elections – up from 9 per cent in the European elections of June 1984.[83] The FN vote in 1986 held up better in some constituencies run by the PCF than in many others governed by the centre-right; gains in Communist-controlled suburbs and losses in the *beaux quartiers* of Paris reflected what Pascal Perrineau called, rather too schematically, the 'proletariani-sation' of the FN vote.[84] While support dropped back among shopkeepers and artisans (14 per cent), farmers and agricultural workers (11 per cent), managers and liberal professionals (9–10 per cent), and white-collar workers (7 per cent), it rose among the unemployed (14 per cent). These early signs of evolution within the FN electorate prompted another commentator to describe the FN vote in 1986 (again too schematically) as no longer one of 'political radicalisation' but rather one of 'desperation'.[85] Where there was remarkable constancy between 1984 and 1986 was in declared voting motivation. In 1986, 60 per cent of FN voters polled by SOFRES cited immigration and 50 per cent *insécurité* as issues of most concern (against 7–16 per cent and 10–31 per cent respectively among voters of other parties).[86]

The final important lesson to emerge from analysis of the FN vote in these elections related to the perception which FN voters had of themselves politically. In June 1984, 39 per cent of those polled by SOFRES had considered themselves closest to the parties of the centre-right, with only 34 per cent expressing a preference for the FN; 10 per cent had signalled a left-wing attachment and 16 per cent no political preference at all. In 1986, those citing the RPR-UDF dropped to 20 per cent, while those declaring a preference for the FN rose to 57 per cent.[87] This suggested the growing acceptability of the FN as a viable political alternative for an increasing number of voters. With two-thirds of its 1984 vote retained, it also suggested the improved prospects for the party of forging a stable support base from its heterogeneous electorate.

Beyond the FN electorate itself, moreover, lay a sizeable reserve of potential support, as suggested by the combined findings of two SOFRES polls from October 1985 and March 1986. Though only 9.8 per cent of the electorate voted for the FN in 1986, 14 per cent of respondents held a positive opinion of the party, 18 per cent wished to see Le Pen play a significant role in the future, and 23 per cent agreed generally with Le Pen's ideas. This latter figure rose to 29 per cent on law and order and to 31 per cent on immigration.[88]

The FN programme in the mid-1980s: change and continuity

The platform on which the FN effected its electoral breakthrough bore little resemblance, in a number of important respects, to that on which it had been launched a decade before. Where immigration had been deemed to warrant only two brief references in 1973,[89] it now constituted the centrepiece of the party's programme. A 15-page chapter in the programme for the 1986 legislative elections held immigrants largely responsible for the ills of contemporary France, from crime and unemployment to economic recession, declining educational standards and the threat to national identity.[90] Adding its voice to a debate whose terms had by now been sharply radicalised, the FN warned of 'an invasion – for the moment peaceful – of French territory' and called for aggressive application of 'the principle of national preference', since 'it is the very existence of the French people that is at stake'. The 'comprehensive and coherent immigration policy' which the FN proposed was summed up thus:

> revision of the Nationality Code, an end to inter-cultural teaching in schools, a block on family reunion, the expulsion of illegal immigrants and delinquents, the return of unemployed immigrants to their countries of origin, the restriction of family allowance and social benefits to French nationals, tighter control over the admission of refugees under the Geneva Convention, the institution of a system to ensure nationals are first in line for employment, and the setting up of a repatriation savings scheme.

The FN called for the scrapping of the renewable 10-year residence and work permit, opposed any move to grant immigrants political rights, and proposed (through revision of the Nationality Code) to abolish automatic access to French nationality, tighten the procedures for naturalisation, and end dual French-Algerian nationality. As it stood, claimed the FN, the Nationality Code created 'more French citizens "despite themselves" or through opportunism than through love of France'.

Spelling out what was to be understood by the term 'immigrant', the FN's 1986 programme returned to the distinction laid down in essence by the Calvez Report of 1969, which had called explicitly for 'a strictly selective immigration policy' based on ethnic criteria.[91] It was necessary, argued the FN in turn, to 'distinguish between foreigners of European origin who can be easily integrated and those of Third World origin who are difficult to assimilate because of both their large numbers and the specific nature of their culture and religion, which predispose them to resist assimilation, a position exacerbated by fundamentalist elements or the promptings of their home governments'. The FN recognised 'the obligations which we have towards the nationals of our European partner states in accordance with Community treaties and in the interests of the solidarity vital for the common defence of Europe'. It proposed that family allowance and associated benefits be open to EEC nationals, while unemployment benefit should be restricted to French citizens and assisted housing reserved first and foremost for French families.[92] It also argued that the right of asylum should be limited to 'genuine refugees, especially those from countries under the yoke of communism and who have historical ties with France'. Finally, it envisaged the repatriation of some two million immigrants and dependants over five years funded by an employment savings scheme for immigrant workers.

On law and order, the FN's 1973 programme had devoted a few lines to denouncing 'irresponsible and partisan elements' within the judiciary and advocating some reforms in the justice system.[93] In 1986, the FN went much further in devoting a chapter of its programme to the escalation of crime and the insufficiency of the penal system.[94] It denounced some of the Socialists' earliest reforms, notably the abolition of capital punishment, of the State Security Court, of the *Loi sécurité et liberté*, and of police powers to stop and search. It cited drug trafficking and terrorism as grave threats to the fabric of French society, and argued a strong link between criminality and immigration. It called for the reinstatement of the death penalty for international drug trafficking and serious terrorist offences; an end to 'no-go' areas in the suburbs of cities such as Lyon and Marseille; a more rigorous prison regime and a building programme to increase capacity by around a quarter; prison sentences for all acts of delinquency, with a requirement that prison terms be served in full; and strict application of the laws on drug consumption. To replace the State Security Court, the FN proposed that a 'central criminal court' be set up with powers to deal with threats to state security, organised crime and large-scale drug trafficking.

In economic terms, too, the 1986 platform owed little to that of 1973. Whereas the FN's first programme bore the stamp of corporatism, that of 1986 was resolutely neo-liberal. Gone were the 'direct and joint responsibilities' of employers' organisations and employees, the empowerment of 'responsible social partners' to resolve conflicts in the workplace, and the role of the state to act as 'arbiter' and 'correct the excesses as required' of employers and the workforce. Gone, too, was the expectation that the government should 'define the overall economic orientation of the country' in consultation with major agencies such as trade unions, consumer interest groups and public-sector representatives.[95] The economics of the FN in the 1980s were not those of social dialogue: they were about deregulation, the free market, competition, enterprise, profit, and rolling back the state.

As part of a 'truly liberal revolution', the 1986 programme called for the abrogation or amendment of the Auroux Laws regulating employer–worker relations; the relaxing of the 39-hour working week; the denationalisation of industries and financial concerns taken into state ownership by the Socialists; and the end of state subsidies to industry. With a view to instituting a 'truly popular capitalism', the FN advocated widespread property-owning and share-owning, proposing that state-controlled companies be privatised and their shares distributed among French families according to the number of children. Taking inspiration explicitly from the sale of council housing by the Thatcher administration in Britain, the programme called for a similar initiative in France. Again drawing inspiration from Thatcher and Reagan both, the FN proposed to phase out income tax and cut public spending in accordance with the bald precept: 'less aid and less tax'. Arguing that the state should be limited to its essential functions of justice, policing, diplomacy and defence, the FN proposed to slash the number of civil servants and open the public sector to direct competition from the private sector.[96]

In setting out to 'defend the French' in 1973, the FN had not identified unemployment as an immediate or even long-term danger; the language was still of 'economic growth', 'development' and 'expansion'. By 1986, unemployment had become 'a worsening social scourge' which, the FN claimed in defiance of official statistics, had already exceeded three million. It located the cause of this unemployment not in international economic conditions but rather in decades of economic mismanagement in France, where the pursuit of an 'egalitarian Utopia' had 'injected the economy with ever increasing doses of *dirigisme*, interventionism, statism, in a word socialism'. Through the 'limitless extension of the welfare state', the virtues of personal endeavour and thrift had given way to a 'dependence mentality'. At the insistence of Marxist trade unions, the French economy had become bogged down in a morass of regulations and obligatory social security charges which left it unable to surmount the economic downturn of the 1970s.

To this economic analysis the FN brought its plan for recovery: the wholesale deregulation of the workplace with the single, overriding exception that French nationals should be systematically prioritised for employment while immigrants (specifically non-EEC nationals) would be progressively removed as a factor in the economy. The FN called for the expulsion of illegal immigrants and severe sanctions against their employers, together with the deportation of unemployed foreigners, who would have their right to unemployment benefit suppressed. It envisaged not that French nationals would simply step into jobs vacated by immigrants but rather that the removal of immigrant labour would provide a stimulus for technological modernisation which would in turn create new job opportunities. The models to be followed in liberalising the workplace were the United States, Japan and Britain. Employers should be free to set their own rates of pay, work practices and working hours, and the terms and duration of employment contracts. The FN called for tax and social security charges to be eased on small and medium-sized business as the sector most adapted for growth in the economic climate of the mid-1980s.[97]

On the three major planks of its 1986 platform, then, the FN showed the extent of its evolution from the programme on which it had campaigned in its earliest years. There were also important areas of continuity: in its anti-communism, its imprecations against moral degeneracy, its promotion of the family, its calls for an integrated European defence strategy and for a modern professional French army on the British model. The 'special complementary allowance' proposed in the 1970s as an incentive for mothers to devote themselves to child-rearing became a 'maternal income' (of 5,000 francs a month for mothers of three or more children), as the later programme sounded yet more acute concern over demographic decline. Measured opposition to abortion in the 1973 programme had quickly given way to outright rejection of the 1975 Veil Law, reiterated now with vehemence 10 years on.

In its earlier programme, the FN had called for 'a truly presidential regime' giving the executive primacy over the legislature; it now complained of an imbalance of power in that direction and called for a strengthened parliament restored to its full deliberative and legislative functions. It proposed expanded use of referenda, with the implementation of a 'referendum by popular initiative' – taking the opportunity to call again here for a referendum on immigration. It had already published, in 1985, a 24-page booklet entitled *Pour un référendum sur l'immigration* through which it sought to raise a national petition with a view to bringing this about.

Just as in the 1970s, a strong theme of the FN's programme in the 1980s was its Europeanism. The earlier call for France to be part of a 'European confederation' was now amplified, with the same central stress on defence. Europe offered a higher plane on which to protect France against the threats – social, cultural, economic, demographic and military – confronting it. On Europe as a political construct the FN's programme was scathing, dismissing the European Parliament as 'an assembly sensitive to Marxist dialectic and responsive to Third World ideology', and the Commission as 'a body under the influence of bureaucratic socialism'; but Europe as a broad cultural community was exalted as 'an ensemble of laws, morals, customs, rules of personal behaviour, in short values which constitute the common storehouse of a civilisation'. Political Europe was a necessary instrument for the preservation of cultural, and ethnic, Europe. Hence the FN's calls in 1986 for a European 'common currency', a 'defence capability and the political will to support it', a 'common police force', and a 'European judiciary tasked with defeating terrorism'. The Europe espoused here was a quasi-Gaullist *Europe des patries* comprising 'the nations held captive' behind the Iron Curtain. The FN advocated a European nuclear strategy centred on France and closer cooperation with the United States in a pact of mutual support.[98] Faced with the conjoined threats of Soviet communism and revolutionary Islamic fundamentalism, Le Pen and his party invoked a history of armed resistance going back to the battle of Marathon, where the Greeks had stemmed the advance of the Persian army in 490 B.C.

The FN in parliament

The FN would implement nothing of this programme during its brief existence as a parliamentary group between 1986 and 1988. Having failed to emerge as the power-broker in a hung assembly, it resigned itself to a posture of opposition, joining with the PS and PCF in voting against the incoming government of Jacques Chirac, which narrowly won the confidence of deputies by 292 to 285 votes. Le Pen made no secret that the FN withheld its support in protest at the 'political apartheid' imposed upon it by the parliamentary centre-right.[99]

Though reduced to a marginal role, the FN could nonetheless use its presence in parliament to project an image of democratic respectability – an image embodied by the group of lawyers, doctors, academics, company directors, journalists and others seated with Le Pen on the FN benches. Among these were a number of former RPR, UDF and CNIP notables (Pascal Arrighi, Charles de Chambrun, Edouard Frédéric-Dupont), other recruits from the centre-right (Bruno Chauvierre, Michel de Rostolan), and respectable professionals (Dr François Bachelot, Guy Le Jaouen). Beyond such figures, the FN group offered a panorama of the French far right, with Le Pen loyalists (Chaboche, Reveau, Peyrat, Bompard), 'solidarists' (Stirbois, Baeckeroot), *Algérie Française* diehards (Holeindre, Sergent, Descaves), a monarchist (Georges-Paul Wagner), right-wing intellectuals (Bruno Gollnisch, Jean-Claude Martinez) and *habitués* of the Nouvelle Droite (Yvon Briant, Bruno Mégret). Catholic fundamentalism was already prominently represented in the FN's European group by Bernard Antony, styling himself Romain Marie.

Unlike the Poujadists in the 1956–58 legislature, these were largely competent politicians, aware of parliamentary procedure and able to contribute to the workings of the National Assembly in full session and in committee (with Jean-Claude Martinez, a specialist in public law and tax, being entrusted notably with preparing reports on the national education budget).[100] Again unlike the Poujadists, they used their parliamentary presence to push forward their agenda, tabling an array of proposals and amendments to articulate their main policies: 'national preference' in employment and housing; a tax on immigrant labour; reform of the Nationality Code; tougher anti-terrorist and anti-drugs legislation, with restoration of the death penalty; a maternal salary; a 'plural vote' in proportion to family size; restrictions on striking in the public sector; and an end to state-subsidised abortion. Despite these periodic sallies, the presence of the FN in the National Assembly was largely unremarkable. In the first 18 months of the legislature, the left-leaning daily *Le Monde* noted the party's 'assiduous' contribution to debates and sustained air of 'parliamentary virtue'.[101]

The only occasion on which FN deputies would depart markedly from this image of Republican correctness was on the night of 9–10 October 1987, when they created a rumpus in the National Assembly over the tabling of a bill to combat drug trafficking. In the same session, two amendments relating to separate legislation were also tabled, one condemning incitement to racism, the other criminalising the defence of crimes against humanity. In an almost empty chamber, FN deputies engaged in a series of blocking manoeuvres and rowdy, intimidating behaviour for some 10 hours before the bill was adopted. Their purpose, they claimed, was to oppose a bill that did not go far enough in tackling the problem of drug trafficking, to highlight parliamentary absenteeism during a vote on such an important issue, and to expose the accepted practice that deputies in attendance (on this occasion eight RPR-UDF, four Socialist and one Communist) could vote electronically on behalf of their absent colleagues. To those who witnessed it and those who reported on it, the behaviour of FN deputies that night seemed a throwback to other manifestations of right-wing anti-parliamentarism, from the inter-war leagues to the Poujadists.[102]

The FN's real grievance lay not in parliamentary procedure but in the fact that it was excluded from the governing majority. Le Pen denounced Prime Minister Chirac as a 'socialist minister of the right' and dismissed his power-sharing with President Mitterrand (the first such arrangement under the Fifth Republic) as 'liberal-socialism'.[103] The FN opposed the government's economic programme, presented by Finance Minister Edouard Balladur, as being insufficiently liberal despite its abolition of the Socialists' wealth tax, emphasis on deregulation and extensive privatisation agenda. The opposition mounted by the FN leadership to the RPR-UDF government, together with Le Pen's occasional verbal intemperance, caused dissension within the parliamentary group and brought about a number of defections (Chauvierre, Le Jaouen, Briant).[104] To the FN group as a whole it was clear that their days in the National Assembly would be numbered, since one of the first steps taken by the Chirac government was to reinstate the two-round system of majority voting for the next legislative elections.

Radicalising the right: the 'original' and the 'copy'

While the FN's programme was nullified by its failure to hold the balance of power, the new RPR-UDF government came to office resolved to recover ground on the right lost to Le Pen. In their joint electoral manifesto, the RPR and UDF had emphasised law and order and immigration control. The 'Platform for Governing Together' which they published in January 1986 pledged a firm line on immigration and reform of the procedures for acquiring French citizenship, while accusing the outgoing Socialists of promoting a climate in which delinquency, crime and racial tensions flourished. To immigrants legally settled in France it offered the simple choice: 'integration or subsidised repatriation'.[105] Going further than its alliance partner, the RPR also proposed – with a strong echo of the FN – that 'benefits promoting population growth should be reserved for nationals only'.[106] This did not find its way into the joint manifesto or the government's programme, but the fact that it could be put forward by France's largest party of the centre-right demonstrated the extent to which policies previously held to be extremist were gaining currency in mainstream political discourse.

Part of the impetus for this was provided by the right-wing press, and especially those publications under the influence of the Nouvelle Droite. On 26 October 1985, *Le Figaro-Magazine* ran its cover page with a bust of Marianne in Muslim attire and the question: 'Will we still be French in thirty years?' Inside was a dossier on immigration which predicted that, by 2015, France would be submerged by an alien, Arab Muslim population and culture. This was presented as the work of Jean Raspail, a writer with close ties to the PFN and GRECE. Other publications bearing the imprimatur of the Nouvelle Droite appeared at the same time, lending a veneer of intellectual credence to the view – propagated by Le Pen and the FN – that French 'national identity' was under threat.

The appointment of the tough neo-Gaullist Charles Pasqua as Interior Minister, and the creation of a special minister with responsibility for public security in the former police chief Robert Pandraud, signalled Chirac's intent to clamp down on immigration and public order issues. Le Pen claimed, plausibly, that Pasqua was 'a bulwark preventing part of the RPR electorate from defecting to the Front National'.[107] The police were given new powers to carry out random identity checks, together with wider powers for the surveillance, arrest and detention of suspected criminals and terrorists. The application of court sentences was stiffened and, with shades of the abolished State Security Court, special tribunals without juries were set up to deal with terrorist offences. An extended maximum sentence for capital offences was brought in, stopping short of the death penalty against which Chirac himself had voted in 1981. Controls on non-EEC foreigners entering France were tightened; so too the conditions governing political asylum. Illegal immigrants could once again be expelled by administrative rather than judicial order – as 101 Malians bundled aboard a charter plane at Orly airport in full view of the national media would discover.

The government also drew up a bill to reform the Nationality Code whereby the children of immigrants would no longer be granted French citizenship automatically at the age of 18 but would have to apply for it, undergoing a proficiency test in French and swearing an oath of allegiance to the Republic. As it stood, the Nationality Code accorded French citizenship either, at birth, to the offspring of at least one French parent (Article 23: *jus sanguinis*), or, at the age of 18, to children born of foreign parents in France who had resided in the country during the five years preceding their majority (Article 44: *jus soli*), unless they chose expressly to refuse it. The bill encountered such opposition that it never went before parliament, being referred instead to a special commission which removed its more controversial proposals;[108] but it showed again the new tenor of public debate on immigration and nationality.

The Chirac government's reforms on law and order and immigration provoked criticism from President Mitterrand, opposition parties, human rights and immigrant organisations, students and a section of the French clergy. The former Socialist minister Yvette Roudy, with little measure in her words, deplored the emergence of 'a fascistic police state' reminiscent of 'the worst days of the Occupation and Pétainist moral order'.[109] Within the French public as a whole, by contrast, the reforms met with little resistance. The campaign for the March 1986 elections had been punctuated by a number of bombings in Paris for which the perpetrators, suspected of belonging to radical Islamist groups, remained at large. In September, a wave of further and bloodier bombings did much to vindicate the government's muscular stance and to heighten public receptivity to a show of force in policing the streets.

Confronted with the spectacle of a government intent on rendering him redundant, Le Pen fell back on his argument that the French would always prefer the 'original' to the 'copy'. The opportunity to test this would be the presidential election due in spring 1988. Though Le Pen's campaign began unofficially in the months following the legislative elections of 1986 (with trips to South East Asia, the United States and Africa to puff up his claim to statesmanship), it was formally launched on 26 April 1987. The management of the campaign was entrusted to Bruno Mégret, the new rival to Stirbois as FN fixer-in-chief. At the head of his small Comités d'Action Républicaine (CAR), Mégret had nothing about him of the extreme-right activist *à la* Stirbois. A highly educated techno-crat, he had occupied posts in the upper echelons of the civil service under Giscard d'Estaing, gravitating politically to the RPR (as a member of its central committee, 1979–81) and ideologically to the Club de l'Horloge (as an influential member, 1975–81). He had stood as an RPR candidate in the 1981 legislative elections before quitting Chirac's party to set up his CAR in 1982 and joining the FN in late 1985, helping to smooth the path of other notables from the centre-right enlisted by Le Pen for the 1986 elections. When Stirbois was killed in a car accident in November 1988, Mégret, in his newly created post of dele-gate-general, would be left unrivalled as the FN's *de facto* deputy leader for the next decade.

The 1988 presidential and legislative elections

Almost a quarter-century after having managed Tixier-Vignancour's campaign and 14 years on from his own abortive bid, Le Pen was again a challenger for France's highest political office. In announcing his candidacy, he addressed a 'French people at risk of being ruined, overrun and enslaved'. He denounced the failure of France's political parties and institutions to resist the 'oligarchies, factions and national or foreign lobbies' dragging the country into the abyss. The 'clinical symptoms of mortal decadence', he claimed, were 'demographic crisis, immigration, unemployment, insecurity, a burdensome administrative and fiscal state, and moral degeneracy'.[110] To this familiar store of evils Le Pen now brought a new addition: the AIDS virus (*le SIDA*). Here was an issue which allowed the FN leader to combine his imprecations against moral dissolution, homosexuality, drug abuse and, above all, immigration. Calling for AIDS sufferers to be confined in '*sidatoriums*', he deemed it 'one more pernicious effect of immigration that this scourge should be visited upon us'.[111]

Running as outsider

Some weeks before its official announcement, Le Pen launched his campaign with a rally in the Zenith concert hall in Paris which attracted some 10,000 flag-waving supporters. Also present were a number of figures from the mainstream right (among them the RPR mayor of Nice, Jacques Médecin, and the president of the CNIP, Philippe Malaud).[112] The rally demonstrated Le Pen's capacity to draw large, enthusiastic crowds and signalled the narrowing gap between the FN and some elements of the centre-right.

The first stage of the campaign proper was a tried and tested one. In summer 1987, Le Pen and his campaign team undertook a *tournée des plages* (tour of the beaches) from Ajaccio to Dunkerque, as in the good old days of Poujadism, *Algérie Française* and the 'TV caravan'. This was followed by an exacting schedule of meetings throughout France in which Le Pen exhibited his considerable talents as an orator, haranguing and amusing his paying audiences. His campaign was marked by its populist tone. Like his early mentor Poujade, Le Pen cast himself as the representative of the people against the establishment, or 'gang of four' (RPR, UDF, PS, PCF). '*Avec Le Pen – Les Français à l'Elysée*' ('With Le Pen – the French in the Elysée'), proclaimed his posters and tracts. Some of these featured a broadly smiling Le Pen against a race-course backdrop, with the (loaded) slogan: 'The Outsider – Let's defend our colours.'

Keen to shed his image of political pariah, the gentrified leader of the FN applied a fastidious attention to wardrobe, diet and hairstyle in his campaign preparations. Similarly, Le Pen's minders were turned out in well-pressed blazers, though the cropped hair remained a distinguishing feature. This was a new improved Le Pen, repackaged for the television age and seeking to broaden his appeal among more moderate conservative voters. In a lacklustre campaign, no candidate came close to rivalling his ability to enthuse audiences at rallies or to boost viewing figures in his periodic television appearances.

The central theme in Le Pen's campaign was '*la préférence nationale*', priority for the French in jobs, housing, education, health care and welfare support. This was a theme that bore the stamp of the Nouvelle Droite, hatched by Jean-Yves Le Gallou and the Club de l'Horloge in the mid-1980s.[113] Le Pen used it to argue for a restrictive revision of the Nationality Code as the first step in preserving '*l'iden-tité nationale*'. More broadly, his campaign called for a law allowing 'referenda by popular initiative'; restoration of the death penalty for murderers, terrorists and drug traffickers; a 'family income' for French parents, with the state funds hitherto covering abortion being reallocated for research into sterility; separate social security systems for French and foreign workers; limitations on the right to strike in the public sector; the reduction and phasing out ('within five to seven years') of income tax; the right of social housing tenants to buy their homes; and the expulsion of illegal and unemployed immigrants together with those convicted of criminal offences. Though the message was still markedly pro-European, calling for closer military and monetary integration, the emphasis remained on the nation state as the irreducible core. With echoes of Pétain, Le Pen called for a '*redressement national*', a purge of leftist schoolbooks imparting 'mistakenly egalitarian' ideas, a tricolour in every classroom, and 'the restoration of moral values marking the line that separates good from evil'.[114]

The devil in the detail

By now Le Pen was guaranteed the close attention of journalists and broadcasters, with an assured share of television and radio airtime. Interest in his private life was heightened in June 1987 when his estranged wife, Pierrette, bared more than her bitterness towards her ex-husband in *Playboy* and brought an element of bedroom farce for a time to his campaign. Le Pen's rise had not been reversed by allegations of torture during the Algerian War, of bribery in his selection of FN candidates, or of tax evasion on the estate which he had inherited by reportedly questionable means. On 13 September 1987, in a televised interview, he subjected his standing in public opinion to a further severe test. Ever since his days as a Poujadist, Le Pen had been accused of, and denied, being anti-Semitic. Asked on this occasion what he thought of Holocaust revisionists, he declared that there were 'a number of questions' in his mind, that he would 'not say that the gas chambers did not exist' but that he thought them to be 'a point of detail in the history of the Second World War'. Pressed by his interviewers, he added that there had been 'hundreds of thousands, perhaps millions of Jews killed along with people who were not Jewish', but that this was not 'a revealed truth in which everyone must believe as a moral obligation'. There were, Le Pen protested, 'historians debating these questions'.[115]

The remarks caused uproar. Le Pen's carefully confected image of respectability was undone at a stroke. Though he declared himself the victim of 'intellectual terrorism' and sought refuge in laboured definitions of the term 'detail',[116] the expression of doubt over the Holocaust played to a pronounced anti-Semitism in some quarters of his party. This was articulated not through the FN's official publications but through sympathetic organs such as the Catholic fundamentalist daily, *Présent*. Brought to the FN by Bernard Antony in 1984 and claiming a readership of 30,000, *Présent* took as its own the trilogy '*Travail, Famille, Patrie*' and located itself in terms of morality 'on the right of the extreme right'.[117] It articulated an anti-Semitism reminiscent of the 1930s and of Vichy, denouncing 'a new intrusion of the Jewish phenomenon' and 'the tendency of Jews to occupy all the key posts in Western nations'. Like the inter-war extreme-right press in its attacks on Léon Blum and the Popular Front, *Présent* vilified Mitterrand's Jewish Minister of Justice, Robert Badinter, as a nomad whose 'heritage disposes him to defend the migrant against the settler, the cosmopolitan against the indigenous, the gypsy stealer of chickens against the farmer's wife,

[. . .] the murderer against the murdered'. Vilified too were other Jewish members of Mitterrand's government (Jack Lang, Charles Fiterman) and other Jews prominent in public life, such as broadcasters ('the Arons, Ben Syouns, Naos, Elkabbashes, Druckers, Grumbachs, Zitrones') and the communist trade union leader, Henri Krasucki. The same organ accused former Health Minister Simone Veil, a Jewish survivor of Auschwitz and author of the 1975 abortion law, of being a 'complete stranger' to Christian morality and an 'evildoer of the worst kind, guilty of the most abominable crime'.[118]

For this architect of liberal reform in sexual mores, the FN coined its own shorthand invective, as 'Giscard's *tricoteuse*', the 'immaculate contraception', or quite simply 'the abortionist'. More generally, Le Pen warned against the 'Jewish international' as a source of 'anti-national sentiment' and denounced the 'hidden forces and vested interests' conspiring against France.[119] Anti-racist legislation (notably the Gayssot Law of 1990, making a crime of Holocaust denial) would restrict the freedom with which those in and around the FN could express anti-Semitic sentiment, but it would not alter their world view. In mounting his opposition to the Maastricht Treaty in 1992, Le Pen would call on France to be rescued 'from the hands of foreigners, from the faceless representatives of global capitalism, from stateless bankers and Brussels technocrats'. This xenophobia infused with coded anti-Semitism had a long history, going back to Drumont, Barrès and Maurras. It revealed in the FN a paranoia undiminished on the French extreme right since the Dreyfus affair and stoked by fear of 'plots', 'treason', 'traitors', 'felony' and 'international conspiracy'.[120]

None of the foregoing would have been out of place half a century before in *L'Action Française* or *Je suis partout*. It is instructive to recall in this context the obituary for François Duprat published in the FN's own organ, *Le National*, in April 1978, which warned of the 'project of genocide' hatched against the French by 'a certain very precise lobby' and praised Duprat's revisionist writings for exposing the 'diet of lies' served up since the Second World War. Though identified by allusion only, the Jews were the object here of a double accusation: that they wielded too much power ('an execrable domination') and constituted a community afforded special protection by anti-racist legislation and the memory of the Holocaust ('a category of privileged residents').[121] In his interview on *L'Heure de vérité* in February 1984, Le Pen would stress that he considered 'Jews to be citizens like any others, but not citizens enjoying superior protection'; if anyone should benefit from superior protection, he added, 'it should be the French'.[122]

The distinction was a pointed one. This designation of Jews as un-French – and by extension anti-French – articulated the long-held view on the extreme right of the Jew as the quintessence of rootless cosmopolitanism.[123] Since his early days as a Poujadist, Le Pen had proved himself a master of provocative insinuation, pushing at the bounds of the acceptable while most often leaving open an escape route from accusations of outright anti-Semitism. In his speech to the FN's Fête des Bleu-Blanc-Rouge in September 1988, before an audience of some 10,000, he inveighed against the 'cosmopolitan mafia' engaged in a struggle to extinguish '*la France française*'. Would the day come, Le Pen asked (alluding to the yellow star imposed on Jews by the Nazis in occupied France), when those who held their Frenchness dear would be 'obliged to wear a tricolour star'?[124]

Much of the anti-Semitism that can be detected in the utterances of Le Pen and the FN is subtext, part of a larger discourse of anti-globalisation, anti-Americanism and anti-Europeanism (since 'the Europe of Brussels' is the 'Trojan horse' of the globalists).[125] The FN has called for suspicion of international organisations in all their forms, 'the UN, UNESCO, the Brussels commission, [. . .] all the agencies and circles, from the Bilderberg to the Trilateral via all kinds of clubs'.[126] The activities of international Jewish organisations such as the B'nai B'rith have aroused particular animosity in FN circles, and the disproportionate influence exerted by Jews in French public life has long been an article of faith in the FN. A SOFRES survey carried out among FN delegates at the party's 1990 congress found 88 per cent in agreement with the proposition 'The Jews have too much power in France'.[127]

In his preface to the FN's 1993 programme, *300 mesures pour la renaissance de la France*, Le Pen denounced the political establishment's 'increasingly servile compliance with foreign powers on the outside and lobbies on the inside'.[128] By then, the deepening of European integration through the Maastricht Treaty was depicted as the latest episode in an international conspiracy working against the nation throughout French history, from the Revolution of 1789 through the Dreyfus affair of the 1890s to the defeat of 1940. Lamenting the baleful effects of another treaty – that of Amsterdam – in May 1998, Le Pen would declare that 'the new slavery today is that of the New World Order, and the new slave traders are the big shots of international finance, of that anonymous and vagrant finance that seeks to destroy nations'.[129] To this vision of global conspiracy the FN leader has held with remarkable doggedness. In his speech in honour of Joan of Arc on 1 May 2004, he would warn of the 'real conspiracy against the Nation' being pursued by 'powerful ideological and financial lobbies'.[130] Again in his pre-election speech on the eve of the European poll of June 2004, Le Pen denounced the process of European integration as the project of 'anti-national lobbies' implemented 'in the interests of supranational financiers'. The 'Great Secret', he thundered, was that France and Europe were already on the way to realising 'the Utopia of a world government'.[131]

This has been the language of anti-Semitism in France for over a century, since the rantings of Drumont and the caricature of a Jewish global conspiracy served up in the infamous *Protocols of the Elders of Zion*. Though there has been no recognised negationist current in the FN since Duprat's demise in 1978, to glimpse the anti-Semitic undercurrents that traverse the party is to apprehend something of the import of Le Pen's remarks about the Holocaust in September 1987. He was taken to court by a number of anti-racist organisations, with the process costing him in financial, and for a time political, terms. His popularity dipped sharply, recovering only in January 1988 when the furore had died down. The incident prompted the departure from the FN of one of its most valued catches from the centre-right, Olivier d'Ormesson, scion of a distinguished family of diplomats, head of Le Pen's election support committee and emblem of respectability for the FN group in the European Parliament. The neo-Gaullist Minister of Social Affairs and future leader of the RPR, Philippe Séguin, announced on television that he would leave his party if it ever made a deal with the FN.[132] Le Pen's belittling of the gas chambers thus nullified d'Ormesson's efforts to bring a respectable aura to the FN leader's presidential campaign. According to the then FN insider Yann Piat, Le Pen confided to his closest associates that, in a political career spanning more than three decades, the 'point of detail' was the most unfortunate remark to have come out of his mouth.[133]

A political 'earthquake'

Yet again Le Pen showed his powers of recovery, leaving onlookers wondering what would be required for him to lose support definitively among French voters. As the polls closed on 24 April 1988, Le Pen greeted the 'earthquake' that had transformed the national political landscape.[134] With 14.4 per cent, the support of 4,376,742 voters, the FN leader achieved a hitherto inconceivable result for a far-right candidate, doubling the number of votes won by his party in 1984. Within 6 per cent of the outgoing Prime Minister, Jacques Chirac (RPR), and only some 2 per cent behind the former Prime Minister, Raymond Barre (UDF), he had redrawn the map of the French right (Table 8.3). More than that, Le Pen's score contributed to a dramatic shift in France's political balance overall, as

Table 8.3 The 1988 presidential election: first round (metropolitan and overseas France)

	Votes cast	%
Mitterrand	10,381,332	34.10
Chirac	6,075,160	19.94
Barre	5,035,144	16.54
Le Pen	4,376,742	14.40
Lajoinie	2,256,261	6.76
Waechter	1,149,897	3.78
Juquin	639,133	2.01
Laguiller	606,201	1.99
Boussel	116,874	0.38

Source: Constitutional Council (La Documentation Française, *Institutions et vie politique sous la Ve République*, Paris, 2003, p. 178).

the official PCF candidate, André Lajoinie, recorded his party's worst presidential performance yet, with just under 6.8 per cent.

While the aggregate of Chirac, Barre and Le Pen gave the right a clear majority over the combined left, Chirac's score of under 20 per cent was the lowest for any leading centre-right candidate under the Fifth Republic, and only marginally higher than that which had seen him eliminated at the first round in 1981. This poor performance was due largely to his inability to see off the challenge from Le Pen, who exceeded even the most generous predictions. The Prime Minister's oscillations over the FN and immigration (refusing a national alliance while countenancing local deals; denouncing racism but 'understanding' FN voters) exacerbated divisions on the centre-right over how to deal with the FN. Chirac's clumsy attempts on occasion to vie with Le Pen cost him support in the centre without winning over FN voters who seemed, as Le Pen claimed, to prefer the 'original' to the 'copy'. The FN leader thus proved the most valuable of allies for Mitterrand. From the moment Le Pen's score was announced, Chirac's prospects of unseating the President collapsed, since he could not hope to recuperate intact an electorate as composite and liable to dispersal as Le Pen's. Chirac lost the second round with 46 per cent to Mitterrand's 54 per cent, demonstrating his failure to secure enough either of the middle ground or of the far-right vote.

Just as for the FN, support for Le Pen was strongest in the built-up, industrialised departments of the north and east, around Paris and Lyon, and along the Mediterranean littoral. The remarkable feature of this election, however, was the progression of the Le Pen vote throughout the length and breadth of France. Le Pen exceeded 10 per cent in 76 of France's 96 metropolitan departments, progressing in rural departments like Lot-et-Garonne (15.41 per cent) and Tarn-et-Garonne (15.18 per cent), where his anti-tax, anti-state message was calculated to strike a chord with the shopkeepers, artisans, farmers and agricultural workers who had constituted the bulk of the Poujadist electorate. In the former heartlands of Poujadism, by contrast, Le Pen achieved his lowest scores (7.1 per cent in Cantal, 7.78 per cent in Creuse, and 5.92 per cent in Chirac's fief of Corrèze), though in each of these he almost doubled the FN's vote. In no department did support for the FN leader in 1988 fail to improve on the party's showing in 1986.[135]

In eight departments across the north-east and south-east, Le Pen polled over 20 per cent (Bas-Rhin, Haut-Rhin, Alpes-Maritimes, Bouches-du-Rhône, Gard, Pyrénées-Orientales, Var and Vaucluse). The most dramatic advances were in Alsace, where support rose from 13.05 to 21.93 per cent (Bas-Rhin) and from 14.46 to 22.15 per cent (Haut-Rhin). With 26.39 per cent in the former Socialist stronghold of Bouches-du-Rhône, Le Pen was only marginally beaten by Mitterrand. In the department's capital, Marseille, the FN leader topped the poll with 28.34 per cent (to Chirac and Barre's *combined* 27.87 per cent), as he did in the other major Mediterranean cities of Nice (25.92 per cent) and Toulon (27.04 per cent). In three other towns destined to become bastions of the FN, Le Pen outpolled all candidates with emphatic scores: 33.77 per cent in Marignane, 29.7 per cent in Vitrolles, and just over 27 per cent in Orange.

Analysis of the Le Pen vote in this election confirmed its heterogeneity, with support of 10 per cent or more in most socio-professional categories. Despite this spread of support, the working-class and lower middle-class components had become more pronounced, leading Pascal Perrineau to discern in this Le Pen vote a synthesis of 'old-style Poujadism and working-class protest'.[136] A Bull/BVA exit poll showed support of 31 per cent among small shopkeepers and artisans, making Le Pen by far the favoured candidate of this category. He drew strong support, too, from liberal professionals (21 per cent), farmers and agricultural workers (18 per cent), and commercial and service-industry employees (21 per cent and 15 per cent respectively). By contrast, support among teachers, social workers and the caring professions represented Le Pen's weakest appeal at 6 per cent.[137]

The FN leader's share of the vote among blue-collar workers (16 per cent) was only marginally lower than that of the PCF candidate, Lajoinie (17 per cent). This statistic concealed the fact that among workers aged under 25, Le Pen attracted 23 per cent to Lajoinie's 4 per cent (and to the 11 per cent of the other extreme-left candidates combined). More tellingly still, the FN leader's appeal to the unemployed (19 per cent) was double that of the PCF candidate (9 per cent), and three times the combined level of the other extreme-left candidates (6 per cent). This capacity to eat into the support of right and left alike was borne out by the provenance of new Le Pen voters in this election. Around a quarter of these new voters were estimated to have come from the left, while another quarter were former abstentionists, with fewer than half being radicalised supporters of the centre-right.[138]

Despite this influx of new voters, there was evidence that the FN was consolidating a stable core electorate, with an estimated 90 per cent of those who had supported the party in 1986 returning a vote for Le Pen. Compared with the earlier estimate of 67 per cent of FN voters from 1984 supporting the party again in 1986, this indicated an increasingly solid bedrock of support – more solid indeed than that of any other political formation.[139] Polls indicated the very high ratio of male to female within the Le Pen electorate, a feature characterising the traditional support base of the extreme right. Another feature of the Le Pen vote less readily characteristic of the extreme-right tradition was its relative youth, with strong support among the 18–24 and 35–49 age groups. Voting motivations followed a now familiar pattern, with a large majority of Le Pen voters citing immigration (74 per cent) and law and order (73 per cent) as their main concerns; the innovation in this election compared with those of 1984 and 1986 was the high proportion of Le Pen voters also citing unemployment as a major concern (73 per cent).[140]

Between the two rounds, the Chirac camp engaged in transparent attempts to court Le Pen voters. In an interview for the magazine *Valeurs actuelles*, Interior Minister Pasqua insisted on the 'shared concerns and shared values' of the FN and the centre-right majority: 'It seems to me quite legitimate that FN voters should be worried about the risks posed by uncontrolled immigration to public order and national identity, and we share those concerns.'[141] This was language worthy of Le Pen – and sharply at odds with Chirac's efforts to dissociate himself from the FN and its values in the run-up to the first round, when his attention

Table 8.4 The 1988 legislative elections: first round (metropolitan France)

	Votes cast	%
PCF	2,680,194	11.2
PS	8,381,827	34.9
RPR	4,614,137	19.2
UDF	4,502,712	18.8
Various right	608,695	2.5
FN	2,353,466	9.8 (1 of 577 seats*)

Source: Interior Ministry (La Documentation Française, *Institutions et vie politique sous la Ve République*, Paris, 2003, p. 175).

Note: * won on second round

had been focused more on wooing the centre-right support of Raymond Barre. The recovery of French hostages in Lebanon and the bloody rescue of gendarmes held captive by New Caledonian separatists could be read, too, as attempts to win over the Le Pen vote. Chirac even reportedly held a secret meeting with Le Pen, organised by Pasqua, to bid for the FN leader's support.[142]

At the same time, the FN was itself divided between those (like Mégret and Le Chevallier) who favoured support for Chirac in return for concessions from the centre-right, and more hard-line elements (such as Stirbois) who pushed for a 'revolutionary' vote in favour of Mitterrand. For his part, Le Pen reiterated his formula from 1981 and called on his supporters to 'vote for Joan of Arc', stressing nonetheless that a vote for Mitterrand would be the worst option.[143] In the event, his electorate split three ways: a third favoured abstention, while around a quarter of those who voted opted for Mitterrand and three-quarters for Chirac.[144]

An unholy alliance

Following the re-elected President Mitterrand's dissolution of the National Assembly, the legislative elections of June 1988, with their return to the two-ballot majority voting system, saw the virtual elimination of the FN from parliament. With 9.8 per cent (2,353,466 votes), the party preserved its 1986 percentage share of the poll but lost over 345,000 votes – and over two million of the votes garnered by Le Pen on 24 April (Table 8.4). In 1984 and 1986, the FN had reserved winnable places on its electoral lists for political worthies drawn from the centre-right, a number of whom had now quit the party. It contested the 1988 elections at short notice, with largely inexperienced and unknown party cadres ill-adapted to campaigning in single-member constituencies.

The most serious hurdle for the FN in these elections, however, was the decision by the RPR and UDF to present a single joint candidate in each constituency in the name of an Union du Rassemblement et du Centre (Union for a Rally of the Centre, URC). In the presidential election, Le Pen had outpolled Chirac and Barre in 124 of France's 555 metropolitan constituencies, but he had exceeded their combined scores in only seven.[145] In the face of the RPR-UDF alliance and a very high abstention rate, the FN was able to secure the requisite 12.5 per cent of registered electors and qualify for the second round in no more than 32 constituencies. It retained only one seat, that of Yann Piat in the southern Var department.

Despite the disadvantages it faced, the FN outpolled the joint forces of the centre-right in nine constituencies (eight of them in Bouches-du-Rhône, the other in Var). Here, in its Mediterranean bastions, it would make its most meaningful impact in these elections. Confronted with a locally powerful FN threatening to maintain its candidates in the second round, the leader of the RPR-UDF alliance in the Provence-Alpes-Côte d'Azur region, Jean-Claude Gaudin, concluded a deal to withdraw from eight constituencies of Bouches-du-Rhône in return for the FN's withdrawal from the other eight. This was a classic case of *désistement* as practised habitually on the left by the PS and PCF. That it was not disavowed by the national RPR-UDF leadership indicated how susceptible the centre-right parties remained to pressure from the FN, despite their firm stance when less was at stake. The previous year, the UDF mayor of Grasse (in the Alpes-Maritimes), Hervé de Fontmichel, had been expelled from the small centrist Radical Party for having won re-election by incorporating six FN candidates into his list.[146]

In the event, the RPR-UDF alliance secured six of the eight seats which it contested in Bouches-du-Rhône, while FN candidates won none of the other eight. This demonstrated clearly the difficulty faced by Le Pen's party in seeking to harness the full centre-right electorate against a left more mobilised for the occasion. In the 3rd constituency of Marseille, the FN candidate, Jean Roussel, contributed to a combined first-round score of 53.82 per cent for the RPR-UDF and FN; but in the second round he could attract only 49.87 per cent, losing by 92 votes to the sitting Socialist deputy. In the city's 8th constituency, the RPR-UDF and FN combined trailed the PS-PCF by 3.65 per cent on the first ballot; but Le Pen lost the run-off by 12.85 per cent to another sitting Socialist deputy. Practically, then, these alliances brought Le Pen and his party no rewards. Symbolically, however, the agreement to allow the FN to represent the broad right (brokered by a UDF baron of Gaudin's standing) marked a further landmark in the party's quest for respectability, bringing about locally what Le Pen craved at the national level. In the neighbouring Var department, moreover, a similar *désistement* helped the FN to retain its single seat.[147]

The loss of its parliamentary group deprived the FN of a prominent public forum for its ideas, and of valuable financial and administrative support. With only a marginally higher score (11.2 per cent), the PCF regained its lead over Le Pen's party and conserved 27 seats. This was due mainly to three factors: the concentration of communist support in some constituencies, the PCF's ability to field local notables as candidates, and the tactical cooperation between the PS and PCF in places to offset the distortive effect of the two-round majority system. That distortive effect played against the FN also in the 1988 cantonal elections, which saw its score drop to 5.35 per cent (fewer than half a million votes) and left the party with only two seats out of over 2,000 at stake across France's departmental councils.[148]

The June 1988 legislative elections served to confirm areas of FN strength, both geographically and within the electorate, notably among working-class voters (19 per cent) and the young (15 per cent of those aged 18–24).[149] The Bouches-du-Rhône department, with its pact between the centre-right parties and the FN, provided an instructive case. Here, on average, some 72 per cent of centre-right voters supported the FN in its second-round contests. Though not high enough to deliver seats, this figure was comparable to the proportion of PS voters willing to back the PCF in run-off contests, thereby confirming a considerable degree of popular legitimacy for the FN in this department.[150] In other locations (Mulhouse, Vichy, Voiron), the FN used its *pouvoir de nuisance* to help defeat prominent RPR-UDF candidates deemed too liberal or too anti-FN.

The FN in the 1980s

The achievement of the period 1981–88 was unprecedented in the history of the extreme right in France. The FN, like the PFN, entered this period as an irrelevant fringe movement; again like the PFN, it might have dwindled to extinction due to lack of momentum and prospects. Instead, the successes achieved from 1984 onward left the FN unrivalled as the major force and pole of attraction on the far right. They vindicated Le Pen's decision to interpret the accession of the left to power as an opportunity to build a base of popular support; they also vindicated the strategy of electoralism which had begun with Isorni's UNIR in 1951 and been pursued by Tixier-Vignancour in the 1960s before becoming the guiding principle of the FN from its creation in 1972. Le Pen's aversion to rigid ideology and ability to harness issues with a mobilising appeal were important factors in the FN's electoral challenge. So too was his insistence on eschewing violent activism, cultivating an image of democratic respectability and opening his party to elements from the traditional right. It was largely the contacts developed with centre-right notables in this period that helped to transform the FN, at least partially, into a legitimate political actor.

The '*quadrille bipolaire*' that had defined the French political landscape in the 1978 legislative elections, with four roughly equal political movements forming opposing coalitions, had already been altered in 1981 with the disjuncture on the left between an ascendant PS and a PCF in decline. The FN introduced a further factor on the right which disrupted the classic profile of the French party system under the Fifth Republic. While the PS consolidated its pre-eminence on the left, space on the right was now disputed by three major forces: the UDF (itself a confederation of several parties), the RPR and the FN. Following its emergence as an electoral threat, the FN posed a constant problem for the centre-right parties, drawing them into more disciplined cooperation with one another and, at the same time, opening damaging divisions over how best to deal with Le Pen and his party. The dividing lines here were between those (Pasqua,

Gaudin) who viewed electoral deals with the FN as preferable to defeat by the left, those (Veil, Séguin) who openly opposed such reasoning, and those (many) *attentistes* who simply hoped that the problem of the FN would go away.

The FN thus became, as Paul Hainsworth has argued, an objective ally to the governing Socialists much as the PCF had served that function for de Gaulle in earlier times.[151] President Mitterrand's intervention to secure media coverage for Le Pen, his reported amusement at the resultant discomfiture of the centre-right, his switch in 1986 to proportional representation, and his periodic pronouncements on sensitive issues such as voting rights for immigrants (notably during the 1988 presidential campaign) can all be read as cynical attempts to exploit the disruptive potential of the FN. Certainly, the view of Le Pen's party as a godsend – a 'historic opportunity for the Socialists', according to Mitterrand's then chief of staff at the Elysée, Pierre Bérégovoy – was readily embraced by a beleaguered Socialist administration in the mid-1980s.[152]

The period 1981–88 proved the FN's ability to contest elections at all levels and to force occasional deals with the centre-right parties. The election of 10 MEPs, 35 parliamentary deputies and 137 regional councillors placed the FN in a quite different category from previous movements on the extreme right in post-war France. Support for the FN was drawn from a wide cross-section of the electorate and marked increasingly by the party's ability to make inroads into the constituencies of right and left alike. Though there was little evidence for direct transfer of voting from the PCF to the FN, it seemed clear that, in certain constituencies, new voters who might once have supported the PCF were now more inclined to vote for the FN. An estimated 14 per cent overall of those voting for the first time in 1986 chose the FN, compared with 8 per cent supporting the PCF.[153] The Communists' participation from 1981 till 1984 in (a highly unpopular) government negated their role as a protest party, while long-term changes within the workforce and the erosion of France's industrial base hit hard a PCF that had long been a natural repository for the industrial working-class vote. In a political climate less defined by class-based allegiances and more conducive to issue-specific voting, the FN showed itself much better able than the archaic-looking PCF to attract new supporters from diverse horizons. Though polls varied at times in their findings, they provided evidence of a growing stability within this composite support base and of an electoral potential beyond the FN's actual achievement.

Whereas studies of voting patterns at sub-departmental and intra-urban levels found that the FN vote was complex and could not always be objectively correlated with the immediate presence of immigrants,[154] surveys repeatedly showed that FN voters were those for whom immigration (along with law and order) was *subjectively* of paramount importance. The 1980s drew the contours of an electoral map that would be replicated in the 1990s, with the FN attracting its strongest support in departments with the highest proportions of North African immigrants. The new terms in which immigration, race and nationality came to be addressed in France, and the new salience of *'insécurité'* as an issue, allowed the FN to find a resonance in public opinion which had eluded it throughout the

1970s. The FN benefited from the difficulties of the left in government and from the radicalisation of the centre-right as it adjusted to its double defeat of 1981 and adopted an aggressive language of opposition on themes dear to Le Pen and his party, themes on which they would in turn take up the running. The FN's impact on the policy agenda and the partial legitimation of its programme from the mid-1980s onward were evident in the Socialists' retreat from their early immigration reforms, their new emphasis on law and order, and the continued hardening of the centre-right's stance in both of these areas.

While the 1980s favoured the emergence and growth of the FN, the same period also highlighted the party's enduring weakness: its inability to impose itself as a necessary ally on the RPR and UDF and thereby overcome the institutional hurdle of the two-round majority voting system. Even on the singular occasion, in June 1988, when it was allowed a clear run by the RPR and UDF at eight parliamentary seats in Bouches-du-Rhône, it failed to secure enough of the centre-right vote to win any of them. The inherently ambiguous nature of the FN vote, too, was demonstrated by a poll showing that one in four Le Pen voters in April 1988 considered the FN leader a danger to democracy. In another poll conducted before the presidential election, only 28 per cent of declared Le Pen supporters wished to see him elected President, with 26 per cent preferring Chirac, 17 per cent Mitterrand, and 10 per cent Barre. This compared with 81 per cent of Barre supporters, 84 per cent of Chirac supporters and 91 per cent of Mitterrand supporters wishing victory for their chosen candidate.[155]

Such findings indicated a strong element of protest in the FN vote and pointed up the limits of the democratic legitimacy which Le Pen and his party had been able to achieve. This was borne out in autumn 1988 when a majority of FN supporters polled by IFOP thought the party to be primarily a vehicle for protest. The same deficit of legitimacy would continue into the 1990s, with a SOFRES poll in March 1990 finding that only 36 per cent of those identifying closely with the FN thought it 'capable of governing France'.[156] This lack of credibility even among its own supporters was only one of the problems confronting the FN. To win seats in the National Assembly in the face of the two-round majority voting system and concerted opposition from the RPR and UDF, the FN had to perform strongly enough to provoke the withdrawal of centre-right candidates, then dispose of a large enough majority to offset the loss of centrist voters and the mobilisation of the left at the second ballot. Yann Piat's election in Var in June 1988 was merely the exception that proved this rule.

9 From strength to strength

The Front National 1988–95

New political variables

That 9.8 per cent and the support of 2.35 million voters in the June 1988 legislative elections could be viewed not as a triumph but as a 'general setback' confirmed the distance which the FN had come in half a decade. That the marginally better result of 11.2 per cent for the PCF could be described as a 'relative recovery' was comment on the political changes of the same period from a somewhat different perspective.[1] The Socialists emerged from these elections without an overall majority but sufficiently strong to allow President Mitterrand to nominate in succession three Socialist Prime Ministers, Michel Rocard (1988–91), Edith Cresson (1991–92) and Pierre Bérégovoy (1992–93). There would be no return to the 'Socialist experiment' of 1981. Instead, Mitterrand's second presidential term would see a quite different experiment in the politics of consensus, adumbrated in his presidential manifesto, the *Lettre à tous les Français* (*Letter to All the French*). This was marked by the minimising of ideological difference and an attempt to broaden the presidential majority towards the centre by offering ministries to a number of centrist figures (Jean-Marie Rausch, Lionel Stoléru, Jean-Pierre Soisson amongst others) and 'non-political' personalities (Bernard Kouchner, Bernard Tapie). The second Rocard government was a model of this new *ouverture* or 'opening out', with little over half of the posts held by Socialists and none at all by Communists.

The minority governments of this period confirmed the Socialists' conversion to cautious reformism and, as the priority of priorities, rigorous economic management. Pale shadows only of the Socialists' earlier agenda could be discerned in the new guaranteed minimum income (*Revenu minimum d'insertion*, RMI), the re-introduction of an attenuated wealth tax (following the abolition of the first in 1986), and an income tax surcharge to help finance the social security system (*Contribution sociale généralisée*, CSG). On most economic indicators (inflation, growth, productivity, budget deficit and trade balance), the results in this period were relatively positive; only rising unemployment continued, as it had done in the period 1981–86, to present an intractable problem. At the same time, a series of financial scandals did little to restore the public's battered faith in politicians. Much more detrimental to the Socialists' electoral prospects in 1993, however, would be the rise of unemployment to over three million just as the last of Mitterrand's Socialist Prime Ministers, Bérégovoy, left office.[2]

Against a Socialist administration converted to market economics, stricter controls on immigration, firmer policies on law and order, and more consensual relations with the centre-right, the FN would have to revise its oppositional stance. The fall of the Berlin Wall in 1989 and the disintegration of the Soviet Union would also undermine the anti-communism that had been central to the party's mission since its formation in 1972. The period following the 1988 elections was one of adjustment to new political variables at home and abroad. It was also a testing period for the FN's internal cohesion.

In September 1988, at the FN's summer school, Le Pen again exceeded the bounds by referring to the centrist minister Michel Durafour as '*Monsieur Durafour-crématoire*', '*four crématoire*' meaning 'crematorium furnace'. This seemed a crude, throwaway remark revealing again Le Pen's provocative impulse and dubious humour; it was in fact part of the FN's new oppositional stance. Having striven to make his party the inevitable pole of attraction for defectors from the RPR-UDF alliance, Le Pen was disconcerted by the readiness of some centre-right figures to collaborate with Mitterrand's policy of opening to the centre. Throughout the summer of 1988, the FN newspaper, *National Hebdo*, had attacked this policy as a Jewish-Masonic plot to expose France to the ravages of international capitalism and subdue it within a 'cosmopolitan world order'. Singled out for special vituperation were prominent Jewish politicians such as Interior Minister Pierre Joxe and Lionel Stoléru, of whom *National Hebdo* wrote in July 1988 that there was something rotten in a French Republic 'where the Stolérus not only exist but prosper'.[3] As the embodiment of the policy of *ouverture*, a UDF-Radical minister in a Socialist-led government, Durafour was part of the same conspiracy denounced by *National Hebdo*. Le Pen's remark had a context and, playing to the hard core of his party, a purpose.

It was a provocative comment too far for some less hard-core elements. Pascal Arrighi and François Bachelot, recruited as part of the FN's drive for respectability in 1986, resigned. They were followed in October by Yann Piat, whose departure cost the FN its only remaining seat in the National Assembly. A month later, Jean-Pierre Stirbois, the party's secretary-general and architect of its electoral breakthrough, was killed in a car crash. At the same time, the FN's public image seemed to be on the wane. The cantonal elections of September 1988 (in which the party won little over 5 per cent) and a number of by-elections suggested declining support, even in relative strongholds such as Seine-Saint-Denis and Bouches-du-Rhône.[4] A poll in December 1988 showed agreement with Le Pen's ideas at 16 per cent, down from 26 per cent in November 1984.[5] More damagingly still, the RPR responded to Le Pen's jibe at Durafour by ruling out any alliance, national or local, with the FN in the forthcoming municipal elections. This closed the loophole which had persisted since 1983 allowing the centre-right parties to condemn the FN nationally while entertaining *ad hoc* deals at the local level.

The 1989 municipal and European elections

Held to elect councils in over 36,000 communes throughout France, the municipal elections of March 1989 challenged the FN's capacity to compete in a significant way. Like cantonal elections, municipal elections are geared to local personalities and issues and unfavourable to parties with weak local implantation. As a result, the FN concentrated on urban communes where it stood the best chance of gaining seats. Fielding lists in 214 of the 392 towns with over 20,000 inhabitants (and 143 of the 219 towns of over 30,000), it won just over 10 per cent of the vote, 2.5 per cent across mainland France as a whole.[6] This superficially poor national result concealed scores of over 20 per cent in towns such as Dreux, Mulhouse, Perpignan and Toulon. With a proportional element at play in the distribution of seats and no possibility of alliance with the RPR and UDF, FN candidates contested the second ballot in all municipalities where they had cleared the qualification bar of 10 per cent on the first round (in 44 towns or urban communes of over 30,000 inhabitants, as opposed to just one in 1983). The FN lists held, and in some cases (Nice, Perpignan, Toulon) even increased, their first-round share of the vote. In Béziers and Mantes-la-Jolie, unofficial deals between centre-right and FN lists resulted in defeat. In other locations, the FN helped to deprive the centre-right of a majority by retaining its candidates in the second round (as in Avignon, Strasbourg, Tourcoing and Maubeuge) or through a poor transfer of support between the rounds (as in Metz, Dunkerque and Beauvais).[7]

In all, the FN won 804 (0.15 per cent) of over half a million seats at stake in mainland France (compared with more than 300,000 – some 60 per cent – for the centre-right lists).[8] Though the left won a much smaller share of the vote and seats than the combined right, the Socialists had cause for satisfaction, with net gains in many large and medium-sized towns and a return to the levels of power which they had won in 1977 but lost in 1983. The PCF, by contrast, merely limited its losses, preserving control of 68 of the 81 medium-to-large towns which it governed and confirming its residual strength at the municipal level. The FN emerged from these elections with councillors in 143 of the 392 towns of over 20,000 inhabitants. Its sole, symbolic victory came in the southern town of Saint-Gilles-du-Gard, where the FN list headed by Charles de Chambrun won 21 of the 29 council seats in a four-way run-off, making this town of over 10,000 inhabitants the first to elect an FN majority and mayor.[9]

In answer to those who were announcing its decline, the FN used the much more favourable format of the European elections of June 1989, conducted by proportional representation, to put itself back on the national electoral map. Despite an abstention rate unprecedented for a national election, the FN won 11.73 per cent (2,129,668 votes), holding its 10 seats in the European Parliament. It finished third behind the UDF-RPR and PS lists, in advance of the Greens, centrists and PCF (the latter, with 7.72 per cent, being reduced to seven seats).[10]

Notable in the distribution of the FN vote were, again, the levels of support in the southern departments of Bouches-du-Rhône (20.76 per cent), Var (22.86 per cent) and Alpes-Maritimes (25.05 per cent). Apart from these outstanding scores, the geographical spread of support for the FN in this election replicated, and in most cases modestly amplified, the party's 1984 performance. Another broad similarity with the FN vote in the previous European elections lay in the return to a somewhat more conservative profile, with a preponderance of voters in the 50–64 age group and an increase in support from women, pensioners and practising Catholics. The strength of support from *petits commerçants*, artisans and small entrepreneurs (18 per cent) accentuated this conservative profile, while it seemed that a significant section of the younger, more working-class electorate which had been drawn to Le Pen in the 1988 presidential election had contributed to the record abstention rate of over 50 per cent.[11]

The most marked difference between both European elections for the FN lay in the party's message. In 1984, the FN had campaigned almost exclusively on national issues: opposition to the 'Socialo-Communist' government, immigration, law and order, unemployment, tax, the defence of private (Catholic) schools, and traditional values. Europe featured barely at all. Following the signing of the Single European Act in 1986, and with the deadline of 1992 set for the removal of barriers to the single internal market, the late 1980s saw momentum gather towards closer economic and political European union. As a consequence, Europe now assumed a much more pressing immediacy for the FN. With the neo-Gaullist leader, Jacques Chirac, evincing a more accommodating attitude to European integration, the field was open for Le Pen – with his 'Europe et Patrie' list – to pose as the most resolute champion of a Europe of nation states. The overtures towards neo-Gaullist voters again paid off, with an estimated 10 per cent of those who had supported Chirac in the first round of the presidential elections a year earlier voting for Le Pen's list.[12]

Ethnic relations: a worsening climate

The 'affaire du foulard'

In autumn 1989, three Muslim schoolgirls were suspended from their state school in Creil, north of Paris, for refusing to remove their Islamic headscarves in class. The headmaster, Ernest Chenière (a future RPR parliamentary deputy), deemed this to be in breach of the Republican principle of secularism (*laïcité*) in state education, a principle going back to the secular laws of the 1880s and the separation of Church and State in 1905. This banal event rapidly assumed the proportions of a national crisis. Against the backdrop of the FN's electoral successes, the vexed debate over immigration and growing concern over Islamic fundamentalism, the *affaire du foulard* (headscarf affair) became a test case in the compatibility or confrontation, depending on viewpoint, of the values of the French Republic with those of Islam. The issue split Socialists, intellectuals and even anti-racist movements, embarrassing the government of Michel Rocard and his Education Minister, Lionel Jospin. When the latter overturned the headmaster's suspension order, he drew criticism from the right, the PCF and some within his own party. His decision was likened by a group of excited intellectuals (including Régis Debray, former adviser to President Mitterrand on the developing world) to appeasement of Nazi Germany at Munich in 1938.[13]

Recognising its potential importance as a precedent, Jospin referred the matter to the Conseil d'Etat (Council of State), France's highest juridical-administrative court. Its finding was that the wearing of the Islamic headscarf did not contravene the law on secularism in schools since it did not necessarily constitute an act of proselytism. This brought the Islamic headscarf into line with the Catholic crucifix and Jewish kippa, both accepted unproblematically in the classroom. It was incumbent on individual schools to determine whether such insignia were being worn in the service of religious propaganda or as a provocation – and if they were, they were to be banned. Hardly a crystal-clear judgement, and one which left largely unresolved a problem that would return to haunt subsequent governments.

The *affaire du foulard* exposed two conflicting conceptions of France and Frenchness: a Jacobin belief in national unity through the one and indivisible Republic, and an argument for a more expansive and pluralistic interpretation of French values and institutions.[14] When it first blew up, it unleashed much sound and fury in the media and in political circles, but elicited relatively little comment from the Muslim community in France. Alec Hargreaves rightly noted that, far from being a trial of strength between ethnic minority groups and the Republic, this was 'first and foremost a Franco-French affair, i.e. a struggle between two different camps within the native population'.[15] The same might be said of almost the entire immigration debate as it had been conducted throughout the 1980s. As such, the *affaire du foulard* was not to be resolved by a simple judgement from the Council of State. At the close of a decade which had seen the issues of immigration and national identity assume unprecedented salience in public debate, it crystallised anxieties that would continue to be played out long after the three pupils from Creil had returned to class.

Following a marked rise in the number of schoolgirls wearing the *foulard* or *hijab*, and in response to demands from head teachers for a clearer ruling, President Mitterrand's successor, Jacques Chirac, would in July 2003 appoint a special commission headed by the former centrist minister Bernard Stasi. The commission published its findings in December 2003, advocating the prohibition of all obvious religious symbols (notably the Islamic headscarf, Jewish kippa and large crucifixes) in state schools and reaffirming the 'strict neutrality' of public services such as hospitals. The commission's proposals were endorsed with some modification by President Chirac, who called for a law to ban 'ostentatious' displays of religious faith in state schools and for a 'secularity code' across the public sector. The so-called 'law on the veil' was passed (with a 494 to 36 majority) in March 2004 and came into effect at the start of the new school year on 2 September 2004.[16]

Throughout the earliest episode of this prolonged 'affair' in 1989, the FN adopted a relatively low profile, secure in the knowledge that it would reap some reward. It did not have to wait long. The first round of a legislative by-election held in Dreux on 26 November 1989 saw the FN candidate, Marie-France

Stirbois, campaigning on an anti-Islamist platform, win 42.49 per cent to the RPR's 24.55 per cent, the PS's 18.12 per cent, and the PCF's 3.89 per cent. She went on to win the seat (against the RPR candidate) with 61.3 per cent of the second-round vote, returning a symbolic FN presence to the National Assembly. At the same time, another by-election in Marseille brought the FN candidate, Marie-Claude Roussel, 47.18 per cent of the run-off vote (against a UDF opponent). These were remarkable results, gained despite the impediment of the two-round majority voting system and against opposition from all parties.[17]

The success of Marie-France Stirbois in Dreux was due largely to the investment in grass-roots campaigning which she and her late husband, Jean-Pierre Stirbois, had made over the preceding decade. It was due also to a hardening of public attitudes. Conducted at the height of the headscarf affair in autumn 1989, an IFOP poll revealed the negative image of Islam held in French public opinion. Among non-Muslim French respondents, 71 per cent associated Islam with fanaticism and 76 per cent with the oppression of women, while 75 per cent were opposed to the Islamic headscarf in school. Two out of three respondents were also against granting voting rights to foreigners in local elections.[18] A SOFRES poll conducted at the same time found those supporting voting rights for immigrants to be as low as 20 per cent, while 83 per cent of respondents were unsympathetic to the wearing of the Islamic headscarf in school (against only 12 per cent in support). Jospin's decision to overrule the headmaster at the centre of the headscarf affair was supported by only 26 per cent, with 66 per cent opposed.[19] Eloquent in themselves, these findings were more instructive still when read in conjunction with a series of BVA polls which showed voting intentions for the FN rising from 8.5 per cent in October 1989 to 18 per cent by May 1990.[20]

Political discourse

In the wake of the *fatwa* issued in 1989 by Iran's Ayatollah Khomeini against Salman Rushdie, the *affaire du foulard* radicalised further the debate on immigration, compounding the discussion of national identity with that of Islamic fundamentalism. It proved an issue where consensus eluded the government even within its own ranks. The Joxe Law of 2 August 1989 had attenuated the 1986 Pasqua Law, re-establishing judicial control over expulsion procedures; this was followed in December 1989 by the creation of an Haut Conseil à l'Intégration (High Council for Integration) charged with advising on the social integration of immigrant communities. At the same time, dissonant voices on the Socialist left warned of the threat of fundamentalism and of the dangers of multiculturalism. Even President Mitterrand, in a televised interview in December 1989, declared that immigration in France had already reached the 'threshold of tolerance' in the 1970s.[21]

The joint policy-making forum of the RPR and UDF, the 'Estates-General of the Opposition', dedicated its April 1990 meeting to an emergency examination of the immigration issue. The RPR stepped up its calls for reform of the Nationality Code and, in autumn 1990, launched a petition against votes for immigrants in municipal elections (for which it claimed 900,000 signatures).[22] Chirac's party contributed only fitfully, with its UDF allies, to a series of discussions with Prime Minister Rocard on his integration strategy. The desecration of a Jewish cemetery in the southern town of Carpentras (Vaucluse) in May 1990 kept the focus of public attention on race relations, and was followed by new legislation (the Gayssot Law) increasing the scope of anti-racist sanctions and making a crime of Holocaust denial.[23]

The Carpentras affair forced the FN onto the defensive for a time – but only for a time. A similarly short-term dip in the FN's popularity resulted from Le Pen's apparently perverse support for Iraq and opposition to UN intervention in Kuwait in 1990. Disturbances in a number of *banlieues* (Vaulx-en-Velin, Sartrouville, Mantes-la-Jolie), combined with political corruption scandals and polls showing deepening distrust of mainstream politicians, soon allowed the FN to recover its impetus.[24] Meanwhile, some hawkish voices on the centre-right (Jean-Claude Gaudin, Michel Poniatowski, Gérard Longuet) continued to argue for an alliance with the FN as a political imperative.[25] Even those who ruled out such an alliance were not averse to stealing part of Le Pen's message. During a dinner-debate in Orléans in June 1991, the leader of the RPR and Mayor of Paris, Jacques Chirac, judged the country to be suffering from an 'overdose' of foreigners. He rehearsed the situation of a 'French worker' living in a council flat in a working-class district of Paris with a high immigrant population 'who struggles along with his wife to make about 15,000 francs, and who sees across the landing a crowded family with a father, three or four wives and twenty-odd kids, who receive 50,000 francs in social security benefits, without working, of course [. . .]. Add to that the noise and the smell, and it's enough to drive the French worker mad.'[26]

As the most powerful figure on the centre-right, twice Prime Minister and a strong contender for the presidency, Chirac drew instant condemnation from anti-racist movements and those concerned about the degeneration of the immigration debate. His presentation of the immigrant – as lazy, scrounging, sexually incontinent, noisy, smelly . . . and Muslim – had all of the demagogic populism normally associated with Le Pen. Far from being an unintended slip, however, these remarks were, Chirac protested, the acknowledgement of a daily reality for 'hundreds of people' and of a problem which the extreme right should not be allowed to 'monopolise'. The list of measures which he then proceeded to outline could have been lifted straight from the programme of the FN: 'control immigration', 'put an end to family reunion', 'conduct a thorough review of the right of asylum', 'open up a debate on the right of foreigners to welfare benefits that are not linked to contributions', 'reform the Nationality Code', 'stop talking about votes for immigrants'.[27]

This was the strongest bid yet by the RPR leader to challenge Le Pen on his own terms. Nor was Chirac alone in raising the rhetorical stakes on immigration. Three months later, the head of the centrist UDF and former President of the Republic, Valéry Giscard d'Estaing, published an article in *Le Figaro-Magazine* luridly entitled 'Immigration or Invasion?' Here Giscard argued that 'the type of problem which we face is changing from being one of *immigration* ("the arrival of foreigners wishing to settle in a country") to being one of *invasion* ("the act of entering and spreading with sudden effect", according to the definition given by Littré)'. Like Chirac, Giscard presented a list of proposals that could have been scripted by Le Pen: the restriction of nationality to a 'blood right'; a 'zero quota' of immigration until the next census; the automatic expulsion of all illegal immigrants; heavier penalties for those employing illegal immigrant labour; a review of the legislation allowing immigrants to bring their families into France; increased powers for mayors to grant or refuse housing to immigrants; and, in the interests of 'French identity', a 'vigorous policy of birth promotion' to redress the 'demographic implosion' by reserving preferential aid through childcare provision and tax concessions to French families or those of EC origin.[28]

Nor were the parties of the left immune to the contagion. In summer 1991, the PCF published a tract which rehearsed some of the worst impressions of immigrants as illegal residents, clandestine workers, delinquents, drug addicts, criminals, and a drain on welfare resources. Even as the PCF was being taken to task by the anti-racist MRAP, the new Socialist Prime Minister, Edith Cresson, proposed in a televised interview that charter flights could be used to deport illegal immigrants and failed asylum seekers. Her remarks were followed by a new package of measures which prioritised the fight against illegal immigration and a clampdown on the employment of clandestine foreign labour.[29]

The FN's '50 Measures'

It was no coincidence, then, that the FN chose November 1991 as the moment to publish its most radical policy document to date on immigration. In the previous two years, Le Pen had seen his parliamentary immunity lifted by the European Parliament and had lost several court judgements in relation to his remarks about the gas chambers and the role of the 'Jewish international' in fostering 'anti-national sentiment'. He was able to shrug off these minor setbacks by pointing now to the excessive statements of the so-called moderate right in Chirac and Giscard.[30] 'Giscard is chasing after Chirac who is chasing after Le Pen', declared the FN's delegate-general, Mégret.[31] Rehearsing the neo-Gramscian rationale of the Nouvelle Droite, Mégret crowed that the FN had so far only 'won the ideological battle, but everyone knows that electoral victories are always preceded by advances made in the domain of ideas'.[32]

As though to prove his point, a poll in October 1991 showed by far the highest recorded approval rating for Le Pen and the FN, with 32 per cent of respondents agreeing with their ideas (up from 18 per cent a year before), and 38 per cent agreeing on the specific question of immigration.[33] On 16 November, Mégret sought to capitalise on this momentum by presenting a policy paper detailing the FN's latest proposals on immigration.[34] Conceived in the form of a 50-point agenda, this called for: the repeal of anti-racist legislation; the restriction of nationality to a blood right; the review of all cases of naturalisation since 1974; the practice of 'national preference' in employment, housing and welfare provision; a special tax on employers using immigrant labour; the restriction of family allowance to French nationals; the conversion of immigrant hostels into housing for French nationals; the expunging of 'cosmopolitan' ideas from school textbooks; quotas for immigrant children in schools; a ban on the building of 'places of worship foreign to French identity'; the expulsion of illegal and unemployed immigrants together with those convicted of crimes; the creation of secure detention centres for immigrants facing deportation.

Accompanied by a panoply of further controls and restrictions, these proposals defied the Constitution of the Fifth Republic and carried sinister echoes of the Vichy regime. They also contravened a number of international conventions ratified by France, in particular the 1966 United Nations Convention on Racial Discrimination. While Mégret's document held immigrants to be the gravest threat to 'French identity' and the 'national community', it included the proviso that, 'since we consider France an intrinsic part of Europe, the measures set out here clearly do not apply to EEC nationals or, more broadly, to those of our European community who share our destiny, culture, religion and civilisation'. The distinctions propounded here were essentially ethnic and cultural, not national. They were foreshadowed in a remark made by Mégret some 10 days earlier, when he had deplored 'the disappearance of human races through widespread interbreeding'.[35]

This remark, like the ensuing '50 Measures', rang with echoes of the Nouvelle Droite. In December 1989, the Club de l'Horloge had launched the association SOS-Identité (a counter to the anti-racist SOS-Racisme) for the defence of French art, architecture, history, local traditions and folklore against a 'multicultural society without national roots'.[36] In the same year, the Club's honorary president, Yvan Blot, had left the RPR to join the FN. By this time too, Le Pen's party had launched its own journal *Identité* on the model of GRECE's *Nouvelle Ecole* and *Eléments* to lend an intellectual gloss to FN policy. The porousness of the borders between the Nouvelle Droite and the FN was demonstrated by high-profile recruits such as Pierre Vial and Jean Varenne (former secretary-general and president of GRECE respectively), Jean-Claude Bardet, Jean-Jacques Mourreau, Philippe Milliau, and others who joined Mégret and Le Gallou in positions of influence within the FN, either on the party's central committee, or on its journal, or in its Institut de Formation Nationale (National Training Institute).[37]

Nation and Europe: redrawing the borders

With their references to 'blood', 'identity', 'community' and the 'natural', Mégret's '50 Measures' invoked some of the principles on which the Nouvelle Droite founded its world view. In their Europeanist perspective, Mégret's proposals drew on the conception elaborated by GRECE of the pre-eminence of European civilisation and the grounding of French national identity in a wider racial and cultural heritage. The Europeanism articulated in the FN's first programme of 1973 had been of a purely geo-strategic character, calling for

European and Atlanticist military cooperation against the global threat of communism. A decade later, with the same perceived threat looming still and France under a Socialist-Communist government, Le Pen had urged the French 'to go beyond patriotism, beyond our respective feelings of national patriotism, to achieve a European patriotism. Which is to say that there will be no Europe unless it is destined to become a Nation.' This call for a 'European patriotism' as the binding agent of a European 'nation' implied an achievable fusion of French and European identity and interests. That it should have issued from a work bearing the defiant title *Les Français d'abord* (*The French First*) pointed up the problematic nature of the relationship in question.[38]

By the early 1990s, the threats facing France, both external and internal, had considerably changed. As late as 1989, the Soviet Union had still provided the most pressing reason for European unity;[39] with its collapse and the effective abandonment of socialism in France, the FN found itself deprived of two of its favoured themes. The threat to national identity (demographic through immigration, political and economic through European integration) now expanded to fill the space vacated by the diminishing spectre of Marx.[40] The FN's growing opposition in the 1990s to the construction of the very Europe which it purported, in another vein, to support laid bare the contradictions at the heart of its Europeanism. In passing from ideology to politics, from the abstractive conception of Europe as a 'common fund of civilisation'[41] to the concrete realities of the European Union as a political and economic entity, the FN's Europeanism turned out to be little more than an empty formula, an aggrandised expression of discriminatory nationalism projected onto the European stage. It thus continued to uphold 'the inviolable principle that our *Europe des patries* can only include those European *patries* sharing a civilisation whose roots are essentially Hellenistic and Christian'.[42] This 'inviolable principle' of neo-Hellenistic culture and Christian religion served for the FN as a criterion to distinguish states belonging within the European community from others, such as Turkey notably.

The FN's relationship to Europe over more than three decades provides a study in ambiguity and contradiction. In the 1980s and early 1990s, it argued for a 'coherent political project' comprising a common European defence and foreign policy, common immigration controls and anti-terrorist jurisdiction, a unified judicial system, a common (as opposed to single) currency, a 'European citizenship', and a policy of 'European preference' to complement that of 'national preference'.[43] The FN came to national political prominence through European elections and sustained its presence in the European Parliament when it could gain only a fleeting foothold in the French National Assembly. At the same time, however, it did all in its power to thwart the major initiatives (Single European Act, Schengen Agreement, Maastricht Treaty) which sought to give political expression to the vision of a unified Europe. Le Pen used the 1989 European elections to publish a book in which he argued forcefully for the principle of subsidiarity. Invoking the 'Gaullist formula', as he put it, he elaborated his notion of a 'confederal' Europe, insisting that an element of supranational control should be applied only in those areas where government authority was best pooled, chief amongst them defence. In no circumstances, however, was national sovereignty to be the price of closer European integration.[44]

This appeal to the neo-Gaullist constituency was strengthened by the presence in fifth place on the FN list for the 1989 European elections of the RPR defector Yvan Blot. In his letter of resignation to Chirac's party, dated 19 May 1989, Blot evoked the rift between his own and the RPR's 'values of patriotism and liberty'.[45] Lending his weight to the FN campaign, he urged neo-Gaullist voters not to betray the General's vision and to support Le Pen's calls for a Europe of nation states. Similarly, before a crowd gathered in Paris on 1 May 1989 to honour Joan of Arc, Le Pen anticipated the European elections as 'first and foremost a battle for France'; the FN, he pledged, would not allow the French to be sold out to a 'cosmopolitan and multi-racial Europe'.[46] Following the elections, Le Pen used the extraordinarily high abstention rate as an argument against 'the Europeanism of Strasbourg and Brussels'. Despite his party's own role in the European Parliament, he dismissed such Europeanism as 'a largely artificial phenomenon created by the globalists [*mondialistes*] for reasons that are yet to be identified and explained to public opinion'.[47]

This went to the core of the FN's difficulty over Europe, that of keeping its Europeanism in line with nationalist dictates and resolving the conflict between two quite distinct discourses on Europe. How could the call for a 'common European identity' be reconciled with the preservation of an authentic 'national identity'? How could the principle of 'national preference' leave room for any meaningful policy of 'European preference'? How could a united Europe of any sort be achieved without some sacrifice of national sovereignty – and without reinforcing the very structures (legislative, administrative, judicial) for which Le Pen reserved increasingly acerbic criticism?[48] Alongside the mythical Europe which the extreme right had long cherished, the FN engaged in a constant denunciation of the real Europe, in its institutions, its policies and its personnel. The shared cultural heritage, the commitment to the defence of 'Western civilisation', were all very well; but they must not intrude upon a national integrity that remained paramount for the FN.

The decision by President Mitterrand to put the ratification of the Maastricht Treaty to referendum in September 1992 forced Le Pen and the FN to forsake their abstractions and pronounce on the closer integration of the real Europe. Denouncing the Maastricht Treaty as a 'national suicide', 'a supranational edifice built on the shattered ruins of the nation', Le Pen and his party mounted a vigorous campaign under the slogan 'No to Maastricht – Yes to a *Europe des Patries!*'[49] Gone was the vision of a common European endeavour and a 'European patriotism' transcending national sentiment. In their place was a hard-right discourse echoing the sentiments that had accompanied French withdrawal from Indo-China and Algeria in the 1950s and 1960s, with Le Pen's party denouncing 'this French capitulation, this national abdication, this sell-out of France'. Maastricht was a 'conspiracy against the peoples and nations of Europe', leaving France at the mercy (more historical echoes, this time of Poujadism) of foreigners, capitalists, bankers and technocrats.[50]

Here was the FN at its most entrenched, mobilising all the symbols of narrow, exclusive nationalism – Vercingetorix, Clovis, Saint Louis, Joan of Arc, Roland at Ronceveaux, the *poilus* of Verdun, 'the betrayed soldiers of Indo-China and Algeria'. The consequences of a 'yes' vote, warned Le Pen, would be 'worse than losing a war', the triumph of a 'global conspiracy' mounted by 'hidden forces and vested interests against our nations', the end of 'eternal France'.[51] Projecting an apocalyptic vision of a post-Maastricht Europe, such pronouncements illustrated well the paranoid tendency on the French extreme right, as the ratification debate became for Le Pen and the FN a platform on which to parade the evils besetting France: 'In concrete terms, it means more immigration, more insecurity, more unemployment, and more taxes […] less democracy and less freedom […] the death-knell of France's History!'[52]

Behind the hysterical language and imagery (Maastricht as a '*coup d'état*', as an AIDS epidemic, as 'the end of France')[53] lay a systematic assault on the whole project of European integration. Backed by the FN's propaganda machine and by the editorials of François Brigneau in *National Hebdo*, the FN's 'Euro-Right' group published, in September 1992, a special issue of its bulletin, *Europe et Patries*, in which it lambasted the EC and its institutions – '*l'Europe de Bruxelles*', a Europe of bureaucrats and bankers. Were Maastricht to be ratified, argued this booklet, France's European partners would conspire to bring about her ruin: Britain and Portugal would serve as conduits for immigrants from ex-colonial territories seeking to exploit their future voting rights in France; Spain and the Netherlands would be open routes for drug trafficking; the power of the German mark would hold the French economy to ransom; Ireland, Greece, Spain and Portugal would soak up subsidies from revenue raised by taxing the French.[54] Among the more extravagant fears expressed here was that, should a future Labour government grant British nationality to members of the Commonwealth, 827 million Indians, 116 million Bangladeshis and 123 million Pakistanis would have the right to vote in France and throughout the EU. Such were the dire consequences of Maastricht, argued Le Pen in a special issue of the bi-monthly *Lettre de Jean-Marie Le Pen*, that it could be compared to the Treaty of Troyes, which had ceded the French throne to Henry V of England in 1420 – a wrong which, he recalled, it had been Joan of Arc's historic mission to right.[55]

Le Pen was somewhat overshadowed by other major protagonists in the anti-Maastricht campaign (notably the dissident neo-Gaullists Philippe Séguin and Charles Pasqua, and the UDF's Philippe de Villiers), as the 'yes' camp scraped a narrow victory (51 per cent). The Maastricht referendum nonetheless marked a critical moment in the FN's evolving relationship with Europe. For it exposed two quite divergent and ultimately irreconcilable postures: a pro-Europeanism rooted in notions of ethnic and cultural kinship, and an anti-Europeanism drawing its rationale from the perceived threat of integration on the Maastricht model and from a deep antipathy to any form of political federalism. The 'coherent political project' which the FN had advocated in the name of Europe was to be achieved, it transpired, without the merest concession on French sovereignty, the French franc, French national borders, France's defence capability and independent foreign policy.[56] By forcing it into a stance of defensive nationalism, Maastricht brought the FN's contradictions to a head and effectively set the party on a course of outright opposition to Europe.

Party structure: continuity and renewal

The replacement at the head of the party apparatus of Jean-Pierre Stirbois by Bruno Mégret had, in late 1988, announced a new phase in the FN's development. The deceased Stirbois was technically replaced as secretary-general by Carl Lang, who assumed a much lower profile than would Mégret in the newly created post of delegate-general. Lang was to take charge of party membership, organisation and internal cohesion, Mégret of political strategy, training, propaganda and communication. The new post of delegate-general offered a means both of dividing responsibilities in a fast-growing party and of tempering the ambitions of a single would-be deputy leader, the role which Stirbois had assumed unchallenged for the previous decade. Beyond this innovation, the party structure remained essentially unchanged through the 1990s, characterised by a highly centralised, top-down leadership. A national congress of federation delegates elected the president and the 120-strong central committee, which in turn elected the 30- then 40-strong political bureau, the party's main decision-making body. In addition, an executive bureau (composed of the president, vice-presidents, secretary-general, delegate-general and treasurer) acted as a steering committee and as the real locus of power within the party.

Under Mégret's guidance, the FN now developed its own in-house think-tank in the form of the Conseil Scientifique (Scientific Council), with its training centre, the Institut de Formation Nationale (National Training Institute), and its review, *Identité*.[57] It also extended its targeted recruitment circles, launching or developing associations for the armed services (Cercle National des Combattants), lycée and university students (Renouveau Etudiant; Cercle National des Etudiants de Paris), businesspeople and professionals (Entreprise Moderne et Libertés), farmers (Cercle National des Agriculteurs de France), and other groups. The FN in the 1990s would boast associations to protect the disadvantaged, the disabled, pensioners, the unemployed, animals and the environment; to promote the rights of repatriates and of French citizens living abroad; to foster solidarity among the 'women of Europe'; and to advance the interests of groups as diverse as taxi drivers, health workers and bank staff. It had lobby groups to campaign against abortion, against the tax system, and even for the protection of Iraqi children (an activity headed by Le Pen's wife since 1991, Jany). It would also support a Comité National des Français Juifs (National Committee of French Jews), a body existing mainly to refute charges of anti-Semitism, and an Alliance Générale contre le Racisme et pour le Respect de l'Identité Française (General Alliance Against Racism and For Respect of French Identity, AGRIF), a Catholic fundamentalist organisation under Bernard Antony dedicated to opposing 'anti-French racism' in all its perceived guises.[58]

The late 1980s and early 1990s would see a sustained push by the FN's propaganda machine to disseminate a plethora of national and regional publications conveying aspects of the party's programme to specific groups.[59] It would be supported by a number of daily and weekly national newspapers (*National Hebdo, Présent, Minute, Rivarol, Le Français*) catering for different tendencies within the party (ultra-conservative, Catholic fundamentalist, monarchist, Nouvelle Droite, etc.). Internal publications such as the *Lettre de Jean-Marie Le Pen* and *Europe et Patries* kept activists informed of party issues and briefed on the activities of its elected officials. A Minitel service would give way to a sophisticated internet service, with numerous websites on the party's personnel, structures, programmes and affiliates. By the early 1990s, the FN's quasi-official organ, *National Hebdo*, claimed a readership of 100,000, while the party boasted a membership of 80,000. A more plausible figure, calculated by Mayer and Rey on the basis of local surveys and delegates to the party's 1990 congress, was around 50,000.[60] Whatever the exact figure, it was clear that the FN by now commanded an extensive support base and fostered an energetic culture of activism at a time when party membership and militancy in general were on the wane. The *Guide du responsable*, published in several volumes by the FN's Editions Nationales in the early 1990s, offered advice to activists on all aspects of implanting and growing a national party from the grass roots. At the same time, the militants' manual produced by the FN's National Training Institute urged 'selfless devotion', 'discipline' and 'exemplary' behaviour to project 'the most positive image possible' of the party.[61]

More amenable than his predecessor to building bridges with the centre-right, and with much better personal connections for that purpose (in the RPR and Club de l'Horloge notably), Mégret took over at a moment when the centre-right parties had ruled out further deals with the FN at all levels. Though a decade under his influence would fail to bring about a reversal of that policy (this proving ultimately a factor in his acrimonious departure), Mégret's tenure as delegate-general marked an important period in the development of the FN's programme, its message, and its claims to legitimacy. The early to mid-1990s would complete the transformation of the party's public image that had been underway since the mid-1980s. Having joined the FN in 1978 and been a leading member of the FNJ, Carl Lang represented the new face of the party leadership: professional, affable, impeccably dressed and mannered, to all appearances a model party official. In 1995, he would be replaced as secretary-general by Bruno Gollnisch, a specialist in international law and Japanese civilisation. Gollnisch had joined the FN in 1983 while lecturing at the University of Lyon-III. Like Mégret, he brought more of the bourgeois intellectual than the street activist to the FN's leadership. He would replace the departing Mégret as delegate-general in 1999, opening the way for Lang's return as secretary-general.

Along with the well-pressed suits came a well-pressed set of ideas. The arrival of Mégret and other *habitués* of the Club de l'Horloge such as Yvan Blot and Jean-Yves Le Gallou modernised the FN's economic outlook, confirming the party in its turn away from neo-corporatism towards the neo-liberal economics for which the 1980s and early 1990s proved a favourable environment. In attacking the early Socialist administration for its misconceived egalitarianism, high taxes and belief in big government, the FN gave expression to a free-market ideology that had been honed by the Club de l'Horloge before the Anglo-Saxon 'New Right' propagated its more high-profile brand of ultra-liberalism. Le Pen's claim to have been a Reaganite before Reagan owed much to the infiltration of the FN by the Club de l'Horloge's ideas. Taking other cues from the Nouvelle Droite, the FN learned at the same time to dress wider aspects of its programme in more respectable garb, resting its anti-immigrant message on cultural and social rather than overtly racial premises. As with GRECE and the Club de l'Horloge, the 'right to difference' became an argument not for egalitarian inclusion within a multicultural, multi-ethnic society but for the selective exclusion of designated groups. The increasing contribution made to the FN in the late 1980s and early 1990s by leading Grécistes such as Pierre Vial and Jean Varenne further encouraged the party to couch its calls for 'national preference' and 'France for the French' in socio-cultural terms, with only the occasional unguarded remark from Le Pen and others allowing a racialist subtext to break through.[62]

For all the FN's new, more respectable image, the early 1990s witnessed an increasingly aggressive stance by the centre-right parties, coupled with attempts (as already seen) to stem and reverse the haemorrhage of support to Le Pen's party. Certain voices, however, such as that of the former Giscardian Interior Minister, Michel Poniatowski, would not be silenced, calling for an alliance with the FN as a policy 'ten times' less dangerous than handing victory to the PS and PCF. At the same time, a mirror image of this debate was to be found within the FN, between those (like Le Pen) favouring a war of attrition with the RPR and UDF, and those (like the FN leader in Nice, Jacques Peyrat) who urged compromise as the only way to end the party's marginality.[63] The auguries for the forthcoming series of elections were difficult to read. On the one hand, a number of prominent figures, including the Abbé Pierre, came out publicly against Le Pen, with other clergymen like the Archbishop of Lyon, Monsignor Decourtray, warning against a 'new Hitler'; on the other hand, as already noted, a poll in October 1991 showed record levels of support for Le Pen, with 32 per cent of respondents agreeing with the FN leader's ideas, rising to 38 per cent on the issue of immigration.[64]

More elections, mixed results

In the regional elections of 22 March 1992, the FN won 13.9 per cent (3,396,141 votes), exceeding its 1986 score of 9.7 per cent and increasing its seats in the regional councils of metropolitan France from 137 to 239.[65] These elections reflected a dramatic slump in support for Mitterrand and the Socialists (18.3 per cent), the continuing decline of the PCF (8 per cent), some erosion of support for the RPR-UDF alliance (33 per cent), the breakthrough of two main ecologist parties (with a combined 13.9 per cent), and a marked advance for the

FN. Le Pen's party was confirmed as France's third political force, behind the RPR-UDF and the PS, its vote falling below 10 per cent in only 31 of metropolitan France's 96 departments (compared with 68 in 1986). The FN outpolled the governing Socialists in four regions: Ile-de-France, Rhône-Alpes, Alsace and Provence-Alpes-Côte d'Azur. The most emphatic of these successes was in Provence-Alpes-Côte d'Azur, where the FN emerged as the strongest party (with 23.26 per cent and 34 of the region's 123 seats); the most symbolic was in Ile-de-France with Paris at its heart, where the FN won 16.22 per cent and 37 seats compared with 14.66 per cent and 32 seats for the governing Socialists.

The system of proportional representation employed for these elections again allowed the FN to convert its support into seats. It increased its representation in all regions of mainland France, winning a seat even in the rural Limousin where it had failed in 1986.[66] This gave the FN real influence in councils with responsibility for economic development, education and training, transport and infrastructure, and culture, *inter alia*. The party had set itself three objectives for these elections: to achieve the 15–20 per cent required to make it a credible contender for a stake in national power; to win the presidency for Le Pen of the Provence-Alpes-Côte d'Azur region; and to play a decisive role in the election of other regional council presidents. It succeeded in none of these. The collapse of the Socialist vote and the weakness of the PCF meant that the RPR-UDF alliance was too strong for the FN to hold the balance of power. In the much less favourable cantonal elections held on the same day, the FN signalled its growing local implantation by fielding candidates for almost all (1,868) of the 1,945 seats at stake. It won 12.2 per cent (over 1.5 million votes), though it failed to translate this on the second ballot into more than a single seat.[67]

The slump of the left, the tactical solidarity of the RPR-UDF, and the problem of the two-round majority voting system were all factors working against the FN as it entered the 1993 legislative elections. Despite its pretensions to legitimacy, it was hampered still by a serious credibility deficit, with 81 per cent of public opinion deeming it 'racist', 78 per cent 'sectarian' and 76 per cent 'incapable of governing France', according to SOFRES polling in October 1991.[68] Opposite a Socialist government mired in scandal, Le Pen's party adopted the slogan '*Mains propres et tête haute*' ('Clean Hands and Head Held High') and made political corruption a theme of its campaign.[69] It struck an aggressive posture towards the centre-right, pledging to retain its candidates in all constituencies where it passed the 12.5 per cent threshold of registered voters. Winning 12.7 per cent of votes cast (3,150,764), it secured a sufficiently high score to make the second round in 56 of France's 577 constituencies (up from 32 in 1988), and, due to the weakness of the Socialist vote, qualified in a further 45 constituencies as the strongest challenger to the RPR-UDF alliance (Table 9.1). The FN contested the second ballot in all but one of these 101 cases, 81 of which were straight run-offs against an RPR-UDF candidate. It won 5.66 per cent of the second-round vote and not a single seat in the National Assembly, with Marie-France Stirbois relinquishing the party's symbolic foothold in Dreux with 49.86 per cent of the

Table 9.1 The 1993 legislative elections: first round (metropolitan France)

	Votes cast	%
PCF	2,273,520	9.1
PS	4,396,109	17.8
Greens/ecologists	1,943,694	7.8
RPR	5,037,382	20.2
UDF	4,812,306	19.4
Various right	1,115,457	4.5
FN	3,150,764	12.7 (0 of 577 seats*)

Source: Interior Ministry (La Documentation Française, *Institutions et vie politique sous la Ve République*, Paris, 2003, p. 175).

Note: * over both rounds

run-off poll (105 votes short of her RPR opponent). In all, RPR, UDF and other centre-right candidates swept 485 of the 577 seats in these elections.[70]

This bleak end result for the FN disguised the importance of these elections in confirming the party's territorial implantation. Though it lost almost a quarter of a million votes from its score in the previous year's regional elections (conducted on a proportional system), it gained over three-quarters of a million votes, almost three percentage points, on its performance in the previous legislative elections of 1988 (conducted on the same two-round majority system). It increased its score in all but two of France's 96 metropolitan departments and recorded impressive gains at the constituency level. In 1988, the FN had won less than 5 per cent in 49 of France's 555 metropolitan constituencies, and 5–10 per cent in 264; in 1993, it fell short of 5 per cent in only 11 and recorded 5–10 per cent in 154. Particularly satisfying for the FN was the fact that it convincingly beat its arch-adversary, the PCF, polling 3.6 per cent more overall and finishing ahead of the PCF in 422 constituencies.[71] The advance which these elections marked for the FN on those of 1988, moreover, was in line with an upward trend in other elections over this period. Between the regional elections of 1986 and those of 1992, the FN had increased its score by over 4 per cent (from 9.7 to 13.9 per cent); between the cantonal elections of 1988 and those of 1992, it had recorded an increase of almost 7 per cent (from 5.35 to 12.2 per cent).[72]

The 1993 legislative elections saw the FN confirm its now established map of support, strongest in and around densely populated urban areas combining post-industrial restructuring with social tensions, high unemployment, high crime rates and large immigrant populations.[73] FN voting was again at its highest in the greater Paris region, in pockets of Nord-Pas-de-Calais, in the north-eastern border territories of Alsace and Lorraine, in the Rhône-Alpes region centred on Lyon, and across the entire Mediterranean arc from

Perpignan to Nice. The FN won 23.51 per cent of the first-round vote in the Alpes-Maritimes department, 21.64 per cent in Var, 21.19 per cent in Bouches-du-Rhône, 20.91 per cent in Vaucluse, and 20.39 per cent in Eure-et-Loir west of Paris (double its score of 1988). In the second round, in addition to Marie-France Stirbois' narrow failure to secure re-election in Dreux, Bruno Mégret won 49.52 per cent in Marignane and Jacques Peyrat 48.42 per cent in Nice, while Le Pen won just over 42 per cent of the second-round vote in the Nice constituency which he contested; in Marseille, Marie-Claude Roussel took 45.28 per cent of the second ballot and Maurice Gros 44.9 per cent, while Jean-Claude Martinez went down with 42.56 per cent in Perpignan. These results (achieved against single candidates from the RPR, UDF, PS and PCF) showed again the FN's capacity in certain locations to hold its own in head-to-head contests with the parties of the centre-right and left, together with the difficulty of prevailing on the crucial second ballot. Projections of the FN's results calculated on a proportional basis suggested that, with this performance, it would have won 64 seats in the National Assembly.[74]

The 1993 elections confirmed the growing trend towards a more popular FN electorate, with support of 18 per cent among blue-collar workers; they also signalled continuing strong support among the former Poujadist electorate of shopkeepers, artisans and small entrepreneurs (15 per cent), farmers and agricultural workers (13 per cent), together with white-collar workers (13 per cent). They suggested again the FN's capacity to secure a substantial proportion of the young vote (18 per cent of those aged under 25). While the FN attracted support of 16 per cent among modestly educated voters, it polled its lowest share of the vote among those with higher education (8 per cent) and saw its support drop concomitantly among senior managers and liberal professionals (6 per cent).[75] In terms of outlook, polls showed FN voters to be the most anxious about their personal and economic welfare and the most politically disenchanted. While the party attracted a quarter of voters 'very worried about their personal and occupational future' and almost 30 per cent of those judging that democracy in France functioned 'very badly', it retained its untouchable image for the great majority of voters. Three-quarters of those interviewed in a pre-election poll declared that they would never 'under any circumstances' vote FN, while the same proportion wished to see the party play no role whatever in governing the country.[76]

An exit poll on voting motivation provided some instructive data on the FN electorate. Asked to select those issues which had been uppermost in determining their vote, FN voters' responses diverged sharply at times from those of centre-right voters and voters across the wider electorate. It is clear from the findings in Table 9.2 that the most powerful mobilising issues for FN voters in 1993 were immigration, employment, and law and order (*la sécurité*). While psephologists continued to caution against simplistic correlations between the presence of immigrants and FN voting,[77] FN voters themselves were emphatic in registering immigration as their single most pressing concern. Though they were in line with other voters in their concern over employment, they were sharply at odds on the importance accorded to immigration and law and order, and in the lack

Table 9.2 Motivational issues in the 1993 legislative elections (% calculated on several prioritised responses)

	Mean	RPR-UDF	FN
Employment	68	67	64
Education and training	42	43	23
Law and order	34	37	57
Social inequalities	32	23	26
Immigration	31	33	72
Construction of Europe	25	27	11
Political corruption	12	15	12
Environment	22	15	10

Source: CSA exit poll (21 March 1993), adapted from P. Perrineau, 'Le Front National: la force solitaire', in P. Habert *et al.*, *Le Vote sanction. Les élections législatives des 21 et 28 mars 1993*, Paris, Département d'Etudes Politiques du *Figaro*/Presses de la Fondation Nationale des Sciences Politiques, 1993, p. 155.

of importance accorded to education. The findings also showed that, despite the FN's strident campaign against Maastricht in 1992 and its use of political corruption as a major campaigning theme in 1993, neither of these issues appeared to exercise a determining influence over its voters. Though the FN electorate was becoming more working-class in its profile, responses on the issue of social inequalities placed its voters on a par here with those of the centre-right (compared with 52 per cent of PCF and 40 per cent of Socialist voters mobilised on this issue). Finally, FN voters showed themselves the least concerned about environmental issues – as they were, in the same poll, about cultural issues.

A year later, the cantonal elections of March 1994 served again to highlight the punitive effects of the two-round majority voting system on a party bereft of allies, combined with the difficulty for the FN of contesting seats at this local level. It won 9.67 per cent of votes cast (just over one million) and qualified to contest 92 run-offs (compared with only 13 in the corresponding elections of 1988). The FN fielded 1,848 candidates in these elections and emerged from the second round winning only three seats out of some 2,000 at stake (with the PCF, by comparison, taking 145 seats in return for its 11.39 per cent share of the first-round vote).[78] This was a stark statement of the FN's continued marginality, despite its tenacious capacity to attract around one voter in 10.

What should have been a much more favourable opportunity presented itself in the European elections of June 1994. These saw the FN mount a vigorously anti-European campaign that sought to appeal to the 49 per cent of voters who had rejected the Maastricht Treaty in the referendum of September 1992. The name of its list proclaimed the FN's programme: 'Contre l'Europe de Maastricht, Allez la France! avec Jean-Marie Le Pen' ('Against the Europe of Maastricht,

Come On France! with Jean-Marie Le Pen'). It declared that it would 'not allow the French to be sacrificed on the altar of a Euro-globalist Utopia, French territory to be invaded and our borders violated, our national heritage to be ruined and the public security of our society imperilled, or the French people to be sucked into the great magma of globalisation'. This was the FN at its most trenchantly anti-European yet, declaring for the first time: 'The future of France does not lie in Europe.'[79]

The problem for the FN was that it was not the only strident voice of nationalism in this election. With 10.52 per cent (2,050,086 votes), it was outpolled by the 'sovereignist' list of Philippe de Villiers, which won 13 seats to the FN's 11 (within an increased French quota of 87). Though this result marked an advance on the 10 seats won by the FN in 1984 and 1989, it was interpreted as evidence that the momentum behind the party's rise had petered out. The competition from de Villiers' list drew off part of the anti-European conservative vote, notably among the rural Catholic constituency, and accentuated the popular, urban character of the FN vote, which for the first time accounted for 21 per cent of blue-collar workers.[80]

Taken together, the regional, cantonal, legislative and European elections of the early 1990s thus confirmed the serious presence and tenacity of the FN, but did not appear to presage any dramatic advance in its electoral fortunes. In each of these elections, the FN failed in its bid to break into the 15–20 per cent range and position itself as a serious contender for a stake in power. Ahead, however, lay major elections that would see Le Pen and the FN nudge closer to achieving this objective, thereby opening a new phase in their ambitions.

The 1995 presidential election

'*Historique*', proclaimed the banner headline of *National Hebdo*.[81] In the first round of the presidential election on 23 April 1995, Le Pen polled fully 15 per cent of the vote, the support of 4,570,838 electors (Table 9.3). In so doing, he surpassed his 1988 performance (14.4 per cent, 4.38 million votes) and set a new record for the far right in a French national election.[82]

In a campaign dominated by unemployment (at 12.2 per cent, 3.26 million) and the associated issues of social deprivation and exclusion, Le Pen's programme *Le Contrat pour la France avec les Français* (*The Contract for France with the French*) was an exercise in outright populism. The FN leader promised to create four million jobs over the seven-year presidential mandate, to repatriate three million immigrants, to ensure priority for French nationals over foreigners in employment, housing, social welfare and education, and to protect French jobs and products against international competition. Extending his concerns notably to the poor, the homeless and low-income families, he pledged an increase in the national minimum wage (SMIC), the introduction of a monthly 'maternal or parental income' (6,000 francs), a house-building programme, a review of family allowances and of the guaranteed minimum income (RMI). His first act as President, he declared, would be to found the Sixth Republic, with a Constitution

Table 9.3 The 1995 presidential election: first round (metropolitan and overseas France)

	Votes cast	%
Jospin	7,097,786	23.30
Chirac	6,348,375	20.84
Balladur	5,658,796	18.58
Le Pen	4,570,838	15.00
Hue	2,632,460	8.64
Laguiller	1,615,552	5.30
De Villiers	1,443,186	4.74
Voynet	1,010,681	3.32
Cheminade	84,959	0.28

Source: Constitutional Council (La Documentation Française, *Institutions et vie politique sous la Ve République*, Paris, 2003, p. 178).

enshrining in law the principle of 'national preference'. Other proposals in Le Pen's programme were to cut employers' taxes, phase out income tax, reduce public expenditure, reinstate the death penalty, introduce proportional representation and a 'referendum by popular initiative', disengage France from the Schengen Convention and Maastricht Treaty, and restore full French border controls.

Public attention in this election was focused on the fratricidal contest between the neo-Gaullist leader, Jacques Chirac, and the outgoing neo-Gaullist Prime Minister, Edouard Balladur, concluding a two-year spell of 'cohabitation' with the ailing President Mitterrand. As a result, Le Pen was able to run a relatively low-key campaign, indicating the extent to which he had become a feature of the electoral landscape. The first round threw up two surprises: the advance by the Socialist Lionel Jospin on the favourite, Chirac, and the 15 per cent polled by Le Pen.

The FN leader's vote was particularly high across the north and north-east, in parts of Ile-de-France and the Rhône valley, and along the Mediterranean coastal belt. Le Pen emerged as the leading candidate of the right in five of France's 22 metropolitan regions (Alsace, Lorraine, Provence-Alpes-Côte d'Azur, Languedoc-Roussillon and Nord-Pas-de-Calais) and in 18 of the 96 metropolitan departments. He improved on his 1988 score in almost two-thirds of departments, outpolling all candidates in Bas-Rhin (25.83 per cent), Haut-Rhin (24.8 per cent), Moselle (23.82 per cent), Vaucluse (23.12 per cent), Var (22.35 per cent), Bouches-du-Rhône (21.42 per cent) and Loire (21.09 per cent). In one department only (Chirac's rural stronghold of Corrèze) did the vote for Le Pen fall below 7 per cent (4.58 per cent).

Among the most striking results were those in the industrialised Rhône-Alpes region and in the mining, steel and textile areas of the north and north-east. Across a swathe of departments north of a line from Rennes to Besançon, Le Pen's share of the vote indicated a marked progression on his 1988 performance.[83] The results recorded in cities and towns confirmed the predominantly urban character of this vote. Le Pen emerged as the leading candidate in a large number of towns, among them Tourcoing (26.99 per cent), Mulhouse (26.72 per cent), Toulon (23.98 per cent), Nice (23.75 per cent) and Marseille (22.32 per cent). Arresting results were achieved in a string of industrial towns and urban constituencies across the north (28 per cent in Oignies, 26.5 per cent in Maubeuge), the north-east (31.23 per cent in Woippy, 29.95 per cent in Stiring-Wendel, 29.46 per cent in Saint-Dizier), and in the central-eastern Rhône-Alpes region (33.5 per cent in La Ricamarie, 33.46 per cent in Le Chambon-Feugerolles, 27.91 per cent in Saint-Priest).

The most remarkable feature of Le Pen's performance was the increase in support from workers and unemployed voters and from those defining themselves as disadvantaged. In these traditionally left-leaning constituencies, Le Pen emerged with a clear lead over *all* candidates. Comparison with the 1988 presidential election showed Le Pen's share of the blue-collar vote up from 16 to 27 per cent, beyond that of Jospin (21 per cent) and almost double that of the PCF candidate, Robert Hue (15 per cent), who polled the same share of this electorate as Chirac.[84] Support for Le Pen also rose markedly among white-collar workers (from 14 to 19 per cent). While Jospin and Hue drew 17 per cent and 13 per cent respectively from those classing themselves as disadvantaged, support for Le Pen here was put as high as 34 per cent. Though polls were at variance in measuring the vote among the unemployed, all showed strong support for Le Pen (BVA crediting him with 18 per cent, IFOP with 24 per cent, SOFRES with 25 per cent, CEVIPOF with 28 per cent, and CSA with all of 31 per cent).[85]

These were telling statistics. Even allowing for (sometimes sizeable) margins of error, they attested an important evolution in the FN electorate. At its emergence in the mid-1980s, the FN had looked to wayward RPR and UDF voters – an older, wealthier, better educated and more strongly Catholic electorate. In 1988, despite signs of a growing appeal among working-class voters, the Le Pen vote was still far from being a vote of the dispossessed.[86] Since then, Le Pen and the FN had consolidated an increasingly popular support base. Though the FN leader continued to attract voters from all social categories, his electorate in 1995 was defined above all by its younger, poorer, less well-educated, working-class components.[87] Le Pen drew 11 per cent and 8 per cent respectively of those defining themselves as 'privileged' or 'well-off', and 19 per cent from the lowest social categories ('*classes populaires*'); he attracted 10 per cent of the upper middle-class and 15 per cent of the lower middle-class vote, with strong support among small shopkeepers and artisans (21 per cent). There was evidence here again of the combined support from shop floor and factory floor described by Pascal Perrineau in the previous presidential election as a fusion of old-style Poujadism and working-class protest.[88] This electorate thus brought together sectors of the working population that had traditionally been on separate sides of the right/left divide, articulating quite different social and economic priorities, with the balance now shifting more towards the working class. In all, an estimated 46 per cent of Le Pen's electorate in 1995 were blue-collar or white-collar workers.[89] This more popular electorate was, moreover, now seen by Le Pen as a natural constituency. Campaigning as a 'man of the people' on the slogan '*Homme du peuple, Homme d'Etat*', he addressed his intended audience: 'I am not appealing to the rich bourgeois of the 16th *arrondissement* [an affluent district of Paris]: I am appealing to those French people whose present lot is miserable, and there are millions of them.'[90]

Le Pen outpolled Hue by a clear margin in some traditional PCF strongholds such as the *départements ouvriers* of Nord, Pas-de-Calais and Seine-Maritime, and by an emphatic margin in other comparable departments, notably Meurthe-et-Moselle, Bouches-du-Rhône and Var. In the traditional PCF bastion of Seine-Saint-Denis in Ile-de-France, Le Pen won 18.8 per cent to Hue's 14 per cent. Rather than a straight transfer of votes from the PCF to the FN (a simplistic conclusion to be resisted), these results and the accompanying polling data suggested that Le Pen had garnered support, often from first-time voters, that might have gone to the PCF in its earlier role as the 'party of the discontents'.[91] With unemployment and social deprivation at the centre of his campaign, Le Pen's incursions into these popular constituencies showed the effect with which he was able to exploit Chirac's campaign theme of '*la fracture sociale*'. By contrast, Le Pen's share of the vote among higher socio-professional categories (senior management, liberal professionals) declined sharply on his 1988 performance, while support among middle-ranking and lower professional categories also dropped significantly (Table 9.4).

Table 9.4 Occupational profile of the Le Pen electorate in 1988 and 1995 (% within each category voting for Le Pen)

	1988	1995
Farmer/agricultural worker	18	14
Shopkeeper/artisan	31	21
Liberal professional/senior manager	17	6
Middle/lower professional	16	10
White-collar worker	14	19
Blue-collar worker	16	27
Unemployed	19	18*

Sources: BVA exit polls, adapted from *Le Monde dossiers et documents: L'élection présidentielle 24 avril–8 mai 1988*, May 1988, pp. 41, 44; *Le Monde dossiers et documents: L'élection présidentielle 23 avril–7 mai 1995*, May 1995, p. 47.

Note: * Other poll findings ranged as high as 31% in this category.

Three further features marked the Le Pen vote in this election: its appeal across different age groups, with notable support among younger voters; its political heterogeneity; and its continuing stability. In 1988, Le Pen drew his highest share of support from the 35–49 age group; in 1995, from the 18–34 group, with a strong showing among first-time voters (21 per cent). Only the Socialist Jospin attracted more first-time voters (23 per cent), while merely 7 per cent opted for the Communist Hue. Le Pen's share of the vote was strongest among young men aged 18–24 (19 per cent), but it was unusually strong too among young women aged 25–34 (16 per cent). This tilt towards youth, in a context of high youth unemployment and widespread disaffection with mainstream political parties, suggested a potential for renewal and growth within the FN electorate. Though Le Pen accused de Villiers of having drawn off a crucial fraction of his support, analysis of both electorates showed them to be quite distinct. Support for de Villiers was largely rural, affluent and more strongly Catholic than Le Pen's electorate, where religion played no defining role. De Villiers achieved his highest share of the poll among the 35–64 age group, where his appeals to traditional French values found their most sympathetic audience. The Le Pen vote again rang with anti-Europeanism as the FN leader attracted 26 per cent of those who had voted 'no' in the Maastricht referendum, compared with only 8 per cent for the 'sovereignist' de Villiers.

Politically, the Le Pen electorate continued to be a hybrid defying easy categorisation. Polling data measuring political affinity showed 30 per cent of Le Pen voters classing themselves on the extreme right, 23 per cent on the right, 7 per cent in the centre, 13 per cent on the left and 5 per cent on the extreme left; a further 22 per cent refused to identify themselves in any of these categories.[92] The same heterogeneous character was evident in the transfer of support on the second ballot. Despite Le Pen's calls for a 'blank' vote, an estimated 50 per cent of his voters transferred to Chirac and 21 per cent to Jospin, while 29 per cent abstained or spoiled their ballot. This was the most evenly redistributed electorate of all candidates eliminated at the first round.[93]

For all its relatively youthful profile and its hybrid character, the Le Pen vote exhibited a strong element of voter loyalty. The IFOP polling agency found that 81 per cent of those who had voted FN in the 1993 legislative elections returned a vote for Le Pen in 1995; at the same time, different polls recorded among Le Pen voters 80–84 per cent of those declaring a partisan attachment to the FN.[94] This represented the highest degree of party identification among supporters of any candidate in this election, while the largest proportion of voters to have selected their candidate some months before the first round was again recorded in Le Pen's electorate (64 per cent). These findings confirmed a pattern already evident in the 1993 legislative elections, where FN voters had exhibited a stronger party loyalty even than the traditionally faithful PCF electorate.[95]

Though Le Pen failed in his bid to reach the second round (where Chirac beat Jospin by 52.64 to 47.36 per cent), his performance in the first round signalled important developments in his electoral appeal. The most significant of these was the growth of a strong leftist current of support for Le Pen. This emerged mainly to the detriment of the Socialist Jospin in areas scarred by the industrial recession of the previous two decades.[96] It was in keeping with the ambition that the FN had set itself as far back as the legislative elections of 1978 and gave some retrospective credence to its boast in the early 1980s that it was the only right-wing party capable of making incursions into the left-wing popular vote.[97] What Pascal Perrineau hastily termed '*gaucho-lepénisme*' was better described by Nonna Mayer as '*ouvriéro-lepénisme*', since the latter focused on the working-class (socio-economic) character of that vote rather than its supposed left-wing (political) provenance. As Mayer argued, the voters making up this new core of the Le Pen electorate were not all predisposed to lean left, but they were demonstrably working-class.[98]

Unemployment, high crime rates, fears over immigration, antipathy to the EU, and political corruption all contributed to the ferment of Le Pen's campaign. In the hierarchy of voters' concerns, however, the same three issues predominated once more, though with a significant change in emphasis. The findings in Table 9.5 showed once again the specificity of the FN voter. Though unemployment emerged for the first time as the prime concern of Le Pen supporters, it fell some way short of the same concern as expressed by other voters. Similarly, on the socio-economic issues of preserving social benefits and purchasing power, Le Pen voters registered below-average concern. On immigration and *insécurité*, by contrast, the proportions were dramatically inverted. Beyond these issues, de Villiers' electorate was the only one to evince more concern than Le Pen's for traditional values, while that of the Trotskyist Arlette Laguiller was the only one to show less concern for the building of Europe. Finally, despite Le Pen's penetration into the most socially and economically fragile constituencies, his voters registered markedly less interest than others in the fight against social exclusion.

Though Le Pen voters were more exercised in this election by unemployment, its importance as a determining issue in their vote was tempered by the very low proportion of those same voters (only 19 per cent as measured by SOFRES-CEVIPOF) with faith in the FN leader's capacity to resolve this problem.[99] Almost twice as many Le Pen supporters (34 per cent) thought Chirac most able to reduce unemployment. By contrast, the proportion of Le Pen voters believing their candidate capable of solving the problems of immigration or of enforcing law and order was fully 85 per cent and 55 per cent respectively. Significantly, this same pattern was reflected among voters at large. Despite the tougher laws on immigration and nationality introduced in 1986 and 1993 by Interior Minister Pasqua,[100] Le Pen remained the politician most readily associated with these issues. In a CSA survey published two weeks before the first round, 36 per cent of respondents judged Le Pen the candidate 'most capable' of dealing with immigration, denoting a much higher confidence in the FN leader on this issue than in any other candidate (Balladur followed on 18 per cent and Chirac on 14 per cent); on his perceived competence to tackle all other issues, by contrast, Le Pen was consistently outdistanced by other candidates.[101] A similar survey published in early March 1995 revealed comparable findings: 44 per cent of those interviewed judged Le Pen's immigration policies to be 'credible', while 40

Table 9.5 Motivational issues in the 1995 presidential election (% calculated on several prioritised responses)

	Mean	Jospin	Chirac	Le Pen
Unemployment	81	85	84	73
Preserving social benefits	37	54	29	25
Fight against exclusion	31	44	30	14
Insécurité	31	19	35	57
Immigration	25	13	25	65
Purchasing power	24	26	24	21
Traditional values	16	10	20	21
Construction of Europe	15	23	20	9

Source: SOFRES post-election poll (20–23 May 1995), adapted from P. Perrineau, 'La dynamique du vote Le Pen: le poids du gaucho-lepénisme', in P. Perrineau and C. Ysmal (eds), *Le Vote de crise. L'élection présidentielle de 1995*, Paris, Département d'Etudes Politiques du *Figaro*/Presses de la Fondation Nationale des Sciences Politiques, 1995, p. 253.

per cent believed in his capacity to enforce law and order; on all other issues, the FN leader's credibility ratings again fell away sharply.[102]

The dynamic brought to the second round by Le Pen's strong showing in the first was similar to that of 1988. Holding the statistical balance with his 15 per cent, the FN leader announced that he would await his party's May Day rally before advising his electorate which way to vote. In the event, he refused to issue any clear recommendation, berating Chirac as being 'like Jospin only worse' and declaring his own intention to cast a blank vote.[103] The theatrical suspense preceding this anti-climax achieved two things: it kept Le Pen at the centre of public attention as potential arbiter of the presidency, and it put both Chirac and Jospin under pressure to respond to the FN leader's agenda (notably on proportional representation for legislative elections, the most pressing of Le Pen's demands). Where Charles Pasqua had appealed between the rounds in 1988 to the 'shared values' of the centre-right and FN, the same Pasqua now called for 'an element of proportional representation so that all political forces should be represented'. Jospin, too, argued the merits of proportionality – in order, he insisted, that ecologists and women might be better represented.[104]

On other issues, the attempt to woo Le Pen voters was more transparent still. The RPR leader, Alain Juppé, declared on national radio that Le Pen's electorate had 'legitimate concerns of which account must be taken', especially in relation to 'law and order in our towns and suburbs and the preservation of a certain form of national identity'.[105] Against the lofty neo-Gaullist Balladur in the first round, Chirac had stressed the fight against social deprivation and exclusion; faced by Jospin in the run-off and with Le Pen menacing in the wings, he turned his attention now to immigration, crime and national identity. Hence his dark warning against 'the flouting of law and order by ethnic or religious groups' in their 'ghettoised' cultures; hence, too, his overtures to Euro-sceptic voters in proposing a review of the Schengen Convention and a further referendum on European integration.[106] At the height of the second-round campaign, the murder of a young Moroccan man by skinheads taking part in the FN's May Day parade prompted an abrupt revision of Chirac's message. References to ethnic and religious subcultures were now excised from his speech, to be replaced by calls for a 'generous policy of integration' for immigrant communities who should not be made 'the cause of all our ills'.[107]

Paradoxically, Le Pen's strong performance in this election was at odds with his weak standing in public opinion as a potential President. Here the pre- and post-election polls yielded some significant findings. In a succession of monthly SOFRES polls carried out between November 1994 and April 1995, Le Pen scored consistently poorly on the question of whether he would make 'a good President', with ratings well below his eventual 15 per cent of the vote (and only 10 per cent in the final such poll before the election).[108] In the IFOP exit poll conducted on 23 April, only 11 per cent of Le Pen voters were motivated by their candidate's 'personality', as opposed to 46 per cent by his 'programme' and 28 per cent by his 'values'.[109]

The conclusion to which these findings pointed was twofold: first, that Le Pen remained seriously hampered by his unpresidential image, even among those who voted for him; second, that the FN leader attracted support much more readily through his policies than through the appeal of his personality, for all his skilful manipulation of the media. A vote for Le Pen, it seemed clear, was not a vote for a genuine *présidentiable* but rather a means of pushing issues of concern – notably immigration and *insécurité* – up the political agenda. Though he had been indispensable to the FN in its electoral rise, did this mean that the party could now envisage a real prospect of success through the force of its policies, once Le Pen had passed the leadership to less charismatic lieutenants? The results of the elections that followed in June 1995 would clearly suggest as much.

10 Pushing the bounds

The Front National 1995–2002

Municipal power: the FN in local government

An immediate test of the FN's electoral standing in the wake of the presidential poll of April 1995 was provided by the municipal elections of 11 and 18 June. For the FN, these presented an opportunity to measure grass-roots strength and to bid for a real stake in local power. Following decentralisation measures implemented by the Socialists in 1981, France's municipal councils had seen their political weight substantially increased as they assumed greater responsibility in areas of public provision such as housing, transport, schools, social services, culture, and some aspects of law enforcement. The larger the town, the larger was the budget which the mayor controlled, and the more significant the personal power that went with it.

The system of apportioning seats in these elections (combining the majority principle with a proportional element) allowed for the representation of smaller lists but made it difficult for such lists to achieve a victory margin. In the case of the FN, the problem was compounded in 1995 by the continued refusal of the RPR and UDF to countenance deals with Le Pen's party. The aim of the FN in embarking on its campaign for these elections was to perform so strongly in many localities as to confront the RPR and UDF with the choice between a deal, as in Dreux in 1983, and defeat.

Accordingly, the FN concentrated its candidates in those predominantly urban areas where it was likely to perform best, capitalising on the major national issues of immigration, unemployment, and law and order. It fielded some 25,000 candidates, around 10,000 more than in 1989, demonstrating the success with which it had expanded its network of militants.[1] With no presence at all in many of the small towns and villages that make up the great majority of over 36,000 communes in France, the FN's performance across the country as a whole was patchy; but its lists exceeded the 10 per cent threshold in 116 of the 226 towns of over 30,000 inhabitants (compared with fewer than half that number in 1989), including 18 towns of over 100,000. This guaranteed the party's presence in many run-off ballots and its representation on numerous town and city councils.[2] Breakdown by size of commune confirmed once again the essentially urban nature of the FN vote: 0.05 per cent support in communes of fewer than 3,500 inhabitants, 0.6 per cent in communes of 3,500–9,000 inhabitants, 5 per cent in communes or towns of 9,000–30,000 inhabitants, and 11.4 per cent in towns and cities of over 30,000 inhabitants. When allowance was made for those locations in which the FN did not run candidates, its score in municipalities of over 9,000 inhabitants averaged some 13 per cent. Its final tally of municipal councillors rose from 804 to 1,249, up from 0.15 per cent to 0.25 per cent of the total number of municipal seats.[3]

In areas where support for Le Pen's presidential candidacy had been particularly strong, the FN recorded a number of spectacular results: 43.04 per cent in the southern town of Vitrolles, 44.03 and 35.15 per cent in the towns of Noyon and Dreux near Paris, and 30.51 per cent in the industrial town of Mulhouse in the east.[4] In these towns, the FN was prevented from taking control at the second ballot only by concerted anti-FN campaigning and (with the exception of Vitrolles) local cross-party pacts between right and left. Even so, the FN won over a third of the second-round vote in each case, narrowly failing to take Noyon with 48.12 per cent.[5] The FN also performed strongly in the major southern towns of Perpignan (32.71 per cent) and Marseille (21.99 per cent), in urban communes with large immigrant populations such as Clichy-sous-Bois (31.66 per cent) in Paris, Vaulx-en-Velin (31.02 per cent) and Saint-Priest (34.46 per cent) in Lyon, and in depressed industrial towns of the north such as Tourcoing (32.46 per cent) and Roubaix (24.34 per cent).

It was in the southern region of Provence-Alpes-Côte d'Azur that real breakthroughs for the FN occurred. With first-round scores of 33.49 per cent in Marignane (a satellite town of Marseille in Bouches-du-Rhône), 31.36 per cent in Orange (Vaucluse) and 31.02 per cent in Toulon (Var), the FN went on to win control of all three of these towns in run-offs against divided opposition. 'Three Stains on France', ran the banner headline of the left-wing daily *Libération* – to which *National Hebdo* riposted with its own provocative headline, 'Three Devils Elected'.[6] For Bruno Mégret, these were three 'liberated towns', the first in the push to 'recapture' France.[7] In addition, the major city of Nice, France's fifth largest with close to 350,000 inhabitants, fell to an independent list headed by Jacques Peyrat, who had resigned from the FN in 1994 after serving for years as the party's local leader in Nice and as an FN parliamentary deputy between 1986 and 1988.

Reviewing his party's gains on the evening of the second round, Le Pen betrayed more disappointment than triumphalism. The FN's progress, he claimed, had been stymied by the 'establishment gang', who had mobilised 'battalions of Beurs' (children born in France of North African immigrants) in a number of towns.[8] In particular, Le Pen railed against the centre-right alliance for preferring defeat at the hands of the Socialists to an agreement with the FN in several locations. Post-election analyses bore out this point, indicating that the FN's presence in the second round had facilitated the left's victory in 27 of the 226 towns of over 30,000 inhabitants.[9]

Despite Le Pen's protestations, the capture of three sizeable towns, especially Toulon with its population of 170,000, marked a further important stage in the FN's progression (the population of Marignane being 33,000 and that of

Orange 28,000). Though the party had consolidated its presence in the European Parliament and throughout France's regional councils, it had failed to make any major impact at the municipal level. In the previous municipal elections of 1989, it had succeeded in winning the small southern town of Saint-Gilles-du-Gard, with its electoral register of barely 7,000, only to lose control again in 1992. The election in June 1995 of an FN city council and mayor in Toulon was of an altogether different order of magnitude.

All of the classic elements favouring FN success were present in Toulon: rundown housing estates, a high crime rate, unemployment above the national average, a large working-class population, conspicuous North African and sub-Saharan African communities, and a strong contingent of *rapatriés* from Algeria. As France's chief garrison port and a city with a culture of patronage and shady dealing in local administration, Toulon provided fertile ground for a campaign which promised to defend the interests of the French, strengthen law and order and eliminate political corruption. Benefiting from a system of apportioning seats that privileged the winning list, the FN now held 41 of the Toulon city council seats, with the remaining 18 divided among the other parties. Le Pen's long-time friend and prized recruit from the centre-right, Jean-Marie Le Chevallier, was elected mayor. Of a total 39 seats on the Marignane town council, the FN gained 27 along with the election as mayor of Daniel Simonpieri, a moderate-seeming exponent of 'light Lepenism'; of 35 seats on the Orange town council, Le Pen's party won 24, with the election as mayor of the former Occident activist and FN veteran, Jacques Bompard.[10]

Having secured these local victories, Le Pen wasted no time in declaring that his party would seek to implement its policy of 'national preference' at the risk of provoking confrontation with central government and infringing the laws of the Republic, which expressly forbade such discrimination. More guarded than their party leader, the newly elected FN mayors stressed their commitment to legality and to implementing FN policies without bringing the weight of the Constitution down upon them. Their avowed priority was to demonstrate that the FN could govern a town as ably as any other party, 'with transparency, honesty and integrity, without back-handers and with the emphasis on efficiency'.[11] As for the exclusion of foreigners, there were means other than a head-on challenge to the law; the mere presence of the party in power, they anticipated, would have a dissuasive effect, discouraging immigrants from settling or remaining in towns under FN control.

The first dissuasive effects of the FN's local successes were registered not among France's immigrant communities but among the French artistic milieux. A number of artists and musicians called for a cultural boycott of Toulon, Orange, Marignane and Nice. This set off a debate in French cultural circles over the justice of ostracising these towns, with leading mainstream politicians coming out on both sides of the argument. At a press conference with his three newly designated mayors, Le Pen condemned those calling for a boycott and vowed that the FN would 'pursue its policies in favour of French men and women who are treated like pariahs in their own country'.[12]

As Michel Samson's investigative study showed, Toulon served as a testing ground for many of these policies and the means of implementing them.[13] There the FN adopted an aggressive approach to government in which Samson saw the imprint of the German political theorist Carl Schmitt and of the FN's militant training programmes overseen by Mégret. It displayed a revanchist attitude towards the previous administration and used the fortnightly council publication, *Le Toulonnais*, for blatantly propagandist purposes. It embarked on a highly publicised dispute with the Châteauvallon cultural centre (too alternative in its programme and leftist in its political sympathies), hijacked the annual Book Festival (again on the grounds of its left-wing bias), and discriminated openly in granting aid to associations engaged in artistic or charitable activities. It installed a regime inspired by anti-communism, militant Catholicism, traditional values (anti-abortion, anti-homosexuality), the cult of order, and a patriotism infused with xenophobia. Hence the withholding of public funds from a synagogue while approving subsidies for Catholic associations and church repairs; hence, too, the organisation of a solemn Mass, with the council in formal attendance, to consecrate Toulon to the Sacred Heart. By such means, Le Chevallier and his team set out to 'return' Toulon to the French. The refusal to grant municipal premises for the annual fête of the populous and ethnically diverse suburb of Sainte-Musse was motivated by no other rationale. 'When one sees the photos published in *Var Matin*, one wonders whether one is in Toulon or in Algeria', observed the mayor. 'One rather has the impression of being in Algeria.'[14]

Like the FN councils of Orange and Marignane, that of Toulon placed a premium on lowering taxes, municipal debt and expenditure while stepping up the fight against crime, mainly through bolstering the municipal police. An important feature of all three councils was their emphasis on a '*politique de proximité*'. By means of a free telephone line and scrupulous attention to processing mail, the Toulon city hall invited communication on matters of everyday material concern. The conspicuous efficiency with which its technical services set about repairing holes in the road or street-sweeping echoed the 'Improving Life in Toulon' programme on which the FN had been elected; it was also ritually reported by *Le Toulonnais* in a monthly column headed 'You requested it' (the apogee of popular consultation being a questionnaire on the action to be taken against dog owners whose pets fouled public footpaths).

This ostentatious accountability in matters of day-to-day material concern demonstrated the FN's populist approach to governing its newly captured towns, with Jacques Bompard's market walkabouts becoming a feature of life in Orange under the FN. Bompard's electoral platform had included pledges to reduce traffic and parking problems and to give the town centre a face-lift. Once installed as mayor, he cleaned up the *centre-ville*, relocated the police headquarters, reduced the municipal payroll from 650 to 520, cut subsidies to a list of welfare support associations (notably those with a multicultural mission), and generally tightened the municipal council's purse-strings.[15] He behaved at times in the manner of a Roman emperor, laying on free public events and insisting that a number of places at other events be reserved 'at the discretion of the mayor' for distribution to 'the people of Orange' (as opposed to 'strangers from outside the town'). To claim this privilege, residents were invited to present themselves at the town hall with their identity card, a utilities bill, a local tax bill, and two signed photographs.[16] Not only *panem et circenses* but an instructive insight into a local variant of '*préférence nationale*'.

The '*politique de proximité*' practised by the FN in local government extended to more politically charged matters too. In July 1996, the Orange council publication, *Orange vérités*, included a cut-out questionnaire on whether a Koranic school should be allowed to open in the town centre. In response to this impromptu municipal 'referendum' (a parody of the FN's calls for fuller use of referenda as an institutional device), the mayor's office reported one response in support, one abstention, and 1,408 negative returns.[17]

No less than in Toulon, the councils of Orange and Marignane took an interventionist role in determining the new cultural complexion of their towns, exerting their influence over artistic events, cinema schedules and library holdings. All three FN mayors cut back or halted subsidies to multicultural associations. The observance of 'national preference' was sometimes symbolic (renaming the Place Nelson Mandela as the Place de Provence), sometimes provocative (naming a crossroads in Toulon after General Salan of OAS renown), sometimes crude (halting kosher and halal alternatives in Marignane's school refectories).[18]

In a municipal by-election in February 1997, the FN added a fourth town to its name, Vitrolles in the greater Marseille conurbation (with close to 40,000 inhabitants). Control of the town was wrested from a Socialist administration charged with financial irregularities. Standing in for her temporarily disqualified husband, the new mayor of Vitrolles, Catherine Mégret, adopted the same belligerent approach as her colleagues in Toulon, Orange and Marignane, sacking municipal employees deemed unsuitable and closing community centres and associations of which the FN administration disapproved. As in Toulon and Orange, the new mayor installed a regime with a tendency to nepotism, notably in appointments to municipal posts. So much for the FN's pledge to eradicate patronage from local government.[19]

In one highly significant measure, Mme Mégret went further than her three fellow FN mayors, introducing a special 5,000-franc allowance for babies born to at least one parent of French nationality or from an EU member state. This was a measure too far for French constitutional law to tolerate, and it was ruled illegal by a court which handed down to Mme Mégret a suspended prison sentence, a fine and a ban from public office for two years. A lengthy appeals process would allow her to be re-elected in March 2001 then unseated in a by-election in October 2002 before having her conviction upheld in January 2003.

The presidential and municipal elections of 1995 thus confirmed the enduring challenge of the FN as a force in French politics. In the space of three months, Le Pen and his party broke considerable new ground in the quest for respectability on which they had been embarked for over two decades. With the support of more than one voter in seven, Le Pen demonstrated again the strength of his appeal in a presidential first ballot which lent itself to the expression of protest, while the party's performance in the municipal elections signalled the effectiveness with which it had adapted to the exigencies of campaigning at the local level. More importantly, these latter successes also pushed a stage further the FN's influence on the public policy agenda. Within months of the election of three high-profile FN mayors, a growing number of centre-right mayors began announcing cutbacks in programmes to support the integration of immigrants and combat social exclusion. Others argued for tougher law and order measures, a clampdown on begging, and even discrimination in favour of French nationals over immigrants in the allocation of social housing and certain welfare benefits. Their rationale for this reassessment of municipal priorities explicitly acknowledged the role played by such issues in generating and sustaining support for the FN.[20]

Indications of a rise in the FN's credibility were also provided by a SOFRES poll published some weeks after the municipal elections. While 72 per cent of those interviewed disavowed Le Pen, 26 per cent declared themselves wholly or partly in agreement with him (marking a clear advance on the 19 per cent recorded in January 1994). This was in line with consistently high levels of public approval for Le Pen's immigration policies specifically, and again suggested a reserve of support far in excess of Le Pen's actual electorate. On the question of whether the FN represented a danger for democracy, 68 per cent replied in the affirmative, marking a drop from 73 per cent in 1994.[21] Though findings in response to such questions require to be interpreted with some caution, they appeared to confirm a slow but sure process of legitimation carried one stage further by the electoral successes of 1995.

The 1997 legislative elections

The first round of the legislative elections on 25 May 1997 set the FN the challenge of replicating the achievements of 1995. These elections (not formally due until March 1998) were called intemperately by President Chirac in a bid to renew his majority and give fresh impetus to his administration. The result was a resounding rejection of neo-Gaullist Prime Minister Alain Juppé and his centre-right government, consigning Chirac to five years of awkward 'cohabitation' with a Socialist-Communist-Green coalition under the new Prime Minister, Lionel Jospin.[22]

With 15.24 per cent in metropolitan France, the FN achieved its strongest ever showing in a national poll, proving itself able for the first time to match Le Pen's share of the presidential ballot (Table 10.1). These elections signalled the FN's growing electoral implantation, with some 625,000 more votes than in 1993, and 1.4 million more than in 1988. They confirmed its position as the third political force in France and the second most powerful party on the right, little more than a percentage point short of the RPR and ahead of the UDF. The 1997 results also showed the FN to be the only major party to have increased its electorate in legislative elections over the decade since 1986,

Table 10.1 The 1997 legislative elections: first round (metropolitan France)

	Votes cast	%	Seats won (577 over 2 rounds for metropolitan and overseas France)
Extreme left	550,106	2.22	–
PCF	2,441,375	9.86	37
PS (+ Left Radicals)	6,357,206	25.66	259
Greens/ecologists	1,583,440	6.39	8
Citizens Movt (MDC)	266,167	1.07	7
Various left	490,124	1.98	9
RPR	4,084,506	16.49	139
UDF	3,685,015	14.88	109
Various/indep. right	1,094,901	4.42	8
FN	3,775,382	15.24	1

Sources: Interior Ministry (La Documentation Française, *Institutions et vie politique sous la Ve République*, Paris, 2003, p. 176); *Le Monde dossiers et documents: Elections législatives 25 mai–1er juin 1997*, June 1997, p. 57.

expanding its national support base from some 2.7 million to almost 3.8 million.[23] As Table 10.1 shows, however, the disparity between strength of support and gains in seats was stark, with a score of over 15 per cent bringing the FN one seat while Jean-Pierre Chevènement's Citizens Movement (MDC) gained seven seats with just over 1 per cent of the first-round vote.

Geographically, the 1997 elections consolidated and in some places extended the ground made by Le Pen in 1995. Again, support for the FN peaked in the urbanised and industrialised departments of the north and north-east and along the Mediterranean coastal belt, with notable results in and around Paris, Marseille and Lyon; again, too, the lowest mainland scores were registered in the rural departments of the Massif Central (Creuse, Corrèze, Cantal) and along parts of the Atlantic seaboard. As in 1995, the FN confirmed its strength in the Mediterranean regions of Provence-Alpes-Côte d'Azur and Languedoc-Roussillon while recording notable gains in a sweep of regions across the north and north-east – Haute-Normandie, Picardie, Champagne-Ardenne, Alsace, Lorraine and Franche-Comté.[24]

Particularly striking was the strength of the FN vote in the 'frontier nationalist' departments of Moselle (Lorraine), Bas-Rhin and Haut-Rhin (Alsace), where support for de Gaulle's brand of nationalism had run high in the 1960s and where Le Pen had made important ground in the 1995 presidential election. The FN recorded scores above its national average in 15 of the 16 constituencies in Alsace, exceeding 20 per cent in 10 of these and raising its vote by some 6 per cent (to 20.8 per cent) across the region as a whole. In the heavily industrialised Moselle department, the FN increased its share of the vote from 15 per cent in 1993 to 20.6 per cent. The gains in certain locations were dramatic. In the mining town of Forbach, the FN's score rose from 14.71 per cent in 1993 to 22.05 per cent, an advance mirrored in other industrial towns such as Sarrebourg (from 13.17 to 20.44 per cent), Rombas (from 14.32 to 20.96 per cent) and Moyeuvre-Grande (from 15.03 to 21.99 per cent). While these results illustrated the growing strength of the FN's challenge in the industrial north-east, advances were also made in more rural areas. In Ardennes, the party increased its vote from 13.2 to 19.7 per cent, and in Jura from 11.5 to 16.2 per cent, winning 17.71 per cent in Dominique Voynet's Green constituency of Dole.

Building on its municipal power bases, the FN recorded its most imposing scores in Provence-Alpes-Côte d'Azur. Of the 40 constituencies across this region, FN candidates registered scores of 20 per cent or more in 34, coming first in eight of these. The performances of Mégret in Marignane-Vitrolles (35.45 per cent), Le Chevallier in Toulon-South (32.39 per cent) and Bompard in Orange (28.79 per cent) confirmed their local '*notabilisation*'. Having contested 570 of the 577 seats at stake, however, the FN managed to convert first-round strength into election only in the constituency of Toulon-South, where Le Chevallier beat the Socialist candidate with 53.16 per cent on the second ballot. For the first time as leader of the FN, Le Pen himself did not contest a seat, preferring to cultivate his presidentialist image and avoid the prospect of a humbling defeat.

The strongest results recorded by FN candidates elsewhere were those of Marie-France Stirbois in Dreux (31.4 per cent), Maurice Gros in Marseille (31.23 per cent), Jean-Claude Lunardelli in Toulon-North (30.04 per cent), and Jean-Jacques Susini in Marseille (30.89 per cent). The decision to field Susini as a candidate in Marseille said much about the FN's appeal in this part of France. An implacable defender of *Algérie Française* and former leader in the OAS, Susini had spent some years as a political exile in Italy, condemned to death for plotting to assassinate de Gaulle after the granting of independence to Algeria.[25] In a city with a large North African immigrant population, high unemployment and crime rates, and a proven susceptibility to the FN's nationalist message, his candidacy was a clear attempt to capitalise on his past notoriety among a *pied-noir* community for whom the Algerian War remained a live issue. Winning almost a third of the first-round vote, Susini justified his selection, outpolling all other candidates in the 4th constituency of Bouches-du-Rhône.

A further notable result was achieved by Le Pen's daughter Marie-Caroline, who topped the poll in Mantes-la-Jolie near Paris with 28.48 per cent.[26] This was the site of the least edifying – and for the FN the most ultimately significant – incident in these elections. On a campaign stop in support of his daughter, Le Pen became involved in an ugly confrontation with demonstrators and was captured on film aggressing the female Socialist candidate and eventual winner of the seat, Annette Peulvast-Bergeal. For this, he would be served with a three-month suspended prison sentence, a fine and a ban from public office for two years (reduced to one on appeal). Though its implications were as yet unclear, this event was to serve as catalyst for the split that would see Mégret and his followers leave the FN and set up their rival party in January 1999.

Despite the robust showing by many FN candidates in the first round of these elections, the isolation of the party was again underlined by the smaller forces on the left whose alliance with the Socialists assured them parliamentary representation on a much narrower share of the vote than that secured by the FN. With a first-round score of under 10 per cent, the PCF went on to take 37 seats in the National Assembly; with barely 7 per cent between them, Green candidates and Chevènement's MDC claimed 15 seats within the combined left's new parliamentary majority.

The results achieved by the FN in 1997 nonetheless confirmed the success with which the party had reinforced its national electoral base. In the legislative elections of 1986 and 1988, the FN had exceeded 10 per cent in a third of metropolitan France's 96 departments, and in 1993 in two-thirds of departments; the 1997 results showed that support now exceeded 10 per cent in three-quarters of departments. The FN emerged as the leading party of the right in 44 constituencies (up from 11 in 1993).[27] It qualified outright for the second round in 133 of the 555 metropolitan constituencies (compared with 56 in 1993), despite a high abstention rate (almost 32 per cent) which raised the qualifying threshold of 12.5 per cent of the electoral register typically to around 20 per cent of actual votes cast. A partial explanation for this performance lay in the FN's increased ability to draw on already elected officials in selecting its candidates. In the 1993 legislative elections, 31 per cent of FN candidates had been regional councillors; in 1997, 38 per cent held office either as regional or municipal councillors, with around a third of those combining both mandates.[28] This showed the FN using to effect the traditional means of sinking political roots in France, including the holding of different elected offices at once (*cumul des mandats*), and again provided an important measure of the progressive institutionalisation of the party.

Two highly significant statistics emerged from the first round. The broad right, including the FN, again won a clear majority of 51 per cent; and the FN's share of the right-of-centre vote rose from 17.9 per cent in 1986, 19.4 per cent in 1988 and 22.2 per cent in 1993 to almost 30 per cent in 1997. Deprived of a prospective alliance, this left the FN in a position to exert the only meaningful influence open to it: that of power-broker and spoiler. It retained its candidates in 132 constituencies, contesting two-way run-offs against a candidate of the left or centre-right in 56 cases and three-way (left-right-FN) *triangulaires* in a further 76. Le Pen urged FN voters to support their own candidate where they could and called on voters elsewhere to defeat or spare centre-right candidates depending on their attitude to the FN, along with their declared positions on '*l'Europe de Maastricht*' and 'the principle of national preference'.[29] The real damage was inflicted by the decision to contest the 76 *triangulaires*, where the presence of FN candidates (who won on average 17 per cent in these three-way run-offs) helped secure 47 seats – and overall victory –

for the left, toppling in the process a number of prominent RPR-UDF candidates.[30] Though subsequent analysis counselled caution in concluding that the FN had been the determining factor in the left's 63-seat majority,[31] Le Pen's party clearly played a role as never before in the outcome of these elections. Even in the 445 constituencies where it did not contest the second round, the FN had an impact on some results through the votes cast by its supporters (only 50 per cent of whom were estimated to have transferred to the RPR-UDF, with 21 per cent supporting PS candidates and 29 per cent abstaining or spoiling their ballot). This followed precisely the same pattern as the redistribution of Le Pen's electorate in the second round of the 1995 presidential election.[32]

The FN electorate in the 1990s

Again the evidence was of a remarkably stable pattern of voting, with an estimated 91 per cent of those who had voted FN in 1993 supporting the party in 1997.[33] Similarly, the highest proportion of those who had determined their choice a month or more before the 1997 elections was to be found among FN voters (72 per cent).[34] Such findings indicated a much stronger allegiance among these voters than was the case in the 1980s, when the FN had struggled with the structural difficulties of forging a settled electorate within a well-established party system.[35] This growing partisan attachment suggested, as Nonna Mayer observed, 'a normalisation and stabilisation of the FN vote, and its progressive shift from a vote of rejection to a vote of adherence'.[36]

Despite the evidence in its favour, this interpretation was open to the objection of a SOFRES-CEVIPOF poll conducted in May 1997 which showed the FN electorate to harbour the lowest proportion of those feeling close to a political party (28 per cent). The FN electorate was likewise found here to have the lowest proportion of those declaring an interest in politics and the highest proportion of those believing politicians to be out of touch with ordinary people.[37] These findings invite us to temper the conclusion that the FN had by 1997 built a partisan electoral base in the conventional sense. Rather than supporting the FN through positive identification, many of these voters appear to have been negatively mobilised, casting what might be crudely described as a serial protest vote over successive elections. Though it would be wrong to reduce the FN's support merely to a protest vote, dissatisfaction with the political provision in general was an important motivation in sustaining it. Beyond the 29 per cent of FN voters whom SOFRES found to have voted *for* their 'chosen candidate' in 1997, 67 per cent voted *against* the 'other candidates'.[38] This was in line with the strikingly low proportion of Le Pen supporters in the 1988 and 1995 presidential elections declaring a wish to see Le Pen elected President (28 per cent as measured by SOFRES in 1988, 27 per cent as measured by IFOP in 1995).[39] A degree of negative voting in first rounds was consistently suggested, too, by the patterns of dispersal for FN voters in second rounds where the FN candidate had been eliminated.

These factors compounded the difficulty of defining the FN electorate in conventional political terms. FN voters did not in their majority class themselves as 'far-right' (15–20 per cent only by one measure), but they did in their majority recognise a vote for Le Pen or the FN as a 'far-right' vote (70–71 per cent). If the party's electorate contained a core of committed right-wing voters, it also – in similar proportion – drew politically alienated voters with no strong affinity to right or left, no fixed ideological compass, a largely 'left-wing' socio-economic profile, and a predisposition to abstention or protest voting.[40] Many of these voters rejected the broad right/left classification by which supporters of other parties were more ready to denote their political allegiance, with 50 per cent of FN voters refusing in a 1997 poll even to describe themselves as being 'on the right'.[41]

In his typology of the FN electorate for the 1997 legislative elections, Pascal Perrineau identified five distinct categories of voter: largely working-class and sociologically left-leaning *nationaux-populistes* (21 per cent); wealthier, national-istic, hard-line conservatives or *droito-frontistes* (20 per cent); conservatives of more pro-European outlook, largely practising Catholic and often former centre-right voters (16 per cent); relatively 'moderate' and pro-European economic liberals, again with a penchant for the centre-right (18 per cent); and, the largest group, socially disadvantaged, politically disenchanted, naturally left-leaning *gaucho-fron-tistes* (25 per cent). While the first two types exhibited the strongest loyalty to the FN, this 'pluralist' electorate as a whole appeared bound mainly by its anti-immi-grant tendencies and by the FN's negative function as a vehicle for protest against the other political parties. In conventional political terms, the most telling conclusion to emerge from this analysis was the almost equal split between right-leaning (54 per cent) and more naturally left-leaning (46 per cent) components.[42]

While such findings indicated that the FN electorate remained highly complex in its political composition, the 1997 elections reaffirmed the trend towards a more working-class support base with a sociological profile marked by masculinity, relative youth, low educational attainment, urban location, and weak (or no) religious attachment. Attracting 18 per cent of male against 12 per cent of female voters, the FN exerted its strongest appeal (19 per cent) among the 25–34 age group, drawing 20 per cent overall of those with only a basic education.[43] Again in 1997 the appeal to economically vulnerable sections of the electorate was strong: according to BVA polling figures, 24 per cent of blue-collar voters, 22 per cent of unemployed voters and 29 per cent of voters classing themselves as disadvantaged supported the FN (compared with 14, 13 and 16 per cent respectively for the PCF).[44] Among blue-collar unemployed voters, support for the FN came close to 40 per cent; among blue-collar workers aged 18–39 with strong working-class family attachments, it ran as high as 47 per cent.[45] In many old industrial areas where the PCF had been or remained domi-nant, the FN emerged as the main party of the right.[46] Polls also suggested growing support for the FN among left-wing trade union members and sympa-thisers, as 11 per cent of those identifying with the communist-leaning CGT and 18 per cent of Force Ouvrière sympathisers voted FN in the first round (compared with only 6 per cent of those identifying with the right-leaning

Table 10.2 Motivational issues in the 1997 legislative elections (% calculated on several prioritised responses)

	Mean	*PCF*	*PS*	*RPR-UDF*	*FN*
Unemployment	75	82	82	71	67
Law and order	35	28	27	39	65
Social inequalities	35	44	48	21	26
Construction of Europe	25	18	31	30	15
Immigration	22	14	15	20	67
Political corruption	13	13	13	11	22

Source: CSA exit poll, *Les Elections législatives du 25 mai 1997. Explication du vote et attentes des électeurs du premier tour (sondage sortie des urnes)*, Paris, May 1997, pp. 4–6.

Confédération Française des Travailleurs Chrétiens, CFTC).[47] Again the combined appeal to factory floor and shop floor was evident, with support of 23 per cent for the FN among shopkeepers, artisans and small entrepreneurs, while support was lower among farmers, liberal professions, management and white-collar workers (10–16 per cent).[48]

As the FN electorate evolved, so too did the motivating factors underlying this vote. In the 1980s, immigration and law and order far outweighed other reasons for voting FN, and the success with which the party made itself a repository of concern on these issues largely explained its electoral advance. During the course of the 1990s, as has been argued, there was evidence of a change. The same ethnocentric and authoritarian tendencies persisted, with immigration and law and order again cited as priority issues by a large majority of FN voters in 1997; the change was that unemployment came to figure also as a prime motivating factor in the FN vote, on a par with both immigration and law and order in the frequency with which it was now cited.

While the figures in Table 10.2 confirmed a broadly familiar pattern, a more extensive attitudinal survey carried out between the two rounds of the 1997 elections yielded further and more telling findings on the specificity of the FN voter. These distinguished the FN electorate sharply from both the wider electorate and that of the centre-right. The findings in Table 10.3 revealed a widespread anxiety on the part of FN voters in relation to France's prospects within Europe and the globalised economy. Significantly, the FN electorate in 1997 accounted for the highest proportion of voters worried about their personal and occupational future. The profile emerging here was of an authoritarian, anti-immigrant, anti-European, protectionist, profoundly pessimistic voter radicalised in their response to the economic and social challenges confronting France in the late 1990s and markedly at variance with other voters across the political spectrum.

Table 10.3 Economic and social attitudes of voters in 1997 (% identifying with each position)

	Mean	*RPR-UDF*	*FN*
Pro EU in context of globalisation	61	72	38
Confident in face of globalisation	41	53	29
Negative about France in EU	43	33	63
Opposed to single currency	36	24	65
Feel more French than European	35	37	53
Pro import controls	55	55	66
Pro discipline as priority in schools	51	58	73
Pro capital punishment	50	54	83
Too many immigrants in France	59	69	94
North Africans can be assimilated	62	61	35
Feel socially disadvantaged	20	10	26
Worried about future	66	54	81

Source: SOFRES-CEVIPOF poll (26–31 May 1997), adapted from P. Perrineau, *Le Symptôme Le Pen. Radiographie des électeurs du Front national*, Paris, Fayard, 1997, p. 116.

The attitudes outlined in Tables 10.2 and 10.3 can be set alongside the plethora of statistics from the 1980s and 1990s signalling the decline of public confidence in politicians and political parties. This was exacerbated in the 1990s by a string of corruption cases featuring politicians of right and left, inviting the FN to seek the moral high ground by adding a strong anti-corruption note to its repertoire. Polls showed an emphatic majority of respondents to be disenchanted with their political leaders and only a minority considering themselves well represented by a political party.[49] Rising levels of abstention also attested this growing alienation from the political system, a sentiment which the FN was able in part to harness. Polling in 1997 found the FN electorate to contain the highest proportion by far of those believing that the democratic process in France was failing (77 per cent) and of those 'with faith in neither the left nor the right to govern the country' (72 per cent).[50]

The FN programme: a 'third way'?

The FN's tenth national congress in Strasbourg in late March 1997 brought together 2,200 delegates from across France to engage in the theatre of tabling their own *projets de loi*, or parliamentary bills, as the sign of a party now ready to assume national power. Coming in the wake of the FN's municipal victory in Vitrolles, the congress was a personal triumph for Bruno Mégret, who appeared to secure his position as the party's rising star and leader-in-waiting. The elections to the FN's central committee saw Mégret (followed by his friend and ally, Jean-Yves Le Gallou) outstrip all other potential leadership contenders. This marked a significant power shift within the FN, confirming Mégret's growing support across the party's base and presaging a potential threat to Le Pen's authority.

The 'bills' over which the congress played out its legislative charade, complete with mock *Assemblée Nationale* imprimatur, contained proposed reforms on the FN's long-standing political priorities ('national preference' in employment, tighter restrictions on nationality, repeal of anti-racist legislation, reinstatement of capital punishment); they also put forward measures which confirmed the more popular socio-economic orientation of the FN in the 1990s (on family housing, apprenticeship schemes, and tariff barriers to protect French jobs and goods).[51] They were drawn up in accordance with the weighty tome which had, since spring 1993, proclaimed itself the FN's *'Programme de gouvernement'*, the *300 mesures pour la renaissance de la France* (*300 Measures for the Rebirth of France*). Produced under the auspices of Mégret and a drafting committee including some of the party's brightest lights (Blot, Gollnisch, Le Gallou, Martinez), this 430-page document replaced the 1986 programme, *Pour la France*.

The *300 mesures* reiterated some of the FN's earliest proposals, as set down in the party's first programme of 1973, such as a 'plural vote' for heads of families with three or more children, and a maternal income to support child-rearing. In other ways, this programme marked a fundamental shift in FN strategy and policy, from the neo-liberal, pro-European line of the 1980s to an anti-European, protectionist, more welfarist agenda. The distillation of the programme that served as the party's manifesto for the 1997 legislative elections – *Le Grand Changement* (*The Great Change*) – struck a resonantly populist note. Particularly prominent was the stress laid on social welfare issues, promoted to chapters 1 ('Jobs for the French'), 2 ('Building a Fraternal Society') and 3 ('The Right to Health') of the 1997 manifesto.[52] In the mid-1980s, taking cues from Ronald Reagan and Margaret Thatcher, Le Pen had accused France's unemployed of being 'social parasites' and decried a society where 'the number of workers is constantly falling while the number of social parasites and dependants is on the increase'. In the same period, he had argued for abolishing the SMIC and statutory working week, clamping down on trade unions, and phasing out the welfare state. The FN discourse of the 1980s rang with calls for deregulation, swingeing tax cuts, and the disengagement of the state from welfare and social security provision.[53]

By the mid-1990s, with growing support among the most economically vulnerable sections of French society, Le Pen and the FN had undergone a conversion – superficially at least – to the politics of social welfare. The 1997 manifesto promised 'a new and wide-ranging social policy', with the buttressing of the social security system, the launch of a national welfare support scheme 'aimed at those most disadvantaged', the raising of the SMIC (from 6,400 to 7,000 francs per month), the introduction of a 'parental income' equivalent to the SMIC, higher family allowances, state-subsidised loans for families purchasing houses, and the protection of gains made in the workplace under the Socialists such as the fifth week of statutory holiday entitlement. The FN anticipated a return to full employment, to be achieved partly through a reallocation of jobs vacated by immigrants and working mothers, together with a reduction of the tax burden on employers, a new emphasis on apprenticeship and the implementation of a strict economic protectionism.

A test of the FN's new orientation presented itself in winter 1995, when the centre-right government of Alain Juppé faced a wave of industrial unrest. Coming out in support of striking public-service workers, Le Pen blamed the turmoil on the 'free trade, suppression of borders and economic globalisation' associated with Maastricht. This was a posture calculated to appeal to the FN's increasingly popular support base, as a poll showed 65 per cent of FN voters to be in sympathy with the striking workers. The FN condemned the 'sell-out' of France's industrial capacity to global competition and called for import tariffs and the withdrawal of France from the single currency project. It sought to capitalise further on popular unrest by setting up a number of trade unions targeting specific groups (police and prison services, transport workers, postal workers, teachers) together with associations for the socially disadvantaged (notably the charitable Fraternité Française) and for occupants of low-rent social housing.[54] In France, such organisations offer access to a range of social and professional elections (conducted largely by proportional representation), allowing FN representatives to press the party's agenda within these different grass-roots fora and to build clientelist links with potential local voters.[55]

While the development of a major social dimension – exclusively for French nationals – marked a clear attempt to court the popular vote, it posed problems for the coherence of the FN's programme. Straining to appeal to its growing working-class constituency while retaining its lower middle-class base of *petits patrons*, the FN found itself caught between its earlier economic liberalism and a *dirigiste* rationale, embracing objectives that could not be easily reconciled.[56] Thus the party rehearsed again its proposals to phase out income tax and inheritance tax, reduce the professional taxes on small- and medium-sized business, cut employers' social security contributions, and free the economy from the state – while defending employees' social benefits, launching trade unions, supporting striking workers, and proposing a new '*taxe de préférence nationale*' on those employing immigrant labour.[57] Nowhere was there any explanation of how the defence of workers' rights and conditions might be reconciled with easing the burden on employers; how a 'parental income', increased family allowances and loan subsidies, together with a huge programme of spending on policing and justice, might be financed alongside a massive reduction (220 billion francs over five years) in public expenditure; or how the proposed national welfare support scheme would be implemented by a party that had long argued for the transfer of health care and welfare provision from the state to the private sector.

The 1990s also saw a clear shift by the FN towards a more stridently protectionist discourse. In the 1980s, with the accession of the Socialists and

Communists to power in France, ultra-liberalism had been a convenient ideological posture against Marxist collectivism; following the collapse of the Soviet Union and the failure of the Socialist project in France, a new imperialist enemy was identified in the very economic liberalism that the FN had championed, a liberalism assuming the menacing form of '*mondialisme*', or the globalised economy. While there had always been a protectionist instinct at the heart of the FN's nationalism, it now promoted this to a first principle of economic policy. Warning against the 'damaging effects of the unbridled free market', it declared: 'The regulation of trade through tariff barriers as a means to overcome the perverse effects of international competition is the central principle of the Front National's economic policy.'[58] The FN called for resistance to American-driven globalisation (with its 'lobbies' and 'vagrant' interests) and for the withdrawal of France from '*l'Europe de Maastricht*' (with its 'single currency as a means of enslavement').[59] As the slogan '3 million unemployed = 3 million immigrants too many' became less compelling (with the FN now suggesting that only a million immigrant jobs might be readily filled by French nationals), Le Pen and his party turned increasingly to Europe as an open door to *mondialisme* and the main culprit for France's economic ills, causing 'unemployment, excessive taxation, bureaucracy and recession'.[60]

Given de Villiers' marginality, Séguin's less oppositional stance on Europe and the PCF's enforced commitment to the Jospin government's line on economic and monetary union, the other major players within the anti-Maastricht camp were now effectively muted. The FN's reaction in July 1997 to the closure of Renault's plant at Vilvoorde – denouncing the 'suicidal strategy of the euro' – showed its own anti-EU animus to be undiminished.[61] As the party inveighed against 'Anglo-Saxon liberal dogmas' and called for protectionist measures, however, the problem lay not just in its deviation from its earlier, radically free-market posture; it lay also in the failure to explain how tariff barriers might be raised against imported goods without exposing French exporters to the same restrictions in return. The FN's 1997 manifesto stated quite simply: 'Taxes will therefore be raised on imports [...]. At the same time, everything will be done to encourage exports [...].'[62]

The 1990s clearly altered the electoral strategy – and with it the ideological contours – of the FN. Toning down its long-standing claim to be a party of the right (the 'social, popular and national right'), it sought more than ever to rally a sociologically diverse electorate with the slogan '*Ni droite, ni gauche – Français!*' ('Neither Right Nor Left – French!').[63] This shift was carefully articulated not as a return to the proto-fascist 'third way' discourse of the inter-war years but as an attempt to reclaim for the FN a Gaullist heritage of popular '*rassemblement*' neglected by Chirac and the RPR. Le Pen's increasingly explicit identification with de Gaulle chimed with Mégret's declared conception of the FN as a 'major rallying force' for the defence of timeless 'Gaullian ideals'.[64]

While the left had represented big government and economic *dirigisme*, the FN's programme had been a paean to neo-liberalism; following the Socialists' conversion to managing capitalism, the FN moved increasingly to claim the less contested ground of state intervention and social protection. In the changed international environment, the battle to be waged was no longer that between the free world and communism but that between the nation and the globalising project, whose cutting edge was free trade. Within the typology of radical-right parties developed by Herbert Kitschelt,[65] this turn away from outright neo-liberalism saw the FN move from 'new radical right' (a category of which it was a prototype for Kitschelt) towards 'welfare chauvinist', combining strong features now of both types in its melding of xenophobic authoritarianism with welfare-oriented social policies and protectionist economics. The programme articulating this change, however, represented less a genuine 'third way' between the free market and *étatisme* than an uneasy amalgam of elements borrowed at will from both.[66]

Strategic dilemmas and dissensions

The 1995 municipal and 1997 legislative elections saw the FN more firmly implanted within the French political landscape. They confirmed the party's electoral progression both locally and nationally, and suggested its capacity to survive the departure of its imposing, but ageing, leader. The FN's score in the legislative elections was more remarkable for being achieved in a climate of mounting public protest. Since August 1996, when Le Pen caused outrage by proclaiming his belief in 'the inequality of races',[67] there had been a rise in anti-FN militancy, with calls for the party to be banned, demonstrations against its meetings, and much debate over the ethics of granting it media coverage. The victory at Vitrolles in February 1997 was followed by the mobilisation of an estimated 50,000 demonstrators against the party's congress in Strasbourg in late March. At the same time, polling showed the proportion of those considering the FN 'a danger for democracy' to be at its highest level since 1983 (75 per cent).[68]

If a factor in Chirac's decision to call a snap election was the hope of capitalising on anti-FN sentiment, it proved a miscalculation.[69] Reviving the old Poujadist slogan '*Sortez les sortants!*', the FN entered the 1997 elections with little prospect of winning seats but well placed to exploit voters' disaffection. It determined to inflict as much damage as possible on the outgoing centre-right coalition, in the hope of provoking the 'implosion of the RPR-UDF bloc' and bringing about a 'recomposition of the broad political landscape'.[70] Le Pen named specific RPR-UDF candidates whom he called on FN voters to defeat in the second round, while *National Hebdo* trumpeted the victory of the left and the centre-right's worst performance under the Fifth Republic in its banner headline, '*La Catastrophe nécessaire*' ('The Necessary Catastrophe').[71]

With its one symbolic seat, the FN found itself arguably in a much more influential position now than it had been with 35 seats in 1986. Studies published before and after the 1997 elections estimated that as many as a quarter of French voters had, at some time, cast a vote for the FN. In addition, polls in the 1990s showed up to a third of those interviewed to be in agreement with Le

Pen's views, notably on immigration and law and order.[72] Given the durability of the social problems that had favoured the rise of the FN, the reservoir of real and potential support remained considerable. The question for the FN was how to convert that support into actual political power – and here divisions were becoming visible over the strategy to be adopted. During the election campaign, a disagreement had occurred within the FN leadership over Le Pen's declared preference for 'a left-wing Assembly' that would prevent Chirac from 'dissolving France in the Europe of Maastricht'. In an unusual display of dissent, this position was contested by both Mégret and Gollnisch, who favoured constructive compromise rather than the wrecking strategy advocated by their leader.[73]

With the left elected to government, the choice facing the FN was between a Lepenist line that argued against offering any 'crutch' to a weakened centre-right, and a Mégrétist line that advocated a rapprochement with the RPR-UDF as a means of bringing the FN into the mainstream of French political life.[74] To that end, Mégret called for a '*discipline nationale*' on the model of the '*discipline républicaine*' long practised by the PS and PCF: tactical cooperation in retaining or withdrawing candidates between the two rounds of elections. There was some precedent for this in the deals struck between the FN and the centre-right in the legislative elections of 1988 in Bouches-du-Rhône and Var, and in governing alliances in regions such as Languedoc-Roussillon and Provence-Alpes-Côte d'Azur between 1986 and 1992. Mégret declared himself ready to resume such cooperation in Bouches-du-Rhône for the 1998 cantonal elections, and proposed that it be extended to challenge the PCF in strongholds such as Seine-Saint-Denis.[75]

Cleaving to an isolationism endemic on the French extreme right, Le Pen was publicly dismissive of such proposals.[76] With the prospect of a five-year 'cohabitation' between a neo-Gaullist President and a Socialist-Communist-Green government, he reasoned that the FN stood to gain from disaffected voters of right and left alike. The evolution of the FN's electorate, with its increasingly working-class character, showed that the party could make serious inroads into traditionally left-wing constituencies and gave force to its '*Ni droite, ni gauche – Français!*' slogan. One of the most avid proponents of this strategy, Le Pen's son-in-law, Samuel Maréchal, then head of the FN youth section (FNJ), ruled out any 'short-term compromise for the sake of five more deputies'.[77] A special three-day seminar held by the FN's political bureau in Strasbourg in mid-July 1997 endorsed the Le Pen line; but there were signs of growing dissension as an influential founding member, Roland Gaucher, published a book criticising the FN as an 'absolutist monarchy' where Le Pen's word went unchallenged by 'a bunch of courtiers paying extravagant homage to him'.[78]

The debate within the FN was reflected by a parallel debate across the centre-right, with voices calling for a more politically pragmatic attitude towards Le Pen's party. Prominent amongst these was de Gaulle's former lieutenant, Alain Peyrefitte, who argued against 'excommunicating' FN voters and suggested that Le Pen's leadership posed the greatest obstacle to an eventual RPR-UDF-FN alliance.[79] Following a dinner with Le Pen, the former RPR security minister, Robert Pandraud, called for 'dialogue' between the centre-right and the FN, just as former Interior Minister Pasqua urged the RPR to debate the question of an alliance. While the secretary-general of the UDF, Claude Goasguen, ventured likewise that the moment was right to end the 'demonisation' of the FN, the former centre-right minister Jean-Pierre Soisson framed the issue starkly: 'When the left unites to win, the right must do so too – the entire right, from the centre to the extreme right.'[80]

These were influential voices within a centre-right alliance obliged now to contemplate the FN as the potential key to electoral victory or defeat. The newly installed leader of the RPR, Philippe Séguin, resisted the idea of an alliance and stressed instead the need to win over FN voters. For that to be achieved, he argued, the centre-right must 'address issues of public concern like the nation and its future, Europe, unemployment […], the future of our suburbs and the increasing number of no-go areas, […] and immigration, that problem which we have allowed to be taken over by slogans and the false truths they convey'.[81]

These remarks were problematic on two counts: they conceded to the FN the right to dictate the political agenda, and they advocated an attempt to woo its voters that had already met with failure. In 1995, Chirac had centred his presidential campaign on the *'fracture sociale'* caused by unemployment and social exclusion – only to see Le Pen emerge as the leading candidate among workers, the unemployed and those classing themselves as disadvantaged. The Pasqua and Debré immigration laws of 1993 and 1997 had similarly failed to stem support for the FN, despite tightening the conditions for entry, residence and naturalisation, increasing police powers, and even calling on French citizens to inform their local authority about foreign visitors lodging with them.[82] If the three major national elections of 1993, 1995 and 1997 had proved anything, it was that attempts to co-opt the FN's mobilising themes did nothing to block the electoral advance of Le Pen and his party, and might even have served to give them increased legitimacy.

An eloquent variation on this problem was provided by former Prime Minister Edouard Balladur in June 1998, when he proposed (to varied reaction on the centre-right) that a commission be set up to discuss one of the FN's key policies, the observance of 'national preference' in the allocation of certain welfare benefits.[83] If the risk of alienating centrist voters through such proposals was difficult to gauge, the risks involved in a pact with the FN were clear. An IFOP poll carried out in July 1997 showed a large majority of RPR (66 per cent) and UDF (77 per cent) supporters opposed to any such alliance. Significantly, the pattern was reversed among FN supporters, with only 6 per cent opposed and 74 per cent in favour.[84]

Raising the pressure: the 1998 regional and cantonal elections

This failure to shake off the extremist label and gain mainstream acceptance would be as much a factor as personal rivalry in the split that occurred between Le Pen and Mégret in December 1998. Compounded by Le Pen's refusal to designate Mégret as his successor elect, their divergence came to a head when the FN seemed poised to exert its strongest influence yet. Winning just over 15 per cent (3,270,118 votes) across metropolitan France in the regional elections of March 1998, the FN took its tally of regional councillors from 239 to 275, ahead of the UDF (262) and only marginally behind the RPR (285). It secured seats in all of France's 21 mainland regions, emerging as the largest single party in the councils of Provence-Alpes-Côte d'Azur (with 37 of 123 seats), Rhône-Alpes (35 of 157 seats), Alsace (13 of 47 seats) and Franche-Comté (9 of 43 seats).[85] In rural regions that had previously proved resistant to the FN and where its favoured issues of immigration and *insécurité* had relatively little resonance, the party also increased its representation (from one to three seats in Limousin and from six to eight in Midi-Pyrénées).

These modest gains in rural regions repaid the FN's efforts to appeal beyond its urban heartlands. In other, more favourable regions, local UDF leaders were forced to conclude hurried deals with FN regional councillors in order to secure governing majorities (Jean-Pierre Soisson in Bourgogne, Jacques Blanc in Languedoc-Roussillon, Charles Baur in Picardie, and Bernard Harang in the Centre region).[86] By this means, the FN was able to increase its administrative role and clientelist profile in a number of regions.[87] Denying any such collusion, Charles Millon was likewise re-elected president of the Rhône-Alpes region with the support of the FN's 35 councillors.[88] These tractations and quasi-tractations provoked yet another anguished and highly publicised debate within the RPR and UDF hierarchies, and prompted *Le Monde* to conclude that Mégret's 'open-handed strategy' was at last prevailing.[89] Up to a point only. In two of France's three largest regions, Ile-de-France and Provence-Alpes-Côte d'Azur, the RPR and UDF opted for defeat rather than alliance with the FN, allowing both assemblies to pass under a Socialist presidency despite the right's overall numerical majority.[90]

In the cantonal elections held at the same time, the FN won 13.7 per cent, over 1.5 million votes. This was the party's strongest share of the vote yet in cantonal elections, allowing it to contest the second round in 316 cantons.[91] In the event, it won only three seats (in Marignane, Noyon and Toulon) to add to the five already held – out of almost 4,000 across metropolitan France's 96 departmental councils (*conseils généraux*).[92] This meagre reward notwithstanding, the regional and cantonal elections confirmed the stabilisation of the FN vote in different electoral contests since the mid-1990s: 15 per cent in the presidential and legislative polls of 1995 and 1997, and now 15 per cent and almost 14 per cent respectively in regional and cantonal polls in 1998. The growing evidence of the FN's institutionalisation appeared to herald its progression beyond the role of protest party to become a firm, and increasingly powerful, fixture within the French political system.[93]

A damaging split

The acrimonious split that ensued between the traditionalist and modernising wings of the FN showed the fragility of a party that had always been an uneasy coalition of diverse tendencies and factions. The catalyst was provided by Le Pen's proposal to entrust leadership of the FN list for the forthcoming European elections of June 1999 not to Mégret but to his own wife Jany, should he fail in his appeal against the two-year ban from public office imposed in April 1998 for the incident at Mantes-la-Jolie during the 1997 legislative election campaign. This was one of a number of provocative gestures by Le Pen in summer and autumn 1998 aimed at undermining Mégret's growing power base within the FN. It was a personal slight too far for a deputy leader already at odds with Le Pen over strategy.[94] The departure in January 1999 of the *'mégrétiste'* faction fragmented the party apparatus, with a large number of the FN's national and local officials defecting to Mégret's breakaway Front National-Mouvement National, to become in October 1999 the Mouvement National Républicain (MNR). Of the 275 regional councillors elected in 1998, just over half (140) joined Mégret, together with 57 of the 96 metropolitan federation secretaries, 52 of the 120-strong central committee, and 14 of the (now) 44 members of the political bureau, where Mégret was replaced as delegate-general by Gollnisch. The party's security service (DPS) also sided with Mégret in 12 of metropolitan France's 22 regions.[95]

The FN retained its old guard (Holeindre, Chaboche, Reveau, Baeckeroot, Brigneau, Bompard, Martine Lehideux and others), the 'solidarist' current (Marie-France Stirbois, Michel Collinot, Bruno Gollnisch), and younger activists who had often come through the ranks of the FNJ (Carl Lang, Martial Bild, Samuel Maréchal, and Le Pen's daughter Marine). The MNR attracted denizens of the Nouvelle Droite such as Jean-Yves Le Gallou and Pierre Vial who had, like Mégret, joined the FN in the mid-1980s with a view to building bridges with the parliamentary right. Such figures had been particularly influential in intellectualising the FN's position on the issues of immigration, identity and 'national preference', and were now denounced by Le Pen as 'extremist' and 'racist'.[96] From the outset, the ultra-nationalist and traditionalist Catholic elements in the FN had existed in uneasy tension with this new breed of technocratic intellectual for whom Mégret had acted as internal leader. The latter also attracted his share of younger sympathisers such as Franck Timmermans, Daniel Simonpieri, Philippe Olivier and Le Pen's daughter Marie-Caroline, along with much of the FNJ and the student Renouveau Etudiant. Of the four towns governed by the FN, only Orange (under Bompard) was retained, with Marignane (under Simonpieri) and Vitrolles (under Catherine Mégret) passing to the MNR, and Toulon being lost with Le Chevallier's subsequent departure from the FN in March 1999.

These developments replayed, in the full glare of the media, the dissensions and internal power struggles that had been a feature of the FN since its formation and which had seen the successive departure of Robert's Ordre Nouveau, Duprat's GNR and Frédriksen's FANE in the 1970s. The history of Le Pen's leadership of the FN, too, had throughout been one of blocking the rise of aspirant successors. He had used Jean-Pierre Stirbois in the late 1970s as a counterweight to the influence of Duprat, only to counter Stirbois' influence in turn by promoting Mégret in the mid- to late 1980s; likewise, the nomination of Gollnisch as party secretary-general in 1995 and the promotion to vice-president of Roger Holeindre in 1997 were clear attempts to counter Mégret's rise. The nomination in October 1998 of the former OAS leader Jean-Jacques Susini as head of the FN's Bouches-du-Rhône federation was inspired by the same desire to contain Mégret even in his electoral heartland.

Herein lay an essential problem for a party that had failed to keep pace organisationally with its electoral evolution. While the FN had been a movement still consigned to the political wilderness in the early 1980s, Le Pen's writ ran unchallenged; but the proliferation of elected officials at European, regional, municipal and now mayoral levels brought a new pluralism to the party's leadership and a challenge to the autocratic style of management that Le Pen had wielded from the outset. Sensing a threat to his authority from the election of three high-profile mayors in 1995, Le Pen had insisted that the latter did not 'own their mayoralties' but had been elected 'on FN lists, on the FN programme, with the patronage of the FN and the FN president'. In December 1998, he rounded likewise on Mégret's mutineers as opportunists who owed their electoral existence to having run on the Le Pen name. 'The legitimacy of the Front National', he insisted, 'resides in its president.'[97]

The formation of the MNR returned the French far right to the situation that had prevailed from 1974 to 1981, with two rival movements (then the FN and PFN) vying for ascendancy and undermining each other's prospects. The 5.7 per cent (just over one million votes) polled by the FN list in the European elections of June 1999 was the lowest score recorded by the party in a national election since 1984. With the 3.28 per cent polled by Mégret's list, the combined score of both movements fell some way short of the 10.5 per cent recorded by the FN in the previous European elections of 1994.[98] This poor showing was due to the deleterious effects of the split, a high abstention rate that reached its peak among Le Pen and FN sympathisers, and the presence of a rival 'sovereignist' list under Pasqua and de Villiers.[99] Polling evidence indicated that, while Mégret's party retained a predominantly male electorate, it exerted a readier appeal among better educated, higher-income categories than among the poorly educated, economically vulnerable constituencies where the FN now found its strongest support.[100] This suggested already the difficulty which Mégret would face in carving out a distinct electoral space for his MNR between the FN and the traditional centre-right. This first electoral contest between the two parties followed months of legal wrangling over the FN's funds, assets and even name, the rights to which Le Pen was finally granted – though too late, he claimed, to allow his party to mount an effective campaign.[101]

The result saw the FN's representation in the European Parliament cut from 11 to five MEPs, though the reduced FN group included a highly symbolic recruit in the grandson, and namesake, of Charles de Gaulle. Placed second on the FN list to make a bizarre 'Le Pen–de Gaulle' leadership tandem, the latter was publicly disowned by his family for defecting from de Villiers to the 'enemies of all that General de Gaulle had embodied'.[102] This minor political coup aside, the collapse of the FN vote was a spectacular reversal for a party that had set its sights on 20 per cent but now found itself overtaken by its old enemy, the PCF (6.8 per cent), and – humiliatingly – by the fringe movement Chasse, Pêche,

Nature et Traditions (Hunting, Fishing, Nature and Tradition, CPNT) (6.77 per cent). More ominously for Le Pen, his list was resoundingly beaten by that of Pasqua and de Villiers, whose Rassemblement pour la France (Rally for France, RPF) secured 13.09 per cent on a nationalist, anti-European platform which drew significant support away from the FN.[103] Though Le Pen resolved with characteristic resilience to rebuild his party's strength for the municipal elections of 2001 and the presidential election of 2002, the schism pitched the FN into a crisis which appeared to herald its demise as a major political force.

In the municipal elections of March 2001 (which saw the centre-right make ground on the left despite the major losses of Paris and Lyon), the FN fielded 1,702 candidates to the MNR's 1,318.[104] Jacques Bompard's FN list was re-elected on the first ballot in Orange (with almost 60 per cent of the vote), while the MNR lists of Daniel Simonpieri and Catherine Mégret won on the second ballot in Marignane and Vitrolles. Only in Toulon did one of the FN's former municipal fiefs fall as Le Pen's erstwhile friend and confidant, Jean-Marie Le Chevallier, facing criticism of his administration, lawsuits and opposition from an FN candidate, was eliminated at the first round with less than 8 per cent support for his list.[105] To those who had argued that the FN would betray itself in power, the re-election of three mayors was a sobering spectacle. It marked a further stage in their '*notabilisation*' and delivered a clear verdict from the voters of Orange, Marignane and Vitrolles on the model of local government practised by the FN and MNR.

Weakened by division and contesting only a fraction of the seats contested by the FN in 1995, both parties won just over 4 per cent (FN) and 3 per cent (MNR) of the vote as a whole in these elections.[106] They nonetheless averaged over 10 per cent, either separately or together, in the municipalities which they contested, indicating tenacious support in areas of strength.[107] In the cantonal elections held at the same time, with some 2,000 seats at stake, the FN fielded 1,667 candidates to the MNR's 1,273. They scored just over 7 per cent and 3 per cent respectively, losing the four renewable seats held between them (in Canisy, Dreux, Toulon and Mulhouse).[108]

The 2002 presidential election: a 'seismic shock'

Nothing in these results, in opinion polls or in events since late 1998 presaged what was to follow in the presidential election of April and May 2002. Bringing to a close the five-year 'cohabitation' between President Chirac and the Socialist-led government of Lionel Jospin, this was an election whose only apparent uncertainty was over which of these two leading candidates would prevail in the second round. The shock on the evening of 21 April, when Le Pen overtook Jospin to qualify instead, was all the greater since no polling agency had considered this a serious prospect. With 16.86 per cent (4,804,713 votes), Le Pen polled 0.68 per cent (194,600 votes) more than the outgoing Prime Minister. Adding the 2.34 per cent (667,026 votes) mustered by Mégret, the combined result for Le Pen and his former deputy in this election was 19.2 per cent, or 5,471,739 votes – the support of almost one in five voters. This represented a share of public support well in excess of that attained in any previous election, with the FN and MNR candidates exceeding the combined Socialist and Communist scores in metropolitan France.[109] For the first time since 1969 there would be no candidate of the left in a presidential run-off; for the first time ever there would be a candidate of the far right.

An indifferent campaign

Despite its dramatic denouement and the presence of a record 16 candidates, the campaign for the first round of this election was a bland affair. The protracted experience of 'cohabitation' left Chirac and Jospin, who had faced each other in the 1995 run-off, unable to project any sense of real choice or change. Polls showed a majority of respondents finding little difference between the two on any issue, from tax and pensions to law and order.[110] In the absence of a genuine debate over issues, the media manufactured interest in novelties such as the young Trotskyist postman, Olivier Besancenot, and the self-styled custodian of country life and traditions, Jean Saint-Josse. To these were added a further two Trotskyist candidates (the perennial Arlette Laguiller and Daniel Gluckstein), a Communist (Robert Hue), a Left Radical (Christiane Taubira), a 'Republican' Socialist (Jean-Pierre Chevènement), centre-rightists of various labels (François Bayrou, Alain Madelin, Christine Boutin), and Greens of different hues (Noël Mamère, Corinne Lepage).

On the far right, Le Pen entered the presidential race facing a direct challenge from Mégret, who ran a campaign promising to 'restore order in France' and rehearsing, at times verbatim, the FN's main proposals on national identity, immigration, law and order, tax, family values and other issues (which Mégret himself had helped to elaborate in the party's 1993 programme, *300 mesures pour la renaissance de la France*).[111] The FN had marked Mégret's departure by preserving the essence of its programme but re-issuing it, in 2001, under the new title *Pour un avenir français* (*For a French Future*). This was the platform on which Le Pen stood in 2002, with a manifesto calling for: French national sovereignty within a Europe of nation states; 'zero tolerance' in law and order, with a referendum on the death penalty, harsher sentencing and increased prison capacity; tighter restrictions on immigration, asylum and nationality; a sharp reduction in taxes and public expenditure; full employment for the French, to be achieved partly through the policy of 'national preference'; an extensive programme of family support, again based on 'national preference' in welfare benefits, housing and the provision of a 'parental income'; and measures to protect the countryside, infused with an appeal to rural anxieties over wider and deeper European integration.[112]

More than that of Mégret, Le Pen's campaign was marked by an acerbic anti-Europeanism. The FN leader's most radical pledge was to pull France out of the EU and reinstate the franc as national currency. The FN's 2001 programme and Le Pen's campaign rang with denunciations of the treaties of Schengen,

Maastricht and Amsterdam as the foundations of 'a supranational entity spelling the end of France'. Where once they had argued for a France bound militarily to Europe, the FN and Le Pen now called for withdrawal from European military cooperation in favour of bilateral accords with individual states.[113] With neither Pasqua nor de Villiers able to muster sufficient support to stand, Le Pen found himself virtually unrivalled in this election as the strident voice of right-wing anti-Europeanism, though there were plenty of competing voices elsewhere. Saint-Josse and Mégret provided anti-EU noises off on the right, while Chevènement, Laguiller, Besancenot, Gluckstein and Hue created a cacophony on the left.

Despite radicalising his stance against Europe and globalisation, the 73-year-old Le Pen conducted this campaign in a relatively emollient style, projecting the image of a senior politician mellowed by the wisdom of years. Claiming that he was and had always been a 'man of the centre-right', he now modified somewhat his proposals on immigration. Though repatriation remained in order for illegal immigrants, those convicted of criminal offences, the long-term unemployed and foreign students on completion of their studies, the FN leader dropped his 1995 pledge to deport three million non-European immigrants over the course of the presidential term.[114] He refused to condemn the booing of the Marseillaise at a recent France-Algeria football match in the Stade de France, interpreting it as an understandable reaction of 'the weak against the strong'. He even expressed a measure of regret now for his notorious remarks about the gas chambers being a 'detail' of history and his reference to '*Durafour-crématoire*' – both, as he put it, 'unfortunate expressions' proving that he was 'not perfect'.[115]

On social issues, too, Le Pen's 2002 campaign reflected some evolution, consolidating the FN's image as a party appealing most strongly to poorer, working-class and dispossessed voters. Where once he had advanced a quasi-Darwinian view of social disparities, Le Pen's platform in 2002 struck a conspicuously inclusive note, with emphasis on equality of opportunity and support for the unemployed, pensioners, the poor, the homeless, the disabled, and others threatened with social or economic exclusion.[116] The formula which he repeated with relish throughout the campaign was that he was 'socially to the left, economically to the right, and nationally French'.[117] Another formula which he felt secure enough to rehearse before several thousand supporters at his final pre-election rally in Paris was the Vichy slogan of '*Travail, Famille, Patrie*', values that had been 'demonised', he intoned, but 'without which there is no viable society'.[118]

The issue which played most to Le Pen's advantage in this election was law and order, pushed to the centre of the campaign by a Chirac anxious to press his Socialist Prime Minister on a vulnerable point. The previous year had seen almost a 10 per cent rise in recorded crime. At the same time, a number of violent incidents (including the murder of a policeman in Vannes and a killing spree by a deranged gunman in the municipal council of Nanterre) put the government's record on law and order under the spotlight.[119] On this issue, which emerged as the prime concern from opinion polls, Le Pen was happy to take up the running from Chirac.[120] In the aftermath of the attacks of 11 September 2001 on the World Trade Center in New York, moreover, equations between *insécurité*, illegal immigration and Islamic fundamentalism found a louder resonance.

It was no surprise when polling showed Le Pen voters to be concerned above all by law and order (74 per cent), followed by immigration (60 per cent) then other issues such as unemployment (31 per cent), the justice system (31 per cent), pensions (22 per cent) and tax (20 per cent).[121] Surveys conducted by the CEVIPOF political research unit found support of 79 per cent for capital punishment among Le Pen voters, compared with 44 per cent in public opinion at large.[122] The link between immigration and the breakdown in law and order was a central feature of the FN's 2001 programme, with immigration deemed a 'mortal threat to civil peace in France'.[123] When invited to identify a single issue of concern rather than several, Le Pen voters privileged immigration, with 96 per cent judging that there were 'too many immigrants' in France, 87 per cent that the French were 'no longer at home' in their own country, and 46 per cent that 'some races are less gifted than others' (a rephrasing of Le Pen's openly stated belief in 'the inequality of races'); to these could be added the 44 per cent of Le Pen voters declaring that Jews had 'too much power' in France.[124] Le Pen voters also articulated a radicalised rejection of landmark reforms introduced by the Jospin government, with emphatic opposition to the 35-hour working week, the single currency, the abolition of military service, the introduction of gender parity in electoral candidacies, and the *pacte civil de solidarité* (PACS) recognising same-sex civil unions.[125] *Sortez les sortants!* writ large.

A 'seismic shock'[126]

In qualifying for the run-off, Le Pen found himself the beneficiary of simple arithmetic. With every one of the five tendencies in Jospin's 'plural left' coalition fielding a candidate, and with no fewer than three Trotskyists contesting ground yet further to the left, it was little wonder that the Socialist front runner saw his support base eroded to 16.18 per cent. His elimination to Le Pen's benefit was not without its irony, since the FN leader had in previous presidential contests banked on the divisions and rivalries of the right rather than those of the left to allow him to squeeze through. Conspiring in Jospin's defeat, too, was an inordinately high abstention rate of 28.4 per cent, including many potential Socialist voters who viewed the first round as a formality. Fighting a lacklustre and tactically poor campaign (which he announced by fax to the press), the Prime Minister fell victim to the prevailing forecasts of first-round success, to the recklessness of the 'plural left', and to his own complacency. The classic imperative for presidential hopefuls is to secure their natural support base in the first round then extend their appeal to the centre and to floating voters in the second. Jospin fought the first round as though it were already the second, seeking to maximise his appeal to the centre and taking for granted much of his traditional support on the left. At his campaign headquarters, copies of his schedule of public meetings to be held *between* the two rounds were arranged in a neat pile on the welcome desk: Montpellier, Lyon, Paris, Toulouse, culminating in a final pre-election rally at Nantes on 3 May. All were abruptly cancelled on the evening of 21 April, when Jospin announced his retirement from political life.

Thus was the outgoing Prime Minister rewarded for the longest-serving government of post-war France, and one whose record of economic and social management was far from negligible. It had notably reduced unemployment from over 12 to almost 9 per cent and extended health cover for the poor, though its landmark reform of the 35-hour working week brought it more brickbats than plaudits and unemployment was again on the rise, together with job insecurity.[127] Combined with Chirac's dismal 19.88 per cent, Jospin's score contributed to the weakest performance on record for the two leading mainstream candidates in a presidential first ballot. This poor showing by the mainstream front runners was to be seen in the light not only of Le Pen's 16.86 per cent but also of the 10 per cent secured jointly by Trotskyist candidates, who capitalised on left-wing disgruntlement at the Prime Minister's accommodation with economic orthodoxy and his perceived neglect of workers' rights and social justice. The picture was completed by a further dispersal of votes among minor candidates and the poorest performance ever (fewer than a million votes) for an official PCF candidate, alienated from much of his natural constituency by his party's participation in the Jospin government (Table 10.4). With under 5 per cent of the vote, Robert Hue did not even qualify for the reimbursement of his campaign costs.

Political opportunism and miscalculation had their part to play in the outcome of the first round. Despite Chirac's stern condemnation of the extreme right, it was partly through the intervention of the RPR that Mégret secured the requisite 500 signatures from elected officials to enable him to stand. While Chirac's party worked behind the scenes to promote Mégret as a useful rival to Le Pen, the Socialist Party was said to be encouraging certain mayors to support the FN leader as the major threat on the right to Chirac. If the PS was rightly to be charged with such a crass error, it was an error compounded by helping the Trotskyist Besancenot and the Left Radical Taubira likewise to secure their 500 signatures.[128]

Le Pen topped the poll in 35 of metropolitan France's 96 departments and in nine of the 22 regions: Alsace (23.44 per cent), Provence-Alpes-Côte d'Azur (23.35 per cent), Languedoc-Roussillon (22.33 per cent), Lorraine (21.24 per cent), Champagne-Ardenne (21.12 per cent), Picardie (20.26 per cent), Franche-Comté (19.98 per cent), Rhône-Alpes (19.83 per cent) and Nord-Pas-de-Calais (19.03 per cent). By contrast, Jospin came first in the single region of Midi-Pyrénées, with Chirac commanding the other 12 (one of them – Bourgogne – by less than 1 per cent over Le Pen). The FN leader claimed first place in 31 of the 38 departments across the above nine regions, demonstrating the geographical coherence of a support concentrated once again mainly east of a line from Caen through Lyon to Montpellier and peaking in the southern departments of Alpes-Maritimes (25.99 per cent) and Vaucluse (25.79 per cent).[129] The dominance of Le Pen over his former deputy and would-be rival, Mégret, was everywhere

Table 10.4 The 2002 presidential election: first round (metropolitan and overseas France)

	Votes cast	%
Chirac	5, 665, 855	19.88
Le Pen	4, 804, 713	16.86
Jospin	4, 610, 113	16.18
Bayrou	1, 949, 170	6.84
Laguiller	1, 630, 045	5.72
Chevènement	1, 518, 528	5.33
Mamère	1, 495, 724	5.25
Besancenot	1, 210, 562	4.25
Saint-Josse	1, 204, 689	4.23
Madelin	1, 113, 484	3.91
Hue	960, 480	3.37
Mégret	667, 026	2.34
Taubira	660, 447	2.32
Lepage	535, 837	1.88
Boutin	339, 112	1.19
Gluckstein	132, 686	0.47

Source: Constitutional Council (La Documentation Française, *Institutions et vie politique sous la Ve République*, Paris, 2003, p. 178).

evident. While the FN leader secured over 10 per cent of the poll in 525 of France's 555 metropolitan constituencies (and over 20 per cent in more than a quarter of these), the MNR leader exceeded 10 per cent in only one, the 12th constituency of Bouches-du-Rhône incorporating his personal power base of Marignane-Vitrolles. In all other locations, Mégret attracted under 6 per cent, and in most cases under 3 per cent, finishing twelfth out of the 16 candidates.[130]

Despite some erosion of support in places, notably to the benefit of far-left candidates in some working-class constituencies of Nord and Seine-Saint-Denis, Le Pen improved his 1995 score by more than 3.5 per cent in over 100 constituencies, a fifth of the electoral map. Many of the gains were made in rural areas where FN voting had previously been weak and where Le Pen ate into the support of the centre-right more than that of the left.[131] A growth of support was recorded in rural areas of north-eastern France, in communes close to large agglomerations, and in more extensive rural areas hitherto resistant to incursions by Le Pen. In Tarn-et-Garonne and Lot-et-Garonne in the agricultural south-west, the FN leader progressed from fourth place in 1995 to first in 2002, with 20.12 and 18.91 per cent respectively. Gains in communes with fewer than 2,000 inhabitants were among the most notable advances made by Le Pen in this election.[132] The 20 per cent of support garnered among farmers and agricultural workers suggested a rural community responsive to the low-tax, anti-European, anti-globalisation aspects of Le Pen's programme at a critical moment in the development of the EU. A marked correlation was detectable between the Le Pen vote and the 'no' vote in the 1992 Maastricht referendum, with almost a third of those who had rejected Maastricht supporting the FN leader in the second round.[133]

This election confirmed Le Pen's support base as predominantly male, working-class, poorly educated, and with weak religious ties. Had only men voted on 21 April 2002, Le Pen would have led the poll by several percentage points over Chirac and Jospin both; had only women voted, he would have been eliminated to Jospin's benefit.[134] The FN leader was credited with support of 20 per cent or more among men, blue-collar workers, white-collar workers, the unemployed, shopkeepers, artisans and small entrepreneurs, farmers and agricultural workers, those with a basic education, non-practising Catholics, and the 50–64 age group (which emerged in this election as the most sympathetic to Le Pen).[135] As in 1988 and 1995, the Le Pen electorate was again characterised in 2002 by its merging of working-class and lower middle-class components. In some polls, support was put as high as 30 per cent among blue-collar workers, almost 32 per cent among shopkeepers, artisans and small entrepreneurs, and 38 per cent among the unemployed.[136] An estimated 26 per cent of those considering themselves disadvantaged voted for Le Pen, along with 31.5 per cent of those feeling that their personal situation had worsened.[137] Tellingly, Le Pen voters were the most politically alienated, with 93 per cent signalling the remoteness of politicians and 77 per cent judging them corrupt (though these sentiments were shared, respectively, by 82 per cent and 58 per cent of public opinion at large).[138] In his declaration on the evening of 21 April, Le Pen stressed again his aspiration to harness this popular, working-class, politically alienated vote. 'Do not be afraid to dream', he urged,

> you the small people, the foot soldiers, the excluded [. . .], the miners, the steelworkers, the women and men who labour in all of those industries that have been ruined by the Euro-globalism of Maastricht. You who work the land in return for a miserable pension and are driven to the brink of ruin and inexistence. You who suffer most from the breakdown of law and order in our suburbs, towns and villages. [. . .] Be assured that, as a man of the people, I can always be relied upon to support those who suffer, since I know what it is to be cold, hungry and poor.[139]

Le Pen progressed in some areas where support for the left declined, reflecting the dissatisfaction of industrial workers and low-wage earners with the outgoing 'plural left' government. He relied mostly, however, on the solid bedrock of his own support, with an estimated 83 per cent of those having voted for him in

1995 returning a vote for him again in 2002. This compared with fidelity rates over the same two elections of only 51 per cent for Chirac and 53 per cent for Jospin.[140] Accordingly, 63 per cent of Le Pen voters had decided on their vote several months before the election (compared to an average of 43 per cent within the electorate at large).[141]

This evidence of strong voter loyalty was again accompanied by a marked ambivalence in the motivations underlying support for Le Pen. Law and order and immigration were by far the most pressing issues at stake in the Le Pen vote of 2002, followed by unemployment. Though Le Pen was seen by voters at large as the politician most able to preserve law and order or deal with immigration, only a minority of his own supporters (45 per cent) approved of his proposal to pull France out of the EU.[142] More soberingly for Le Pen, fewer than half of his voters (41–46 per cent) wished to see him elected President, and over a quarter (29 per cent) saw his presence in the second round as a danger for democracy. Within the wider electorate, CEVIPOF polling found only 13–15 per cent who believed that Le Pen had 'what it takes to be President of the Republic', against 81 per cent for the incumbent Chirac.[143]

Imposing though his results appeared, moreover, Le Pen's overall perfor-mance in the first round of this election did not mark a significant advance. Despite the public anguish provoked by his presence in the run-off and far-fetched comparisons with Germany in 1933, the FN leader did not, as some commentators claimed, 'come so close to securing power'.[144] In simple statistical terms, he increased his 1995 showing by less than 2 per cent, fewer than a quarter of a million votes; in the 14 years since the presidential election of 1988, Le Pen's share of the ballot had risen by precisely 2.46 per cent, a long way short of half a million votes. As a proportion of the electoral register, unaffected by fluctuating abstention, Le Pen's gain over this period was almost non-existent, rising from 11.47 per cent in 1988 to 11.66 per cent in 2002. The Republic was hardly more in danger now than it had been at any time since the FN's break-through in the mid-1980s.

Even adding Mégret's 2.34 per cent, the aggregate gain since 1995, at 4.2 per cent, was considerably less than a million votes. If one takes account of the 4.74 per cent won by de Villiers on an essentially far-right platform in 1995, then the total far-right vote in 2002 actually *dropped* from 19.74 per cent to 19.2 per cent (with a loss of over half a million votes). This was to be compared with Jospin's loss of over 7 per cent, or almost 2.5 million votes, between the same two elec-tions. The mechanics of the 2002 presidential election turned not on the dynamism of the far right but on the self-destruction of the left.

Rather the 'crook' than the 'fascist'

This did not prevent the second round from being played out as a crucial test of France's commitment to Republican values. In the two weeks between the rounds, French streets became the theatre for a sustained display of opposition to Le Pen, culminating on May Day when coordinated anti-Le Pen demonstrations involving an estimated 1.5 million people took place across the country.[145] Such was the level of concerted opposition to the FN leader within the political establishment, the media and public opinion that his adversary, Chirac, became little more than an idle spectator, watching events unfold without the need even to campaign. His uninspiring record as President and equally uninspiring programme – including rash promises to drive taxes down and police numbers up – were nowhere put to the test. The one occasion which would have placed the incumbent in the spotlight opposite his challenger, the traditional televised debate, was summarily cancelled. Dogged by allegations of corruption from his time as RPR leader and Mayor of Paris, Chirac spared himself any embarrassing public probing by refusing to debate with Le Pen, restricting himself instead to platitudes about 'national cohesion', a society 'anchored in humanism' and a 'moral union to defend the values of the Republic'.[146] The man who had argued the equation between immigrants and unemployment before Le Pen, who had lamented the 'noise' and 'smell' of foreigners in France's social housing estates, who had worn his anti-Lepenism as a badge of honour while denouncing the 'overdose' of immigrants in France, became now the embodiment of the 'moral imperative of tolerance and respect for others'.[147]

Faced with the scale of opposition ranged against him, Le Pen did not perform well between the two rounds. Whereas his campaign for the first ballot had focused on projecting a calm, moderate, reasonable image, interviews now showed him defiant and irascible, condemning the 'lynch mob' that had taken to the streets.[148] Though his campaign team had been astute enough to prepare separate manifestos to cater for the eventuality of a run-off against either Chirac or Jospin, Le Pen now cut the figure of a man who had gone beyond his comfort zone as eternal loser and who could not strike the posture of a serious contender for power.

The second round held no surprise. Where Chirac had been uncertain of beating Jospin, he won an implausible 82.21 per cent against Le Pen (a margin of victory eclipsing de Gaulle's 55.2 per cent to Mitterrand's 44.8 per cent in 1965). With an abstention rate of just over 20 per cent (down by some 8 per cent from the first round), Chirac found his support massively swollen by former abstentionists and, in particular, by left-wing voters who chose what they perceived as the lesser of two evils, *l'escroc* (the crook) rather than *le facho* (the fascist). Polling found that 71 per cent of Chirac's second-round electorate voted 'to block Le Pen' and only 29 per cent because they thought Chirac 'a good candidate'.[149] Having been supported by fewer than 14 per cent of registered voters in the first round, Chirac achieved in the second what no other President before him could boast: the endorsement of a clear majority (fully 62 per cent) of the electoral register. On entering this election, Le Pen had wished above all to topple Chirac; instead, he assured the President's re-election by a margin from the realm of dreams.

With 17.79 per cent (5,525,032 votes), Le Pen increased his own first-round tally by some 720,000 votes – compared with an increase of almost 20 million for Chirac, just under half of the entire French electorate. A major lesson of the second round was not that Le Pen failed to improve significantly on his first-round score, falling far short of the 30 per cent target which he set himself; it was rather that he sustained his first-round support, attracting over one voter in six despite the most extensive public protest ever mounted against a political figure in France. Though Mégret had been the only candidate on the evening of the first round to call on support for Le Pen, the FN leader did not simply hold his first-round vote and add that of Mégret, as the figures superficially suggested. CEVIPOF polling found that 78 per cent of Le Pen voters held firm, while 15 per cent transferred to Chirac and 7 per cent abstained. At the same time, an estimated 55 per cent only of Mégret's negligible electorate switched to Le Pen, with 32 per cent preferring Chirac and 13 per cent abstaining. A substantial component of Le Pen's second-round support was therefore drawn from beyond the confines of his own and of Mégret's first-round electorate. The FN leader was found to have attracted a second-round vote from supporters of most other candidates, notably the anti-European Saint-Josse (10 per cent), the 'traditional values' candidate Boutin (9 per cent), the Communist Hue (6 per cent), the Trotskyist Laguiller (5 per cent), and some first-round abstentionists (5 per cent).[150] Combining Le Pen's support of over 5.5 million on 5 May with more than a million voters estimated to have voted for him on 21 April only, the figure for those supporting Le Pen in one or both rounds of this election can thus be put at over 6.5 million.

Geographically, Le Pen's vote on 5 May largely replicated that of 21 April, with high points in the southern departments of Bouches-du-Rhône (27.46 per cent), Alpes-Maritimes (28.68 per cent), Var (28.69 per cent) and Vaucluse (29.64 per cent). In only one of France's 96 metropolitan departments, Chirac's fief of Corrèze, did Le Pen's score dip (just) below 10 per cent. He achieved 20 per cent or more in over a third of the 555 metropolitan constituencies, and improved on his first-round score, if only marginally, in almost half of them.[151] Again the FN leader recorded above-average support among men (22 per cent), shopkeepers, artisans and small entrepreneurs (20 per cent), white-collar workers (20 per cent), low-wage earners (20 per cent), and – especially – blue-collar workers (33 per cent). Support for Le Pen was again marked among those with a basic education (22 per cent), residents of low-rent social housing (27 per cent), and those feeling that their personal situation had worsened (30 per cent). With Chirac as his sole opponent, Le Pen's support held up well among younger voters (21–22 per cent of 18–34-year-olds), while he retained above-average support too among the over-65s (20 per cent). As in the first round, a strong motivating factor in the Le Pen vote was law and order, cited by 72 per cent of his supporters as opposed to 32 per cent of Chirac's.[152]

The 2002 legislative elections: towards a 'UMP state'

The 2002 presidential election saw Chirac reinstated for a five-year rather than seven-year term. This was the result of a constitutional reform approved by referendum in September 2000 and aimed at reducing the likelihood of further power-sharing between right and left by synchronising the presidential and legislative timetables. The presidential election had been due to follow the legislative elections scheduled for March, but the order had been reversed as part of Jospin's strategy to oust Chirac and return a left-wing majority in the wake of his own anticipated victory.

Once re-elected, Chirac proceeded to form an interim government, appointing as his new Prime Minister the largely unknown senator and president of the unglamorous Poitou-Charentes region, Jean-Pierre Raffarin, from the small centre-right Démocratie Libérale (DL) party, an offshoot of the UDF.[153] This was an attempt by Chirac to 'reach down' to the France that had just re-elected him, through a reassuringly centrist, provincial figure called on to embody *la France d'en bas* (grass-roots France) rather than Parisian technocracy. With barely a month separating the presidential and legislative polls, Chirac was anxious to capitalise on his triumph and, after five years of cramping 'cohabitation', secure a 'clear and coherent majority' to support him through his new presidential term.[154] This call for a presidential majority – opposite a demoralised Socialist Party that had warned against further 'cohabitation' before helping to reinstall Chirac in the Elysée – effectively took the place of a legislative programme. The appointment of the energetic Nicolas Sarkozy as Interior Minister was designed to ward off the challenge from the FN on the issue of law and order which had dominated the first round of the presidential election, and which emerged again as the voters' prime concern in the legislative campaign.[155]

The innovation of the June 2002 elections for the centre-right was the hasty formation of an umbrella Union pour la Majorité Présidentielle (Union for the Presidential Majority, UMP), to become in November 2002 the Union pour un Mouvement Populaire (Union for a Popular Movement, UMP) under Chirac's neo-Gaullist lieutenant, Alain Juppé. In its first incarnation, the UMP was conceived as a body to oversee the nomination of joint candidates, but it marked the most decisive step yet towards the establishment of a single, broad party of the centre-right. It had at its core the RPR and absorbed much of the UDF, DL and other smaller centre-right formations. Though a rump UDF under François Bayrou resisted absorption and contested some seats under its own banner, the UMP ran single candidates in almost all of France's 577 constituencies, thereby minimising the risk of damaging 'primaries' on the right. Mindful of the 47 seats won by the left in triangular contests in 1997, the UMP anticipated anxiously the FN's capacity to maintain candidates through to the second round. Extrapolations from Le Pen's presidential performance suggested that this could be the case in enough constituencies (up to 237) to jeopardise a centre-right victory, though the official line laid down by Chirac was that no deals should be done with either Le Pen's or Mégret's party.[156] This was in response to a more conciliatory FN, calling now for constructive cooperation with the UMP when in 1997 it had revelled in its power to wreck the electoral prospects of the RPR and UDF.[157]

In the event, the FN vote fell far short of Le Pen's presidential score. With 11.34 per cent (2,862,960 votes), the party qualified to retain its candidates in only 37 of the 566 constituencies which it contested (with nine three-way run-offs), compared with the 132 second ballots (and 76 three-way run-offs) contested in 1997.[158] On that occasion, with over 15 per cent, the FN had matched its leader's performance in the preceding presidential poll; now it reverted to the experience of 1988, with a wide gap between the achievement of Le Pen and that of his party. Whereas Le Pen's presence in the presidential run-off should have been a major asset to the FN in these elections, it proved more of a liability, given the groundswell of popular opposition which he had faced and the extent of his second-round defeat. In June 2002, the split between the FN and the MNR also proved more damaging than in the presidential poll, with much of the FN's constituency apparatus and locally elected base having defected with Mégret. This was to little avail, since the MNR (fielding symbolically one candidate more than the FN)[159] secured a derisory 1.09 per cent nationally, just over a quarter of a million votes, and failed to retain any of its 567 candidates for the second round (Table 10.5).

Even in its isolated bastion of Marignane-Vitrolles, the only constituency where the MNR outpolled the FN, Mégret was eliminated with 18.58 per cent of the vote (short of the 12.5 per cent of the electoral register required to take him through). This represented little more than half of Mégret's first-round score in the same constituency in 1997 (35.45 per cent), with 13.25 per cent of the vote now going to the rival FN candidate. The results of the presidential and legislative polls confirmed Mégret's failure to launch a credible alternative to the FN. Despite trading on essentially the same policies, the MNR leader suffered from a debilitating lack of personal charisma and from the poor electoral appeal of his technocratic style alongside Le Pen's sonorous populism.

Both the FN and the MNR were hit hard by the massive abstention rate of over 35 per cent, the highest for any legislative first ballot under the Fifth Republic, confirming that the citizens' mobilisation of April had run its course. This despite the unprecedented range of choice on offer, with the number of candidates increased (by the strong presence of far-left parties and competition on the far right) to an average of almost 15 per seat. It was notable that, in their selection of candidates, both the FN and the MNR bowed to the new legislation on gender parity and fielded some 49 per cent and 40 per cent of women respectively. This was a development most uncharacteristic of extreme-right parties, calculated both to project a softer image and to avoid the financial penalties incurred by breaching the new law. Le Pen would subsequently point to this law as a reason for the FN's relatively modest performance, claiming that the party had been obliged to field women 'to the detriment of better placed men'.[160]

Analysis carried out by CEVIPOF showed the dispersal of Le Pen's first-round presidential vote, with 44 per cent supporting the FN, 1 per cent the MNR, 21 per cent the centre-right, 6 per cent the left, and an estimated 28 per cent abstaining or spoiling their ballot. The FN also suffered from a *vote utile*, or tactical vote, which played to the benefit of the UMP as a means of avoiding a further period of unpopular 'cohabitation'. Finally, the speed with which the interim Raffarin government moved to reassure public opinion on the salient issues of law and order, illegal immigration and taxation deprived the FN of

Table 10.5 The 2002 legislative elections: first round (metropolitan France)

	Votes cast	%
Far left (Lutte Ouvrière/LCR)	622,451	2.47
PCF	1,216,178	4.82
PS	6,086,599	24.11
Various/indep. left	964,341	3.82
Greens/ecologists	1,434,121	5.68
UMP	8,408,023	33.30
UDF	1,226,462	4.85
Various/indep. right	1,323,793	5.23
FN	2,862,960	11.34 (0 of 577 seats*)
MNR	276,376	1.09

Source: Interior Ministry (La Documentation Française, *Institutions et vie politique sous la Ve République*, Paris, 2003, p. 176).

Note: * over both rounds

powerful oppositional themes. Polling indicated a 58–60 per cent rate of approval among far-right voters for the early pledges and measures of the new government, a confidence level comparable to that registered within the electorate as a whole.[161]

Trends detected in the presidential election were confirmed. The FN once again drew its strongest share of the vote from men (13 per cent), white-collar workers (20 per cent), shopkeepers and artisans (12 per cent), those with the most basic education (15 per cent), and the unemployed (30 per cent). The FN's share of support among blue-collar workers, who abstained in large numbers, dropped sharply while remaining significant at 15 per cent.[162] Geographically, the well-established contours of the FN vote were again in evidence, with support strongest along the entire Mediterranean littoral, in the industrial north and north-east, and in the greater Paris and Lyon conurbations.

On the second ballot, demobilised FN supporters helped swell the abstention rate to a new record of nearly 40 per cent. Polling data indicated that, where FN candidates had been eliminated, around half of the party's first-round voters abstained, while 40 per cent voted for the centre-right and 10 per cent for the left.[163] In those constituencies where FN candidates remained in contention, they had little prospect of success faced with a UMP standing firm against deals and a 'united left' around the Socialist Party replacing the fissiparous 'plural left' of 21 April. Jacques Bompard (with 42.37 per cent) lost his duel against the outgoing UMP-RPR deputy in Orange, as did Marine Le Pen (32.3 per cent) against the Socialist incumbent in Lens; Bruno Gollnisch went down in a three-way contest in Lyon (21.29 per cent), along with Marie-France Stirbois in Nice (20.13 per cent) and Jean-Claude Martinez in Sète (17.15 per cent). The FN found itself in the familiar position of having not a single parliamentary seat to show for its first-round score of 11.34 per cent, while the PCF, with only 4.82 per cent, retained its parliamentary group with 21 seats in the National Assembly.

In sum, these elections were marked by the reasserted hegemony of the mainstream parties, with the Socialists performing strongly and the non-Communist far left collapsing from over 10 per cent in the presidential poll to under 3 per cent. Where Chirac and Jospin had mustered a combined 36 per cent on 21 April, the PS and UMP secured over 57 per cent on 9 June. The main comfort derived by Le Pen on the evening of the second round was one of *Schadenfreude*: that of seeing the chief architects of Jospin's 'plural left' government (Martine Aubry, Robert Hue, Jean-Pierre Chevènement, Dominique Voynet) defeated one by one in their parliamentary fiefs. There was less consolation to be found elsewhere, as the hastily launched presidential party secured 369 of the centre-right's 399 seats in the new National Assembly, against 178 for the parties of the left. For only the third time under the Fifth Republic (after the Gaullists in 1968 and the Socialists in 1981), a single political formation claimed an absolute majority in the National Assembly.

The overwhelming dominance of the UMP in these elections, like that of Chirac in the second round of the presidential contest, belied the fragmentation and volatility that had become features of the French electoral landscape, with unprecedented numbers of candidates, the relative success of fringe movements, record abstention rates and strong elements of protest voting. It inaugurated what amounted to a 'UMP state', surpassing even the so-called 'UDR state' through which the Gaullists had consolidated their hold on power following their landslide in 1968.[164] The President's party now controlled not only the Elysée and National Assembly but also the Senate and Constitutional Council, together with most regional and departmental councils throughout France. In seven weeks, the presidentialism of the Fifth Republic had been extravagantly bolstered and its electorally weakest incumbent gifted more power than that enjoyed even by his illustrious predecessor, de Gaulle.

11 Looking back and forward

The Front National since 2002

The 2004 regional elections: a '21 April in reverse'

The period following the 2002 presidential and legislative elections saw Le Pen bask in his new notoriety while his party projected itself bullishly as the major force of opposition in France. With no elections scheduled for two years, the FN concentrated on completing its structural recovery from the split of 1999. At the party's triennial congress in April 2003, Le Pen was re-elected unopposed as president. This deferred the thorny question of the leadership succession until, at the earliest, the next congress due in spring 2006 but set back until autumn 2007, after the presidential and legislative elections of spring and summer 2007.[1] With that prospect in view, the most significant internal development was the promotion within the party leadership of Le Pen's youngest daughter, Marine. Nominated at her father's urging to a vice-presidency with a seat on the FN's key executive bureau, Marine Le Pen emerged almost overnight as a potential rival to the long-serving Bruno Gollnisch and Carl Lang, the party's delegate-general and secretary-general.[2] Having attracted media attention in support of her father's presidential bid in 2002, she had gone on to win almost 25 per cent of the vote in the first round of the legislative elections in the mining town of Lens in Pas-de-Calais, a former left-wing stronghold. Relishing her new-found celebrity, the 35-year-old Marine made no secret of her ambition to give the FN a more modern and respectable image and to rescue it from its isolation on the far right, with Italy and Austria offering lessons in how this might be achieved.

The first 18 months of the Raffarin government saw its early popularity give way to widespread disgruntlement over resurgent unemployment and proposed reforms to state welfare provision. With unemployment by March 2004 at 9.8 per cent (some 2.4 million),[3] the economy stalled, and the budget deficit and national debt in breach of the EU's stability pact, the new government drew criticism for its poor economic performance. It also incurred public anger over its programme of reforms to health care, pensions, unemployment benefits, and education. As the first mid-term test of the Raffarin government's standing, the regional elections of March 2004 were preceded by widespread public protests against belt-tightening measures already in place or projected.

These elections reasserted the volatility of contemporary French politics over any illusion of stable alignment, with the combined left of Socialists, Communists and Greens sweeping all but two (Alsace and Corsica) of metropolitan France's 22 regional councils, and with left-leaning lists also gaining the four overseas regions. Though losses for the centre-right had been anticipated, the extent of the rout (with the loss of 12 of the 14 regions under its control) invited comparison with the triumph of Chirac and the UMP and the humiliation of the Socialists less than two years before. A headline in *Le Monde* proclaimed 'The 21 April in reverse for Jacques Chirac'.[4]

Essentially, regional elections are a local affair on a grander scale with little direct bearing on national politics, appointing councils for six years with responsibility in matters of regional development, education and training, transport and infrastructure, culture and tourism. The timing of these elections, however, turned them into a mid-term referendum on the Raffarin government. This first electoral test of the UMP as a settled party was a calamitous failure, with all but one of the 19 centre-right ministers who ran for election figuring on defeated lists in their respective regions.[5] That the Socialists, by their own avowal, did not even have a coherent project to offer underlined the extent to which this was a *vote-sanction*.[6]

The most emblematic defeat of all was that of the Prime Minister in the Poitou-Charentes region which he had run for 14 years (1988–2002) and which fell to the Socialists' rising star, Ségolène Royal. Another major casualty was former President Valéry Giscard d'Estaing, ousted from his long-time personal fief in the Auvergne. A year before, President Chirac had enjoyed dizzying popularity for his opposition to the American-led invasion of Iraq; now, an embattled Chirac was obliged to reshuffle his government, retaining Raffarin as Prime Minister in defiance of public opinion and moving Nicolas Sarkozy to the Finance Ministry, Dominique de Villepin to the Interior Ministry, and Jean-Louis Borloo to an enlarged Ministry of Labour and Social Cohesion. The most telling of these appointments was that of Sarkozy, an able, hyper-active, popular politician who had made no secret of his ambition to succeed Chirac in the Elysée. Already guilty of *lèse-majesté* for having supported Balladur against Chirac in the 1995 presidential election, Sarkozy was moved from Interior to Finance Minister in a bid both to redress France's ailing balance sheet and to expose to potential public ire the President's most serious rival on the centre-right.

A new record for the FN

With the left still in disarray following the catastrophe of 2002, these elections appeared to offer the FN an unusually promising conjuncture. Since the turn of the year, polls had signalled the intention of a growing majority of voters to protest against the Raffarin government.[7] The election campaign followed the conviction in January 2004 of Chirac's former Prime Minister and heir apparent, Alain Juppé, in a high-profile political corruption scandal.[8] It also followed the highly charged public debate in December 2003 over the banning of Islamic headwear and other conspicuous religious symbols in state schools.

The immediate run-up to the poll was marked by growing fears over terrorism as a previously unknown group threatened attacks on the French rail network and train bombings in Madrid attributed to Al-Qaida claimed almost 200 lives.[9]

Whereas the regional elections of 1986, 1992 and 1998 had been contested in one round on a strictly proportional basis, the March 2004 elections employed a new two-round system combining majority and proportional elements. Only those lists winning 10 per cent or more of the vote in the first round were allowed to proceed to the second, where they could fuse with smaller lists having scored over 5 per cent. In the second round, the best placed list would secure 25 per cent of the seats outright (effectively guaranteeing it a majority), with the rest distributed proportionally above a 5 per cent threshold on the basis of performance within individual departments. The new system was promoted as a means of producing clear majorities and bringing regional assemblies closer to their electorate. More precisely, it represented an attempt to reduce the influence – both numerical and political – of the FN within France's regional councils following its role as arbiter in a number of regions in 1998.[10]

In the first round, the FN attracted its strongest support ever in a regional poll. With 15.11 per cent across metropolitan France, it dropped slightly from its 15.27 per cent of 1998; but in actual votes cast (with turnout up from 58 to 62 per cent), it added almost 300,000 votes to its tally (which rose from 3.27 to just under 3.56 million).[11] It passed to the second round in 17 of the 22 metropolitan regions, falling little short of the qualifying threshold in the central and western regions of Auvergne, Limousin, Brittany and Pays de la Loire, and failing also in Corsica. Though it lost some ground in its heartland of Provence-Alpes-Côte d'Azur (down from 26.6 to 22.95 per cent, a drop due in part to competition from the MNR), it scored well in other established areas of strength – Alsace (18.58 per cent), Rhône-Alpes (18.21 per cent), Languedoc-Roussillon (17.17 per cent) – and improved its standing in most regions. Particularly strong results were recorded in the northern industrial regions of Picardie (22.94 per cent, a rise of almost 4.5 per cent), Champagne-Ardenne (19.72 per cent) and Lorraine (17.58 per cent). In Nord-Pas-de-Calais, where the FN raised its score from 15.3 to 17.94 per cent, the party's secretary-general, Carl Lang, finished second to the Socialist-alliance list, pushing into third place the UMP list headed by the government minister Jean-Paul Delevoye. In all but four other mainland regions, the FN claimed third place behind Socialist-led and UMP-led lists, confirming its place as France's third political force, well ahead of the UDF, PCF, Greens and other parties.

Mégret's MNR, by contrast, ran lists in 13 regions and scored above 2 per cent in only five of these, with a high point of 2.94 per cent in Provence-Alpes-Côte d'Azur. Finishing last in all but two of the regions contested, the MNR lost all of the seats which it had held since breaking away from the FN in 1999. Its only meaningful contribution was to divert enough of the far-right vote to hasten the FN's exit in Auvergne, Brittany and Pays de la Loire. In Pays de la Loire notably, the 2.55 per cent won by the MNR candidate consigned Le Pen's son-in-law, Samuel Maréchal, to elimination with 9.71 per cent, just 0.29 per cent short of the qualifying threshold.

In Alsace, where the MNR did not present a list, the FN was challenged by the far-right regionalist movement Alsace d'Abord (Alsace First, AA), led by the former FN parliamentary deputy Robert Spieler. Launched in 1989 on Spieler's departure from the FN, AA played on the same themes of immigration and insecurity as the FN, calling for regional over national preference ('*la préférence communautaire*') in economic development, jobs, health care, cultural identity etc. Its charter cast in regional terms many of the FN's national policies and was markedly more pro-European in tone. Each denouncing the other as a movement of dangerous extremists, the FN and AA attracted fully 28 per cent between them (18.58 per cent and 9.42 per cent respectively), marginally exceeding the combined score of Le Pen and Mégret for this region in the 2002 presidential election. Their acrimonious relationship precluded any alliance for the second round, where the FN won 22 per cent and eight of the 47 seats in a three-way run-off against the UMP-UDF and PS-Green lists.[12]

In all, the FN won 12.78 per cent across metropolitan France in the second round of these elections, withstanding efforts by centre-right leaders to dislodge FN voters and securing seats in all of the regions contested. Though it registered almost the same support in these 17 regions as it had across all of France's 26 metropolitan and overseas regions in 1998 (some 3.2 million votes), it saw its cohort of regional councillors cut by the new voting system from 275 in 1998 to 156 (out of a total 1,829). In reality, this represented a rise from the much reduced figure of 130 with which the FN had been left following the defection in 1999 of most of its sitting regional councillors to the MNR.[13] In the 17 regions where it remained in contention, the FN held its vote almost intact between the two rounds, compensating for losses in some regions with gains in others and proving once again the tenacity of its support base. Though the victory of the left was sufficiently sweeping in most regions to offset the FN's strong presence, Le Pen's party drew significant support away from the centre-right in Picardie, Rhône-Alpes and Provence-Alpes-Côte d'Azur. In Champagne-Ardenne, where the Socialist-led alliance won just under 42 per cent and the UMP-led alliance just under 40 per cent, the FN struck its most convincing pose as arbiter with 18.28 per cent of the second-round vote.

The same tenacity was evident in the cantonal elections held alongside the regional poll to elect around half of France's 4,038 departmental councillors. Winning almost 12.5 per cent of the first-round vote in metropolitan France (just over 1.5 million), the FN confirmed its now solid implantation at the departmental level. It qualified for the second round in 281 cantons and contested 278 of these, winning just under 5 per cent and contributing to the swing that saw control at the departmental level shift to the left by 51 to 49 councils.[14] The role of the FN in these elections was restricted to that of spoiler, since it managed to elect a councillor to only one of the 2,034 seats at stake, raising the party's total to two seats in all. The peculiar fact was that this was achieved in Orange-East by Marie-Claude Bompard, wife of Jacques Bompard, the mayor of Orange and sitting departmental councillor for Orange-West. Marie-Claude Bompard secured almost 40 per cent in the first round and won the second with 55.4 per cent against her Socialist opponent. Set alongside the 60 per cent of the first-round vote with which her husband had been re-elected mayor at the head of the FN municipal list in 2001, and the 40 per cent recorded in Orange by the FN regional list led by Guy Macary, this result confirmed Orange as the town in France voting furthest to the right (in the most far-right department of Vaucluse, with its 28.49 per cent support overall for the FN regional list).[15]

A more eccentric situation still arose in the neighbouring Bouches-du-Rhône. Like Orange, Marignane was a town won by the FN in 1995 and retained in 2001 by its mayor, Daniel Simonpieri, following his defection to Mégret's MNR. The second round of the cantonal election here witnessed an unprecedented run-off between two far-right candidates, the incumbent Simonpieri (now standing as an independent) and the FN challenger, Léonard Faraci. With all other candidates eliminated, this extraordinary contest saw Simonpieri re-elected with 72.75 per cent against Faraci's 27.25 per cent. Once re-elected, Simonpieri joined the UMP group in the departmental council, adopting his fourth political label in six years. This did not alter the fact that, for the first time in a run-off ballot, every one of the (11,961) votes was cast in the name of a far-right candidate, projecting Marignane as a close rival to Orange in its voting tendency.[16]

1984–2004: twenty years on

Following hard on the regional and cantonal polls of March, the European elections of 13 June 2004 were something of a landmark for the FN. Twenty years on from its breakthrough in the European elections of June 1984, they offered an opportunity to measure the strength and durability of its support. They were also seen by the FN as a means of redeeming its poor performance in the corresponding elections of 1999, following the party's split, when it had recorded its lowest score in a European poll and seen its representation in Strasbourg cut from 11 to five MEPs.

In its programme, the FN set out the case against a 'federal Europe, the last stage on the road to world government'. Such a Europe would reduce France to the status of a 'rump state like Alabama or Dakota, lost in a vast Federation that would itself be a puppet of the New World Order' and its pernicious 'lobbies'. Between full independence and 'absorption into the Euro-globalist magma', it argued, no middle way was now possible.[17] The FN's proposals were to withdraw France completely from the EU, breaking all institutional ties stretching back to the Treaty of Rome in 1957, and to reassert full French sovereignty in political, economic, fiscal, judicial and other domains. With Gaullist overtones, the FN called for the reversion of Europe to an essentially economic market, for inter-governmental cooperation on the basis of nation states only, and for a 'grand political project' that would revitalise France's international standing by drawing on francophone influence across the world. It returned to its old idea of a common – rather than single – European currency as an economic instrument with which to rival the power of the 'dollar god', and it voiced shrill opposition to the possible accession of Turkey to the EU.

Despite this uncompromising message, the FN's campaign was notable less for its policies than for a number of incidents casting adverse attention on its leader. In early April 2004, Le Pen was convicted by a Paris court of incitement to racial hatred, fined and ordered to pay damages to the anti-racist Ligue des Droits de l'Homme. The judgement was in response to remarks published in *Le Monde* in which the FN leader had reportedly asserted that the massive explosion of the Muslim population ('from five million to 25 million') would ultimately render the French cowering outcasts in their own land.[18] Le Pen was already under suspension of his European mandate following a series of court rulings and appeals relating to the disorderly incident at Mantes-la-Jolie in 1997.[19] When in late April 2004 he visited England to help launch the European election campaign of the British National Party (BNP), he was dogged by protesters and publicly warned by the Home Secretary, David Blunkett, not to provoke racial tension. Then in June the old ghost of Le Pen's past in Algeria returned to haunt him with a court case in response to renewed allegations of torture during his military service in Algiers in 1957.[20]

Like the regional elections of March, the European elections of June 2004 were contested according to a new system less favourable to the FN. Whereas in previous European elections seats had been allocated proportionally on a national basis, the system devised for these elections divided France into eight inter-regional constituencies. In the newly enlarged Europe of 25 member states, the number of French MEPs was reduced from 87 to 78, to be drawn pro rata from the eight constituencies. On 13 June, the FN won 9.81 per cent (1,684,792 votes) and seven seats – two in the south-east (Jean-Marie Le Pen, Lydia Schenardi) and in the north-west (Carl Lang, Chantal Simonot), one in the east (Bruno Gollnisch), in the south-west (Jean-Claude Martinez) and in Ile-de-France (Marine Le Pen). This represented an advance on the 5.7 per cent and five seats won in 1999, but fell far short of the party's aspirations.[21]

Shedding close to two million votes in the space of a few weeks, the FN saw its support drop to 12.86 per cent in the north-west, 12.18 per cent in the south-east, 12.17 per cent in the east and 8.58 per cent in Ile-de-France. It was hampered by competition from Philippe de Villiers' 'sovereignist' Mouvement pour la France (Movement for France, MPF), which won 6.67 per cent, and to a much lesser degree by Charles Pasqua's Rassemblement pour la France (RPF), which mustered 1.7 per cent, while Mégret's MNR barely registered its presence with 0.31 per cent. More significantly, the FN vote was depressed by a record abstention rate of 57.2 per cent and by the unpopularity of its radical stance on Europe, even among many of its own supporters.

A year later, the apathy that had attended these elections would be replaced by a vexed national debate over the EU constitutional treaty and the future direction of Europe. Though Le Pen's proposal to withdraw France from the EU had been supported by only 45 per cent of his own electorate in April 2002, opposition to the EU constitution in the referendum of 29 May 2005 won the support of an estimated 92–96 per cent of FN sympathisers.[22] Just as in the Maastricht referendum of 1992, the FN campaigned vigorously for a 'no' vote, opposing the proposed constitution as a charter for unfettered economic liberalism and the Islamicisation of the EU through the eventual accession of Turkey. Alongside the PCF, the Trotskyist LCR, a large component of the PS, and de Villiers' MPF, the FN found itself now for the first time on the winning side as the French voted by some 55 to 45 per cent against the constitution. Since the determining margin of 2.74 million votes in this referendum was much less than the 3.56 million secured by the FN in the regional elections of 2004, Le Pen and his party were prompt in claiming to have made a decisive contribution to defeating the constitution and effectively arresting the process of European integration.[23]

After the distortive outcome of the 2002 presidential election, the regional, cantonal and European elections of 2004 restored a more nuanced picture of the FN's place in the French political landscape, while the referendum of May 2005 allowed it to revel in a rare celebration of victory. These polls showed that the party had recovered from its scission and prevailed to the near-eclipse of Mégret's MNR, just as it had once seen off opposition from an earlier breakaway rival in the PFN. The regional elections of March 2004 confirmed the FN's standing as France's third political force, capable of sustaining a serious challenge at this median level between the national and the local. They also demonstrated again the recovery powers of the party less than two years on from the nationwide campaign of vilification mobilised against its leader in 2002.

In concrete terms, the main lesson of the 2004 elections was that no region now lay beyond the appeal of the FN, which recorded over 8 per cent in every one of France's 21 mainland regions. High scores in Nord-Pas-de-Calais, Picardie, Champagne-Ardenne, Lorraine, Rhône-Alpes and elsewhere confirmed the FN's solid electoral presence in areas of de-industrialisation and its capacity to exploit the symptoms of urban anomie. There was another, less prominent but no less significant feature of the FN's performance in these elections: its gradual implantation in regions hitherto resistant to the party's appeal (Bourgogne, Aquitaine, Midi-Pyrénées, Basse-Normandie, Pays de la Loire). In seeking to extend its electoral geography, the FN showed that it could feed off disenchantment of different sorts, running on unemployment, immigration and insecurity in the industrial north and east, on anxieties over European enlargement in the agricultural south-west, or on the defence of rural life in the south. The village of Camembert in Basse-Normandie, famed for its creamy cheese, is no recession-scarred urban enclave; but over a quarter of its 185 inhabitants voted for the FN in the first round of the 2004 regional elections. In nearby Sap-André, with its 127 inhabitants, support for the FN was almost 40 per cent; in the tiny commune of Ménil-Bérard (68 inhabitants), it reached 42 per cent, in Ménil-Broût (181 inhabitants) 38 per cent, and in Ferrières-la-Verrerie (195 inhabitants) 35 per cent. Such scores are worthy of note since they give the lie to any notion that the FN is confined for support to its urban bastions. In the sleepy village of Saint-Hippolyte-le-Graveyron in the southern Vaucluse department (with its electoral register of 166), support for Le Pen's party in the first round of the March 2004 cantonal election reached all of 50 per cent.[24]

Ambiguous auguries

As the FN adjusted to its gains and losses in 2004, the auguries for its future role in French politics remained ambiguous. It had proved its capacity to combine a strong, recurrent element of protest with a strikingly high degree of voter allegiance; it had also shown, in the regional and cantonal elections, that even an Interior Minister as resolute about law and order and immigration control as Nicolas Sarkozy could not stem its support. Yet in the 20 years since its electoral breakthrough, the FN had failed in its essential mission: that of becoming more than a spoiler, a '*minorité de blocage*', and of attaining real power in more than a few local instances.[25] It had succeeded as a focus for negative mobilisation but not as a positive alternative.

This raises the broader institutional difficulty by which the FN has throughout been critically impeded. Under the system of proportional representation introduced exceptionally for the legislative elections of 1986, the FN won 35 of the 577 seats in the National Assembly. Since the return to the two-round majority system in 1988, the party has at no time held more than a token seat (winning one seat in 1988 and 1997, and no seat at all in 1993 and 2002). Nor has the FN enjoyed any representation in the 321-strong, indirectly elected upper house of the Senate. By 2006, the party had lost control of all of the towns which it had governed; and following the defection of Jacques and Marie-Claude Bompard in Orange, it no longer held any of the 4,038 seats across France's departmental councils (the *conseils généraux*, elected by a two-round majority system in single-member 'cantons').

Despite some isolated successes, the FN has thus been precluded from an institutional status commensurate with its electoral support. Had the proportional system used in 1986 been applied in 1997, the FN would have won an estimated 77 seats in the National Assembly, making it an indispensable ally in the formation of a right-of-centre majority.[26] The strong showing of the FN in the regional elections of March 1998, and the subsequent deals struck with the UDF in several regions, demonstrated how susceptible some centre-right leaders remained to the siren calls of Le Pen's party when it effectively turned support into seats.[27] Hence the crucial role played by the electoral system in blocking the FN's progress in legislative elections and in sparing the centre-right the potential choice at the national level between defeat and a pact with the devil. Despite enjoying substantial representation at the European, regional and (in places) municipal levels, the FN emerged in 1997 from its strongest ever performance in a legislative poll with a single seat which it subsequently lost on a technical irregularity. Since then, the isolation of the party has been increased and its electoral progress further impeded. The creation in 2002 of the UMP formalised the centre-right's strategy of exclusion and constituted the most potentially far-reaching outcome of the FN's impact on the French party system. The new electoral rules introduced for both the regional and the European elections of 2004 were another example of systemic change provoked by the FN, designed as they were to reduce the party's capacity to exploit the two types of election which had hitherto proved most fruitful in converting its support into representation.

The second difficulty by which the FN has been critically hampered lies in the nature and extent of the legitimation which it has been able to achieve. For all its sustained momentum, the FN has failed to go beyond its electoral ceiling of 15 per cent and graduate to being a potential party of government. In his own analysis of his failure to make a better contest of the 2002 presidential run-off, Le Pen identified the FN's 'credibility deficit' and absence of a 'culture of government'.[28] The trajectory of the party following its national breakthrough in 1984 was one of almost constant progression; but with this progress came a hardening of public rejection. Between the early 1980s and the late 1990s, the number of those in SOFRES polls for whom the FN represented 'a danger for democracy' rose inexorably, from 38 per cent in 1983 to 75 per cent in 1997; as Le Pen entered the run-off for the 2002 presidential election, the figure stood at 70 per cent. Similarly, the proportion of those declaring that they would never vote for the FN rose over the same period to reach 72 per cent in 2002. This marked a degree of ostracism far exceeding that of any other party, including the PCF and other far-left movements such as the Trotskyist LCR.[29] Asked to position Le Pen politically at the time of the 2002 presidential election, 84 per cent of respondents in a CEVIPOF poll defined him as 'extreme-right', with 60 per cent of his own supporters concurring. Accordingly, the idea of deals between the centre-right and the FN has been massively rejected by public opinion, while that of a 'Republican front' between centre-right and centre-left against the FN has found majority approval.[30] After more than two decades in the political spotlight, this ostracism remains the most intractable problem confronting the FN today.

Beyond these proven difficulties lie a number of imponderables: the capacity of the centre-right (or in turn the centre-left) to deliver on electoral promises and retain its fragile 'unity'; the future shape of European integration and expansion; the pace of France's recovery from chronic unemployment (which remained above or about 10 per cent, close to 2.5 million, throughout 2005);[31] the fight against crime and delinquency; the management of ethnic relations in a climate of tension over the integration of immigrant communities and radical Islamism; and the waxing or waning of public faith in political elites, an impressive number of whom have in recent years been arraigned before French justice in high-profile corruption scandals. All of these issues could have a determining impact on the FN's prospects for future growth, despite – or, inversely perhaps, because of – its political isolation.[32]

The riots in rundown, largely immigrant-populated suburbs of many towns and cities across France in November 2005, prompting a national state of emergency, provided a conducive platform for the FN's anti-immigrant and strong-arm law and order message and showed how quickly events can turn in the party's favour. On 15 December 2005, *Le Monde* led its front page with the results of a TNS-SOFRES poll showing support for 'Le Pen's ideas' at 24 per cent, with only 39 per cent of respondents finding them 'unacceptable' alongside 43 per cent considering them 'excessive'.[33] This marked a clear drop on previous measures of the FN's beyond-the-pale image in public opinion. The same poll reaffirmed a trend evident in previous polls: that when explicit reference to Le Pen and the FN is removed, support for their ideas rises disproportionately. Thus

73 per cent of respondents declared that 'traditional values' were neglected, 70 per cent that the justice system was 'not sufficiently severe on delinquents', and 63 per cent that there were 'too many immigrants in France', with 48 per cent stating that they no longer felt 'truly at home in France'.

Le Pen has long projected the FN not as a party which could be elected to power in normal circumstances but as a force of last resort, with himself as prov-idential saviour in waiting. Like 'firefighters or paramedics', he has predicted, the FN's 'mission' will be to answer the call 'when there is no one else left in charge'.[34] Though an unbridgeable gulf remains between that prospect and the support levels recorded above, there is capital to be made from events such as those of November 2005 by a party poised to profit from social unrest. Three decades on from the end of '*les trente glorieuses*', France remains in a period of economic, social and political readjustment, and the FN has forged the bulk of its support from the most vulnerable socio-professional categories: those of low educational and occupational attainment, blue-collar and white-collar workers, shopkeepers, artisans and small entrepreneurs, and the unemployed.

Après-Le Pen: *storm clouds gathering*

Le Pen incarnates the history of the FN but its future lies with others. Perhaps the most significant feature of the 2004 elections for the party was that they raised more pointedly than ever the question of the 75-year-old Le Pen's succession. In the weeks preceding the official start of the regional campaign, media attention was focused on Le Pen's likely exclusion from the poll, as a court in Nice judged him ineligible to lead the FN list in Provence-Alpes-Côte d'Azur since he was not registered as a resident taxpayer or voter in the region. When a Marseille court upheld this ruling, Le Pen adopted the familiar posture of persecuted victim and denounced the 'totalitarian methods' of 'an administration under the orders of Raffarin and Chirac'. He was replaced by the head of the FN group in the Provence-Alpes-Côte d'Azur council, Guy Macary, a 74-year-old lawyer, *pied-noir*, former paratrooper and long-time FN representative in the region.[35]

Despite this unexpected exclusion (from which Mégret also suffered in Champagne-Ardenne), the name Le Pen continued to dominate coverage of the FN's campaign as his daughter, Marine, became the new face of the party in heading its list in Ile-de-France, France's most populous region with Paris at its heart.[36] A lawyer and mother of three young children, divorced and remarried to the FN's elections coordinator, Eric Iorio, Marine Le Pen did not fit the classic profile of the extreme-right bruiser or ideologue. As head of the FN's legal department and of the youth movement Générations Le Pen, she seemed ready to challenge or at least moderate some of the party's more hard-line tenets. This, together with the scarcely veiled nepotism from which she benefited, alienated some of the party's older guard and laid the ground for what threatened to be a bitter struggle for control of the FN following the departure of Le Pen senior.

The 2004 regional elections were seen as the first skirmish in this impending contest and marked an inauspicious start to Marine Le Pen's leadership bid.

While Bruno Gollnisch benefited from a rise in FN support of over 41,000 in Rhône-Alpes (securing 18.21 per cent) and Carl Lang from an increase of over 53,000 in Nord-Pas-de-Calais (17.94 per cent), the Ile-de-France list fell back by over 71,000 from its 1998 score (from 16.3 to 12.26 per cent), finishing fourth behind the PS-alliance, UMP and UDF lists. As a result, the 10.11 per cent and 15 seats (out of 209) won by Marine Le Pen's list on the second ballot were over-shadowed by the 19.73 per cent and 16 seats (out of 113) delivered by Lang and the 15.28 per cent and 18 seats (out of 157) won by Gollnisch. These results reflected the pecking order that had emerged from the elections to the FN's central committee at the party's twelfth national congress in Nice in 2003. There, Gollnisch and Lang had retained their positions as first and second in the poll of federation delegates, while Marine Le Pen had slipped from tenth place at the Paris congress in 2000 to 34th place in Nice. Despite her father's protestations that her result in the regional elections signified 'remarkable progress', it was a disappointment and an undeniable reversal.[37]

More potentially serious than this setback to the Le Pens' dynastic aspirations was the appearance during the European election campaign of fault lines within the FN reminiscent of those that had torn the party apart in January 1999. These surfaced over Le Pen's decision in drawing up his list of candidates to demote the long-serving Marie-France Stirbois to the benefit of the younger Lydia Schenardi, widow of the recently deceased FN regional councillor for Provence-Alpes-Côte d'Azur, Jean-Pierre Schenardi. The declared reason was to temper the 'old-fashioned image' (*dixit* Le Pen) of a party with 'a lot of elderly women' in its ranks;[38] again, however, the incident gave evidence of Le Pen's high-handed style of leadership and his penchant for nepotism. As Gollnisch came out uncharacteristically against Le Pen's decision, others in the party seized the moment to mark their distance from the FN leader. Chief amongst these were an embittered Marie-France Stirbois, the head of the FN's Catholic funda-mentalist current, Bernard Antony, and the mayor of Orange, Jacques Bompard, who defied Le Pen by opening a meeting of his think-tank Esprit Public (Public Spirit) to all components of the far right, including Mégrétists.[39] A few barbed exchanges via the media, for all their pettiness, were of real significance. Within an FN culture intolerant of *lèse-majesté*, they marked the growth of a vocal current of dissent that would find more focused expression some weeks later.[40]

In late August 2004, the FN's traditional summer school *(université d'été)* was held over three days in Enghien-les-Bains, a small spa town in the Ile-de-France region known for the healing properties of its water. It did not heal the growing rift between the Lepenists and the 'Orangists', the faction taking shape around Bompard and Mme Stirbois, who took the extraordinary step of holding a rival summer school in Orange at precisely the same time (which attracted some 400 participants, including a number of senior FN figures). The two conferences set out quite divergent visions of the FN's future. While announcing some 'internal reform', Le Pen promised essentially more of the same, arguing that 'the Front National has always been a hierarchical and disciplined party, which has been a fundamental necessity for maintaining unity and assuring its survival and progress within an environment that is massively hostile to it'. From his platform in Orange, by contrast, Bompard called for an intellectual and organisational reform of a party that had 'transformed itself over time into a kind of Fort Chabrol'. The days of the *'Duce'*, the *'Führer'*, the *'Caudillo'*, the *'Conducator'*, of the *'Caesar imperator'*, he insisted provocatively, were over. The FN did not need a single leader 'playing at being a general' from his headquarters in Paris; it needed 'hundreds of leaders' out harvesting grass-roots support in the constituencies.[41]

A master of the *politique de proximité*, Bompard argued (in a swipe at Marine Le Pen) that FN cadres would be better occupied running a commune of 2,000 inhabitants than jockeying for position within the upper echelons of the party. Politics was not about being a 'professional talker' but about being a 'practitioner', about 'getting one's hands dirty' and making a difference on the ground. The state funds which the FN received, Bompard protested, should not be channelled into the party's central reserves to be squandered on futile presidential election campaigns but should go to support the work of local branches. After delivering this unequivocal challenge to Le Pen's leadership style and to the FN's top-down structure, the mayor of Orange promptly left to inaugurate a garlic fair in his constituency.

The dissidence emanating from Orange in summer 2004 appeared to presage a new period of tension within the FN and a potentially serious threat to Le Pen's authority as leader. Whereas in the leadership clash of late 1998 Le Pen had represented the old guard of the FN against the would-be moderniser Mégret, it was now members of the old guard itself who were fomenting dissent. They resented the growing influence of Marine Le Pen and her presumption to soften some of the FN's long-held policies (on issues as charged as abortion, same-sex marriage and the euro)[42] and to manoeuvre it closer to the mainstream, thereby undermining the specific identity of the party led by her father since 1972. The destructive effects of the split of January 1999 imposed caution even on the autocratic Le Pen, who was prevailed upon not to exclude Bompard and Mme Stirbois from the FN at that point and to impose instead a temporary exclusion from the party's political bureau. Clouds were nonetheless gathering once again over a party that had weathered its share of storms already.

Vichy: an enduring reference

On 7 January 2005, the Pétainist weekly *Rivarol* published an interview in which the FN leader was invited to give his *tour d'horizon* of the year ahead. After a series of questions ranging over the EU constitutional treaty, the dangers of Turkish accession, and events in the Ukraine and Ivory Coast, the interview turned to the forthcoming commemorations to mark the end of the Second World War and the torrent of 'propaganda' that would accompany them. 'In France at least', averred Le Pen, 'the German occupation was not particularly inhumane even if there were some blunders, as was inevitable in a country of 550,000 square kilometres.' He went on to suggest that the Gestapo had acted as a force for civil protection in occupied France and to cast doubt on the official version of the massacre at Oradour-sur-Glane in June 1944, in which 642 French civilians, mostly women and children, were slaughtered by soldiers from the SS Das Reich Division. Le Pen lamented 'the wall of silence erected around all of these questions for decades' and held in place by a series of 'liberticide laws' that made it impossible to challenge established orthodoxies: 'It is not only from the European Union and globalism that we must free our country, but also from the lies about its history, lies that are protected by exceptional measures.'[43]

In delivering himself of these reflections, Le Pen was assured the approval of a small but appreciative audience, the few thousand readers of a weekly founded in 1951 to keep alive the flame of Vichy and press for the rehabilitation of Marshal Pétain, still then incarcerated on the Ile d'Yeu.[44] He might have known, however, that his remarks would filter out to a much wider audience; and there a purpose can be divined beyond the FN leader's habitual taste for provocation and defying the *politiquement correct*. To argue that the Occupation had not been so brutal was to offer a mitigating judgement on the regime that signed up to collaboration with the occupying forces, and to lessen the opprobrium associated with that one brief period in the twentieth century when government in France fell under the sway of the extreme right.[45]

In these few remarks, Le Pen provided eloquent testimony of his own political lineage and of the enduring importance of Vichy as the most potent reference still on the French far right. He also kept faith with part of the FN's founding mission as the voice of the 'national', 'social', 'popular' right.[46] From the earliest, the FN offered a spiritual home to former Vichyites and collaborationists, including LVF and Waffen-SS veterans (together, it should be said, with some former resisters and offspring of resisters). It lent itself to the cause of rehabilitating Vichy, with Le Pen upholding the defence of Pétain as the 'shield' to de Gaulle's 'sword'; he even took up the call, in 1973, for the Marshal's remains to be transferred to Douaumont near Verdun in a 'gesture of reconciliation'.[47] In its values, policies and discourse, the FN has since preserved its affinities with Vichy, whether in its conception of the nation and the family, its views on morality, education, women and abortion, its authoritarianism, its anti-communism, its exclusionary policy of 'national preference', or the anti-Semitism that breaks occasionally to the surface. Echoes of Vichy proliferate in the FN's imprecations against '*la décadence*', '*l'égalitarisme*' and '*le cosmopolitisme*'; in its fear of international conspiracies, notably '*l'internationale juive*'; in its calls for national regeneration ('*redressement national*' being a formula borrowed directly from the lexicon of Pétain); and in its open espousal of the Vichy trilogy '*Travail, Famille, Patrie*'.[48]

Le Pen's remarks to *Rivarol* represented more, however, than a simple reaffirmation of his spiritual affinity with Vichy. In denouncing the 'lies about [our] history' and the 'injustice of the justice system', he conjured up the ghosts of Jacques Isorni, Maurice Bardèche and other apologists of the Etat Français, using the very terms in which Bardèche first openly defied the post-war Republican consensus in his *Lettre à François Mauriac* (1947) and *Nuremberg ou la terre promise* (1948).[49] Le Pen in turn has spent more than half a century chipping away at that same post-war consensus and at the verdicts of 1945.[50] With laws brought in to counter historical revisionism, Le Pen would be more constrained than was Bardèche. His method has been not to deny but to minimise, to raise questions, to cast doubt. So it was with his description in 1987 of the Holocaust as a 'point of detail' and his reference to the 'historians debating these questions'; so too now with his assertion that 'there would be much to say on the drama of Oradour-sur-Glane' if 'the truth' on this as on other matters were allowed to be told.[51] In justifying these remarks before a meeting of party activists, Le Pen argued (again with a clear ring of Bardèche) that Oradour-sur-Glane should be judged in the context of Dresden and Hiroshima.[52]

Only some weeks before Le Pen's interview with *Rivarol*, the FN delegate-general, Bruno Gollnisch, used a similar method to cast doubt on the findings of the post-war tribunals and the official version of the Holocaust. There was no longer, he claimed, 'any serious historian who accepts in their entirety the conclusions of the Nuremberg tribunals'. While acknowledging the 'crimes that were undoubtedly committed by the National Socialist regime', including 'deportations on grounds of race', the FN second-in-command urged that the 'drama of the concentration camps' should be 'freely discussed'. In particular, historians should seek to determine with precision 'the actual number of those killed', for which Gollnisch reportedly advanced his own estimate of 'several hundred thousand for sure'.[53]

These remarks were made in response to a report into historical revisionism at the University of Lyon-III, where Gollnisch lectured in international law and Japanese civilisation. Like those of Le Pen, they were uttered in the run-up to the sixtieth anniversary of the liberation of Auschwitz on 27 January 2005. In seeking to open a breach in the established consensus around the Occupation, the Nuremberg trials and the Holocaust, Le Pen and Gollnisch remained true to their roots on the ultra-nationalist, neo-Pétainist right. To the *nostalgiques de Vichy* in and around the FN, they sent an unequivocal message, and to the wider public a more insidious one. Gollnisch was suspended as a result from his lectureship, and both he and Le Pen faced judicial investigation.[54]

The long view

This study has sought to provide a long view of the extreme right in modern France, tracing a history both of continuity and of change. When the FN promotes the instincts of the people over oligarchic elites, it echoes Maurice Barrès; when it calls for a strong executive with recourse to popular referenda, it evokes General Boulanger; when it denounces 'anti-French racism' and raises the alarm against France's enemies within, we hear Charles Maurras; when it inveighs against the confiscation of democracy or the 'fiscal inquisition', it is redolent of Poujadism. The discourse of Le Pen and the FN is a compendium of ideas, fears and prejudices that have a long pedigree. The cry of 'France for the French' reverberates across the twentieth century from Drumont through Pétain to Le Pen, just as the equation between 'national unemployment' and 'foreign invasion' resonated already in the Chamber of Deputies in the 1930s.[55]

Despite these fixed historical reference points, and despite the abiding importance of history – with all its unrighted wrongs – for some within the FN's ranks, the party today has little in common with the style, methods or programme of the inter-war leagues, the PPF or RNP, of post-war neo-fascist groups, or of later movements such as Jeune Nation or Occident. It is a party which is only remotely recognisable as that formed under the auspices of Ordre Nouveau in 1972. It has held fast to some core values while modifying or renouncing others, and it has privileged the exploitation of contemporary social and political issues over the perpetuation of ideology. Using all of the modern communication methods at its disposal, it has transformed itself from a marginal irrelevance into France's third political party. Most importantly of all, for a party with its roots set deep in the anti-republican nationalist right, it has stayed true to its founding mission to compete at all levels in the democratic process.

In retaining this commitment to electoralism, the FN has repudiated a central component of its extreme-right heritage and pursued the path taken by Isorni's UNIR in 1951, by the Poujadists in 1956 and by Tixier-Vignancour in the 1960s. Le Pen, it is worth recalling, played a part in each of these early engagements with democracy, just as he has steered the FN on the same electoralist course since its launch. 'There is only one way forward, the way of elections, the way of legality.' Le Pen is as clear in asserting this today as he was in the run-up to the FN's first electoral debacle of 1973.[56] In a series of perceptive articles published in *Le Monde* in 1976, Bernard Brigouleix detected a 'process of modernisation' at work across the French extreme right, a recognition of the need to 'adapt to the new political conditions' of the 1970s. While the names of Barrès, Maurras, Brasillach, Céline and Drieu continued to resonate, and while Pétain remained a powerful focus of allegiance, the emphasis was shifting towards 'a more normal participation in politics'. The greatest obstacle to this enterprise, as Brigouleix noted, lay in the factionalism which continued to characterise this atomised and deeply divided political 'family'.[57]

The achievement of the FN has been to pursue this modernising agenda while bringing together historically irreconcilable elements of the extreme right. After more than two decades of meaningful electoral challenge, moreover, the FN has broken the pattern which previously defined the extreme right, that of periodic surges followed by a return to marginality. While many smaller movements have preferred to retain their ideological identity at the cost of terminal isolation on the margins of the right, the FN has made a principle of pragmatism. It has welded together a coalition of far-right militants of diverse persuasions with traditionalist conservatives and defectors from the centre-right. Though it attracted veterans of collaboration, neo-fascists and neo-Nazis, some of whom later deserted while others made their accommodation with *Realpolitik*, descriptions of the FN today as 'fascist' or 'Nazi' do more to confound than to advance our understanding of this party and its significance within contemporary French politics.

The FN: a fascist party?

It has been argued that the FN represents a resurgence in modern guise of historical fascism, that it is a 'mass party' akin to Doriot's PPF which 'shares a core of basic characteristics with interwar fascism, and possesses others in embryonic form'.[58] Its policies have been denounced as 'fascist' and its activists as 'Nazi thugs' and 'Storm Troopers'.[59] That the FN is stridently nationalist, authoritarian and populist has been evidenced in the foregoing chapters; that it is neither doctrinally nor programmatically 'fascist' is equally evident. The very eclecticism of the party – in terms of the members, factions and ideological currents it has absorbed – makes it a hybrid construct that fits no pre-defined mould. Broadly, Le Pen and his party are the inheritors of an authoritarian, populist, reactionary nationalism running, *mutatis mutandis*, from Boulangism through Maurrassism to Pétainism and down to the present. Combined with this historical legacy is a more contemporary sensibility deriving from the post-war ideological synthesis developed by Europe-Action and the Nouvelle Droite and responsive to the changed circumstances of France in the modern world, stressing national, racial and cultural identity within a French and a wider European perspective. It is easy enough to detect echoes of fascism in the FN's discourse (exclusionary nationalism, anti-egalitarianism, anti-liberalism, anti-communism among others); but none of these is the preserve of fascism, and other features which are integral to historical fascism (rejection of democracy, the single-party state, political violence, militarism, corporatism, anti-conservatism, the 'leadership cult' in a real sense) cannot be inferred from the FN's programme. To see that programme merely as a 'mask' for a cryptofascist agenda that would lead to 'salutes and the stamping of boots'[60] is to discount the FN's long-term adaptation to the political and institutional imperatives of the Fifth Republic, its progressive rapprochement with much of the centre-right, and the powerful moderating influence on far-right and far-left parties alike of the democratic consensus in France and western Europe today.

Though at variance with much of the Fifth Republic's underlying value system and some of its institutional practices, the FN, unlike so many of its precursors, does not call the Republic as such into question. In January 1994, a special issue of *Identité* devoted to 'The Modernity of the Front National' boasted the party's achievement in representing the age-old values of the nationalist right 'within the framework of the Republic and of the democratic principle of popular sovereignty'.[61] Republics, of course, can take very different forms, as can popular sovereignty. Such terms as used by the far right (or far left) need to be interpreted with circumspection, and the strategy of covert infiltration developed in the 1960s continues to prompt caution. As it can be read off the page, however, the FN's programme is no charter for the overthrow of democracy and installation of a fascist state, in line either with classic inter-war fascism or with post-war neo-fascism as defined by Bardèche. Some of the institutional changes which the FN advocates call – rhetorically at least – not for less but for more democratic pluralism, notably through a re-empowered National Assembly elected by proportional representation and referenda by popular initiative at both local and national levels.[62] The 'Sixth Republic' for which Le Pen campaigned as a presidential candidate in 1995 was to be 'a truly democratic Republic', with 'a parliamentary system reformed to make it truly representative', decentralisation of decision-making by a state reduced to its regalian functions, the 'protection of liberties' and 'assurance of equality of rights' for all French citizens.[63] Just words perhaps, with no guarantee of what inflection the FN might bring to them if elected to power; but they declare a broad commitment to 'the Republic' that would have been inconceivable even for the party's immediate predecessor, Ordre Nouveau. Le Pen would later temper his calls for a Sixth Republic, projecting himself in spring 2005 as the very custodian of the Fifth Republican Constitution against the threat posed by a European Constitution.[64] Similarly, in April 2006, he would tax Chirac with violating Article 21 (on the Prime Minister's executive function) and Article 39 (on parliamentary process) of the Constitution by overruling the government and effectively annulling a controversial employment law reform (the *Contrat première embauche*, CPE) in response to public opposition. The President, Le Pen charged, was guilty of breaching 'the fundamental laws of the Republic' and of flouting 'the rule of law'.[65]

This avowed, and at times even fastidious, obeisance to the Republic is to be interpreted always within the terms of an exclusive nationalism that conceives 'the nation' as an organically homogeneous, rather than a genuinely pluralistic, community. The FN's is a selective conception of a selective Republic. It is a Republic which invokes '*la souveraineté du peuple*' but which is based on a strictly reductive definition of that '*peuple*': *liberté, égalité, fraternité* may be retained, but as '*l'égalité des citoyens*' and '*la liberté et la fraternité nationale*' (equality, liberty and fraternity for *French citizens/nationals*), not as the founding principles of a universalist '*idéologie des droits de l'homme*'. This crucial distinction was articulated by Mégret shortly after his departure from the FN in 1999, as he sought to reclaim the party's programme (the drafting of which he himself had led) for his breakaway movement. The same Mégret, while protesting his 'attachment to democratic principles' and to 'the institutional principles of the Republic', made no secret of his adoption of '*la République*' as a concept seized from 'the enemy' and pressed into the service of the nationalist cause.[66]

Nor does the FN's proclaimed observance of Republican laws and institutions redress its defining tendency towards authoritarianism, which sits at odds with the argument for a more democratically elected and empowered National Assembly. At odds, too, with the FN's calls for more democratic pluralism are the discriminatory elements of its programme and its open disregard for minority rights, manifest in its approach to local government as it withheld subsidies from associations of which it disapproved, censored library holdings and cultural activities, and sought (in Vitrolles) to apply its policy of 'national preference' in the allocation of family allowance. Though partisan choices have always been a feature of local government in France, not least in PCF-controlled municipalities, the FN pushed these at times to new bounds.

A survey of delegates at the FN's national congress in 1990, on the question of the best political system for France, found support of 10 per cent for a 'popular democracy', 16 per cent for a 'monarchy', 32 per cent for the 'republic', and 38 per cent for an 'authoritarian government'.[67] This authoritarian tendency, with its emphasis on hierarchy, order and a strong presidentialist executive, accords more easily with models of direct than of liberal democracy; it remains to the fore in the FN's preference for '*l'Etat*' and '*la Nation*' over '*la République*' in articulating its conception of the French polity, and in its sympathy for the plebiscitary republic over other types.[68] There is more here, however, of Boulangism than of fascism. The authoritarianism explicit in the FN's programme envisages the reinforcement of existing hierarchies (political institutions, justice system and police, Catholic Church and nuclear family, traditional moral code), not the creation of a single-party dictatorship. It is, as Roger Griffin has argued, 'reformist' rather than 'revolutionary', and therefore excluded both from identification with historical fascism and from Griffin's influential definition of generic fascism.[69] Le Pen has ably exploited the highly personalised nature of the Fifth Republic's presidential system to disseminate his message and amplify his support base; but the pens and key rings bearing his name on stalls at FN rallies are a frivolous parody of the leadership cult in the fascist tradition.[70]

A less 'extreme' extreme right?

The FN has contrived to adapt its appeal to different audiences across the social and political spectrum, responding to changing public anxieties and further blurring its ideological contours. Its message too has become gradually less 'extreme', as some of its foremost concerns (on Europe, 'economic patriotism', law and order, immigration, national identity, Islamic radicalism) have moved to the very centre of mainstream political debate. Even its trademark policy of 'national preference', the single most pressing constitutional amendment proposed by the FN, has found some resonance on the centre-right (in pronouncements notably by former President Giscard d'Estaing and former Prime Minister Balladur).[71] The vote against the EU constitutional treaty in May 2005 and the rioting in largely immigrant-populated suburbs of French towns in November 2005 allowed the FN to claim vindication for its warnings against the dangers of European integration and against ghettoised ethnic communities as 'a mortal threat to civil peace in France'.[72] At the same time, the hard line adopted by Interior Minister Sarkozy (calling troublesome youths 'riff-raff' (*racaille*), moving to deport foreigners convicted of involvement in the riots, and proposing to take an 'industrial powerhose' to criminal elements in some suburbs) delivered a muscular message to Le Pen sympathisers and made the FN leader's interventions seem moderate by comparison.[73] The subsequent stress placed on immigration control by the government and the rhetorical contest on law and order between prospective candidates for the 2007 presidential election (chiefly Sarkozy and the new Socialist pretender, Ségolène Royal) brought the wry comment from the FN's Carl Lang that the 'Lepenisation of minds' was progressing apace – and that a few more months of the campaign would see Le Pen stand as 'a candidate for the centre-left'.[74]

Though blocked from playing an institutional role in proportion to its electoral strength, the FN has thus achieved much of its early objective – as theorised by the Nouvelle Droite and articulated by Le Pen in the 1970s – to wage a 'battle of ideas' and 'exert pressure on all the other parties, and on French political life'.[75] It is here, in its impact on the political agenda, that the real significance of the FN lies. Though it was not at first the only party to invoke immigration or law and order, it has been the most forceful and effective in exploiting these issues and in dictating the terms in which they are addressed. That, however, is only part of the picture. Just as the centre-right and elements of the left have shifted towards the FN on these and other issues, the FN too has moved some way towards the centre-right. Where it has had the opportunity to govern alone (locally), the FN has at times tested the bounds of constitutionality in implementing its programme; where it has been a partner or would-be partner in government (locally and regionally), it has shown itself ready to moderate its position and to sign up as required to Republican norms (witness the formal declaration of allegiance to the Republic and its anti-discriminatory values signed by FN representatives in the Bourgogne regional council in spring 1998).[76] There is insufficient evidence to assess how far the FN might, if more fully involved in public administration, replicate the process of 'deradicalisation' undergone by some other parties of left and right, such as the PCF in France or the Alleanza Nazionale (formerly MSI) in Italy;[77] but it was notable that, in seeking to build alliances with the UDF and RPR within regional councils in 1998, the FN was prepared to omit its cherished policy of 'national preference' from the six-point '*programme minimum*' on which it proposed to cooperate with the centre-right. The resulting 'programme' was a conspicuously anodyne document calling for commitment to lower taxes, increased emphasis on law and order, defence of 'French cultural identity', improved occupational training schemes, appointments on a proportional basis to posts in regional administration, and greater governing transparency.[78]

While the distinction between mainstream right and FN may be upheld in the UMP's resolve to avoid the compromises once made by the RPR and UDF, it is a distinction increasingly more of degree than of kind. It is also an arguably lesser distinction than that which separates the FN from those radical activist groups on the outer fringes of the extreme right who are the real outsiders to the prevailing democratic order. As is evident from attendance at any FN rally, the party serves as a gravitational centre for some of these extra-systemic movements; but Le Pen and the FN today sustain at best a strained relationship with 'revolutionaries' who refuse to compromise with democracy, who reject 'the games played by politicians' and dismiss the FN as just another 'soft', 'Republican' party.[79]

Giovanni Sartori's classic definition of the 'anti-system party' (as one abiding by 'a belief system that does not share the values of the political order within which it operates') is only partially applicable to an FN which, though critical of elements within the Constitution, nonetheless protests its constitutionalism and enacts this generally in its political behaviour.[80] To that degree, Michael Minkenberg is justified in classifying parties like the FN as '"extreme" not in terms of being against or outside the existing constitutional order but in terms of being extreme within that order'.[81] Such a judgement may risk overstating a compliance with 'the system' that owes arguably more to convenience than to conviction; but it has the merit of distinguishing the FN from extreme-right movements which parade their fascist heritage, reject democracy outright or appeal to violence as a political medium.[82] This distinction raises questions over the precise spatial positioning of the FN today in terms of the border separating mainstream from extreme right: if Le Pen's party still sits furthest to the right of all the major parties, its 'extremism' has been progressively attenuated and, within the wider context of contemporary French politics, much relativised. Though spatial boundaries can shift or blur in relation to different issues, Robert Andersen and Jocelyn Evans argue convincingly that the FN vote is best located not in a separate extreme-right bloc but 'on the radical wing of the right bloc *in toto*', with ideological disparities between 'moderate-right' and 'extreme-right' (as represented by FN voters at least) being ultimately 'a matter of intensity rather than direction'.[83]

The tenacity with which Le Pen and his party have maintained their political pressure on the centre-right despite the institutional obstacles ranged against them was acknowledged in June 2005 when the new Prime Minister, Dominique de Villepin, invited the FN to participate in cross-party consultations in the wake of the EU constitutional treaty referendum of May. The invitation was extended to all parties which had qualified for broadcasting time in the referendum campaign and was intended to elicit views on such issues as economic harmonisation within the euro zone and technological development in Europe; but it marked a lifting of the *cordon sanitaire* that had been kept largely in place around the FN since Chirac's election to the presidency in 1995.[84] The participation of two of the FN's MEPs, Carl Lang and Jean-Claude Martinez, furnished a divided Socialist Party with the pretext to boycott the talks and caused the anti-racist MRAP to issue a communiqué denouncing this 'affront to democracy'. The same recognition of the FN, however, had already been evident in 2003 when Interior Minister Sarkozy had involved the party in consultations over voting system reforms, and when the Stasi Commission on secularism had formally canvassed the FN's views.[85]

These stand as significant markers of a political legitimacy built up through sustained engagement in the democratic process, and through the electoral (and wider popular) support which the FN can claim for its ideas. It has been estimated that, in the 10 years following the party's breakthrough in 1984, up to one in four French voters at some time cast a vote for the FN.[86] SOFRES polls measuring agreement with Le Pen's ideas peaked at 32 per cent in 1991 and remained above 20 per cent throughout most of the 1990s; the level recorded as Le Pen contested the presidential election in 2002 stood at 28 per cent, with a 40 per cent approval rating for his ideas on law and order and justice.[87] Again in 2002, 45 per cent of respondents in a SOFRES poll judged that Le Pen played 'a useful role in political and social debate in France', while an IFOP poll in April 2006 found 34 per cent considering 'the extreme right' (synonymous mainly with Le Pen) to be 'in tune with [their] concerns' and 63–67 per cent acknowledging its 'useful contribution to political debate' on law and order and immigration.[88] In 1995 and 2001, the FN proved capable not only of winning and exercising local power but of being re-elected (as either FN or MNR) in three of the four towns which it had governed; and in 2002, an estimated 6.5 million voters supported Le Pen in at least one of the two rounds of the presidential election.[89]

All of this makes the FN an important voice within the French polity. The questions it raises are real, and they require real answers. To identify it with a 'politics of fascism'[90] rooted in the 1930s forecloses discussion of the FN's significance within France today and disqualifies it as a political interlocutor. By refusing to confront the FN leader in the traditional presidential debate in 2002, Chirac neglected an opportunity to expose the fallacy in so much of what Le Pen proposes; by harping on moral denunciation, the PS and PCF have failed to develop a political strategy for winning back working-class voters from the FN. The refusal to engage in political argument with Le Pen and his party, like the periodic calls for them to be banned or silenced, represents an abdication. Worse, it allows the FN to exploit such ostracism to political effect.[91]

Nor is it helpful to characterise the FN as a party essentially unchanged since its launch in the backwash of de Gaulle's presidency in 1972. In the intervening years, the FN has changed radically – in its personnel and much of its programme, as in its electoral impact and political significance. Even since its split in 1999, the FN has undergone further change, cultivating a 'moderate' image on immigration and Islam by comparison with some of the more extremist pronouncements of Mégret and his acolytes in the MNR or of de Villiers and his MPF.[92] While the FN still proposes to remove illegal immigrants, those convicted of crimes, the unemployed and foreign students on completion of their studies, it has moved beyond the simplistic equation between immigration and unemployment, and the systematic repatriation of legally resident and legally employed immigrants no longer features expressly in its programme. In 2003 as in 1991, Le Pen opposed the US-led invasion of Iraq, while appearances in June 2006 by Marine Le Pen on Beur FM radio and by Louis Aliot on Al-Jazeera television signalled a new strategy of engagement with the communities of North African origin in France. Under Marine Le Pen's influence, too, the explicit 'republicanising' of the FN ('the only party today defending Republican principles') has gained new impetus. The launch of Le Pen senior's 2007 presidential campaign on 20 September 2006 at Valmy, that revered shrine to the Revolution and the Republic, was a symbolically charged gesture to project the FN as a Republican party at one with French history (despite dissenting voices within its monarchist and traditionalist Catholic components). So too the invocation by Le Pen of '*la liberté, l'égalité, la fraternité*' and the expansive appeal to all French people, including '*Français d'origine étrangère*', those of foreign origin.[93] None of this is to deny the strong neo-fascist influence within the early FN, or its ambivalent relationship with democracy, or the formative role played by the Doriotist Victor Barthélemy and other former collaborationists (as discussed in

Chapters 6 and 7); nor is it to neglect those policies or utterances that continue to locate Le Pen and his party on the far right of French politics; but it is no more adequate to define the FN today by reference to 1972 than to define the present-day PS or PCF through their radically reformist 'Common Programme' of that same year.

By developing a strong and relatively stable electoral constituency, winning significant representation in the European Parliament and (briefly) the National Assembly, and participating in government at the regional and municipal levels, the FN has since the mid-1980s undergone a process of 'normalisation' and institutional adaptation. More than a third of FN candidates in the 1997 legislative elections already held elected office as regional or municipal councillors, with a third again of these combining both mandates. By such measures, the FN has shown itself an adept exemplar of the new far right cultivated in western Europe since the 1980s, not that of brown shirts but that of smart suits, administrative competence and a professed commitment to modern democratic norms.[94] As with the Freiheitliche Partei Österreichs (FPÖ) or the Alleanza Nazionale (AN) in Austria and Italy, the issues on which the FN has come to prominence, and the wider social, economic and political environment in which it has grown, are profoundly different from the conditions that gave rise to fascism in inter-war Europe.[95]

Despite attracting more than one vote in seven over three consecutive presidential elections, Le Pen has failed, unlike his counterparts in Austria and Italy, to impose his party as a partner in national government. The FN may make a virtue of necessity by promoting itself as the 'outsider', but its real ambition is to be on the inside. As the oldest major right-of-centre party in France and the third most important political force after the UMP and PS, the FN today is, as Alistair Cole has acutely observed, a 'reluctant anti-establishment party',[96] an extra-parliamentary force only too keen to be a parliamentary player. In an interview with the present author in April 2005, Le Pen complained that, while former left-wing radicals were allowed to effect their transition to more moderate politics, right-wing nationalists were definitively branded as irredeemable extremists. Disingenuous perhaps, self-serving certainly; but the remark conveyed the importance of legitimation, of distancing the FN from a neo-fascist legacy and moving it closer to democratic 'normality'.

Looking back and forward

As this study reaches its conclusion, the FN finds itself at a critical juncture. It is divided in its leadership between Le Pen loyalists and those, such as the dissenting 'Orangist' faction around Jacques Bompard, who have tired of Le Pen's high-handed style and of the FN's failure to develop a genuine culture of government from the local level up.[97] Brandishing the Resistance credentials of her parents, Marie-France Stirbois demanded an explanation of Le Pen for his comments about the Occupation to *Rivarol* in January 2005, while Bernard Antony warned against 'obsession with the past' and Bompard called for an extraordinary party congress.[98] The eventual decision to respond to Bompard's persistent provocations by excluding him from the FN's political bureau in September 2005 was less a solution than a reaffirmation of the problem. The mayor of Orange left the FN and immediately switched his allegiance to Philippe de Villiers and the MPF.[99] Excluded temporarily from the FN in October 2005, Marie-France Stirbois died in April 2006 without making her peace with the party whose electoral legitimation she had personified – as a regional, departmental and municipal councillor, a parliamentary deputy and an MEP by turns between 1986 and 2004.[100]

The FN is further divided between a dwindling old guard keeping faith with the historical legacy of the extreme right and a new generation for whom this has much less compelling significance, between those bent on fighting still the lost battles of the past (collaboration, the *épuration*, decolonisation) and younger cadres anxious to project the image of a modern, forward-looking party. In the words of former secretary-general Carl Lang, the FN today comprises 'a tenth of activists and officials wishing to talk about [the Second World War], a tenth believing it shameful to call into question the official version of History, and the rest who wish to move on to other matters'.[101] Prominent among the latter group is Le Pen's daughter Marine, who publicly rebuked Gollnisch for his remarks about the Holocaust then reacted to her father's about the Occupation by distancing herself for a time from the party machine in protest that her attempt to 'de-demonise' the FN had been sabotaged. Le Pen's subsequent designation of Gollnisch as heir apparent suggested that the modernising project advocated by his daughter was, for the moment at least, stalled – though the replacement as secretary-general in October 2005 of Carl Lang by the youthful Louis Aliot, a close associate of Marine Le Pen and product of Générations Le Pen, was characteristic of an FN leader ever anxious to unsettle the ambitions of any would-be successor.[102] By April 2006, Marine Le Pen had re-emerged as a declared candidate for the leadership succession, with her book *A contre flots* doubling as a personal political testimony and a partial defence of Le Pen *père*.[103]

For more than two centuries, the extreme right in France has defined itself through rejection. Rejection of the Revolution and of the values it promoted, of the Republic and parliamentary democracy; rejection of elements deemed a threat to the national community and of moves to diversify and dilute that community; rejection of the Liberation and of the cultural hegemony of the left sealed by the defeat of fascism; rejection of the post-war geopolitical order and of decolonisation; rejection even of the official verdicts of history. Le Pen and the FN have in turn built much of their political capital on rejection: not of the democratic Republic, which they have endorsed explicitly and through sustained participation, but of the type of society into which contemporary France has evolved and of those political forces which have presided over that evolution. Immigration, unemployment, social degeneration, crime and public disorder, lax morality, national decline, economic and cultural globalisation, the encroachments of Europe and of foreign influence in every guise – all are so many symptoms of a decadent modernity fostered by 'the real left and the false right'.[104] An image favoured by Le Pen to sum up his long political career is that of the 'lookout on the watchtower',[105] warning of the dangers on the horizon and nursing the remote fantasy that a crisis of sufficient proportions might call him, in the manner of a Pétain or a de Gaulle, to 'save' France. This explains in part his dogged refusal to relinquish the leadership of the FN when a better political instinct might have counselled the handover to a younger, and less objectionable, aspirant following the presidential election of 2002. With almost 18 per cent in the second round of that election, Le Pen marked a high point for the politics of rejection that defined his personal commitment over more than half a century. How to build on that and reduce the rejection from which the FN itself continues to suffer as a far-right party seeking popular acceptance is the challenge that will fall, after Le Pen's fifth and surely final presidential campaign in 2007, to his eventual successor.

Appendix

Votes for the FN and Le Pen, 1973–2004

Table A.1 Votes for the FN and Le Pen, 1973–2004 (national total in first ballots or single-round elections)

Year	Election	%	Votes	Seats
1973	Legislative	0.46	108,616	–
1974	Presidential	0.75	190,921	–
1978*	Legislative	0.29	82,743	–
1981*	Legislative	0.18	44,414	–
1984	European	10.95	2,210,334	10 MEPs
1986	Legislative	9.80	2,699,307	35 deputies
1986	Regional	9.70	2,654,390	137 councillors
1988	Presidential	14.40	4,376,742	–
1988	Legislative	9.80	2,353,466	1 deputy
1989	European	11.73	2,129,668	10 MEPs
1992	Regional	13.90	3,396,141	239 councillors
1993	Legislative	12.70	3,150,764	–
1994	European	10.52	2,050,086	11 MEPs
1995	Presidential	15.00	4,570,838	–
1997	Legislative	15.24	3,775,382	1 deputy
1998	Regional	15.27	3,270,118	275 councillors
1999**	European	5.70	1,005,113	5 MEPs
2002	Presidential (1st round)	16.86	4,804,713	–
2002	Presidential (2nd round)	17.79	5,525,032	–
2002	Legislative	11.34	2,862,960	–
2004	Regional	15.11	3,557,240	156 councillors
2004	European	9.81	1,684,792	7 MEPs

Sources: Interior Ministry and *Le Monde* figures mainly. Legislative and regional results are for metropolitan France, presidential and European results for metropolitan and overseas France.

Notes:

* Elections in which the extreme right was also represented by the PFN.

** First election following the FN's split and the formation of Bruno Mégret's rival Mouvement National/MNR.

Notes

Introduction

1 *Le Monde*, 16 and 17 July 2002, and 8, 10, 12–13 December 2004.
2 R. Gildea, *France since 1945*, Oxford, Oxford University Press, 1996, p. 75.
3 Le Pen, pre-election rally, Salle Equinoxe, Paris, 18 April 2002.
4 *Rivarol*, no. 2698, 7 January 2005, pp. 6–7.
5 Front National, *Pour un avenir français. Le Programme de gouvernement du Front National*, Paris, Editions Godefroy de Bouillon, 2001, pp. 137, 186.
6 H. Coston *et al.*, *Partis, journaux et hommes politiques d'hier et d'aujourd'hui*, Paris, Lectures Françaises, 1960.
7 J.-Y. Camus and R. Monzat, *Les Droites nationales et radicales en France. Répertoire critique*, Lyon, Presses Universitaires de Lyon, 1992.
8 *Le Monde*, 23–24 January and 3 February 2005; *Assemblée Nationale: Compte Rendu Analytique Officiel*, 2ème Séance du mardi 1er février 2005 (www.assemblee-nationale.com/12/cra/2004-2005/130.asp).
9 C. Mudde, *The Ideology of the Extreme Right*, Manchester, Manchester University Press, 2000, p. 11.
10 For some of the terminological difficulties in defining contemporary 'extreme-right' parties, see R. Eatwell, 'Introduction: The New Extreme Right Challenge', in R. Eatwell and C. Mudde (eds), *Western Democracies and the New Extreme Right Challenge*, London, Routledge, 2004, pp. 1–16; Mudde, *The Ideology of the Extreme Right*, pp. 1–24; also E. Carter, *The Extreme Right in Western Europe: Success or Failure?*, Manchester, Manchester University Press, 2005, pp. 14–23.
11 Though no substantive distinction is observed here between these two terms, and though they are often used interchangeably by commentators, the less loaded 'far right' will at times be preferred for reasons of emphasis to 'extreme right'. In such cases, 'far right' is used as a somewhat more embracive term to include that wider area of right-wing political identification where pronounced positions (conservatism, nationalism, authoritarianism, cultural separatism, etc.) shade into extremism. The term 'far right' will also be used in relation to a contemporary FN which has undergone a sustained process of political institutionalisation and electoral endorsement and whose relative 'extremism' or 'anti-system' character, it will be argued, can no longer be as consistently attested as that of other movements examined here.

1 The Vichy regime

1 R. O. Paxton, *Vichy France: Old Guard and New Order 1940–1944*, New York, Columbia University Press, 2001, p. 32; J. Jackson, *France: The Dark Years 1940–1944*, Oxford, Oxford University Press, 2001, pp. 132–33.

2 France also concluded an armistice with Italy, to which it ceded a small occupation zone in the south-east of the country.

3 P. Pétain, *Discours aux Français: 17 juin 1940–20 août 1944*, ed. J.-C. Barbas, Paris, Albin Michel, 1989, p. 65.

4 Pétain, *Discours aux Français*, p. 95.

5 Pétain, *Discours aux Français*, p. 96.

6 Though this was the term by which the Vichy project was best known, Pétain used it only sparingly, preferring '*rénovation*' (renewal) or '*redressement*' (recovery) to '*révolution*'.

7 By contrast, the tricolour flag and Marseillaise were retained as enduring symbols of nationhood, though the latter would be rivalled by the popular Pétainist hymn '*Maréchal, nous voilà!*'

8 Pétain, *Discours aux Français*, pp. 89, 90, 152.

9 Pétain, *Discours aux Français*, p. 150.

10 The new constitution which the law anticipated would 'guarantee the rights of work, family and *patrie*' and be 'ratified by the Nation and applied by the Assemblies it shall have created' (D. Rémy (ed.), *Les Lois de Vichy*, Paris, Romillat, 1992, p. 31). It was never promulgated.

11 Around a quarter of deputies and senators were absent from the vote of 10 July 1940. The French Communist Party (PCF) played no part in the proceedings, having been dissolved and seen its deputies expelled from parliament following the Nazi–Soviet pact of August 1939.

12 Henri du Moulin de Labarthète, quoted in M. O. Baruch, *Le Régime de Vichy*, Paris, La Découverte, 1996, p. 17; Rémy, *Les Lois de Vichy*, pp. 31–47.

13 In defiance of these celebrations in 1939, Maurras and his Action Française had staged a counter-commemoration, that of Marat's assassin, Charlotte Corday, and of the Vendée uprising of 1793 (H. Rousso, *Le Syndrome de Vichy de 1944 à nos jours*, Paris, Seuil, 1990, p. 100).

14 D. Rossignol, *Histoire de la propagande en France de 1940 à 1944. L'utopie Pétain*, Paris, Presses Universitaires de France, 1991, pp. 97–99. The future President François Mitterrand was among those awarded the *Francisque*, a fact that would cause him no little embarrassment in the last years of his presidency as his youth in the service of Vichy came under scrutiny. See P. Péan, *Une jeunesse française. François Mitterrand 1934–1947*, Paris, Fayard, 1994.

15 Pétain, *Discours aux Français*, p. 363.

16 R. Jeanneret, *Maréchal Pétain. Maximes et principes extraits des messages au peuple français, choisis et classés pour servir à l'éducation morale et civique de la jeunesse en conformité avec les programmes de 1941*, Tours, Mame, n.d. [1942].

17 J.-P. Azéma, *From Munich to the Liberation, 1938–1944*, trans. J. Lloyd, Cambridge, Cambridge University Press, 1984, p. 67.

18 Baruch, *op. cit.*, pp. 61–62; Jackson, *France: The Dark Years*, p. 124.

19 Paxton, *Vichy France*, pp. 151–65; Jackson, *France: The Dark Years*, pp. 155–56.

20 On youth policy and culture, see W. D. Halls, *The Youth of Vichy France*, Oxford, Clarendon Press, 1981.

21 B. M. Gordon, *Collaborationism in France during the Second World War*, Ithaca, Cornell University Press, 1980, pp. 234–38, 242–43, 272–73.

22 Secrétariat Général à la Jeunesse: Direction de la Propagande, *Qu'est-ce que la Révolution Nationale?*, Paris, 1941, p. 13.

23 The last woman guillotined in France was an abortionist sentenced under Vichy. The law of October 1940 barring married women from public-sector employment would be suspended through economic necessity in September 1942, and in February 1944 married women even became liable for labour service in Germany (Jackson, *France: The Dark Years*, pp. 331–32).

24 On Vichy and eugenics, see W. H. Schneider, *Quality and Quantity: The Quest for Biological Regeneration in Twentieth-Century France*, Cambridge, Cambridge University

Press, 1990, pp. 256–86. A similar pre-marital examination would be retained as 'a veritable measure of public health' by the post-war provisional government and the Fourth Republic (*ibid.*, pp. 287–88).

25 Declaration by Pétain to the American press corps, 22 August 1940, quoted in J. Plumyène and R. Lasierra, *Les Fascismes français 1923–1963*, Paris, Seuil, 1963, p. 148.

26 Pétain, *Discours aux Français*, pp. 127–30, 246–52. On economic policy under Vichy, see R. F. Kuisel, *Capitalism and the State in Modern France*, Cambridge, Cambridge University Press, 1983, pp. 128–56.

27 Pétain, *Discours aux Français*, pp. 130, 136–39, 249; Kuisel, *op. cit.*, p. 145.

28 Rémy, *Les Lois de Vichy*, pp. 51–53.

29 Pétain, *Discours aux Français*, p. 72.

30 Rémy, *Les Lois de Vichy*, pp. 48–50, 55–56. This figure represented around a quarter of all Jews naturalised between 1927 and 1940 (D. Peschanski, 'Exclusion, persécution, répression', in J.-P. Azéma and F. Bédarida (eds), *Le Régime de Vichy et les Français*, Paris, Fayard, 1992, p. 226).

31 F. Kupferman, *Le Procès de Vichy: Pucheu, Pétain, Laval*, Brussels, Editions Complexe, 1980, pp. 86–87.

32 Rémy, *Les Lois de Vichy*, pp. 87–91, 116–27; Baruch, *op. cit.*, p. 25.

33 Rémy, *Les Lois de Vichy*, pp. 127–29; Paxton, *Vichy France*, pp. 178–79.

34 D. Peschanski, *Vichy 1940–1944. Contrôle et exclusion*, Brussels, Editions Complexe, 1997, p. 143.

35 Paxton, *Vichy France*, p. 179.

36 Peschanski, *Vichy 1940–1944*, pp. 157–58.

37 Reproduced in Baruch, *op. cit.*, p. 25.

38 Rémy, *Les Lois de Vichy*, p. 87.

39 I. Ousby, *Occupation: The Ordeal of France 1940–1944*, London, Pimlico, 1999, pp. 99–100.

40 Rémy, *Les Lois de Vichy*, p. 91.

41 J. F. Sweets, *Choices in Vichy France: The French under Nazi Occupation*, Oxford, Oxford University Press, 1994, pp. 99–127; Peschanski, 'Exclusion, persécution, répression', pp. 214–15; Jackson, *France: The Dark Years*, pp. 151, 633–35.

42 A. Chebel d'Appollonia, *L'Extrême-droite en France. De Maurras à Le Pen*, Brussels, Editions Complexe, 1988, p. 232.

43 P. Burrin, *Living with Defeat: France under the German Occupation 1940–1944*, trans. J. Lloyd, London, Arnold, 1996, p. 134.

44 M. R. Marrus and R. O. Paxton, *Vichy France and the Jews*, Stanford, Stanford University Press, 1995, pp. 250–52; Jackson, *France: The Dark Years*, pp. 217–19, 360. Bousquet was assassinated in 1993 while awaiting trial for his role as chief of police under Vichy.

45 Burrin, *Living with Defeat*, p. 156.

46 Over 50,000 of almost 76,000 Jews deported from France were foreign (Peschanski, 'Exclusion, persécution, répression', p. 226).

47 Burrin, *Living with Defeat*, pp. 156–59.

48 Baruch, *op. cit.*, p. 58.

49 Rémy, *Les Lois de Vichy*, pp. 68–70.

50 Pétain, *Discours aux Français*, p. 82.

51 Following the suspension of their trial in spring 1942, the main defendants were re-imprisoned then deported to Germany.

52 Paxton, *Vichy France*, p. 171.

53 Peschanski, 'Exclusion, persécution, répression', pp. 209–10.

54 Pétain, *Discours aux Français*, p. 88.

55 W. R. Tucker, *The Fascist Ego: A Political Biography of Robert Brasillach*, Berkeley, University of California Press, 1975, p. 239.

56 S. G. Payne, *A History of Fascism 1914–1945*, London, Routledge, 2001, pp. 312–17, 397–98.

57 All of these terms featured in the rationale for the Etat Français as set out in the *Journal Officiel* of 11 July 1940 (quoted in Baruch, *op. cit.*, pp. 15–16; emphases added). Unless thus indicated, emphases in quotations reflect the texts cited in this study.

58 Peschanski, *Vichy 1940–1944*, p. 145.

59 Secrétariat Général à la Jeunesse, *Qu'est-ce que la Révolution Nationale?*, pp. 3, 7, 21–22.

60 J. Algazy, *La Tentation néo-fasciste en France de 1944 à 1965*, Paris, Fayard, 1984, p. 43.

61 R. Rémond, *Les Droites en France*, Paris, Aubier Montaigne, 1982, pp. 125–40.

62 M. Winock, *Nationalisme, antisémitisme et fascisme en France*, Paris, Seuil, 1990, p. 17.

63 S. M. Osgood, *French Royalism since 1870*, The Hague, Martinus Nijhoff, 1970, pp. 51–52.

64 P. Milza, *Fascisme français: passé et présent*, Paris, Flammarion, 1987, p. 78.

65 Z. Sternhell, *La Droite révolutionnaire 1885–1914. Les origines françaises du fascisme*, Paris, Seuil, 1978, pp. 146–76.

66 Chebel d'Appollonia, *L'Extrême-droite en France*, p. 69; Winock, *Nationalisme, antisémitisme et fascisme en France*, pp. 43, 44, 354.

67 K. Passmore, 'The Croix de Feu and Fascism: A Foreign Thesis Obstinately Maintained', in E. J. Arnold (ed.), *The Development of the Radical Right in France: From Boulanger to Le Pen*, London, Macmillan, 2000, p. 111.

68 Rémond, *Les Droites en France*, p. 207; Algazy, *La Tentation néo-fasciste en France*, p. 34.

69 Chebel d'Appollonia, *L'Extrême-droite en France*, pp. 64–93.

70 C. Prochasson, 'Elusive Fascism: Reflections on the French Extreme Right at the End of the Nineteenth Century', in Arnold (ed.), *op. cit.*, p. 71; G. Wright, *France in Modern Times: From the Enlightenment to the Present*, New York, Norton, 1981, p. 260.

71 Prochasson, 'Elusive Fascism', p. 74.

72 Winock, *Nationalisme, antisémitisme et fascisme en France*, pp. 198, 202.

73 Winock, *Nationalisme, antisémitisme et fascisme en France*, pp. 44, 117–44, 173.

74 Jackson, *France: The Dark Years*, p. 178; Winock, *Nationalisme, antisémitisme et fascisme en France*, pp. 123–24.

75 Winock, *Nationalisme, antisémitisme et fascisme en France*, p. 46.

76 Zay's very name proclaimed him an alien for the nationalist right: arriving as a young man in Paris, Maurras had been famously dismayed to find so many names containing the letters 'K', 'W' or 'Z'.

77 Other such headlines ('The Jewish Revolution Crows Victory', 'The Great Jewish Offensive') adorned *L'Action Française* throughout June 1936 (J. Verdès-Leroux, *Refus et violences. Politique et littérature à l'extrême droite des années trente aux retombées de la Libération*, Paris, Gallimard, 1996, p. 59).

78 Paxton, *Vichy France*, pp. 177–78.

79 Winock, *Nationalisme, antisémitisme et fascisme en France*, p. 206.

80 Winock, *Nationalisme, antisémitisme et fascisme en France*, p. 149.

81 L. Rebatet, *Les Mémoires d'un fasciste*, vol. 1: *Les Décombres 1938–1940*, Paris, Société Nouvelle des Editions Jean-Jacques Pauvert, 1976, p. 54.

82 Winock, *Nationalisme, antisémitisme et fascisme en France*, pp. 170–71; Algazy, *La Tentation néo-fasciste en France*, pp. 40–41.

83 R. Kedward, *La Vie en bleu: France and the French since 1900*, London, Penguin/Allen Lane, 2005, p. 217. The same Céline liked to spell 'I hate you' (*'Je vous hais'*) as *'Je vous Zay'* (Paxton, *Vichy France*, p. 153 n. 35).

84 Rémond, *Les Droites en France*, p. 235.

85 *Le Petit Marseillais*, 9 February 1941, quoted in J.-P. Azéma, 'Vichy', in M. Winock (ed.), *Histoire de l'extrême droite en France*, Paris, Seuil, 1993, p. 196; Rebatet, *op. cit.*, pp. 523, 532.

86 P. Ory, *Les Collaborateurs 1940–1945*, Paris, Seuil, 1976, p. 125; Jackson, *France: The Dark Years*, p. 610.

87 Milza, *Fascisme français*, pp. 226–32.

88 Burrin, *Living with Defeat*, pp. 19–20.

89 Paxton, *Vichy France*, pp. 29–33, 136–39.

90 Paxton, *Vichy France*, pp. 234–41.

91 S. Hoffmann, *Decline or Renewal? France since the 1930s*, New York, Viking Press, 1974, pp. 5–6.

92 Pétain, *Discours aux Français*, p. 86.

93 Winock, *Nationalisme, antisémitisme et fascisme en France*, p. 173.

94 Pétain, *Discours aux Français*, p. 95; Burrin, *Living with Defeat*, p. 151.

95 Burrin, *Living with Defeat*, pp. 177–90. On the evolution of public opinion under Vichy, see P. Laborie, *L'Opinion française sous Vichy*, Paris, Seuil, 1990. For an insightful study of French attitudes under the Occupation, see also R. Gildea, *Marianne in Chains: In Search of the German Occupation 1940–1945*, London, Macmillan, 2002.

96 According to Baruch, the number of hostages executed by autumn 1941 stood at 123; by autumn 1942, it had risen to some 1,500 (*op. cit.*, p. 104).

97 Pétain, *Discours aux Français*, pp. 164–72. On this insidious aspect of life under Vichy, see A. Lefébure, *Les Conversations secrètes des Français sous l'Occupation*, Paris, Plon, 1993.

98 Rémy, *Les Lois de Vichy*, pp. 139–40, 146–47.

99 Secrétariat Général de l'Information, *Mardi 12 août 1941: Le Maréchal Pétain décide*, Lyon, 1941.

100 For some pointers to this debate, see Azéma and Bédarida (eds), *op. cit.*, pp. 251–63; Milza, *Fascisme français*, pp. 221–75; M. Cointet-Labrousse, *Vichy et le fascisme*, Brussels, Editions Complexe, 1987, pp. 94–132, 197–248; also the contributions by Burrin, Jackson and Chebel d'Appollonia in Arnold (ed.), *op. cit.*, pp. 135–92.

101 Kupferman, *op. cit.*, p. 91. The defence of having acted as a 'shield' to France was also made by Pétain in his final message to the French on 20 August 1944, before his enforced evacuation to Sigmaringen in Germany (Pétain, *Discours aux Français*, p. 341).

102 M. Larkin, *France since the Popular Front: Government and People 1936–1986*, Oxford, Clarendon Press, 1988, p. 83.

103 Azéma, *From Munich to the Liberation*, pp. 50–51.

104 S. Hoffmann, 'Collaborationism in France During World War II', *Journal of Modern History*, vol. 10, no. 3, 1968, pp. 375–95.

105 Rémy, *Les Lois de Vichy*, p. 31. For the last and most 'Republican' version of Vichy's draft constitution dating from autumn 1943, see J. Godechot (ed.), *Les Constitutions de la France depuis 1789*, Paris, Garnier-Flammarion, 1979, pp. 343–55.

106 Rémy, *Les Lois de Vichy*, pp. 33–34; Paxton, *Vichy France*, pp. 29–33.

107 P. Burrin, 'The Ideology of the National Revolution', in Arnold (ed.), *op. cit.*, p. 136.

108 Jackson, *France: The Dark Years*, p. 79.

109 Kuisel, *op. cit.*, p. 131; also Milza, *Fascisme Français*, pp. 230-37.

110 S. Hoffmann, Foreword to Marrus and Paxton, *op. cit.*, p. x.

111 Kuisel, *op. cit.*, pp. 144–46; also Hoffmann, *Decline or Renewal?*, p. 5; M. Anderson, *Conservative Politics in France*, London, Allen & Unwin, 1974, pp. 68–69; A.-G. Slama, 'Vichy était-il fasciste?', *Vingtième Siècle*, no. 11, 1986, pp. 50–51.

112 Azéma, 'Vichy', p. 205; Pétain, *Discours aux Français*, pp. 94–96.

113 Hoffmann, 'Collaborationism in France During World War II', pp. 382–89.

114 R. Soucy, 'The Nature of Fascism in France', *Journal of Contemporary History*, vol. 1, no. 1, 1966, pp. 27–55.

115 Rebatet, *op. cit.*, p. 598.

116 F. Grover, *Drieu La Rochelle*, Paris, Gallimard, 1962, pp. 49–51; R. Soucy, *Fascist Intellectual: Drieu La Rochelle*, Berkeley, University of California Press, 1979, p. 83.

117 Soucy, *Fascist Intellectual*, pp. 26, 66–67, 91–92.

118 Tucker, *The Fascist Ego*, p. 231; Verdès-Leroux, *Refus et violences*, pp. 97–98, 156–58, 160, 162; B. Laguerre, 'Brasillach', in J. Julliard and M. Winock (eds), *Dictionnaire des intellectuels français*, Paris, Seuil, 1996, p. 182; Jackson, *France: The Dark Years*, pp. 202–

3. For some of Brasillach's early impressions of Nazi Germany, see *Notre avant-guerre*, Paris, Plon, 1941, pp. 264–78.
119 Soucy, *Fascist Intellectual*, p. 205.
120 Soucy, *Fascist Intellectual*, p. 72; Tucker, *The Fascist Ego*, p. 109.
121 Soucy, *Fascist Intellectual*, p. 205.
122 Tucker, *The Fascist Ego*, p. 101.
123 Soucy, *Fascist Intellectual*, pp. 181–87, 237, and 'The Nature of Fascism in France', pp. 54–55; Tucker, *The Fascist Ego*, pp. 147–49, 166–71.
124 Ory, *op. cit.*, p. 211.
125 Soucy, *Fascist Intellectual*, p. 101.
126 Grover, *op. cit.*, p. 55.
127 Burrin, *Living with Defeat*, pp. 432, 521 n. 18; H. R. Kedward, *Occupied France: Collaboration and Resistance 1940–1944*, Oxford, Blackwell, 1993, pp. 43–44. Jackson calculates that the combined membership of all such movements between 1940 and 1944 did not exceed 220,000 (*France: The Dark Years*, p. 194).
128 Burrin, *Living with Defeat*, pp. 432–33.
129 Gordon, *op. cit.*, pp. 19–20.
130 On the PPF, see Gordon, *op. cit.*, pp. 130–65; Milza, *Fascisme français*, pp. 159–78, 252–56; R. Soucy, *French Fascism: The Second Wave 1933–1939*, New Haven, Yale University Press, 1995, pp. 204–79.
131 S. Berstein and P. Milza, *Dictionnaire historique des fascismes et du nazisme*, Brussels, Editions Complexe, 1992, p. 524.
132 Anderson, *op. cit.*, pp. 216–20.
133 Anderson, *op. cit.*, p. 219.
134 Anderson, *op. cit.*, p. 218; Berstein and Milza, *op. cit.*, pp. 524–25; Burrin, *Living with Defeat*, p. 521 n. 18.
135 A. Chebel d'Appollonia, 'Collaborationist Fascism', in Arnold (ed.), *op. cit.*, pp. 185–86.
136 On military collaboration, see J. G. Shields, 'Charlemagne's Crusaders: French Collaboration in Arms, 1941–1945', *French Cultural Studies*, vol. 18, no. 1, 2007, pp. 83–105.
137 P. Randa, *Dictionnaire commenté de la collaboration française*, Paris, Jean Picollec, 1997, pp. 357, 371.
138 Published in *L'Œuvre* of 4 May 1939.
139 Plumyène and Lasierra, *op. cit.*, p. 155.
140 On the Cagoule, or Comité Secret d'Action Révolutionnaire (Secret Committee for Revolutionary Action, CSAR), see Anderson, *op. cit.*, pp. 224–30.
141 On the RNP, see Gordon, *op. cit.*, pp. 90–129; Milza, *Fascisme français*, pp. 256–59.
142 Plumyène and Lasierra, *op. cit.*, pp. 154–55; Berstein and Milza, *op. cit.*, p. 578; Jackson, *France: The Dark Years*, p. 143.
143 Berstein and Milza, *op. cit.*, p. 578.
144 Berstein and Milza, *op. cit.*, p. 578; Burrin, *Living with Defeat*, p. 521 n. 18.
145 Milza, *Fascisme français*, pp. 265–66.
146 Chebel d'Appollonia, 'Collaborationist Fascism', p. 182.
147 M. Bardèche, *Qu'est-ce que le Fascisme?*, Paris, Les Sept Couleurs, 1961, p. 77. A reactionary monarchist, Marshal Mac-Mahon was elected President in 1873 by a 'Moral Order' coalition of monarchists and conservatives, only to resign in 1879 rather than work with a Republican majority in both chambers.
148 Plumyène and Lasierra, *op. cit.*, p. 150.
149 On the Milice, see Gordon, *op. cit.*, pp. 166–95; Milza, *Fascisme français*, pp. 268–75.
150 Baruch, *op. cit.*, p. 85.
151 Gordon, *op. cit.*, pp. 181, 183; Ory, *op. cit.*, pp. 250–51; Burrin, *Living with Defeat*, p. 443.
152 Gordon, *op. cit.*, p. 168.

153 Gordon, *op. cit.*, p. 166.
154 Burrin, *Living with Defeat*, pp. 427, 521 n. 18; Jackson, *France: The Dark Years*, pp. 192, 201.
155 Jackson, *France: The Dark Years*, pp. 192, 195.
156 Algazy, *La Tentation néo-fasciste en France*, p. 52; Jackson, *France: The Dark Years*, pp. 198–212, 307–8.
157 Jackson, *France: The Dark Years*, pp. 171, 198.
158 Jackson, *France: The Dark Years*, p. 185; Azéma, *From Munich to the Liberation*, p. 69.
159 Tucker, *The Fascist Ego*, p. 237.
160 A. S. Milward, *The New Order and the French Economy*, Oxford, Oxford University Press, 1970, p. 41.
161 Chebel d'Appollonia, 'Collaborationist Fascism', pp. 178, 186–87; Verdès-Leroux, *Refus et violences*, p. 170; Soucy, *Fascist Intellectual*, p. 77.
162 Vichy nonetheless provided Doriot with some subsidies, just as it gave official approval for the anti-Bolshevik 'crusade' undertaken by the LVF.
163 L. Joly, 'Darquier de Pellepoix, "champion" des antisémites français (1936–1939)', *Revue d'Histoire de la Shoah*, no. 173, 2001, pp. 45, 47; Randa, *op. cit.*, pp. 114–18.
164 Schneider, *op. cit.*, pp. 258–63; Jackson, *France: The Dark Years*, pp. 358–60.
165 Gordon, *op. cit.*, p. 290.
166 J. Jackson, 'Vichy and Fascism', in Arnold (ed.), *op. cit.*, p. 168.
167 Rebatet, *op. cit.*, p. 133; Marrus and Paxton, *op. cit.*, p. 42; Ory, *op. cit.*, p. 160. On some of the divisions and generational tensions within the French extreme right dating from the 1930s, see Verdès-Leroux, *Refus et violences*, pp. 37–141.
168 Hoffmann, 'Collaborationism in France During World War II', p. 392.
169 Baruch, *op. cit.*, pp. 30–31; Jackson, *France: The Dark Years*, p. 159.
170 Azéma, *From Munich to the Liberation*, p. 60.
171 Jackson, *France: The Dark Years*, pp. 567–69.
172 Hoffmann, *Decline or Renewal?*, pp. 3–25.
173 Laborie, *op. cit.*, pp. 256–57.
174 Verdès-Leroux, *Refus et violences*, pp. 155, 160.
175 Hoffmann, *Decline or Renewal?*, p. 21.
176 Slama, 'Vichy était-il fasciste?', p. 43.
177 R. Griffin, *The Nature of Fascism*, London, Routledge, 1991, p. 47.
178 R. Eatwell, 'On Defining the "Fascist Minimum": The Centrality of Ideology', *Journal of Political Ideologies*, vol. 1, no. 3, 1996, pp. 303–19; also Payne, *op. cit.*, pp. 3–19, and Griffin, *The Nature of Fascism*, pp. 26-55.
179 Griffin, *The Nature of Fascism*, p. 135. On Vichy as 'a regime of moderate right authoritarianism (though with increasing right radical overtones)', see Payne, *op. cit.*, pp. 397–402; also R. O. Paxton, *The Anatomy of Fascism*, London, Penguin, 2004, p. 218.
180 Bardèche, *Qu'est-ce que le Fascisme?*, pp. 74–80.
181 D. Thomson, *Democracy in France since 1870*, London, Cassell, 1989, p. 220.
182 Jackson, *France: The Dark Years*, pp. 1, 234. The figure for French workers in Germany, combining volunteers and conscripts, varies from source to source, with Paxton putting it at almost 1.4 million by November 1943 (*Vichy France*, p. 366).
183 Peschanski, 'Exclusion, persécution, répression', pp. 217–18; Jackson, *France: The Dark Years*, pp. 260–61.
184 J.-P. Rioux, 'La délation', *Le Monde dossiers et documents: Les Français sous l'Occupation*, no. 262, February 1998, p. 6.
185 *Le Monde*, 17 November 2004.
186 Paxton, *Vichy France*, p. 297.
187 Rémy, *Les Lois de Vichy*, pp. 229–31; Gordon, *op. cit.*, pp. 293–94.
188 Paradoxically, the year 1942–43 was also the period when some of the most committed French ideologues, such as Brasillach and Drieu, disenchanted by the

failure of collaboration, began to lose faith in the fascism which they had previously championed.

189 Rémy, *Les Lois de Vichy*, pp. 188, 198–200.

190 Godechot, *Les Constitutions de la France depuis 1789*, pp. 340–55.

191 Paxton, *Vichy France*, pp. 324–25; Burrin, *Living with Defeat*, pp. 172–73.

192 Jackson, *France: The Dark Years*, p. 227.

193 Rémy, *Les Lois de Vichy*, pp. 221–23. The duration was reducible to compensate for time already spent in the armed forces or the Chantiers de la Jeunesse.

194 Rémy, *Les Lois de Vichy*, p. 210.

195 By the end of November 1942, all of these assets had been lost: the southern zone had been occupied, the armistice army dissolved and the fleet (or what was left of it after Mers El-Kébir) scuttled, while the overseas territories were now largely in Allied hands.

196 Azéma, *From Munich to the Liberation*, p. 125.

197 Paxton, *Vichy France*, pp. 113–24.

198 R. O. Paxton, *Parades and Politics at Vichy: The French Officer Corps under Marshal Pétain*, Princeton, Princeton University Press, 1966, pp. 229–43; Burrin, *Living with Defeat*, pp. 119–29; Jackson, *France: The Dark Years*, pp. 178–81.

199 Paxton, *Vichy France*, pp. 304–5.

200 Pétain, *Discours aux Français*, pp. 336–37; Paxton, *Vichy France*, p. 325.

201 Ory, *op. cit.*, p. 255.

202 Gordon, *op. cit.*, p. 294; Ousby, *op. cit.*, pp. 283–86.

203 Marrus and Paxton, *op. cit.*, pp. 166, 168–69. It is estimated that some 3,000 internees died from the atrocious conditions alone (*ibid.*, p. 176).

204 Jews in the occupied zone were also subject to a special curfew, restrictions on hours of shopping and the use of public transport, and a ban from public places of assembly such as cinemas, theatres and restaurants.

205 Paxton, *Vichy France*, pp. 295–97; Jackson, *France: The Dark Years*, pp. 215–19, 359.

206 The meticulous work done by Serge Klarsfeld in the 1970s produced these figures, which have since been accepted as definitive. For some essential statistics relating to the deportation of Jews, see S. Klarsfeld, 'Convois pour la mort', *Le Monde dossiers et documents: Les Français sous l'Occupation*, no. 262, February 1998, p. 4; also *Le Monde*, 17 November 2004 and 26 January 2005.

207 Paxton, *Vichy France*, pp. 173–85.

208 Kedward, *Occupied France*, p. 28. This historic French anti-Semitism had religious, economic and racial as well as political roots. For an extensive discussion, see Winock, *Nationalisme, antisémitisme et fascisme en France*, pp. 79–223.

209 Peschanski, *Vichy 1940–1944*, p. 147.

210 Jackson, *France: The Dark Years*, p. 355; Marrus and Paxton, *op. cit.*, p. 47.

211 Hoffmann, Foreword to Marrus and Paxton, *op. cit.*, pp. xi, xii; Jackson, *France: The Dark Years*, pp. 355–60.

212 Jackson, *France: The Dark Years*, pp. 106, 203–4. Such figures as Rebatet and Céline saw themselves as part of an Aryan elite to which the Nazis had, in fact, no intention of admitting them.

213 Marrus and Paxton, *op. cit.*, pp. 20, 95.

214 Paxton, *Vichy France*, p. 178.

215 Jackson, *France: The Dark Years*, p. 354.

216 La Documentation historique et philosophique, *Le Gouvernement Pétain. Ce qu'il a fait sans nous. Ce qu'il ne peut continuer sans nous*, Paris, Collection Possibilités Françaises, n.d. [1941], p. 20.

217 Sweets, *op. cit.*, pp. 124–27; R. Poznanski, *Être juif en France pendant la Seconde Guerre mondiale*, Paris, Hachette, 1994, pp. 537–40.

218 Burrin, *Living with Defeat*, pp. 156–57.

219 Schneider, *op. cit.*, p. 262.

220 A. Kaspi, 'Vichy et les Juifs', in J.-F. Sirinelli (ed.), *Dictionnaire historique de la vie politique française au XXe siècle*, Paris, Presses Universitaires de France, 1995, p. 1056.

221 Burrin, *Living with Defeat*, pp. 156, 486 n. 17.

222 Marrus and Paxton, *op. cit.*, p. 261.

223 P. Bezbakh, *Histoire de la France contemporaine de 1914 à nos jours*, Paris, Bordas, 1990, p. 137; Marrus and Paxton, *op. cit.*, p. 262.

224 Correspondence with the author, 4 August 2005.

225 For how little such 'exemptions' could be worth, see Gildea, *Marianne in Chains*, pp. 233–34.

226 Marrus and Paxton, *op. cit.*, pp. 346–56. On the question of how much Vichy knew about the purpose of the deportations, Robert Paxton tersely observes: 'They did not know what we know, but they knew enough' (correspondence with the author, 4 August 2005).

227 *Au Pilori*, 19 November 1942, quoted in D. Pryce-Jones, 'Paris During the German Occupation', in G. Hirschfeld and P. Marsh (eds), *Collaboration in France: Politics and Culture During the Nazi Occupation 1940–1944*, Oxford, Berg, 1989, p. 28.

228 Randa, *op. cit.*, p. 397.

229 Pryce-Jones, 'Paris During the German Occupation', pp. 28–29.

230 Marrus and Paxton, *op. cit.*, pp. 211–12; Ory, *op. cit.*, p. 282.

231 Pryce-Jones, 'Paris During the German Occupation', pp. 20, 28–29; Ory, *op. cit.*, pp. 116–27, 283–84; Algazy, *La Tentation néo-fasciste en France*, p. 52; Jackson, *France: The Dark Years*, pp. 201–4

2 The Vichy legacy

1 Hoffmann, 'Collaborationism in France During World War II', p. 393.

2 Godechot, *Les Constitutions de la France depuis 1789*, pp. 389–91.

3 Gildea, *France since 1945*, p. 60; Paxton, *Vichy France*, p. 346.

4 A. Cole and P. Campbell, *French Electoral Systems and Elections since 1789*, Aldershot, Gower, 1989, pp. 69, 78.

5 F. Duprat, *Les Mouvements d'extrême-droite en France depuis 1944*, Paris, Albatros, 1972, pp. 16–17; H. R. Lottman, *The People's Anger: Justice and Revenge in Post-Liberation France*, London, Hutchinson, 1986, pp. 272–73.

6 J.-P. Rioux, *La France de la Quatrième République*, vol. 1, Paris, Seuil, 1980, p. 54; Jackson, *France: The Dark Years*, pp. 577–78; Gildea, *France since 1945*, p. 58.

7 Kupferman, *op. cit.*, pp. 86–87.

8 Pétain, *Discours aux Français*, pp. 94–96.

9 Kupferman, *op. cit.*, pp. 90–93.

10 On Laval's trial and execution, see Kupferman, *op. cit.*, pp. 128–54.

11 For the list, see Randa, *op. cit.*, pp. 699–704.

12 Alibert and Darquier de Pellepoix were also tried and sentenced to death (*in absentia*) in 1947.

13 Jackson, *France: The Dark Years*, p. 587.

14 Randa, *op. cit.*, pp. 705–6.

15 A. Y. Kaplan, 'Literature and Collaboration', in D. Hollier (ed.), *A New History of French Literature*, Cambridge (Massachusetts), Harvard University Press, 1989, p. 970.

16 J.-P. Rioux, 'Des clandestins aux activistes (1945–1965)', in M. Winock (ed.), *op. cit.*, p. 218. On this counter-culture, see N. Hewitt, *Literature and the Right in Postwar France: The Story of the 'Hussards'*, Oxford, Berg, 1996, pp. 42–73.

17 For an inventory of extreme-right publications in the immediate post-war years, see Coston *et al.*, *op. cit.*, pp. 173–90.

18 Algazy, *La Tentation néo-fasciste en France*, p. 66; Milza, *Fascisme français*, p. 293.

19 Bardèche, *Qu'est-ce que le Fascisme?*, pp. 98–99.

20 Jackson, *France: The Dark Years*, p. 49.

21 Osgood, *op. cit.*, pp. 182–85.

22 Algazy, *La Tentation néo-fasciste en France*, pp. 64–70. Algazy's invaluable documentary study provides a rich source of extracts from the writings of extreme-right groups and individuals in the post-war years.

23 M. Bardèche, *Lettre à François Mauriac*, Paris, La Pensée Libre, 1947, pp. 12, 14, 19, 58, 138, 142, 166. A similar defence of state anti-Semitism was put forward by others such as Rebatet and Brasillach (Tucker, *The Fascist Ego*, pp. 167–68).

24 Bardèche, interview with Joseph Algazy, *La Tentation néo-fasciste en France*, p. 207.

25 M. Bardèche, *Nuremberg ou la terre promise*, Paris, Les Sept Couleurs, 1948, pp. 14, 17, 23, 30–32, 146, 193–94; Algazy, *La Tentation néo-fasciste en France*, p. 210.

26 G. Desbuissons, 'Maurice Bardèche: un précurseur du "révisionnisme"', *Relations internationales*, no. 65, 1991, pp. 23–37.

27 A. Y. Kaplan, *Reproductions of Banality: Fascism, Literature, and French Intellectual Life*, Minneapolis, University of Minnesota Press, 1986, p. 178.

28 Bardèche, *Qu'est-ce que le Fascisme?*, p. 98.

29 Algazy, *La Tentation néo-fasciste en France*, pp. 72–90; Chebel d'Appollonia, *L'Extrême-droite en France*, pp. 282–85.

30 Coston *et al.*, *op. cit.*, p. 179. There was nothing new about this slogan, which went back to Drumont and had served as a rallying cry in the 1930s.

31 Duprat, *op. cit.*, pp. 33–35.

32 Algazy, *La Tentation néo-fasciste en France*, p. 77.

33 Duprat, *op. cit.*, pp. 36–37; Algazy, *La Tentation néo-fasciste en France*, pp. 74–80.

34 'Negroes, Jews and Mongols', in Binet's terms (Algazy, *La Tentation néo-fasciste en France*, p. 73).

35 Algazy, *La Tentation néo-fasciste en France*, pp. 99, 105.

36 Algazy, *La Tentation néo-fasciste en France*, pp. 90–92, 98–112, 139–56, 380–83; Duprat, *op. cit.*, pp. 41–42; Chebel d'Appollonia, *L'Extrême-droite en France*, pp. 285–87. Like fascist groups before and after them, Luca's various movements paraded as 'socialist' in their rejection of 'banks, trusts and Judeo-capitalist exploitation' and in their declared ambition to bring about a classless society based on a new hierarchical order, that of race and nation.

37 Milza, *Fascisme français*, pp. 276–94.

38 Algazy, *La Tentation néo-fasciste en France*, pp. 68, 73–75.

39 Algazy, *La Tentation néo-fasciste en France*, p. 80.

40 On the Malmö conference, see A. Del Boca and M. Giovana, *Fascism Today*, trans. R. H. Boothroyd, London, Heinemann, 1970, pp. 82–84; Milza, *Fascisme français*, pp. 281–82.

41 Del Boca and Giovana, *op. cit.*, pp. 84–86; Camus and Monzat, *op. cit.*, pp. 252–54.

42 Milza, *Fascisme français*, pp. 283–84. For a review of some of these groups and their programmes, see Algazy, *La Tentation néo-fasciste en France*, pp. 59–94.

43 Despite the objective weakness of the extreme right, Algazy points to 1947 as the year when the French press began to carry dire warnings of a fascist revival (*La Tentation néo-fasciste en France*, p. 92).

44 The weekly *Rivarol* drew collaborationist journalists such as Lucien Rebatet and the former editor of *Je suis partout*, Pierre-Antoine Cousteau. Serving as a vehicle for pro-Vichy, anti-Resistance sentiment, it enjoyed an estimated circulation of some 45,000 in 1952 (Milza, *Fascisme français*, p. 295). Today, with a circulation of several thousand, it remains one of the principal conduits for anti-immigrant and anti-Semitic nationalism in the French press (Camus and Monzat, *op. cit.*, pp. 478–79).

45 Anderson, *op. cit.*, p. 271.

46 J.-M. Le Pen, *Les Français d'abord*, Paris, Carrère-Lafon, 1984, p. 32.

47 Le Pen, *Les Français d'abord*, p. 34. On Le Pen's childhood, see G. Bresson and C. Lionet, *Le Pen. Biographie*, Paris, Seuil, 1994, pp. 7–37.

48 Bresson and Lionet, *op. cit.*, pp. 52–78.

49 Le Pen, *Les Français d'abord*, pp. 37–39; R. Mauge, *La Vérité sur Jean-Marie Le Pen*, Paris, Editions France-Empire, 1988, pp. 64–71; P. Buisson and A. Renault (eds), *L'Album Le Pen. Images d'un Français*, Paris, S.E.R.P., 1988, pp. 18–23. The political aspect of these activities, Le Pen would nonetheless recall, consisted of combating the Marxist influence within the UNEF.

50 *Le Monde*, 17 March 1951.

51 Le Pen, *Les Français d'abord*, p. 68.

52 Bresson and Lionet, *op. cit.*, pp. 54–55, 66, 76.

53 Le Pen, interview with the author, 15 April 2005; Bresson and Lionet, *op. cit.*, p. 54.

54 Those like Claude Chabrol who knew Le Pen during his student days would recall his pronounced anticlericalism (Bresson and Lionet, *op. cit.*, p. 41).

55 Osgood, *op. cit.*, pp. 58–64, 198–99.

56 Milza, *Fascisme français*, p. 292.

57 Le Pen, *Les Français d'abord*, p. 39.

58 Bresson and Lionet, *op. cit.*, p. 41; Mauge, *op. cit.*, pp. 100–101.

59 Bresson and Lionet, *op. cit.*, pp. 48–49, 70–71; Algazy, *La Tentation néo-fasciste en France*, pp. 228–29.

60 *Le Monde*, 17 and 18 June 1951; J. Isorni, *Ainsi passent les républiques*, Paris, Flammarion, 1959, pp. 8–17; Duprat, *op. cit.*, pp. 47–48. In an interview with the author on 15 April 2005, Le Pen confirmed his participation on behalf of Isorni in this so-called 'Battle of Wagram'.

61 Still in existence today, this organisation campaigned for a review of Pétain's case and the transfer of his remains to Douaumont near Verdun. The ADMP attracted former Vichy officials such as Admiral Auphan, François Lehideux, Jean Borotra and General Weygand, along with future members of the FN and the wider far right.

62 Algazy, *La Tentation néo-fasciste en France*, p. 114.

63 Isorni, *Ainsi passent les républiques*, pp. 17–19; Algazy, *La Tentation néo-fasciste en France*, p. 82.

64 The other two UNIR deputies, also former Vichy officials, were Roger de Saivre and Paul Estèbe, with Commander Loustaunau-Lacau elected as a quasi-UNIR candidate (J. Isorni, *Le Silence est d'or ou la parole au Palais-Bourbon*, Paris, Flammarion, 1957, p. 165 n. 2; Duprat, *op. cit.*, pp. 47–48).

65 Gildea, *France since 1945*, p. 62.

66 Rousso, *op. cit.*, p. 70.

67 J.-Y. Camus, 'Nostalgia and Political Impotence', in Arnold (ed.), *op. cit.*, pp. 199–201.

68 Algazy, *La Tentation néo-fasciste en France*, pp. 82–83.

69 Coston *et al.*, *op. cit.*, pp. 37, 41, 197.

70 Camus, 'Nostalgia and Political Impotence', p. 201.

71 Algazy, *La Tentation néo-fasciste en France*, pp. 275–77; Camus and Monzat, *op. cit.*, pp. 76–79.

72 Algazy, *La Tentation néo-fasciste en France*, p. 279. Both Sicard and Augier would be expounding these views still in the 1960s, the former in his *Histoire de la collaboration* (Paris, L'Esprit Nouveau, 1964), the latter in *Les Volontaires* (Paris, Presses de la Cité, 1963) and *Les Hérétiques* (Paris, Presses de la Cité, 1965).

73 Despite Mutter's credentials as a former Resistance chief, *Paroles Françaises* became a forum for the range of extreme-right positions being articulated in the late 1940s and early 1950s. It boasted a circulation of 100,000 at its peak in 1947–48 (Algazy, *La Tentation néo-fasciste en France*, pp. 67–70).

74 Gildea, *France since 1945*, p. 19; A. Clayton, *The Wars of French Decolonization*, London, Longman, 1994, p. 74.

75 Gildea, *France since 1945*, pp. 19–20.

76 Mauge, *op. cit.*, p. 73.
77 Le Pen, *Les Français d'abord*, p. 40.
78 Le Pen, *Les Français d'abord*, pp. 42–43. 'Mendès cobbled together a peace settlement and sold out in Indo-China for reasons of political expediency at home' (*ibid.*, p. 44).
79 Mauge, *op. cit.*, pp. 103–4.
80 Bresson and Lionet, *op. cit.*, p. 99.
81 Le Pen, *Les Français d'abord*, p. 45.
82 Le Pen, *Les Français d'abord*, p. 45. On the JIP, see Bresson and Lionet, *op. cit.*, pp. 105–17.
83 Mauge, *op. cit.*, p. 101; Bresson and Lionet, *op. cit.*, pp. 107–10

3   The Poujadist movement

1 P. Poujade, *A l'heure de la colère*, Paris, Albin Michel, 1977, pp. 13–82.
2 S. Hoffmann, 'Protest in Modern France', in M. A. Kaplan (ed.), *The Revolution in World Politics*, New York, John Wiley & Sons, 1962, pp. 69–80, and 'Paradoxes of the French Political Community', in S. Hoffmann *et al.*, *In Search of France: The Economy, Society, and Political System in the Twentieth Century*, New York, Harper & Row, 1965, pp. 3–12.
3 M. S. Lipsedge, 'The Poujade Movement', *Contemporary Review*, February 1956, p. 85; J.-P. Rioux, *La France de la Quatrième République*, vol. 2, Paris, Seuil, 1983, p. 79.
4 The complexity of the tax system and potential for fraud were illustrated by the 'twenty-four different taxes for the café proprietor, and twenty-five for the owner of a small garage' (Lipsedge, 'The Poujade Movement', p. 85).
5 P. Poujade, *L'Histoire sans masque. Autobiographie*, Cestas, Elytis Edition, 2003, pp. 183–90.
6 S. Hoffmann, *Le Mouvement Poujade*, Paris, Armand Colin, 1956, p. 191; A. Knapp and V. Wright, *The Government and Politics of France*, 4th edn, London, Routledge, 2001, p. 165.
7 Poujade, correspondence with the author, 15 August 2003; *A l'heure de la colère*, p. 150.
8 Coston *et al.*, *op. cit.*, p. 243; Duprat, *op. cit.*, p. 75; Bresson and Lionet, *op. cit.*, pp. 119–20.
9 Poujade, *A l'heure de la colère*, pp. 145–47.
10 S. Fitzgerald, 'The Anti-Modern Rhetoric of Le Mouvement Poujade', *Review of Politics*, vol. 32, no. 2, 1970, p. 177; J. Touchard, 'Bibliographie et chronologie du Poujadisme', *Revue française de science politique*, January–March 1956, p. 36. For an overview, see R. Eatwell, 'Poujadism and Neo-Poujadism: From Revolt to Reconciliation', in P. G. Cerny (ed.), *Social Movements and Protest in France*, London, Pinter, 1982, pp. 70–78.
11 Hoffmann, *Le Mouvement Poujade*, pp. 159–60, 205–8; P. M. Williams, *Crisis and Compromise: Politics in the Fourth Republic*, London, Longmans, 1964, pp. 507–8.
12 Hoffmann, *Le Mouvement Poujade*, p. 30. Hoffmann records 2,785 meetings held by the Poujadists in the same period, while Duprat claims that they held over 2,000 meetings in the three weeks preceding the elections alone (*op. cit.*, p. 75).
13 A poll published in *L'Express* recorded a 66 per cent rate of dissatisfaction with the outgoing National Assembly (Rioux, *La France de la Quatrième République*, vol. 2, p. 84).
14 Reproduced in Hoffmann, *Le Mouvement Poujade*, p. 145.
15 Reproduced in Hoffmann, *Le Mouvement Poujade*, p. 170.
16 J.-P. Rioux, 'La révolte de Pierre Poujade', *L'Histoire*, no. 32, March 1981, p. 11.
17 Reproduced in Hoffmann, *Le Mouvement Poujade*, pp. 153–54.
18 Rémond, *Les Droites en France*, p. 252. On the politicisation of the UDCA, see Hoffmann, *Le Mouvement Poujade*, pp. 71–74.
19 P. M. Williams (with D. Goldey and M. Harrison), *French Politicians and Elections 1951–1969*, Cambridge, Cambridge University Press, 1970, p. 46.

20 Williams, *French Politicians and Elections*, p. 47; Poujade, *A l'heure de la colère*, pp. 136–42, 164–65; C. Prieur, 'La campagne électorale dans l'Aveyron', in M. Duverger *et al.* (eds), *Les Elections du 2 janvier 1956*, Paris, Armand Colin, 1957, pp. 338–39.

21 Hoffmann, *Le Mouvement Poujade*, p. 202.

22 For an analysis of the Poujadist vote, see Hoffmann, *Le Mouvement Poujade*, pp. 189–208.

23 S. M. Lipset, *Political Man: The Social Bases of Politics*, London, Heinemann, 1983, pp. 159–61; Williams, *French Politicians and Elections*, pp. 61–62; D. MacRae, *Parliament, Parties, and Society in France 1946–1958*, New York, St. Martin's Press, 1967, pp. 268–73.

24 C. Brindillac and A. Prost, 'Géographie des élections législatives du 2 janvier 1956', *Esprit*, vol. 24, no. 236, 1956, pp. 443–48.

25 Williams, *Crisis and Compromise*, p. 165 n. 21; *L'Observateur*, 12 January 1956.

26 Poujade, *A l'heure de la colère*, p. 163; Hoffmann, *Le Mouvement Poujade*, pp. 115–31.

27 *Paris Match*, 21 January 1956, pp. 56–57.

28 *Paris Match*, 7 and 14 January 1956, pp. 44–49 and 64–67 respectively.

29 Isorni, *Ainsi passent les républiques*, p. 75.

30 D. Borne, *Petits bourgeois en révolte? Le Mouvement Poujade*, Paris, Flammarion, 1977, pp. 152–53.

31 *Le Monde*, 10 March 1956; Isorni, *Ainsi passent les républiques*, p. 75.

32 J. G. Shields, 'An Enigma Still: Poujadism Fifty Years On', *French Politics, Culture and Society*, vol. 22, no. 1, 2004, pp. 47–50.

33 Notably Pierre Durand, Alain Jamet, Dominique Chaboche, Jean-Pierre Reveau, André Dufraisse and Jean-François Galvaire.

34 Bresson and Lionet, *op. cit.*, pp. 131, 136, 144.

35 For vivid accounts of this incident, which included the firing of blanks from a gun in the public gallery, see *Le Figaro* and *New York Herald Tribune* of 16 February 1956. In the 11 constituencies in question, the Poujadists had fallen foul of the 1951 electoral law governing alliances (or *apparentements*) between lists. Though technically at fault, 10 of the 11 Poujadist deputies were summarily replaced by candidates whom they had defeated – a procedure described by *Le Figaro* (8 February 1956) as 'a clumsy political ploy' and by the *Manchester Guardian* (15 February 1956) as 'a deplorable device to distort the expression of the popular will'. Only one replacement, the future Gaullist minister Jean Chamant, refused to accept a seat gained in this way, insisting on an election which he duly won.

36 *Le Monde*, 29 January 1956; Poujade, *A l'heure de la colère*, p. 161. 'They want to make us sit on the extreme right, whereas in fact it is on the extreme left that we should be' (*L'Express*, 4 January 1956).

37 Quoted in Bresson and Lionet, *op. cit.*, p. 135.

38 Bresson and Lionet, *op. cit.*, pp. 139–41.

39 Poujade, interview with the author, 18 April 1995, and *A l'heure de la colère*, pp. 202, 228; Bresson and Lionet, *op. cit.*, pp. 136–45; Mauge, *op. cit.*, p. 118.

40 Bresson and Lionet, *op. cit.*, p. 145.

41 Tixier-Vignancour had been a high-ranking official in the Vichy Ministry of Information before being involved with a number of extreme right-wing organisations in the post-war years. For Poujade's unfavourable judgement of him, see *A l'heure de la colère*, pp. 162, 197, 202, 228. Frédéric-Dupont was a political grandee of the Paris left bank who had been prominent in the anti-parliamentary agitation of 6 February 1934. He offered himself as an early mentor to Le Pen and would feature much later on the FN's list of candidates for the 1986 legislative elections, winning a seat in Paris alongside Le Pen.

42 Duprat, *op. cit.*, pp. 76–77; Bresson and Lionet, *op. cit.*, pp. 147–49.

43 Borne, *Petits bourgeois en révolte?*, pp. 156–57; Duprat, *op. cit.*, p. 77.

44 In correspondence with the author dated 22 August 2003, five days before his death aged 82, Poujade recalled with rancour still this betrayal. There ensued a lifelong rift,

with Le Pen dismissing Poujade as a 'providential man who fled from providence' and Poujade denouncing Le Pen as a dangerous extremist (Le Pen, *Les Français d'abord*, pp. 46–47; Poujade, *L'Histoire sans masque*, p. 213).

45 Poujade, *A l'heure de la colère*, pp. 184–221.

46 Poujade, *A l'heure de la colère*, pp. 224–25.

47 Isorni, *Ainsi passent les républiques*, p. 77; Duprat, *op. cit.*, p. 78; Coston *et al.*, *op. cit.*, p. 237.

48 On the splits provoked by de Gaulle within the Poujadist ranks, see *Le Monde*, 8–9 June and 24 September 1958.

49 H. Portelli, *La Politique en France sous la Ve République*, Paris, Grasset, 1987, p. 315. Long before Le Pen and the FN, Poujade warned of 'the suicide of France through the Common Market' (Coston *et al.*, *op. cit.*, p. 240 n. 30).

50 Poujade, *A l'heure de la colère*, pp. 223–24; Coston *et al.*, *op. cit.*, p. 244.

51 Portelli, *La Politique en France sous la Ve République*, p. 317.

52 *Le Monde*, 13 December 1955; Hoffmann, *Le Mouvement Poujade*, p. 354.

53 *Le Monde*, 15–16 January 1956; also *L'Express*, 9 January 1956.

54 Algazy, *La Tentation néo-fasciste en France*, p. 129; Lipset, *op. cit.*, p. 157.

55 *L'Express*, 9 January 1956.

56 P. Poujade, *J'ai choisi le combat*, Saint-Céré, Société Générale des Editions et des Publications, 1955, pp. 66, 152.

57 *Le Monde*, 10 January 1956.

58 Milza, *Fascisme français*, pp. 63–66; Poujade, *J'ai choisi le combat*, p. 124.

59 Poujade, *J'ai choisi le combat*, p. 136. The chapter 'Mendès et sa clique' (*ibid.*, pp. 109–16) contains the most bilious attack on Mendès-France and his policies.

60 Poujade, *J'ai choisi le combat*, p. 114.

61 P. Birnbaum, *Un mythe politique: 'la République juive'. De Léon Blum à Pierre Mendès France*, Paris, Fayard, 1988, pp. 179–83.

62 Poujade, *J'ai choisi le combat*, pp. 115–16.

63 Poujade, *J'ai choisi le combat*, p. 110.

64 *Le Monde*, 20 January 1956; also Poujade, *J'ai choisi le combat*, pp. 229–30.

65 Hoffmann, *Le Mouvement Poujade*, pp. 226–27; Touchard, 'Bibliographie et chronologie du Poujadisme', p. 30.

66 Hoffmann, *Le Mouvement Poujade*, p. 226.

67 G. Dupeux, 'Les plates-formes des partis', in Duverger *et al.* (eds), *op. cit.*, p. 62.

68 *Le Monde*, 15–16 January 1956.

69 Hoffmann, *Le Mouvement Poujade*, p. 226; also Poujade, *J'ai choisi le combat*, p. 132.

70 Sternhell, *La Droite révolutionnaire*, pp. 177–214.

71 R. Magraw, *France 1815–1914: The Bourgeois Century*, London, Fontana, 1983, pp. 261–67.

72 Hoffmann, *Le Mouvement Poujade*, p. 280; Touchard, 'Bibliographie et chronologie du Poujadisme', p. 30; Bresson and Lionet, *op. cit.*, pp. 127–28.

73 Poujade, *J'ai choisi le combat*, p. 229.

74 E. Renan, 'Qu'est-ce qu'une nation?', in H. Psichari (ed.), *Œuvres complètes de Ernest Renan*, vol. 1, Paris, Calmann-Lévy, 1947, p. 904.

75 Renan, 'Qu'est-ce qu'une nation?', p. 904; Hoffmann, *Le Mouvement Poujade*, pp. 226–27.

76 Reproduced in Poujade, *J'ai choisi le combat*, pp. 231–32.

77 Winock, *Nationalisme, antisémitisme et fascisme en France*, p. 170.

78 Plumyène and Lasierra, *op. cit.*, p. 234; Hoffmann, *Le Mouvement Poujade*, p. 227; C. Guy, *Le Cas Poujade*, Givors, André Martel, 1955, p. 80.

79 Guy, *op. cit.*, p. 80; Hoffmann, *Le Mouvement Poujade*, pp. 225–27.

80 P. Poujade, 'Notre "apolitisme"', *Le Monde*, 29 December 1955; also *J'ai choisi le combat*, pp. 247–48.

81 Poujade, *J'ai choisi le combat*, p. 26.

82 Touchard, 'Bibliographie et chronologie du Poujadisme', p. 28. 'To resist is therefore the sacred duty, as indicated in the Constitution, the real one, that of [17]89' (Poujade, *J'ai choisi le combat*, p. 244).
83 Poujade, *J'ai choisi le combat*, pp. 43, 250; *Le Monde*, 20 January 1956.
84 Lipset, *op. cit.*, pp. 158–62.
85 Poujadist poster, reproduced in Hoffmann, *Le Mouvement Poujade*, p. 174.
86 Prieur, 'La campagne électorale dans l'Aveyron', p. 344.
87 Hoffmann, *Le Mouvement Poujade*, p. 230. Hoffmann notes that references to the Resistance were toned down during the election campaign in deference to the divisions of opinion that persisted among the French.
88 Poujade, *J'ai choisi le combat*, pp. 123–24, 141–42, 240, and *A l'heure de la colère*, pp. 86–87. Cf. Rebatet, *op. cit.*, p. 523; Bardèche, *Qu'est-ce que le Fascisme?*, p. 98.
89 Poujade, *J'ai choisi le combat*, p. 202; Hoffmann, *Le Mouvement Poujade*, p. 229.
90 Poujade, *J'ai choisi le combat*, p. 142.
91 Poujade, *A l'heure de la colère*, pp. 188, 214. This is a point which Poujade stressed to the author in an interview on 18 April 1995.
92 Poujade, *J'ai choisi le combat*, p. 124.
93 Hoffmann, *Le Mouvement Poujade*, p. 242.
94 Poujade, *A l'heure de la colère*, pp. 153, 155; Duprat, *op. cit.*, p. 78. This slogan would much later give Le Pen a ready-made formula in campaigning for a Sixth Republic to replace the Fifth.
95 P. Campbell, 'Le Mouvement Poujade', *Parliamentary Affairs*, vol. 10, no. 3, 1957, pp. 362, 364; also Hoffmann, *Le Mouvement Poujade*, pp. 251–54.
96 On echoes of Alain in Poujadism, see Hoffmann, *Le Mouvement Poujade*, pp. 211–13, 228, 388.
97 Poujade, *A l'heure de la colère*, p. 171; also Plumyène and Lasierra, *op. cit.*, pp. 229–32.
98 Touchard, 'Bibliographie et chronologie du Poujadisme', p. 30.
99 Williams, *Crisis and Compromise*, p. 163.
100 Touchard, 'Bibliographie et chronologie du Poujadisme', p. 32. On the early communist influence and subsequent 'purge', see Hoffmann, *Le Mouvement Poujade*, pp. 38–40, 58–61, 349–56.
101 Milza, *Fascisme français*, p. 301.
102 Duprat, *op. cit.*, p. 60; also Milza, *Fascisme français*, pp. 307–8; Touchard, 'Bibliographie et chronologie du Poujadisme', p. 43.
103 Poujade claimed that he employed these former collaborationists in defiance of their unjust ostracism by the post-war press establishment: 'My opinion on them was clear: either they acted against France and should have been shot, or they had paid their debt and should not be barred from working and becoming part of society again' (*A l'heure de la colère*, p. 151).
104 Hoffmann, *Le Mouvement Poujade*, p. 225.
105 Hoffmann, *Le Mouvement Poujade*, p. 354.
106 Plumyène and Lasierra, *op. cit.*, p. 238.
107 W. Rochet, 'Le caractère fasciste du "mouvement" poujadiste', *Les Cahiers du communisme*, March 1956, pp. 194–211.
108 On Poujade and Dorgères, see Hoffmann, *Le Mouvement Poujade*, pp. 337–41; Plumyène and Lasierra, *op. cit.*, pp. 234–37.
109 Poujade, *A l'heure de la colère*, pp. 224–33, and *L'Histoire sans masque*, pp. 121–33.
110 Williams, *Crisis and Compromise*, p. 162; Poujade, *L'Histoire sans masque*, p. 86.
111 Duprat, *op. cit.*, pp. 76–78.
112 Hoffmann, *Le Mouvement Poujade*, pp. 388, 392–95. In his later campaigning for *Algérie Française*, Poujade would boast of bringing together 'huge gatherings of communists and royalists alike' (*A l'heure de la colère*, p. 225).
113 Hoffmann, *Le Mouvement Poujade*, pp. 363–65.
114 Algazy, *La Tentation néo-fasciste en France*, p. 105.

115 Algazy, *La Tentation néo-fasciste en France*, pp. 111–12.

116 Dupeux, 'Les plates-formes des partis', p. 63.

117 *Le Monde*, 5 January 1956; also *L'Express*, 4 January 1956.

118 Algazy, *La Tentation néo-fasciste en France*, p. 153.

119 M. Bardèche, 'Histoire du Mouvement Poujade', *Défense de l'Occident* (spec. no. 'Le Poujadisme'), no. 33, May 1956, pp. 3–27.

120 Poujade, *A l'heure de la colère*, p. 20.

121 On the Republican idealism inherent in Poujadism, see Hoffmann, *Le Mouvement Poujade*, pp. 228–34.

122 G. Warner, 'France', in S. J. Woolf (ed.), *Fascism in Europe*, London, Methuen, 1981, p. 314.

123 Shields, 'An Enigma Still: Poujadism Fifty Years On', pp. 47–48.

124 Bardèche, *Qu'est-ce que le Fascisme?*, p. 108.

125 Poujade, *A l'heure de la colère*, p. 161.

126 Hoffmann, *Le Mouvement Poujade*, p. 388; also pp. 389–90, 251–54.

127 J.-C. Petitfils, *L'Extrême droite en France*, Paris, Presses Universitaires de France, 1983, p. 89.

128 Poujade denounced with equal vehemence 'atrocious Anglo-American capitalism and vile Russian dictatorship' (Hoffmann, *Le Mouvement Poujade*, p. 410).

129 Hoffmann, *Le Mouvement Poujade*, p. 154; also pp. 235–40.

130 Plumyène and Lasierra, *op. cit.*, pp. 241–42, 248.

131 Campbell, 'Le Mouvement Poujade', p. 365.

132 Campbell, 'Le Mouvement Poujade', p. 365.

133 J. Stoetzel and P. Hassner, 'Résultats d'un sondage dans le premier secteur de la Seine', in Duverger *et al.* (eds), *op. cit.*, pp. 226–27.

134 *Le Monde*, 12 January 1956.

135 Rioux, *La France de la Quatrième République*, vol. 2, pp. 79–80.

136 P.-H. Simon, 'L'Appel du vide', *Le Monde*, 25 January 1956; Wright, *France in Modern Times*, p. 405.

137 Rioux, 'Des clandestins aux activistes', p. 227.

138 Milza, *Fascisme français*, p. 308.

139 *Rivarol*, quoted in Hoffmann, *Le Mouvement Poujade*, p. 365.

4 Algeria: another war, another 'fascism'

1 Duprat, *op. cit.*, pp. 60, 62.

2 P. Hainsworth, 'The Extreme Right in Post-War France: The Emergence and Success of the Front National', in P. Hainsworth (ed.), *The Extreme Right in Europe and the USA*, London, Pinter, 1992, p. 32.

3 So named, it is thought, because of the shoes that distinguished the European settlers from the sandal-wearing or barefoot North African population.

4 Wright, *France in Modern Times*, p. 431; Algazy, *La Tentation néo-fasciste en France*, pp. 221–22.

5 P. Montagnon, *La Guerre d'Algérie: genèse et engrenage d'une tragédie*, Paris, Pygmalion/Gérard Watelet, 1984, pp. 127–28.

6 Montagnon, *op. cit.*, pp. 217–18.

7 Gildea, *France since 1945*, p. 21.

8 Algazy, *La Tentation néo-fasciste en France*, p. 97.

9 Del Boca and Giovana, *op. cit.*, p. 181.

10 Anderson, *op. cit.*, pp. 280–81. For the same estimate of a thousand extreme-right groups active in the early 1960s, see R. Chiroux, *L'Extrême-droite sous la Ve République*, Paris, Librairie Générale de Droit et de Jurisprudence, 1974, p. 92.

11 Algazy, *La Tentation néo-fasciste en France*, p. 223.

12 Algazy, *La Tentation néo-fasciste en France*, p. 172.
13 Del Boca and Giovana, *op. cit.*, p. 175.
14 Hoffmann, 'Paradoxes of the French Political Community', in Hoffmann *et al.*, *In Search of France*, p. 83.
15 Algazy, *La Tentation néo-fasciste en France*, p. 124.
16 Radio-televised broadcast of 16 September 1959.
17 *L'Espoir Nationaliste*, quoted in Algazy, *La Tentation néo-fasciste en France*, p. 172.
18 Milza, *Fascisme français*, p. 312; Rioux, 'Des clandestins aux activistes', p. 233.
19 Duprat, *op. cit.*, pp. 56–58, 70–74, 87–93.
20 Algazy, *La Tentation néo-fasciste en France*, pp. 120, 160, 168; Milza, *Fascisme français*, pp. 296–97.
21 Del Boca and Giovana, *op. cit.*, p. 180.
22 Milza, *Fascisme français*, pp. 319–20.
23 Duprat, *op. cit.*, p. 73.
24 Algazy, *La Tentation néo-fasciste en France*, pp. 119–20, 161–66.
25 Chiroux, *op. cit.*, p. 120 n. 419.
26 Algazy, *La Tentation néo-fasciste en France*, p. 284.
27 Algazy, *La Tentation néo-fasciste en France*, pp. 192–99.
28 A.-M. Duranton-Crabol, 'Du combat pour l'Algérie française au combat pour la culture européenne', in J.-P. Rioux and J.-F. Sirinelli (eds), *La Guerre d'Algérie et les intellectuels français*, Brussels, Editions Complexe, 1991, p. 72.
29 Algazy, *La Tentation néo-fasciste en France*, p. 196.
30 A.-M. Duranton-Crabol, *Visages de la Nouvelle Droite. Le GRECE et son histoire*, Paris, Presses de la Fondation Nationale des Sciences Politiques, 1988, pp. 22–25.
31 Algazy, *La Tentation néo-fasciste en France*, p. 124.
32 Coston *et al.*, *op. cit.*, p. 214 n. 21; also Duprat, *op. cit.*, p. 88.
33 Coston *et al.*, *op. cit.*, p. 214; Algazy, *La Tentation néo-fasciste en France*, p. 159.
34 Algazy, *La Tentation néo-fasciste en France*, p. 165.
35 Algazy, *La Tentation néo-fasciste en France*, pp. 182–92; Milza, *Fascisme français*, pp. 311, 315–17.
36 Algazy, *La Tentation néo-fasciste en France*, p. 183 n.
37 Gordon, *op. cit.*, p. 337.
38 Algazy, *La Tentation néo-fasciste en France*, p. 188.
39 Algazy, *La Tentation néo-fasciste en France*, p. 186.
40 Del Boca and Giovana, *op. cit.*, p. 175.
41 Chiroux, *op. cit.*, p. 77 n. 292.
42 Algazy, *La Tentation néo-fasciste en France*, pp. 234–35.
43 *Qu'est-ce que le Fascisme?*, pp. 9, 54.
44 Algazy, *La Tentation néo-fasciste en France*, pp. 214–20, and *L'Extrême-droite en France de 1965 à 1984*, Paris, L'Harmattan, 1989, p. 167.
45 *Qu'est-ce que le Fascisme?*, pp. 10, 12, 33.
46 Algazy, *La Tentation néo-fasciste en France*, pp. 200, 242–43.
47 *Qu'est-ce que le Fascisme?*, p. 14.
48 *Qu'est-ce que le Fascisme?*, p. 15.
49 On Italy and Germany, see *Qu'est-ce que le Fascisme?*, pp. 15–56.
50 *Qu'est-ce que le Fascisme?*, pp. 26, 28.
51 *Qu'est-ce que le Fascisme?*, p. 44.
52 *Qu'est-ce que le Fascisme?*, pp. 30–31, 53–54. Bardèche's remarks here are at odds with his reported claim elsewhere that there was no policy of systematic extermination of the Jews (Algazy, *La Tentation néo-fasciste en France*, p. 210).
53 *Qu'est-ce que le Fascisme?*, p. 32.
54 *Qu'est-ce que le Fascisme?*, p. 94.
55 *Qu'est-ce que le Fascisme?*, pp. 76, 95–97.
56 *Qu'est-ce que le Fascisme?*, pp. 33, 74.

57 *Qu'est-ce que le Fascisme?*, pp. 93, 112.
58 *Qu'est-ce que le Fascisme?*, pp. 106–8, 112–15.
59 E. Weber, 'Nationalism, Socialism, and National-Socialism in France', *French Historical Studies*, vol. 2, no. 3, 1962, p. 292.
60 *Qu'est-ce que le Fascisme?*, pp. 106–8, 143.
61 *Qu'est-ce que le Fascisme?*, pp. 93–94, 106–8, 165. The 'anger of the nation', Bardèche insists, 'is the very blood that irrigates fascism'.
62 *Qu'est-ce que le Fascisme?*, pp. 55-56, 177.
63 *Qu'est-ce que le Fascisme?*, pp. 50, 75; Del Boca and Giovana, *op. cit.*, p. 180.
65 On the 'revisionist strategy for dehistoricising fascism' pioneered by Bardèche and pursued by others, see R. Griffin, 'Plus ça change! The Fascist Pedigree of the Nouvelle Droite', in Arnold (ed.), *op. cit.*, pp. 217–52.
65 *Qu'est-ce que le Fascisme?*, pp. 108, 194–95.
66 *Qu'est-ce que le Fascisme?*, pp. 115–21, 123–32, 149–50.
67 *Qu'est-ce que le Fascisme?*, pp. 112–15.
68 *Qu'est-ce que le Fascisme?*, pp. 120–21.
69 Algazy, *La Tentation néo-fasciste en France*, pp. 213–14.
70 Algazy, *La Tentation néo-fasciste en France*, p. 213.
71 M. Bardèche, 'Le drame de l'Algérie', *Défense de l'Occident*, no. 32, April 1956, pp. 3–9.
72 Algazy, *La Tentation néo-fasciste en France*, pp. 80, 302.
73 Duranton-Crabol, 'Du combat pour l'Algérie française au combat pour la culture européenne', pp. 66–71.
74 Algazy, *La Tentation néo-fasciste en France*, pp. 144, 151.
75 Del Boca and Giovana, *op. cit.*, p. 181.
76 *Le Monde*, 20–21 November 1960.
77 Le Pen, *Les Français d'abord*, p. 50.
78 Algazy, *La Tentation néo-fasciste en France*, p. 237.
79 Algazy, *La Tentation néo-fasciste en France*, pp. 228–29.
80 Wright, *France in Modern Times*, p. 437. For a much smaller figure of 415 dead and 1,145 injured, see Del Boca and Giovana, *op. cit.*, p. 196.
81 Rousso, *op. cit.*, p. 97.
82 Chiroux, *op. cit.*, p. 77 n. 292.
83 Le Pen, *Les Français d'abord*, p. 50.
84 Chiroux, *op. cit.*, p. 77 n. 292; Montagnon, *op. cit.*, pp. 217–18.
85 Williams, *Crisis and Compromise*, p. 162.
86 Rousso, *op. cit.*, p. 97; Gildea, *France since 1945*, p. 26.
87 *Le Monde*, 17 October 1997.
88 R. J. Golsan (ed.), *The Papon Affair: Memory and Justice on Trial*, New York, Routledge, 2000, pp. 223–42; W. B. Cohen, 'The Sudden Memory of Torture: The Algerian War in French Discourse, 2000–2001', *French Politics, Culture and Society*, vol. 19, no. 3, 2001, p. 92 n. 19. The government-commissioned Geronimi report in 1999 arrived at a figure of 48 documented deaths attributable to police actions on the night of 17–18 October 1961 (*Le Monde*, 13 August 1999).
89 On Papon's long administrative career (spanning the Popular Front, Vichy, the Fourth and Fifth Republics), see *Le Monde*, 23 April 1994.
90 Anderson, *op. cit.*, p. 288.
91 Duprat, *op. cit.*, p. 115.
92 Plumyène and Lasierra, *op. cit.*, p. 291.
93 Milza, *Fascisme français*, p. 323; Algazy, *La Tentation néo-fasciste en France*, pp. 233–34, 237–38.
94 Del Boca and Giovana, *op. cit.*, p. 197.
95 Reproduced in Algazy, *La Tentation néo-fasciste en France*, pp. 224–25.

96 Del Boca and Giovana, *op. cit.*, p. 197; Algazy, *La Tentation néo-fasciste en France*, p. 234.

97 Algazy, *La Tentation néo-fasciste en France*, p. 235. A notable exception was again Bardèche, who took up the opposite position of sympathising with the Algerian Arabs and castigating the Israelis for 'disembowelling hundreds of Arab women and children without incurring any criticism' ('Le drame de l'Algérie', p. 6).

98 Le Pen, *Les Français d'abord*, pp. 47–51.

99 P.-H. Simon, 'Situations exceptionnelles', *Le Monde*, 30 May 1957.

100 Bresson and Lionet, *op. cit.*, pp. 177–78. For a statement of Le Pen's subsequent position, see his letter in *Le Monde* of 17 July 2002.

101 Larkin, *op. cit.*, p. 260.

102 Bresson and Lionet, *op. cit.*, pp. 174–75, 183–84, 190–91.

103 Le Pen, *Les Français d'abord*, pp. 48–49; Bresson and Lionet, *op. cit.*, p. 184.

104 Bresson and Lionet, *op. cit.*, p. 184.

105 Bresson and Lionet, *op. cit.*, pp. 187–90.

106 Le Pen, *Les Français d'abord*, p. 48.

107 *Journal Officiel*, quoted in Bresson and Lionet, *op. cit.*, p. 191.

108 Verdès-Leroux, *Refus et violences*, p. 80 n. 2.

109 Bresson and Lionet, *op. cit.*, pp. 193–95.

110 Bresson and Lionet, *op. cit.*, pp. 195–96, 279–82. For a time in the 1970s, Le Pen would cut an idiosyncratic figure by wearing an eye patch.

111 Bresson and Lionet, *op. cit.*, p. 200.

112 Le Pen, *Les Français d'abord*, p. 49; Bresson and Lionet, *op. cit.*, pp. 203–8.

113 La Documentation Française, *Institutions et vie politique sous la Ve République*, Paris, 2003, p. 174. Unless otherwise indicated, results for national elections under the Fifth Republic are cited from this source.

114 Bresson and Lionet, *op. cit.*, pp. 208–10, 225.

115 Le Pen, *Les Français d'abord*, pp. 49–51.

116 Bresson and Lionet, *op. cit.*, pp. 218–29.

117 Rioux, 'Des clandestins aux activistes', p. 236; Milza, *Fascisme français*, pp. 317–18; Bresson and Lionet, *op. cit.*, pp. 213–14, 229.

118 Algazy, *La Tentation néo-fasciste en France*, p. 227.

119 Duprat, *op. cit.*, pp. 99–102; Bresson and Lionet, *op. cit.*, pp. 230–31.

120 On Le Pen's stance following the January 1961 referendum and his measured support for the OAS, see Bresson and Lionet, *op. cit.*, pp. 232–52.

121 Bresson and Lionet, *op. cit.*, p. 206. Skorzeny had led the German commando unit that sprang Mussolini from captivity in 1943 and subsequently organised the escape into exile of numerous Nazis through his ODESSA network (Del Boca and Giovana, *op. cit.*, pp. 79–82).

122 *Combat*, 9 February 1956.

123 Bresson and Lionet, *op. cit.*, p. 247.

124 Front National, *Pour un avenir français*, pp. 61, 144.

125 Anderson, *op. cit.*, p. 287.

126 Milza, *Fascisme français*, p. 325.

127 W. R. Tucker, 'The New Look of the Extreme Right in France', *Western Political Quarterly*, vol. 21, no. 1, 1968, p. 87.

128 Algazy, *La Tentation néo-fasciste en France*, p. 222.

129 Chiroux, *op. cit.*, p. 80.

130 Bresson and Lionet, *op. cit.*, p. 276.

131 Chiroux, *op. cit.*, p. 87 n. 318; Gildea, *France since 1945*, p. 28.

132 Duprat, *op. cit.*, p. 119.

133 Duprat, *op. cit.*, p. 64.

134 Algazy, *La Tentation néo-fasciste en France*, p. 233. Bringing together revolutionaries and extreme reactionaries, the OAS never developed a coherent doctrine and 'was

obliged to be vague, in order to avoid offending one or other of its many factions' (Del Boca and Giovana, *op. cit.*, p. 196).
135 Bresson and Lionet, *op. cit.*, p. 257.

5 The extreme right in the 1960s

1 On the PPNS, see Algazy, *La Tentation néo-fasciste en France*, pp. 252–64.
2 Algazy, *La Tentation néo-fasciste en France*, p. 248.
3 Algazy, *La Tentation néo-fasciste en France*, pp. 249–51.
4 Milza, *Fascisme français*, pp. 315–17; Del Boca and Giovana, *op. cit.*, p. 191.
5 Anderson, *op. cit.*, p. 287; Algazy, *La Tentation néo-fasciste en France*, pp. 225–26.
6 Duprat, *op. cit.*, p. 122; Algazy, *L'Extrême-droite en France*, pp. 33–34.
7 Algazy, *La Tentation néo-fasciste en France*, p. 267.
8 Duranton-Crabol, 'Du combat pour l'Algérie française au combat pour la culture européenne', p. 63.
9 P. Fysh and J. Wolfreys, *The Politics of Racism in France*, London, Macmillan, 1998, p. 94.
10 Algazy, *La Tentation néo-fasciste en France*, pp. 266, 283.
11 Camus and Monzat, *op. cit.*, p. 45.
12 *Europe-Action*, May 1963, quoted in Algazy, *La Tentation néo-fasciste en France*, pp. 280–81.
13 Algazy, *La Tentation néo-fasciste en France*, pp. 265–68.
14 Algazy, *La Tentation néo-fasciste en France*, p. 269.
15 Camus and Monzat, *op. cit.*, p. 45.
16 Algazy, *La Tentation néo-fasciste en France*, pp. 282–83.
17 Duranton-Crabol, 'Du combat pour l'Algérie française au combat pour la culture européenne', pp. 65, 73. With François d'Orcival, Laroche published a paean to Smith's regime entitled *Rhodésie, pays des lions fidèles* (*Rhodesia, the Country of Faithful Lions*) (Paris, La Table Ronde, 1966).
18 Duranton-Crabol, *Visages de la Nouvelle Droite*, pp. 27–28.
19 Algazy, *La Tentation néo-fasciste en France*, pp. 269–70; Duranton-Crabol, *Visages de la Nouvelle Droite*, p. 27.
20 Chebel d'Appollonia, *L'Extrême-droite en France*, pp. 309–10.
21 Duranton-Crabol, *Visages de la Nouvelle Droite*, p. 25.
22 Algazy, *La Tentation néo-fasciste en France*, pp. 270–71.
23 Algazy, *La Tentation néo-fasciste en France*, pp. 271–74.
24 J. Brunn, *La Nouvelle Droite. Le dossier du 'procès'*, Paris, Nouvelles Editions Oswald, 1979, p. 43
25 Algazy, *La Tentation néo-fasciste en France*, p. 273.
26 Anderson, *op. cit.*, p. 285; Algazy, *La Tentation néo-fasciste en France*, p. 283.
27 Duprat, *op. cit.*, p. 133.
28 Algazy, *La Tentation néo-fasciste en France*, pp. 284–85.
29 Duranton-Crabol, *Visages de la Nouvelle Droite*, p. 29.
30 Duprat, *op. cit.*, p. 134; Duranton-Crabol, *Visages de la Nouvelle Droite*, p. 30.
31 Algazy, *La Tentation néo-fasciste en France*, pp. 286–87.
32 Cole and Campbell, *op. cit.*, p. 96.
33 Milza, *Fascisme français*, pp. 324–25.
34 Bresson and Lionet, *op. cit.*, pp. 256, 258.
35 Tucker, 'The New Look of the Extreme Right in France', p. 90.
36 Williams, *Crisis and Compromise*, p. 161.
37 Bresson and Lionet, *op. cit.*, p. 257; Duprat, *op. cit.*, pp. 127–28.
38 P. Rees, *Biographical Dictionary of the Extreme Right since 1890*, New York/London, Harvester Wheatsheaf, 1990, p. 390.

39 C. Ysmal, 'La stratégie des formations politiques devant la perspective de l'élection présidentielle', in Centre d'Etude de la Vie Politique Française (CEVIPOF), *L'Election présidentielle des 5 et 19 décembre 1965*, Paris, Armand Colin/Fondation Nationale des Sciences Politiques, 1970, p. 71.

40 Anderson, *op. cit.*, p. 290; Bresson and Lionet, *op. cit.*, p. 266.

41 Duprat, *op. cit.*, pp. 128–30.

42 *Le Nouveau Candide*, 3 December 1964, quoted in Algazy, *L'Extrême-droite en France*, pp. 21–22.

43 Bresson and Lionet, *op. cit.*, p. 269.

44 Chiroux, *op. cit.*, pp. 90, 118–19.

45 Chiroux, *op. cit.*, p. 115.

46 Tucker, 'The New Look of the Extreme Right in France', p. 96; Duprat, *op. cit.*, p. 128; Anderson, *op. cit.*, p. 290.

47 Algazy, *L'Extrême-droite en France*, p. 22.

48 Bresson and Lionet, *op. cit.*, pp. 269–70, 370.

49 Algazy, *L'Extrême-droite en France*, p. 22.

50 R.-G. Schwartzenberg, *La Campagne présidentielle de 1965*, Paris, Presses Universitaires de France, 1967, p. 60; Bresson and Lionet, *op. cit.*, p. 267; Duprat, *op. cit.*, p. 131; Chiroux, *op. cit.*, p. 91 n. 334.

51 Bresson and Lionet, *op. cit.*, pp. 263–65.

52 Schwartzenberg, *op. cit.*, pp. 67–68, 71 n. 4, 80 n. 2.

53 Bresson and Lionet, *op. cit.*, pp. 114, 250, 266; Algazy, *L'Extrême-droite en France*, p. 21.

54 J.-L. Tixier-Vignancour, *J'ai choisi la défense*, Paris, La Table Ronde, 1964. On Tixier-Vignancour's campaign, see R. Cayrol and J.-L. Parodi, 'Propagandes', in CEVIPOF, *L'Election présidentielle des 5 et 19 décembre 1965*, pp. 203–6.

55 J.-L. Parodi, 'Thèmes', in CEVIPOF, *L'Election présidentielle des 5 et 19 décembre 1965*, p. 238 n. 8.

56 Duprat, *op. cit.*, pp. 253–54. Others on the extreme right used the same anti-constitutional argument against de Gaulle (Schwartzenberg, *op. cit.*, pp. 44–45).

57 Schwartzenberg, *op. cit.*, p. 113.

58 Schwartzenberg, *op. cit.*, pp. 111–12; Bresson and Lionet, *op. cit.*, p. 265; Parodi, 'Thèmes', in CEVIPOF, *L'Election présidentielle des 5 et 19 décembre 1965*, pp. 255–56.

59 Chiroux, *op. cit.*, p. 111.

60 Parodi, 'Thèmes', in CEVIPOF, *L'Election présidentielle des 5 et 19 décembre 1965*, p. 256.

61 Schwartzenberg, *op. cit.*, pp. 120–21.

62 Tucker, 'The New Look of the Extreme Right in France', p. 92; Parodi, 'Thèmes', in CEVIPOF, *L'Election présidentielle des 5 et 19 décembre 1965*, p. 256.

63 Tucker, 'The New Look of the Extreme Right in France', p. 91

64 Chiroux, *op. cit.*, p. 111 n. 374.

65 Tixier-Vignancour, interview with *Minute*, 24 April 1964, quoted in Algazy, *L'Extrême-droite en France*, p. 22.

66 Bresson and Lionet, *op. cit.*, p. 265. Tixier-Vignancour had already hinted that this post would go instead to the former Prime Minister and diehard partisan of *Algérie Française*, Georges Bidault, then still in exile (Anderson, *op. cit.*, p. 291).

67 Tucker, 'The New Look of the Extreme Right in France', p. 90.

68 Schwartzenberg, *op. cit.*, p. 113.

69 Schwartzenberg, *op. cit.*, p. 113; Algazy, *L'Extrême-droite en France*, p. 21; Anderson, *op. cit.*, p. 290.

70 Ysmal, 'La stratégie des formations politiques', in CEVIPOF, *L'Election présidentielle des 5 et 19 décembre 1965*, p. 73; Parodi, 'Thèmes', in *ibid.*, p. 255.

71 Bresson and Lionet, *op. cit.*, p. 273; Ysmal, 'La stratégie des formations politiques', in CEVIPOF, *L'Election présidentielle des 5 et 19 décembre 1965*, p. 72.

72 Chiroux, *op. cit.*, pp. 94–96, 99–101, 112–13.

73 Schwartzenberg, *op. cit.*, p. 44.
74 Chiroux, *op. cit.*, p. 118.
75 Schwartzenberg, *op. cit.*, p. 23.
76 Duprat, *op. cit.*, p. 128.
77 Duprat, *op. cit.*, pp. 129–31.
78 Chiroux, *op. cit.*, p. 103; Duprat, *op. cit.*, pp. 253–54.
79 Anderson, *op. cit.*, p. 290.
80 E. Deutsch *et al.*, *Les Familles politiques aujourd'hui en France*, Paris, Editions de Minuit, 1966, pp. 64, 70; also Chiroux, *op. cit.*, pp. 90–91, 104.
81 Deutsch *et al.*, *op. cit.*, p. 125.
82 R. Cayrol and J.-L. Parodi, 'Relais', in CEVIPOF, *L'Election présidentielle des 5 et 19 décembre 1965*, pp. 130–32.
83 Anderson, *op. cit.*, p. 291.
84 Tucker, 'The New Look of the Extreme Right in France', pp. 93–94; Schwartzenberg, *op. cit.*, p. 115; Duprat, *op. cit.*, p. 121.
85 Parodi, 'Thèmes', in CEVIPOF, *L'Election présidentielle des 5 et 19 décembre 1965*, pp. 278–79.
86 Schwartzenberg, *op. cit.*, p. 80 n. 2.
87 Cayrol and Parodi, 'Propagandes', in CEVIPOF, *L'Election présidentielle des 5 et 19 décembre 1965*, pp. 206, 216.
88 Bresson and Lionet, *op. cit.*, pp. 262–63.
89 Duprat, *op. cit.*, p. 129; Chiroux, *op. cit.*, p. 106.
90 This attitude would find its most perverse expression in the 1997 legislative elections. See Chapter 10.
91 Bresson and Lionet, *op. cit.*, pp. 268–69, 273–75.
92 Bresson and Lionet, *op. cit.*, p. 276.
93 Chiroux, *op. cit.*, p. 121.
94 Tucker, 'The New Look of the Extreme Right in France', p. 95.
95 Algazy, *L'Extrême-droite en France*, pp. 24–35.
96 Duprat, *op. cit.*, p. 254; F. Goguel, 'Analyse des résultats', in CEVIPOF, *L'Election présidentielle des 5 et 19 décembre 1965*, p. 396.
97 A. Hauriou, 'La fin des extrémismes?', *Le Monde*, 25 December 1965.
98 Anderson, *op. cit.*, p. 292; Chiroux, *op. cit.*, pp. 111–12.
99 Duprat, *op. cit.*, p. 254.
100 Chiroux, *op. cit.*, pp. 123–29; La Documentation Française, *Institutions et vie politique*, p. 174.
101 In an interview with the author on 15 April 2005, Le Pen identified his support for Tixier-Vignancour in 1965 and his decision not to stand himself as the major regret of his political life, robbing the nationalist right of a 'historic opportunity' to unify definitively around a common leader and programme. It would be a further seven years before this project would be undertaken with the launch of the FN in 1972.
102 Gaultier had also been a member of the PPF and served as an official under Paul Marion at Vichy (Randa, *op. cit.*, p. 164).
103 Bresson and Lionet, *op. cit.*, p. 254.
104 *Le Monde*, 23–24 November 1969; Mauge, *op. cit.*, pp. 185–87; Algazy, *L'Extrême-droite en France*, p. 73.
105 Bresson and Lionet, *op. cit.*, p. 277.
106 Algazy, *L'Extrême-droite en France*, p. 24.
107 Algazy, *L'Extrême-droite en France*, p. 26.
108 Duprat, *op. cit.*, pp. 132–35; Algazy, *L'Extrême-droite en France*, pp. 27, 31.
109 Algazy, *L'Extrême-droite en France*, pp. 33, 35; Duprat, *op. cit.*, p. 133.
110 Tucker, 'The New Look of the Extreme Right in France', p. 95; Algazy, *L'Extrême-droite en France*, pp. 29–30. The MNP set up a France-Rhodesia Committee in

support of Ian Smith's regime and of 'all the white communities of southern Africa', under the presidency of the Waffen-SS veteran Marc Augier (alias Saint-Loup) (Algazy, *L'Extrême-droite en France*, p. 32).

111 Algazy, *L'Extrême-droite en France*, pp. 31–33.
112 Algazy, *L'Extrême-droite en France*, p. 36.
113 For the REL's programme, see Duprat, *op. cit.*, pp. 259–63.
114 Duprat, *op. cit.*, p. 136; Algazy, *L'Extrême-droite en France*, pp. 36–37.
115 Duprat, *op. cit.*, pp. 135–37, 265–67.
116 Algazy, *L'Extrême-droite en France*, pp. 38–39.
117 Duprat, *op. cit.*, pp. 124–25. Sidos and Venner had collaborated at the head of Jeune Nation and the Parti Nationaliste. Besides the personal rivalry between the two, the catalyst for this split was the stance taken by the FEN's *Cahiers universitaires* in autumn 1963 against military service in 'the Gaullist army that sold out French Algeria'.
118 Algazy, *L'Extrême-droite en France*, p. 45.
119 Duprat, *op. cit.*, p. 132; Algazy, *L'Extrême-droite en France*, p. 60.
120 Milza, *Fascisme français*, p. 331; Algazy, *L'Extrême-droite en France*, pp. 45, 55. In this spirit, Occident allied itself to the United Front of Support for South Vietnam set up by the former OAS activist Roger Holeindre.
121 J.-C. Cambadélis and E. Osmond, *La France blafarde. Une histoire politique de l'extrême droite*, Paris, Plon, 1998, p. 64.
122 Duprat, *op. cit.*, p. 126; Algazy, *L'Extrême-droite en France*, p. 46.
123 Duprat, *op. cit.*, p. 142.
124 Algazy, *L'Extrême-droite en France*, pp. 47–48.
125 Algazy, *L'Extrême-droite en France*, p. 49.
126 Extracts from *Occident-Université* and *Le Soleil*, quoted in Algazy, *L'Extrême-droite en France*, pp. 47–51. The *Protocols of the Elders of Zion* was a document first published in Russia in 1905, then widely republished in the 1920s, supposedly confirming a Jewish conspiracy to dominate the world. It is generally held to have been forged by the Tsarist secret police to legitimise anti-Semitic pogroms.
127 On the political evolution of these erstwhile radicals, see F. Charpier, *Génération Occident. De l'extrême droite à la droite*, Paris, Seuil, 2005.
128 Algazy, *L'Extrême-droite en France*, pp. 51, 58–59.
129 Duprat, *op. cit.*, p. 256.
130 Quoted in Algazy, *L'Extrême-droite en France*, pp. 61–62. An instance of Occident's ideological confusion was signalled in the report, which detected in some militants a shift of support towards the 'nationalist aspects and anti-Arab imperatives' of Zionism following the Six Day War of June 1967.
131 Cambadélis and Osmond, *op. cit.*, pp. 71–73.
132 Duprat, *op. cit.*, p. 158.
133 Duprat, *op. cit.*, p. 159.
134 Algazy, *L'Extrême-droite en France*, pp. 57–58.
135 Justice Minister René Capitant, quoted in Algazy, *L'Extrême-droite en France*, p. 58.
136 Duprat, *op. cit.*, pp. 177–79; Algazy, *L'Extrême-droite en France*, pp. 58, 64; Cambadélis and Osmond, *op. cit.*, p. 75.
137 *Le Monde*, 30 June 1973.

6 The Nouvelle Droite and Ordre Nouveau

1 Brunn, *op. cit.*, p. 55.
2 A. de Benoist, *Vu de droite. Anthologie critique des idées contemporaines*, Paris, Copernic, 1979, p. 19. When in 1991 the then deputy leader of the FN, Bruno Mégret, remarked that 'electoral victories are always built on ground won first by ideas', he

was merely reiterating this founding principle of the Nouvelle Droite (P. Perrineau, 'Le Front national: 1972–1992', in Winock (ed.), *op. cit.*, p. 294). Elsewhere, the same Mégret would acknowledge the effectiveness of the Gramscian idea of cultural hegemony and its successful implementation by the French Socialist Party in relation to the rights of man (*La Flamme. Les voies de la renaissance*, Paris, Editions Robert Laffont, 1990, pp. 21–41).

3   'Pour un "Gramscisme de droite"' was the title of GRECE's 16th national conference in November 1981 and of an article by de Benoist in a 1977 number of *Eléments* (Duranton-Crabol, *Visages de la Nouvelle Droite*, p. 249; A. Douglas, '"La Nouvelle Droite": G.R.E.C.E. and the Revival of Radical Rightist Thought in Contemporary France', *Tocqueville Review*, vol. 6, no. 2, 1984, p. 383 nn. 3 and 5).

4   A. Rollat, *Les Hommes de l'extrême droite: Le Pen, Marie, Ortiz et les autres*, Paris, Calmann-Lévy, 1985, pp. 155–57.

5   Duranton-Crabol, *Visages de la Nouvelle Droite*, p. 141. For a discussion of de Benoist's project in relation to that of Maurras, see Rémond, *Les Droites en France*, pp. 284–89.

6   A. de Benoist, *Les Idées à l'endroit*, Paris, Editions Libres-Hallier, 1979, pp. 57, 74.

7   Algazy, *La Tentation néo-fasciste en France*, p. 121.

8   De Benoist, *Vu de droite*, p. 16; Douglas, '"La Nouvelle Droite"', p. 362.

9   Editorial article, 'France's "Aryans"', *Patterns of Prejudice*, vol. 13, no. 4, 1979, p. 10; I. R. Barnes, 'The Pedigree of GRECE–I', *Patterns of Prejudice*, vol. 14, no. 3, 1980, p. 21.

10   Brunn, *op. cit.*, pp. 386–87; Algazy, *L'Extrême-droite en France*, p. 244; Camus and Monzat, *op. cit.*, p. 76.

11   Duranton-Crabol, *Visages de la Nouvelle Droite*, pp. 35–36, 56, 58, 250–51; Brunn, *op. cit.*, pp. 375–79.

12   Duranton-Crabol, *Visages de la Nouvelle Droite*, p. 39.

13   Brunn, *op. cit.*, p. 380.

14   Brunn, *op. cit.*, pp. 45–46. For an example of such correspondence, see Roger Lemoine's 'Letter to the Editor', *Patterns of Prejudice*, vol. 14, no. 2, 1980, p. 55.

15   Duranton-Crabol, *Visages de la Nouvelle Droite*, pp. 30, 38.

16   Brunn, *op. cit.*, p. 368.

17   D. Johnson, 'The New Right in France', in L. Cheles *et al.* (eds), *Neo-Fascism in Europe*, London, Longman, 1991, pp. 240–41.

18   Brunn, *op. cit.*, p. 380.

19   M. Billig, *L'Internationale raciste. De la psychologie à la 'science' des races*, Paris, Maspero, 1981, pp. 128–49. The author is grateful to Professor Billig for providing a copy of this out-of-print book.

20   De Benoist, *Vu de droite*, p. 144.

21   Brunn, *op. cit.*, pp. 140–41; also de Benoist, *Les Idées à l'endroit*, pp. 159–62.

22   The winter 1972–73 issue of *Nouvelle Ecole* was devoted to Dumézil and Indo-European studies. For an overview, see also the section 'Le monde des Indo-Européens' in de Benoist's *Vu de droite*, pp. 32–37.

23   Brunn, *op. cit.*, p. 143.

24   Rollat, *op. cit.*, pp. 147–48; Douglas, '"La Nouvelle Droite"', p. 369.

25   Brunn, *op. cit.*, p. 143.

26   Griffin, *The Nature of Fascism*, p. 169.

27   Duranton-Crabol, *Visages de la Nouvelle Droite*, pp. 50–54.

28   De Benoist appropriated the rightist label with some elaborate qualification in his *Vu de droite* (pp. 15–16, 24–25).

29   An instructive statement of the 'organic economics' advocated by GRECE was contained in the article 'Economie organique et société marchande' (*Eléments*, March 1979), reproduced in Brunn, *op. cit.*, pp. 56–69.

30   Douglas, '"La Nouvelle Droite"', pp. 377–78; Brunn, *op. cit.*, p. 68.

31 Rollat, *op. cit.*, p. 149; also de Benoist, *Les Idées à l'endroit*, p. 99.
32 Billig, *L'Internationale raciste*, pp. 128–38; M. Vaughan, '"Nouvelle Droite": Cultural Power and Political Influence', in D. S. Bell (ed.), *Contemporary French Political Parties*, London, Croom Helm, 1982, pp. 58–59; Duranton-Crabol, *Visages de la Nouvelle Droite*, p. 249.
33 *Le Monde*, 30 May 2000.
34 De Benoist, *Vu de droite*, p. 16; Brunn, *op. cit.*, p. 138; L. Pauwels, 'La nouvelle droite', in J.-P. Apparu (ed.), *La Droite aujourd'hui*, Paris, Albin Michel, 1979, p. 170.
35 De Benoist, 'Les idées de la "nouvelle droite"', in Apparu (ed.), *op. cit.*, pp. 117–22; Brunn, *op. cit.*, pp. 137–40; Vaughan, '"Nouvelle Droite": Cultural Power and Political Influence', p. 59; also de Benoist, *Les Idées à l'endroit*, pp. 99–100.
36 De Benoist, *Vu de droite*, pp. 16, 25, and *Les Idées à l'endroit*, p. 99; Brunn, *op. cit.*, pp. 96, 141.
37 M. Bardèche, 'Les silences de la Nouvelle Droite', *Défense de l'Occident*, no. 170, December 1979, pp. 19–20.
38 De Benoist, 'Les idées de la "nouvelle droite"', p. 120.
39 Brunn, *op. cit.*, p. 141; M. Bardèche, 'La "Nouvelle Droite"', *Défense de l'Occident*, no. 167, July–August 1979, p. 10.
40 M. Vaughan, 'Neither New nor Right', *West European Politics*, vol. 4, no. 3, 1981, p. 306.
41 Brunn, *op. cit.*, p. 96.
42 De Benoist, *Les Idées à l'endroit*, p. 147.
43 De Benoist, *Les Idées à l'endroit*, pp. 145–56.
44 See *Le Monde*, 22 June 1979.
45 M. Billig, *Psychology, Racism and Fascism* (Searchlight booklet), Birmingham, A. F. & R. Publications, 1979, pp. 11–26, and *L'Internationale raciste*, pp. 126–28. As Billig noted, all three journals carried advertisements for each other and shared patrons, editorial advisers and occasionally contributors; de Benoist was on the Advisory Board of *Neue Anthropologie* and, in 1976, contributed an article on 'The Misfortunes of the Highly Gifted' (*Psychology, Racism and Fascism*, p. 24).
46 Billig, *L'Internationale raciste*, pp. 129–31.
47 De Benoist, *Les Idées à l'endroit*, p. 153, and *Vu de droite*, p. 180.
48 Billig, *L'Internationale raciste*, pp. 130–45.
49 J.-J. Moureau, 'L'eugénisme: survol historique' (*Nouvelle Ecole*, no. 14, January–February 1971), reproduced in Brunn, *op. cit.*, pp. 97–134.
50 On self-creation and will, see de Benoist, *Les Idées à l'endroit*, pp. 93–100, and 'Les idées de la "nouvelle droite"', p. 122; on inherited intelligence, see de Benoist, *Vu de droite*, pp. 175–80; also Brunn, *op. cit.*, pp. 91–92.
51 De Benoist, *Vu de droite*, p. 83.
52 On Nietzsche, see de Benoist, *Vu de droite*, pp. 81–88; on the three stages of egalitarianism, see T. Sheehan, 'Paris: Moses and Polytheism', in A. Montagu (ed.), *Sociobiology Examined*, Oxford, Oxford University Press, 1980, p. 353.
53 Brunn, *op. cit.*, pp. 7–14, 95.
54 Quoted in Duranton-Crabol, *Visages de la Nouvelle Droite*, pp. 141–42; see also Brunn, *op. cit.*, pp. 379–80.
55 Duranton-Crabol, *Visages de la Nouvelle Droite*, pp. 42–43. By 1979, Alain de Benoist put the membership of GRECE at 'several thousand, organised in regional branches' (*Les Idées à l'endroit*, p. 19); for varying estimates of membership, see Barnes, 'The Pedigree of GRECE–I', p. 21; Camus and Monzat, *op. cit.*, p. 268.
56 Brunn, *op. cit.*, pp. 380, 385.
57 Duranton-Crabol, *Visages de la Nouvelle Droite*, pp. 164, 254–58; Brunn, *op. cit.*, pp. 369–73.
58 On *Le Figaro-Magazine* as a 'research and energy centre' for the Nouvelle Droite, see Pauwels, 'La nouvelle droite', pp. 169–71.

59 Duranton-Crabol, *Visages de la Nouvelle Droite*, p. 192; Douglas, '"La Nouvelle Droite"', p. 379.

60 'La "Nouvelle Droite"' and 'Les silences de la Nouvelle Droite', *Défense de l'Occident*, nos. 167 (pp. 3–16) and 170 (pp. 12–30).

61 Barnes, 'The Pedigree of GRECE–I', p. 21; Sheehan, 'Paris: Moses and Polytheism', p. 355 n. 2.

62 De Benoist, *Les Idées à l'endroit*, pp. 25–26.

63 Rollat, *op. cit.*, p. 153; Vaughan, '"Nouvelle Droite": Cultural Power and Political Influence', pp. 55–56; C. Ysmal, 'Le Giscardisme face aux nouvelles idéologies', in P. Bacot and C. Journès (eds), *Les nouvelles idéologies*, Lyon, Presses Universitaires de Lyon, 1982, p. 157.

64 J. G. Shields, 'Immigration Politics in Mitterrand's France', in G. Raymond (ed.), *France During the Socialist Years*, Aldershot, Dartmouth, 1994, pp. 224–27.

65 Duranton-Crabol, *Visages de la Nouvelle Droite*, p. 127; Douglas, '"La Nouvelle Droite"', p. 380.

66 M. Poniatowski, *L'Avenir n'est écrit nulle part*, Paris, Albin Michel, 1978, pp. 86–95.

67 Poniatowski, *op. cit.*, pp. 144–61.

68 Louis Pauwels, quoted in Bardèche, 'La "Nouvelle Droite"', p. 11.

69 See, for example, the verbatim replication in Poniatowski's book (p. 92) of passages from de Benoist's *Vu de droite* (p. 35).

70 Duranton-Crabol, *Visages de la Nouvelle Droite*, pp. 128, 189; Rollat, *op. cit.*, p. 152; Ysmal, 'Le Giscardisme face aux nouvelles idéologies', pp. 156–57.

71 The book was published by Plon (Paris, 1979) under the collective pseudonym 'Maiastra'.

72 V. Giscard d'Estaing, *Démocratie française*, Paris, Fayard/Livre de poche, 1976, p. 66.

73 Duranton-Crabol, *Visages de la Nouvelle Droite*, p. 130. Alain Rollat records that the subscription list of the journal *Eléments* rose from 2,000 to 6,000 between 1979 and 1981 (*op. cit.*, p. 152).

74 Bardèche, 'Les silences de la Nouvelle Droite', p. 29.

75 Brunn, *op. cit.*, p. 385.

76 For an overview of these movements, see Duprat, *op. cit.*, pp. 167–92, and Algazy, *L'Extrême-droite en France*, pp. 69–88.

77 Formed in February 1968 and still active today, L'Œuvre Française has proved one of the most durable movements on the French extreme right.

78 Algazy, *L'Extrême-droite en France*, pp. 74–76; Duprat, *op. cit.*, pp. 182–84; Camus and Monzat, *op. cit.*, pp. 286–89.

79 Algazy, *L'Extrême-droite en France*, p. 75.

80 While an estimated 88 per cent of extreme-right voters supported Pompidou, diehard anti-Gaullists like Jacques Isorni sided *faute de mieux* with Poher, while others such as Henry Coston came out against both candidates (Chiroux, *op. cit.*, pp. 196–209).

81 Algazy, *L'Extrême-droite en France*, pp. 87–88.

82 Algazy, *L'Extrême-droite en France*, pp. 89–90; Camus and Monzat, *op. cit.*, p. 53. A prominent Vichyite, Jeantet had been one of François Mitterrand's sponsors for the award of the *Francisque* in November 1943 (A. Cole, *François Mitterrand: A Study in Political Leadership*, London, Routledge, 1994, p. 185 n. 11).

83 *Pour un Ordre nouveau*, June 1972 supplement, quoted in Algazy, *L'Extrême-droite en France*, p. 89.

84 Algazy, *L'Extrême-droite en France*, pp. 89–90. The MSI was formed in 1946 to perpetuate the Fascist legacy within the new democratic structures of the post-war Italian state (R. Chiarini, 'The "Movimento Sociale Italiano": A Historical Profile', in Cheles *et al.* (eds), *op. cit.*, pp. 19–42).

85 *Pour un Ordre nouveau*, quoted in Algazy, *L'Extrême-droite en France*, p. 90, and in Rollat, *op. cit.*, pp. 52–53.

86 Algazy, *L'Extrême-droite en France*, pp. 90–91; Cambadélis and Osmond, *op. cit.*, p. 78.
    Jean-François Galvaire, who emerged as leader in the first phase of Ordre
    Nouveau's existence, had begun his political career as a Poujadist militant in support
    of Le Pen's election campaign in 1956; he succeeded Le Pen as head of the
    Poujadist youth movement (UDJF) before going on to play a leading role in Tixier-
    Vignancour's ARLP.

87 Algazy, *L'Extrême-droite en France*, pp. 91–97; Milza, *Fascisme français*, pp. 337–38;
    Duprat, *op. cit.*, pp. 193–98.

88 For a vivid account of the meeting, see *Le Monde*, 15 May 1970; also Rollat, *op. cit.*,
    pp. 50–51.

89 Cambadélis and Osmond, *op. cit.*, p. 82.

90 Algazy, *L'Extrême-droite en France*, p. 93.

91 Algazy, *L'Extrême-droite en France*, pp. 89–90, 96; Cambadélis and Osmond, *op. cit.*, p.
    79. The links between Ordre Nouveau and the MSI were fostered largely through
    the latter's youth wing, the Fronte della Gioventù.

92 Cambadélis and Osmond, *op. cit.*, pp. 86–87; also Milza, *Fascisme français*, pp. 339–40.

93 Duprat, *op. cit.*, p. 199; Algazy, *L'Extrême-droite en France*, p. 115; Camus and Monzat,
    op. cit., p. 53. Cambadélis and Osmond estimate that Ordre Nouveau's membership
    never exceeded 2,500 (*op. cit.*, p. 95).

94 Algazy, *L'Extrême-droite en France*, pp. 99–100. For broadly similar findings, see
    Duprat, *op. cit.*, pp. 279–80; Milza, *Fascisme français*, p. 340.

95 Political charter of Ordre Nouveau, reproduced in Duprat, *op. cit.*, pp. 275–77.

96 Rollat, *op. cit.*, p. 49.

97 Chiroux, *op. cit.*, p. 210 n. 726; Algazy, *L'Extrême-droite en France*, pp. 98, 104–5;
    Duprat, *op. cit.*, p. 204.

98 Cambadélis and Osmond, *op. cit.*, p. 85.

99 Rollat, *op. cit.*, p. 52; Cambadélis and Osmond, *op. cit.*, pp. 83–84.

100 Algazy, *L'Extrême-droite en France*, pp. 102–4; Cambadélis and Osmond, *op. cit.*,
    pp. 83–85; Duprat, *op. cit.*, p. 203.

101 Algazy, *L'Extrême-droite en France*, pp. 114–15.

102 Duprat, *op. cit.*, pp. 199–200; Algazy, *L'Extrême-droite en France*, pp. 106–7.

103 Algazy, *L'Extrême-droite en France*, pp. 106–10; Cambadélis and Osmond, *op. cit.*,
    pp. 85–86.

104 *Pour un Ordre nouveau*, quoted in Algazy, *L'Extrême-droite en France*, pp. 110–11; Rollat,
    op. cit., p. 55.

105 Algazy, *L'Extrême-droite en France*, pp. 112–13.

106 F. Bergeron and P. Vilgier, *De Le Pen à Le Pen. Une histoire des nationaux et des nationalistes
    sous la Ve République*, Saint-Brieuc, Dominique Martin Morin, 1986, pp. 96–97; also
    Algazy, *L'Extrême-droite en France*, pp. 112, 145; Camus and Monzat, *op. cit.*, p. 36.

107 Rollat, *op. cit.*, p. 55.

108 Though there was no common ground between Ordre Nouveau's activism and
    GRECE's project of cultural infiltration, the latter was not above engaging the
    former's militants as a security service.

7 The Front National 1972–81

1 Algazy, *L'Extrême-droite en France*, p. 117.

2 Chiroux, *op. cit.*, pp. 236–37. As early as 1959, Charles Luca's MPF had lamented in
   similar terms the failure of extreme-right groups to 'unite, or choose a leader, or elaborate a doctrine, or accept a framework of common action that would have allowed
   them to become a political force' (Algazy, *La Tentation néo-fasciste en France*, p. 153).

3 Algazy, *L'Extrême-droite en France*, p. 116.

4 Perrineau, 'Le Front national: 1972–1992', p. 244.

5 *Le Monde*, 9 November 1972, 6 and 27 February 1973; Algazy, *La Tentation néo-fasciste en France*, p. 160.
6 A photograph of the event is reproduced in D. Bariller and F. Timmermans (eds), *20 ans au Front. L'Histoire vraie du Front National*, Paris, Editions Nationales, 1993, p. 15.
7 *Le Monde*, 9 November 1972.
8 *Ordre Nouveau Hebdo*, October 1972, quoted in Fysh and Wolfreys, *op. cit.*, p. 97.
9 Algazy, *L'Extrême-droite en France*, p. 117.
10 Williams, *Crisis and Compromise*, p. 160.
11 Algazy, *L'Extrême-droite en France*, p. 117.
12 *Le Monde*, 9 November 1972.
13 *Le Monde*, 22 December 1972.
14 Chiroux, *op. cit.*, p. 217.
15 For a complete list of the FN candidates and their results, see Chiroux, *op. cit.*, pp. 218–31; also *Le Monde*, 27 December 1972; Bresson and Lionet, *op. cit.*, p. 363.
16 *Le Monde*, 9 November 1972, 22 December 1972, and 6 March 1973.
17 *Défendre les Français. C'est le programme du Front National*, supplement to *Front National*, no. 3, February 1973. The author is grateful to Georges Moreau of the FN for providing a rare copy of this original programme.
18 *Le Monde*, 28 February 1973.
19 J.-Y. Camus, 'Origine et formation du Front National (1972–1981)', in N. Mayer and P. Perrineau (eds), *Le Front National à découvert*, Paris, Presses de la Fondation Nationale des Sciences Politiques, 1989, p. 20.
20 Reproduced in Duprat, *op. cit.*, pp. 275–77.
21 C. Calvez, 'Le Problème des travailleurs étrangers', *Journal Officiel de la République Française. Avis et Rapports du Conseil Economique et Social*, no. 7, 27 March 1969, p. 316.
22 *Le Monde*, 27 February 1973.
23 Calvez, 'Le Problème des travailleurs étrangers', p. 316.
24 Chiroux, *op. cit.*, pp. 214–16.
25 Quoted in Algazy, *L'Extrême-droite en France*, p. 119.
26 Algazy, *L'Extrême-droite en France*, p. 122.
27 Cambadélis and Osmond, *op. cit.*, p. 94.
28 *Le Monde*, 30 June 1973; Bresson and Lionet, *op. cit.*, pp. 365–66.
29 Algazy, *L'Extrême-droite en France*, p. 124. According to J.-Y. Camus, Ordre Nouveau counted some 1,850 members when it was banned (*Le Front National. Histoire et analyses*, Paris, Editions Olivier Laurens, 1996, p. 24).
30 *Le Monde*, 15 January 1974.
31 Algazy, *L'Extrême-droite en France*, pp. 134–35, 195–99. Together with its allies in the GUD, Faire Front was opposed not only by the left but also by the extreme-right GAJ, also an offshoot of Ordre Nouveau.
32 Cambadélis and Osmond, *op. cit.*, pp. 97–98; Randa, *op. cit.*, pp. 38–39.
33 On the FN structure which Barthélemy helped to fashion, see Fysh and Wolfreys, *op. cit.*, pp. 97–98, 135–41.
34 Rollat, *op. cit.*, p. 72.
35 Algazy, *L'Extrême-droite en France*, pp. 160–70.
36 On Frédriksen and the FANE, see Algazy, *L'Extrême-droite en France*, pp. 172–87.
37 Algazy, *L'Extrême-droite en France*, p. 164; Cambadélis and Osmond, *op. cit.*, p. 99.
38 Rollat, *op. cit.*, p. 72.
39 Bresson and Lionet, *op. cit.*, pp. 370–71.
40 Algazy, *L'Extrême-droite en France*, p. 211.
41 Rollat, *op. cit.*, p. 63; electoral tract quoted in Algazy, *L'Extrême-droite en France*, p. 211.
42 Algazy, *L'Extrême-droite en France*, pp. 198–99, 210; on the CDPU, see *ibid.*, pp. 151–60.
43 P. Perrineau, 'Les étapes d'une implantation électorale (1972–1988)', in Mayer and Perrineau (eds), *op. cit.*, p. 39.
44 Cambadélis and Osmond, *op. cit.*, pp. 99–100.

45 B. Brigouleix, 'L'extrême droite à la recherche d'un avenir. III – S'organiser', *Le Monde*, 15 June 1976.

46 Algazy, *L'Extrême-droite en France*, pp. 202–3.

47 Rollat, *op. cit.*, p. 65.

48 Algazy, *L'Extrême-droite en France*, p. 205; Camus and Monzat, *op. cit.*, p. 57.

49 On the affinities between GRECE and the PFN, see Rollat, *op. cit.*, pp. 163–67. The prime mover of GRECE, Alain de Benoist, would feature on the PFN's list for the European elections of 1979 (*ibid.*, p. 77).

50 Camus and Monzat, *op. cit.*, pp. 56–57.

51 Bresson and Lionet, *op. cit.*, pp. 376, 378, 381–82.

52 Portelli, *La Politique en France sous la Ve République*, p. 323; S. Dumont *et al.*, *Le Système Le Pen*, Antwerp, Editions EPO, 1985, pp. 145–46; Bresson and Lionet, *op. cit.*, pp. 383–85.

53 Dumont *et al.*, *op. cit.*, pp. 144–47; Bresson and Lionet, *op. cit.*, p. 386; Algazy, *L'Extrême-droite en France*, p. 218.

54 Bresson and Lionet, *op. cit.*, p. 386.

55 Bresson and Lionet, *op. cit.*, pp. 379–80. A different stroke of fortune in September 1976 had made Le Pen the chief legatee of the wealthy industrialist Hubert Lambert, bringing a large (and contested) inheritance to the FN leader.

56 It was suspected in some circles that Duprat was in the employ of the French security services and was murdered by fellow right-wing extremists; other accusations pointed to extreme-left groups, and yet others to Jewish self-defence groups (Rollat, *op. cit.*, pp. 73–74; Algazy, *L'Extrême-droite en France*, pp. 168–69).

57 Quoted in Rollat, *op. cit.*, pp. 74–75. For *Minute*, Duprat's death was 'part of a plot to exterminate the nationalist right through assassinating its leaders and provoking a murderous vendetta among its different tendencies' (Algazy, *L'Extrême-droite en France*, p. 168).

58 Camus and Monzat, *op. cit.*, pp. 34–37.

59 Algazy, *L'Extrême-droite en France*, pp. 144–51.

60 On the contribution made by Antony to the FN, see Rollat, *op. cit.*, pp. 197–205.

61 Rollat, *op. cit.*, pp. 76–77, 80–81.

62 On the 1979 European elections, see Bresson and Lionet, *op. cit.*, pp. 388–94.

63 Portelli, *La Politique en France sous la Ve République*, p. 324.

64 Bresson and Lionet, *op. cit.*, p. 398; Cambadélis and Osmond, *op. cit.*, pp. 110–11.

65 Portelli, *La Politique en France sous la Ve République*, p. 326.

66 Portelli, *La Politique en France sous la Ve République*, p. 326; *Le Monde dossiers et documents: Les élections législatives de juin 1981*.

67 Cambadélis and Osmond, *op. cit.*, pp. 111–12.

68 Bresson and Lionet, *op. cit.*, pp. 373–75.

69 Camus, 'Origine et formation du Front National (1972–1981)', p. 28.

70 Bariller and Timmermans, *20 ans au Front*, p. 36; Bresson and Lionet, *op. cit.*, pp. 381–82.

71 C. Wihtol de Wenden, *Les Immigrés et la politique. Cent cinquante ans d'évolution*, Paris, Presses de la Fondation Nationale des Sciences Politiques, 1988, p. 206.

72 Algazy, *L'Extrême-droite en France*, pp. 122–23.

73 *Le Monde*, 26 September 1973.

74 Dumont *et al.*, *op. cit.*, pp. 119–20; Bresson and Lionet, *op. cit.*, pp. 365–66; Algazy, *L'Extrême-droite en France*, pp. 216–17.

75 Bresson and Lionet, *op. cit.*, p. 385.

76 Algazy, *L'Extrême-droite en France*, p. 219.

77 Wihtol de Wenden, *op. cit.*, p. 206.

78 *Le Monde*, 15 June 1979; P. Weil, *La France et ses étrangers. L'aventure d'une politique de l'immigration 1938–1991*, Paris, Calmann-Lévy, 1991, pp. 107–38.

79 Algazy, *L'Extrême-droite en France*, pp. 220–22.

80 Algazy, *L'Extrême-droite en France*, p. 223.
81 See, for example, Bresson and Lionet, *op. cit.*, p. 371.
82 J.-M. Le Pen, 'Le Front national', in Apparu (ed.), *op. cit.*, pp. 173–81.
83 Rollat, *op. cit.*, p. 69.
84 *Le Monde*, 26 September 1973.
85 Algazy, *L'Extrême-droite en France*, p. 166.
86 *Droite et démocratie économique. Doctrine économique et sociale du Front National*, 2nd edn (first published 1978), Paris, National Hebdo, 1984.
87 J.-M. Le Pen, *L'Espoir*, Paris, Albatros, 1989, p. 117; see S. Bastow, 'Front National Economic Policy: From Neo-Liberalism to Protectionism', *Modern and Contemporary France*, vol. 5, no. 1, 1997, pp. 61–63.
88 Bresson and Lionet, *op. cit.*, pp. 136–38, 385, 396; Camus and Monzat, *op. cit.*, pp. 73–74; Algazy, *L'Extrême-droite en France*, p. 90; Jackson, *France: The Dark Years*, p. 620.
89 *Pour un Ordre nouveau*, June 1973, quoted in Algazy, *L'Extrême-droite en France*, p. 123.
90 Bresson and Lionet, *op. cit.*, pp. 376, 382; Algazy, *L'Extrême-droite en France*, p. 219; Rollat, *op. cit.*, p. 69.

8   The Front National 1981–88

1 La Documentation Française, *Institutions et vie politique*, p. 179. Having failed to secure an alliance with the FN, the PFN could not put together a viable list for these elections.
2 Perrineau, 'Les étapes d'une implantation électorale', pp. 39–40, 43–44.
3 For full results, see *Le Monde*, 19 June 1984.
4 The term *'employé'* translates inadequately as 'employee'. Designating clerical and routine non-manual workers, it is translated here as 'white-collar workers', distinct from 'blue-collar workers' (*'ouvriers'*) and white-collar professionals or managers.
5 BVA poll published in *Le Monde dossiers et documents: l'élection présidentielle 24 avril–8 mai 1988*, May 1988, p. 44.
6 P. Perrineau, *Le Symptôme Le Pen. Radiographie des électeurs du Front national*, Paris, Fayard, 1997, p. 102.
7 J. Marcus, *The National Front and French Politics*, London, Macmillan, 1995, p. 57.
8 Perrineau, 'Les étapes d'une implantation électorale', p. 41. Another notable result was 13.3 per cent in the Grande-Synthe suburb of Dunkerque.
9 Rollat, *op. cit.*, p. 88.
10 Bresson and Lionet, *op. cit.*, p. 399.
11 Camus, *Le Front National*, pp. 48–49; Perrineau, *Le Symptôme Le Pen*, p. 33.
12 P. Martin, *Les Elections municipales en France depuis 1945*, Paris, La Documentation Française, 2001, pp. 112–14; Rollat, *op. cit.*, p. 90; Bresson and Lionet, *op. cit.*, p. 401.
13 F. Gaspard, *Une petite ville en France*, Paris, Gallimard, 1990, p. 119. When Gaspard published her book in 1990, the immigrant population of Dreux stood at 28 per cent and was made up of 67 different nationalities (*ibid.*, pp. 117, 131).
14 Martin, *Les Elections municipales en France depuis 1945*, pp. 115, 120.
15 E. Plenel and A. Rollat, *L'Effet Le Pen*, Paris, La Découverte/*Le Monde*, 1984, p. 99.
16 J.-P. Stirbois, *Tonnerre de Dreux. L'avenir nous appartient*, Paris, Editions National Hebdo, 1988, pp. 72–78.
17 Rollat, *op. cit.*, pp. 95–97.
18 SOFRES, *Opinion publique 1985*, Paris, Gallimard, 1985, pp. 182–83.
19 Le Pen, *Les Français d'abord*, pp. 15–16, 211–46.
20 E. Faux *et al.*, *La Main droite de Dieu. Enquête sur François Mitterrand et l'extrême droite*, Paris, Seuil, 1994, pp. 21–24; Le Pen, *Les Français d'abord*, pp. 201–10; Bresson and Lionet, *op. cit.*, pp. 405–8.
21 Cambadélis and Osmond, *op. cit.*, p. 226.

22 Bresson and Lionet, *op. cit.*, p. 409; Rollat, *op. cit.*, pp. 99, 107; Camus, *Le Front National*, p. 54. Cambadélis and Osmond credit the FN with around 20,000 members in early 1985 and some 30,000 by late 1986 (*op. cit.*, p. 248).

23 SOFRES, *Opinion publique 1985*, pp. 200–201.

24 SOFRES, *Opinion publique 1985*, pp. 182–83. In May 1984, other SOFRES findings showed 18 per cent of respondents declaring themselves 'very or somewhat sympathetic to Jean-Marie Le Pen', while levels of support for Le Pen's ideas on immigration, law and order, and anti-communism reached 28 per cent, 26 per cent and 25 per cent respectively (*ibid.*, pp. 178, 180).

25 Algazy, *L'Extrême-droite en France*, pp. 260, 262.

26 Le Pen, *Les Français d'abord*, p. 231; cf. Poujade, *A l'heure de la colère*, p. 151.

27 Bresson and Lionet, *op. cit.*, pp. 136–37, 385 n. 1; Camus and Monzat, *op. cit.*, pp. 83–84; Fysh and Wolfreys, *op. cit.*, pp. 127–28, 187; Jackson, *France: The Dark Years*, p. 620. For the positions held by Dufraisse, Gaucher, Malagutti and others within the FN in the 1980s, see Le Pen's 1988 presidential programme, *République Française. Passeport pour la victoire*, Limoges, NPC, 1988, pp. 141–53.

28 Camus and Monzat, *op. cit.*, pp. 85–88; Algazy, *L'Extrême-droite en France*, pp. 260–61.

29 Camus, *Le Front National*, p. 53; Dumont *et al.*, *op. cit.*, p. 216; Bresson and Lionet, *op. cit.*, pp. 410–12; Rollat, *op. cit.*, pp. 99–100.

30 Bresson and Lionet, *op. cit.*, pp. 416–19.

31 Rollat, *op. cit.*, pp. 99, 107; Dumont *et al.*, *op. cit.*, p. 214; Fysh and Wolfreys, *op. cit.*, p. 53.

32 As this book goes to press, Lang has been replaced by Louis Aliot as secretary-general of the party (a post he had held since 1999, and before that from 1988 to 1995), and Bild continues as deputy delegate-general (since 1999) to Bruno Gollnisch.

33 Camus, *Le Front National*, p. 54 n. 21.

34 *Le Monde dossiers et documents: Les élections législatives de juin 1981*, June 1981, pp. 137–38.

35 P. Favier and M. Martin-Roland, *La Décennie Mitterrand*, vol. 1, Paris, Seuil, 1990, p. 114.

36 J. W. Friend, *The Long Presidency: France in the Mitterrand Years 1981–1995*, Boulder, Westview Press, 1998, p. 67.

37 In 1981, SOFRES recorded 62 per cent of French opinion in favour of the death penalty and 33 per cent opposed (Perrineau, 'Le Front national: 1972–1992', p. 248).

38 Friend, *op. cit.*, p. 84.

39 J. Jaffré, 'L'état d'esprit des Français à travers les sondages d'opinion', in S. Berstein *et al.* (eds), *Les Années Mitterrand. Les années du changement (1981–1984)*, Paris, Perrin, 2001, p. 771; also Favier and Martin-Roland, *op. cit.*, vol. 1, p. 179.

40 Friend, *op. cit.*, p. 84. In October 1985, the then leader of the opposition, Jacques Chirac, would complain of 12,500 prisoners freed since 1981, among them many repeat offenders (*Le Monde*, 29 October 1985).

41 SOFRES, *Opinion publique 1984*, Paris, Gallimard, 1984, p. 26; SOFRES, *Opinion publique 1985*, pp. 109, 119.

42 The National Institute of Statistics and Economic Studies (INSEE) recorded 3.68 million immigrants (almost 6.8 per cent) in the March 1982 census; the Ministry of the Interior, basing its calculation on valid residence permits with no allowance for deaths, departures or naturalisations, put the figure at 4.46 million (8.2 per cent) in December 1982.

43 G. Dreyfus-Armand and T. Caudron, 'Les immigrés dans la société 1981–1984', in Berstein *et al.* (eds), *op. cit.*, p. 557.

44 Gildea, *France since 1945*, pp. 138–39.

45 Weil, *op. cit.*, Annex VI, pp. 374–75.

46 Calvez, 'Le Problème des travailleurs étrangers', p. 316.

47 A. G. Hargreaves, *Immigration, 'Race' and Ethnicity in Contemporary France*, London, Routledge, 1995, pp. 188–97.

48 M. A. Schain, 'Immigrants and Politics in France', in J. S. Ambler (ed.), *The French Socialist Experiment*, Philadelphia, Institute for the Study of Human Issues, 1985, pp. 166–90.
49 Hargreaves, *Immigration, 'Race' and Ethnicity in Contemporary France*, pp. 55–57.
50 Dreyfus-Armand and Caudron, 'Les immigrés dans la société 1981–1984', pp. 554–55.
51 A. Hochet, 'L'immigration dans le débat politique français de 1981 à 1988', *Pouvoirs*, no. 47, 1988, p. 24.
52 SOFRES, *Opinion publique 1984*, p. 125; SOFRES, *Opinion publique 1985*, pp. 84, 102, 109; *Le Monde*, 23 April 1985.
53 Dreyfus-Armand and Caudron, 'Les immigrés dans la société 1981–1984', pp. 560–65; Gildea, *France since 1945*, p. 144.
54 Friend, *op. cit.*, pp. 54–60.
55 SOFRES, *Opinion publique 1984*, pp. 36, 50, 73–74; SOFRES, *Opinion publique 1985*, pp. 132, 143.
56 *Le Monde*, 7 September 1984.
57 *Lettre de Matignon*, no. 123, 15 October 1984.
58 *Le Monde*, 29 October 1985.
59 *Lettre de Matignon*, no. 127, 12 November 1984, and no. 158, 1 July 1985; *Le Monde*, 12 July 1985 and 29 October 1985.
60 SOFRES, *Opinion publique 1984*, pp. 85–87; P. Perrineau, 'Glissements progressifs de l'idéologie', in E. Dupoirier and G. Grunberg (eds), *Mars 1986: la drôle de défaite de la gauche*, Paris, Presses Universitaires de France, 1986, pp. 42–43; P. Ignazi, 'Un nouvel acteur politique', in Mayer and Perrineau (eds), *op. cit.*, pp. 67–69.
61 See, for example, SOFRES, *Opinion publique 1985*, pp. 11–29.
62 J. Jaffré, 'Front national: la relève protestataire', in Dupoirier and Grunberg (eds), *op. cit.*, p. 215.
63 A.-M. Duranton-Crabol, 'L'extrême droite', in Berstein *et al.* (eds), *op. cit.*, p. 751.
64 *Le Monde*, 21 September 1982 and 14 December 1983.
65 Duranton-Crabol, 'L'extrême droite', p. 750.
66 A. Stevens, 'France', in J. Lodge (ed.), *Direct Elections to the European Parliament 1984*, London, Macmillan, 1986, p. 111.
67 SOFRES, *Opinion publique 1985*, p. 191. This rose to over one in four FN supporters.
68 SOFRES, *Opinion publique 1985*, pp. 178, 180, 184.
69 M. A. Schain, 'The National Front in France and the Construction of Political Legitimacy', *West European Politics*, vol. 10, no. 2, 1987, p. 244; Ignazi, 'Un nouvel acteur politique', pp. 68–69.
70 *Le Monde dossiers et documents: L'élection présidentielle 26 avril–10 mai 1981*, May 1981, p. 48.
71 Weil, *op. cit.*, Annex VI, pp. 373, 375.
72 Rollat, *op. cit.*, p. 91; Plenel and Rollat, *L'Effet Le Pen*, p. 239.
73 Dreyfus-Armand and Caudron, 'Les immigrés dans la société 1981–1984', p. 561; C. Lanzmann, 'Entretien avec Gaston Defferre, ministre de l'intérieur et de la décentralisation, maire de Marseille', *Les Temps modernes*, vol. 40, nos. 452–54, 1984, pp. 1561–80.
74 SOFRES, *Opinion publique 1985*, pp. 180–81.
75 Schain, 'The National Front in France and the Construction of Political Legitimacy', p. 237.
76 Perrineau, 'Les étapes d'une implantation électorale', pp. 43–44.
77 Perrineau, 'Les étapes d'une implantation électorale', p. 45; Hainsworth, 'The Extreme Right in Post-War France', p. 42.
78 Favier and Martin-Roland, *op. cit.*, vol. 2, pp. 308–9.
79 Unless otherwise specified, analysis of these elections is based on results published in *Le Monde dossiers et documents: Les élections législatives du 16 mars 1986*, March 1986, and *Le Monde*, 18 March 1986.

80 Shields, 'Immigration Politics in Mitterrand's France', p. 234.
81 P. Perrineau, 'Le Front national: un électorat de la crainte', *CFDT Aujourd'hui*, no. 88, February 1988, pp. 29–31.
82 Jaffré, 'Front national: la relève protestataire', pp. 213–14; Perrineau, *Le Symptôme Le Pen*, p. 102.
83 BVA poll in *Le Monde dossiers et documents: L'élection présidentielle 24 avril–8 mai 1988*, p. 44; also Perrineau, *Le Symptôme Le Pen*, p. 102.
84 Perrineau, 'Les étapes d'une implantation électorale', pp. 48–49; also Jaffré, 'Front national: la relève protestataire', p. 226.
85 *Le Monde dossiers et documents: L'élection présidentielle 24 avril–8 mai 1988*, p. 44; Jaffré, 'Front national: la relève protestataire', p. 223.
86 Jaffré, 'Front national: la relève protestataire', p. 216.
87 Jaffré, 'Front national: la relève protestataire', p. 227. For a poll recording partisan attachment among 65 per cent of FN voters in 1986, see Perrineau, 'Le Front National: un électorat de la crainte', p. 27.
88 Jaffré, 'Front national: la relève protestataire', pp. 218–19.
89 Front National, *Défendre les Français*, pp. 13, 20.
90 Front National, *Pour la France. Programme du Front National*, Paris, Albatros, 1985, pp. 110–24.
91 Calvez, 'Le Problème des travailleurs étrangers', p. 316.
92 On family allowance, the 1986 programme was inconsistent, proposing on one page that it be open to EEC nationals, then on another that it be reserved strictly for French nationals (*Pour la France*, pp. 122, 139).
93 These included reform of the prison service, a review of legal aid, fewer rights of appeal, and a right for poorer victims of crime to seek redress through the courts at no personal cost (*Défendre les Français*, pp. 16–17, 31).
94 *Pour la France*, pp. 97–109.
95 *Défendre les Français*, pp. 3, 26–28. These references had already been eliminated from the party's 1978 economic programme, *Droite et démocratie économique* (as discussed in Chapter 7).
96 *Pour la France*, pp. 38, 61–85.
97 *Pour la France*, pp. 151–62.
98 *Pour la France*, pp. 178–92.
99 Bresson and Lionet, *op. cit.*, p. 438.
100 *Le Monde*, 11–12 October 1987.
101 *Le Monde*, 11–12 October 1987; also 4 May 2002.
102 *Le Monde*, 11–14 October 1987. In a discussion with the author (20 July 2003), one of the main protagonists in this incident, Pierre Descaves, shrugged it off as an amusing diversion.
103 Bresson and Lionet, *op. cit.*, p. 440.
104 Bresson and Lionet, *op. cit.*, pp. 440–42.
105 Rassemblement pour la République/Union pour la Démocratie Française, *Plate-forme pour gouverner ensemble*, Paris, 1986, p. 14.
106 Rassemblement pour la République, *Le Renouveau: Pacte RPR pour la France*, Paris, 1985, p. 85.
107 On this and other aspects of the pressure exerted by the FN, see P. Fysh, 'Government Policy and the Challenge of the National Front – The First Twelve Months', *Modern and Contemporary France*, no. 31, 1987, pp. 9–20.
108 Hargreaves, *Immigration, 'Race' and Ethnicity in Contemporary France*, pp. 169–73.
109 *Le Monde*, 27 May 1986.
110 J.-M. Le Pen, 'Déclaration officielle à la candidature présidentielle', 26 April 1987, reprinted in *Les Cahiers FN-INFOS*, July 1987.
111 Bresson and Lionet, *op. cit.*, pp. 449–50.
112 Bresson and Lionet, *op. cit.*, p. 447.

113 J.-Y. Le Gallou and the Club de l'Horloge, *La Préférence nationale. Réponse à l'immigration*, Paris, Albin Michel, 1985.

114 *République Française. Passeport pour la victoire*, pp. 50–52; *Le Monde dossiers et documents: L'élection présidentielle 24 avril–8 mai 1988*, pp. 12–13.

115 Bresson and Lionet, *op. cit.*, p. 452.

116 Bresson and Lionet, *op. cit.*, pp. 453–57.

117 Camus and Monzat, *op. cit.*, pp. 476–77; Fysh and Wolfreys, *op. cit.*, p. 129.

118 Quoted in Algazy, *L'Extrême-droite en France*, pp. 260–61.

119 E. Plenel and A. Rollat, *La République menacée. Dix ans d'effet Le Pen*, Paris, *Le Monde*-Editions, 1992, p. 380; *Le Monde*, 25 August 1992; *Libération*, 24 August 1992.

120 *Le Monde*, 17–18 May and 25 August 1992.

121 Rollat, *op. cit.*, pp. 74–75.

122 Le Pen, *Les Français d'abord*, p. 232.

123 'And what is cosmopolitanism if not the wish to erase difference and identity and propagate a melting-pot of intermixing and interbreeding, with the eradication of culture and ethnicity?' A people thus bereft of its culture becomes 'a docile flock rushing headlong to the slaughterhouse' (Mégret, *La Flamme. Les voies de la renaissance*, pp. 36, 50).

124 *Le Monde*, 20 September 1988.

125 Le Pen, closing speech of the FN's June 2004 European election campaign, Paris, 10 June 2004.

126 *National Hebdo*, 26 October–1 November 1995, quoted in Fysh and Wolfreys, *op. cit.*, p. 131.

127 *Le Monde*, 8–9 April 1990. A CSA poll in May 1990 found the response to this proposition in public opinion at large to be 17 per cent in agreement and 69 per cent in disagreement (*Le Monde*, 18 May 1990).

128 Front National, *300 mesures pour la renaissance de la France. Programme de gouvernement*, Paris, Editions Nationales, 1993, preface.

129 Le Pen, speech in honour of Joan of Arc, Paris, 1 May 1998.

130 Le Pen, speech in honour of Joan of Arc, Paris, 1 May 2004.

131 Le Pen, closing speech of the FN's June 2004 European election campaign, Paris, 10 June 2004.

132 Bresson and Lionet, *op. cit.*, pp. 453–58; Fysh and Wolfreys, *op. cit.*, p. 58.

133 Bresson and Lionet, *op. cit.*, p. 453.

134 *Le Monde dossiers et documents: L'élection présidentielle 24 avril–8 mai 1988*, p. 59.

135 Unless otherwise specified, analysis of these elections is based on results and BVA polling data published in *Le Monde dossiers et documents: L'élection présidentielle 24 avril–8 mai 1988*.

136 Perrineau, *Le Symptôme Le Pen*, p. 53.

137 *Le Monde dossiers et documents: L'élection présidentielle 24 avril–8 mai 1988*, p. 41. This poll is used here since it allows useful comparison across the candidates.

138 *Le Monde dossiers et documents: L'élection présidentielle 24 avril–8 mai 1988*, pp. 44, 86; N. Mayer, 'Le vote FN de Passy à Barbès (1984–1988)', in Mayer and Perrineau (eds), *op. cit.*, pp. 262–63.

139 *Le Monde dossiers et documents: L'élection présidentielle 24 avril–8 mai 1988*, p. 44; Mayer, 'Le vote FN de Passy à Barbès', p. 261; Schain, 'The National Front in France and the Construction of Political Legitimacy', p. 245.

140 *Le Monde dossiers et documents: L'élection présidentielle 24 avril–8 mai 1988*, p. 44; Perrineau, *Le Symptôme Le Pen*, p. 102.

141 *Le Monde dossiers et documents: L'élection présidentielle 24 avril–8 mai 1988*, p. 61.

142 On this alleged episode, recounted in a book by the journalist Eric Zemmour, see *Le Monde*, 18 January 2002. While reportedly confirming this version of events to *Le Monde*, Le Pen subsequently denied that Chirac had made any such blatant overture (interview with the author, 15 April 2005).

143 G. Ivaldi, 'La scission du Front national', *Regards sur l'actualité*, May 1999, p. 21 n. 6; Bresson and Lionet, *op. cit.*, pp. 460–61.

144 Bresson and Lionet, *op. cit.*, pp. 42, 82; Perrineau, 'Les étapes d'une implantation électorale', pp. 51, 56.

145 Perrineau, 'Les étapes d'une implantation électorale', p. 54.

146 Fysh and Wolfreys, *op. cit.*, p. 58.

147 It would hold this seat only until October 1988, when Yann Piat would leave the party over disagreement with Le Pen.

148 *Le Monde dossiers et documents: Les élections législatives 21–28 mars 1993*, March 1993, p. 70; *Le Monde*, 19 March 1994.

149 Perrineau, *Le Symptôme Le Pen*, p. 102.

150 D. B. Goldey and R. W. Johnson, 'The French Presidential Election of 24 April–8 May and the General Election of 5–12 June 1988', *Electoral Studies*, vol. 7, no. 3, 1988, p. 220.

151 P. Hainsworth, 'The Triumph of the Outsider: Jean-Marie Le Pen and the 1988 Presidential Election', in J. Howorth and G. Ross (eds), *Contemporary France: A Review of Interdisciplinary Studies*, vol. 3, London, Pinter, 1989, pp. 168–69.

152 Faux *et al.*, *op. cit.*, pp. 26–28; Duranton-Crabol, 'L'extrême droite', pp. 756–61.

153 Perrineau, 'Le Front national: un électorat de la crainte', pp. 24–25.

154 See, for example, Mayer, 'Le vote FN de Passy à Barbès', pp. 249–67; P. Perrineau, 'Le Front national: un électorat autoritaire', *Revue politique et parlementaire*, vol. 87, no. 918, 1985, pp. 24–31.

155 Goldey and Johnson, 'The French Presidential Election of 24 April–8 May', p. 203; N. Mayer and P. Perrineau, 'Why Do They Vote For Le Pen?', *European Journal of Political Research*, vol. 22, no. 1, 1992, p. 133.

156 Mayer and Perrineau, 'Why Do They Vote For Le Pen?', p. 133.

9   The Front National 1988-95

1 *Le Monde dossiers et documents: Les élections législatives 5–12 juin 1988*, June 1988, pp. 33, 38.

2 For an overview of government in the period 1988–93, see Cole, *François Mitterrand: A Study in Political Leadership*, pp. 43–52; Friend, *op. cit.*, pp. 113–41.

3 Fysh and Wolfreys, *op. cit.*, pp. 128–29.

4 *Le Monde*, 24 January 1989.

5 N. Mayer and P. Perrineau, 'La puissance et le rejet ou le lepénisme dans l'opinion', in SOFRES, *L'Etat de l'opinion 1993*, Paris, Seuil, 1993, p. 65.

6 P. Perrineau, 'Le Front national, d'une élection l'autre', *Regards sur l'actualité*, May 1990, p. 29.

7 Martin, *Les Elections municipales en France depuis 1945*, pp. 139, 142.

8 *Le Monde dossiers et documents: Spécial élections municipales*, April 1989, p. 40.

9 *Le Monde dossiers et documents: Spécial élections municipales*, April 1989, pp. 6, 24. On these elections, see also Martin, *Les Elections municipales en France depuis 1945*, pp. 125–44; A. Cole, 'The French Municipal Elections of 12 and 19 March 1989', *Modern and Contemporary France*, no. 39, October 1989, pp. 23–34.

10 La Documentation Française, *Institutions et vie politique*, p.179; *Le Monde*, 20 June 1989. This was the tenth time that French voters had been summoned to the polls in little over a year, following presidential, legislative, cantonal (involving half of the constituencies) and municipal elections, plus a referendum on New Caledonia. Record abstention rates were ascribed, not unreasonably, to voter fatigue and the variability of the stakes in these polls.

11 Perrineau, *Le Symptôme Le Pen*, p. 102, and 'Le Front national, d'une élection l'autre', p. 31.

12 SOFRES, *L'Etat de l'opinion 1990*, Paris, Seuil, 1990, p. 181.

13 Fysh and Wolfreys, *op. cit.*, pp. 175–76.

14 A. Cole, *French Politics and Society*, London, Prentice Hall, 1998, pp. 229–31.

15 Hargreaves, *Immigration, 'Race' and Ethnicity in Contemporary France*, p. 129.
16 See *Le Monde*, 12 December 2003; *Le Monde*, *Libération* and *Le Figaro* of 18 December 2003; *Le Monde*, 31 August 2004.
17 *Le Monde dossiers et documents: Elections législatives 21–28 mars 1993*, pp. 97, 137.
18 *Le Monde*, 30 November 1989.
19 SOFRES, *L'Etat de l'opinion 1990*, p. 239.
20 P. Bréchon and S. K. Mitra, 'The National Front in France: The Emergence of an Extreme Right Protest Movement', *Comparative Politics*, vol. 25, no.1, October 1992, p. 66.
21 *Le Monde*, 12 December 1989 and 16 July 1991.
22 A. Knapp, *Gaullism since de Gaulle*, Aldershot, Dartmouth, 1994, p. 125.
23 J. G. Shields, 'Antisemitism in France: the Spectre of Vichy', *Patterns of Prejudice*, vol. 24, nos. 2–4, 1990, pp. 5–17.
24 SOFRES, *L'Etat de l'opinion 1996*, Paris, Seuil, 1996, p. 322; Perrineau, *Le Symptôme Le Pen*, pp. 65–70.
25 Plenel and Rollat, *La République menacée*, pp. 382–83.
26 *Le Monde*, 21 June 1991.
27 *Le Monde*, 22 June 1991.
28 *Le Figaro-Magazine*, 21 September 1991, pp. 48–57.
29 MRAP, 'Non à la dérive du débat politique', communiqué dated 5 July 1991; *Le Monde*, 10, 14–15 July 1991.
30 Plenel and Rollat, *La République menacée*, pp. 341, 380–82.
31 *Libération*, 21–22 September 1991.
32 Perrineau, *Le Symptôme Le Pen*, pp. 71–72.
33 *Le Monde*, 29 May 2002; Perrineau, *Le Symptôme Le Pen*, pp. 72, 191–92.
34 B. Mégret, 'Contribution au règlement du problème de l'immigration: 50 mesures concrètes', paper presented to the FN conference 'Immigration: les solutions', Marseille, 16 November 1991. The proposals were subsequently disseminated by the FN in the form of a 50-point questionnaire (*Immigration: 50 mesures concrètes. Les Français ont la parole*).
35 Plenel and Rollat, *La République menacée*, p. 384.
36 *L'Evénement du jeudi*, 21–27 December 1989, p. 60.
37 Fysh and Wolfreys, *op. cit.*, pp. 102–3; Camus and Monzat, *op. cit.*, pp. 109, 111.
38 Le Pen, *Les Français d'abord*, p. 163; also pp. 155, 164. The discussion here draws in places on C. Fieschi *et al.*, 'Extreme Right-Wing Parties and the European Union', in J. Gaffney (ed.), *Political Parties and the European Union*, London, Routledge, 1996, pp. 235–53.
39 J.-M. Brissaud, *L'Europe face à Gorbatchev: une stratégie impériale contre l'impérialisme*, Paris, G.D.E., 1989.
40 See the article by Yvan Blot in *Présent*, 26 April 1991 (quoted in Perrineau, *Le Symptôme Le Pen*, p. 70); also J.-M. Le Chevallier, *Immigration en Europe: attention, danger*, Paris, G.D.E., 1989.
41 *République Française. Passeport pour la victoire*, p. 58.
42 *300 mesures pour la renaissance de la France*, p. 365. See the eulogy of Athens in J.-M. Le Pen, *Europe: discours et interventions 1984–1989*, ed. J.-M. Brissaud, Paris, G.D.E., 1989, p. 149.
43 *300 mesures pour la renaissance de la France*, pp. 362–65, 371–72; Le Pen, *L'Espoir*, pp. 86, 96, 97, 100, and *Pour la France*, p. 191.
44 Le Pen, *L'Espoir*, pp. 85–112.
45 *Le Monde*, 23 May 1989.
46 *Le Monde*, 3 May 1989.
47 *Le Monde*, 20 June 1989.
48 P. Pujo, 'Jean-Marie Le Pen entre la France et l'Europe', *Aspects de la France*, 20 April 1989, 'Le Front national devra choisir', *ibid.*, 11 May 1989, and 'L'Europe de Jean-Marie Le Pen', *ibid.*, 15 June 1989.

49 *Le Monde*, 17–18 May and 25 August 1992.
50 *Le Monde*, 17–18 May 1992. By contrast, Poujade's UDCA came out in favour of a 'yes' vote (*Le Monde*, 20–21 September 1992).
51 *Le Monde*, 25 August and 8 September 1992; *Libération*, 24 August and 7 September 1992. See, in similar vein, J. Ploncard d'Assac, 'Maastricht, un complot maçonnique contre les nations', *Minute-La France*, 19–25 August 1992.
52 *Le Monde*, 7 July 1992; the Maastricht Treaty meant 'more immigration, more insecurity, more drugs, and more AIDS' (*Le Monde*, 25 August 1992).
53 *Le Monde*, 29 August and 15 September 1992; also the interview with Le Pen in *Le Quotidien de Paris*, 5 September 1992.
54 *Maastricht – Avant d'aller voter. Les questions que vous vous posez. Les réponses que vous recherchez*, special issue of *Europe et Patries*, no. 46, September 1992, pp. 8–9, 12–13, 15, 18–19.
55 *La Lettre de Jean-Marie Le Pen*, no. 160, July 1992, p. 2.
56 *300 mesures pour la renaissance de la France*, pp. 366–70.
57 An insight into the National Training Institute's work can be had from the 158-page handbook which it produced for party activists (Front National: Institut de Formation Nationale, *Militer au Front*, Paris, Editions Nationales, 1991).
58 Camus and Monzat, *op. cit.*, pp. 113–29, 377–78; G. Ivaldi, 'Les formations d'extrême droite: Front national et Mouvement national républicain', in P. Bréchon (ed.), *Les Partis politiques français*, Paris, La Documentation Française, 2001, pp. 30–31.
59 For some of these publications, see Camus and Monzat, *op. cit.*, pp. 130–48.
60 N. Mayer and H. Rey, 'Avancée électorale, isolement politique du Front national', *Revue politique et parlementaire*, vol. 95, no. 964, 1993, p. 47. René Monzat also estimated a membership close to 50,000 in the 1990s (*Le Monde*, 28–29 April 2002). By 2002, following the party's costly split in 1999, the FN would claim 40,253 members (Front National, *Français passionnément. Front National, une force pour la France*, n.d. [2002], p. 12).
61 *Militer au Front*, pp. 48–49, 52–56. The author is grateful to the FN's former secretary-general, Carl Lang, for providing a copy of volume 1 of *Le Guide du responsable* on the FN's organisation.
62 D. S. Bell, *Parties and Democracy in France: Parties under Presidentialism*, Aldershot, Ashgate, 2000, pp. 142–48. On 'indiscretions' by Le Pen and Catherine Mégret in particular, see *Le Monde*, 1–2 September 1996 and 2 July 1997.
63 Plenel and Rollat, *La République menacée*, pp. 384, 387; Marcus, *The National Front and French Politics*, p. 70.
64 Plenel and Rollat, *La République menacée*, pp. 386–87; Perrineau, *Le Symptôme Le Pen*, pp. 72, 191–92.
65 Analysis of these elections is based on results published in *Le Monde dossiers et documents: La France dans ses régions*, April 1992. Through defections provoked largely by some of Le Pen's public utterances, the FN's actual tally of regional councillors going into these elections was lower than 100 (*Le Monde*, 24 March 1992).
66 By contrast, the FN lost its representation in the Corsican regional assembly, with only 3.6 per cent of the poll.
67 N. Mayer, 'Des élections sans vainqueur', *French Politics and Society*, vol. 10, no. 2, 1992, p. 9; P. Bréchon, *La France aux urnes. Cinquante ans d'histoire électorale*, Paris, La Documentation Française, 1993, p. 53; *Le Monde dossiers et documents: Elections législatives 21–28 mars 1993*, p. 70.
68 Mayer, 'Des élections sans vainqueur', pp. 4–5. In the same poll, two-thirds of respondents continued to see the FN as 'a danger for democracy'.
69 On the scandals besetting the Socialist administration, see Friend, *op. cit.*, pp. 131–41.
70 On this election, see *Le Monde dossiers et documents: Elections législatives 21–28 mars 1993*; P. Habert *et al.*, *Le Vote sanction. Les élections législatives des 21 et 28 mars 1993*, Paris, Département d'Etudes Politiques du *Figaro*/Presses de la Fondation Nationale des Sciences Politiques, 1993.

71 Mayer and Rey, 'Avancée électorale', pp. 42–43.
72 Mayer, 'Des élections sans vainqueur', p. 9; *Le Monde*, 19 March 1994.
73 For an overview of this map, see *Le Monde*, 28–29 April 2002; also Perrineau, *Le Symptôme Le Pen*, pp. 45, 52, 77, 83, 97.
74 Mayer and Rey, 'Avancée électorale', p. 48.
75 Perrineau, *Le Symptôme Le Pen*, p. 102.
76 Mayer and Rey, 'Avancée électorale', p. 48.
77 For example, P. Perrineau, 'Le Front national: la force solitaire', in Habert *et al.*, *op. cit.*, p. 144 n. 1, and *Le Symptôme Le Pen*, pp. 145–51.
78 *Le Monde*, 19, 22, 23 and 29 March 1994; P. Martin, 'Les élections cantonales des 20 et 27 mars 1994', *Regards sur l'actualité*, June 1994, pp. 47–56. In addition to the three seats won here, the FN held another which was not due for renewal in these elections.
79 Perrineau, *Le Symptôme Le Pen*, p. 79.
80 La Documentation Française, *Institutions et vie politique*, p.180; Perrineau, *Le Symptôme Le Pen*, pp. 79–80, 102.
81 *National Hebdo*, 27 April–3 May 1995.
82 Unless otherwise specified, analysis of the 1995 election is based on results and BVA polling data published in *Le Monde dossiers et documents: L'élection présidentielle 23 avril–7 mai 1995*, May 1995.
83 Le Pen's score rose by 4–5 per cent in the departements of Aisne, Eure, Haute-Marne, Meuse, Seine-Maritime and Vosges, and by 3–4 per cent in Aube, Bas-Rhin, Marne, Meurthe-et-Moselle, Moselle, Nord, Oise, Orne and Pas-de-Calais.
84 BVA poll published in *Le Monde dossiers et documents: L'élection présidentielle 23 avril–7 mai 1995*, pp. 47–48, 50. This poll allows useful comparison of the candidates and facilitates cross-reference with the 1988 election.
85 For the IFOP and CSA polls, see *Libération*, 25 April, and *Le Parisien*, 24 April 1995; for SOFRES, see Perrineau, *Le Symptôme Le Pen*, p. 102; and for CEVIPOF, see N. Mayer, 'Les hauts et les bas du vote Le Pen 2002', *Revue française de science politique*, vol. 52, nos. 5–6, 2002, p. 508.
86 N. Mayer, *Ces Français qui votent Le Pen*, Paris, Flammarion, 2002, p. 93.
87 On some of the changes in Le Pen's electorate between 1988 and 1995, see N. Mayer, *Ces Français qui votent FN*, Paris, Flammarion, 1999, pp. 75–97.
88 Perrineau, *Le Symptôme Le Pen*, p. 53.
89 P. Perrineau, 'La dynamique du vote Le Pen: le poids du gaucho-lepénisme', in P. Perrineau and C. Ysmal (eds), *Le Vote de crise. L'élection présidentielle de 1995*, Paris, Département d'Etudes Politiques du *Figaro*/Presses de la Fondation Nationale des Sciences Politiques, 1995, p. 249.
90 *Le Monde*, 14 April 1995.
91 Mayer and Perrineau, 'Why Do They Vote For Le Pen?', p. 134; Perrineau, 'La dynamique du vote Le Pen', p. 255; N. Mayer, 'The Front National Vote in the Plural', *Patterns of Prejudice*, vol. 32, no. 1, 1998, p. 11 n. 24.
92 G. Le Gall, 'Présidentielle et municipales 95: victoire de Jacques Chirac et retour à un équilibre électoral', *Revue politique et parlementaire*, vol. 97, no. 977, 1995, p. 40.
93 SOFRES poll published in *Le Monde*, 24 May 1995.
94 In addition to BVA figures, see again here the IFOP poll in *Libération*, 25 April 1995, and the CSA poll in *Le Parisien*, 24 April 1995; also Perrineau, 'La dynamique du vote Le Pen', p. 254 n. 1.
95 Mayer and Rey, 'Avancée électorale', p. 47; Ivaldi, 'Les formations d'extrême droite', p. 17.
96 Perrineau, 'La dynamique du vote Le Pen', pp. 254–57.
97 Algazy, *L'Extrême-droite en France*, pp. 262–63.
98 Mayer, *Ces Français qui votent FN*, pp. 23–24, 85–89, 214–19.

99 P. Martin, 'Qui vote pour le Front National français?', in P. Delwit *et al.* (eds), *L'Extrême droite en France et en Belgique*, Brussels, Editions Complexe, 1998, pp. 137–38.
100 In his two periods as Interior Minister (1986–88 and 1993–95), Pasqua tightened entry and residence requirements, asylum law and procedures for acquiring French citizenship.
101 *La Tribune Desfossés*, 11 April 1995.
102 *Infomatin*, 1 March 1995.
103 *Le Monde dossiers et documents: L'élection présidentielle 23 avril–7 mai 1995*, p. 54.
104 *Le Monde*, 25, 26 and 27 April 1995.
105 *Le Monde*, 26 April 1995.
106 Jacques Chirac, speech in the Parc des Expositions, Orléans, 25 April 1995.
107 Jacques Chirac, speech in Metz, 3 May 1995.
108 G. Le Gall, 'Présidentielle 95: une opinion indécise', *Revue politique et parlementaire*, vol. 97, no. 976, 1995, p. 14.
109 *Libération*, 25 April 1995.

10 The Front National 1995–2002

1 *Libération*, 20 June 1995; J. Marcus, 'Advance or Consolidation? The French National Front and the 1995 Elections', *West European Politics*, vol. 19, no. 2, 1996, p. 312.
2 Martin, *Les Elections municipales en France depuis 1945*, pp. 139, 148, 156; *Le Monde*, 13 June 1995.
3 Le Gall, 'Présidentielle et municipales 95', p. 41; Ivaldi, 'Les formations d'extrême droite', p. 17. It is difficult to arrive at a representative percentage for the FN vote in municipal elections, or even to determine with precision the number of FN councillors elected. This is due partly to the very uneven distribution of FN lists, and partly to the tendency of FN sympathisers in certain localities to stand as 'independents' or as part of broader right-wing lists. The official Interior Ministry figure for FN (as distinct from 'extreme-right') councillors elected in June 1995 was 992, up from 489 in 1989 (*Le Monde*, 21 June 1995); other estimates put the number much higher (almost 2,000 according to *Libération*, 20 June 1995).
4 Results for the first round of these elections are taken from *Le Monde*, 13 June 1995. The scores noted here were far in excess of Le Pen's 28.48 per cent in Vitrolles, 28.94 per cent in Noyon, 23.61 per cent in Dreux, and 26.72 per cent in Mulhouse.
5 The second-round results for the FN in these towns were 42.89 per cent in Vitrolles, 48.12 per cent in Noyon, 39.31 per cent in Dreux, and 34.46 per cent in Mulhouse (*Le Monde*, 20 June 1995).
6 *Libération*, 19 June 1995; *National Hebdo*, 22–28 June 1995.
7 Fysh and Wolfreys, *op. cit.*, p. 196.
8 *Le Monde*, 20 June 1995.
9 *Le Monde*, 22 June 1995.
10 *Le Monde*, 20 June 1995. For a discussion of the FN in Toulon, Orange, Marignane and later Vitrolles, see P. Davies, *The National Front in France: Ideology, Discourse and Power*, London, Routledge, 1999, pp. 166–220.
11 *Le Monde*, 18–19, 21, 22 June 1995; *Libération*, 20 and 22 June 1995.
12 *Le Monde*, 23 June 1995.
13 *Le Front National aux affaires. Deux ans d'enquête sur la vie municipale à Toulon*, Paris, Calmann-Lévy, 1997.
14 Samson, *Le Front National aux affaires*, pp. 39, 70–72.
15 *Le Monde*, 23 February 2001 and 3 April 2004.
16 Davies, *op. cit.*, pp. 168, 182–83, 186–87.
17 Davies, *op. cit.*, pp. 187–89.
18 Davies, *op. cit.*, pp. 189, 217–18; *Le Monde*, 18 June 2005.

19 *Le Monde*, 10 January 1998.

20 *Le Monde*, 12–13 November 1995.

21 *Le Monde*, 20 July 1995.

22 J. G. Shields, 'Europe's Other Landslide: The French National Assembly Elections of May–June 1997', *The Political Quarterly*, vol. 68, no. 4, 1997, pp. 412–24.

23 M. A. Schain, 'The National Front and the French Party System', *French Politics and Society*, vol. 17, no. 1, 1999, p. 1.

24 Unless otherwise specified, analysis of these elections is based on detailed results published in *Le Monde dossiers et documents: Elections législatives 25 mai–1er juin 1997*, June 1997.

25 *Le Monde*, 3 May 1997.

26 Other impressive results were achieved by the FN in Maubeuge (25.89 per cent), Nice (25.88 per cent), Cannes (27.62 per cent) and La Valette-du-Var (26.36 per cent).

27 N. Mayer, 'Du vote lepéniste au vote frontiste', *Revue française de science politique*, vol. 47, nos. 3–4, 1997, p. 438; Schain, 'The National Front and the French Party System', p. 7.

28 Ivaldi, 'Les formations d'extrême droite', p. 17.

29 *Le Monde*, 28 and 31 May 1997.

30 *Libération*, 3 June 1997; Ivaldi, 'Les formations d'extrême droite', p. 17 n. 4. FN candidates in *triangulaires* carried most of their voters into the second round, and even attracted an estimated 11 per cent of abstentionists and 7 per cent of PCF voters from the first round.

31 G. Courtois, 'La gauche ne doit pas sa victoire de 1997 au FN', *Le Monde*, 25 March 1998.

32 SOFRES polls cited in *Le Monde*, 24 May 1995, and in Perrineau, *Le Symptôme Le Pen*, p. 96; also in *Libération*, 3 June 1997. In the 1993 legislative elections, by contrast, an estimated 62 per cent of FN voters fell in behind the RPR-UDF, 29 per cent abstained or spoiled their ballot, and only 9 per cent voted for the left in the second round (*Le Monde*, 29 May 1997).

33 CSA exit poll, *Les Elections législatives du 25 mai 1997. Explication du vote et attentes des électeurs du premier tour*, Paris, May 1997, p. 18; also BVA exit poll, *Elections législatives – mai 1997. Sondage à la sortie des bureaux de vote*, Paris, May 1997, p. 7, and IPSOS poll, *Le Point*, 2 June 1997, p. 68. The author is grateful to Nonna Mayer for making available the full data of the CSA and BVA polls; for extracts, see *Le Parisien*, 26 May 1997, and *Le Figaro*, 3 June 1997.

34 BVA exit poll, p. 9. Also notable was the high proportion of FN voters (59 per cent) who had 'always known' how they would vote (CSA exit poll, p. 15).

35 Both the CSA (p. 18) and BVA (p. 7) polls detected a very high degree of voter loyalty in the FN electorate; similar results were yielded by the IPSOS poll in *Le Point*, 2 June 1997, p. 68.

36 CSA exit poll, p. 13; N. Mayer, 'Le Front national n'est plus le premier parti ouvrier de France', *Le Monde*, 5 June 1997; M. A. Schain, 'The Normalization of the National Front', *French Politics and Society*, vol. 15, no. 2, 1997, pp. 9–12.

37 Perrineau, *Le Symptôme Le Pen*, p. 116.

38 SOFRES, *La Signification du vote des Français aux élections législatives*, Paris, June 1997, p. 25. Again the author is grateful to Nonna Mayer for the results of this poll. The CSA exit poll (p. 13) found 46 per cent of FN voters supporting their chosen candidate and 54 per cent either voting against other candidates or refusing to justify their vote.

39 Mayer and Perrineau, 'Why Do They Vote For Le Pen?', p. 133; *Libération*, 25 April 1995.

40 Mayer, *Ces Français qui votent Le Pen*, pp. 34–36, 43–46, 53, 447; Perrineau, *Le Symptôme Le Pen*, p. 212.

41 Perrineau, *Le Symptôme Le Pen*, p. 116.

42 Perrineau, *Le Symptôme Le Pen*, pp. 212–26.

43 BVA exit poll, p. 6. The FN's appeal was stronger among non-practising Catholics and those espousing no religion than among regularly or irregularly practising Catholics (SOFRES-CEVIPOF poll, *Libération*, 3 June 1997; Perrineau, *Le Symptôme Le Pen*, p. 102).

44 BVA exit poll, pp. 6, 8. The CSA exit poll (p. 18) put support for the FN among blue-collar workers at 25 per cent and among the unemployed at 23 per cent.

45 Mayer, 'The Front National Vote in the Plural', p. 11, and *Ces Français qui votent FN*, p. 24; also *ibid.*, pp. 75–97.

46 Schain, 'The Normalization of the National Front', p. 10.

47 CSA poll reported in *Le Monde*, 12 June 1997.

48 BVA exit poll, p. 6.

49 See, for example, Mayer, *Ces Français qui votent FN*, pp. 138–39.

50 SOFRES-CEVIPOF poll in *Libération*, 3 June 1997. For a developed discussion of these issues, see J. G. Shields, 'Political Representation in France: A Crisis of Democracy?', *Parliamentary Affairs*, vol. 59, no. 1, 2006, pp. 118–37.

51 The author is grateful to Nonna Mayer for providing copies of these 'bills'.

52 *Le Grand Changement. Et si on essayait le Front National?*, Paris, 1997. In the *300 mesures pour la renaissance de la France*, these concerns occupied chapters 10, 11 and 12, with the more traditional emphasis on 'Immigration' and 'Famille' in chapters 1 and 2.

53 Le Pen, *Les Français d'abord*, pp. 129–31, 137–39; also J.-M. Le Pen, *La France est de retour*, Paris, Carrère-Lafon, 1985, pp. 199, 207, 211–13; Front National, *Pour la France*, chapters 4–7 and 12.

54 Perrineau, *Le Symptôme Le Pen*, pp. 87–89; Schain, 'The National Front and the French Party System', pp. 5–6.

55 On the FN's attempts to infiltrate council housing associations, industrial tribunals, professional organisations and other bodies, see *Le Monde*, 29 May 1996, 10 January 1998, 5–6 April 1998, and 27 April 2002.

56 On the divergent profiles of these two constituencies, see Mayer, *Ces Français qui votent Le Pen*, pp. 334–37.

57 *Le Monde*, 2 April 1997.

58 *300 mesures pour la renaissance de la France*, p. 127; *Le Grand Changement*, p. 50.

59 Le Pen, closing speech, FN's tenth national congress, Strasbourg, 31 March 1997; speech in honour of Joan of Arc, Paris, 1 May 1997.

60 *300 mesures pour la renaissance de la France*, p. 250; *Le Grand Changement*, pp. 9, 24, 55.

61 *Le Monde*, 27–28 July 1997.

62 *Le Grand Changement*, p. 50.

63 *Défendre les Français*, p. 4; *Le Monde*, 9 November 1972 and 27 February 1973. See the book by Le Pen's son-in-law and former head of the FNJ, Samuel Maréchal, *Ni droite, ni gauche . . . Français! Contre la pensée unique: l'autre politique*, Paris, Première Ligne, 1994.

64 Le Pen, *L'Espoir*, pp. 98–100; *Le Monde*, 12 May 1998.

65 H. Kitschelt (with A. J. McGann), *The Radical Right in Western Europe: A Comparative Analysis*, Ann Arbor, University of Michigan Press, 1997.

66 On aspects of FN economic policy, see Bastow, 'Front National Economic Policy: From Neo-Liberalism to Protectionism'; also S. Bastow, 'The Radicalization of Front National Discourse: A Politics of the "Third Way"?', *Patterns of Prejudice*, vol. 32, no. 3, 1998, pp. 55–68; J.-P. Roy, 'Le programme économique et social du Front National en France', in Delwit *et al.* (eds), *op. cit.*, pp. 85–100.

67 *Le Monde*, 1–2 September 1996. The FN mayor of Vitrolles, Catherine Mégret, subsequently incurred a lawsuit for reiterating Le Pen's remarks in an interview published by the German newspaper *Berliner Zeitung* (*Le Monde*, 2 July 1997).

68 Perrineau, *Le Symptôme Le Pen*, p. 93; Mayer, 'The Front National Vote in the Plural', p. 22.

69 In his televised broadcast to announce the dissolution of the National Assembly, Chirac was much preoccupied by the FN, denouncing it in all but name and calling for France to rediscover its 'civic and moral bearings' (*Le Monde*, 23 April 1997).

70 *Le Monde*, 3 June 1997.
71 *National Hebdo*, 5–11 June 1997.
72 Le Gall, 'Présidentielle et municipales 95', p. 41; Mayer, 'The Front National Vote in the Plural', p. 20; Perrineau, *Le Symptôme Le Pen*, pp. 193–99.
73 *Le Monde*, 21, 22 and 24 May 1997.
74 *Le Monde*, 15–16 and 17 June 1997.
75 *Le Monde*, 6, 11, 15–16 June 1997, and 20 January 1998; also Ivaldi, 'Les formations d'extrême droite', p. 18 n. 5.
76 *Le Monde*, 17 June 1997; *Libération*, 16 June 1997.
77 *Le Monde*, 15–16 June 1997.
78 *La Montée du FN, 1983–1997*, Paris, Jean Picollec, 1997. A former youth leader in Marcel Déat's collaborationist RNP, Gaucher had served on the FN's political bureau and was still a regional councillor for Franche-Comté (*Le Monde*, 18 July 1997; Bresson and Lionet, *op. cit.*, p. 385 n. 1).
79 *Le Figaro*, 2 June 1997; *Le Monde*, 17 June and 8 July 1997.
80 *Le Monde*, 24 June 1997, and 1, 19, 20–21 July 1997.
81 *Le Monde*, 8 July 1997. For other reactions on the centre-right, see *Le Monde*, 2, 3, 26 July 1997.
82 This latter requirement was dropped from the Debré bill before it passed into law. On the Debré Law, see F. Julien-Laferrière, 'La "Loi Debré" sur l'immigration', *Regards sur l'actualité*, June 1997, pp. 27–39.
83 *Le Monde*, 17 June 1998.
84 *Le Nouvel Observateur*, 10–16 July 1997.
85 *Le Monde*, 17 and 18 March 1998.
86 Soisson, Blanc and Baur would retain their seats until March 2004. The furore over the 'deal' in the Centre region was such that the assembly quickly became ungovernable and, with Harang opposed by some of his own centre-right colleagues, the presidency passed to the Socialists.
87 On the case of Bourgogne, for example, see *Le Monde*, 23 May 1998.
88 Millon's election would subsequently be annulled by the Council of State and the presidency passed to the UDF's Anne-Marie Comparini in January 1999.
89 *Le Monde*, 22–23 March 1998; for the repercussions of the FN's strong showing, see the issues of 17–28 March.
90 *Le Monde*, 25 March 1998.
91 *Le Monde*, 17 March 1998 and 26 March 2004; *Le Figaro*, 29 March 2004.
92 *Le Monde*, 24 March 1998.
93 G. Ivaldi, 'Le Front national à l'assaut du système', *Revue politique et parlementaire*, vol. 100, no. 995, 1998, pp. 5–22.
94 On the Le Pen–Mégret split, see Ivaldi, 'La scission du Front national'; also M. Darmon and R. Rosso, *Front contre Front*, Paris, Seuil, 1999.
95 On the effects of the split, see *Le Monde*, 12 January 1999 and 27 April 2002; A. Laurent and P. Perrineau, 'L'extrême droite éclatée', *Revue française de science politique*, vol. 49, nos. 4–5, 1999, pp. 633–41; Darmon and Rosso, *op. cit.*, p. 106; Ivaldi, 'La scission du Front national', p. 25 n. 13.
96 Ivaldi, 'La scission du Front national', pp. 19–20, 26 n. 16. Having taken his distance from Le Pen, the founder of the Club de l'Horloge, Yvan Blot, subsequently denounced Mégret's betrayal and returned to the FN in February 1999.
97 Ivaldi, 'La scission du Front national', p. 24.
98 La Documentation Française, *Institutions et vie politique*, p.180; *Le Monde*, 15 June 1999.
99 *Le Monde*, 15 June 1999; Mayer, *Ces Français qui votent Le Pen*, p. 318.
100 Mayer, *Ces Français qui votent Le Pen*, pp. 316–17, 322–23; Ivaldi, 'La scission du Front national', p. 30 n. 25.
101 *Le Monde*, 15 June 1999.

102 See the letter by the de Gaulle family in *Le Monde*, 19 May 1999. The other four FN seats went to Le Pen, Jean-Claude Martinez, Bruno Gollnisch and Carl Lang. By falling short of 5 per cent, Mégret's party failed to win a single seat and lost out on reimbursement of its campaign costs.

103 *Le Monde*, 16 June 1999; G. Ivaldi, 'L'extrême-droite renforcée mais toujours isolée', *Revue politique et parlementaire*, vol. 104, nos. 1020–21, 2002, p. 134 n. 1.

104 G. Le Gall, 'L'étrange consultation électorale de 2001 ou l'invention d'une défaite', *Revue politique et parlementaire*, vol. 103, no. 1011, 2001, p. 4; *Libération*, 9 March 2001.

105 For full results of both rounds, see *Le Monde*, 13 and 20 March 2001.

106 G. Grunberg, 'Les élections locales françaises de mars 2001: un échec pour la majorité', *French Politics, Culture and Society*, vol. 19, no. 3, 2001, p. 26.

107 J. Jaffré, 'Le retournement électoral', *Le Monde*, 29 March 2001. Particularly strong results in some small towns across France testified to the local penetration of the FN: e.g. 30.18 per cent in Noyon (Oise), 34.3 per cent in Bollène (Vaucluse), 35.81 per cent in Cluses (Haute-Savoie).

108 Mayer, *Ces Français qui votent Le Pen*, p. 324; *Le Monde*, 20 March 2001; Le Gall, 'L'étrange consultation électorale de 2001', p. 17.

109 *Le Monde*, 24 April 2002.

110 Mayer, 'Les hauts et les bas du vote Le Pen 2002', p. 516.

111 *Remettons la France à l'endroit avec Bruno Mégret*, official presidential campaign statement, April 2002. On some of the overlaps between Le Pen's and Mégret's discourse, see Mayer, *Ces Français qui votent Le Pen*, pp. 322, 428 n. 12.

112 *Jean-Marie Le Pen – La France et les Français d'abord!*, official presidential campaign statement, April 2002.

113 *Pour un avenir français*, pp. 144, 161.

114 *Français passionnément – Le Pen président*, official presidential campaign statement, April 1995.

115 *Le Monde*, 3–4 February 2002.

116 *Pour un avenir français*, pp. 345–64.

117 This became the slogan of Le Pen's official campaign statement for the second round (*La France retrouvée*).

118 Le Pen, pre-election rally, Salle Equinoxe, Paris, 18 April 2002.

119 Mayer, *Ces Français qui votent Le Pen*, pp. 351–52.

120 On the primacy of law and order as a public concern, see the IPSOS poll in *Le Figaro*, 23 April 2002, and the Louis Harris poll in *Libération*, 23 April 2002.

121 IPSOS poll in *Le Figaro*, 23 April 2002; for comparable figures, see the CSA poll in P. Martin, 'L'élection présidentielle et les élections législatives françaises de 2002', *French Politics, Culture and Society*, vol. 21, no. 1, 2003, p. 16.

122 Mayer, 'Les hauts et les bas du vote Le Pen 2002', p. 506.

123 *Pour un avenir français*, pp. 61–62, 206–8.

124 Mayer, 'Les hauts et les bas du vote Le Pen 2002', pp. 505–6.

125 Mayer, *Ces Français qui votent Le Pen*, pp. 356–58.

126 This was the most common of the images of natural disaster that abounded in reports of the first round (as, for example, in *Le Monde*, 23 and 26 April 2002).

127 Mayer, 'Les hauts et les bas du vote Le Pen 2002', pp. 515, 519 n. 1.

128 *Les dossiers du Canard enchaîné: Manufacture française de candidats*, December 2001, p. 70; A. Cole, 'A Strange Affair: The 2002 Presidential and Parliamentary Elections in France', *Government and Opposition*, vol. 37, no. 3, p. 325 n. 22; G. Le Gall, 'Consultations électorales du printemps 2002: enseignements et spécificités', *Revue politique et parlementaire*, vol. 104, no. 1019, 2002, p. 40. While indirect support is difficult to verify, Le Pen denied having received any direct support from the PS, deeming it 'too sectarian to adopt such an intelligent attitude' (interview with the author, 15 April 2005).

129 For full results of the first round, see *Le Monde*, 23 April 2002.

130 P. Perrineau, 'La surprise lepéniste et sa suite législative', in P. Perrineau and C. Ysmal (eds), *Le Vote de tous les refus. Les élections présidentielle et législatives de 2002*, Paris, Presses de la Fondation Nationale des Sciences Politiques, 2003, p. 208. At the departmental level, Mégret's performance was comparable to that of the Communist Robert Hue, who did not reach 10 per cent in any department (having achieved this in almost a third of departments in 1995).

131 Perrineau, 'La surprise lepéniste et sa suite législative', pp. 209, 211–12.

132 Mayer, 'Les hauts et les bas du vote Le Pen 2002', pp. 508, 510–11.

133 IPSOS poll in *Le Figaro*, 23 April 2002; Ivaldi, 'L'extrême-droite renforcée mais toujours isolée', p. 143.

134 Mayer, 'Les hauts et les bas du vote Le Pen 2002', p. 509.

135 Polls conducted by IPSOS, Louis Harris and CEVIPOF concurred broadly on these findings (*Le Figaro*, 23 April 2002; *Libération*, 23 April 2002; Perrineau, 'La surprise lepéniste et sa suite législative', pp. 208–10). This somewhat older peak in support was due in part to voters who had remained loyal to Le Pen since 1988.

136 IPSOS and Louis Harris polls in *Le Figaro* and *Libération* of 23 April 2002.

137 Louis Harris poll, *Libération*, 23 April 2002. The IPSOS poll (*Le Figaro*, 23 April 2002) showed support for Le Pen at 23 per cent among low-income earners.

138 Mayer, 'Les hauts et les bas du vote Le Pen 2002', pp. 515–16.

139 *Le Monde*, 23 April 2002.

140 Louis Harris poll, *Libération*, 23 April 2002; also the IPSOS poll in *Le Figaro*, 23 April 2002, and the CEVIPOF poll in Perrineau, 'La surprise lepéniste et sa suite législative', p. 212. Mégret accounted for a further 5–8 per cent of this confirmed core of former Le Pen voters (Ivaldi, 'L'extrême-droite renforcée mais toujours isolée', p. 136).

141 IPSOS poll, *Le Figaro*, 23 April 2002.

142 Mayer, *Ces Français qui votent Le Pen*, pp. 354, 359, 377–78.

143 Perrineau, 'La surprise lepéniste et sa suite législative', pp. 212–15; Mayer, *Ces Français qui votent Le Pen*, pp. 374, 376.

144 N. Atkin and F. Tallett, 'Towards a Sixth Republic? Jean-Marie Le Pen and the 2002 Elections', *The Right in France: From Revolution to Le Pen*, London, I. B. Tauris, 2003, p. 294.

145 *Le Monde*, 2 and 3 May 2002; Mayer, *Ces Français qui votent Le Pen*, pp. 366–70.

146 Perrineau, 'La surprise lepéniste et sa suite législative', p. 214.

147 *Le Monde*, 21 June 1991 and 25 April 2002; Wihtol de Wenden, *op. cit.*, p. 206.

148 Mayer, *Ces Français qui votent Le Pen*, p. 370.

149 Mayer, *Ces Français qui votent Le Pen*, p. 378. A SOFRES poll published in *Le Monde* four days before the first round found only 8 per cent of respondents judging Chirac to be 'honest' (*Le Monde*, 17 April 2002).

150 Perrineau, 'La surprise lepéniste et sa suite législative', pp. 215–16; Mayer, *Ces Français qui votent Le Pen*, pp. 365–66. For broadly comparable findings, see the IPSOS poll in *Le Figaro*, 7 May 2002.

151 For results of the second round, see *Le Monde*, 7 May 2002; also Ivaldi, 'L'extrême-droite renforcée mais toujours isolée', p. 143; H. Portelli, 'L'élection présidentielle des 21 avril et 5 mai 2002', *Regards sur l'actualité*, no. 284, 2002, p. 71.

152 Louis Harris poll in *Libération*, 7 May 2002. These findings tally broadly with those indicated by IPSOS (Ivaldi, 'L'extrême-droite renforcée mais toujours isolée', p. 139) and CEVIPOF (Perrineau, 'La surprise lepéniste et sa suite législative', p. 210), the latter placing second-round support for Le Pen among the unemployed at 30 per cent.

153 Raffarin had been a minister for small business in Alain Juppé's 1995–97 administration.

154 *Le Monde*, 1 June 2002.

155 Perrineau, 'La surprise lepéniste et sa suite législative', p. 218.

156 *Le Monde*, 1, 2–3, 9–10 June 2002.

157 See the articles by G. Ivaldi and O. Pognon in *Le Figaro*, 18–19 May 2002.

158 *Le Monde*, 18 June 2002.

159 *Le Monde*, 2–3, 11 June 2002.

160 M. Sineau, 'La parité en peau de chagrin (ou la résistible entrée des femmes à l'Assemblée nationale)', *Revue politique et parlementaire*, vol. 104, nos. 1020–21, 2002, p. 213; Mayer, *Ces Français qui votent Le Pen*, p. 358.

161 Perrineau, 'La surprise lepéniste et sa suite législative', pp. 217–19; Mayer, *Ces Français qui votent Le Pen*, pp. 382–84; *Le Monde*, 12 June 2002.

162 IPSOS poll in Ivaldi, 'L'extrême-droite renforcée mais toujours isolée', p. 139; H. Portelli, 'Les élections législatives des 9 et 16 juin 2002', *Regards sur l'actualité*, no. 284, 2002, p. 74.

163 CEVIPOF statistics cited in *Libération*, 18 June 2002.

164 The UDR was the acronym for the Gaullist Union des Démocrates pour la République.

11 The Front National since 2002

1 *Le Monde*, 28–29 and 30 August 2005.

2 *Le Monde*, 19 April 2003.

3 *Le Monde*, 2–3 May 2004.

4 *Le Monde*, 30 March 2004. For the composition and presidencies of the 26 regional councils, see *Le Monde*, 1 and 4–5 April 2004.

5 *Le Monde*, 30 and 31 March 2004. The sole exception was François Loos in the Alsatian department of Bas-Rhin.

6 See the interview with the PS leader, François Hollande, in *Libération*, 3–4 April 2004; also *Libération*, 29 March 2004.

7 *Le Monde*, 23 January and 18 March 2004; *Le Figaro*, 22 March 2004.

8 Juppé was convicted of diverting funds from the Paris municipality to finance the RPR during Chirac's tenure of the Paris mayorship in the late 1980s and early 1990s. The UMP leader was given an 18-month suspended prison sentence and barred from public office for 10 years (later reduced to 14 months and one year on appeal). Only Chirac's presidential immunity prevented him from being part of the same investigation.

9 *Le Monde*, 4, 5, 6 and 12, 13, 14–15 March 2004.

10 *Le Monde*, 21–22 and 28–29 March 2004.

11 *Le Monde*, 18 March 1998 and 23, 25 March 2004. For full results of both rounds of the 2004 elections, see *Le Monde*, 23 and 30 March 2004.

12 On relations between the FN and AA, see *Le Monde*, 19 and 26 March 2004.

13 *Le Monde*, 28–29 March and 4–5 April 2004.

14 *Le Monde*, 23, 26, 30, 31 March 2004, and 7 April 2004. Previously, the right had held 59 councils to the left's 41.

15 *Le Monde*, 24 March 2004; *Le Figaro*, 25 March 2004.

16 In the first round, Simonpieri and Faraci had together attracted 7,952 (some 55 per cent) of the 14,410 votes cast across eight candidates.

17 Front National, *Programme du Front National: Europe*, n.d. [2002].

18 *Le Monde*, 19 April 2003. The conviction was upheld by an appeals court (*Le Monde*, 26 February 2005).

19 Sentenced to a year's ineligibility, Le Pen was replaced in the European Parliament by Marie-France Stirbois (*Le Monde*, 12 April 2003).

20 *Le Monde*, 18 June 2004.

21 Results for these elections are taken from *Le Monde*, 15 June 2004.

22 Mayer, *Ces Français qui votent Le Pen*, pp. 377–78; *Le Monde*, 31 May 2005; *Libération*, 31 May 2005.

23 On the 2005 referendum, see *Le Monde*, 31 May and 1, 2, 3 June 2005.

24 *Le Monde*, 28–29 and 30 March 2004; *Libération*, 23 March 2004; Vaucluse Prefecture figures for March 2004 cantonal elections.
25 On this point, see Perrineau, 'L'extrême droite s'ancre solidement dans le paysage politique', *Le Figaro*, 23 March 2004.
26 *Le Monde*, 5 June 1997.
27 J.-P. Moinet, 'La notabilisation du FN: engrenage et dangers', *Revue politique et parlementaire*, vol. 100, no. 995, 1998, pp. 23–26.
28 *Le Monde*, 19 April 2003.
29 Mayer, *Ces Français qui votent Le Pen*, pp. 372, 373, 376, 453; *Le Monde*, 29 May 2002.
30 Mayer, *Ces Français qui votent Le Pen*, pp. 331, 385–86.
31 *Le Monde*, 8 November 2005.
32 On some of these issues, see Shields, 'Political Representation in France'.
33 The same poll showed a reduced proportion of 66 per cent considering the FN 'a danger for democracy in France' (*Le Monde*, 15 December 2005). In the corresponding poll a year later, support for 'Le Pen's ideas' rose to 26 per cent, while the proportion of respondents judging them 'unacceptable' dropped from 39 to 34 per cent (*Le Monde*, 15 December 2006).
34 *Le Monde*, 4 May 1999; Fysh and Wolfreys, *op. cit.* (2nd edn, 2003), p. 235.
35 *Le Monde*, 17, 19, 20, 24, 25 February 2004.
36 See the flurry of profiles of Marine Le Pen in the British press (*Financial Times*, 28–29 February 2004; *Independent*, 20 March 2004; *Sunday Telegraph Magazine*, 21 March 2004; *Daily Telegraph*, 24 March 2004).
37 *Le Monde*, 19 and 22 April 2003, and 25 March 2004.
38 *Le Monde*, 7 May 2004; *Libération*, 18 May 2004.
39 *Le Monde*, 22 and 23–24 May 2004; *Libération*, 21, 22–23, 24 May 2004. The rift between Bompard and the Le Pens went back to acerbic public exchanges in early 2003 (*Le Monde*, 14 February 2003).
40 *Libération*, 15 June 2004; *Le Figaro*, 30 August 2004; *Le Monde*, 18 September 2004.
41 *Le Monde*, 25 and 31 August 2004, and 4 September 2004; *Le Figaro*, 30 August 2004; *Libération*, 31 August 2004.
42 For a surprisingly indulgent comment by Le Pen on same-sex marriages, see *Le Monde*, 4 June 2004; and for a response by Marie-France Stirbois, *Libération*, 15 June 2004.
43 *Rivarol*, no. 2698, 7 January 2005, pp. 6–7.
44 Opening its columns to former journalists from the collaborationist *Je suis partout*, such as Pierre-Antoine Cousteau and Lucien Rebatet, *Rivarol* would become a forum for historical revisionism and for resistance to the 'occupation' of France by Jews, immigrants and foreign influence (Algazy, *La Tentation néo-fasciste en France*, pp. 130–32; Camus and Monzat, *op. cit.*, pp. 478–79).
45 In an interview with the author on 15 April 2005, Le Pen insisted that his remarks about the Occupation had been off the record and that he would have removed them from the published transcript had he seen a copy in advance. He also observed caustically that he was now under judicial investigation for 'expressing an opinion' about the Occupation more than half a century after the general amnesty extended to actual collaborators in 1953.
46 *Le Monde*, 9 November 1972 and 27 February 1973.
47 *Le Monde*, 28 February 1973; Bresson and Lionet, *op. cit.*, p. 54.
48 For a few examples, see Le Pen's programme for the 1988 presidential election, *République Française. Passeport pour la victoire*, pp. 50–51; the 1991 document 'Contribution au règlement du problème de l'immigration: 50 mesures concrètes'; and Le Pen's official campaign statement for the 2002 presidential election, *Jean-Marie Le Pen – La France et les Français d'abord!*; also *Le Monde*, 15 July 1997, 3–4 February 2002, and 20 April 2002.
49 *Lettre à François Mauriac*, pp. 12, 58; *Nuremberg ou la terre promise*, pp. 9, 14, 17.
50 See, for example, *Les Français d'abord*, pp. 29, 31–32.

51 Le Pen was implicitly subscribing here to a revisionist claim that the fire in the church at Oradour-sur-Glane which killed almost all of the women and children of the village was due to the explosion of an arms cache concealed there by the local Resistance.

52 *Libération*, 17 January 2005. The fire-bombing of Dresden in particular has become a favoured counter-argument to the condemnation of Nazi war crimes. On the commemoration of this event, and the attempt by the German NPD to exploit it, see *Le Monde*, 13–14 and 15 February 2005; *Libération*, 14 February 2005.

53 *Le Monde*, 13 October 2004 and 6–7 March 2005; also *Le Monde*, 15 October 2004 and the letter from Gollnisch published in the issue of 23 October 2004.

54 *Le Monde*, 16–17 January, 4 February, 6–7 and 10 March 2005, and 16 September 2006.

55 Winock, *Nationalisme, antisémitisme et fascisme en France*, pp. 44–45.

56 Le Pen, interview with the author, 15 April 2005. In the 1970s, Le Pen's legalism was more circumscribed; he advocated the army's intervention should a radical turn to the left bring 'misery, famine and the threat of terror' to France (*Le Monde*, 26 September 1973).

57 B. Brigouleix, 'L'extrême droite à la recherche d'un avenir', *Le Monde*, 12, 13–14, 15 June 1976.

58 J. Wolfreys, 'Neither Right Nor Left? Towards an Integrated Analysis of the Front National', in Atkin and Tallett (eds), *op. cit.*, pp. 261–76.

59 See the extracts quoted in R. Griffin (ed.), *International Fascism: Theories, Causes and the New Consensus*, London, Arnold, 1998, pp. 301–3.

60 J. Wolfreys, 'An Iron Hand in a Velvet Glove: The Programme of the French Front National', *Parliamentary Affairs*, vol. 46, no. 3, 1993, pp. 415–29.

61 Quoted in *Le Monde*, 28–29 April 2002. Unlike many of its predecessors, the FN also acknowledges the Revolution of 1789 as an integral component of France's long and variegated political heritage.

62 In an interview on institutional reform published in *Le Monde* of 14 July 2005, Le Pen lamented 'the progressive erosion of democracy' in France, the lack of popular representation and the draining of power from the national parliament to Europe. His proposed solutions were proportional representation for elections at all levels, the restoration of full legislative powers to the National Assembly, and a return to the seven-year presidential mandate and to the President as supreme custodian of national sovereignty.

63 *Le Contrat pour la France avec les Français*, pp. 3–5, 49–52.

64 *Le Monde*, 2 March 2005.

65 Front National, *Pôle Communication: la lettre de diffusion. www.frontnational.com*, 10 April 2006. See Marine Le Pen's description of the FN as 'the only party today defending Republican principles' (*Le Monde*, 5 July 2006).

66 *Le Monde*, 19 May and 3–4 October 1999; Fysh and Wolfreys, *op. cit.* (2nd edn, 2003), pp. 234–35.

67 SOFRES poll published in *Le Monde*, 8–9 April 1990.

68 *Pour un avenir français*, pp. 165–84.

69 See *The Nature of Fascism*, pp. 26, 161, and *International Fascism*, pp. 37, 288, 291; also R. Griffin (ed.), *Fascism*, Oxford, Oxford University Press, 1995, p. 312. See also Payne, who defines the FN as a 'rightist-nationalist movement' (*op. cit.*, p. 510).

70 For a discussion germane to the argument advanced here, see S. Hazareesingh, *Political Traditions in Modern France*, Oxford, Oxford University Press, 1994, pp. 140–49.

71 This central component of the FN's programme was echoed by the RPR as early as 1985 (*Le Renouveau: Pacte RPR pour la France*, p. 85). See also the proposals of Giscard (*Le Figaro-Magazine*, 21 September 1991) and Balladur (*Le Monde*, 17 June 1998), and

the response by some centre-right mayors to the FN in local government (*Le Monde*, 12–13 November 1995).

72 *Pour un avenir français*, pp. 61, 144.

73 *Le Monde*, 1, 6–7 and 11 November 2005. Sarkozy blended his tough talk with calls for positive discrimination towards ethnic minorities and possible voting rights for non-French immigrants in local elections (*Le Monde*, 25, 26 and 28 October 2005).

74 Reported in *The Scotsman*, 3 June 2006. On the '*lepénisation*' of centre-right government policy since 2002, in relation to immigration and law and order notably, see *Le Monde*, 27 December 2005.

75 Le Pen, 'Le Front national', p. 177. See Chapter 7.

76 *Le Monde*, 23 May 1998.

77 For a discussion of 'deradicalisation' on the classic model developed by Robert Michels, see M. A. Schain, 'The Impact of the French National Front on the French Political System', in M. Schain *et al.* (eds), *Shadows over Europe: The Development and Impact of the Extreme Right in Western Europe*, New York, Palgrave Macmillan, 2002, pp. 223–43.

78 *Le Monde*, 18 March 1998.

79 R. Griffin, 'Net Gains and GUD Reactions: Patterns of Prejudice in a Neo-Fascist *Groupuscule*', *Patterns of Prejudice*, vol. 33, no. 2, 1999, p. 35; *Le Monde*, 30 July 2002; also interview with Fabrice Robert of Bloc Identitaire, *Monde et Vie*, no. 763, 13 May 2006, p. 16.

80 G. Sartori, *Parties and Party Systems*, Cambridge, Cambridge University Press, 1976, p. 133.

81 M. Minkenberg, 'The New Right in France and Germany: *Nouvelle Droite*, *Neue Rechte*, and the New Right Radical Parties', in P. H. Merkl and L. Weinberg (eds), *The Revival of Right-Wing Extremism in the Nineties*, London, Frank Cass, 1997, pp. 77, 84.

82 For a discussion of these points, see P. Hainsworth, 'Introduction: The Extreme Right', in P. Hainsworth (ed.), *The Politics of the Extreme Right: From the Margins to the Mainstream*, London, Pinter, 2000, pp. 4–9; H.-G. Betz, 'Introduction', in H.-G. Betz and S. Immerfall (eds), *The New Politics of the Right: Neo-Populist Parties and Movements in Established Democracies*, London, Macmillan, 1998, pp. 2–9.

83 R. Andersen and J. Evans, 'Contemporary Developments in Political Space in France', in J. Evans (ed.), *The French Party System*, Manchester, Manchester University Press, 2003, pp. 183–84; J. Evans, 'Introduction', in *ibid.*, pp. 7-8; R. Andersen and J. Evans, 'Values, Cleavages and Party Choice in France, 1988-1995', *French Politics*, vol.1, no.1, 2003, pp. 83-114.

84 It was under President Mitterrand and the neo-Gaullist Prime Minister Balladur that the FN had last been involved in a similar consultation in 1993.

85 *Le Monde*, 28 June 2005; *Libération*, 27 June 2005. Even as de Villepin was hosting the FN at the Hôtel Matignon, Sarkozy, now back at the Interior Ministry, was cranking up the rhetoric on law and order in the *banlieues* as part of an openly declared strategy to court the FN vote (*Le Monde*, 23 June 2005; *Libération*, 19 July 2005).

86 Le Gall, 'Présidentielle et municipales 95', p. 41; Mayer, 'The Front National Vote in the Plural', p. 20.

87 In the same survey, 35 per cent of respondents agreed with Le Pen's defence of traditional values, 27 per cent with his proposals on immigration and tax, and 26 per cent with his criticism of the political class (*Le Monde*, 29 May 2002).

88 G. Le Gall, 'Pourquoi le 21 avril?', in SOFRES, *L'Etat de l'opinion 2003*, Paris, Seuil, 2003, p. 89; IFOP/Acteurs Publics poll, *Les Français et l'extrême droite*, Paris, 21 April 2006.

89 Marignane and Vitrolles were won in the name of the MNR in 2001, but with essentially the same administration as that set in place by the FN.

90 N. Hewlett, *Modern French Politics: Analysing Conflict and Consensus since 1945*, Cambridge, Polity Press, 1998, p. 191.

91 See the poll results in *Le Monde*, 29 May 2002, 15 December 2005 and 15 December 2006.
92 Fysh and Wolfreys, *op. cit.* (2nd edn, 2003), pp. 234–36; *Le Monde*, 23 March 1999, 30 May 2000, 7 February and 26 April 2006.
93 Le Pen, speech to launch 2007 presidential campaign, Valmy, 20 September 2006.
94 On the process of 'normalization' at work on the contemporary extreme right in France, Italy and Austria, see Paxton, *The Anatomy of Fascism*, pp. 185–88.
95 For a thoughtful discussion of the differences between historical fascism and contemporary parties such as the FN, see D. Prowe, '"Classic" Fascism and the New Radical Right in Western Europe: Comparisons and Contrasts', *Contemporary European History*, vol. 3, no. 3, 1994, pp. 289–313; also, on the FN as a party 'alien to the fascist imprint', P. Ignazi, 'The Extreme Right: Defining the Object and Assessing the Causes', in Schain *et al.* (eds), *op. cit.*, pp. 21-37.
96 Cole, *French Politics and Society*, p. 175.
97 See the interview with Bompard in *Le Monde*, 4 February 2005.
98 *Libération*, 18 January and 14 June 2005; *Le Monde*, 19 January and 4 February 2005; *Le Nouvel Observateur*, 20–26 January 2005.
99 *Le Monde*, 11–12 September and 23–24 October 2005, and 11 April 2006; see also the defection to the MPF in March 2006 of Marie-Christine Bignon, FN mayor of Chauffailles, a town of some 4,500 inhabitants in Saône-et-Loire (*Le Monde*, 22 March 2006).
100 See the obituary in *Le Monde*, 19 April 2006.
101 *Le Monde*, 4 February 2005.
102 *Le Monde*, 18, 27 January, 2 March and 30 August 2005; *Libération*, 1, 19–20 March 2005; *Le Monde*, 13 October 2005.
103 *Le Monde*, 16–17 April 2006.
104 Le Pen, pre-election rally, Salle Equinoxe, Paris, 18 April 2002.
105 Le Pen, interview with the author, 15 April 2005.

Bibliography

Algazy, J., *La Tentation néo-fasciste en France de 1944 à 1965*, Paris, Fayard, 1984.

Algazy, J., *L'Extrême-droite en France de 1965 à 1984*, Paris, L'Harmattan, 1989.

Andersen, R., and Evans, J., 'Contemporary Developments in Political Space in France', in J. Evans (ed.), *The French Party System*, Manchester, Manchester University Press, 2003.

Andersen, R., and Evans, J., 'Values, Cleavages and Party Choice in France, 1988-1995', *French Politics*, vol.1, no. 1, 2003, pp. 83-114.

Anderson, M., *Conservative Politics in France*, London, Allen & Unwin, 1974.

Apparu, J.-P. (ed.), *La Droite aujourd'hui*, Paris, Albin Michel, 1979.

Arnold, E. J. (ed.), *The Development of the Radical Right in France: From Boulanger to Le Pen*, London, Macmillan, 2000.

Aron, R., *France Steadfast and Changing: The Fourth to the Fifth Republic*, Cambridge (Massachusetts), Harvard University Press, 1960.

Atkin, N., and Tallett, F. (eds), *The Right in France: From Revolution to Le Pen*, London, I. B. Tauris, 2003.

Azéma, J.-P., *From Munich to the Liberation, 1938–1944*, trans. J. Lloyd, Cambridge, Cambridge University Press, 1984.

Azéma, J.-P., 'Vichy', in M. Winock (ed.), *Histoire de l'extrême droite en France*, Paris, Seuil, 1993.

Azéma, J.-P., and Bédarida, F. (eds), *Le Régime de Vichy et les Français*, Paris, Fayard, 1992.

Backes, U., 'L'extrême droite: les multiples facettes d'une catégorie d'analyse', in P. Perrineau (ed.), *Les Croisés de la société fermée. L'Europe des extrêmes droites*, Paris, Editions de l'Aube, 2001.

Bardèche, M., *Lettre à François Mauriac*, Paris, La Pensée Libre, 1947.

Bardèche, M., *Nuremberg ou la terre promise*, Paris, Les Sept Couleurs, 1948.

Bardèche, M., 'Histoire du Mouvement Poujade', *Défense de l'Occident* (spec. no. 'Le Poujadisme'), no. 33, May 1956, pp. 3–27.

Bardèche, M., 'Le drame de l'Algérie', *Défense de l'Occident*, no. 32, April 1956, pp. 3–9.

Bardèche, M., *Qu'est-ce que le Fascisme?*, Paris, Les Sept Couleurs, 1961.

Bardèche, M., 'La "Nouvelle Droite"', *Défense de l'Occident*, no. 167, July–August 1979, pp. 3–16.

Bardèche, M., 'Les silences de la Nouvelle Droite', *Défense de l'Occident*, no. 170, December 1979, pp. 12–30.

Bariller, D., and Timmermans, F. (eds), *20 ans au Front. L'Histoire vraie du Front National*, Paris, Editions Nationales, 1993.

Barnes, I. R., 'The Pedigree of GRECE–I', *Patterns of Prejudice*, vol. 14, no. 3, 1980, pp. 14–24.

Baruch, M. O., *Le Régime de Vichy*, Paris, La Découverte, 1996.

Bastow, S., 'Front National Economic Policy: From Neo-Liberalism to Protectionism', *Modern and Contemporary France*, vol. 5, no. 1, 1997, pp. 61–72.

Bastow, S., 'The Radicalization of Front National Discourse: A Politics of the "Third Way"?', *Patterns of Prejudice*, vol. 32, no. 3, 1998, pp. 55–68.

Bell, D. S., 'The Extreme Right in France', in M. Kolinsky and W. E. Paterson (eds), *Social and Political Movements in Western Europe*, London, Croom Helm, 1976.

Bell, D. S., 'The French National Front', *History of European Ideas*, vol. 18, no. 2, 1994, pp. 225–40.

Bell, D. S., *Parties and Democracy in France: Parties under Presidentialism*, Aldershot, Ashgate, 2000.

Bell, D. S., and Criddle, B., 'Presidentialism Restored: The French Elections of April–May and June 2002', *Parliamentary Affairs*, vol. 55, no. 4, 2002, pp. 643–63.

Bergeron, F., and Vilgier, P., *De Le Pen à Le Pen. Une histoire des nationaux et des nationalistes sous la Ve République*, Saint-Brieuc, Dominique Martin Morin, 1986.

Berstein, S., and Milza, P., *Dictionnaire historique des fascismes et du nazisme*, Brussels, Editions Complexe, 1992.

Berstein, S., Milza, P., and Bianco, J.-L. (eds), *Les Années Mitterrand. Les années du changement (1981–1984)*, Paris, Perrin, 2001.

Betz, H.-G., *Radical Right-Wing Populism in Western Europe*, London, Macmillan, 1994.

Betz, H.-G., and Immerfall, S. (eds), *The New Politics of the Right: Neo-Populist Parties and Movements in Established Democracies*, London, Macmillan, 1998.

Bezbakh, P., *Histoire de la France contemporaine de 1914 à nos jours*, Paris, Bordas, 1990.

Billig, M., *Psychology, Racism and Fascism* (Searchlight booklet), Birmingham, A. F. & R. Publications, 1979.

Billig, M., *L'Internationale raciste. De la psychologie à la 'science' des races*, Paris, Maspero, 1981.

Birnbaum, P., *Un mythe politique: 'la République juive'. De Léon Blum à Pierre Mendès France*, Paris, Fayard, 1988.

Blinkhorn, M. (ed.), *Fascists and Conservatives: The Radical Right and the Establishment in Twentieth-Century Europe*, London, Unwin Hyman, 1990.

Borne, D., *Petits bourgeois en révolte? Le Mouvement Poujade*, Paris, Flammarion, 1977.

Bourderon, R., 'Le régime de Vichy était-il fasciste? Essai d'approche de la question', *Revue d'Histoire de la Deuxième Guerre Mondiale*, no. 91, 1973, pp. 23–45.

Brasillach, R., *Notre avant-guerre*, Paris, Plon, 1941.

Bréchon, P., *La France aux urnes. Cinquante ans d'histoire électorale*, Paris, La Documentation Française, 1993.

Bréchon, P., and Mitra, S. K., 'The National Front in France: The Emergence of an Extreme Right Protest Movement', *Comparative Politics*, vol. 25, no. 1, October 1992, pp. 63–82.

Bréchon, P. (ed.), *Les Partis politiques français*, Paris, La Documentation Française, 2001.

Bresson, G., and Lionet, C., *Le Pen. Biographie*, Paris, Seuil, 1994.

Brigouleix, B., 'L'extrême droite à la recherche d'un avenir', *Le Monde*, 12, 13–14, 15 June 1976.

Brindillac, C., and Prost, A., 'Géographie des élections législatives du 2 janvier 1956', *Esprit*, vol. 24, no. 236, 1956, pp. 437–61.

Brissaud, J.-M., *L'Europe face à Gorbatchev: une stratégie impériale contre l'impérialisme*, Paris, G.D.E., 1989.

Brissaud, J.-M. *et al.*, *La France en danger. Non à l'Europe de Maastricht*, Limoges, Editions Nationales, 1994.

Brunn, J., *La Nouvelle Droite. Le dossier du 'procès'*, Paris, Nouvelles Editions Oswald, 1979.

Buisson, P., and Renault, A. (eds), *L'Album Le Pen. Images d'un Français*, Paris, S.E.R.P., 1988.

Burrin, P., 'Le fascisme', in J.-F. Sirinelli (ed.), *Histoire des droites en France*, vol. 1: *Politique*, Paris, Gallimard, 1992.

Burrin, P., *Living with Defeat: France under the German Occupation 1940–1944*, trans. J. Lloyd, London, Arnold, 1996.

Burrin, P., *Fascisme, nazisme, autoritarisme*, Paris, Seuil, 2000.

Burrin, P., 'The Ideology of the National Revolution', in E. J. Arnold (ed.), *The Development of the Radical Right in France: From Boulanger to Le Pen*, London, Macmillan, 2000.

BVA, *Elections législatives – mai 1997. Sondage à la sortie des bureaux de vote*, Paris, May 1997.

Calvez, C., 'Le Problème des travailleurs étrangers', *Journal Officiel de la République Française. Avis et Rapports du Conseil Economique et Social*, no. 7, 27 March 1969.

Cambadélis, J.-C., and Osmond, E., *La France blafarde. Une histoire politique de l'extrême droite*, Paris, Plon, 1998.

Campbell, P., 'Le Mouvement Poujade', *Parliamentary Affairs*, vol. 10, no. 3, 1957, pp. 362–67.

Camus, J.-Y., 'Origine et formation du Front National (1972–1981)', in N. Mayer and P. Perrineau (eds), *Le Front National à découvert*, Paris, Presses de la Fondation Nationale des Sciences Politiques, 1989.

Camus, J.-Y., *Le Front National. Histoire et analyses*, Paris, Editions Olivier Laurens, 1996.

Camus, J.-Y., 'Nostalgia and Political Impotence: Neo-Nazi and Extreme Right Movements in France, 1944–64', in E. J. Arnold (ed.), *The Development of the Radical Right in France: From Boulanger to Le Pen*, London, Macmillan, 2000.

Camus, J.-Y., and Monzat, R., *Les Droites nationales et radicales en France. Répertoire critique*, Lyon, Presses Universitaires de Lyon, 1992.

Canard enchaîné (Le), *Les dossiers du Canard enchaîné: Manufacture française de candidats*, Paris, December 2001.

Carroll, D., *French Literary Fascism: Nationalism, Anti-Semitism, and the Ideology of Culture*, Princeton, Princeton University Press, 1995.

Carter, E., *The Extreme Right in Western Europe: Success or Failure?*, Manchester, Manchester University Press, 2005.

Cautrès, B., and Mayer, N. (eds), *Le nouveau désordre électoral*, Paris, Presses de la Fondation Nationale des Sciences Politiques, 2004.

Centre d'Etude de la Vie Politique Française (CEVIPOF), *L'Election présidentielle des 5 et 19 décembre 1965*, Paris, Armand Colin/Fondation Nationale des Sciences Politiques, 1970.

Charpier, F., *Génération Occident. De l'extrême droite à la droite*, Paris, Seuil, 2005.

Chebel d'Appollonia, A., *L'Extrême-droite en France. De Maurras à Le Pen*, Brussels, Editions Complexe, 1988.

Chebel d'Appollonia, A., 'Collaborationist Fascism', in E. J. Arnold (ed.), *The Development of the Radical Right in France: From Boulanger to Le Pen*, London, Macmillan, 2000.

Cheles, L., Ferguson, R., and Vaughan, M. (eds), *Neo-Fascism in Europe*, London, Longman, 1991.

Chirac, J., *Discours à Metz*, 3 May 1995.

Chirac, J., *Discours au Parc des Expositions*, Orléans, 25 April 1995.

Chiroux, R., *L'Extrême-droite sous la Ve République*, Paris, Librairie Générale de Droit et de Jurisprudence, 1974.

Clayton, A., *The Wars of French Decolonization*, London, Longman, 1994.

Cohen, W. B., 'The Sudden Memory of Torture: The Algerian War in French Discourse, 2000–2001', *French Politics, Culture and Society*, vol. 19, no. 3, 2001, pp. 82–94.

Cointet-Labrousse, M., *Vichy et le fascisme: les hommes, les structures et les pouvoirs*, Brussels, Editions Complexe, 1987.

Cole, A., 'The French Municipal Elections of 12 and 19 March 1989', *Modern and Contemporary France*, no. 39, October 1989, pp. 23–34.

Cole, A., *François Mitterrand: A Study in Political Leadership*, London, Routledge, 1994.

Cole, A., *French Politics and Society*, London, Prentice Hall, 1998.

Cole, A., 'A Strange Affair: The 2002 Presidential and Parliamentary Elections in France', *Government and Opposition*, vol. 37, no. 3, 2002, pp. 317–42.

Cole, A., and Campbell, P., *French Electoral Systems and Elections since 1789*, Aldershot, Gower, 1989.

Commissariat Général à la Famille, *L'Ecole et la Famille*, Paris, Office de Propagande Générale, n.d. [1942].

Coston, H. *et al.*, *Partis, journaux et hommes politiques d'hier et d'aujourd'hui*, Paris, Lectures Françaises, 1960.

CSA, *Les Elections législatives du 25 mai 1997. Explication du vote et attentes des électeurs du premier tour (sondage sortie des urnes)*, Paris, May 1997.

Darmon, M., and Rosso, R., *Front contre Front*, Paris, Seuil, 1999.

Davies, P., *The National Front in France: Ideology, Discourse and Power*, London, Routledge, 1999.

De Benoist, A., *Les Idées à l'endroit*, Paris, Editions Libres-Hallier, 1979.

De Benoist, A., 'Les idées de la "nouvelle droite"', in J.-P. Apparu (ed.), *La Droite aujourd'hui*, Paris, Albin Michel, 1979.

De Benoist, A., *Vu de droite. Anthologie critique des idées contemporaines*, Paris, Copernic, 1979.

Del Boca, A., and Giovana, M., *Fascism Today*, trans. R. H. Boothroyd, London, Heinemann, 1970.

Delwit, P., De Waele, J.-M., and Rea, A. (eds), *L'Extrême droite en France et en Belgique*, Brussels, Editions Complexe, 1998.

Desbuissons, D., 'Maurice Bardèche: un précurseur du "révisionnisme"', *Relations internationales*, no. 65, 1991, pp. 23–37.

Deutsch, E., Lindon, D., and Weill, P., *Les Familles politiques aujourd'hui en France*, Paris, Editions de Minuit, 1966.

Documentation Française (La), *Institutions et vie politique sous la Ve République*, 3rd edn, ed. J.-L. Parodi, Paris, La Documentation Française, 2003.

Documentation historique et philosophique (La), *Le Gouvernement Pétain. Ce qu'il a fait sans nous. Ce qu'il ne peut continuer sans nous*, Paris, Collection Possibilités Françaises, n.d. [1941].

Douglas, A., '"La Nouvelle Droite": G.R.E.C.E. and the Revival of Radical Rightist Thought in Contemporary France', *Tocqueville Review*, vol. 6, no. 2, 1984, pp. 361–87.

Dreyfus-Armand, G., and Caudron, T., 'Les immigrés dans la société 1981–1984', in S. Berstein, P. Milza and J.-L. Bianco (eds), *Les Années Mitterrand. Les années du changement (1981–1984)*, Paris, Perrin, 2001.

Dumont, S., Lorien, J., and Criton, K., *Le Système Le Pen*, Antwerp, Editions EPO, 1985.

Dupeux, G., 'Les plates-formes des partis', in M. Duverger, F. Goguel and J. Touchard (eds), *Les Elections du 2 janvier 1956*, Paris, Armand Colin, 1957.

Duprat, F., *Les Mouvements d'extrême-droite en France depuis 1944*, Paris, Albatros, 1972.

Duranton-Crabol, A.-M., *Visages de la Nouvelle Droite. Le GRECE et son histoire*, Paris, Presses de la Fondation Nationale des Sciences Politiques, 1988.

Duranton-Crabol, A.-M., 'Du combat pour l'Algérie française au combat pour la culture européenne', in J.-P. Rioux and J.-F. Sirinelli (eds), *La Guerre d'Algérie et les intellectuels français*, Brussels, Editions Complexe, 1991.

Duranton-Crabol, A.-M., 'L'extrême droite', in S. Berstein, P. Milza and J.-L. Bianco (eds), *Les Années Mitterrand. Les années du changement (1981–1984)*, Paris, Perrin, 2001.

Duverger, M., Goguel, F., and Touchard, J. (eds), *Les Elections du 2 janvier 1956*, Paris, Armand Colin, 1957.

Eatwell, R., 'Poujadism and Neo-Poujadism: From Revolt to Reconciliation', in P. G. Cerny (ed.), *Social Movements and Protest in France*, London, Pinter, 1982.

Eatwell, R., 'The Nature of the Right, 2: The Right as a Variety of "Styles of Thought"', in R. Eatwell and N. O'Sullivan (eds), *The Nature of the Right: European and American Politics and Political Thought since 1789*, London, Pinter, 1989.

Eatwell, R., *Fascism: A History*, London, Chatto & Windus, 1995.

Eatwell, R., 'On Defining the "Fascist Minimum": The Centrality of Ideology', *Journal of Political Ideologies*, vol. 1, no. 3, 1996, pp. 303–19.

Eatwell, R., and Mudde, C. (eds), *Western Democracies and the New Extreme Right Challenge*, London, Routledge, 2004.

Elgie, R., *Political Institutions in Contemporary France*, Oxford, Oxford University Press, 2003.

Evans, J., 'Le vote gaucho-lepéniste: le masque extrême d'une dynamique normale', *Revue française de science politique*, vol. 50, no. 1, 2000, pp. 21–51.

Evans, J., and Ivaldi, G., 'Les dynamiques électorales de l'extrême droite européenne', *Revue politique et parlementaire*, vol. 104, no. 1019, 2002, pp. 67–83.

Evans, J. (ed.), *The French Party System*, Manchester, Manchester University Press, 2003.

Faux, E., Legrand, T., and Perez, G., *La Main droite de Dieu. Enquête sur François Mitterrand et l'extrême droite*, Paris, Seuil, 1994.

Favier, P., and Martin-Roland, M., *La Décennie Mitterrand*, vol. 1, Paris, Seuil, 1990.

Fieschi, C., *Fascism, Populism and the French Fifth Republic: In the Shadow of Democracy*, Manchester, Manchester University Press, 2004.

Fieschi, C., Shields, J., and Woods, R., 'Extreme Right-Wing Parties and the European Union', in J. Gaffney (ed.), *Political Parties and the European Union*, London, Routledge, 1996.

Fitzgerald, S., 'The Anti-Modern Rhetoric of Le Mouvement Poujade', *Review of Politics*, vol. 32, no. 2, 1970, pp. 167–90.

Flood, C., 'National Populism', in C. Flood and L. Bell (eds), *Political Ideologies in Contemporary France*, London, Pinter, 1997.

Friend, J. W., *The Long Presidency: France in the Mitterrand Years 1981–1995*, Boulder, Westview Press, 1998.

Front National, *Défendre les Français. C'est le programme du Front National*, supplement to *Front National*, no. 3, February 1973.

Front National, *Droite et démocratie économique. Doctrine économique et sociale du Front National*, 2nd edn (first published 1978), Paris, National Hebdo, 1984.

Front National, *Pour la France. Programme du Front National*, Paris, Albatros, 1985.

Front National, *Pour un référendum sur l'immigration*, Paris, n.d. [1985].

Front National, *Immigration: 50 mesures concrètes. Les Français ont la parole*, Paris, n.d. [1991].

Front National, *Maastricht – Avant d'aller voter. Les questions que vous vous posez. Les réponses que vous recherchez*, spec. no. of *Europe et Patries*, no. 46, September 1992.

Front National, *300 mesures pour la renaissance de la France. Programme de gouvernement*, Paris, Editions Nationales, 1993.

Front National, *'Tournons la page'. En avant pour la 6ᵉ République*, Paris, n.d. [1995].

Front National, *Le Grand Changement. Et si on essayait le Front National?*, Paris, 1997.

Front National, *Pour un avenir français. Le Programme de gouvernement du Front National*, Paris, Editions Godefroy de Bouillon, 2001.

Front National, *Français passionnément. Front National, une force pour la France*, Paris, n.d. [2002].

Front National, *Programme du Front National: Europe*, Paris, n.d. [2002].

Front National: Institut de Formation Nationale, *Militer au Front*, Paris, Editions Nationales, 1991.

Front National: Secrétariat Général du Front National, *Le Guide du responsable*, vol. 1: *Organisation*, Paris, Editions Nationales, n.d.

Fysh, P., 'Government Policy and the Challenge of the National Front – The First Twelve Months', *Modern and Contemporary France*, no. 31, 1987, pp. 9–20.

Fysh, P., and Wolfreys, J., *The Politics of Racism in France*, London, Macmillan, 1998/ Palgrave Macmillan, 2003.

Gaffney, J. (ed.), *The French Presidential and Legislative Elections of 2002*, Aldershot, Ashgate, 2004.

Gaspard, F., *Une petite ville en France*, Paris, Gallimard, 1990.

Gaucher, R., *La Montée du FN, 1983–1997*, Paris, Jean Picollec, 1997.

Gildea, R., *France since 1945*, Oxford, Oxford University Press, 1996.

Gildea, R., *Marianne in Chains: In Search of the German Occupation 1940–1945*, London, Macmillan, 2002.

Giscard d'Estaing, V., *Démocratie française*, Paris, Fayard/Livre de poche, 1976.

Godechot, J. (ed.), *Les Constitutions de la France depuis 1789*, Paris, Garnier-Flammarion, 1979.

Goldey, D. B., and Johnson, R. W., 'The French Presidential Election of 24 April–8 May and the General Election of 5–12 June 1988', *Electoral Studies*, vol. 7, no. 3, 1988, pp. 195–223.

Golsan, R. J. (ed.), *The Papon Affair: Memory and Justice on Trial*, New York, Routledge, 2000.

Gordon, B. M., *Collaborationism in France during the Second World War*, Ithaca, Cornell University Press, 1980.

Griffin, R., *The Nature of Fascism*, London, Routledge, 1991.

Griffin, R., 'Net Gains and GUD Reactions: Patterns of Prejudice in a Neo-Fascist *Groupuscule*', *Patterns of Prejudice*, vol. 33, no. 2, 1999, pp. 31–50.

Griffin, R., 'Plus ça change! The Fascist Pedigree of the Nouvelle Droite', in E. J. Arnold (ed.), *The Development of the Radical Right in France: From Boulanger to Le Pen*, London, Macmillan, 2000.

Griffin, R. (ed.), *Fascism*, Oxford, Oxford University Press, 1995.

Griffin, R. (ed.), *International Fascism: Theories, Causes and the New Consensus*, London, Arnold, 1998.

Grover, F., *Drieu La Rochelle*, Paris, Gallimard, 1962.

Grunberg, G., 'Les élections locales françaises de mars 2001: un échec pour la majorité', *French Politics, Culture and Society*, vol. 19, no. 3, 2001, pp. 17–31.

Guy, C., *Le Cas Poujade*, Givors, André Martel, 1955.

Guyomarch, A., and Machin, H., 'François Mitterrand and the French Presidential and Parliamentary Elections of 1988: Mr Norris Changes Trains?', *West European Politics*, vol. 12, no. 1, 1989, pp. 196–210.

Habert, P., Perrineau, P., and Ysmal, C. (eds), *Le Vote sanction. Les élections législatives des 21 et 28 mars 1993*, Paris, Département d'Etudes Politiques du *Figaro*/Presses de la Fondation Nationale des Sciences Politiques, 1993.

Hainsworth, P., 'The Triumph of the Outsider: Jean-Marie Le Pen and the 1988 Presidential Election', in J. Howorth and G. Ross (eds), *Contemporary France: A Review of Interdisciplinary Studies*, vol. 3, London, Pinter, 1989, pp. 160–72.

Hainsworth, P., 'The Extreme Right in Post-War France: The Emergence and Success of the Front National', in P. Hainsworth (ed.), *The Extreme Right in Europe and the USA*, London, Pinter, 1992.

Hainsworth, P., 'Introduction: The Extreme Right', in P. Hainsworth (ed.), *The Politics of the Extreme Right: From the Margins to the Mainstream*, London, Pinter, 2000.

Hainsworth, P., 'The Front National: From Ascendancy to Fragmentation on the French Extreme Right', in P. Hainsworth (ed.), *The Politics of the Extreme Right: From the Margins to the Mainstream*, London, Pinter, 2000.

Halls, W. D., *The Youth of Vichy France*, Oxford, Clarendon Press, 1981.

Hanley, D., *Party, Society and Government: Republican Democracy in France*, New York and Oxford, Berghahn Books, 2002.

Hargreaves, A. G., *Immigration, 'Race' and Ethnicity in Contemporary France*, London, Routledge, 1995.

Hazareesingh, S., *Political Traditions in Modern France*, Oxford, Oxford University Press, 1994.

Hewitt, N., *Literature and the Right in Postwar France: The Story of the 'Hussards'*, Oxford, Berg, 1996.

Hewitt, N., *The Life of Céline: A Critical Biography*, Oxford, Blackwell, 1999.

Hewlett, N., *Modern French Politics: Analysing Conflict and Consensus since 1945*, Cambridge, Polity Press, 1998.

Hirschfeld, G., and Marsh, P. (eds), *Collaboration in France: Politics and Culture During the Nazi Occupation 1940–1944*, Oxford, Berg, 1989.

Hochet, A., 'L'immigration dans le débat politique français de 1981 à 1988', *Pouvoirs*, no. 47, 1988, pp. 23–30.

Hoffmann, S., *Le Mouvement Poujade*, Paris, Armand Colin, 1956.

Hoffmann, S., 'Protest in Modern France', in M. A. Kaplan (ed.), *The Revolution in World Politics*, New York, John Wiley & Sons, 1962.

Hoffmann, S., 'Collaborationism in France During World War II', *Journal of Modern History*, vol. 10, no. 3, 1968, pp. 375–95.

Hoffmann, S., *Decline or Renewal? France since the 1930s*, New York, Viking Press, 1974.

Hoffmann, S. *et al.*, *In Search of France: The Economy, Society, and Political System in the Twentieth Century*, New York, Harper & Row, 1965.

Husbands, C. T., 'The Support for the Front National: Analyses and Findings', *Ethnic and Racial Studies*, vol. 14, no. 3, 1991, pp. 382–416.

Hutton, P. H., 'Popular Boulangism and the Advent of Mass Politics in France, 1886–90', *Journal of Contemporary History*, vol. 11, no.1, 1976, pp. 85–106.

IFOP/Acteurs Publics, *Les Français et l'extrême droite*, Paris, April 2006.

Ignazi, P., 'Un nouvel acteur politique', in N. Mayer and P. Perrineau (eds), *Le Front National à découvert*, Paris, Presses de la Fondation Nationale des Sciences Politiques, 1989.

Ignazi, P., 'The Extreme Right: Defining the Object and Assessing the Causes', in M. Schain, A. Zolberg and P. Hossay (eds), *Shadows over Europe: The Development and Impact of the Extreme Right in Western Europe*, New York, Palgrave Macmillan, 2002.

Ignazi, P., *Extreme Right Parties in Western Europe*, Oxford, Oxford University Press, 2003.

Isorni, J., *Le Silence est d'or ou la parole au Palais-Bourbon*, Paris, Flammarion, 1957.

Isorni, J., *Ainsi passent les républiques*, Paris, Flammarion, 1959.

Ivaldi, G., 'Le Front national à l'assaut du système', *Revue politique et parlementaire*, vol. 100, no. 995, 1998, pp. 5–22.

Ivaldi, G., 'La scission du Front national', *Regards sur l'actualité*, May 1999, pp. 17–32.

Ivaldi, G., 'Les formations d'extrême droite: Front national et Mouvement national républicain', in P. Bréchon (ed.), *Les Partis politiques français*, Paris, La Documentation Française, 2001.

Ivaldi, G., 'L'extrême-droite renforcée mais toujours isolée', *Revue politique et parlementaire*, vol. 104, nos. 1020–21, 2002, pp. 133–49.

Jackson, J., 'Vichy and Fascism', in E. J. Arnold (ed.), *The Development of the Radical Right in France: From Boulanger to Le Pen*, London, Macmillan, 2000.

Jackson, J., *France: The Dark Years 1940–1944*, Oxford, Oxford University Press, 2001.

Jaffré, J., 'Front national: la relève protestataire', in E. Dupoirier and G. Grunberg (eds), *Mars 1986: la drôle de défaite de la gauche*, Paris, Presses Universitaires de France, 1986.

Jaffré, J., 'L'état d'esprit des Français à travers les sondages d'opinion', in S. Berstein, P. Milza and J.-L. Bianco (eds), *Les Années Mitterrand. Les années du changement (1981–1984)*, Paris, Perrin, 2001.

Jeanneret, R., *Maréchal Pétain. Maximes et principes extraits des messages au peuple français, choisis et classés pour servir à l'éducation morale et civique de la jeunesse en conformité avec les programmes de 1941*, Tours, Mame, 1942.

Jenkins, B., *Nationalism in France: Class and Nation since 1789*, London, Routledge, 1990.

Johnson, D., 'The New Right in France', in L. Cheles, R. Ferguson and M. Vaughan (eds), *Neo-Fascism in Europe*, London, Longman, 1991.

Joly, L., 'Darquier de Pellepoix, "champion" des antisémites français (1936–1939)', *Revue d'Histoire de la Shoah*, no. 173, 2001, pp. 35–61.

Julien-Laferrière, F., 'La "Loi Debré" sur l'immigration', *Regards sur l'actualité*, June 1997, pp. 27–39.

Kaplan, A. Y., *Reproductions of Banality: Fascism, Literature, and French Intellectual Life*, Minneapolis, University of Minnesota Press, 1986.

Kaplan, A. Y., 'Literature and Collaboration', in D. Hollier (ed.), *A New History of French Literature*, Cambridge (Massachusetts), Harvard University Press, 1989.

Karapin, R., 'Radical-Right and Neo-Fascist Political Parties in Western Europe', *Comparative Politics*, vol. 30, no. 2, 1998, pp. 213–34.

Kaspi, A., 'Vichy et les Juifs', in J.-F. Sirinelli (ed.), *Dictionnaire historique de la vie politique française au XXe siècle*, Paris, Presses Universitaires de France, 1995.

Kedward, H. R., *Occupied France: Collaboration and Resistance 1940–1944*, Oxford, Blackwell, 1993.

Kedward, R., *La Vie en bleu: France and the French since 1900*, London, Penguin/Allen Lane, 2005.

Kitschelt, H. (with A. J. McGann), *The Radical Right in Western Europe: A Comparative Analysis*, Ann Arbor, University of Michigan Press, 1997.

Knapp, A., *Gaullism since de Gaulle*, Aldershot, Dartmouth, 1994.

Knapp, A., and Wright, V., *The Government and Politics of France*, 4th edn, London, Routledge, 2001.

Kuisel, R. F., *Capitalism and the State in Modern France*, Cambridge, Cambridge University Press, 1983.

Kupferman, F., *Le Procès de Vichy: Pucheu, Pétain, Laval*, Brussels, Editions Complexe, 1980.

Laborie, P., *L'Opinion française sous Vichy*, Paris, Seuil, 1990.

Laguerre, B., 'Brasillach', in J. Julliard and M. Winock (eds), *Dictionnaire des intellectuels français*, Paris, Seuil, 1996.

Lanzmann, C., 'Entretien avec Gaston Defferre, ministre de l'intérieur et de la décentralisation, maire de Marseille', *Les Temps modernes*, vol. 40, nos. 452–54, 1984, pp. 1561–80.

Larkin, M., *France since the Popular Front: Government and People 1936–1986*, Oxford, Clarendon Press, 1988.

Laurent, A., and Perrineau, P., 'L'extrême droite éclatée', *Revue française de science politique*, vol. 49, nos. 4–5, 1999, pp. 633–41.

Le Chevallier, J.-M., *Immigration en Europe: attention, danger*, Paris, G.D.E., 1989.

Le Gall, G., 'Présidentielle 95: une opinion indécise', *Revue politique et parlementaire*, vol. 97, no. 976, 1995, pp. 10–17.

Le Gall, G., 'Présidentielle et municipales 95: victoire de Jacques Chirac et retour à un équilibre électoral', *Revue politique et parlementaire*, vol. 97, no. 977, 1995, pp. 27–41.

Le Gall, G., 'L'étrange consultation électorale de 2001 ou l'invention d'une défaite', *Revue politique et parlementaire*, vol. 103, no. 1011, 2001, pp. 2–32.

Le Gall, G., 'Consultations électorales du printemps 2002: enseignements et spécificités', *Revue politique et parlementaire*, vol. 104, no. 1019, 2002, pp. 35–43.

Le Gall, G., 'Pourquoi le 21 avril?', in SOFRES, *L'Etat de l'opinion 2003*, Paris, Seuil, 2003.

Le Gallou, J.-Y., and the Club de l'Horloge, *La Préférence nationale. Réponse à l'immigration*, Paris, Albin Michel, 1985.

Le Pen, J.-M., 'Le Front national', in J.-P. Apparu (ed.), *La Droite aujourd'hui*, Paris, Albin Michel, 1979.

Le Pen, J.-M., *Les Français d'abord*, Paris, Carrère-Lafon, 1984.

Le Pen, J.-M., *La France est de retour*, Paris, Carrère-Lafon, 1985.

Le Pen, J.-M., 'Déclaration officielle à la candidature présidentielle', 26 April 1987, reprinted in *Les Cahiers FN-INFOS*, July 1987.

Le Pen, J.-M., *Il est temps que le peuple parle*, official presidential campaign statement, Paris, April 1988.

Le Pen, J.-M./Front National, *République Française. Passeport pour la victoire*, Limoges, NPC, 1988.

Le Pen, J.-M., *Europe: discours et interventions 1984–1989*, ed. J.-M. Brissaud, Paris, G.D.E., 1989.

Le Pen, J.-M., *L'Espoir*, Paris, Albatros, 1989.

Le Pen, J.-M./Front National, *La Lettre de Jean-Marie Le Pen*, no. 160, July 1992.

Le Pen, J.-M., *Discours de clôture*, 1995 presidential election campaign, Bois de Boulogne, Paris, 20 April 1995.

Le Pen, J.-M., *Français passionnément – Le Pen président*, official presidential campaign statement, Paris, April 1995.

Le Pen, J.-M./Front National, *Le Contrat pour la France avec les Français. Le Pen Président*, Paris, 1995.

Le Pen, J.-M., *Discours à Paris*, 1 May 1997.

Le Pen, J.-M., *Discours de clôture*, tenth FN national congress, Strasbourg, 31 March 1997.

Le Pen, J.-M., *Discours à Paris*, 1 May 1998.

Le Pen, J.-M., *Discours de clôture*, 2002 presidential election campaign, Salle Equinoxe, Paris, 18 April 2002.

Le Pen, J.-M., *Jean-Marie Le Pen – La France et les Français d'abord!*, official presidential campaign statement (first round), Paris, April 2002.

Le Pen, J.-M., *La France retrouvée*, official presidential campaign statement (second round), Paris, April–May 2002.

Le Pen, J.-M., *Discours à Paris*, 1 May 2004.

Le Pen, J.-M., *Discours de clôture*, 2004 European election campaign, Paris, 10 June 2004.

Le Pen, J.-M., *Discours à Valmy*, 20 September 2006.

Le Pen, M., *A contre flots*, Paris, Grancher, 2006.

Lefébure, A., *Les Conversations secrètes des Français sous l'Occupation*, Paris, Plon, 1993.

Lettre de Matignon, no. 123, 15 October 1984.

Lettre de Matignon, no. 127, 12 November 1984.

Lettre de Matignon, no. 158, 1 July 1985.

Lipsedge, M. S., 'The Poujade Movement', *Contemporary Review*, February 1956, pp. 83–88.

Lipset, S. M., *Political Man: The Social Bases of Politics*, London, Heinemann, 1983.

Lottman, H. R., *The People's Anger: Justice and Revenge in Post-Liberation France*, London, Hutchinson, 1986.

MacRae, D., *Parliament, Parties, and Society in France 1946–1958*, New York, St Martin's Press, 1967.

Magraw, R., *France 1815–1914: The Bourgeois Century*, London, Fontana, 1983.

Marcus, J., *The National Front and French Politics: The Resistible Rise of Jean-Marie Le Pen*, London, Macmillan, 1995.

Marcus, J., 'Advance or Consolidation? The French National Front and the 1995 Elections', *West European Politics*, vol. 19, no. 2, 1996, pp. 303–20.

Maréchal, S., *Ni droite, ni gauche . . . Français! Contre la pensée unique: l'autre politique*, Paris, Première Ligne, 1994.

Marrus, M. R., and Paxton, R. O., *Vichy France and the Jews*, Stanford, Stanford University Press, 1995 (first published 1981).

Martin, P., 'Les élections cantonales des 20 et 27 mars 1994', *Regards sur l'actualité*, June 1994, pp. 47–56.

Martin, P., 'Qui vote pour le Front National français?', in P. Delwit, J.-M. De Waele and A. Rea (eds), *L'Extrême droite en France et en Belgique*, Brussels, Editions Complexe, 1998.

Martin, P., *Les Elections municipales en France depuis 1945*, Paris, La Documentation Française, 2001.

Martin, P., 'L'élection présidentielle et les élections législatives françaises de 2002', *French Politics, Culture and Society*, vol. 21, no. 1, 2003, pp. 1–19.

Mauge, R., *La Vérité sur Jean-Marie Le Pen*, Paris, Editions France-Empire, 1988.

Mayer, N., 'Le vote FN de Passy à Barbès (1984–1988)', in N. Mayer and P. Perrineau (eds), *Le Front National à découvert*, Paris, Presses de la Fondation Nationale des Sciences Politiques, 1989.

Mayer, N., 'Des élections sans vainqueur', *French Politics and Society*, vol. 10, no. 2, 1992, pp. 1–12.

Mayer, N., 'Du vote lepéniste au vote frontiste', *Revue française de science politique*, vol. 47, nos. 3–4, 1997, pp. 438–53.

Mayer, N., 'The French National Front', in H.-G. Betz and S. Immerfall (eds), *The New Politics of the Right: Neo-Populist Parties and Movements in Established Democracies*, London, Macmillan, 1998.

Mayer, N., 'The Front National Vote in the Plural', *Patterns of Prejudice*, vol. 32, no. 1, 1998, pp. 3–24.

Mayer, N., *Ces Français qui votent FN*, Paris, Flammarion, 1999.

Mayer, N., *Ces Français qui votent Le Pen*, Paris, Flammarion, 2002.

Mayer, N., 'Les hauts et les bas du vote Le Pen 2002', *Revue française de science politique*, vol. 52, nos. 5–6, 2002, pp. 505–20.

Mayer, N., and Perrineau, P., 'Why Do They Vote For Le Pen?', *European Journal of Political Research*, vol. 22, no. 1, 1992, pp. 123–41.

Mayer, N., and Perrineau, P., 'La puissance et le rejet ou le lepénisme dans l'opinion', in SOFRES, *L'Etat de l'opinion 1993*, Paris, Seuil, 1993.

Mayer, N., and Rey, H., 'Avancée électorale, isolement politique du Front national', *Revue politique et parlementaire*, vol. 95, no. 964, 1993, pp. 42–48.

Mayer, N., and Perrineau, P. (eds), *Le Front National à découvert*, Paris, Presses de la Fondation Nationale des Sciences Politiques, 1989.

Mégret, B., *La Flamme. Les voies de la renaissance*, Paris, Editions Robert Laffont, 1990.

Mégret, B., 'Contribution au règlement du problème de l'immigration: 50 mesures concrètes', paper presented to the FN conference 'Immigration: les solutions', Marseille, 16 November 1991.

Mégret, B., *Remettons la France à l'endroit avec Bruno Mégret*, official presidential campaign statement, Paris, April 2002.

Mény, Y., and Surel, Y. (eds), *Democracies and the Populist Challenge*, Basingstoke, Palgrave, 2002.

Merkl, P. H., and Weinberg, L. (eds), *Right-Wing Extremism in the Twenty-First Century*, London, Frank Cass, 2003.

Michels, R., *Political Parties: A Sociological Study of the Oligarchical Tendencies of Modern Democracy*, New York, Free Press, 1962 (first published 1911).

Milward, A. S., *The New Order and the French Economy*, Oxford, Oxford University Press, 1970.

Milza, P., *Fascisme français: passé et présent*, Paris, Flammarion, 1987.

Milza, P., 'Le Front national: droite extrême . . . ou national-populisme?', in J.-F. Sirinelli (ed.), *Histoire des droites en France*, vol. 1: *Politique*, Paris, Gallimard, 1992.

Milza, P., *L'Europe en chemise noire. Les extrêmes droites européennes de 1945 à aujourd'hui*, Paris, Fayard, 2002.

Minkenberg, M., 'The New Right in France and Germany: *Nouvelle Droite, Neue Rechte*, and the New Right Radical Parties', in P. H. Merkl and L. Weinberg (eds), *The Revival of Right-Wing Extremism in the Nineties*, London, Frank Cass, 1997.

Minkenberg, M., and Schain, M., 'The Front National in Context: French and European Dimensions', in P. H. Merkl and L. Weinberg (eds), *Right-Wing Extremism in the Twenty-First Century*, London, Frank Cass, 2003.

Mitterrand, F./Parti Socialiste, *110 Propositions pour la France*, Paris, 1981.

Mitterrand, F./Parti Socialiste, *Lettre à tous les Français*, Paris, 1988.

Moinet, J.-P., 'La notabilisation du FN: engrenage et dangers', *Revue politique et parlementaire*, vol. 100, no. 995, 1998, pp. 23–26.

Monde (Le) dossiers et documents: L'élection présidentielle 26 avril–10 mai 1981, Paris, May 1981.

Monde (Le) dossiers et documents: Les élections législatives de juin 1981, Paris, June 1981.

Monde (Le) dossiers et documents: Les élections législatives du 16 mars 1986, Paris, March 1986.

Monde (Le) dossiers et documents: L'élection présidentielle 24 avril–8 mai 1988, Paris, May 1988.

Monde (Le) dossiers et documents: Les élections législatives 5–12 juin 1988, Paris, June 1988.

Monde (Le) dossiers et documents: Spécial élections municipales, Paris, April 1989.

Monde (Le) dossiers et documents: La France dans ses régions, Paris, April 1992.

Monde (Le) dossiers et documents: Elections législatives 21–28 mars 1993, Paris, March 1993.

Monde (Le) dossiers et documents: L'élection présidentielle 23 avril–7 mai 1995, Paris, May 1995.

Monde (Le) dossiers et documents: Elections législatives 25 mai–1er juin 1997, Paris, June 1997.

Monde (Le) dossiers et documents: Les Français sous l'Occupation, no. 262, Paris, February 1998.

Montagnon, P., *La Guerre d'Algérie: genèse et engrenage d'une tragédie*, Paris, Pygmalion/Gérard Watelet, 1984.

Mudde, C., 'The War of Words Defining the Extreme Right Party Family', *West European Politics*, vol. 19, no. 2, 1996, pp. 225–48.

Mudde, C., *The Ideology of the Extreme Right*, Manchester, Manchester University Press, 2000.

Nolte, E., *Three Faces of Fascism: Action Française, Italian Fascism, National Socialism*, trans. L. Vennewitz, London, Weidenfeld & Nicolson, 1965.

Ory, P., *Les Collaborateurs 1940–1945*, Paris, Seuil, 1976.

Osgood, S. M., *French Royalism since 1870*, The Hague, Martinus Nijhoff, 1970.

Ousby, I., *Occupation: The Ordeal of France 1940–1944*, London, Pimlico, 1999.

Passmore, K., 'The Croix de Feu and Fascism: A Foreign Thesis Obstinately Maintained', in E. J. Arnold (ed.), *The Development of the Radical Right in France: From Boulanger to Le Pen*, London, Macmillan, 2000.

Pauwels, L., 'La nouvelle droite', in J.-P. Apparu (ed.), *La Droite aujourd'hui*, Paris, Albin Michel, 1979.

Paxton, R. O., *Parades and Politics at Vichy: The French Officer Corps under Marshal Pétain*, Princeton, Princeton University Press, 1966.

Paxton, R. O., *Vichy France: Old Guard and New Order 1940–1944*, New York, Columbia University Press, 2001 (first published 1972).

Paxton, R. O., *The Anatomy of Fascism*, London, Penguin, 2004.

Payne, S. G., *A History of Fascism 1914–1945*, London, Routledge, 2001.

Péan, P., *Une jeunesse française. François Mitterrand 1934–1947*, Paris, Fayard, 1994.

Perrineau, P., 'Le Front national: un électorat autoritaire', *Revue politique et parlementaire*, vol. 87, no. 918, 1985, pp. 24–31.

Perrineau, P., 'Glissements progressifs de l'idéologie', in E. Dupoirier and G. Grunberg (eds), *Mars 1986: la drôle de défaite de la gauche*, Paris, Presses Universitaires de France, 1986.

Perrineau, P., 'Le Front national: un électorat de la crainte', *CFDT Aujourd'hui*, no. 88, February 1988, pp. 22–32.

Perrineau, P., 'Les étapes d'une implantation électorale (1972–1988)', in N. Mayer and P. Perrineau (eds), *Le Front National à découvert*, Paris, Presses de la Fondation Nationale des Sciences Politiques, 1989.

Perrineau, P., 'Le Front national, d'une élection l'autre', *Regards sur l'actualité*, May 1990, pp. 17–32.

Perrineau, P., 'Le Front national: 1972–1992', in M. Winock (ed.), *Histoire de l'extrême droite en France*, Paris, Seuil, 1993.

Perrineau, P., 'La dynamique du vote Le Pen: le poids du gaucho-lepénisme', in P. Perrineau and C. Ysmal (eds), *Le Vote de crise. L'élection présidentielle de 1995*, Paris, Département d'Etudes Politiques du *Figaro*/Presses de la Fondation Nationale des Sciences Politiques, 1995.

Perrineau, P., *Le Symptôme Le Pen. Radiographie des électeurs du Front national*, Paris, Fayard, 1997.

Perrineau, P., 'La surprise lepéniste et sa suite législative', in P. Perrineau and C. Ysmal (eds), *Le Vote de tous les refus. Les élections présidentielle et législatives de 2002*, Paris, Presses de la Fondation Nationale des Sciences Politiques, 2003.

Perrineau, P. (ed.), *Les Croisés de la société fermée. L'Europe des extrêmes droites*, Paris, Editions de l'Aube, 2001.

Perrineau, P., and Ysmal, C. (eds), *Le Vote de crise. L'élection présidentielle de 1995*, Paris, Département d'Etudes Politiques du *Figaro*/Presses de la Fondation Nationale des Sciences Politiques, 1995.

Perrineau, P., and Ysmal, C. (eds), *Le Vote de tous les refus. Les élections présidentielle et législatives de 2002*, Paris, Presses de la Fondation Nationale des Sciences Politiques, 2003.

Peschanski, D., 'Exclusion, persécution, répression', in J.-P. Azéma and F. Bédarida (eds), *Le Régime de Vichy et les Français*, Paris, Fayard, 1992.

Peschanski, D., *Vichy 1940–1944. Contrôle et exclusion*, Brussels, Editions Complexe, 1997.

Pétain, P., *Discours aux Français: 17 juin 1940–20 août 1944*, ed. J.-C. Barbas, Paris, Albin Michel, 1989.

Petitfils, J.-C., *L'Extrême droite en France*, Paris, Presses Universitaires de France, 1983.

Pierce, R., 'The French Election of January 1956', *Journal of Politics*, vol. 19, no. 3, 1957, pp. 391–422.

Plenel, E., and Rollat, A., *L'Effet Le Pen*, Paris, La Découverte/*Le Monde*, 1984.

Plenel, E., and Rollat, A., *La République menacée. Dix ans d'effet Le Pen*, Paris, *Le Monde*-Editions, 1992.

Plumyène, J., and Lasierra, R., *Les Fascismes français 1923–1963*, Paris, Seuil, 1963.

Poniatowski, M., *L'Avenir n'est écrit nulle part*, Paris, Albin Michel, 1978.

Portelli, H., *La Politique en France sous la Ve République*, Paris, Grasset, 1987.

Portelli, H., 'Les élections législatives de mars 1993', *Regards sur l'actualité*, April 1993, pp. 23–31.

Portelli, H., 'L'élection présidentielle des 21 avril et 5 mai 2002', *Regards sur l'actualité*, no. 284, 2002, pp. 65–71.

Portelli, H., 'Les élections législatives des 9 et 16 juin 2002', *Regards sur l'actualité*, no. 284, 2002, pp. 73–77.

Poujade, P., *J'ai choisi le combat*, Saint-Céré, Société Générale des Editions et des Publications, 1955.

Poujade, P., *A l'heure de la colère*, Paris, Albin Michel, 1977.

Poujade, P., *L'Histoire sans masque. Autobiographie*, Cestas, Elytis Edition, 2003.

Poujade, P. *et al.*, *Notes et essais sur le 'Poujadisme'*, Saint-Céré, Les Cahiers du Poujadisme, no. 1, n.d. [1956].

Poznanski, R., *Être juif en France pendant la Seconde Guerre mondiale*, Paris, Hachette, 1994.

Prieur, C., 'La campagne électorale dans l'Aveyron', in M. Duverger, F. Goguel and J. Touchard (eds), *Les Elections du 2 janvier 1956*, Paris, Armand Colin, 1957.

Prochasson, C., 'Elusive Fascism: Reflections on the French Extreme Right at the End of the Nineteenth Century', in E. J. Arnold (ed.), *The Development of the Radical Right in France: From Boulanger to Le Pen*, London, Macmillan, 2000.

Prowe, D., '"Classic" Fascism and the New Radical Right in Western Europe: Comparisons and Contrasts', *Contemporary European History*, vol. 3, no. 3, 1994, pp. 289–313.

Pryce-Jones, D., 'Paris During the German Occupation', in G. Hirschfeld and P. Marsh (eds), *Collaboration in France: Politics and Culture During the Nazi Occupation 1940–1944*, Oxford, Berg, 1989.

Randa, P., *Dictionnaire commenté de la collaboration française*, Paris, Jean Picollec, 1997.

Rassemblement pour la République, *Le Renouveau: Pacte RPR pour la France*, Paris, 1985.

Rassemblement pour la République/Union pour la Démocratie Française, *RPR-UDF: Plate-forme pour gouverner ensemble*, Paris, 1986.

Rebatet, L., *Les Mémoires d'un fasciste*, vol. 1: *Les Décombres 1938–1940*, Paris, Société Nouvelle des Editions Jean-Jacques Pauvert, 1976 (first published 1942).

Rees, P., *Biographical Dictionary of the Extreme Right since 1890*, New York/London, Harvester Wheatsheaf, 1990.

Rémond, R., *Les Droites en France*, Paris, Aubier Montaigne, 1982.

Rémy, D. (ed.), *Les Lois de Vichy*, Paris, Romillat, 1992.

Renan, E., 'Qu'est-ce qu'une nation?', in H. Psichari (ed.), *Œuvres complètes de Ernest Renan*, vol. 1, Paris, Calmann-Lévy, 1947, pp. 887–906.

Rioux, J.-P., *La France de la Quatrième République*, 2 vols, Paris, Seuil, 1980, 1983.

Rioux, J.-P., 'La révolte de Pierre Poujade', *L'Histoire*, no. 32, March 1981, pp. 6–15.

Rioux, J.-P., 'Des clandestins aux activistes (1945–1965)', in M. Winock (ed.), *Histoire de l'extrême droite en France*, Paris, Seuil, 1993.

Rioux, J.-P., and Sirinelli, J.-F. (eds), *La Guerre d'Algérie et les intellectuels français*, Brussels, Editions Complexe, 1991.

Rochet, W., 'Le caractère fasciste du "mouvement" poujadiste', *Les Cahiers du communisme*, March 1956, pp. 194–211.

Rollat, A., *Les Hommes de l'extrême droite: Le Pen, Marie, Ortiz et les autres*, Paris, Calmann-Lévy, 1985.

Rossignol, D., *Histoire de la propagande en France de 1940 à 1944. L'utopie Pétain*, Paris, Presses Universitaires de France, 1991.

Rousso, H., *Le Syndrome de Vichy de 1944 à nos jours*, Paris, Seuil, 1990.

Roy, J.-P., 'Le programme économique et social du Front National en France', in P. Delwit, J.-M. De Waele and A. Rea (eds), *L'Extrême droite en France et en Belgique*, Brussels, Editions Complexe, 1998.

Samson, M., *Le Front National aux affaires. Deux ans d'enquête sur la vie municipale à Toulon*, Paris, Calmann-Lévy, 1997.

Sartori, G., *Parties and Party Systems: A Framework for Analysis*, Cambridge, Cambridge University Press, 1976.

Schain, M. A., 'Immigrants and Politics in France', in J. S. Ambler (ed.), *The French Socialist Experiment*, Philadelphia, Institute for the Study of Human Issues, 1985.

Schain, M. A., 'The National Front in France and the Construction of Political Legitimacy', *West European Politics*, vol. 10, no. 2, 1987, pp. 229–52.

Schain, M. A., 'The Immigration Debate and the National Front', in J. T. S. Keeler and M. A. Schain (eds), *Chirac's Challenge: Liberalization, Europeanization, and Malaise in France*, London, Macmillan, 1996.

Schain, M. A., 'The Normalization of the National Front', *French Politics and Society*, vol. 15, no. 2, 1997, pp. 9–12.

Schain, M. A., 'The National Front and the French Party System', *French Politics and Society*, vol. 17, no. 1, 1999, pp. 1–16.

Schain, M. A., 'The Impact of the French National Front on the French Political System', in M. Schain, A. Zolberg and P. Hossay (eds), *Shadows over Europe: The Development and Impact of the Extreme Right in Western Europe*, New York, Palgrave Macmillan, 2002.

Schain, M., Zolberg, A., and Hossay, P. (eds), *Shadows over Europe: The Development and Impact of the Extreme Right in Western Europe*, New York, Palgrave Macmillan, 2002.

Schneider, W. H., *Quality and Quantity: The Quest for Biological Regeneration in Twentieth-Century France*, Cambridge, Cambridge University Press, 1990.

Schwartzenberg, R.-G., *La Campagne présidentielle de 1965*, Paris, Presses Universitaires de France, 1967.

Secrétariat Général à la Jeunesse: Direction de la Propagande, *Qu'est-ce que la Révolution Nationale?*, Paris, 1941.

Secrétariat Général de l'Information, *Mardi 12 août 1941: Le Maréchal Pétain décide*, Lyon, 1941.

Sheehan, T., 'Paris: Moses and Polytheism', in A. Montagu (ed.), *Sociobiology Examined*, Oxford, Oxford University Press, 1980.

Shields, J. G., 'Antisemitism in France: The Spectre of Vichy', *Patterns of Prejudice*, vol. 24, nos. 2–4, 1990, pp. 5–17.

Shields, J. G., 'Immigration Politics in Mitterrand's France', in G. Raymond (ed.), *France During the Socialist Years*, Aldershot, Dartmouth, 1994.

Shields, J. G., 'Europe's Other Landslide: The French National Assembly Elections of May–June 1997', *The Political Quarterly*, vol. 68, no. 4, 1997, pp. 412–24.

Shields, J. G., 'An Enigma Still: Poujadism Fifty Years On', *French Politics, Culture and Society*, vol. 22, no. 1, 2004, pp. 36–56.

Shields, J. G., 'Political Representation in France: A Crisis of Democracy?', *Parliamentary Affairs*, vol. 59, no. 1, 2006, pp. 118–37.

Shields, J. G., 'Charlemagne's Crusaders: French Collaboration in Arms, 1941–1945', *French Cultural Studies*, vol. 18, no. 1, 2007, pp. 83–105.

Simmons, H. G., *The French National Front: The Extremist Challenge to Democracy*, Boulder, Westview Press, 1996.

Sineau, M., 'La parité en peau de chagrin (ou la résistible entrée des femmes à l'Assemblée nationale)', *Revue politique et parlementaire*, vol. 104, nos. 1020–21, 2002, pp. 211–18.

Slama, A.-G., 'Vichy était-il fasciste?', *Vingtième Siècle*, no. 11, 1986, pp. 41–53.

SOFRES, *Opinion publique 1984*, Paris, Gallimard, 1984.

SOFRES, *Opinion publique 1985*, Paris, Gallimard, 1985.

SOFRES, *L'Etat de l'opinion 1990*, Paris, Seuil, 1990.

SOFRES, *L'Etat de l'opinion 1993*, Paris, Seuil, 1993.

SOFRES, *L'Etat de l'opinion 1996*, Paris, Seuil, 1996.

SOFRES, *La Signification du vote des Français aux élections législatives*, Paris, June 1997.

SOFRES, *L'Etat de l'opinion 2003*, Paris, Seuil, 2003.

Soucy, R., 'The Nature of Fascism in France', *Journal of Contemporary History*, vol. 1, no. 1, 1966, pp. 27–55.

Soucy, R., *Fascist Intellectual: Drieu La Rochelle*, Berkeley, University of California Press, 1979.

Soucy, R., *French Fascism: The Second Wave 1933–1939*, New Haven/London, Yale University Press, 1995.

Sternhell, Z., *La Droite révolutionnaire 1885–1914. Les origines françaises du fascisme*, Paris, Seuil, 1978.

Sternhell, Z., *Neither Right Nor Left: Fascist Ideology in France*, trans. D. Maisel, Princeton, Princeton University Press, 1986.

Stevens, A., 'France', in J. Lodge (ed.), *Direct Elections to the European Parliament 1984*, London, Macmillan, 1986.

Stirbois, J.-P., *Tonnerre de Dreux. L'avenir nous appartient*, Paris, Editions National Hebdo, 1988.

Stoetzel, J., and Hassner, P., 'Résultats d'un sondage dans le premier secteur de la Seine', in M. Duverger, F. Goguel and J. Touchard (eds), *Les Elections du 2 janvier 1956*, Paris, Armand Colin, 1957.

Sweets, J. F., *Choices in Vichy France: The French under Nazi Occupation*, Oxford, Oxford University Press, 1994.

Taguieff, P.-A., 'Un programme "révolutionnaire"?', in N. Mayer and P. Perrineau (eds), *Le Front National à découvert*, Paris, Presses de la Fondation Nationale des Sciences Politiques, 1989.

Taguieff, P.-A., *Sur la Nouvelle Droite. Jalons d'une analyse critique*, Paris, Descartes & Cie, 1994.

Thomson, D., *Democracy in France since 1870*, London, Cassell, 1989.

Thomson, D. (ed.), *France: Empire and Republic 1850–1940. Historical Documents*, London, Macmillan, 1968.

Tixier-Vignancour, J.-L., *J'ai choisi la défense*, Paris, La Table Ronde, 1964.

Touchard, J., 'Bibliographie et chronologie du Poujadisme', *Revue française de science politique*, January–March 1956, pp. 18–43.

Tucker, W. R., 'Politics and Aesthetics: The Fascism of Robert Brasillach', *Western Political Quarterly*, vol. 15, no. 4, 1962, pp. 605–17.

Tucker, W. R., 'The New Look of the Extreme Right in France', *Western Political Quarterly*, vol. 21, no. 1, 1968, pp. 86–97.

Tucker, W. R., *The Fascist Ego: A Political Biography of Robert Brasillach*, Berkeley, University of California Press, 1975.

Vaughan, M., 'Neither New nor Right', *West European Politics*, vol. 4, no. 3, 1981, pp. 302–7.

Vaughan, M., '"Nouvelle Droite": Cultural Power and Political Influence', in D. S. Bell (ed.), *Contemporary French Political Parties*, London, Croom Helm, 1982.

Verdès-Leroux, J., *Refus et violences. Politique et littérature à l'extrême droite des années trente aux retombées de la Libération*, Paris, Gallimard, 1996.

Warner, G., 'France', in S. J. Woolf (ed.), *Fascism in Europe*, London, Methuen, 1981.

Weber, E., 'Nationalism, Socialism, and National-Socialism in France', *French Historical Studies*, vol. 2, no. 3, 1962, pp. 273–307.

Weil, P., *La France et ses étrangers. L'aventure d'une politique de l'immigration 1938–1991*, Paris, Calmann-Lévy, 1991.

Wihtol de Wenden, C., *Les Immigrés et la politique. Cent cinquante ans d'évolution*, Paris, Presses de la Fondation Nationale des Sciences Politiques, 1988.

Williams, P. M., *Crisis and Compromise: Politics in the Fourth Republic*, London, Longmans, 1964.

Williams, P. M. (with D. Goldey and M. Harrison), *French Politicians and Elections 1951–1969*, Cambridge, Cambridge University Press, 1970.

Winock, M., *Nationalisme, antisémitisme et fascisme en France*, Paris, Seuil, 1990.

Winock, M. (ed.), *Histoire de l'extrême droite en France*, Paris, Seuil, 1993.

Wolfreys, J., 'An Iron Hand in a Velvet Glove: The Programme of the French Front National', *Parliamentary Affairs*, vol. 46, no. 3, 1993, pp. 415–29.

Wolfreys, J., 'Neither Right Nor Left? Towards an Integrated Analysis of the Front National', in N. Atkin and F. Tallett (eds), *The Right in France: From Revolution to Le Pen*, London, I. B. Tauris, 2003.

Wright, G., *France in Modern Times: From the Enlightenment to the Present*, New York, Norton, 1981.

Ysmal, C., 'Le Giscardisme face aux nouvelles idéologies', in P. Bacot and C. Journès (eds), *Les nouvelles idéologies*, Lyon, Presses Universitaires de Lyon, 1982.

Interviews

Poujade, Pierre, UDCA president, Labastide L'Evêque, 18 April 1995; Saint-Céré, 20 July 2003.

Perinet, André, UDCA national delegate, Paris, 21 April 1995.

Hainaut, Guilbert, MNR official and electoral candidate, Paris, 9 April 1999.

Moreau, Georges, FN official and electoral candidate, Paris, 14 April 1999.

Descaves, Pierre, FN *bureau politique* member and former FN parliamentary deputy (Oise), Saint-Céré, 20 July 2003.

Jalkh, Jean-François, FN *bureau politique* member and former FN parliamentary deputy (Seine-et-Marne), telephone, 16 March 2004.

Le Pen, Jean-Marie, FN president, Paris, 15 April 2005.

Index